FLORIDA

JASON FERGUSON

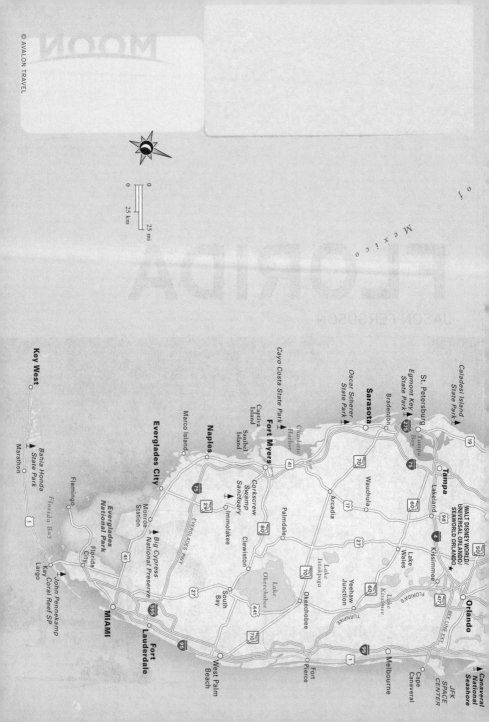

MOON

FLORIDA

JASON FERGUSON

0   25 mi

0   25 km

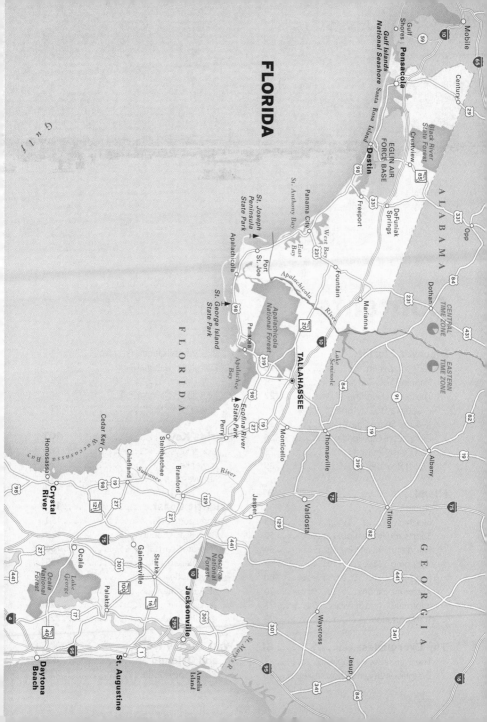

Contents

Ask longtime residents of Florida how they feel about their state, and they'll get a gleam in their eyes. They'll lean in a little closer—as if they're about to reveal a treasured secret—and tell you about a spot off a nearby river, along a beautiful beach, or amid the buzzing electricity of the city. This spot, they'll say, could only be found in Florida. And it's places like that, wonderful locales so numerous that it seems nearly every resident has his or her own private collection, that continue to make Florida one of the most unique places in all of the United States, if not the world.

Florida's history has long been one of people laying odds that the allure of a tropical paradise in the continental United States will remain endlessly attractive. And those people have been right more often than they've been wrong. From Henry Flagler constructing railways down the Atlantic coast that would eventually give rise to the cities of Palm Beach and Miami to Walt Disney furtively buying up marshland south of the once-sleepy town of Orlando in order to ensure a cohesive and holistic experience for visitors to

Clockwise from top left: Ron Jon Surf Shop in Cocoa Beach; Fort Myers Beach; an enthusiastic seabird; Disney's iconic Cinderella Castle in the Magic Kingdom; Florida oranges; Tikis welcome guests to Cocoa Beach.

his theme park, Florida's development as a state has been inextricably intertwined with its attraction as a tourist destination. It's remarkable that, even as development seems destined to take over the state, there are always—no matter where you are—expansive and extensive examples of Florida's wild and natural beauty.

Discover what has drawn people to the Sunshine State for centuries. Sitting on the beach watching the sun rise above the Atlantic with nothing but the squawks of gulls and the waves disturbing the peace, you can imagine how every group of newcomers must have felt, whether the first Europeans, the post-colonial settlers, or the retirees from the Northern United States. The sense of boundless opportunity, the awe-inspiring natural beauty, the numerous opportunities for recreation and relaxation, the sun, the sand, the swamps....

Florida still inspires even the most hard-hearted souls with its beguiling promise: paradise the way it ought to be, if you know where to look.

Clockwise from top left: the marina in downtown St. Petersburg; white-sand dunes at St. Andrews State Park; Ca' d'Zan Mansion in Sarasota; Purple Gallinule in Everglades National Park.

10 TOP
EXPERIENCES

1 **Living It Up in Miami's South Beach:** Whether it's the pastel art deco buildings, the velvet-ropes-and-bottle-service clubs, the shopping, the dining, the stylish multicultural crowds, or even the beautiful beach itself, South Beach neatly encapsulates a uniquely modern Florida experience (page 36).

2 **Theme Parks in Orlando:** With **Walt Disney World** (page 239), **Universal Orlando Resort** (page 267), and **SeaWorld Orlando** (page 280) all within a few minutes of one another, the city has become synonymous with roller-coaster escapism.

3 **Beaches:** Florida is home to some of the best beaches in the United States, with stretches of soft, white sand and crystal-blue waters (page 29).

>>>

4 **Everglades National Park:** This expansive and wild national park (page 83) encompasses one of the last and largest unspoiled natural areas in the state, perfect for **canoeing, kayaking, camping,** and **wildlife watching.**

5 **Free-Wheeling Key West:** The historic homes and buildings of Old Town gorgeously evoke a long-gone, Hemingway-esque version of the island, while the gloriously libertine bars, clubs, tourist traps, and restaurants along this strip highlight the louche Margaritaville it has become (page 133).

>>>

6 **Freshwater Springs:** There are dozens of freshwater springs throughout Florida, many open to the public in the form of state or municipal parks. They're excellent for **swimming, snorkeling,** and **nature watching** (pages 295, 348, 453, and 465).

>>>

7 Surfing on the Atlantic Coast: Florida is one of the best places in the eastern United States to catch some waves (page 213).

>>>

8 Art Deco Architecture: Tour the stunning art deco buildings of Miami's South Beach (page 36).

<<<

9 Sunset: Florida's Gulf Coast waters offer superlative sunset views, best taken in aboard a boat. The colors are particularly lovely from Key West, with water on all sides (page 137).

>>>

10 **Dining and Dancing in Little Havana:** Miami's vibrant Calle Ocho is the historic heart of country's Cuban-American population, with a robust selection of restaurants and nightlife options (page 44).

Planning Your Trip

Where to Go

Miami

Informed by the culture of its substantial Latin American population, by the tropical sea breezes that blow in over Biscayne Bay, and by its stature as the state's **largest metropolitan area,** Miami manages to be urban and stylish while maintaining the laissez-faire sort of cool that comes with year-round gorgeous weather. With skyscrapers, condominiums, and burgeoning art districts crowding the downtown area, **art deco architecture** and fashion-forward clubbing in **South Beach,** the lush, wealthy beauty of **Coconut Grove** and **Coral Gables,** and suburbs extending until the wilderness of the Everglades stops them, Miami neatly summarizes all the dreams and nightmares that people have about Florida.

The Everglades

The Florida Everglades comprise nearly 4,000 square miles of wetlands, swamps, scrub forests, and rivers. The majority of **hiking, canoeing,** and **kayaking trails** are easily accessible, and **the Oasis Visitor Center, Shark Valley Visitor Center,** and **Flamingo Visitor Center** offer exhibits and knowledgeable staff. In the small town of **Everglades City,** you'll find the teeny-tiny **Ochopee Post Office,** the stunning and unique **Big Cypress Gallery.**

Florida Keys

For much of Florida's early history, this island archipelago was Florida's **pioneer paradise,** the place where rogues and adventurers headed on their boats as a way to escape the demands

Quiet beaches can still be found in busy destinations.

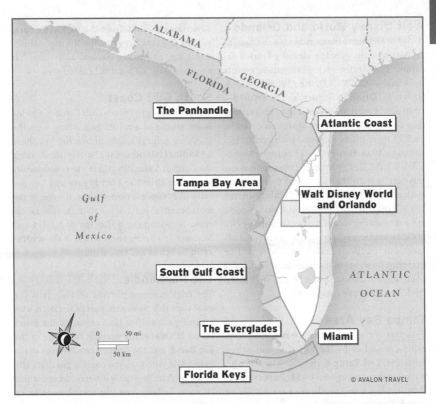

The Panhandle

Atlantic Coast

Gulf
of
Mexico

Tampa Bay Area

Walt Disney World and Orlando

South Gulf Coast

ATLANTIC
OCEAN

The Everglades

Miami

Florida Keys

© AVALON TRAVEL

(and occasionally the laws) of the mainland. Amazingly, decades of tourism have done little to alter the fundamental character of the Florida Keys. **Key West** is the libertarian heart of the Keys, a city as devoted to **bacchanalian pleasures** as it is proud of its beautiful and historic scenery. That spirit carries over to the natural on- and offshore wonders found by divers, boaters, and other nature lovers on **Islamorada** and **Marathon.**

Atlantic Coast

Fort Lauderdale has recovered from its role as the preferred destination for collegiate spring-breakers and has evolved into a cultured, mellow place with vibrant nightlife and arts scenes that complement its beautiful public beaches. Farther north, **Palm Beach** has maintained

its status as the richest town in Florida for almost 100 years. Its sister city of **West Palm Beach** offers a more urban experience and relaxed atmosphere. The beaches and fishing in **Fort Pierce** contrast with the slightly uptight oceanfront vibe in **Vero Beach.** These two cities along the **Treasure Coast** are as unique as they are different from other locales in South Florida. Farther north, the generally laid-back atmosphere that comes with living on the coast is a little more evident. Whether you're staring in awe at the rockets of the **Kennedy Space Center,** the race cars of **Daytona International Speedway,** or historic **St. Augustine** (the oldest continually inhabited city in the United States), you still can't help but notice that it's the area's natural beauty that is by far its primary attraction.

Walt Disney World and Orlando

A visit to Orlando's theme parks is a fundamental part of many people's idea of a Florida vacation. Thankfully, each of the major resorts in Orlando—the **Walt Disney World Resort, Universal Orlando Resort,** and SeaWorld—continue to meet and exceed the expectations that come with that idea. More importantly, each of them offers something different. And although Walt Disney World is interchangeable with the idea of a trip to Orlando in many travelers' minds, the fact is that even without the land of theme parks south of downtown, the city of Orlando and the Central Florida region are a compelling vacation destination. The city of Orlando offers a diverse array of **cultural attractions, outdoor activities,** and **nightlife action.** The sights in its immediate area, most notably the historic and upscale city of **Winter Park,** are also quite compelling.

Tampa Bay Area

This part of the state literally has it all. Urban explorers will enjoy the nightlife and urban scruffiness of **Tampa** and the historic and walkable downtown area of **St. Petersburg.** Families flock to the theme park thrills of **Busch Gardens** and the gorgeous beaches that stretch for miles south of **Clearwater.** Outdoor adventures abound, from the backwater rural vibe of **Crystal River** to the hiking, nature-watching, and other natural activities that abound along this beautiful coastal area.

South Gulf Coast

Traveling along the south Gulf Coast of Florida is something of a mixed bag. Along with the stunning natural beauty of beaches like those on **Sanibel Island** and the barrier islands along the coast of **Sarasota,** there are economically struggling cities like **Fort Myers** and tony locales like **Naples.** Nonetheless, it's one of the most beautiful parts of the state. Art lovers will enjoy browsing the **galleries** of Naples and Sarasota and beach bums will love the **white-sand beaches** and blue waters.

The Panhandle

The northernmost portion of Florida is the most capital-S, Southern, part of the state, with a rural pastoralism that connects the horse farms of **Ocala,** the marshy coastline of the **Big Bend,** and the scrappy beach towns of the Panhandle. Although you could argue that a trip to the Panhandle is quite different from a trip to Ocala or **Tallahassee,** the area shares a sensibility and charm that's quite different from the rest of the state.

When to Go

The question of when to go to Florida depends on where you're planning to go and what you're planning to do. As a general rule, holiday weekends—regardless of the time of year—are busy throughout the state.

Miami, South Atlantic Coast, and the Keys

One of Florida's most popular **winter** destinations, this area hosts several big events, like **Art Basel** in Miami. It is a prime destination for senior-citizen **snowbirds** who spend the season here, along with weekend warriors seeking a respite from the cold weather. Accordingly, **hotel rates** approach high rates in winter, if you can find a vacancy. Those rates plummet during the **summer,** which also brings stiflingly hot and humid weather and the threat of **hurricanes.**

South Gulf Coast

Just like Miami and South Florida, this part of the state fills up with snowbirds and frozen Midwesterners during the **winter.** Unfortunately, although hotel rates go down in the **summer** (again, watch out for hurricanes), many businesses simply close up shop May-October, as it's not worth it for them to stay open to cater to the small number of tourists who visit.

Walt Disney World

There used to be a time when you could recommend the slow season to visitors who had flexible schedules. Theoretically, there still is a slower season at the Orlando parks: **Labor Day-Christmas,** particularly the first few weeks of a new school year. But even that small window of time has begun to see capacity crowds at many of the area's attractions. Still, even though you are unlikely to find any mind-blowing deals or be able to experience Disney World without having to stand in long lines, that period of time, as well as the gap of **Easter-Memorial Day,** are still considered some of the best times to see the parks. The crowds may still be large, but the weather is nearly perfect and the likelihood of a hurricane ruining your vacation is next to nil.

Tampa, Orlando, and the North Atlantic Coast

A visit to beach towns like New Smyrna Beach or Daytona Beach on the north Atlantic coast will find you among large crowds during **summer, spring break,** or any other time when schools aren't in session. Cities like **Tampa** and **Orlando** have activities year-round. The oppressive humidity can make a visit in July or August a withering experience, while the cool, dry weather in the winter makes these areas much more pleasant.

Before You Go

If you're visiting Florida during the high season, December-March, it's imperative that you make **hotel reservations** as early as possible, especially in snowbird cities like Miami, Fort Lauderdale, and Naples. Not only will you be able to save money, but you also won't run the risk of not finding any place to stay. Likewise with **car rentals,** as rates tend to escalate rapidly during the winter months as availability decreases. The reverse is true in the summer, as deals abound in South Florida (especially for rental cars). If your visit is going to be focused on the **theme parks of Orlando,** room availability is always tight on the weekends and any other time school is out. Early reservations are imperative. Also, considerable **discounts** can be had on **admission tickets** to the theme parks by purchasing them online before you arrive.

International visitors will need a **passport** in order to visit Florida. The state has several major **airports** with Miami and Orlando international airports being the busiest. The smaller, regional airports might get you closer to your destination than one of the major airports, but tickets tend to be more expensive. **Rental car** companies have offices at the major airports and driving is the easiest way to get around the state.

a Snowy Egret on a Sanibel Island Beach

The Best of Florida in 14 Days

Florida is big: From the western tip of the Panhandle to the Atlantic coastal city of Jacksonville is about 360 miles, while the peninsula extends southward from the Georgia border until the state ends at the tip of Key West, nearly 500 miles away. To that end, I've broken the state's sights down into manageable sections. While most of these excursions will still require careful planning, lots of driving, and an eye on the clock, they will enable you to get a taste of some of the most unique places that Florida has to offer.

The state covers more than 65,000 square miles, so attempting to see it all at one time is not practical. If your time in the state is limited, here's a (pretty intense) itinerary that will allow you to see some of Florida's best sights in two weeks.

Days 1-2
MIAMI

Start in **Miami** and spend your daylight hours

exploring the **Design District,** the Cuban American community of **Little Havana,** and the galleries and historic sights of **Coconut Grove** and **Coral Gables.** Grab dinner at one of the many excellent restaurants at **South Beach** and spend the night partying with the beautiful people along Ocean Drive.

Once you've shaken off the night before with a *café Cubano,* hit **Miami Beach,** where the sunbathers next to you might be famous. In the afternoon and evening, walk the sidewalks of **Collins Avenue** and **Ocean Drive** to shop, eat, and gawk at the art deco buildings.

Days 3-4
THE EVERGLADES AND THE KEYS

Slather yourself in sunscreen and bug spray and head south to **Everglades National Park.** Spend the day exploring the swamps and nature trails that are accessible from the convenient

a lifeguard tower in South Beach

the beach at Bahia Honda State Park

Ernest Coe Visitor Center. When dusk falls, point your car south for a three-hour drive to Key West, where you'll be able to whoop it up in the clubs and bars of **Duval Street.**

Spend the early morning strolling the sidewalks of **Key West,** exploring the historic buildings and soaking up the tropical vibe before the sun makes the heat and humidity unbearable. After lunch, make your way about an hour north to **Bahia Honda State Park** to take in the rustic oceanfront scenery and beautiful beach area.

Days 5-6
SOUTH GULF COAST
Get up early for the three-hour drive from Miami to **Sanibel Island,** which will take you through the northern edge of the Everglades via "Alligator Alley." These are some of the most beautiful beaches in Florida. You'll want to allow yourself a relaxing day here to enjoy them completely and to explore the **J. N. "Ding" Darling National Wildlife Refuge** on the island.

From Sanibel, it's about a half hour to **Fort Myers,** where you can spend a leisurely few hours exploring the **Edison & Ford Winter Estates.**

Then hit the road again for the 90-minute drive to **Sarasota,** where you can catch an opera performance, stroll the downtown art galleries, or gawk at the gaudy architecture of circus magnate John Ringling's mansion. For fans of serious American architecture, a trip to Sarasota would be incomplete without exploring the scores of gorgeous and innovative buildings in the area, many of which were designed by a confederacy of architects known as the Sarasota School.

Days 7-8
TAMPA BAY AREA
Take a day to relax and enjoy some peaceful and natural scenery. Make for the isolated **Egmont Key State Park,** which you can only access via the town of St. Pete Beach, about an hour north of Sarasota. Excellent snorkeling that can be found just offshore of this wildlife refuge. There's a good chance that you'll wind up swimming alongside one of the pods of dolphins that frequent the area. Plan on spending the night at the gorgeous, historic, and pink **Don CeSar Beach Resort** on St. Pete Beach.

From St. Pete Beach, it's about a half hour to

St. Petersburg proper, where you should definitely take in the **Salvador Dalí Museum** and the walkable waterfront area.

Take the hour drive to **Tampa,** where you'll want to explore the historic district of **Ybor City** and enjoy its vibrant restaurant and nightlife scene.

Day 9
WALT DISNEY WORLD

Depart Tampa as early as possible and head for the **Walt Disney World Resort,** which is only about an hour to the east. Spend one day exploring the fairy-tale fantasies of the **Magic Kingdom**, the eco-minded **Animal Kingdom**, or the international food-and-drink possibilities in the **World Showcase** section of **Epcot Center.**

Days 10-11
THE PANHANDLE AND NORTH FLORIDA

Wake up early for a 90-minute drive to **Crystal River,** a small rural town on the Gulf Coast with a network of warm waterways, like the **Three Sisters Spring,** that are a favorite of manatees. Spend the morning canoeing or kayaking,

keeping an eye out for the sea cows that lumber along just beneath the surface. Afterward, buckle in for the six-hour drive to **Destin** along scenic, rural US-98. You'll arrive fairly late, so enjoy a seafood dinner and sunset.

The next morning, spend a few hours relaxing on Destin's white-sand beaches (the best in the Panhandle) before preparing for a long drive back to the eastern coast. Arrive in Tallahassee in the mid-afternoon, but before checking into your hotel and scoping out the **Florida State Capitol,** take a dip in the cool, freshwater springs at **Edward Ball Wakulla Springs State Park.** Duly relaxed, you'll be ready to take on the crowds of **Florida State University** students and government officials crowding the city's restaurants and bars.

Days 12-14
ATLANTIC COAST

Continuing east, **Daytona Beach** is about 2.5 hours away from Tallahassee. The city's legendary **Daytona 500** race kicks off the stock-car season every year. The city is the site of the racing organization's birth. Even if there's no competition

Ybor City in Tampa

Daytona International Speedway

Sure, some people want to come to Florida to relax, or to retire. Others might want to get their pulses racing with a little more activity than a day at the beach or the back nine. This quick itinerary focuses on a handful of exciting and unique attractions on **Florida's Atlantic Coast.**

DAY 1

For National Association of Stock Car Auto Racing (**NASCAR**) fans, Daytona Beach is the ultimate pilgrimage. The city's legendary **Daytona 500** race kicks off the stock-car season every year, and the city is the site of the racing organization's birth. Even if there's no race happening, the Daytona 500 Experience is an essential stop for fans of the sport, as it combines Hall of Fame tributes with racing simulations as well as the opportunity for well-heeled guests to drive a stock car on the hallowed track.

DAY 2

If the speed of a race car isn't quite fast enough for you, try the nearly 8 million pounds of thrust that propel the space shuttle into orbit at nearly 3,100 mph. At least you can get a sense of it at the **Kennedy Space Center Visitors Center**, about 90 minutes south of Daytona Beach, which offers exhibits and simulators as well as tours of the NASA facilities.

DAY 3

Instead of watching it or dreaming about it, why not get into some action yourself? Florida's mid-

Kennedy Space Center

Atlantic coast is home to some of the best surfing in the state. If you happened to have missed the innumerable billboards for **Ron Jon Surf Shop** around the state, just know that even if you show up in Cocoa Beach with no board, there's a 24-hour store here that can serve your needs. In fact, there are two 24-hour shops (the other is Cocoa Beach Surf Company), which gives you some indication as to how seriously this part of the state takes its wave-riding.

happening, visit the beach here, which is car-centric, allowing visitors to bring their automobiles onto the sand.

About an hour south of Daytona, via a scenic drive along State Road A1A, is **Merritt Island National Wildlife Refuge.** The natural surroundings here still look pretty much the same today as they did millennia ago. Explore the beautiful beaches, take a hike on the trails, or fish along Mosquito Lagoon.

If nature walks or quiet beaches aren't your speed, get a sense of the nearly eight million pounds of thrust that propel the space shuttle into orbit at the **Kennedy Space Center Visitor Complex,** which offers exhibits and simulators as well as tours of the National Aeronautics and Space Administration (NASA) facilities. Spend the night in nearby **Titusville** and enjoy the excellent food and locally brewed beer at **Playalinda Brewing.**

Spend your final day in Florida relaxing on the secluded and near-perfect beach at **Blind Creek Park,** just south of **Fort Pierce,** about a two-hour drive from Merritt Island. From there, you'll only be about two hours away from Miami International Airport, where you can catch a late flight home, exhausted and exhilarated.

Glimpses of Old Florida

Florida seems to reinvent itself on a daily basis, with bulldozers and construction cranes as much a fixture of the landscape as plastic pink flamingos and palm trees. Nonetheless, the state's history manages to persevere, much to the chagrin of developers. This five-day itinerary focuses on the state's evolution from vast natural landscapes and colonial exploration to tourist-baiting attractions.

Day 1

Any tour of Old Florida should start in **St. Augustine,** the oldest continuously inhabited city in the United States. The compact and quite walkable **Old City** is very well-preserved. St. Augustine not only gives insight into early Spanish rule in Florida, but the grounds of **Flagler College**—formerly the site of Henry Flagler's first big venture in Florida, the Ponce de Leon Hotel—are ground zero for the state's evolution as a tourist destination.

Day 2

To get a glimpse of some really old Florida, head for **Merritt Island National Wildlife Refuge,** about 90 minutes south of St. Augustine. Although the refuge serves as a security buffer for the high-tech goings-on at Kennedy Space Center, the expanses of terrain here—on the beaches, hiking trails, or many fishing spots—are undeveloped and largely unspoiled.

Flagler College in St. Augustine

the pier in Cedar Key

Day 3

From Merritt Island, visit the old-school Orlando theme park **Gatorland,** a great example of a pre-Disney take on the idea of a tourist attraction. Nearby, the quaint and beautiful city of **Winter Park** (about 30 minutes away, just north of Orlando) proudly displays its historic architecture in the form of expansive mansions and the retail shops that line its brick-paved Park Avenue.

Day 4

An hour away from Orlando, the lakeside city of **Mount Dora** is, for many people, Old Florida personified. Although the city has few actual historic sights, its rural location and charming downtown area—filled with antiques stores—evoke the wholesome pace of the state's Cracker interior, albeit with a dash of cosmopolitan flair.

Day 5

Although it's three hours away from Mount Dora and located approximately in the middle of no-where, the Gulf coastal fishing village of **Cedar Key** is a must-see for those interested in glimpsing Florida's past. The dockside shops and restaurants have a salt-worn atmosphere that reflects decades of daily service to the anglers who keep the marina area busy, while the small downtown boasts hotels and other buildings that have been in continuous operation for nearly a century.

Day 6

Ybor City, 2.5 hours south of Cedar Key, is one of the oldest neighborhoods in Tampa, and although today it's best known for its rowdy nightlife, its history as the **cigar-rolling capital of the United States** is omnipresent. Several cigar factories are still active, and the spacious brick warehouses, though excellent for nightclubs, retain their historic appearance. You can almost smell the redolent aroma of tobacco leaves emanating from the bricks. Many of the area's ethnic enclaves had roots in Ybor, but the influence of early Cuban immigrants—including one Jose Martí, who rallied for Cuban independence in the factories of Ybor—is unmistakable.

Gulf Coast Getaway

A trip to Florida would be absolutely incomplete without getting wet in **Florida's Gulf Coast.** This quick itinerary allows you to experience some of the unique water-based attractions that you can only find in the Sunshine State. There is fantastic **snorkeling** all along Florida's coastline, but if you make your home base in Tampa Bay, you'll also be able to take in some unique underwater sights like **manatees** and the **sponge divers** of **Tarpon Springs.**

Day 1

From downtown Tampa, the excellent **Caladesi Island State Park** is about 45 minutes away. In addition to beautiful and award-winning beaches, Caladesi offers calm waters that are excellent for snorkeling.

Day 2

To get to **Egmont Key State Park,** you have to take a **ferry** from Fort DeSoto Park or board a scheduled cruise from the town of St. Pete Beach. While Egmont Key's isolated nature is necessary in part due to the fact that it's a wildlife refuge, the small bit of hassle you'll have to endure is worth it for the excellent snorkeling that can be found just offshore. In addition to sighting schools of beautiful tropical fish, there's a good chance that you'll wind up swimming alongside one of the pods of dolphins that frequent the area.

Day 3

IF YOU'RE HERE DURING THE WINTER
Visit **Crystal River,** a small rural town on the Gulf coast with a network of warm waterways like the **Three Sisters Spring** that are a favorite of manatees. You can spend the morning **canoeing** and **kayaking** the area, keeping an eye out for the **sea cows** that lumber along just beneath the surface. Heading back toward Tampa, the small fishing village of **Tarpon Springs** is about an hour away. There you can be immersed

Crystal River is one of the best spots for manatee-viewing.

Best Beaches

Blind Creek Park near Fort Pierce is among the best beaches in Florida.

Between the peninsular coastlines, barrier islands, and the archipelago of the Florida Keys, you're never more than a couple of hours away from an afternoon of castle building, shell collecting, or simply whiling away worries.

- **Bahia Honda State Park** (Florida Keys): The Keys may seem to be lacking in the beach department—that is, until you hit Bahia Honda, one of the best beach areas in the state. The park offers three gorgeous beaches and snorkeling just a few hundred feet offshore.

- **Bill Baggs Cape Florida State Park** (Miami): There's a mid-19th-century lighthouse at this park. Despite the allure of historical exploration, most visitors to this Key Biscayne park head right for the calm, blue waters and mile-long beach.

- **Blind Creek Park** (Atlantic Coast): At the end of a nearly hidden driveway along State Road A1A south of Fort Pierce is a tiny parking lot for Blind Creek Park. There's a 335-foot beach here that's usually quite empty, which is surprising given the tropical blue waters and wide stretch of sand.

- **Caladesi Island State Park** (Tampa Bay): The four miles of beaches on Caladesi Island are only accessible by boat. Such limited (meaning smaller crowds) access would make it a prime beach-going spot, even if those four miles weren't some of the most beautiful and pastoral stretches of white sand you'd ever seen.

- **Canaveral National Seashore** (Atlantic Coast): There are 24 miles of undeveloped beach in this government-owned park. You can thank the security needs of NASA for the isolation. Kennedy Space Center's launchpads are visible from the southernmost beach.

- **Cayo Costa State Park** (South Gulf Coast): This beach consistently pops up on state and national "best beach" lists. The soft white sand and crystal-blue Gulf waters are a huge part of Cayo Costa's appeal. It's only accessible by boat, which nearly ensures that a day spent here is a special one indeed.

- **Fort Lauderdale Beachfront** (Atlantic Coast): With broad stretches of sand, blue-green Atlantic waters, and ample facilities, the city oceanfront understandably draws the crowds, but they don't detract from the beach's beauty.

- **Fort Myers Beach** (South Gulf Coast): Enjoy the casual and welcoming atmosphere at Fort Myers Beach, which couples large and accessible swathes of white sand and a laid-back, beach-bum vibe.

- **Grayton Beach** (Panhandle): The white-sand beaches of Florida's Panhandle are legendary—and quite popular. While there are many secluded beach access areas along north Gulf coast, the funky, artsy community of Grayton Beach—and the relaxing and comfortable vibe at Grayton Beach State Park—makes this a unique and beautiful beach destination.

- **Siesta Key** (South Gulf Coast): The curving coastline of Crescent Beach at Siesta Key is legendary for its white sand and wide and spacious stretches. It's quite popular, thanks to those expanses of sand and gentle, blue Gulf waters that are shallow and calm.

fish on a reef in South Florida

in the village's rich Greek history, which includes the legacy industry of sponge diving. At the very least you can get some really yummy spanakopita.

IF YOU'RE HERE DURING THE SUMMER
The **reefs** along **Treasure Coast** are about three hours from Tampa. There are excellent **diving** and **snorkeling** opportunities along the Treasure Coast. The expansive **Vero Beach Reef** runs from Sebastian Inlet in the north all the way to Fort Pierce Inlet. It is largely unbroken, quite close to shore, and about 0.5 mile wide. Intrepid divers can spot dozens of species of tropical fish, corals, turtles, manatees, rays, and even sharks. The best reef ledges are in the Vero Beach area, with enormous outcroppings and deep caves that provide superlative diving opportunities.

Miami

Highlights

★ **Ocean Drive:** This is the heart of South Beach, where **art deco buildings** house the hippest nightclubs. This part of town is as beautiful during the day as it is decadent at night (page 36).

★ **Pérez Art Museum Miami:** A robust and forward-looking collection that's housed in a gorgeous building has given Miami its first truly world-class museum (page 40).

★ **Design District:** One of Miami's oldest neighborhoods is also one of Miami's premier spots for contemporary art and furnishings. This is a historic and artistic alternative to South Beach (page 43).

★ **Little Havana:** Little Havana is the heart of the U.S. Cuban American community (page 44).

★ **Vizcaya Museum and Gardens:** The 34-room Gilded Age mansion and its 10 acres of botanical gardens have long been an icon of Miami's historical opulence (page 47).

★ **Coral Castle:** This half-acre castle was crafted by hand from local materials as an homage to true romance (page 49).

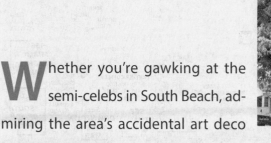

Whether you're gawking at the semi-celebs in South Beach, admiring the area's accidental art deco heritage, digging into some *ropa vieja* in Little Havana, or relaxing on some of the nation's best beaches, Miami offers a vacation that's as tropical as it is urbane.

Between cop shows and glossy magazines, the concept of contemporary Miami has been all but reinvented over the past couple of decades. The southernmost American city is no longer thought of as "God's waiting room," and instead it's now on par with Los Angeles and New York City as one of the country's most exciting, cosmopolitan, and fashion-forward metropolises.

Unlike Manhattan or Hollywood, though, Miami earned its star status somewhat quickly, managing to forge a much stronger and rawer personality, steeped in Latin American culture and Old Florida languor. Although the area's nouveau-riche tendencies show through in its sprawling rapid development and trend-chasing attitude, what makes Miami great today is what's always made it great: near-perfect weather, a hodgepodge of global influences, and a sense that it's possible to do anything here as long as you're a big dreamer and a smooth talker.

As a result, Miami manages to combine fast-paced luxury with old-school Florida style. So, yes, you can certainly indulge in a vacation here that's filled with nothing but $25 cocktails, velvet-rope parties, and platinum-card-straining shopping sprees. But you can just as easily spend your time admiring the offerings of top-notch galleries and museums, exploring the multiple cultural and ethnic enclaves throughout the area, soaking up rays on the beach, or wandering through peaceful low-key neighborhoods like Coral Gables and Coconut Grove, which are flecked with gorgeous architecture and hidden historic treasures.

PLANNING YOUR TIME

You can easily get your fill of South Beach and Miami Beach in a day, but an extended

---

Previous: The Miami River flows through the heart of downtown; colorful Miami Beach. **Above:** the Bay of Pigs memorial in Little Havana.

Miami

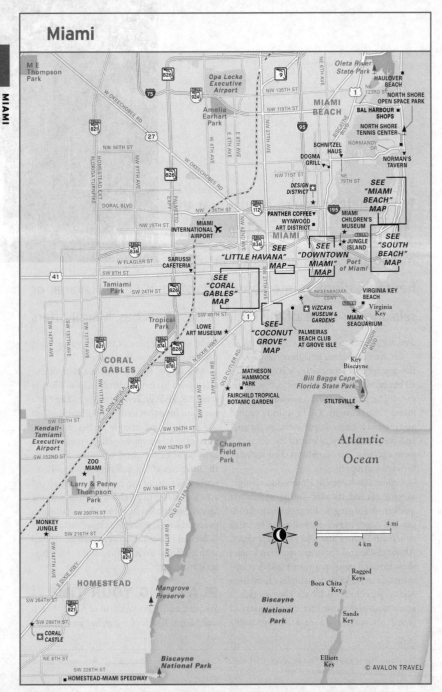

Two Days in Miami

Though it's tough to pack in a good sampling of everything that Miami has to offer in just two days, it's definitely possible to get a feel for the variety of the city.

DAY 1

You should definitely stay in South Beach. If you're on a budget, the stylish hostel-but-not-a-hostel vibe at **Freehand** is an excellent and quite convenient option just outside of South Beach proper. For a more purely indulgent South Beach experience, book a suite at the **Setai.**

Spend your first morning snapping photos of the beautiful art deco buildings along Ocean Drive and soak up some rays on the beach at **Lummus Park.** Dedicate an hour or so to the great organic and local brunch fare at **Essensia,** then head to the mainland to walk around **Little Havana,** grabbing a *café Cubano* and a pastry at **Versailles.**

Hopefully by now you've worked up enough of an appetite to dig into the modern soul food on offer at **Yardbird Southern Table & Bar,** because you're going to need to load up before you indulge in South Beach's legendary nightlife at clubs like **Astor Social Club** or a live venue like the **Fillmore Miami Beach.**

DAY 2

Drive the hour or so south to Homestead to walk around the magnificently weird **Coral Castle.** After you've witnessed the bizarre, romantic majesty there, head back to **Wynwood** to browse the art galleries and boutiques. Make sure to refuel at **Panther Coffee** and then head over to the **Design District** to window-shop for budget-busting decor.

Hit Coral Gables for an excellent dinner at **Ortanique** and a theater show on the Miracle Mile.

weekend in the area will allow you to soak up the art deco architecture, explore the museums and shopping opportunities, hit a few stylish nightclubs, and sleep it all off on the beach. Devote one day to the beach areas and another to the sights of downtown Miami and Little Havana for a concise sampler of what Miami is all about. For a long four-day weekend, tack on a day to explore the sights south of Miami and another for shopping and strolling around Coconut Grove and Coral Gables. A week in Miami is really the minimum needed to get a true taste of the city and its peculiar blend of go-go mobility and tropical languor.

ORIENTATION

Miami-Dade County is a sprawling metropolis, but it is fairly easy to navigate. The municipalities of Miami, Coral Gables, and Coconut Grove are on the mainland, while the city of Miami Beach is on the other side of Biscayne Bay.

The barrier island of Miami Beach—the "billion-dollar sandbar"—is punctuated at its southern tip by South Beach, a semiofficial designation of the area south of Dade Boulevard. Everything north of that part is generally referred to as North Beach or plain old Miami Beach.

Downtown Miami hugs Biscayne Bay along north-south Biscayne Boulevard, and the 10 or so blocks south of 1st Street are generally seen as the main business district. Continuing a few miles along the shores of Biscayne Bay to the southwest is Coconut Grove.

Little Havana is almost due west from downtown along 8th Street, and Coral Gables is slightly southwest of Little Havana. SW 57th Avenue is generally seen as the westernmost border of central Miami. The town of Homestead is approximately 20 miles southsouthwest of central Miami via US-1.

Central Miami—including Little Havana, Coconut Grove, and downtown—is possessed of a remarkably straightforward grid layout. With a midpoint at the intersection of north-south Miami Avenue and east-west Flagler Street, all streets are numerically named, so if you're in the 1100 block of NW 33rd Avenue, you're 10 blocks north of Flagler Street and 33 blocks west of Miami Avenue. This naming system does not extend to Coral Gables.

Sights

SOUTH BEACH

South Beach, or SoBe, has become shorthand for "stylish." While the style referred to involves shimmery and sheer clothing and lots of chrome and glass, the fact is that South Beach is one of the hottest international vacation destinations, drawing celebrities from New York, Hollywood, Europe, and Latin America for tropical bacchanalia that are impossibly glamorous and ineffably decadent. Every casual visitor to SoBe tries to rub off a little of that magic, and, in terms of sheer numbers, tourists outnumber the fashionistas on almost any day of the week. As a result, during the peak winter season, parking in South Beach is a nightmare, getting a reservation at a hot restaurant is almost impossible, and hotel rates are extremely high.

Even during the summer—theoretically the slow season—finding a comfortable spot at the large beach area is a daunting task. And parking is still a challenge. To avoid dealing with parking, rent a bike from the city's public bike-rental program, **DecoBike** (305/532-9494, www.decobike.com, from $4/half hour), which has automated pickup/drop-off kiosks throughout Miami Beach. A free iPhone app makes the process even easier.

★ Ocean Drive

The vintage cars parked along **Ocean Drive** complement the beautiful **art deco buildings** of the area, the crown jewel of Florida's architecture, and were you anywhere but South Beach, the effect would be a bit of historical charm. The crush of tourists and celebrity-spotters that descend on the area during the day are replaced at night by stylish

Ocean Drive in South Beach

South Beach

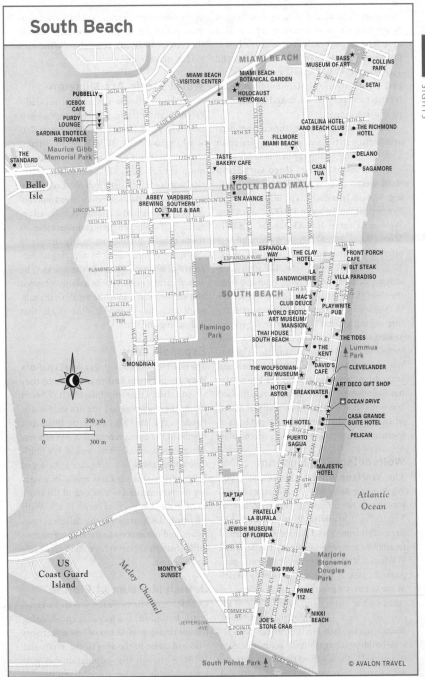

MIAMI BEACH

BASS MUSEUM OF ART ★

■ COLLINS PARK

● SETAI

MIAMI BEACH VISITOR CENTER

MIAMI BEACH BOTANICAL GARDEN

★ HOLOCAUST MEMORIAL

PUBBELLY ▼
ICEBOX CAFE ▼
PURDY LOUNGE ▼
SARDINIA ENOTECA RISTORANTE ▼

CATALINA HOTEL AND BEACH CLUB ●   ■ THE RICHMOND HOTEL

FILLMORE MIAMI BEACH ▼

● DELANO

● SAGAMORE

THE STANDARD ●

Maurice Gibb Memorial Park

VENETIAN WAY

Belle Isle

TASTE BAKERY CAFE ▼

CASA TUA ▼

SPRIS ▼

LINCOLN ROAD MALL

ABBEY YARDBIRD BREWING SOUTHERN CO. TABLE & BAR ▼▼

EN AVANCE ▼

ESPANOLA WAY ★

THE CLAY HOTEL

▼ FRONT PORCH CAFE
▼ BLT STEAK
▼ VILLA PARADISO

LA SANDWICHERIE ▼

SOUTH BEACH

MAC'S CLUB DEUCE ▼

PLAYWRITE PUB ▼

WORLD EROTIC ART MUSEUM/ MANSION ★

Flamingo Park

THAI HOUSE SOUTH BEACH ▼

THE TIDES ▼

● THE KENT

Lummus Park

● MONDRIAN

THE WOLFSONIAN-FIU MUSEUM ★

DAVID'S CAFE ▼

— CLEVELANDER

HOTEL ASTOR ●

BREAKWATER ▼

ART DECO GIFT SHOP

✚ OCEAN DRIVE

THE HOTEL ●

CASA GRANDE SUITE HOTEL ●

PELICAN —

PUERTO SAGUA ▼

MAJESTIC HOTEL ●

Atlantic Ocean

TAP TAP ▼

FRATELLI LA BUFALA ▼

JEWISH MUSEUM OF FLORIDA ★

US Coast Guard Island

Meloy Channel

MONTY'S SUNSET ▼

BIG PINK ▼

Marjorie Stoneman Douglas Park

PRIME 112 ▼

NIKKI BEACH ▼

COMMERCE ST
JOE'S STONE CRAB ▼

South Pointe Park ⚑

© AVALON TRAVEL

0   300 yds
0   300 m

club-goers and action seekers, resulting in South Beach's most dynamic yet crowded area. The actual beach of South Beach is at **Lummus Park** (Ocean Dr. between 5th and 15th Sts., 305/673-7730, www.miamibeachfl. gov). Despite its size, the Lummus Park beach is often incredibly crowded, and it is great for people watching.

To truly appreciate the stunning art deco architecture in the area while also getting an understanding of the lay of the land, start your journey at the **Art Deco Gift Shop** (1001 Ocean Dr., 305/531-3484, www.mpdl. org, 9:30am-7pm daily). The **Miami Design Preservation League** (MDPL, Art Deco Welcome Center, 1001 Ocean Dr., 2nd Fl., Miami Beach, 305/672-2014, www.mdpl.org) offers a **walking tour** (10:30am Fri.-Wed., 10:30am and 6:30pm Thurs., $25 adults, $20 seniors, students, and military veterans) from the shop that points out and contextualizes the numerous examples of art deco architecture on and around Ocean Drive. There are guided and non-guided tours, as well as bike tours and even cell phone tours, too. The stories of how these 1930s icons were rescued from dilapidation and decay are legendary, but the effect of seeing so many refurbished treasures in one place—especially at night, when many of them are lit with clean lines of green, pink, and purple neon—is spectacular.

Wolfsonian-FIU Museum

The **Wolfsonian-FIU Museum** (1001 Washington Ave., 305/531-1001, http://wolf-sonian.org, noon-6pm Sat.-Tues., noon-9pm Thurs.-Fri., $10 adults, $5 seniors and children, children 5 and under free) opened in 1992 as a means to display the Mitchell Wolfson Jr. collection of decorative and propaganda arts. It has since grown to be one of the country's preeminent institutions focused on the history and cultural role of industrial design. The imposing, seven-story, 56,000-square-foot Mediterranean revival-style building is huge, but the actual museum is confined to the top three floors. Visitors can see a variety of materials from the arts and

crafts movement, examples of Italian art nouveau, political propaganda, and other objects that reflect Wolfson's belief that "What man makes, makes man."

World Erotic Art Museum

Near the Wolfsonian is a museum dedicated to an entirely different sort of artistry. The **World Erotic Art Museum** (1205 Washington Ave., 305/532-9336, http:// weam.com, 11am-10pm Mon.-Thurs., 11am-midnight Fri.-Sun., $15) documents centuries' worth of erotic art, from pre-Columbian sculptures and classical nudes to examples of pop-culture sexuality. The museum is well organized, if a bit cramped, and is notable for the fact that it doesn't continually attempt to apologize for its contents by applying unnecessary academic context to the works. The owner-curators clearly have a sense of humor and an eye for art, so while much in the museum is tasteful—if graphic—there's a lot that is shocking and witty.

Española Way

The peach-colored buildings along **Española Way** are beautiful and charming, but they weren't always that way. Like much of South Beach, the neighborhood was in a state of disrepair in the late 1970s and early 1980s. But thanks to the entrepreneurial vision of a few daring souls—and, some would say, multiple appearances as settings for episodes of Miami Vice—the area has made an amazing turnaround and is now one of the more comfortably hip parts of South Beach. With a friendly, inclusive vibe, the galleries, boutiques, and restaurants in the area maintain a funky, historical atmosphere that's accessible and relaxing.

Jewish Museum of Florida

Decades ago, Miami Beach was nicknamed "Little Jerusalem" as a way of acknowledging the enormous population of Jewish retirees who had come to the area in the 1960s and 1970s. Although that population has gotten noticeably smaller since Miami Beach's

Miami Beach

© AVALON TRAVEL

star-powered revival in the 1980s and 1990s, the influence of the Jewish community on the greater Miami area is still quite strong. Part of Florida International University, the **Jewish Museum of Florida** (301 Washington Ave., 305/672-5044, http://jewishmuseum.com, 10am-5pm Tues.-Sun., $12 families, $6 adults, $5 seniors and students, children 5 and under free) documents not only the history of Jews in Miami but also throughout the state, from early settlements in the Panhandle and Key West up to today, when the Miami metro area represents the single largest per capita concentration of Jews outside of Israel. The main exhibit is *Mosaic: Jewish Life in Florida*, a well-organized and informative collection of more than 500 artifacts, photos, articles of clothing, and religious implements. There are also occasional traveling exhibits on display.

MIAMI BEACH

If South Beach is your glamorous high school crush all decked out in next year's hot fashions and partying until breakfast, **Miami Beach** is your grandparents. The high-rise condos along the beach house battalions of retirees, and although the area is home to plenty of high-dollar apartment towers catering to young professionals, the difference between this quiet and slightly worn-looking area and the vibrant environment of South Beach couldn't be starker. As a result, it can also be somewhat more enjoyable. The beaches are far more accessible and often quite a bit less crowded (though never ever empty), and there are pockets of hipness with excellent friendly shops and restaurants.

Miami Beach Botanical Garden

Despite its small size, the five-acre **Miami**

Beach Botanical Garden (2000 Convention Center Dr., 305/673-7256, www.mbgarden. org, 9am-5pm Tues.-Sun., free) is a quiet pastoral reprieve from the buzz of Miami Beach, with several distinct horticultural areas dedicated to banyans, palms, vines, bromeliads, and other tropical plants native to South Florida. The small Japanese garden is beautiful, meditative, and infused with a little bit of Miami Beach hipness.

Holocaust Memorial

The **Holocaust Memorial** (1933 Meridian Ave., 305/538-1663, www.holocaustmemorialmiamibeach.org, 9am-9pm daily, free) is, appropriately, a pensive and elegiac place. The centerpiece is a 42-foot bronze sculpture of an arm extending skyward from the ground; the arm is surrounded by scores of vivid sculptures of people, some climbing the arm, others lying around the ground of the plaza surrounding the primary sculpture. The work, designed by Kenneth Treister, is intense and captivating. To view the sculpture, you pass by a black granite wall that retells the atrocities of the Holocaust, and then walk through an enclosed passage constructed of Jerusalem stone to view the sculpture. Another black granite wall on the opposite side is engraved with the names of Holocaust victims.

DOWNTOWN MIAMI

The actual "downtown" part of Miami may not seem worth your attention unless you're in town to make a deal. The enormous skyscrapers and apartment buildings are all business, and with the exception of the Jewelry District, there's not much to see for the casual traveler. However, the addition of the Pérez Museum of Art has breathed some new life into the area, and just outside of the downtown core is the famous Design District, filled with galleries and decor boutiques.

★ Pérez Art Museum Miami

The **Pérez Art Museum Miami** (PAMM, 101 W. Flagler St., 305/373-5000, www.pamm.org, 10am-6pm Tues.-Wed. and Fri.-Sun., 10am-9pm Thurs., $12 adults, $8 children, students, and seniors, military and children under 7 free) is, technically, a new museum, having opened in its current downtown location in December 2013. However, the PAMM has a history that dates back to the 1980s, when the Miami-Dade Cultural Center was opened on Flagler Street and began hosting high-profile traveling art exhibits. In the mid-1990s,

the Pérez Art Museum Miami

Downtown Miami

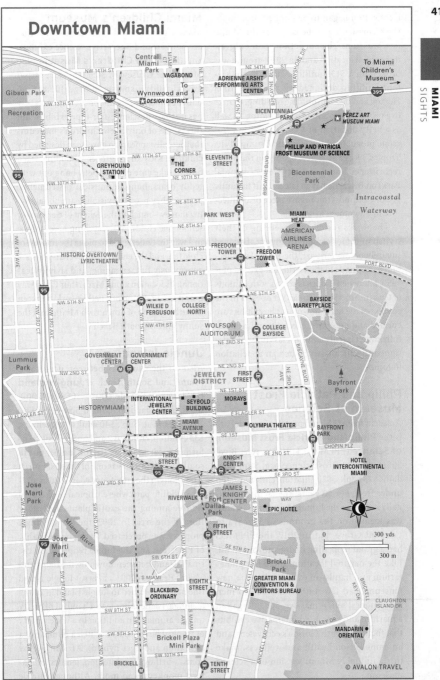

© AVALON TRAVEL

a collection began to be curated, leading to the rechristening of the center as the Miami Art Museum. The collection soon outgrew its original location and, in 2010, ground was broken on a $131-million, 200,000-square-foot building designed by the Swiss firm Herzog and de Meuron. The building, thanks to a mix of public and private funding, as well as a hefty donation of $35 million from real estate mogul (and the "Donald Trump of the Tropics") Jorge M. Pérez, opened in the newly rechristened Museum Park (née Bicentennial Park) on Biscayne Bay in late 2013. It instantly became the most impressive piece of architecture in downtown Miami.

The works inside are deserving of their stylish and modern environment. Focused squarely on modern art, the PAMM's collection barely nods to the world that existed pre-1950, and when it does (such as with exhibits of Cuban American classics), it does so in the context of the here-and-now. The exhibits are curated and presented carefully and respectfully, and it is truly a world-class museum, designed specifically with such an appellation in mind.

Philip and Patricia Frost Museum of Science

Adjacent to PAMM and part of Museum Park is the **Philip and Patricia Frost Museum of Science** (PPFMOS, 1101 Biscayne Blvd, 305/434-9600, frostscience.org, 9am-6pm daily, $28 adults, $20 children, children 2 and under free). For 50 years, the facility (originally known as the Junior Museum of Miami) was located on the grounds of Vizcaya in Coconut Grove, but in 2017, the PPFMOS had a grand reopening in downtown Miami. Like the original location, there is a planetarium and hands-on exhibits, but the new museum bears few similarities to its former, more modest self. A massive, 500,000-gallon aquarium and expanded interactive exhibits that focus on South Florida's ecosystem, and an emphasis on health and wellness, make this a uniquely Miami version of a science museum.

Miami Children's Museum

Many cities have kid-centric museums that are built around interactive science exhibits, and the **Miami Children's Museum** (980 Macarthur Causeway, 305/373-5437, http://miamichildrensmuseum.org, 10am-6pm daily, $20, children under 1 free) certainly has its share of science-fair-type exhibits. But this is one of only a few children's museums that actually appears to have been designed by children. Kids can go grocery shopping, learn how to take care of their pets, hang out with teddy bears, bang on musical instruments, pretend they're on television, learn about saving money—much to the delight of elementary school-age children. Everything here is done in a way that's designed to pique the interest of children, and the child's-eye-level displays are enormously fun, engaging, and slyly educational. Its location along Macarthur Causeway puts it in something of a netherworld between the urban throb of downtown Miami and the sunny glitz of South Beach.

Jungle Island

Also on the causeway between downtown Miami and South Beach is **Jungle Island** (1111 Parrot Jungle Trail, 305/400-7000, www.jungleisland.com, 10am-5pm Mon.-Fri., 10am-6pm Sat.-Sun., $40 adults, $38 seniors, $33 children, children 2 and under free). In its former incarnation as Parrot Jungle, out in southeast Miami, it was one of the first tourist attractions in the area, founded in 1936 as a 22-acre wildlife park where tropical birds could fly free among the exotic plants and other flora of the area. In 2002, the Parrot Jungle property was purchased by the municipality of Pinecrest, and the Jungle reopened on the small island between downtown Miami and Miami Beach in 2003 as Parrot Jungle Island (the name shortened to Jungle Island in 2007).

Jungle Island is home to a handful of pretty unique animals. In addition to a wide variety of tropical birds, you can catch a glimpse of a liger (lion and tiger hybrid), African pygmy goats, warthogs, a white lion, lemurs, alligators, monkeys, and more. Although Jungle

Island doesn't have the same Old Florida charm as Parrot Jungle, the daily "Winged Wonders" show and the unique interactive animal experiences (available for an additional fee) provide a unique opportunity for visitors who want to spend a half day looking at animals without driving all the way out to the Miami Zoo.

Freedom Tower

The **Freedom Tower** (600 Biscayne Blvd.) was built in 1925 as the home of the Miami Daily News and commandeered by the United States government in the 1970s for use as a processing center for the thousands of Cuban refugees who came to Miami after Fidel Castro took over. It was here that many of these refugees were given basic medical and dental care, put in touch with family members who had already immigrated, and given relief aid as they started their new life in the United States. The processing center was closed in the mid-1970s and fell into considerable disrepair in the ensuing decades. A recent effort by Miami's Cuban-American community—spearheaded by a $4.1 million investment by noted anti-Castro activist Jorge Mas Canosa—has taken great steps not just to renovate it but to restore it to its former glory. The building

was designated a National Historic Landmark in October 2008, and it is currently owned by Miami-Dade College, housing an art gallery, museum, library, and the offices of the Mas Canosa-founded Cuban-American National Foundation.

★ Design District

In 1921, pineapple plantation owner T. V. "The Pineapple King" Moore opened a large furniture store on NE 40th Street meant to provide furnishings for his farm workers who resided in the Buena Vista area. From that furniture store, the Buena Vista neighborhood soon became the part of Miami where residents went to buy their home decor from any of the dozens of businesses that had popped up in the area. This was the first incarnation of the **Design District** (NE 36th St. to NE 42nd St. between NE 2nd Ave. and N. Miami Ave., 305/722-7100, www.miami-designdistrict.net), which, like much of Miami, fell on incredibly hard times in the late 1970s and early 1980s. However, the efforts of visionary developers like Craig Robins—inspired by what had taken place in South Beach—transformed the area from a dilapidated warehouse district into a locus of contemporary decor and art that's as

Miami's Design District

Little Havana

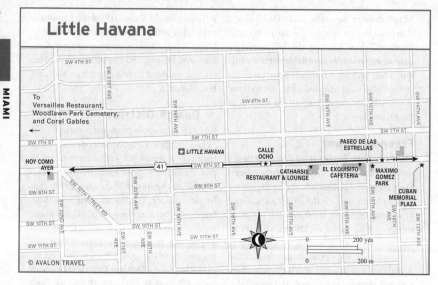

To
Versailles Restaurant,
Woodlawn Park Cemetery,
and Coral Gables

© AVALON TRAVEL

recognized for its retail offerings as it is for its historic flavor. The shops are pricey, and many of them sell items and services that are intended for living spaces rather than carry-on souvenir bags. But even if you only take home inspiration about how to rethink your own domicile, a visit to the district will have been more than worth your while.

TOP EXPERIENCE

★ LITTLE HAVANA

At first, this area was known as the Shenandoah and Riverside neighborhoods and offered inexpensive housing and a bit of a blank slate for exiles and refugees to start new lives. As more and more Cubans immigrated to Miami, the area began to take on a more definitive identity. Some observers have gone as far as to say that walking along Little Havana's Calle Ocho is a reasonable facsimile for a stroll through the Cuban capital, but nobody's going to mistake the low-slung mid-20th-century buildings here for the crumbling majesty of Habana Vieja anytime soon. Still, what Little Havana lacks in architectural beauty, it more than makes up for in its vibrant sense of community.

Calle Ocho

The heart of Little Havana is **Calle Ocho,** the 23-block-long stretch of SW 8th Street that serves as Main Street for Miami's Cuban community. For a day-tripper, that may be something of an esoteric thing to take in, but that doesn't stop the busloads of tourists from trying as they unload at **Maximo Gomez Park** (801 SW 15th Ave. at Calle Ocho) to watch the old-timers playing dominoes.

There are very few sights along Calle Ocho (or in Little Havana, for that matter), but the **Cuban Memorial Plaza** (Calle Ocho at 13th Ave.) is beautiful and poignant, with four blocks of various monuments to fallen heroes of Cuban history, as well as the **Paseo de las Estrellas** (Calle Ocho between 14th and 16th Aves.), a "walk of the stars" honoring the successes of famous Cuban actors, musicians, artists, and writers. Despite the lack of attractions, a great way to spend your time in Little Havana is to simply park your car and take a half day to wander up and down Calle Ocho, stopping into places like the dozen or so cigar shops that line the street. The one thing you'll quickly realize is that Calle Ocho—and, more generally, Little Havana—is not a tourist-ready trapped-in-amber re-creation of a mystical Cuban homeland, but a busy communal neighborhood filled with folks shopping, running errands, and living their lives.

Woodlawn Park Cemetery

As mentioned, Little Havana is a neighborhood filled with people going about their daily business, so it goes without saying that a visit to the **Woodlawn Park Cemetery** (3260 SW 8th St., 305/445-9508, www.caballerorivero-woodlawn.com, 8am-sunset daily) should be undertaken respectfully. Still, history buffs will find much to appreciate, from the Gothic statuary and numerous beautiful grave markers to the final resting places of three former presidents of Cuba, other Cuban notables such as Antonio Prohias (creator of the *Spy vs. Spy* comics), and the touching Unknown Cuban Freedom Fighter Memorial.

CORAL GABLES

As you drive along 22nd Street from the southern edge of Little Havana, the canopy of banyan trees hanging over the street becomes a little thicker. Eventually the street changes names, first to Coral Way and then, after you cross SW 37th Avenue, to the famous **Miracle Mile,** Coral Gables's historic and upscale shopping district. Although the Mile isn't the only thing to see in **Coral Gables,** the atmosphere it projects as a moneyed oasis in the heart of rough-and-tumble Miami is quite appropriate. In addition to the Mile, make sure to explore the neighborhood that houses the Venetian Pool and the Biltmore Hotel.

Venetian Pool

Situated in the heart of a residential neighborhood near the historic Biltmore Hotel is the **Venetian Pool** (2701 DeSoto Blvd., 305/460-5306, www.coralgables.com, hours vary, but generally 11am-6:30pm Mon.-Fri., 10am-4:30pm Sat.-Sun., $15 adults, $10 children Mar.-May and Sept.-Nov., $20 adults, $15 children June-Labor Day, children under 3 not admitted). Carved out of an abandoned limestone quarry in the 1920s, the pool is fed by a freshwater aquifer that pumps more than 820,000 gallons of spring water into it every day; at night, the pool is drained in an environmentally friendly manner, allowing it to be refilled with clean water daily. While the pool itself is a beautiful thing, the ornate observation towers and lush tropical foliage of the surrounding grounds make for a sublimely transporting experience for nonswimmers. Make sure to check out the beautiful **De Soto Fountain,** just on the other side of the

Coral Gables's Venetian Pool

Coral Gables

© AVALON TRAVEL

main parking lot of the Venetian Pool, but don't jump in!

Lowe Art Museum

The deceptively small **Lowe Art Museum** (1301 Stanford Dr., 305/284-3535, www. lowemuseum.org, 10am-4pm Tues.-Sat., noon-4pm Sun., $12.50 adults, $8 children and seniors, children under 12 free) is located on the campus of the University of Miami and houses a surprisingly large

and diverse permanent collection of more than 15,000 works ranging from Greco-Roman antiquities and classical European art to impressive photography exhibits and well-curated exhibits focusing on African, Asian, Latin American, and South Pacific art. Although the exhibit space isn't quite as large as some other Florida museums, the well-organized museum has considerable depth, seeming to prefer to expend its energies on procurement and organization

Coconut Grove

rather than dedicating hundreds of square feet to single pieces of art.

COCONUT GROVE

Home to one of Miami's most iconic locations—the elegant and expansive Vizcaya Museum and Gardens—Coconut Grove has long been one of the city's most desirable neighborhoods. Although some parts have a feel of upscale mediocrity (especially the CocoWalk area), other parts, like **Billy Rolle Domino Park** (Elizabeth St. and Grand Ave.), evince the strong influence of the Bahamian community that is so vibrant here. This combination, along with the tropical foliage, historic architecture, and bayside charm of the area make Coconut Grove a neighborhood that is both unique to Miami as well as uniquely Miami.

The Barnacle
Historic State Park

It's easy to be convinced that Miami's history only reaches back as far as the art deco

buildings of South Beach, but the mansion at the heart of **The Barnacle Historic State Park** (3485 Main Hwy., 305/442-6866, www. floridastateparks.org, 9am-5pm Wed.-Mon., $2) provides a different sort of perspective on the area's growth. Built in 1891 by yacht builder Ralph Munroe as one of the first homes in the Coconut Grove area, the house is highly unique, crafted from timber collected from wrecked sea vessels and designed in a way that can only be described as "whimsical." Opening out onto Biscayne Bay, the grounds are equally gorgeous, spreading out over five acres of hardwood hammocks and sea breezes. There are guided tours of the property Friday-Monday at 10am, 11:30am, 1pm, and 2:30pm.

★ Vizcaya Museum
and Gardens

Designed by Beaux-Arts-trained painter Paul Chaflin as a winter residence for early Miami developer James Deering, the 1916 estate at **Vizcaya Museum and Gardens** (3251 S. Miami Ave., 305/285-9133, http://

vizcayamuseum.org, 9:30am-4:30pm daily, $18 adults, $12 seniors, $10 students, $6 children 6-12, children 5 and under free) is one of the Miami area's most beautiful sights. Deering himself lived here for a little less than a decade. But the house, known as Villa Vizcaya, has all the elegance and opulence of a Gilded Age masterpiece, with 34 rooms decorated in various sumptuous European antiques that reflect the mishmash of Mediterranean revival and Italian Renaissance revival architecture that Chaflin employed in the house's construction. The 10 acres of formal botanical gardens are decorated with antique statuary shrouded by dense tropical foliage, making for something of a mysterious walk-through experience.

Fairchild Tropical Botanic Garden

When international horticulturist and "plant explorer" David Fairchild retired to Miami in the mid-1930s, he had amassed a lifetime's worth of knowledge on rare and exotic plants from around the world. That knowledge and some of his samples went into the creation of the **Fairchild Tropical Botanic Garden** (10901 Old Cutler Rd., 305/667-1651, www.fairchildgarden.org, garden 7:30am-4:30pm daily; conservatory and science village complex 9:30am-4:30pm daily, $25 adults, $18 seniors, $12 children, children 5 and under free). The facility has grown considerably since it first opened in the late 1930s, adding auditoriums, an educational "science village," and several labs and greenhouses along the way. Today, it's a preeminent destination for plant lovers and is one of the best botanical gardens in a state filled with botanical gardens. More than 4,000 plants are on display throughout its 83 acres, including palms, orchids, and bromeliads, as well as more exotic species like rare Asian fruit trees, all of which are well-maintained and informatively marked. Visitors in a hurry should avail themselves of the 45-minute guided tram tour. But the best way to take in these beautiful gardens is to devote half a day to lazily wandering the grounds.

KEY BISCAYNE

Key Biscayne is a 14-square-mile island that's just a few minutes from downtown Miami via the Rickenbacker Causeway. The relaxed outdoors vibe is a marked contrast to the glitzy pulse of South Beach and the all-business tone of central Miami. Most visitors head straight for one of the beaches or the activities at the **Bill Baggs Cape Florida State Park** (1200 S. Crandon Blvd., www.floridastateparks.org, 8am-sunset daily, $8/carload or $4/single-occupant vehicle), but there are a couple of other notable sights here as well.

Miami Seaquarium

The small and somewhat worn **Miami Seaquarium** (4400 Rickenbacker Causeway, 305/361-5705, http://miamiseaquarium.org, 9:30am-6pm daily, $40 adults, $30 children, children 2 and under free) was one of the first big attractions in Miami. But it's beginning to show the cracks and creaks of its 50-year history. Still, the park is compact enough to visit in half a day, allowing visitors to peek into the half-dozen animal exhibits or take in one of the four trained-sea-mammal shows. Additionally, the park's Dolphin Harbor area offers small-group dolphin-interaction experiences starting at $139.

Stiltsville

If you look out into the water at the southern tip of Key Biscayne, you're likely to see the unusual sight of seven houses situated in the middle of Biscayne Bay. Those houses are all that remains of **Stiltsville,** which began with the construction of a fishing shack in the 1920s. Soon after, other buildings, like the Calvert Club and Party Central, were built as a way for moneyed Miamians to escape the hustle and bustle of city life and many of the pesky vice laws that were less easily enforced several yards away from land. The houses of Stiltsville have figured prominently in Miami's underground lore (Carl Hiaasen wrote of activities there in three of his books). Today most of the old social clubs are gone, and the remaining Stiltsville houses have barely escaped being demolished by the National Park Service, which, in an odd turn, now owns and maintains them.

SOUTH OF MIAMI
Monkey Jungle

You really have to love a place with a slogan like "Where humans are caged and monkeys run wild." For decades, **Monkey Jungle** (14805 SW 216th St., 305/235-1611, www.monkeyjungle.com, 9:30am-5pm daily, $29.95 adults, $23.95 children, children 2 and under free) has made it clear where its priorities lie when it comes to choosing between the needs of visitors and the needs of the hundreds of primates who freely roam this 30-acre reserve. There are more than 30 species of primates at this family-owned operation, and although they're not all always visible, visitors are certainly assured of seeing most of them, including Java monkeys, tamarins, spider monkeys, and gibbons. Kids love being able to feed the monkeys (food boxes are available for purchase), and the shows are entertaining if not the most informative. Many of the areas inside the park are unshaded, so it's best to visit early in the morning.

Zoo Miami

A more traditional zoological experience can be had at **Zoo Miami** (12400 SW 152nd St, 305/251-0400, www.miamimetrozoo.com, 9:30am-5:30pm daily, $21.95 adults, $17.95 children, children 2 and under free), a 740-acre facility that is quite exceptional. It's the only tropical zoo in the United States, and is focused primarily on tropical animals from Asia, Africa, South America, and Australia. Most of the creatures here are likely to be familiar—giraffes, kangaroos, rhinoceroses, lions, tigers, elephants—but there are many unique mammals as well, such as okapis, tapirs, a New Guinean singing dog, and a Visayan warty pig. The birds here are also amazing, thanks to the tropical tilt of the zoo's curation, with colorful toucans, cuckoos, flamingos, storks, and more. With 300-plus visitor accessible acres, this park is massive (it was built on a former Naval Air Station). Thankfully, in addition to a three-mile-long walking path that gets you into the heart of the exhibits, there's also an elevated monorail to quickly get visitors from one area of the park to another, with stunning views of the animals below. If you're an animal lover, the zoo is definitely worth the half-hour voyage from central Miami.

★ Coral Castle

India has the Taj Mahal, Miami has the **Coral**

Coral Castle boasts unique structures and a unique history.

Castle (28655 S. Dixie Hwy., Homestead, 305/248-6345, www.coralcastle.com, 8am-6pm Sun.-Thurs., 8am-9pm Fri.-Sat., $15 adults, $12 seniors, $7 children, children 6 and under free). Built as an homage to a lost love, this highly unique architectural oddity is probably one of my favorite places in all of Miami, although not everyone may appreciate the bizarre romantic beauty of the place. While Latvian immigrant Ed Leedskalnin didn't have the armies of laborers and acres of marble that Shah Jahan was able to utilize in the construction of the Taj Mahal, the love-lorn creator of the Coral Castle did have access to 1,100 tons of coral and a friend with a tractor. Somehow, the tubercular, five-foot, 100-pound Leedskalnin managed to construct this enormous assemblage of coral-stone buildings and sculptures all by himself, often in the middle of the night, and the final product is remarkable indeed.

Visitors are free to wander the three-acre site. Although you can take in the structures in as little as 30 minutes, the unique nature of Coral Castle invites a much more leisurely exploration. For first-time visitors, a guided tour (which lasts about an hour and is free) is strongly recommended. As the carving at the entrance gate proclaims, "You will be seeing unusual accomplishment."

Beaches

SOUTH BEACH

When people talk about going to the beach at South Beach, they're most likely talking about heading to **Lummus Park** (Ocean Dr. between 5th St. and 15th St., 305/673-7730, www.miamibeachfl.gov). The beach is long and wide, with crystal-blue waters gently lapping the soft white sands. And those sands are often packed—packed—with people. With the nexus of South Beach's dining and nightlife just a few steps away, the beach is crowded both day and night, and for those looking for an overload of people watching, this is definitely the beach to go to.

Seekers of quietude would likely be better served heading for **South Pointe Park** (1 Washington Ave.), which, due to numerous rocky outcroppings and some incredibly rough waters kicked up by the combination of tides and passing cruise ships, is often pretty deserted. It's a scenic beach that's much better for picnics and relaxing than it is for swimming and sunbathing, although the waves often lure surfers into tempting fate among the rocks.

NORTH MIAMI BEACH

Families will generally find more appropriate beaches north of South Beach. Areas like **Indian Beach Park** (4601 Collins Ave.) and **Collins Park** (201 21st St.) are spacious and often considerably less crowded than the beaches to the south. Both have parking lots ($3/hour) and restroom/shower facilities. The Miami Beach boardwalk starts at Collins Park and continues for 20 blocks north, allowing easy access to parts of the beach that are blocked by the many condominiums along Collins Avenue.

The best beach in the immediate area, though, is the one found at **North Shore Open Space Park** (7900 Collins Ave.), which is remarkably uncrowded and even somewhat rustic in spots thanks to overgrowing sea grape trees and spacious swaths of sand. The water is beautiful and blue, and there are picnic tables, grills, restroom/shower facilities, and, somewhat amazingly, plenty of nearby metered parking spaces ($3/hour).

Those looking to avoid public nudity should avoid heading farther north to

Haulover Beach (10800 Collins Ave., parking $5/car). The large beach park is beautiful and popular, and the northernmost portion of it is clothing optional.

KEY BISCAYNE

Reopened after a long restoration effort that was necessary after years of neglect, **Virginia Key Beach** (3701 Rickenbacker Causeway, 7am-sunset daily, $5/car weekdays, $8/car weekends) is a historic beach park with a mile of narrow shoreline, smooth shallow waters, restroom/shower facilities, picnic area, and even a carousel. The beach area is natural, and a copse directly abuts the shoreline.

A better beach option in the area is the **Bill Baggs Cape Florida State Park** (1200 S. Crandon Blvd., www.floridastateparks. org, 8am-sunset daily, $8/carload or $4/single-occupant vehicle), with its wide and expansive beach that stretches along a mile of Atlantic Ocean coastline. The waters are blue and calm, while the natural areas throughout the park are rough and pastoral. An array of facilities—including water-bike rentals—are available. Make sure to dedicate half an hour or so to exploring the mid-19th-century lighthouse here.

SOUTH OF MIAMI

Windsurfers love the action at **Matheson Hammock Park** (9610 Old Cutler Rd., www. miamidade.gov, sunrise-sunset daily, $5/ car Mon.-Fri., $7/ car Sat.-Sun.). Although the air currents are active, the waters are calm and shallow, making it a favorite with families who love to spread out on the large beach. There's a saltwater lagoon where water cycles through as the tides come in and out; it makes for a great enclosed area for kids to splash around in. Beyond the beach, this park has expansive nature areas, with mangroves, ponds, and lush tropical foliage.

Collins Park

Sports and Recreation

PARKS

Bayfront Park

In downtown, **Bayfront Park** (301 N. Biscayne Blvd.) is probably best known for its two concert spaces: the Bayfront Park Amphitheater and the Tina Hills Pavilion. But the 32-acre park is also an excellent urban park space, redesigned in the early 1980s by Isamu Noguchi to incorporate historical monuments, sculptures, fountains, and scenic walking trails.

Kennedy Park

Near Coconut Grove, the lush scenery and kid-friendly playgrounds at **Kennedy Park** (2600 S. Bayshore Dr.) make it a popular destination for families on the weekends. Dogs are also welcome in a delineated off-leash area. The views out onto Biscayne Bay are fantastic, and there are often food and drink vendors set up nearby to provide the opportunity for a great picnic day.

Biscayne National Park

Biscayne National Park (9700 SW 328 St., Homestead) is actually a 200-square-mile park, most of which is in the waters of Biscayne Bay and thickets of shorefront mangrove. The coral reefs just off shore are ideal for snorkeling and scuba diving. Boat charters ($35 adults, $25 children) and canoe (from $12 per person per hour) and kayak (from $16 pp/hour) rentals are available inside the park.

SPAS

Miami Beach

The best spas in Miami Beach are all located at hotels. **The Setai** (2001 Collins Ave., 305/520-6000, www.thesetaihotel.com) has a spa that offers a modern take on South Pacific atmosphere, while the spa at **The Standard** (40 Island Ave., 305/673-1717, http://standardhotels.com) is more focused on holistic treatments, with yoga and meditation classes as well as a Center for Integral Living.

Miami

The cream of the crop of Miami spas is the five-star spa at the **Mandarin Oriental** (500 Brickell Key Dr., 305/913-8288, www.mandarinoriental.com). Spread out over 15,000 square feet, the spa is as decadent as it is meditative, with 17 different treatment rooms and offerings that range from massages and manicures to Pilates and belly dance classes.

Down in Coconut Grove, the **Spa Terre** at the Grove Isle Hotel & Spa (4 Grove Isle Dr., Coconut Grove, 305/858-8300, www.groveisle.com) is quite a bit smaller, but it has a solid array of services that include massages, body masks, facials, and herbal therapies.

GOLF

There are dozens of excellent golf courses in the Miami area, so golfers should have no problem finding a place to tee off. If you are staying downtown or at the beach, the **Biltmore Golf Course** (1210 Anastasia Ave., Coral Gables, 305/460-5364, www.biltmorehotel.com, $200) is a good option; the scenery is beautiful, the play reasonably challenging, and winding down in one of the Biltmore Hotel's luxurious lounges is enough of an experience to make even a middling day of golf seem like an excellent one. Even more convenient is **Miami Beach Golf Club** (2301 Alton Rd., Miami Beach, 305/532-3350, www.miamibeachgolfclub.com, $100-200), which is scenic even though it isn't on the beach.

TENNIS

At the northern end of Miami Beach, the **North Shore Park Tennis Center** (501 72nd St., Miami Beach, 305/604-4080, http://gsibollettieri.com, 8am-9pm Mon.-Fri., 8am-8pm Sat.-Sun., $8/hr., $1.50 light fee) has 10 clay courts and two hard courts, all of which are lit at night. The Bollettieri Tennis Training Academy holds daily classes here. Also in the area is the **Penny Sugarman Tennis Center at Sans Souci** (1795 Sans Souci Blvd., North Miami, 305/893-7130, www.northmiamifl. gov, 9:30am-4:30pm Mon.-Fri., $4 pp). It has 13 lit courts, one of which is clay and the others Laykold surfaced.

SPECTATOR SPORTS
Professional Sports
Miami has teams in almost every national professional league. The two-time National Football League Super Bowl-winning **Miami Dolphins** play August-January at **Hard Rock Stadium** (2269 Dan Marino Blvd., Miami Gardens, 954/452-7000, www.miamidolphins.com, from $30), which has also hosted five Super Bowls, two World Series, and three Bowl Championship Series final games. The 2012 and 2013 back-to-back National Basketball Association champions **Miami Heat** play November-April at the **American Airlines Arena** (601 N. Biscayne Blvd., 786/777-1135, www.nba.com, from $20).

Two-time Major League Baseball World Series winners, the **Miami Marlins** (800/279-4444, http://miami.marlins.mlb.com) play their games March-October at **Marlins Park** (501 NW 16 Ave., 305/480-1300, from $25).

Homestead-Miami Speedway (1 Speedway Blvd., Homestead, 305/230-5000, www.homesteadmiamispeedway.com) hosts the final races of all three National Association of Stock Car Auto Racing (NASCAR) series in November.

College Sports
The Atlantic Coast Conference's **University of Miami Hurricanes** (www.hurricane-sports.com) play football at **Hard Rock Stadium** (2269 Dan Marino Blvd., Miami Gardens, 954/452-7000), while the basketball team plays its home games at the **University of Miami Watsco Center** (1245 Dauer Dr., Coral Gables, 305/284-8686). The **Florida International University's Golden Panthers** (FIU, www.fiusports.com) play their Sun Belt conference football games in FIU's **Riccardo Silva Stadium** (11200 SW 8th St.). Basketball games are also played on campus at the 6,000-seat **U.S. Century Bank Arena.**

The Miami Heat play at the American Airlines Arena.

Entertainment and Events

NIGHTLIFE

Although it's possible to enjoy a "South Beach" club experience anywhere from Scranton, Pennsylvania, to Spokane, Washington, the only place where those high-priced drinks, billowing linens, rooftop bars, and plush surroundings truly make sense is in the ultra-lounges in and around the Collins Avenue and Ocean Drive area. It's here that the global elite—but mainly those aspiring to emulate the global elite—come to party in clubs that are as swank and sumptuous as they are tropical and decadent. Of course, the roster of "it" places in Miami Beach is reshuffled on a regular basis, and the club that had three-block-long lines a few months ago may well be straining for attention today. But if you want to get a taste of what partying and dancing in South Beach is like, you'll have no shortage of opportunities. Keep in mind, though, that much of the true ultra-luxe experience is kept behind closed doors that no amount of bouncer-flattering will open; while many spots will gladly charge outrageous entrance fees and bottle prices, they are trading on South Beach's reputation, rather than offering truly unique glamour. In all honesty, you'll be much better off choosing to not go clubbing along Ocean Drive; central Miami has several fantastic nightspots, most of which are decidedly cooler, as well as more low-key and welcoming than the velvet ropes and shiny shirts of South Beach.

South Beach

There are plenty of places in Miami Beach where you can be surrounded by folks willing to pay for overpriced drinks in crowded, tropical, glamorous locales. Celebrity DJs can be found spinning in lavishly decorated clubs like the somewhat dated but still busy **LIV** (4441 Collins Ave., 305/674-4680, www.liv-nightclub.com, 11pm-5am Wed.-Sun.), while the vibe at South Beach legends like **Nikki Beach** (1 Ocean Dr., 305/538-1231, www.nikkibeachmiami.com, 11pm-5am Wed.-Sun.) is all indulgent luxury, complete with beds to lounge on while enjoying high-priced drinks and surprisingly decent food. (You'll need to make a reservation for a bed, and there's also a one-bottle-of-champagne drink minimum.) And while this is what South Beach is best known for, this whole VIP-bottle-service scene has seen better days, and is often more hassle than it could possibly be worth.

Not everyone wants to spend the night (and early morning) dancing, and although it doesn't have a reputation as a live-music haven, Miami Beach does have a few decent venues to see bands perform. High-gloss dance clubs like LIV occasionally feature big-name live bands, but the main venue for touring acts is the beautifully renovated Jackie Gleason Theater, now known as **Fillmore Miami Beach** (1700 Washington Ave., 305/673-7300, http://fillmoremb.com, hours vary per show), which features concerts, comedians, and theater performances.

There are also quite a few bars in Miami Beach where the main attraction is, well, the bar. Neighborhood bars like **Purdy Lounge** (1811 Sunset Harbor Dr., 305/531-4622, www.purdylounge.com, 3pm-5am Mon.-Fri., 6pm-5am Sat.-Sun.) and **Mac's Club Deuce** (222 14th St., 305/531-6200, 8am-5am daily) eschew glamour and rope lines for inexpensive drinks and a no-bull atmosphere. And the cozy hotel basement that houses **Beaches Bar & Grill** (4299 Collins Ave., 305/672-1910, 11am-5am daily) may be the only place on Miami Beach where you can queue up Merle Haggard on the jukebox; note that although food is served here, you'd be much better off eating at one of the area's many fine restaurants. Pub lovers should check out the expansive Irish-themed **Playwright Pub** (1265 Washington Ave., 305/534-0667, www.playwrightirishpub.com, 11am-5am daily), which

Mac's Club Deuce provides a nightlife alternative to velvet ropes.

has plenty of room to spread out and multiple TVs on which to watch the big game—especially if that big game involves an Irish soccer team. The best bar in South Beach, though, is probably **Abbey Brewing Co.** (1115 16th St., 305/538-8110, http://abbeybrewinginc.com, 1pm-5am daily), a tiny hallway of pure beer heaven. In addition to a wide range of European craft beers and American microbrews, the Abbey also serves up a selection of its own award-winning beers. The staff knows beer, and although the space can turn from cozy to cramped pretty quickly, there's a feeling of knowing camaraderie among the hopheads gathered here.

Tucked away from the neon clang of South Beach on the property of the cozy (and inexpensive!) Freehand hotel, the **Broken Shaker** (2727 Indian Creek Dr, 786/671-8927, 6pm-2am Mon.-Thurs., 6pm-3am Fri., 1pm-3am Sat., 1pm-2am Sun.) is not only one of the best craft cocktail bars in Miami Beach, but is also one of the best bars in the entire greater Miami area. Since it's exponentially smaller

than most other SoBe venues, it can fill up quite quickly, but it never feels overcrowded or uncomfortable, thanks to the fact that entrance and capacity are controlled at the door. If you encounter a line, don't worry, it's worth it; the vibe is surprisingly friendly, defying yet another Miami Beach stereotype, and drinks—while definitely not inexpensive—are both reasonably priced and immaculately and creatively constructed.

Central Miami

One of the best dingy punk-rock bars in the entire southeastern United States is **Churchill's Pub** (5501 NE 2nd Ave., 305/757-1807, www.churchillspub.com, 11am-5am daily). Despite its location on one of the rougher edges of the Little Haiti neighborhood, Churchill's is routinely packed with regulars and music fans who flock to hear punk, garage rock, metal, and even jazz artists in a super-friendly, dive-bar atmosphere.

For almost the exact opposite experience, head for **Bardot** (3456 N. Miami Ave., 305/576-5570, www.bardotmiami.com, 8pm-3am daily), one of the most unusual and schizophrenic music venues around. On some nights, Bardot feels like a swank VIP room airdropped from South Beach, with bottle service, plush surroundings, and beautiful people drinking beautiful drinks. Other nights, thanks to the presence of great regional and national indie/underground bands playing on the club's stage, it feels like the coolest music bar around. Most nights, though, it's a slightly puzzling combination of the two, positively wonderful and quintessentially Miami.

In downtown Miami, nightlife can be hit-or-miss. There are a few gems in the area, most notably two excellent craft cocktail bars, **The Corner** (1035 N. Miami Ave., 305/961-7887, www.thecornermiami.com, 4pm-5am Mon.-Thurs., 4pm-8am Fri.-Sat., 7pm-5am Sun.) and **Blackbird Ordinary** (759 SW 1st Ave., 305/671-3307, www.blackbirdordinary.com, 3pm-5am Mon.-Fri., 5pm-5am Sat.-Sun.). Both are pricey, hip, comfortable, and worth it for their skilled mixologists, who combine small-batch spirits and seasonal/local ingredients in custom recipes that will almost certainly have you rethinking your booze-and-chaser expectations. If you're in downtown, Blackbird Ordinary is more convenient, but the Corner is just on the west side of I-95, in the Overtown neighborhood.

Believe it or not, it is possible to find a place to dance in Miami that isn't on South Beach. Downtown, the **Vagabond** (30 NE 14th St., 305/379-0509, http://thevagabondmiami. com, 10pm-3am Tues., 10pm-5am Thurs.-Sat.) sometimes sports some serious lines out front, but once inside, the mixture of funk, hip-hop, and rock booming out of the PA makes for a good time; its even got a pretty amazing brunch. Little Havana's **Hoy Como Ayer** (2212 SW 8th St., 305/541-2631, www. hoycomoayer.us, 9pm-3am Wed.-Sun.) unsurprisingly dishes up hot Latin pop and salsa to a packed dance floor.

If you like it when your favorite bar has a food truck outside, then you'll love **The Wynwood Yard** (56 NW 29th St, 305/251-0366, thewynwoodyard.com, Mon. noon-

11 pm, Tues.-Thurs. 11am-11pm, Fri.-Sun. 11am-2am), which is basically a lush garden courtyard outfitted with some awnings and picnic tables, a substantial bar in the center, and ringed by a dozen or so food trucks. Food trucks rotate through on a regular basis, so check the website to see who'll be on site when you want to visit, but, this being Miami, there almost certainly will be something to your liking. Drinks are reasonably priced, but not terribly fancy, and the vibe is much more neighborhood gathering (think dogs, strollers, etc.) than raging night out.

Casinos

Thanks to Florida's rules on casino games, there are no **casinos** that are convenient to any of the most-traveled areas of Miami. The only legal casino action can be found at current or former dog tracks, jai alai arenas, and Native American reservations. The state's rules restrict the types of games that each of these venues can have. The two closest gaming options to downtown are both located near the airport: **Casino Miami Jai-Alai** (3500 NW 37th Ave., 305/633-6400, www.

The Wynwood Yard

casinomiamijaialai.com, 10am-4am Mon.-Fri., 24 hours Sat.-Sun.) offers slots, poker, dominoes, and digital roulette and blackjack tables; **Magic City Casino** (450 NW 37th Ave., 305/649-3000, www.magiccitycasino.com, 10am-4am Sun.-Thurs., 10am-5am Fri.-Sat.) has roulette, craps, and baccarat, as well as live greyhound races.

Out west, at the edge of the Everglades, is **Miccosukee Resort & Gaming** (500 SW 177th Ave., 305/222-4600, www.miccosukee.com, 24 hours daily). It's not at all worth the drive, but if you're headed out to the northern Everglades on the Tamiami Trail, it's a fine place to stop and gamble a few hours away.

THE ARTS
Performing Arts
The crown jewel of Miami's performing arts scene is the **Adrienne Arsht Performing Arts Center** (1300 Biscayne Blvd., 305/949-6722, www.arshtcenter.org), which opened in 2006 and, at 570,000 square feet, is the third-largest performing arts center in the United States. There are two principal venues in the center: an opera house and a concert hall, each of which can seat over 2,000 people. Additionally, there are two smaller performance spaces that hold about 200 people. With so much real estate, the Arsht Center doesn't conform to the same "on-season" intensity as many Florida performing arts centers. Instead, it hosts high-profile performances throughout the year. Of course, winter sees a greater percentage of those, as the New World Symphony, Miami City Ballet, Florida Grand Opera, and the Concert Association of Florida all call the center home. But throughout the year a diverse slate of local arts groups and nationally known artists and performers can be seen here.

The beautiful **Olympia Theater** (174 E. Flagler St., 305/374-2444, www.olympiatheater.org) is located in a gorgeous Jazz Age movie theater and hosts performances by local dance troupes, touring jazz and world musicians, and occasional Broadway-style extravaganzas.

Theater buffs should head for Coral Gables, where they'll have plenty to choose from, including the slate of contemporary plays put on at **GableStage** (1200 Anastasia Ave., Coral Gables, 305/445-1119, www.gablestage.org) and the musicals at the **Ring Theatre** (1312 Miller Dr., Coral Gables, 305/284-3355, www.as.miami.edu/ringtheatre). The beautifully restored art deco **Miracle Theatre** (280 Miracle Mile, Coral Gables, 305/444-4181, www.actorsplayhouse.org) is the home of the Actors' Playhouse, which performs a seasonal selection of musicals, classics, and contemporary theater productions.

Galleries
The greatest concentration of art galleries in Miami can be found in the **Wynwood Art District** (between NW 20th St. and NW 36th St., east of I-95). There are more than 40 galleries in this neighborhood, which is also known as "Little San Juan." On the second Saturday of the month, the district hosts an art walk, which allows casual art fans to explore galleries like the ultramodern **Fredric Snitzer Gallery** (2247 NW 1st Pl., 305/448-8976, http://snitzer.com, 10am-5pm Tues.-Sat., free) and more unique outposts like the 3.2-acre **Bakehouse Art Complex** (561 NW 32nd St., 305/576-2828, www.bacfl.org, noon-5pm daily, free).

FESTIVALS AND EVENTS
Art Festivals
Although **Art Basel** (www.artbasel.com, Dec.) is consistently referred to as a "sister festival" to the original prestigious Art Basel in Switzerland, it could be argued that this younger sibling has eclipsed its predecessor in terms of both its impact on the art world and on the Miami social scene. For three days Miami Beach becomes the beating heart of the visual arts world as more than 200 galleries from around the world converge on museums and other display spaces throughout the area (as well as Wynwood, the Design District, and other locations) to exhibit the best in

contemporary art. Those exhibits are complemented by scores of installations, parties, and innovative art shows that, for a weekend at least, gives the lie to stereotypical notions of Miami's lack of culture.

There are several other worthwhile arts festivals throughout the year as well, and though the **Coconut Grove Arts Festival** (Coconut Grove, 305/447-0401, www.cgaf.com, Feb.) comes nowhere close to emulating Art Basel's intensity, it does allow notable local and regional artists an opportunity to shine on a level playing field.

Film Festivals

Sponsored by Miami-Dade College, the annual **Miami International Film Festival** (citywide, 305/237-3456, www.miamifilmfestival.com, Mar.) is a robust film festival that usually shows around 100 features, many of which are international films with a special focus on Latin American themes and filmmakers.

The **Miami Gay & Lesbian Film Festival** (citywide, www.mglff.com, Apr.) is put on in conjunction with the Fort Lauderdale Gay & Lesbian Film Festival and typically screens 20 features and an equal number of shorts.

Film buffs with short attention spans—or a taste for experimental films—will want to attend the **Miami Short Film Festival** (citywide, www.miamishortfilmfestival.com, Nov.).

Other Festivals

In a town as diverse as Miami, it's unsurprising that there are a number of excellent cultural heritage festivals in the area throughout the year. The biggest is **Calle Ocho** in March, which takes place logically enough on Calle Ocho in Little Havana. It's an enormous street party that brings in big names in Latin music, scores of food vendors, arts and crafts booths, and an enormously festive atmosphere.

Sponsored by the Food Network, the **South Beach Wine & Food Festival** (citywide, South Beach, 877/762-3933, www.sobefest.com, Feb.) is a cornucopia of celebrity chef sightings, culinary seminars, wine tastings, progressive dinners, and scores of food-oriented events that appeal to gourmets and casual food fans alike. Many of the events are pricey, but the festival is to foodies what Sundance is to film fanatics.

The **Winter Music Conference** (WMC, Miami Beach Convention Center, 1901 Convention Center Dr., South Beach, 954/563-4444, http://wintermusicconference.com, Mar.) brings the world of dance and electronic music to South Beach for 10 days of club-hopping and networking. Although theoretically a professional conference, the DJ sets, parties, and events spill out all over Miami Beach and Miami.

In recent years, WMC's star has been somewhat eclipsed in electronic music circles by the three-day **Ultra Music Festival** (866/433-4594, www.ultramusicfestival.com, Mar.), which typically occurs near the tail end of WMC. This annual festival, which began in 1999, takes place in downtown's Bayfront Park. It is absolutely massive, bringing hundreds of thousands of music fans out to see a huge slate of the biggest acts in electronic music, as well as a wide selection of crossover pop and alternative artists.

Shopping

As a prime destination for the well-to-do, it's not all that surprising that the Miami area has plentiful opportunities for visitors to part with their cash. Shops and boutiques abound throughout South Beach but are highly concentrated around the Lincoln Road area. Those looking for a deal on jewelry should head straight for the downtown Jewelry District.

Worth a voyage into Little Haiti is the excellent **Sweat Records** (5505 NE 2nd Ave., 786/693-9309, http://sweatrecordsmiami.com, noon-10pm Mon.-Sat., noon-5pm Sun.), which specializes in indie and underground vinyl (it does have some CDs, too). It also sells turntables and accessories, posters, and, thanks to the inclusion of Miami's only vegan coffee bar, excellent coffee and vegan snacks. Sweat regularly holds in-store concerts by local and touring bands.

SHOPPING DISTRICTS
Downtown
There are lots of places to spend money in downtown Miami. The **Bayside Marketplace** (401 Biscayne Blvd., 305/577-3344, www.baysidemarketplace.com, 10am-10pm Mon.-Thurs., 10am-11pm Fri.-Sat., 11am-9pm Sun.), near the Port of Miami, is geared toward cruise ship passengers. This mall has Foot Locker, Skechers, Gap, and other chain stores. There's also a Hard Rock Cafe and Hooters on-site. There are a handful of decent, if not adventurous, locally owned restaurants here, as well as a couple of interesting, smaller boutiques like **Passage to India** (305/375-9504), which has jewelry, clothing, and accessories with a South Asian flair. Passage to India also has a branch on Washington Avenue in South Beach.

A much more interesting (and expensive) foray downtown would be the four-block area known as the **Jewelry District**. One of the largest jewelry districts in the United States,

there are hundreds of retailers and wholesalers jammed into the area bounded by North Miami Avenue, NE 2nd Avenue, East Flagler Street, and NE 2nd Street. The international distributors here provide much of the stock for jewelry stores throughout the Caribbean and Latin America. The historic **Seybold Building** (36 NE 1st St., 305/374-7922, www.seyboldjewelry.com, 9:30am-5:30pm Mon.-Sat.) is a 10-story jewelry haven with nearly 300 jewelers on-site. Next door, the three-story **International Jewelry Center** (22 NE 1st St., 305/373-9898, http://ijcmiami.com, hours vary by merchant) is smaller but still grand in scale, with jewelers and precious-metal merchants tucked into the cavernous and luxurious building. There are still scores of interesting shops beyond the walls of these massive buildings, including Jewelry District legend **Morays** (50 NE 2nd Ave., 305/374-0739, www.moraysjewelers.com, 10:30am-5pm Mon.-Fri.) and the bling-y flair on offer at **Haimov Jewelers** (33 NE 1st St., 305/381-8901, www.haimov.com, 9am-5pm Mon.-Fri.).

Lincoln Road Mall
Only in South Beach would you have to traverse a velvet rope and then be deemed worthy of entrance into a clothing store. There are several such shops in and around the Lincoln Road pedestrian mall, like **Alchemist** (438 Lincoln Rd., 305/531-4653, http://shopalchemist.com, 10am-10pm daily), which features designer brands like Givenchy and Chanel. There are quite a few other—somewhat less exclusive—shops in the mall, such as Athleta, H&M, and Taschen, as well as a Shake Shack and more than a dozen other restaurants.

Miracle Mile
The founding concept behind the **Miracle Mile** was to allow Coral Gables shoppers to be able to get their hands on anything they could possibly need within just a few blocks. While

the current incarnation of the Mile caters to a more selective audience, the pedestrian-friendly neighborhood has scores of unique businesses like the **Paris-Claire Salon** (345 Miracle Mile, 305/448-5514, http://parisclaire-salon.com, 10am-6pm Tues.-Thurs. and Sat., 1pm-9pm Fri.), **Klein Jewelers** (85 Merrick Way, 305/444-0042, www.kleinjewelers.com, 10am-5pm Mon.-Fri., 10am-1pm Sat.), **Grand Oriental Rug Gallery** (383 Aragon Ave., 305/442-4502, www.grandorientalruggallery.com, 10am-7pm Mon.-Thurs., 10:15am-7pm Fri., 11am-6pm Sat.), and more.

MALLS
CocoWalk

There are only a few dozen shops in **CocoWalk** (3015 Grand Ave., Coconut Grove, 305/444-0777, www.cocowalk.net, 10am-10pm Sun.-Thurs., 10am-11pm Fri.-Sat.), but the open-air mall has somehow managed to make itself a minor tourist destination. While the shops are mostly familiar—Gap, Victoria's Secret, Duffy's Sports Grill—shoppers seem to enjoy the midrange shops.

Bal Harbour Shops

For a truly exclusive mall-going experience, **Bal Harbour Shops** (9700 Collins Ave., Bal Harbour, 305/866-0311, http://balharbour-shops.com, 10am-9pm Mon.-Sat., noon-6pm Sun.) is the place to go. From the moment you pay to park—yes, paid parking at a mall—and

the Miracle Mile in downtown Coral Gables

then step into the lushly landscaped open-air property, it's clear why this mall is considered one of the most luxurious contained shopping experiences in the South. Anchored by Saks and Neiman Marcus, and hosting outposts for Tiffany, Jimmy Choo, Giorgio Armani, Bulgari, Chanel, Prada, Versace, and even more top-name designers, Bal Harbour is definitely not for the bargain hunter.

Food

With restaurants focused on everything from greasy-spoon fare to paradigm-busting celebrity chef outposts, eating in Miami has evolved over the last 30 years. With its new-found culinary focus, Miami restaurants also find themselves heaving under the weight of long wait times. Make reservations for early in the evening. It may throw you off of "Miami time," but you'll be able to eat without an incredible wait.

SOUTH BEACH

Unsurprisingly, the heavily touristed South Beach has more than its fair share of restaurants. Competition here is pretty fierce, so there's not a lot of tolerance for slack kitchens and unimaginative chefs. There's a surprising amount of diversity in these restaurants, and it's just as easy to get a well-done, simple sandwich or a plate of eggs and bacon as it is to get a dinner that's an exemplar of modern

Best Restaurants

★ **Joe's Stone Crab:** The lines can be long, but the fresh crab claws are an essential Florida dish (page 63).

★ **Yardbird Southern Table & Bar:** You may balk at paying big bucks for chicken and waffles, but the fresh, locally sourced Southern fare is well worth the price (page 64).

★ **Tap Tap:** This low-key Hatian diner is a South Beach institution, revered as much for its friendly vibe as its excellent food (page 65).

★ **Panther Coffee:** Skip the chains and get an exceptional Panther cold brew instead; beans are roasted on site (page 66).

★ **Versailles:** This Little Havana cornerstone was founded as a French restaurant, but it serves the best Cuban food in the U.S. (page 67).

★ **Ortanique:** The emphasis on fresh, local produce and seafood makes this Caribbean spot stand out (page 69).

cuisine. What's not so easy is finding someplace cheap to eat. A handful of affordable and decent options have been included here, but plan on allocating a big line item in your vacation budget for food. Don't worry, though. It'll be worth it.

Breakfast and Light Bites

You won't be the first tourist ever to start your day at the **News Cafe** (800 Ocean Dr., 305/538-6397, www.newscafe.com, 24 hours daily, from $6) by lining up for a table and then having a grumpy member of the waitstaff take your order. It's something of a rite of passage in South Beach. And no, you can't leave a bad tip; the gratuity is included in the bill. The breakfast menu of bagels, pastries, pancakes, and egg dishes is served around the clock, and a News Cafe espresso drink is best enjoyed on the outdoor patio, whether it's midmorning or after midnight. Later in the day, a standard selection of burgers, pastas, sandwiches, and salads is available, but the Middle Eastern platters make the grunting tableside service worthwhile.

Although located on the relatively less busy western side of South Beach, the **Taste** Bakery & Cafe (900 Alton Rd., 305/695-9930, www.taste-bakery.com, 6am-8pm Mon.-Fri., 7am-7pm Sat., 8am-6pm Sun., from $5) can get pretty packed pretty quickly. The breakfast fare is standard, with bagels, egg sandwiches, and pastries. The vibe is friendly and casual, and during cooler months the outdoor seating is a hit. Panini sandwiches stand out on the lunch menu, but all of the menu items are fresh and well prepared.

Breakfast at the **Front Porch Cafe** (1418 Ocean Dr., 305/531-8300, www.frontporch-oceandrive.com, 7am-6pm Mon.-Thurs., 7am-8pm Fri.-Sun., from $6) is a casual and slightly groggy affair as diners tuck into challah-bread French toast, stuffed omelets, and massive pancakes. Located in the Penguin Hotel, the Front Porch is busy every day but is particularly popular for its weekend brunch offerings, so be prepared to wait a bit on Saturday and Sunday mornings.

La Sandwicherie (229 14th St., 305/532-8934, www.lasandwicherie.com, 10am-5am daily, from $6) is a fantastic French-inspired deli located right next to a tattoo shop off the main drag of Ocean Drive. The prime location and late-night hours make it a preferred destination for famished club kids, but a nosh on the Camembert- or prosciutto-stuffed French bread sandwiches or the legendary croque monsieur is great any time of the day.

The **BLT Steak** (1440 Ocean Dr., 305/673-0044, www.thebetsyhotel.com, 8:30am-2:30pm and 6pm-10pm Sun.-Thurs., 8:30am-2:30pm and 6pm-11pm Fri.-Sat., from $30) chain has a location in South Beach, in the cozy and comfortable dining room of the Betsy Hotel. It's fine as high-priced steak house chains go, but what really recommends this place is the alfresco dining right on the Ocean Drive strip. This may not make for a romantic dinner, given the evening crowds of partiers on South Beach, but it's perfect for breakfast or brunch, given the relative quiet of the area in the morning hours.

Late-Night Dining

Both a visual landmark and a late-night-noshing standby, the **11th Street Diner** (1065 Washington Ave., 305/534-6373, www.eleventhstreetdiner.com, 24 hours daily, from $5) is situated in an authentic 1940s-era dining car that was relocated from Pennsylvania to South Beach back in the early 1990s. The menu goes far beyond standard diner fare, including an array of fresh salads, European-style hot sandwiches, and a dizzying selection of gourmet hamburgers, along with fish, poultry, beef, and pasta entrées that bear little resemblance to greasy-spoon meals.

Big Pink (157 Collins Ave., 305/531-0888, http://mylesrestaurantgroup.com, 8am-midnight Mon.-Wed., 8am-2am Thurs., 8am-5:30am Fri.-Sun., from $3) specializes in comfort food—the kind that tastes great after a night of dancing and drinking and the kind that helps mitigate the morning-after effects of such a night . Menu items include burgers, pizzas, sandwiches, pasta dishes, ample steaks, mouth-watering fried chicken, buckets of fried food (including corn dogs!), and even a homemade TV dinner. The playful atmosphere is decidedly loose by South Beach standards (the menu insists you clean your plate), but if the dining room is not your speed, Big Pink also delivers to nearby hotels.

Unlike many 24-hour spots, the round-the-clock menu at **David's Cafe** (1508 Collins Ave., 305/674-4545, www.davidscafe.com, 24 hours daily, from $5) isn't breakfast fare, but instead focuses on legendary Cuban lunch food. While David's does serve an excellent breakfast in the morning, the restaurant's Cuban sandwich and *ropa vieja* are what draw the constant crowds. There aren't that

La Sandwicherie is a great spot to grab a bite.

The Best Cuban Sandwich in Miami

The quickest way to start an argument in Miami is to posit that you know the place that prepares the best Cuban sandwich. Whether it's someone proclaiming the excellence of one prepared in an off-the-beaten-path bodega near Little Havana or the accolades given to the massively popular **David's Cafe** in Miami Beach (1058 Collins Ave., 305/534-8735, www.davidscafe.com, 24 hours daily, from $5), the Great Cuban Debate is a discussion that will likely never be resolved. In fact, the only thing more difficult than coming up with an answer to the "Which one is best?" question would have to be actually finding a Cuban sandwich in Miami that's subpar. Even some chain stores manage to make a decent (OK, edible) Cuban in the 305 area code because they know that to do otherwise would just be foolish. But still, for my money, one of the best places in Miami to get a Cuban isn't in Little Havana. Instead, head for the Wynwood district downtown and **Enriqueta's Sandwich Shop** (2830 NE 2nd Ave., 305/573-4681, 6am-4pm Mon.-Fri., 6am-2pm Sun., from $4). Breakfast in the form of steak and eggs is available throughout the day, but it's the sandwiches here that are the true prize, made with fresh bread and a nearly perfect combination of salty ham, succulent roasted pork, pickles, and tangy mustard. In addition to the tried-and-true recipe, Enriqueta's also offers a Cuban stuffed with *croquetas* (breaded and fried ham).

Another excellent choice is **Sarussi Cafeteria** (6797 SW 8th St., 305/264-5464, 7am-10:30pm daily, from $6), which slathers a "secret" mojo sauce on its ham-stacked Cubans. The sandwiches here are so good that they caught the eye of the Travel Channel's *Man v. Food*. They are locally feted as well.

many surprises on the menu, although the potency and rich flavor of David's *café Cubano* may startle those used to mediocre espressos, but the restaurant does the basics very well. Service can be hit-or-miss. There's also a location on Meridian Avenue (1654 Meridian Ave., 305/672-8707, 24 hours daily).

Steak and Seafood

★ **Joe's Stone Crab** (11 Washington Ave., 305/673-0365, www.joesstonecrab.com, 5pm-10pm Mon., 11:30am-2pm and 5pm-10pm Tues.-Thurs., 11:30am-2pm and 5pm-11pm Fri.-Sat., 4pm-10pm Sun., from $11) is so dedicated to its mission of serving fresh stone crab that the restaurant isn't even open outside of stone-crab season (Oct.-May). However, when the owners do open their doors, navigating the queue of people waiting for entry to this Miami Beach institution can be more daunting than traversing the velvet rope at one of South Beach's glamorous nightclubs. The effort and the expense are worth the wait, as the crab claws selected by the kitchen are simply some of the finest in the world. There are other excellent seafood selections available as

well, but you've waited this long to try the crab claws, so why bother?

While it doesn't have the same reputation as Joe's, the crab claws and other raw-bar fare offered at **Monty's Sunset** (300 Alton Rd., 305/673-3444, www.montyssobe.com, 5:30pm-11pm Sun.-Thurs., 5:30pm-midnight Fri.-Sat., from $15) are still quite good, cost about half as much, and don't require scheduling your entire vacation around them. There's a no-frills attitude at Monty's that's quite refreshing for South Beach, and the pool (yes, the pool) can occasionally be the site of some drunken shenanigans.

All the steaks at **Prime 112** (112 Ocean Dr., 305/532-8112, http://mylesrestaurant-group.com, noon-3pm and 5:30pm-midnight Mon.-Thurs., noon-3pm and 5:30pm-1am Fri., 5:30pm-1am Sat., 5:30pm-midnight Sun., from $25) are dry-aged at least three weeks and served as classic cuts—filet mignon, New York strip, rib eye, and Porterhouse—in the classic steak-house style, including potatoes and other sides. However, Prime 112 doesn't feel like a stuffy old-school steak house with its comfortable modern decor and a large variety of nonsteak dishes, including seafood, chicken and waffles, and Kobe beef hot dogs.

Although **Grillfish** (1444 Collins Ave., 305/538-9908, www.grillfish.com, 11:30am-11pm Mon.-Sat., from $20) has only one location in South Beach, it feels more like a franchise-ready concept than a truly unique dining experience. The expansive list of mojito concoctions is thoughtful, the fish is fresh, and the preparations are solid if somewhat uninspired.

American

Breakfast and brunch are a big hit at the **Icebox Cafe** (1657 Michigan Ave., 305/538-8448, http://iceboxcafe.com, 8am-4pm and 6pm-11pm Mon.-Fri., 9am-4pm and 6pm-11pm Sat.-Sun., from $19), but lunch and dinner are also great. Although it is a little pricey, the frequently changing selection of fresh fish dishes, steaks, gourmet burgers, and even a few Southeast Asian delicacies is dependably excellent.

Hotel restaurants are normally known for superlative farm-to-table dining experiences, but **Essensia** (3025 Collins Ave., 305/908-5458, www.essensiarestaurant.com, 7am-10pm daily, from $26) at the Palms hotel on Collins Avenue has staked a claim as one of the best and most innovative restaurants in the Miami area. Guided by the hands of chef Julie Frans, the emphasis here is on locally sourced, organic ingredients prepared in a way that emphasizes their essences. While the menu (especially the breakfast/brunch selection) is extensive, Frans's recipes are notably unfussy, and most consist of just a small handful of ingredients without a lot of overwhelming saucing or seasoning. It's an approach that works as well for a quinoa salad as it does for a breakfast of steak and eggs or a dinner of ricotta ravioli.

Speaking of farm-to-table, the recent trend toward farm-fresh ingredients and rustic preparations has also resulted in a concurrent explosion of restaurants focused on Southern food. Restaurants are serving up organic, farm-fresh plates of fried chicken, gravy,

grits, and ribs. ★ **Yardbird Southern Table & Bar** (1600 Lenox Ave., 305/538-5220, www.runchickenrun.com, 11:30am-11pm Mon.-Thurs., 11:30am-midnight Fri., 10am-midnight Sat., 10am-11pm Sun., from $20) has a plate that is beautiful to behold: the Chicken 'n' Watermelon 'n' Waffles. The fried chicken at Yardbird is a near-perfect thing, but when combined with the restaurant's hot-sauce honey, a cheddar-cheese-infused waffle, and a chunk of peppery, spiced watermelon, you'll quickly forget that you paid $36. The bar not only has an amazing selection of bourbons, but a bar staff that also understands how to turn your drink into something truly magical.

Asian

Doraku Sushi (1104 Lincoln Rd., 305/695-8383, http://dorakusushi.com, noon-11pm Mon.-Thurs., noon-midnight Fri., 3pm-midnight Sat., 3pm-10:30pm Sun., from $7) is a very hip sushi spot that manages not to get too full of itself, and service is usually quite friendly and unpretentious. The cool, contemporary interior gives it a fashionable vibe, and even though Doraku's famed conveyor-belt sushi-delivery system is now gone, the same precision and generosity that went into the construction of its famous rolls and sushi is still present.

Pubbelly (1418 20th St., 305/532-7555, www.pubbelly.com, 6pm-11pm Sun.-Thurs., 6pm-midnight Fri.-Sat., small plates $7-18) offers a unique, small-plate take on Asian fusion that rewards groups of adventurous eaters who want to try everything. A wide range of dumplings, bao, rice dishes, sushi, dim sum plates, and more is available, and although it can get pricey, it's well worth the expense, as Pubbelly takes care that everything on offer is unique in preparation and presentation. Be sure to try the kimchi fried rice, the soft shell chili crab, and any of the excellent desserts.

Thai House South Beach (1137 Washington Ave., 305/531-4841, http://thaihousesobe.com, noon-midnight daily, from $13) has friendly service in a comfortable and stylish dining room (and it also delivers), with a selection of standard Thai fare like pad Thai, curries, and tofu dishes augmented by specialties like the aptly named volcano chicken.

Italian

Neapolitan-style pizzas are the specialty at **Fratelli La Bufala** (437 Washington Ave., 305/532-0700, www.fratellilabufala.eu, noon-midnight Mon.-Thurs., noon-2am Fri.-Sun., from $11). The restaurant, known as FLB, also serves up excellent soups, salads, and decadently rich pasta dishes, as well as a great selection of antipasto plates. And yes, FLB is a chain, but unless you're from Italy it's unlikely you've run into one of its locations.

Located in a residence that has been transformed into a restaurant, **Casa Tua** (1700 James Ave., 305/673-1010, www.casatualifestyle.com, 11:30am-3pm and 6:30pm-11:30pm daily, from $31) is a unique and romantic restaurant that specializes in contemporary interpretations of northern Italian comfort food. The ambiance inside is exceptional, but sitting at one of the outdoor patio tables makes for a delightful and scenic meal. Reservations are imperative.

Spris (721 Lincoln Rd., 305/673-2020, www.sprispizza.com, noon-1am Sun.-Thurs., noon-2am Fri.-Sat., from $9) is routinely awarded the coveted title of Miami's Best Pizza, although the thin-crust concoctions served up may leave fans of Chicago-style pizza scratching their heads as to what the fuss is about. Regardless, the wide variety of gourmet pies at Spris—there are 30 different combinations on the menu—are served in a casual but classy location with plenty of outdoor seating on the Lincoln Road pedestrian mall.

Although it has turned into a chain, with locations throughout South Florida and Southern California, **Pizza Rustica** (863 Washington Ave., 305/674-8244, http://pizzarustica.com, 11am-6am daily, from $3) got its start in South Beach, serving up massive slices of gourmet pizza with fresh ingredients piled high on some amazing crust.

Sardinia Enoteca Ristorante (1801 Purdy Ave., 305/531-2228, www.sardinia-ristorante.com, noon-midnight daily, from $16) has a massive menu filled with innovative takes on traditional Italian country fare. With a wide variety of fresh and cured meats, local seafood, and a selection of olive oil and vinegar that seems nearly as large as the restaurant's prodigious wine list, one won't be at a loss for options. Amazingly, the kitchen is able to get food out quickly and excellently, although the warm and romantic atmosphere definitely encourages extended visits.

Other International

Puerto Sagua (700 Collins Ave., 305/673-1115, 7:30am-2am daily, from $9) has been in this neighborhood since before South Beach was used as an adjective. The old-school diner specializes in Spanish and Cuban cuisine, heavy on fish and chicken dishes. The paella is legendary, and the formally dressed waiters deliver friendly service.

The blindingly bright decor inside ★ **Tap Tap** (819 5th St., 305/672-2898, www.taptap-miamibeach.com, 5pm-11pm Mon.-Thurs., 5pm-midnight Fri.-Sat., 5pm-10pm Sun., from $9) gives this Haitian diner a festive and friendly feel. Although it's not conveniently located, Tap Tap is a South Beach institution among Haitians and non-Haitians alike. The goat-based dishes are the fulcrum of the menu, but other fare like pumpkin soup and conch salads are available for those who just can't bring themselves to dig into a plate of succulent goat flesh.

MIAMI BEACH
Breakfast

Roasters 'n Toasters (525 Arthur Godfrey Rd., 305/531-7691, www.roastersntoasters.com, 6:30am-3:30pm daily, from $7) is a New York-style deli chain that has taken over the location that was formerly home to Miami Beach deli institution Arnie and Richie's. While the new location doesn't have quite as much vintage charm, the food is quickly attracting its own crowd. Breakfast includes bagels, egg platters, frittatas, blintzes, and smoked fish platters.

American

Norman's Tavern (6770 Collins Ave., 305/868-9248, noon-5pm daily, from $12) is about as unpretentious as they come in Miami Beach. Traditional fried bar snacks along with steaks, chops, chicken, and seafood are surprisingly excellent considering that they're served in a tavern-style environment that, as the night goes on, seems more focused on the party than on the plates.

Asian

The "Indo" in **Indomania** (131 26th St., 305/535-6332, www.indomaniarestaurant. com, 6pm-10pm Tues.-Thurs., 6pm-11pm Fri.-Sat., from $16) refers to Indonesia, making the cuisine stand out in a crowded Miami dining scene. Fried rice and noodle dishes may seem the most familiar. Digging in to a chicken curry or stewed-beef rice plate—which come with an array of delectable and unusual side dishes, some of which are Dutch—is a thoroughly unique experience. The dining room is quite small, albeit contemporary and unpretentious.

Latin

For a diner-style Cuban meal, head for the straightforward atmosphere of the **Latin Cafe** (441 W. 41st St., 305/531-1057, 6:30am-8pm Mon.-Fri., 7am-6pm Sat., 8am-3pm Sun., from $5). Cuban coffee in the morning is a real eye-opener, and the lunch sandwiches and pork-centric dinner entrées are basic but quite satisfying.

Italian

With outdoor seating and a reputation for some of the best homemade pasta in Miami, **Café Prima Pasta** (414 71st St., 305/867-0106, www.cafeprimapasta.com, 5pm-midnight daily, from $14) can sometimes require a bit of a wait, especially on weekend evenings. The delay, however, is more than worth it, as the food—fresh and richly seasoned traditional Italian fare—almost never disappoints. Despite the bustling crowds inside and out, Café Prima still dishes up a good bit of atmosphere too.

DOWNTOWN AND LITTLE HAVANA
Breakfast and Light Bites

If you are a coffee aficionado, head directly to ★ **Panther Coffee** (2390 NW 2nd Ave., 305/677-3952, www.panthercoffee.com, 7am-9pm Mon.-Sat., 8am-9pm Sun.) in the Wynwood neighborhood. Although there are a few other coffee specialists in downtown (most notably Eternity Coffee Roasters in the Brickell neighborhood), Panther is a Miami institution. It brews and serves coffee, and its on-site roasted beans are the heart of many of Miami's best restaurants' cups of coffee. Incredibly knowledgeable and personable baristas pour fantastic cups of whatever concoction you desire. Make sure you try one of the cold-brew coffees. Panther also serves pastries, sandwiches, and craft beers, but really, the excellent coffee is the reason you need to go here.

American

There are several places in town where you can get a standard white-tablecloth lobster dinner, but **Luke's Lobster** (701 S. Miami Ave., 786/837-7683, 11am-9:30pm Mon.-Sat., noon-8pm Sun., from $13) has a much more low-key take, delivering lobster rolls that—while maybe not up to the standards of discerning Mainers—are definitely way better than you'd expect some 1,700 miles from Kennebunk. Excellent bread (essential for a good roll), sweet coleslaw, shockingly wonderful clam chowder, and a cooler full of beer are on hand to complement the lobster, shrimp, and crab rolls (try the "Trio" sampler plate of all three). The vibe here is casual and friendly.

If you're looking for a hot dog in Miami, the place to go is **Dogma Grill** (7030 Biscayne Blvd., 305/759-3433, www.dogmagrill.com, 10am-9pm Mon.-Sat., from $4). In addition to all-beef dogs, Dogma also serves turkey and

Versailles restaurant is a Little Havana icon.

in the heart of Little Havana. Originally a French restaurant (hence the name), Versailles is the heart and stomach of the Cuban community, and its legendary status should allow it to coast on reputation alone. But the food is excellent and always well prepared, and there is an extensive menu that goes far beyond sandwiches and *ropa vieja*. *Bistec de Palomillo* (butterflied steak), breakfast tortas, *lechon asado* (marinated pork), *boliche* (stuffed beef roast), and other Cuban staples are served in massive portions delivered by well-dressed waiters who are far more formal than the clientele. Even if you're not hungry, if you happen to be in Little Havana, you should make a point to stop at Versailles's walk-up window and grab a *cafecito*.

While it doesn't get quite the same amount of attention as Versailles, the **El Exquisito Restaurant** (1510 SW 8th St., 305/643-0227, www.elexquisitomiami.com, 7am-midnight daily, from $6) is a great and inexpensive choice for solid Cuban food in Little Havana. With a tiny dining room and friendly staff, Exquisito turns out all the basics along with a few specials like spicy shrimp with rice and a bistec de palomilla. The place is light on flair and high on quality, with excellent—and dirt-cheap—café Cubanos.

Of course, Little Havana is a great neighborhood to explore authentic Latin fare, but the incredibly popular **Catharsis Restaurant & Lounge** (1644 SW 8th St, 305/479-2746, http://catharsisrestaurant.com, 5pm-10:30pm Thurs., 5pm-midnight Fri.-Sat., from $16) has done pretty well for itself by serving Italian food with a Cuban flair. In fact, it's done so well that the restaurant is only open three nights a week. The place is routinely packed, both for dishes like grilled fish flavored with a guava sauce and served with truffle-infused potatoes and for the live music that keeps the place humming into the late-night hours.

European
Tutto Pasta (1751 SW 3rd Ave., 305/857-0709, www.tuttopasta.com, 11:30am-10:30pm

chicken dogs as well as soy-based franks for vegetarians. They're all grilled to order, but the dogs themselves are almost secondary to the infinite ways they can be dressed. A full salad bar-type setup is available so you can add fresh vegetables, herbs, and salsa, as well as a few different cheeses to your plain dog. The inventions that come out of the kitchen—like the Pitchfork (bacon, grilled onions, barbecue sauce, and cheddar cheese), Pomodoro (chopped tomatoes, garlic, basil, olive oil, and Parmesan cheese), or El Macho (jalapeños, diced tomatoes, onions, cheddar cheese, spicy brown mustard, and a spicy salsa and cream concoction)—are what truly sets this place apart from other hot-dog joints.

Cuban and Latin
A favorite among tourists and locals alike, ★ **Versailles** (3555 SW 8th St., 305/444-0240, www.versaillesrestaurant.com, 8am-2am Mon.-Thurs., 8am-3am Fri., 8am-4:30am Sat., 9am-1am Sun., from $5) is a richly decorated but completely casual Cuban restaurant

Mon.-Sat., from $9) is a friendly neighborhood restaurant serving Italian standards in a classy, comfortable environment. Pasta is freshly made on-site and can be sampled in the dozen or so pasta-based dishes on the menu, including some unusual choices like ravioli stuffed with veal, pumpkin, or even pear.

The blue-and-white decor of the **Schnitzel Haus** (1085 NE 79th St., 305/754-8002, www. schnitzelhausmiami.com, 5pm-11pm Sun.-Thurs., 5pm-midnight Fri.-Sat., from $11) may put you in the mood for Greek food, but the quirky design touches are just part of what makes this German restaurant in North Miami a unique proposition. Eleven different schnitzels and half a dozen grilled-sausage platters battle for space on the menu along with horseradish-topped beef brisket, sauerbraten, potato pancakes, and more authentic German fare. The atmosphere is a bit odd, but the service is unflaggingly friendly, if not downright festive.

In the Design District, **Mandolin Aegean Bistro** (4312 NE 2nd Ave., 305/576-6066, www.mandolinmiami.com, noon-11pm Mon.-Sat., noon-10pm Sun., from $15) serves great Mediterranean food that moves well beyond the standard gyros and spanakopita, although, the spanokopita and gyros are fantastic. If you're in the mood for a sandwich, you should really try the grilled cheese, which is built on *Kefolograviera* (a Greek sheep's milk cheese) and accented with Turkish chorizo. Main courses are fairly straightforward (kebabs, moussaka, lamb chops), but one of the best ways to eat at Mandolin is to order a variety of its starters, which range from *kefte* (lamb meatballs) and fried calamari to shrimp ouzo and grilled chorizo.

COCONUT GROVE, CORAL GABLES, AND KEY BISCAYNE
American
The Seven Dials (2030 S. Douglas Rd., Coral Gables, 786/542-1603, lunch noon-3pm Mon.-Fri., 11:30am-3pm Sun. dinner 5pm-10pm Mon.-Sat., entrees from $15) is technically

a gastropub, which means it's cozy and the dishes tend toward freshly rethought classics. However, the comfortable vibe here, combined with an excellent kitchen, has made it one of the best restaurants in Coral Gables; delightfully unstuffy, while squarely focused on delivering exceptional food and drink. A good portion of the menu is deeply inspired by British pub fare, and the Scotch egg, fish-and-chips, Welsh rarebit, and bangers and mash sit perfectly alongside avocado-mustard potato salad, salt-and-pepper chicken wings, a decadent burger, and a Gulf shrimp-stocked bouillabaisse. The combination of items equals a bill of fare that's perfectly tuned to complement your drinking, but also meticulously and thoughtfully crafted so that each dish can stand on its own.

Monty's (2550 S. Bayshore Dr., Coconut Grove, 305/856-3992, 4pm-11pm daily, from $9) is legendary for its stone crabs, but most of the other seafood selections are excellent as well. While many of the preparations are fairly straightforward, the kitchen clearly takes pride in its work preparing fresh seafood (a marina is just steps away) and preferring to broil or grill your catch rather than fry it. In the spring and fall, outdoor dining is a great casual option, while the somewhat more upscale indoor dining room is a year-round choice.

Red Fish Grill (9610 Old Cutler Rd., Coral Gables, 305/668-8788, www.redfishgrill.net, 6pm-10pm daily, from $15) doesn't have the best or the most innovative seafood in the Miami area, but the setting in the heart of the wild nature of Matheson Hammock Park is definitely one of the most beautiful in town. With outdoor seating only adding to the exceptionally romantic atmosphere, you may be able to overlook the middling fish and seafood dishes.

Latin and Caribbean
One of the best Spanish restaurants in Miami is **Xixón Spanish Cuisine** (2101 SW 22nd St., Coral Gables, 305/854-9350, www.xixoncafe.com, 11am-10pm Mon.-Thurs.,

11am-11pm Fri.-Sat., noon-5pm Sun., from $18), located just outside the heart of Coral Gables on Coral Way. Dedicated to delivering an authentic Spanish dining experience from the menu to the service, the primary dining room is airy and open, with a tapas bar as its centerpiece. There's also a beautiful wine cellar where you can nosh on small plates and sample a wide variety of wines by the ounce, thanks to single-serve Enoteca machines. Xixón takes wine-pairing seriously. If you're in doubt as to which glass will go best with your tapas or paella, just ask and you'll be expertly guided in the right direction. Despite the fact that Xixón doesn't open before 11am any day of the week, it has a limited breakfast menu to get your day started right. There's also a delicatessen here to grab some great food to go.

The Caribbean-fusion fare at ★ **Ortanique** (278 Miracle Mile, Coral Gables, 305/446-7710, http://ortaniquerestaurants.com, 6pm-10pm Mon.-Wed., 6pm-11pm Thurs.-Sat., 5:30pm-9:30pm Sun., from $31) has made the restaurant one of Coral Gables's most noteworthy dining destinations. Bringing the flavors of the Bahamas, Jamaica, and Haiti together in light, spicy-sweet masterpieces is no mean feat, but chef Cindy Hutson has received nothing but glowing praise for the concoctions that come out of Ortanique's kitchen. Fresh vegetables, fruits, and seafood form the cornerstones of most meals, and though it is quite pricey, the intimate atmosphere and inventive menu make it top-shelf dining.

Other International
Le Bouchon du Grove (3430 Main Hwy, Coconut Grove, 786/475-5126, breakfast and lunch: 9:30am-3pm Mon.-Fri, 8:30am-3pm Sat.-Sun, dinner: 6pm-11pm Sun.-Thurs.., 6pm-midnight Fri.-Sat., from $14) is well-known for delivering high-quality French classics in a bistro-style environment that, while quite cozy, is neither uncomfortable nor overly pretentious.

PokéBao (153 Giralda Ave., 786/801-1951, pokebaomiami.com, 11am-9pm daily, from $13) already has a little bit of culture clash in its very name, and yes, you can not only enjoy Hawaiian-style poké bowls filled with fresh tuna, vegetables, and toppings, but also get those ingredients—and others—stuffed into Chinese bao. However, the pan-globalism doesn't stop there; while the emphasis is certainly on Asia-Pacific cuisine, a good bit of Latin American flair also pops up on the

Ortanique offers great dining on Coral Gables's Miracle Mile.

ingredient list, thanks to mojo pork shoulder, crispy whitefish, fish tacos, *vaca frita* (fried beef), and more.

Maroosh Mediterranean (223 Valencia Ave., Coral Gables, 305/476-9800, www.maroosh.com, 11:30am-10pm Tues.-Thurs., noon-11:30pm Fri.-Sat., noon-10pm Sun., from $16) serves hummus, kibbe, falafel, lemon chicken, and other Middle Eastern standards in a dimly lit, intimate environment that on weekends is interrupted by the gyrations of a belly dancer.

Accommodations

To get the most out of a visit to Miami, stay on Miami Beach, since the concentration of restaurants and nightlife is at its highest here and you will only be a few minutes' drive from the sights of mainland Miami. However, the vast majority of hotels in the area have peak-season rates that will make your wallet weep. It's not cheap to stay in Miami, but visiting doesn't necessarily have to be a budget-buster. During the **high season (Dec.-Mar.)** it's possible (not necessarily likely) to snag a decent room in the vicinity of South Beach for under $200, with the rates decreasing the farther north you go. During the **summer,** those rates can sometimes be reduced by as much as half. Those who choose to stay downtown tend to be business travelers, so there are often incredible deals to be found for weekend stays in the area's chain hotels, which are just a short cab ride away from South Beach.

SOUTH BEACH
Under $100

With a history that dates back to the 1930s (gangster Al Capone ran a gambling operation out of here), it's remarkable that the **Clay Hotel** (1438 Washington Ave., 305/534-2988, www.clayhotel.com, $99 d) has managed to maintain its art deco charm while offering clean, decent accommodations at very low rates. Part of the Clay is set up as a dorm-style hostel. The audience skews pretty young and draws a lot of party-ready kids from Latin America. The atmosphere is exceedingly friendly, and the operators run a pretty tight ship. Hotel rooms have private baths as well as telephones, TVs, air-conditioning, and even mini fridges. Rooms are small but tidy and surprisingly modern. The Clay has a full kitchen and laundry facilities available to guests.

$150-200

South Beach is a great place to stay if you want to spend a lot of money on a room, only to have the hotel staff treat you rudely. **The Kent** (1131 Collins Ave., 305/604-5068, www.thekenthotel.com, from $159 d) completely inverts the equation, putting an emphasis on friendly customer service and cheap rooms. While the stylish and modern guest rooms aren't the largest on South Beach, neither do they raise the "Is this a room or a closet?" question that some art deco hotels around here do.

$200-300

Although South Beach's reputation as a vacation destination for the rich and famous leads most folks to assume that hotel accommodations in the area are universally high-priced, it's important to remember that South Beach wasn't always such a glamorous outpost. There are quite a few hotels in the area that could easily be considered a bargain. Guest rooms in most of them are quite small, and the decor is usually not the most sumptuous, but the art deco architecture and central location of places like the **Majestic Hotel** (660 Ocean Dr., 305/455-3270, www.majesticsouthbeach.com, from $229 d) manage to more than make up for its relative lack of glamour. Guest rooms are clean and bright, with reasonably up-to-date furnishings, and some of the guest rooms even have great ocean views.

Best Accommodations

★ **Casa Grande Suite Hotel:** This hotel offers all-suite accommodations and it's probably one of the best deals on South Beach (page 72).

★ **Setai:** With two entirely different lodging experiences on the same property, visitors can choose between chic suites and spacious condo-style rooms (page 74).

★ **Freehand:** The stylish hostel-but-not-a-hostel vibe at Freehand makes it an excellent budget option just outside of South Beach proper (page 74).

★ **EPIC Hotel:** It combines hip design, luxurious touches, exemplary service, and surprisingly large guest rooms (page 76).

★ **Mandarin Oriental:** From the open-yet-intimate lobby and the award-winning restaurants to the excellent spa and beautiful guest rooms, the Mandarin delivers five-star luxury (page 77).

★ **Hotel St. Michel:** This small, European-style hotel has an excellent location in the middle of downtown (page 77).

The **Villa Paradiso** (1415 Collins Ave., 305/532-0616, from $249 d) is a bargain. With its location right on Collins Avenue, the guest rooms are surprisingly calming, with views of the lush, quiet courtyard. More like cute studio apartments than standard motel rooms, the suites are good for those looking for a comfortable and inexpensive place to stay in the heart of South Beach.

Possessed of a similar charm is the **Richmond Hotel** (1757 Collins Ave., 305/538-2331, from $229 d), a family-owned establishment in a pink-lit art deco beauty of a building. There's a lushly landscaped pool and courtyard area that feels completely isolated from the buzz of Collins Avenue, and guests can walk right from the pool to the beach. Guest rooms are simple and a little frumpy, but they're clean and comfortable and come with all the modern conveniences.

The Catalina Hotel & Beach Club (1732 Collins Ave., 305/674-1160, www.catalina-hotel.com, from $249 d) is a blast out of the 1960s retro-futurist past. Combining both the ornamental excess and the plasticky colors of jet-age chic with a refined modern touch (and Tempur-Pedic mattresses), the Catalina

exudes the sort of visual decadence that so many visitors to South Beach are searching for. With more than 130 guest rooms spread over two buildings, it doesn't quite feel like a boutique hotel, but its individualistic flair makes it seem far more intimate than it really is. Guest rooms are beautifully appointed with upscale fixtures and flat-screen TVs, and the three restaurants (Kung Fu Sushi, Red Bar & Cafe, and Maxine's Bistro & Bar) and two swimming pools round out the fun and glamour combination.

For a while, many visitors to the **Hotel Astor** (956 Washington Ave., 305/531-8081, www.hotelastor.com, from $219 d) never made it past the restaurant in the basement; the Metro Kitchen + Bar was a preferred spot for B-list celebs and those who sought them out. Even though the Metro is closed, getting booked into one of the gorgeous and intimate guest rooms at the Astor is still pretty easy. The 40 freshly renovated guest rooms in this 80-year-old art deco building are beautiful (although the views generally aren't) and they are incredibly comfortable, with adjustable lighting, soft mattresses, and upscale appointments. Even better, despite the Astor's relatively central location and the popularity of its lounge and courtyard, the guest rooms manage to be pretty quiet.

In 1999, designer Todd Oldham reimagined the art deco classicism of the Tiffany Hotel into the directly named **The Hotel** (801 Collins Ave., 305/531-2222, www.thehotelofsouthbeach.com, from $249 d). Whether his work was a success depends completely on whether you prize style or square footage as a hotel's most important feature. The Hotel has the former in spades; all the originality Oldham saved in coming up with the Hotel's name was obviously directed into the modern, quirky elegance of the facility's public areas and the 53 cute, well-appointed, and quiet guest rooms, each of which seems to have been individually decorated. Nearly all of the guest rooms push the definition of "cozy" into laughable territory. Still, with the clubs and restaurants of South Beach within steps of the front door, and the hotel's own rooftop Spire Bar a nightlife destination of its own, you're not likely going to be spending that much time in your room anyway.

Need a little more space to stretch out in your room? The ★ **Casa Grande Suite Hotel** (834 Ocean Dr., 305/672-7003, www.casagrandesuitehotel.com, from $229 d) offers, as the name implies, all-suite accommodations, and it's probably one of the best deals on South Beach. Located right across Ocean Drive from Lummus Park, it's right in the heart of the action, both during the day and at night. So, it's not the quietest place to stay, nor will you experience anything remotely approaching beach-bum solitude, but if the raucous energy of South Beach is why you're here in the first place, you can do a whole lot worse than the Casa Grande. The smallest rooms here are studio apartment-sized, clocking in at 600-plus square feet, while the one-bedroom suites are around 850 square feet. While none of the rooms are particularly character-rich when it comes to decor, they're all furnished nicely (if sparsely), with modern accents and comfortable bedding. As if that weren't enough, all the rooms come with full kitchens. Did I mention that this was an incredible deal?

Like Diesel jeans? You might want to stay at the **Pelican** (828 Ocean Dr., 305/673-3373, www.pelicanhotel.com, from $299 d). If the Italian stylists behind Diesel know anything, it's how to make something aggressively cool and fashion-forward accessible to the masses. Having the Diesel brand behind the design decisions at the Pelican is as awesome as it is odd. Each of the rooms here is put together with its own self-contained theme—"Birth of the Bubbles," "Best Whorehouse," "Me Tarzan, You Vain"—and each one of them is whimsical without being overly cute. More importantly, each room is interesting without being uncomfortable. Very few of the lower-priced rooms (in the "deluxe queen-size" category) are spacious, but neither are they overly cramped. Stepping up a couple of notches to the king-size suites like "Executive Fifties" makes for a more indulgent experience. Regardless of their design or price, all of the rooms come with flat-screen TVs, complimentary Wi-Fi, fridges, safes, and nicely appointed bathrooms.

Over $300

One of the most photographed hotels in South Beach is undoubtedly the **Breakwater** (940 Ocean Dr., 305/532-2362, www.breakwater-southbeach.com, from $339 d), thanks to its imposing and beautiful art deco exterior, which is highlighted by equally unmissable neon signage and accented by swaying palms out front. Add on the beach-view rooftop terrace, complete with bed seating and crisp, white umbrellas, and this is a property that is visual shorthand for "South Beach." Thanks to a comprehensive renovation that concluded in 2011, the interior delivers on what the street view promises, with luxurious and stylish lodging ranging from smallish-but-comfortable rooms (at about 300 square feet) to somewhat larger 550-square-foot suites. If you're looking for a splurge, plunk down for the privacy and poshness of one of the rooftop suites. All rooms feature minibars, flat-screen TVs, and posh bathrooms, while the more expensive suites also have sitting areas and terraces with whirlpool tubs. There is also a decent fitness center on-site with a small lap pool. Wi-Fi is complimentary throughout the property.

Blessed with a great location on Collins Avenue in the heart of South Beach, the **Blue Moon Hotel** (944 Collins Ave., 305/673-2262, www.bluemoonhotel.com, from $329 d) was "rescued" in 2012 by the Marriott chain and reimagined as part of the chain's "Autograph Collection." After coming under Marriott's wing, the Blue Moon underwent a light facelift, and its rooms were slightly refreshed, but nothing monumental enough to warrant a near doubling of the room rates. All the guest rooms are spacious and stylishly appointed, with flat-screen TVs, in-room safes, minibars, and coffee-makers, while the somewhat larger "deluxe" guest rooms are more conveniently located, with better views and slightly larger floor plans. There's not a whole lot to differentiate the Blue Moon from South Beach's art deco hotels, but it's still a very nice hotel. The Blue Moon may not be an optimal selection for families as all guest rooms have only one queen-size bed.

The **Clevelander** (1020 Ocean Dr., 877/532-4006, www.clevelander.com, from $379 d) is best known for its late-night parties and raucous poolside scene. So despite its classy art deco exterior, those seeking a peaceful evening of rest in a historic building should look elsewhere. Those choosing to indulge (or overindulge) themselves will find copious opportunities and won't mind stumbling back to guest rooms that still show their age despite attempts to dress them up with flat-screen TVs and nice linens.

Miami Beach's **Mondrian** (1100 West Ave., 305/514-1500, www.morganshotelgroup.com, from $349 d) is only the third hotel to bear the name, and unsurprisingly it both meets and exceeds the expectations people tend to have about this stylish brand. Opened at the beginning of 2009, the Mondrian doesn't mimic its Los Angeles forebear but instead embraces its South Beach environment with billowing cabana-style tents, gorgeous views of the bay from its Sunset Lounge (the Mondrian isn't located on the beach), and a stylish neo-tropical decor that's as bracingly modern as it is sumptuous and comfortable. The Marcel Wanders-designed hotel even features an enormous vending machine in the lobby that, instead of chocolate bars or sundries, dispenses jewelry, Rolls Royce rentals, and designer sunglasses. The guest rooms are, of course, breathtakingly modern, with whimsical design-forward features accenting luxury touches like flat-screen TVs and down-stuffed duvets.

Guest rooms at **The Tides** (1220 Ocean Dr., 305/604-5070, www.tidessouthbeach.com, from $409 d) are among the most expensive in South Beach, but they're also some of the largest. The 12-story art deco building contains only 45 guest rooms, all of which are oceanfront suites. The guest rooms are decadent and luxurious, with large flat-screen TVs, complimentary Wi-Fi, and in-room espresso makers. The smallest guest rooms—the lower-floor studio suites—are still quite spacious at 550 square feet. The art deco charm at the Tides is present in all the guest rooms courtesy of faux-vintage furnishings (all of the style, twice the comfort). In the larger suites, the amenities and square footage increase, with some including Sub-Zero refrigerator-equipped kitchens, advanced audio-visual technology, and individual decor touches.

Although the stark white decor, haughtily glamorous staff, and sky-high rates at the **Delano** (1685 Collins Ave., 305/672-2000, www.morganshotelgroup.com, from $419 d) have come to define the South Beach hotel experience, they've also become somewhat clichéd. The well-heeled still pack the hotel almost every night, but much of the electricity of South Beach has moved to smaller, hipper, and, yes, friendlier places. Still, if you've got money to burn, the staff at the Delano will gladly (or at least quickly) take it from you. Despite their monochrome color scheme, the guest rooms feel rather cramped, although they are, admittedly, incredibly gorgeous and stylish.

The beautiful guest rooms at the all-suite **Sagamore** (1671 Collins Ave., 305/535-8088, www.sagamorehotel.com, from $429 d) are a far better investment, and they're a half block away. Although the hotel is quite pricey, the staff at Sagamore seem glad to see you, and when you step into your suite you'll feel as if you got your money's worth. Like a true boutique hotel, the Sagamore is impossibly stylish, with public areas that blend dark wood floors, stark white furnishings, and contemporary sculpture. Guest rooms feature large flat-screen TVs, whirlpool baths, tile floors, and upscale appointments. Celebrity sightings are quite common, but even without the A-list, the Sagamore's bar is a pleasure to hang out in, especially early in the evening before the crowds descend.

The ★ **Setai** (2001 Collins Ave., 305/520-6500, www.thesetaihotel.com, from $599 d) offers two entirely different lodging experiences on its property. The main building is an 8-story art deco building with interiors that are lavish, sleek, and minimalist, while the adjacent tower building is a 40-story condo hotel. Although the tower guest rooms are more spacious, they're also considerably more expensive, and while the guest rooms in the art deco building are far from cheap, they're a much better value as they're both charming and contemporary. All of the guest rooms are suites, ranging from studios to two-bedrooms. Studios in the art deco building have black-granite tubs, espresso machines, and flat-screen TVs, while the one- and two-bedroom suites in the tower add on full kitchens and living areas. Musicians may want to consider splurging on the four-bedroom penthouse suite: for only $25,000 per night they can not only sleep like kings but also avail themselves of the Lenny Kravitz-designed rooftop recording studio.

The **Royal Palm** (1545 Collins Ave., 786/276-0177, www.royalpalmmiamibeach. com, from $399 d) is a large, relatively modern high-rise hotel with over 400 guest rooms, many of which are suites. The guest rooms are equipped with new bathroom fixtures and

Upscale lodgings like the Setai are abundant in Miami Beach.

flat-screen TVs, and the "resort" features two outdoor pools, beachfront cabanas, two bars, a restaurant, a fitness center, and the availability of various water activities. This property has no connection with the Royal Palm Hotel that was Henry Flagler's first hotel in the city, opened when Flagler extended his Florida East Coast Railway into Miami in 1897.

MIAMI BEACH
Under $150

Located just a block from the ocean and facing the Intracoastal Waterway, the beautifully updated 1930s-era building of the ★ **Freehand** (2727 Indian Creek Dr., 305/531-2727, www.thefreehand.com, dorms from $45 pp, private from $200) is as convenient as it is isolated. Formerly the Indian Creek Hotel, the Freehand was created as an upscale hostel in 2012. It's one of the best values on Miami Beach and one of the coolest places to stay. The vibe here is relaxed and unpretentious. Both the coed dorms and the private rooms are bright and comfortable.

Staying in one of the quad dorms allows for just enough interaction with fellow travelers to give you plenty of good stories to go home with. This modern interpretation of the hostel moves beyond the stereotypes of budget-squeezed backpackers without turning its back on folks looking for an affordable place to stay. The same designers behind New York's stunning Ace Hotel are responsible for the casual, colorful, and worldly decor here. The onsite bar, the Broken Shaker, is one of the best craft cocktail bars in Miami.

The 53 small guest rooms at the motel-style **Beach Place Hotel** (8601 Harding Ave., 305/866-3313, www.beachplacemiami. com, from $129 d), renovated in 2012, are clean and equipped with fresh new furnishings. The hotel is just across the street from the beaches at North Shore Park.

$200-300

The **Alexander Hotel** (5225 Collins Ave., 305/865-6500, www.alexanderhotel.com, from $229 d) was one of the first condo-hotels

the stylish and affordable Freehand hotel in Miami Beach

to be built in Miami Beach back in the early 1980s, and despite a 2013 multimillion-dollar renovation to the property, there's a chance that you may end up with a room with older furnishings. Even the most dated guest room at the Alexander will still be a nice one, as they're all quite spacious. In either one- or two-bedroom configurations, the smallest guest room is 1,000 square feet. All units have full kitchens, private bedrooms, and balconies that look out onto either the ocean or the Intracoastal Waterway. The public spaces exude a rich elegance thanks to antiques and other decor that came from the Cornelius Vanderbilt mansion.

The **Mimosa Hotel** (6525 Collins Ave., 305/867-5000, www.themimosa.com, from $199 d) is a fine, small-scale option for those who want to enjoy the relative quietude of Miami Beach but don't feel like staying in a massive condo-hotel. Located right on the beach near the beach park at 64th Street and boasting only 60 guest rooms, the Mimosa isn't quite a cozy boutique hotel, but the service and space are far more intimate than at most of Miami Beach's other waterfront lodgings. The standard guest rooms are clean and stylish, if a bit small, with modern minimalist furnishings and comfortable queen beds. There are also several different-size suites, some with kitchenettes.

At the confusing intersection of Arthur Godfrey Road and Collins Avenue, **Circa 39** (3900 Collins Ave., 305/538-4900, www. circa39.com, from $199 d) sits right on the southern end of Miami Beach. It is still far enough away from the buzz of South Beach to feel like something of a respite from the rush. The building has plenty of SoBe charm, combining late 1930s architecture with modern amenities. Although Circa 39 doesn't trip over itself to be the hippest spot in town, the courtyard garden, comfortable restaurant, and pool area exude a relaxed sort of cool. Guest rooms are clean and reasonably spacious, with the standard array of amenities.

Just like its next-door neighbor, the Rat Pack fave Fontainebleau, the mammoth

Eden Roc (4525 Collins Ave., 305/531-0000, www.edenrocmiami.com, from $299 d) has been updated from its faded 1950s glory to resemble something approaching a modern hotel. Although it still maintains much of its original post-deco exterior, instead of offering quaint retro-styled lodging, the interior spaces are sleek and modern. The hotel is often home to conventioners or special events, so the public areas can sometimes be a bit congested. The 630 guest rooms are large, modern, and stylish, if a bit anonymous. There is a Nobu restaurant on site.

The Palms (3025 Collins Ave., 305/534-0505, www.thepalmshotel.com, from $299 d) is a large, traditional hotel with 243 guest rooms spread over 11 floors. This being Miami Beach, "traditional" is a somewhat flexible term, and the Palms offers a unique combination of art deco simplicity, luxe filigree, and contemporary style. Guest rooms are available in standard, suite, and penthouse configurations. Make sure to splurge for an oceanfront room, as the views from the large windows, which have no balconies, are fairly spectacular. With a spa, restaurant, and poolside bar as well as nine meeting rooms, the Palms is far from cozy, but the guest rooms are comfortable and possessed of enough personality to warrant the cost.

Over $300

With an in-between location alongside the causeway between downtown Miami and Miami Beach, **The Standard** (40 Island Ave., 305/673-1717, http://standardhotels. com, from $399 d) is a typically impressive property from Andre Balázs, the trendsetting hotelier. Guest rooms are labeled in whimsical but declarative fashion, with the "Missionary" referring to the small basic guest rooms, "Dry," "Lush," and "Wet" indicating views of the courtyard, gardens, or the Intracoastal Waterway, respectively, each of which is available in "medium" or "large" sizes. The spa aspect of the hotel is played up via outdoor tubs, waterfall showerheads, organic minibar snacks, and decor

that's all about clean lines, mod cons, and comfort.

CENTRAL MIAMI
$150-200

Fortune House Hotel Suites (185 SE 14th Terr., 305/349-5200, www.fortunehousehotel. com, from $199 d) is a reasonably priced downtown condo-hotel that provides good value, especially for extended-stay visitors. While far from luxurious and not even all that modern, the standard suites are spacious, with full kitchens and washer-dryer combos. Stepping up to the "executive" suites, you'll get more contemporary furnishings and balconies that provide great nighttime views of the city or Biscayne Bay.

$200-300

The **Hotel InterContinental Miami** (100 Chopin Plaza, 305/577-1000, www.icmiami-hotel.com, from $279 d) offers chain-hotel luxury aimed at business travelers who can't justify the splurge at the handful of truly upscale hotels downtown. The lobby area is decadent and quite fancy, but guest rooms are unimaginative, although they are equipped with the requisite level of mass-market plushness one expects from the brand. With three decent restaurants, two bars, a spa, laundry service, and a heated outdoor pool, there's not much need for a short-stay executive to leave the premises, but there's little here to tempt other travelers.

Over $300

The ★ **EPIC Hotel** (270 Biscayne Blvd., 305/424-5226, www.epichotel.com, from $299 d) is a Kimpton Hotels property that definitely maintains the chain's reputation for combining hip design, modern luxurious touches, exemplary service, and surprisingly large guest rooms. Even the most basic guest rooms are around 475 square feet, with gorgeous views and private balconies; as you go up the chain of guest-room quality, there are loft-style junior suites (700 square feet) and one-bedroom suites (950 square feet). All 400 guest rooms are painted in muted clean colors, appointed with sleek indulgent furnishings, and boast touches like soaking tubs, flat-screen TVs, and more. The hotel is pet friendly, has an on-site marina, a spa, and an excellent restaurant named Area 31.

If you're going to spring for a luxury downtown hotel with Asian touches, you may as well go for a few nights at the ★ **Mandarin Oriental** (500 Brickell Key Dr., 305/913-8288, www.mandarinoriental.com, from $479 d). Although you can occasionally stumble onto somewhat lower rates on the weekends and during the melting humidity of hurricane season, those rates could hardly be called a bargain. Still, from the open-yet-intimate lobby area and the award-winning restaurants to the excellent spa and beautiful guest rooms, the Mandarin more than delivers on the pricey deal. Guest rooms are spectacularly simple, with clean modern lines and minimalist furnishings that manage to be simultaneously unobtrusive and sumptuous; although the standard hotel rooms are slightly on the small side, the suites range in size from 625 square feet all the way up to the 2,365 square feet for the deluxe Oriental Suite (which includes an eight-person dining room and a private theater). Though the hotel is downtown, the Mandarin is less focused on the needs of business travelers than on the needs of those who can do without the glitz and noise of South Beach.

COCONUT GROVE AND CORAL GABLES
$150-200

The ★ **Hotel St. Michel** (162 Alcazar Ave., Coral Gables, www.boutiquehotelcoralgables. com, 305/444-1666, from $179 d) is a small, European-style hotel with an excellent location in the middle of downtown Coral Gables, just a couple of blocks from the Miracle Mile. The 27 cozy guest rooms are decked out with beautiful antiques and turn-of-the-century decor that's heavy on the dark wood and brass. The effect is sublimely romantic and utterly transportive. Although the restaurants along

the Mile are just a few steps away, the hotel's restaurant is excellent, and a small lobby-area lounge is a great place to unwind with a glass of wine after a long day.

$200-300

Once famous—or infamous—as a hangout for some notorious "cocaine cowboys" in the early 1980s, **The Mutiny Hotel** (2951 S. Bayshore Dr., Coconut Grove, 305/441-2100, www.providentresorts.com, from $219 d) is a great option for travelers looking for a charming, stylish, and affordable place in Coconut Grove. The furnishings are intentionally dated, reflecting the nautical and Caribbean colonial theme of the property's name, but they're also well-maintained, clean, and quite comfortable. All the guest rooms are large suites with full kitchens, and the Mutiny's location right on Biscayne Bay makes for some beautiful scenery.

The **Sonesta Coconut Grove** (2889 McFarlane Rd., 305/529-2828, www.sonesta. com, from $239 d) offers standard mid-scale accommodations as well as one- and two-bedroom suites in a contemporary high-rise building that overlooks Biscayne Bay. Guest rooms are modern and well-maintained, if unspectacular, and there is a pool, rooftop fitness center, and two squash courts on the premises.

The **Palmeiras Beach Club at Grove Isle** (4 Grove Isle Dr., Coconut Grove, 305/858-8300, www.palmeirasbeachclub. com, from $329 d) is a self-contained escape, seemingly expressly designed for those celebrating special occasions. Thanks to its island location in Biscayne Bay and a generally insulated atmosphere, you could stay for your entire Miami vacation without venturing past the security gate until it's time to depart. Given the gorgeous views, comfortable guest rooms, and ample facilities that include tennis, an exceptional spa, a very nice restaurant, and a (small) private beach, you may want to do exactly that. However, the Palmeiras feels more like a gated community than a hotel or resort.

Over $300

For travelers who want some of the stylishness of a South Beach hotel but can do without the space constraints that come with art deco architecture, the 179 guest rooms at Coconut Grove's **Mayfair Hotel & Spa** (3000 Florida Ave., 305/441-0000, www.mayfairhotelandspa.com, from $229 d) manage to exude a bit of boutique-style hipness while also being exceptionally large. Still, the size and beauty of the guest rooms don't quite justify the high room rates. After all, you're in Coconut Grove, not on Collins Avenue. But, if a bit of low-key relaxation is in order, the sumptuous guest rooms and 4,500-square-foot spa may be just the ticket.

The **Biltmore Hotel & Resort** (1200 Anastasia Ave., Coral Gables, 305/445-1926, www.biltmorehotel.com, from $329 d) is a superlative and classic hotel that excels in every respect. From exemplary front-door service and sumptuous public areas to modern well-appointed guest rooms and exceptional golf, tennis, and recreational facilities, the Biltmore maintains the same level of quality it did when it opened in 1926. The only drawback to staying at the Biltmore is its location; it's really not convenient to anything. However, with four restaurants, four bars, 10 tennis courts, a golf course, and even a wine cellar on-site, it's quite possible that you'd never even want or need to leave this postcard-perfect property. It's said that the spirit of Al Capone is one of several ghosts that roam the halls, especially near the suite that bears his name. The hotel's enormous swimming pool was for decades the largest in the United States and the site where Olympic champion Johnny Weissmuller broke a world record.

Information and Services

TOURIST INFORMATION

The **Greater Miami Convention and Visitors Bureau** (701 Brickell Ave., Suite 700, 800/933-8448, www.miamiandbeaches.com, 8:30am-6pm Mon.-Fri.) is a good source of information for advance planning, and it has an information counter open 24 hours a day at Miami International Airport's Concourse E. The **Miami Beach Chamber of Commerce** operates both a tourist hotline (305/673-7400) and an enormous and well-stocked **Visitors Center** (1920 Meridian Ave., 305/674-1300, www.miamibeachchamber.com, 9am-6pm Mon.-Fri., 10am-4pm Sat.-Sun.). Both visitors bureaus sell the **Go Miami pass,** which provides entry to major attractions as well as dining deals.

EMERGENCY AND MEDICAL SERVICES

In the event of an emergency, dial 911, a free call from any phone. For less pressing medical needs, call **Physician Referral Service** (305/324-8717), which will connect you with an appropriate doctor. In Miami Beach, the **Mt. Sinai Medical Center** (4300 Alton Rd., 305/674-2121, www.msmc.com) is the most convenient hospital. The **University of Miami Hospital** (1400 NW 12th Ave., 305/325-5511, http://umiamihospital.com) is located just to the west of the main downtown area, which also makes it close to Coral Gables, Coconut Grove, and Little Havana.

ATMS

ATMs are abundant throughout Miami and Miami Beach. The only heavily touristed area where you might have trouble finding an ATM is Little Havana. There is a branch of **U.S. Century Bank** (468 NW 27th Ave., 305/642-6990, www.uscentury.com) in West Little Havana, which has an ATM.

Transportation

GETTING THERE
Car

The 230-mile drive from Orlando to Miami takes about three hours on **Florida's Turnpike,** and costs about $15 in tolls. For a more scenic route through the heart of Old Florida, you can take **US-27** south from Kissimmee (near Disney World) through the cow pastures and orange groves of the state's inner corridor, before it curves east toward Fort Lauderdale and Miami; the road terminates as North 36th Street in midtown Miami. This route is 233 miles and takes about 4.5 hours.

It's 270 miles from Tampa to Miami, via **I-75.** This route takes about four hours and passes by Sarasota, Venice, Fort Myers, and Naples before curving east through the northernmost sections of the Everglades and terminating in Fort Lauderdale; there, you'll need to jump on **I-95** for the remaining 45-minute drive into Miami.

I-95 also connects Miami to the entire eastern coast of the U.S., terminating in Maine.

Air

Miami International Airport (MIA, 4200 NW 21st St., 305/876-7000, www.miami-airport.com) is continually duking it out with Orlando International for the title of Florida's busiest airport, but without a doubt MIA is the more international of the two. The airport is not only served by multiple daily flights by all major low-cost and cut-rate American carriers—including dozens of direct flights from around the country—but is also the primary point of entry for travelers entering the United States from South America and the Caribbean. It is the third-busiest international gateway after Los Angeles's LAX and New York's JFK. The airport, a hub for American Airlines, is located only about eight miles from downtown Miami. Taxis ($32 flat rate for 1-5 people to South Beach, $26.50 flat rate for 1-5 people to North Miami Beach, $21.70 flat rate for 1-5 people to downtown and Coconut Grove) and shuttles are available (from $10 pp to hotels) in the ground transportation area. Ride-share services like Lyft and Uber also operate from MIA, but their legality seems to be constantly in flux.

Despite the proximity and the wide availability of service at MIA, many travelers have begun using **Fort Lauderdale-Hollywood International Airport** (FLL, 320 Terminal Dr., Ft. Lauderdale, 866/435-9355, www.broward.org/airport) instead. Although it's almost an hour away from downtown Miami, FLL has carved out a niche catering to low-cost carriers and is far easier to navigate than the labyrinthine and somewhat outdated facilities at MIA. Taxis can run upwards of $75 to Miami, but shuttle services are available in the ground transportation area from around $40.

Train and Bus

Amtrak (305/835-1221, www.amtrak.com) runs its Silver Star and Palmetto services from Miami north through Jacksonville, Orlando, and Tampa.

The **Tri-Rail** (8303 NW 37th Ave., $7-10) commuter train connects Palm Beach and Broward Counties with Miami. 2017 has seen the debut of high-speed rail in Florida, in the form of the privately owned **Brightline,** which connects Miami and other major cities in South Florida to Orlando; the ride from Miami to Orlando is projected to take just three hours, and the route is expected to be complete in 2018. Amtrak, Tri-Rail, and Brightline all terminate at the Miami Central Station, at Miami International Airport.

The Miami **Greyhound** station (4111 NW 27th St., 305/871-1810, www.greyhound.com) is open 24 hours.

GETTING AROUND
Car

Central Miami, including Coral Gables

and Coconut Grove, as well as the southern parts of the area, are best seen by car. The Dolphin Expressway (State Road 836/I-395) runs east-west from South Beach all the way out to the edge of the Everglades. For, north-south travels (especially to Coral Gables and Homestead), take the South Dixie Highway (US-1). Several of the city's main arteries, including the Dolphin Expressway, Florida's Turnpike, and other routes, are toll roads, and many of these have unmanned toll plazas. But don't think you're getting away with anything by flying through the E-Pass lane, as you'll still get a bill (at a higher rate!) sent to you thanks to the toll-by-tag system.

Miami is about 30 miles south of Fort Lauderdale. Within the Miami area, distances are fairly short: downtown to Miami Beach is just a hop over a mile-long causeway; Coconut Grove is about 5 miles to the southwest; and Coral Gables is about 3 miles southwest of the Grove. Coral Gables is about 5 miles from downtown Miami, and Homestead is 30 miles southwest of downtown Miami.

Rental cars are available at Miami International Airport and Fort Lauderdale-Hollywood International Airport. Rates are extremely competitive: you can easily get a seven-day rental for under $150. This will leave you with funds to cover the numerous parking-garage fees and meter feedings you'll encounter throughout the area. Most of the major car rental agencies also have offices in downtown Miami. Street parking in Miami Beach is always difficult to find.

Bike and on Foot

South Beach is best seen on foot or by bicycle, which is a good thing, since finding parking is an abominable proposition. Bike traffic is better tolerated throughout South Beach

than anywhere else in Miami. In fact, central Miami and its outlying areas can be pretty dangerous for bikers (and pedestrians) who are unfamiliar with the rhythms and rules of Miami roads. Bike rentals are available via the city's **Deco Bike** (305/532-9494, www.deco-bike.com, rates from $4/half hour) service.

Public Transportation

In a theme that you'll find recurs throughout Florida, public transportation in Miami is not the ideal choice for moving around the city. Although Miami-Dade's network of buses and trains is more advanced than any other Florida city, that's really not saying very much. The **Metrorail/Metrobus** system (www.miamidade.gov, Metrorail 5am-midnight daily, Metrobus hours vary, with several routes running 11pm-6am or 24 hours daily, one-way fares range from $2-4) is almost completely useless unless you're traveling to and from downtown and Coral Gables. The downtown **Metromover** (www.miamidade.gov, 5am-midnight daily, free) is an elevated train that runs in a 4.5-mile loop, which is great for getting around to the limited sights and restaurants of the downtown area.

Taxis and Ride-Sharing Services

Taxis are readily available throughout Miami Beach, Coconut Grove, and Coral Gables. Finding a cab downtown may be a difficult proposition outside the immediate vicinity of a hotel. Call **Yellow Cab** (305/444-4444) or **Central** (305/532-5555) to have one dispatched to your location. It costs $2.95 to start the meter and fares add $2.40 for each mile. Lyft, Uber, and other ride-sharing services operate throughout the Miami-Dade area.

The Everglades

Highlights

★ **Ten Thousand Islands National Wildlife Refuge:** The 35,000 acres of undeveloped swamps, marshland, and waterways are perfect for adventurous types willing to get their feet wet (page 88).

★ **Ochopee Post Office:** At 61 square feet—just enough room for a clerk and a tiny bit of equipment—it's the smallest fully operational post office in the United States (page 94).

★ **Big Cypress Gallery:** Clyde Butcher's photographs of the Everglades are worldrenowned. His gallery is a place to buy everything from prints to books to coffee mugs (page 96).

★ **Shark Valley Visitor Center:** The most popular of all of the area visitors centers, Shark Valley offers tram rides, a bike trail, and other ways to gingerly experience the 'Glades firsthand (page 98).

★ **Pa-hay-okee Overlook:** This short boardwalk gives you stunning vistas without hours of backcountry walking (page 102).

★ **Hiking:** The Royal Palm Visitor Center is the starting point for two of the Everglades' most popular trails, **Anhinga Amble** and **Gumbo Limbo** (page 102).

★ **Canoeing and Kayaking:** From the southernmost point on the Florida mainland, boat excursions allow unparalleled access into some remote and unspoiled waters of Florida Bay (page 103).

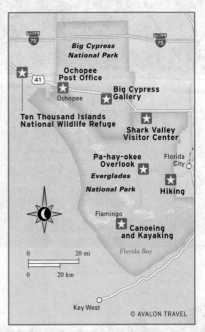

The Everglades are huge. There's a whole lot of natural beauty to absorb here—and almost all of it can be explored and enjoyed in relative peace and quiet.

There's a small creek behind an elementary school in Orlando that is as inconspicuous as they come. But the trickle of Shingle Creek is the humble origin of one of the world's most treasured wetland ecosystems. Those headwaters merge into the Kissimmee River, which flows into Lake Okeechobee, which discharges into the Everglades, a vast expanse of marshes, swamps, islands, forests, and the waterways of mainland Florida's southernmost points. Comprising essentially all of the wetlands and prairies south of Lake Okeechobee and sandwiched between Naples in the west and Miami in the east, the area covers nearly 4,000 square miles. Despite the best efforts of voracious real-estate developers, most of the Everglades remain wild. Although, decades of agriculture, drainage, attempts at "taming" the land, and nearby population growth have dramatically (and in some cases, permanently) altered the ecosystems for the worse.

PLANNING YOUR TIME

It's important to keep in mind that, basically, what you're here to see is a relatively undisturbed swamp, along with the various ecosystems within it. This means that facilities are few and far between, and access to the heart of the park is largely limited to what you're able to see from within a small boat. For that reason, people usually have to decide between undertaking a backwater adventure or availing themselves of the easily accessible visitors centers inside the park. The visitors centers not only provide maps and guidance but provide relatively populous landmarks that help to ensure you won't be unintentionally spending the night in the swamp. Under all circumstances, you should make sure your car's gas tank is topped off, you've brought in plenty of water, sunscreen, and bug repellent, and that you make every effort to ensure that no members of your group wander off on their own; all that swamp can start to look the same after a while.

Previous: Alligators abound in the Everglades; Airboats are a classic way to get around. **Above:** Everglades swamp.

The Everglades

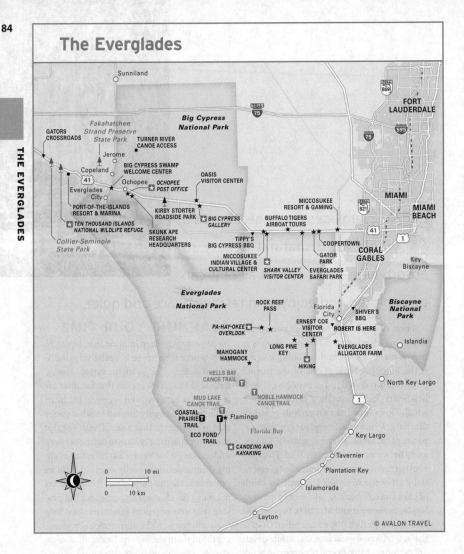

If you're coming to the southern Everglades via Florida City and Homestead, you'll need to dedicate a full day to making the 30-plus-mile journey from the park's entrance all the way to the far reaches of the Flamingo Visitor Center. This will give you time not only to take in the multiple stops along the way, but also give you time to return and get back to civilization before nightfall.

FEES AND PERMITS

It costs $25 per vehicle to access Everglades National Park via any of the visitors centers. Pedestrians and bicyclists can enter for $8 each. This admission fee allows entrance for seven consecutive days. Annual passes cost $40. There is no entrance fee for Big Cypress National Preserve. Campground fees vary depending on the site, but typically are in the $16-20 range, with the exception of the sites

© AVALON TRAVEL

Two Days in the Everglades

Clyde Butcher's Big Cypress Gallery

Thanks to the limited points of access available to enter the Everglades, this vast park can be neatly, though superficially, explored in two days.

DAY 1

If you're camping, plan on staying at **Monument Lake Campground,** which is about halfway between Miami and Naples. This will allow you to spend the two halves of your first day exploring sites on either side: **Everglades City** and **Chokoloskee** to the east, **Shark Valley Visitor Center** and Clyde Butcher's **Big Cypress Gallery** to the west.

If you're not camping, try to book the **cottage at Clyde Butcher's Big Cypress Gallery** or get a room in Everglades City at **Ivey House,** a great lodge-style hotel that can also help arrange canoe/kayak rentals.

DAY 2

The next day, wake up early and head to the southern area of Everglades National Park near Florida City. Book a room in **Homestead** and plan on spending the entire day taking in the park's vast wilderness, whether by hiking along popular trails like the easily accessible **Anhinga Trail** and **Gumbo Limbo Trail,** or exploring the 16-mile **Turner River Loop** bike trail.

near Flamingo that have electrical hookups (those cost $30).

Permits are required for fishing; no hunting is allowed in either park. Pets are permitted in both parks, however, they are typically prohibited on any of the trails or waterways.

VISITORS CENTERS

Visitors centers are located throughout the Everglades. These centers are staffed by knowledgeable National Park Service staff who can provide information, insight, and directions, and check in campers and hikers to the park. Also, the centers have bathrooms and air-conditioning!

There are two visitors centers in Big Cypress National Preserve, the **Oasis Visitor Center** (52105 Tamiami Trail E., 239/695-1201, www.nps.gov/bicy, 9am-4:30pm daily, free) in the eastern part of the preserve and

Big Sugar and the Everglades

Almost half of the sugar consumed in the United States comes from cane fields growing in and around the Everglades. Thanks to rich, organic peat deposits, sugarcane farming has a long history in the area dating back to the late 19th century. However, the last 50 years have seen a comingling of industrial agriculture, poor government planning, and rampant development conspiring to devastate the ecosystems that make up the 'Glades. For years, the term "Big Sugar" referred to the web of plantation-style sugar-growers throughout the area who worked together to set prices and controlled the line of production from field to refinery with an iron fist. Now, though, "Big Sugar" basically means two companies, Fanjul Corp. (operated by the Fanjul family, and comprising Domino Sugar, Florida Crystals, and other brands) and U.S. Sugar. Even if the names have changed, the game has remained the same.

The power wielded by Big Sugar has resulted in immense damage to the Everglades, both from chemical runoff of fertilizers and pesticides, but also due to years of damming, dredging, and water-redirection projects undertaken by the U.S. Army Corps of Engineers and the South Florida Water Management District in order to make the region arable and, in many cases, open for residential development. (And that's to speak nothing of the economic impact of having thousands of plantation-wage workers in the employ of a single industry.) Those projects have starved the Everglades of the one thing it needs to survive: a constant flow of water. The results have been predictably devastating, and, for the last 30 years, one of the clarion calls of the Florida environmental movement. However, those calls have gone largely unheeded, greeted with complex and incredibly expensive half-measures that seek to chip away at the problem without offending the Fanjuls or U.S. Sugar.

In 2008, Governor Charlie Crist proposed a purchase and shutdown of U.S. Sugar by the state of Florida. Although this move would help the huge company in the short term, it was a dramatic and major move to help the Everglades in the long term. The proposal has been reworked and stripped down in the intervening years to further favor the sugar industry while doing little in the way of actively healing the Everglades. There's still hope among Florida environmentalists that bits and pieces of the deal will eventually happen in a helpful way. But what one day looked like hope for an Everglades free of the sugar industry has now been transformed into a more pragmatic return to trying to contain the damage this industry wreaks on one of America's most important natural treasures.

Big Cypress Swamp Welcome Center (33000 Tamiami Trail E., 239/695-4758, www.nps.gov/bicy, 9am-4:30pm daily, free), which is in the western portion of the preserve, near the park boundary.

There are four visitors centers in Everglades National Park. The **Gulf Coast Visitor Center** (815 Oyster Bar Ln., 239/695-3311, www.nps.gov/ever, 9am-4:30pm daily, free) is located in Everglades City and provides watercraft access to the Ten Thousand Islands area. The **Shark Valley Visitor Center** (36000 SW 8th St., 305/221-8776, www.nps.gov/ever, 9:15am-5:15pm daily) is closer to Miami but is still along the Tamiami Trail. In the southern portions of the Everglades, which will also likely be accessed by visitors coming from Miami, the **Main Visitor Center** (40001 SR-9336, Homestead, 305/242-7700, 9am-5pm daily, $10 per vehicle, $5 for pedestrians/cyclists) is located at the main entrance of the park. The **Flamingo Visitor Center** (1 Flamingo Lodge Hwy., 941/695-2945, 7:30am-5pm Nov.-Apr.) is much farther to the southwest, at the main park's road terminus. Both parks are technically open 24 hours a day.

PLANTS AND ANIMALS

The main reason people set foot within the vast expanses of the Everglades is to get a look at wild, natural Florida. And the Everglades does not disappoint. Of course, the one

Marjory Stoneman Douglas

The Everglades are often referred to as "the river of grass." That designation comes from a landmark 1947 book by Marjory Stoneman Douglas, *The Everglades: River of Grass*. Until Douglas's book was published, most people perceived the Everglades as a useless wasteland of swamps that needed to, at least, be tamed, and, if possible, paved over. And, for a few decades both before and after the book, that was the primary act of engagement by the government and developers in south Florida. Dredging, draining, canal digging, rerouting, and all other manner of attempts to bring the 'Glades under control were utilized. But Douglas was adamant—and correct—in her assertions that the Everglades was an active and vital (if slow-moving) river that should be protected and respected as much as the Mississippi. Although the book itself was a semi-scholarly work, its impact was profound among the general public, thanks mostly to Douglas's tireless advocacy for protection and restoration of the Everglades, a cause she championed until her death in 1998 at the stunning age of 108. Although the Everglades still suffers undue abuse at the hands of agriculture and development interests, there are now substantial speed bumps in place to prevent the area's wholesale destruction. Change is slow and somewhat modest, but without Douglas, it's likely that the Everglades wouldn't have even survived the 1950s.

animal instantly associated with the area is the American Alligator, which is not only a large beast (some grow up to around 16 feet), but also a stealthy predator. Some backwater boaters are frequently surprised when they discover that they've paddled within inches of one of these prehistoric marvels. Gators tend to hug the shoreline and prefer the cover of mangroves, so spotting them can sometimes be a challenge. One can also see American Crocodiles in the Everglades, however, they tend to only be found in the southernmost area, around Flamingo.

The most abundant animal type in the Everglades are birds. Dozens of species call the 'Glades home, including spoonbills, wood storks, egrets, and bald eagles. During migration season, dozens more non-native species can be seen as well.

Mangroves and sawgrass all but define the plant life of the Everglades. It seems that if you're not confronted with an endless, uninterrupted expanse of the former, you're being hemmed in by the dense thickets of the latter. However, slash pine trees and saw palmetto trees are also quite common, as are tiny pockets of hardwood hammocks that house an abundance of animal life, such as raccoons, rabbits, and deer. And, of course, anyone who's seen the movie *Adaptation* knows South Florida and the Everglades are perfect growing areas for orchids. Almost 50 different species of the fragile, beautiful flowers grow throughout the 'Glades.

The Everglades via Naples

The Everglades region doesn't actually start until you're halfway across the state from Naples. However, as soon as the city's suburbs begin retreating into your rearview mirror, a landscape nearly as expansive and wildly natural begins to quickly unfold. As you head eastward into the Everglades, you'll encounter the grassy marshes of the **Ten Thousand Islands National Wildlife Refuge, and** the swampy forests of **Big Cypress Bend** and the **Collier-Seminole State Park**. However, most importantly, you'll almost immediately begin experiencing the vast openness and seemingly infinite calm of this part of the state. Herons and egrets are more common than cars, and buildings can be spaced miles apart from one another. Even though the transition from the upscale shops and restaurants of Naples is certainly gradual, it's nonetheless shocking not just how completely different this part of the state is from the rest of Florida, but also how unique it is on this planet. And, this is just the beginning.

SIGHTS AND RECREATION
★ Ten Thousand Islands National Wildlife Refuge

The entirety of the **Ten Thousand Islands National Wildlife Refuge** (3860 Tollgate Blvd., Suite 300, 239/353-8442, www.fws.gov/floridapanther, sunrise-sunset daily, free) is massive, covering more than 35,000 acres of mangrove swamps, tiny keys, grassy marshes, and tropical hardwood hammocks. Nearly all of those acres are completely undeveloped. In fact, the only signs of human life here are a short, rough hiking trail that's about a mile long, and a two-story observation tower that provides some stunning panoramas of the marshlands. This tower and trail are easily accessed via a parking lot right alongside the Tamiami Trail, just as you enter the wildlife refuge area heading east from Naples. The other, oh, 34,990 acres are best explored by

hikers, hunters, anglers, and boaters. There are boat launches that get you into the refuge's waterways in the tiny fishing village of Goodland (near Marco Island) and at the **Port-of-the-Islands Resort & Marina** (525 Newport Dr., 239/389-0367), just on the edge of the refuge. Primitive camping can be done on the coastal beach areas that are only accessible by boat. Hunting is limited to about 4,000 acres of the refuge, and even there, it's restricted to ducks and coots only.

Collier-Seminole State Park

Collier-Seminole State Park (20200 E. Tamiami Trail, 239/394-3397, www.floridastateparks.org, 8am-sunset daily, $5 per vehicle, $2 pedestrians and bicyclists) is a great way to take in the natural offerings of the Everglades in a way that allows both for independent exploration and somewhat more structured sightseeing. There are more than 7,000 acres of mangrove swampland in the park, and there are several biking and hiking trails that can give you a taste of that vastness. There is also a 13-mile-long kayaking trail that takes you through a mangrove forest along the Black Water River. Camping is incredibly popular here (especially during the cooler months, when the weather is

an observation tower in Ten Thousand Islands National Wildlife Refuge

Indian Villages

As you drive along the Tamiami Trail through the Everglades, you'll come across signs marked "Indian Village." Off to one or another side of the road (usually the northern end), there will be a chickee hut (or a concentration of several), and it will often be behind a privacy fence. Please be aware that these are private residences of local members of the Miccosukee and Seminole tribes, and you should refrain from photographing the residences or the people within. If you're interested in the public face of the local Native American tribes, the Miccosukee tribe welcomes visitors to the **Miccosukee Indian Village and Cultural Center** (Mile Marker 70, Tamiami Trail, 305/552-8365, www.miccosukee.com, 9am-5pm daily, adults $8, children $5, children under 5 free). This facility is geared toward tourists, complete with alligator wrestling and airboat rides ($16).

less oppressive and the mosquitos are less overwhelming). There are 120 tent and RV campsites with water, power, and restrooms, as well as two small primitive campsites, one of which is only available by boat. It's worth checking out the nightly campfire circle/slide show, where park rangers teach about the local wildlife.

Fakahatchee Strand Preserve State Park

The long and narrow swath of land that makes up the **Fakahatchee Strand Preserve State Park** (137 Coastline Dr., 239/695-4593, www.floridastateparks.org, 8am-sunset daily, $5 per vehicle, $2 pedestrians and bicyclists) is a beautiful and largely inaccessible piece of the Everglades. The 100 square miles of forest is four times longer than it is wide. It is primarily a slough that may look like a swamp but is actually a slow-moving, freshwater river. In the mucky ground of the strand grow an astonishing number and variety of plant life, including more orchids and bromeliad species than anywhere else in North America, as well as native royal palm trees and bald cypress trees. In fact, this is one of the only places in the world where both tree types exist. All that flora means lots of fauna, and terrapins, alligators, and bears. Even a few stray Florida panthers have been spotted in the area, along with, of course,

voluminous numbers of bird species, including the roseate spoonbill. Given the less-than-solid swamplike terrain, navigating the Fakahatchee Strand can be kind of tough on foot. However, there is a fantastic boardwalk trail located at Big Cypress Bend that takes you on a nearly mile-long path through the deepest part of the slough, where you can see much of the flora and fauna mentioned. This boardwalk is an absolute favorite among visitors to the Everglades.

FOOD AND ACCOMMODATIONS

There are not too many places to eat or stay in this part of the Everglades, and, in fact, the **Port of the Islands Resort** (25000 Tamiami Trail E., 239/394-3005, http://poiresort.com, from $99 d) is the only hotel around for miles. The harbor view from the marina is exceptional. The hotel's location makes access to the waters of the Ten Thousand Islands National Wildlife Refuge incredibly easy. Although this resort's restaurant is closed during the summer, many of the rooms are efficiencies with small kitchens. Alternately, the closest (and, honestly, the only) restaurant is just down the road at **Gators Crossroads** (19800 Tamiami Trail E., 239/393-4116, noon-8pm daily, from $8). It's a basic bar-and-grill with great burgers; it's a preferred stop of motorcyclists making their way through the 'Glades.

Everglades City and Chokoloskee

Everglades City is the biggest city in the Everglades, but that's not to say it's big. Were it a town along a busy road, you could blink and miss it, as it's only got about a dozen roads and just about twice that many businesses. It's an outpost in the truest sense of the word, established as a marina and fishing village by the hardy souls who explore the waters in and around the Ten Thousand Islands. **Chokoloskee** is even smaller. It is a literal end-of-the-road community that's seldom visited by outsiders but is adored by the anglers who call it home.

SIGHTS
Museum of the Everglades

The **Museum of the Everglades** (105 W. Broadway, 239/695-0008, www.colliermuseums.com, 9am-5pm Tues.-Sat., free) is home to several well-curated permanent exhibits that do a marvelous job of illustrating just how difficult life was for settlers in this area throughout the years. Focusing primarily on the southwestern region of the Everglades, this museum packs plenty of information and

perspective into its well-designed exhibition space and a nicely designed art gallery. The physical struggles and environmental challenges that have confronted everyone from the earliest Native Americans to contemporary residents are nicely illuminated, and show that, unlike many other places in Florida where human development has tamed Mother Nature, the Everglades is one place where she fights back quite a bit harder.

Gulf Coast Visitor Center

Like the rest of the visitors centers throughout Everglades National Park, the **Gulf Coast Visitor Center** (815 Oyster Bar Ln., 239/695-3311, www.nps.gov/ever, 9am-4:30pm daily, free) is designed to give guests relatively easy access to some largely inaccessible areas, such as the waterways and tiny islands of the Ten Thousand Islands. Via the park's boat tours and canoe rentals ($32/day), you can make your way through the 99-mile Wilderness Waterway Trail. The guided boat tours are given on pontoons that hold about two dozen passengers. Well-versed naturalists lead the

The Museum of the Everglades documents the area's unique history.

Everglades City and Chokoloskee

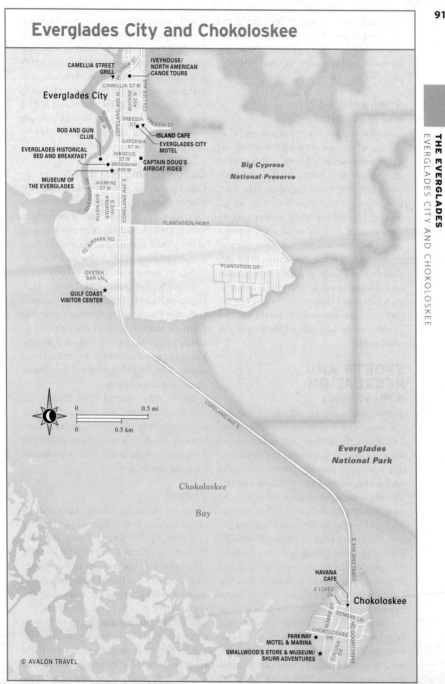

Everglades City

CAMELLIA STREET GRILL
IVEYHOUSE/NORTH AMERICAN CANOE TOURS
CAMELLIA ST W
COLONIA ST
CAMELLIA ST W
BUCKNE AVE N
COLLIER AVE
FREESIA ST
FREESIA ST
ROD AND GUN CLUB
COPELAND AVE N
N STORTER DR
GARDENIA ST W
ISLAND CAFE
EVERGLADES CITY MOTEL
EVERGLADES HISTORICAL BED AND BREAKFAST
HIBISCUS ST W
BROADWAY AVE W
CAPTAIN DOUG'S AIRBOAT RIDES
MUSEUM OF THE EVERGLADES
JASMINE ST W
RIVERSIDE DR
ALLEN AVE
STORTER AVE S
COPELAND AVE S
PLANTATION PKWY
EC AIRPARK RD
PLANTATION DR
OYSTER BAR LN
GULF COAST VISITOR CENTER

Big Cypress National Preserve

COPELAND AVE S

Everglades National Park

Chokoloskee Bay

0   0.5 mi
0   0.5 km

© AVALON TRAVEL

COPELAND AVE S

HAVANA CAFE
S LOPEZ LN
Chokoloskee
MAMIE ST
DEMERE LN
CHOKOLOSKEE DR
PARKWAY MOTEL & MARINA
CALUSA DR
SMALLWOOD DR
SMALLWOOD'S STORE & MUSEUM/SHURR ADVENTURES

tours and put the array of flora and fauna into perspective. The center's main building also has some interesting nature exhibits, information on Everglades National Park, and picnic areas.

Smallwood's Store and Museum

Located at the end of a rutted dirt road that, itself, is off the end of an isolated residential street, **Smallwood's Store and Museum** (360 Mamie St., 239/695-2989, www.smallwoodstore.com, 10am-5pm daily Dec.-Apr., 10am-4pm Fri.-Tues. May-Nov., $2) is an authentic, turn-of-the-20th-century trading post, situated on stilts above a sandy beach on Chokoloskee Bay. The site is pretty amazing, as it's where the earliest settlers to the area traded with local Native Americans and managed to learn how to survive in this unforgiving wilderness. The memorabilia here help tell that story. The near-isolation of the location provides all the background illustration you could need.

SPORTS AND RECREATION
Airboat Rides

Airboat tours are an incredibly popular and super-fun way to see the Everglades. But, given the delicate ecosystems here, it's quite hard to unreservedly recommend this method of touring. It's not only quite loud and disruptive but polluting and potentially destructive to plant life as well. As such, airboats aren't allowed within the confines of Everglades National Park and the Ten Thousand Islands National Wildlife Refuge. However, airboat operators are plentiful outside the parks' boundaries. If this is the way you choose to explore the area, **Captain Doug's Family of Airboat Tours** (www.captaindougs.net) can take care of you. Captain Doug is Doug House and has been operating airboat tours in the 'Glades since the early 1980s, and although he's retired, he lends his legacy and reputation to his son's operation—**Captain Mitch's Airboat Tours** (www.captainmitchs.com)—as well as his son-in-law's—**Captain Bruce's Original Everglades Airboat Tours** (www.evergladescity-airboattours.com). Mitch handles grassland tours, while Bruce specializes in mangrove waterway tours; rates are typically the same—about $40 for adults, and $20 for kids—so if you can't decide which is the right tour for you, you can call 800/282-9194 for guidance.

Canoeing and Kayaking

Canoe rentals are available at the **Gulf Coast Visitor Center** (815 Oyster Bar Ln., 239/695-3311, www.nps.gov/ever, 9am-4:30pm daily, $32/day), but you may have better luck at some of the private operators in the area, as these rentals run out quickly during peak season.

North American Canoe Tours (107 Camellia St., Everglades City, 239/695-3229, http://evergladesadventures.com) operates out of the Ivey House Inn. Its daytime, sunset, and overnight tours (from $124/day for non-Ivey House guests) have a decidedly eco-friendly bent and can be enjoyed in either kayaks or canoes. Rentals ($35/day for non-Ivey House guests) are also available.

Shurr Adventures (360 Mamie St., 239/695-2576, http://shurradventures.net, kayak trips from $80) focuses on kayak tours through the diverse ecosystems of the Ten Thousand Islands. It also offers a backcountry mangrove tour.

Fishing

There are numerous fishing charters available in the area. **Everglades Kayak Fishing** (239/695-9107), **Capt. Tony Polizos** (239/695-2608), and **Capt. Nick Varallo** (239/695-2536) operate out of Everglades City. Despite what they'd have you believe, most of these charters are essentially the same, offering anglers the opportunity to choose between flats and deepwater fishing excursions that will yield cobia, redfish, tarpon, and snook, among others. Most charters are geared toward small groups (2-5 people) and prices typically begin around $350 for a half day of fishing. If you have specific needs, it's always best to call the captain before booking.

Aerial Tours
An exciting way to see the Everglades is by air. **Wings-Ten Thousand Island Aero Tours** (650 E C. Airpark Rd., Everglades City, 239/695-3296, www.wingsaerotours.com) offers flights ranging from 20 to 90 minutes; you'll cruise in an Alaska floatplane over the sawgrass and swamps at a low enough altitude to see a good bit of wildlife. It's not up close and personal, but it's quite exhilarating.

FOOD
Everglades City
If you're in Everglades City and hungry for anything besides seafood or swamp food you're going to be out of luck. Thankfully, there are a handful of spots that can fry up water creatures with the best of 'em. The ★ **Camellia Street Grill** (208 Camellia St., 239/695-2003, 11am-10pm daily, from $10) is probably the best, with some quirky decor, great riverfront views, a friendly staff, and some incredible homemade sangria. For homestyle breakfasts and a decent lineup of burgers and sandwiches, head for the **Island Cafe** (305 Collier Ave., 239/695-0003, 6am-10pm daily, from $5). The restaurant at **The Rod and Gun Club** (200 Riverside Dr., 239/695-2101, everglades-rodandgunclub. com, lunch from $13, dinner from $21, cash only) is a great choice as well, as it serves up excellent seafood, steak, and sandwiches in a classic Old Florida environment.

Chokoloskee
This small fishing village's main restaurant isn't a seafood shack or a diner, but a friendly and cute Cuban restaurant. The **Havana Café** (191 Smallwood Dr., 239/695-2214, https://havanacafeoftheeverglades.com, 7am-3pm Sun.-Thurs. and 7am-8pm Fri.-Sat. Oct.-mid-Apr., from $8) serves breakfast, lunch, and dinner menus that include a selection of Cuban classics and American standards. On a (relatively) cool winter day, the outdoor patio is a great place to relax while you eat.

ACCOMMODATIONS
Everglades City
Many of the accommodations in Everglades City evoke the atmosphere of a classic fish camp. **The Rod and Gun Club** (200 Riverside Dr., 239/695-2101, everglades-rodandgunclub. com, $110 d) is the fanciest of the bunch, with more of a relaxed, hunting-lodge vibe.

The rustic cabins and cottages at ★ **Ivey House** (107 Camellia St., 239/695-3299, http:// iveyhouse.com, $115 d) are even less glamorous, but the staff here is remarkably friendly and quite helpful. The onsite charter and rental service make it something of a one-stop shop for those embarking upon a backcountry adventure.

For more standard accommodations, the motel-style lodgings at **Everglades City Motel** (310 Collier Ave., 239/695-4224, www. evergladescitymotel.com, from $90) and the villas and hotel rooms at **Captain's Table** (102 E. Broadway, 239/695-4211, $75 d) are good options.

Chokoloskee
The four very basic rooms at the waterfront **Parkway Motel & Marina** (1180 Chokoloskee Dr., 239/695-3261, www.parkwaymotelandmarina.net, $99 d) are just about your only option for an overnight stay in Chokoloskee.

INFORMATION AND SERVICES
The folks at the **Naples, Marco Island, Everglades Convention and Visitors Bureau** (239/225-1013, www.paradisecoast. com) are a great resource for information and planning tips. They can be reached over the phone or online, but have no public office.

GETTING THERE
Everglades City is located about five miles south of the Tamiami Trail (US-41) via County Road 29. It's about a 45-minute drive

from Naples to Everglades City. The only way to get to Chokoloskee is via County Road 29 through Everglades City; the road changes names from County Road 29 to Collier Avenue, to Copeland Avenue, to Smallwood Avenue. The road terminates in Chokoloskee.

Big Cypress National Preserve

Although not technically part of the Everglades, the nearby Big Cypress Swamp covers an impressive 720,000 acres, most of which are under the protection of the Big Cypress National Preserve, which was the first property in the National Park System to be designated as a National Preserve. As with Everglades National Park, human access is limited by the terrain, but it's far drier than the 'Glades (relatively speaking), and visitors will find that much more of the park can be used for camping, hiking, and hunting. Ochopee is the only real town along this stretch of the Tamiami Trail.

SIGHTS AND RECREATION
Big Cypress Swamp Welcome Center
The **Big Cypress Swamp Welcome Center** (33000 Tamiami Trail, Ochopee, 9am-4:30pm daily, except Christmas Day) has a small wildlife exhibit and a brief movie about the history and natural beauty of the preserve. This is where you need to be if you want to pick up maps, register with rangers, or pick up a camping or Off-Road Vehicle permit.

★ Ochopee Post Office
A post office? Yes, a post office. **Ochopee Post Office** (38000 Tamiami Trail E., 10am-4:15pm Mon.-Fri., 10:15am-11:30am Sat.) is the smallest post office in the United States. This tiny building is only 61 square feet. Although there's not much more inside than a desk, a scale, a computer, and a chair for the (necessarily) good-spirited clerk, that's enough for it to act as a fully functional post office for the few permanent residents of Ochopee.

The tiny Ochopee Post Office is the smallest in the United States.

Skunk Ape Research Headquarters

While cryptozoologists and Bigfoot hunters have typically focused their efforts on the forests of the Pacific Northwest, there's a legend in southwest Florida about the "Skunk Ape"—a very Bigfoot-like creature—that has persisted since the 1960s. Although reports have been sporadic and inconsistent throughout the years, it seems that the biggest differentiator for the Everglades version of the Bigfoot is its powerful and quite nasty odor. Hence the "Skunk Ape" moniker. Brothers Dave and Jack Shealy head up the **Skunk Ape Research Headquarters** (40904 Tamiami Trail E., 239/695-2275, www.skunkape.info, 7am-7pm daily, adults $5, children under 5 free) in Ochopee. They gather the evidence about Skunk Apes and present it to visitors to make up their own minds. Unsurprisingly, they also sell quite a few T-shirts, bumper stickers, and other Skunk Ape-related memorabilia items. The Shealys also run a campground, a Miss Skunk Ape contest, and Skunktoberfest. A stop here is an essential voyage into classic, kitschy Floridiana. Just be careful!

Kirby Storter Roadside Park

Lots of folks pull off of the Tamiami Trail at **Kirby Storter Roadside Park** (US-41/Tamiami Trail, between HP Williams Roadside Park and Monument Lake Campground, sunrise-sunset daily, free) to avail themselves of the restrooms and picnic tables. However, going just a little bit farther into the park along the boardwalk trail is an incredibly rewarding experience. The approximately 0.5-mile-long boardwalk provides incredible views of the cypress swamp and the vast expanses of marshlands that make up the Big Cypress Preserve. Bird-watching is excellent, and there's a small chickee hut about halfway down the trail that provides respite from the sun.

Oasis Visitor Center

The **Oasis Visitor Center** (52105 Tamiami Trail E., 239/695-1201, www.nps.gov/bicy, 9am-4:30pm daily, free) is the second of two visitors centers in the Big Cypress National Preserve, and, like the Big Cypress Swamp Welcome Center, it has sparkling-clean restrooms, incredibly helpful park rangers, and a couple of small educational and art exhibits inside the (blissfully) air-conditioned main

Skunk Ape is the Everglades' answer to Bigfoot.

building. A big draw for Oasis is the roadside boardwalk, which sits above a narrow canal with some resident alligators and cormorants, making for some good photo opportunities.

★ Big Cypress Gallery

A stop into **Clyde Butcher's Big Cypress Gallery** (52388 Tamiami Trail E., 239/695-2428, www.clydebutchersbigcypressgallery.com, 9:30am-4:30pm daily, free) should be an all-but-essential part of anyone's Big Cypress itinerary. Located just 0.5 mile west of the Big Cypress Visitor Center, the gallery displays Butcher's stunning black-and-white photography, and covers nearly 40 years of amazing visual documentation of wild and natural Florida. As the property is also home to Butcher's studio, odds are he'll be around and more than willing to provide visitors to the area plenty of insight into his work. Every Saturday at 11am, weather permitting, there are guided swamp walks on the property behind the gallery. Also worth noting, there's a bungalow available for overnight stays, which is just about the only place to spend the night in the area if you didn't bring camping gear.

Turner River Canoe Access

One of the best (and safest) places to put in your canoe or kayak in this part of the Everglades is the **Turner River Canoe Access** (entry point at US-41 west of Turner River Rd., 239/695-2000, www.nps.gov/bicy). However, even non-boaters find this park a good spot to stop, as there's a boardwalk nature trail. For those who don't even want to get out of their car, the Turner River Loop Drive is one of the better scenic drives in the Everglades.

HIKING TRAILS

There are three primary and well-marked **hiking trails** within the preserve, all of which are part of the Florida Trail. The most popular is the 6.5-mile trail that connects Loop Road in the south and US-41. During the winter,

when the bugs are more tolerable and the ground is dry, this trail can get busy. The vast expanses of prairie still make it feel quite isolated. There's a much longer and more challenging trail with a trailhead at the visitors center, which winds nearly 28 miles through slash pine copses, hardwood hammocks, and lots and lots of dry prairie land.

SCENIC DRIVES

One of the biggest draws in Big Cypress is a drive along the 27-mile **Loop Road** (off US-41/Tamiami Trail, just at the Miami-Dade County line). The well-marked and generally smooth road makes its way through dense forest canopies filled with dwarf cypress and slash pine trees. The pastoral setting is as relaxing as the frequent wildlife-spotting is invigorating. The drive along the shorter **Turner River Loop**, a 16-mile loop that starts at **H. P. Williams Roadside Park** (Hwy. 41 and Turner River Rd.), is a great option for bird-watchers, as the open spaces and watering areas are popular with migrating (and native) bird species.

FOOD

Joanie's Blue Crab Cafe (39395 Tamiami Trail E., 239/695-2682, http://joaniesbluecrab-cafe.com, 11am-5pm daily, from $12) is the best restaurant in Ochopee (granted, it's one of only two restaurants in Ochopee). Still, Joanie's is an essential stop, and the food is good. The small menu focuses on true swamp fare, with frog legs, fried gator, garlic blue crabs, Indian fry bread, and a few other dishes. Everything on the menu is excellent and portions are huge. The bar does incredible business serving up ice-cold beer and live music to weary travelers and hardworking locals.

The other restaurant in Ochopee is **Tippy's Big Cypress BBQ** (39025 SW 8th St./US-41, 305/559-6080, www.tippysoutpost.com, 7am-11pm Mon.-Thurs., 6am-midnight Sat.-Sun., hours highly variable), which isn't much more than a chickee hut with a smoker and a couple of tables, but the barbeque is excellent, served with a limited selection of sides.

ACCOMMODATIONS

Non-camping accommodations in this area are pretty much limited to the **Swamp Cottage & Bungalow** (52388 Tamiami Trail E., 239/695-2428, www.clydebutchersbigcypressgallery.com/swamp-cottage, from $295) at Clyde Butcher's Big Cypress Gallery. It offers two standalone two-bedroom houses with an incredible, immersed-in-the-swamp atmosphere. Please keep in mind that reservations for either can be something of a challenge.

If you've brought your own camping gear—whether it's a tent or an RV—you'll have a much better selection. The **Skunk Ape Headquarters Campground** (40904 Tamiami Trail E., 239/695-2275, www.skunkape.info, tent camping $20/night, RV camping $25/night) is the most mainstream of the bunch and also the kitschiest. It's a pretty typical roadside campground. To get a slightly wilder experience, the **Burns Lake**

Campground & Backcountry Access (check in at Oasis Visitor Center, no phone, Aug. 29-Jan. 6, $16/night) has a dozen or so primitive campsites surrounding Burns Lake (which should really be called Burns Pond). It can feel a little busy in the camping area since it's so wide-open, but campers can easily make their way into the vast expanses of flatwood hammocks just behind their campsites. **Monument Lake Campground** (check in at Oasis Visitor Center, no phone, Aug. 28-Apr. 15, $16/night) offers a similar setup, although it has real restrooms, a cold-water shower, and picnic/barbeque facilities. It's also the site of the 1936 Seminole Conference, where Florida's governor met with Seminole tribe leaders in an attempt to offer them aid.

GETTING THERE

Ochopee is situated right along the Tamiami Trail (US-41), about 35 miles (30 minutes) east of Naples, 8 miles (about 10 minutes) from Everglades City, and 10 miles (about 15 minutes) from the eastern boundary of Big Cypress.

Joanie's Blue Crab Cafe is an essential stop in Ochopee.

Everglades National Park via Miami

This part of the Everglades is often the only part of the Everglades that many visitors see. Being so close to Miami, tourists make the short drive here for a day trip. The airboat operators and kitschy "alligator wrestling" shows of the Miccosukee tribe are unique to the area and give a glimpse of the vast natural expanses. For a deeper look, visit the popular Shark Valley Visitor Center and discover some of the lesser-traveled canoe and kayak trails.

SIGHTS AND RECREATION

★ Shark Valley Visitor Center

For many visitors—especially those coming from Miami—a trip to the Everglades means a beeline to the **Shark Valley Visitor Center** (36000 SW 8th St., 305/221-8776, www.nps.gov/ever, 9:15am-5:15pm daily, $25 for seven-day automobile pass, $8/person on bike or foot). By far the most developed and the busiest of all the park's visitor centers, Shark Valley is right on the heavily traveled Tamiami Trail that links downtown Miami and Naples. Paying the $10 gate fee gets you into the center (and the rest of Everglades National Park). You'll have to pay additional fees for the tram rides ($19 adults, $12 children) and bike rentals ($8/hour). The center offers boat cruises, guided walking tours, and two-hour tram tours. A popular 15-mile bike trail loop originates here, and bikes can be rented right where the trams depart. Shark Valley offers a sort of one-stop-shopping for the Everglades experience. Due to the crowds, you should definitely arrive early, as the parking lots can fill up pretty quickly. Also, reservations for tram tours can and should be made in advance.

Miccosukee Resort and Gaming

For those who like to gamble, **Miccosukee Resort and Gaming** (500 SW 177th Ave., 305/222-4600, http://500nations.com, open 24 hours daily) awaits you. This hotel and casino has a 32-table poker room and a deafening assortment of more than 1,900 slot machines. In keeping with its original roots as a bingo hall (the only type of gambling the state of Florida used to allow the Native American tribes to offer), there's a ridiculously huge "high-stakes" bingo room with more than 1,000 seats. It's far less upscale than the gaming resorts operated by the nearby Seminole tribe. Those with an aversion to cigarette smoke should know that the air recirculation system leaves quite a bit to be desired.

Airboat Rides

Just outside the boundaries of the Everglades National Park, there are several airboat tour operators. Lots of tourists from Miami make their way here to experience the Everglades. Airboats are loud and can be disruptive and potentially an ecological hazard. However, they are also a blast to ride in and their usage is just as much a real part of the Everglades as fried gator tails and the Skunk Ape. Of all the tourist-friendly airboat outfits on the eastern edge of the park, **Coopertown** (22700 SW 8th St./US-41, 305/226-6048, www.coopertownairboats.com, 8am-6pm daily, tour tickets: adults $22, children 7-11 $11, children under 7 free) is the most interesting, since it's a fish camp that dates back to 1945. It is possibly the oldest continually operating business in this part of the Everglades, and you should definitely see it while you have a chance; the National Park Service recently bought the property and gave the original owners a 10-year-lease through 2026, leaving its fate beyond that date unknown. Other airboat operators in the area include **Buffalo Tiger's Airboat Tours** (29701 SW 8th St., 305/559-5250, www.buffalotigersairboattours.com, 9am-5pm daily, airboat rides from $50 for adults, children 6-10 $10, children under 6 free), **Gator Park** (24050 SW 8th St./US-41, 305/559-2255, www.gatorpark.com, 9am-5pm daily, adults $22.99, children $11.99, admission includes park entrance, airboat ride, and wildlife show), and **Everglades Safari Park** (26700 SW 8 St., 305/226-6923, www.evergladessafaripark.com, 9am-5pm daily, tour tickets adults $25, children 5-11 $12, children under 5 free). If you come prepared with the knowledge that it's going to be a loud, crowded, half-hour boat ride, taking an airboat tour through the swamp can certainly make for a memorable morning.

FOOD

There are restaurants at **Coopertown** (22700 SW 8th St./US-41, 305/226-6048, www.coopertownairboats.com, 8am-6pm daily, $8) and **Everglades Safari Park** (26700 SW 8th St., 305/226-6923, www.evergladessafaripark.com, 9am-5pm daily, $8) that serve standard burgers-and-fries fare with an expected selection of gator tail and frog legs. Of the two, Coopertown is definitely better, with an authentic Old Florida vibe that comes from being around since the 1940s. Everglades Safari Park is a little more modern, with a greater emphasis on airboat rides.

ACCOMMODATIONS

The **Miccosukee Resort** (500 SW 177th Ave., 305/222-4600, www.miccosukee.com, $99 d) is just about the only place to overnight in this part of the Everglades. Although the focus here is on the casino, the rooms are decent enough, if dated. If you're continuing on to Miami, the closest lodgings are some chain hotels near the Dolphin Mall, including a **Courtyard by Marriott** (11275 NW 12th St., Miami, 305/994-9343, www.marriott.com, $169 d), which is clean and well-kept, but not particularly interesting.

GETTING THERE

It's 40 miles (less than an hour) from South Beach to the Shark Valley Visitor Center. It's a 75-mile drive to get from Naples to Shark Valley via the Tamiami Trail (US-41), which takes about 90 minutes.

Everglades National Park via Homestead

There are vast expanses of the Everglades to the south of the Tamiami Trail (US-41). The southern portions of Everglades National Park offer visitors incredible opportunities for canoeing, kayaking, and other sorts of exploration. These areas aren't as easily accessed as the northern and western portions of the Everglades. Once you're in this part of the 'Glades, it's all Everglades National Park, so all of the (limited) facilities are operated by the park.

Thanks to the lack of civilization, this region presents some of the most idyllic and isolated ways to experience the Everglades. With multiple canoe trails, hiking trails, and camping facilities, this area is geared toward outdoor activities, so visitors can fully appreciate the wild expanses of the Everglades.

FLORIDA CITY

The last outpost of civilization you'll experience before heading into Everglades National Park is Florida City, a tiny little town that most people breeze through on their way to the Florida Keys. It's not much more than a few gas stations and a 24-hour Starbucks, but as you head west off of US-1 toward the Everglades, you'll see that Florida City has a little more to offer than being just a spot to refuel between Miami and Key Largo.

Everglades Alligator Farm

You're going to see a lot of signs for **Everglades Alligator Farm** (40351 SW 192nd Ave., Homestead, 305/247-2628, www.everglades.com, 9am-6pm daily, $19.50 adult, $14.50 child, airboat rides additional cost) on your way to Everglades National Park. You can't fault the folks at Everglades Alligator Farm for doing whatever they can to lure people down a very long dirt road (past a giant prison) to check out their collection of alligators and snakes. The crew here does a great job of providing a couple of hours' worth of entertainment by hosting interesting shows. There are three snake and three alligator shows every day, as well as gator feedings at noon and 3pm. The farm allows guests to wander the grounds and feed the lounging gators food that is accessible from $0.25 gumball machines.

Visitors can also take hourly airboat rides into the waterways. These rides don't go into Everglades National Park, as airboats are prohibited within park property. Despite how loud, disruptive, and polluting they are, airboats are as much a part of Florida as palm trees and oranges. If it seems like an appealing way to speed through the swamps, by all means, go for it.

If you hang around the farm long enough to get hungry, there's a tiny concession where you can grab a freshly grilled burger—a hamburger, not a gator burger.

Everglades Outpost Wildlife Rescue

The primary mission of **Everglades Outpost Wildlife Rescue** (35601 SW 192nd Ave., Homestead, 305/247-8000, www.evergladesoutpost.com, 10am-5pm Fri.-Tues., $10 donation requested) is the rescue and rehabilitation of exotic animals. Although it's not a tourist attraction per se, the Outpost welcomes visitors (and donations) as it attempts to raise awareness. Visitors are welcome to tour the facilities and observe the range of animals currently being cared for. Due to the rescue-and-release nature of the Outpost's mission, the exact population varies. You may be able to see a tiger, a lemur, or a parrot, or you may end up seeing a donkey or a camel. Regardless of the wildlife you encounter, the energy and enthusiasm of the volunteer staff is infectious enough that you may end up "adopting" one of the patients here by way of helping to provide the funds needed for its continued care and relocation.

VISITORS CENTERS

Ernest Coe Visitor Center

The **Ernest Coe Visitor Center** (40001 SR-9336, Homestead, 305/242-7700, www.nps.gov/ever, 9am-5pm daily, $25 per vehicle for 7-day pass, $8 per person for pedestrians and cyclists), also known as the Main Visitor Center, is at the main entrance to the park. It is therefore the most popular of all the visitors centers, as well as the most expansive and well-staffed. If you've never been to the 'Glades, this is an ideal place for a park ranger to give you tips on navigating the park, and there are also some excellent exhibits that detail the flora, fauna, and history of the Everglades. The admission fee paid at the main gate grants you entrance to the entire Everglades National Park.

Royal Palm Visitor Center

The **Royal Palm Visitor Center** (four miles west of the park entrance on Main Park Rd., 305/242-7700, 8am-4:15pm daily, admission included with park entrance fee) is the starting point for two of the park's most popular walking trails: the Anhinga Amble Trail and the Gumbo Limbo Trail. The 0.8-mile-long **Anhinga Amble Trail** is thick with visible wildlife. You'll almost certainly see alligators and, in the winter, dozens of species of birds, including the trail's namesake, which will likely be spotted using its long neck to assist it in hunting for fish. The **Gumbo Limbo Trail** is half as long. Instead of wading through swampy marsh grass, walkers along this trail will be strolling through a lush hardwood hammock. Both of these trails are well maintained and wheelchair accessible. Aside from the trails, on-site rangers, and clean restrooms, there is little else at this center.

Flamingo Visitor Center

About an hour south of the park's main entrance, and at the end of the park's main paved road, is the **Flamingo Visitor Center** (1 Flamingo Lodge Hwy., 941/695-2945, www.nps.gov/ever, 8am-4:30pm daily Jan.-mid-Apr., admission included with park entrance fee). Flamingo feels like a weird outpost of civilization in a wildlife area. There's really not much here for the casual tourist besides the imposing visitors center and the marina, but it feels like a bustling metropolis compared to the still and quiet throughout the rest of Everglades National Park.

In addition to an educational area inside the center, there's a marina from which you can take **boat tours** ($32 adults, $12 children) of Florida Bay or rent canoes or kayaks ($16 for two hours, $30/day) to take on the beautiful, mangrove-thick **water trails.** The short **Eco Pond Trail** (0.5 mile) here is pleasant and wheelchair accessible. For boaters, Flamingo is often just the beginning of a journey, as it's from here that you can set off into the waters of Florida Bay and its numerous tiny keys for some real explorations. You can buy beer and Moon Pies at the marina.

The visitors center is staffed intermittently mid-April-December and does not have regular visiting hours.

MAIN PARK ROAD

There's not a whole lot of proper sightseeing within Everglades National Park, but the National Park Service has done a good job at balancing visitors' desires to see *something* with the low-impact mission of the park itself. The result is a handful of minimally equipped pullovers along **Main Park Road** where you can walk along a boardwalk, have a picnic, or just stare off into the vast expanses of the Everglades. There's only one road in and out of Everglades National Park, which means you're going to pass by all of these sights anyway, so take time to check them out.

Long Pine Key

Long Pine Key is a great stop, about four miles along Main Park Road, for biking, hiking, and picnicking. It's also a very popular campsite. The unnamed 14-mile loop bike trail takes you through slash pine and prairies, but there's not a whole lot of shade. Hikers and day-trippers should head for the

The Royal Palm Visitor Center provides access to two great walking trails.

(also unnamed) 0.5-mile multipurpose trail, which offers a similarly diverse look at the area's ecology. There are picnic tables in the shade, and clean, well-maintained restroom facilities.

Rock Reef Pass

The sign just before **Rock Reef Pass**, about 11 miles along Main Park Road, reminds you just how flat and near-swampy this part of the state is. It states, "Elevation: Three Feet." This is practically mountainous for the Everglades, as much of the area is actually at or below sea level. The high altitude of Rock Reef Pass makes for a unique ecological combination of pine forest and marshes filled with dwarf cypress trees. There's a very short boardwalk here that allows you to get out into areas that alternate between tinderbox trails in the dry winter and foot-deep swamp in the summer rainy season.

★ Pa-hay-okee Overlook

Situated at 12.5 miles down Main Park Road, the elevated boardwalk at **Pa-hay-okee Overlook** is considerably longer than the one at Rock Reef Pass (about 750 ft.). It offers much more magnificent and expansive vistas onto the grassy infinity of the Everglades.

It's also much more popular. So, during the busy season, there is the distinct possibility of a packed parking lot and cattle-chute movement along the boardwalk. This seldom actually happens, though, but for the most quietude and the best chance of having these beautiful views to yourself, make sure to get here early in the day. This boardwalk is wheelchair accessible.

Mahogany Hammock

Mahogany Hammock, which is about 20 miles along Main Park Road, offers another boardwalk-through-the-'Glades experience. Although this particular loop trail (0.5 mi) is quite short, the density of mahogany trees (and the shade they provide!) makes it unique and a nice, quick stop. Mahogany's boardwalk rewards visitors who look up into the mahogany canopy, where they're likely to see migratory birds.

SPORTS AND RECREATION
★ Hiking

Everglades National Park offers a variety of different **hiking** experiences, from easily accessed, elevated boardwalks and quick, shaded loops to more challenging and lengthy forays

the boardwalk at Rock Reef Pass

into the more ecologically imposing areas of the park.

The two trails from the **Royal Palm Visitor Center** (four miles west of the park entrance on Main Park Rd., 305/242-7700, 8am-4:15pm daily), the **Anhinga Amble** (0.8 mi) and **Gumbo Limbo** (0.4 mi), are by far the most popular non-boardwalk trails in Everglades National Park, and not just because they're the closest to the main entrance. Both trails manage to be easily navigable while taking hikers through the stunning variety of Everglades terrain. Even during the hottest summer months, you're likely to see a decent array of wildlife (especially alligators). During the winter months, bird-watching is incredible. If you have to pick, take the Anhinga Trail; even though this easy loop trail is just under a mile long, it provides a great (if quick) look at some amazing natural beauty.

Other quick and gorgeous trails include the mangrove-lined, waterfront **Bayshore Trail** (2 mi), which starts at Flamingo Campground, and the **Eco-Pond Trail** (0.5 mi), a loop of bird-watching heaven, which starts from the Flamingo Visitor Center.

Hikers looking for something more challenging will want to explore the **Coastal Prairie Trail** (5.6 mi), which starts from Flamingo Campground, and is such a tough slog that park rangers discourage casual visitors from taking it on. The campground at the end, at Clubhouse Beach, is well worth the struggle through muck and brush that it takes to get there. Another good trail for experienced hikers (and those unafraid to spend the majority of their hike under the brutal Florida sun) is the walk along the **Old Ingraham Highway** (22 mi). This used to be the chief thoroughfare, until Main Park Road was built in the 1960s. It's wide and fairly well-graded, making it a popular trail for bicyclists as well. The trailhead is near Royal Palm Visitor Center.

Hikers should always be prepared with sunscreen, lots of water, and bug repellent, and should always be on the lookout for venomous snakes. In the summer, mosquitos and other flying insects can make hiking a challenge.

★ Canoeing and Kayaking

By far, the best way to experience the Everglades is in a boat. Canoe and kayak rental opportunities abound, and there are several boat trails throughout the park. While many rental agencies offer guided tours, the quietude of solo exploration has its

Pa-hay-okee Overlook provides exceptional views.

advantages. By all means, unless you're hauling a lot of gear, a kayak is far better suited to the narrow waterways of the 'Glades, as you'll appreciate the navigational flexibility when making your way through a dense thicket of mangroves. Also, for overnight boaters, there are several Seminole-style "chickees" located throughout the park that provide an elevated and roofed camping area right on the water.

Experienced boaters will want to explore the 3-6 miles of twists and turns of **Hell's Bay Canoe Trail,** a challenging run that announces its intentions with a comically difficult put-in and a trail that can take up to six hours to navigate completely; oddly, it's quite popular! Another challenging trail is the 8-mile **West Lake Canoe Trail,** which runs mainly through open waters but also takes boaters through some impressive (and occasionally claustrophobic) mangrove tunnels. There are easier options, too: **Nine Mile Pond Trail** is only 3.5 miles long (the pond it's named after is located 9 miles from the former site of a visitors center), and is well marked, guiding paddlers through mangrove tunnels and several wider marshes. It's best explored during the summer, when water levels are higher. Even easier is the 2-mile loop of the **Noble Hammock Canoe Trail,** which only takes about an hour to traverse. The **Mud Lake Canoe Trail** is also very popular as it is close to the Flamingo Visitor Center, and quite short.

Serious canoers and kayakers will want to plan their Everglades adventure around exploring the **Wilderness Waterway.** The trail is 99 miles long, and gets boaters into some of the most isolated and beautiful areas of the Everglades. Running along the western edge of the 'Glades along Cape Sable, from Flamingo all the way north to Chokoloskee, this part of the Everglades is known as **the Ten Thousand Islands.** Some of the waterway is in Everglades National Park, while some of it traverses through Ten Thousand Islands National Wildlife Refuge. There may not be an actual 10,000 islands, but it sure does seem like it. The vast majority of the small outcroppings of scrub and sand are tiny, although some of them house chickee huts for overnight camping. Make sure to have up-to-date nautical and tide charts, as some parts of the waterway are nigh unnavigable without them. Information on

Everglades National Park provides amazing opportunities for wildlife viewing.

specific put-in points is available at Ernest Coe Visitor Center.

If you don't want to do the entire 99 miles, shorter one- and two-night trips can be planned. Consult with a ranger at one of the park's visitors centers first. If you decide to take on the whole thing, be advised that even under the best conditions, this is a hugely challenging affair that can take more than a week to complete.

From **Flamingo Visitor Center** (1 Flamingo Lodge Hwy., 941/695-2945, 7:30am-5pm Nov.-Apr.), boaters can also explore the waters of **Florida Bay** and its numerous keys. Canoers and kayakers probably don't want to go any farther than the chickees on **Shark Point Key,** as the open water of Florida Bay can be daunting, and the density of islands decreases noticeably past here, but there are also chickees far out in the bay on Little Rabbit and Johnson Keys.

Hunting

Hunting is illegal within Everglades National Park, but there are several private hunting preserves in the area. **Everglades Adventures** (28965 Obern Rd., Clewiston, 863/983-8999, www.huntsflorida.com) is one of the largest.

FOOD

There are a number of decent restaurants in Homestead. **Shiver's Bar-B-Q** (28001 S. Dixie Hwy., 305/248-2272, http://shiversbbq. com, 11am-10pm daily, from $7) is something of a local legend, having served up excellent ribs, pulled pork, and chicken for almost 60 years. Another fantastic option to grab a great meal is **Chefs on the Run** (10 E. Mowry Dr., 305/245-0085, 12pm-8pm Tues.-Sat., from $9), a cozy, table-service spot in "downtown" Homestead that serves up a nice array of fresh and hearty Cuban, Caribbean, and even Asian and Vietnamese dishes. As the name implies, the food here is chef driven, so while the high-variety menu may seem inconsistent, the dishes are almost always excellent.

Closer to the main entrance of Everglades National Park in Florida City is ★ **Robert Is Here** (19200 SW 344th St., Homestead, 305/246-1592, www.robertishere.com, 8am-7pm daily Nov.-Aug.). While it's not a restaurant per se, it's undoubtedly the best place to eat anywhere near the park. Starting out as little more than a far-flung produce stand, it's an essential stop for locals and tourists alike to stock up on fresh fruits, vegetables, snacks, and milkshakes that almost make the drive worth it on their own. Try the key lime milkshake for a quintessential South Florida delicacy. Robert is justifiably proud of his wide selection of hard-to-find "weird tropical fruit" like lychee, guanabanas, sapotes, starfruit, and tamarind. You can pick up jams and jellies as well as gift baskets and a decent selection of grab-and-go snacks for the road. There's also a petting zoo, but this is probably the only place in Florida where a live emu is the third (or fourth) most interesting reason to visit.

ACCOMMODATIONS
Hotels

There are a handful of decent and inexpensive hotels in downtown Homestead that provide relatively quick access to the Everglades. Of them, the **Hotel Redland** (5 S. Flagler Ave., 305/246-1904, www.hotelredland. com, $99 d) and the **Floridian Hotel** (990 N. Homestead Blvd., 305/ 247-7020, $75 d) are the best. The Redland is situated in a beautiful, historic building and feels more like a bed-and-breakfast than a typical hotel. The Floridian is a fairly standard, clean, and comfortable motel that looks like some conscientious local owners took over from a national chain, updating its amenities (there's a sparkling pool and decent Wi-Fi) and keeping the property well-maintained. There are also a number of budget motel chains with locations in the area.

Camping

Camping with a camper, tent, or in a chickee is your only choice for staying within the park's boundaries. There are two easily accessible campgrounds within Everglades

National Park, both of which welcome tent campers and RVs. During the summer rainy season, the National Park Service typically allows camping for free, but the sites get quickly waterlogged.

In the eastern portion of the park, **Long Pine Key Campground** (approx. six miles from park entrance, 305/242-7700, $16/site, $30 group site) has 108 drive-up sites and one group site. Restrooms, water, and RV dump stations are available, but there are no showers. Sites are available on a first-come, first-served basis.

★ **Flamingo Campground** (reservations 877/444-6777, $16/site, $30 group site) is the largest and most popular campground in this part of Everglades National Park, with 234 drive-up sites, 40 walk-up single sites, and 3 walk-up group sites. Its popularity is due to its proximity to the Flamingo Visitor Center. The end-of-the-road isolation of this part of the park has considerable appeal. This campground may feel busy or even a little overcrowded (especially over the winter holidays), but just a quick walk or bike ride away puts you in some of the most pristine natural quietude you've ever experienced.

There are also 47 backcountry campsites, ranging from chickees along the Wilderness Waterway and in Florida Bay to "beach" sites in Cape Sable and standard ground sites, which are only accessible by boat. Wilderness permits are required for all backcountry camping ($10 processing fee, plus $2 pp/day camping fee). The three beach sites at Cape Sable are the largest, accommodating around 150 people. They're as beautiful as they are rustic and are often uncrowded. Call 305/242-7700 for more information on backcountry campsites.

GETTING THERE

It's about 35 miles (30 minutes) to get to Homestead and Florida City from Miami, and then another 15 miles (30 minutes) west into the park.

Florida Keys

Look for ★ to find recommended
sights, activities, dining, and lodging.

Highlights

★ **John Pennekamp Coral Reef State Park:** Some of the best snorkeling in all of the United States can be found within the vast boundaries of this state park, with sights like vibrant coral reefs and the *Christ of the Abyss* statue (page 112).

★ **Crane Point Hammock:** This expansive, accessible tropical ecosystem takes in mangroves, hammocks, and wetlands, providing nature lovers ample opportunity to explore some of the most beautiful scenery in the Keys (page 125).

★ **Pigeon Key Historic District:** Pigeon Key was used as a base of operations for Henry Flagler's railroad crew as they connected Key West to the mainland via train. Today, it offers a look at life in the Keys in the first half of the 20th century (page 126).

★ **National Key Deer Refuge:** This wildlife refuge is dedicated to the tiny Key deer that live on Big Pine Key (page 130).

★ **Bahia Honda State Park:** This state park is home to the best beaches in the Keys. Rugged naturalism and pastoral oceanside beauty make this park popular and unique (page 131).

★ **Duval Street:** The nightlife scene along Key West's Duval Street is legendary. By day, the buildings and shopping encapsulate the Key West experience (page 133).

★ **Southernmost Point:** At this buoy on the southern tip of Key West, you're closer to Cuba than you are to Miami (page 138).

★ **Dry Tortugas National Park:** Visitors flock to the seven islands of this national park for the pristine natural environment as well as snorkeling and boating (page 151).

The Florida Keys archipelago is more than a chain of islands; it's a place where visitors and residents live on a mainland version of "island time." The natural beauty demands a certain slow pace.

That same beauty makes you feel as if you're wasting time if you're not diving, fishing, or exploring all that the Keys have to offer.

Although Key West gets the majority of the Keys's spotlight, it's important to remember there are almost 1,700 other islands in this tropical archipelago. Granted, most of them are tiny, uninhabited spits of sand and mangrove. But quite a few offer their own unique character. The Keys are roughly divided into the Upper Keys (Largo and Islamorada) and the Lower Keys (Marathon and below, including Key West).

The historic architecture and bustling counterculture in Key West belies its reputation as a soused-and-sunburned Margaritaville. To be sure, this southernmost island is the best known and most visited of all the Keys. While you could certainly restrict a Keys trip to the sights and sounds of Duval Street, to do so would be to miss out on the island's tropical charm.

The craggy shores and equally craggy characters that inhabit Key Largo are far from the image conjured by the classic film of the same name, and they probably represent the spirit of the "Conch Republic" as well or better than heavily trafficked Key West. Throughout the Keys, though, the primary attractions are the water-related activities: snorkeling, boating, and fishing. But the onshore wildlife, historic houses, and museums on the islands also provide their own unique pleasures.

PLANNING YOUR TIME

The 140-mile drive from the southern edge of Miami to downtown Key West only takes about three hours. So, it's quite possible to "see" the Florida Keys in a jam-packed day that has you eating breakfast in Key Largo,

---

Previous: the old Bahia Honda Bridge; The Seven Mile Bridge connects the upper keys and the lower keys. **Above:** Fort East Martello documents Key West's nautical past.

Florida Keys

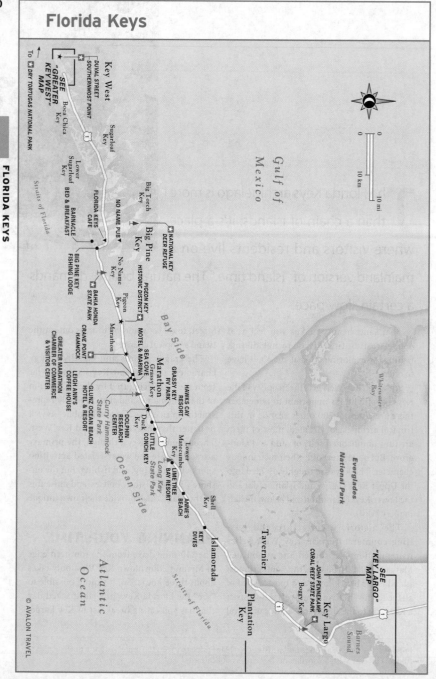

Two Days in the Florida Keys

The original *African Queen* is docked in Key Largo.

If you've got only a couple of days to explore the Keys from a home base in Miami, this itinerary will help you hit the highlights without too much pressure. After all, it's the Keys; nobody should be feeling too stressed down here:

DAY 1

Start your first day with breakfast in **Key Largo** at **Mrs. Mac's Kitchen,** and then head immediately to **John Pennekamp Coral Reef State Park.** Get there early to take one of the 9am **snorkeling tours** that will take you out to some of the most beautiful coral reefs in North America.

Head out of the park around noon, stopping to look at the *African Queen* (from the Humphrey Bogart movie of the same name). Grab lunch at the **Key Largo Conch House.**

Head south for the hour-ish drive to **Marathon,** where you can spend the afternoon exploring the **Pigeon Key Historic District,** a ghost town dating from the days when Henry Flagler's railway was being constructed. Have dinner and a drink at the nearby **Sunset Grille,** where you can watch a gorgeous sunset over the **Seven Mile Bridge.** Spend the night at one of the cute and romantic cottages at **Little Conch Key.**

DAY 2

Get fresh pastries and coffee at **Leigh Ann's Coffee House** in Marathon, then head toward **Bahia Honda State Park,** home of the Keys' most beautiful beaches.

After a few hours of soaking in some rays, drive 30 minutes to the **National Key Deer Refuge** on **Big Pine Key,** where you'll have a unique opportunity to see the tiny, endangered deer.

Lunch at the out-of-the-way **No Name Pub** will fortify you for the short drive to **Key West.** Once you're in Key West, head immediately for the **Southernmost Point** of the continental United States. Next, you can explore the shops, restaurants, and sights of **Duval Street.**

Take your happy hour break with a craft beer at the supposedly haunted **The Porch,** and then walk a few blocks over to **Blue Heaven,** the most tourist-friendly and personality-rich restaurant in all of Key West. Spend the rest of the evening checking out the bars of Duval Street, and crash at the retro-luxe **Orchid Key Inn.**

lunch in Marathon, and wind up the day with dinner and drinks along Key West's Duval Street. Such an itinerary is ill-advised for all but the most time-pressed traveler. The whole point of making your way to the Keys is to experience the laid-back tropical vibe, and rushing through the islands is almost as bad as not seeing them at all.

If time is a factor, you should make a beeline directly for Key West for a weekend; two full days should allow you to take in the historic sights, do some snorkeling, and enjoy a couple of beautiful sunsets before hitting the bars along Duval Street. The Key Largo and Marathon areas are both worth a day or so each. Diving the reefs or heading out for some sportfishing requires at least a day dedicated to each.

Upper Keys

Heading out of the sprawling suburbs and scrappy towns of South Miami and onto the Overseas Highway on the way to the Keys, the transformation of the atmosphere, topography, and attitude is both immediate and overwhelming. As the worn-out gas stations and fast-food outlets of Florida City recede in the rearview, an open expanse of sea and a slender road spread out in front of you. This is the **Upper Keys,** most folks' first introduction to the island archipelago. Comprised of all the islands north of Marathon and including the famous Key Largo and snorkeling and diving paradise of Islamorada, these islands are a bit more developed than some of the Lower Keys, but they still manage to retain all the friendly, relaxed beauty expected of the Florida Keys.

KEY LARGO

The largest and longest of all the Florida Keys, hence the name, **Key Largo** was made internationally famous in the 1948 Bogie-Bacall film of the same name. Even before that movie (which, incidentally, was filmed almost entirely on a Hollywood soundstage), the island had an excellent reputation among sportfishing enthusiasts and intrepid vacationers. Today, Key Largo still welcomes thousands of anglers as well as snorkelers and scuba divers who are eager to explore the underwater beauty of John Pennekamp Coral Reef State Park. The town itself is small-town Florida through and through, despite quite a bit of it given over to tourist paraphernalia.

★ John Pennekamp Coral Reef State Park

John Pennekamp Coral Reef State Park (102601 Overseas Hwy., 305/451-6300, http://pennekamppark.com, 8am-sunset daily, $8/carload, $4/single-occupant vehicle, $2 pedestrians/bicyclists) has three beaches, which is about three more than many other state parks in the Keys have. Almost every single one of the park's beaches are jam-packed with people during the busy season. It also has some picnic areas, campsites, and a unique visitors center with a massive saltwater aquarium as its centerpiece.

The primary attraction at Pennekamp lies a few miles away from shore in clear, shallow waters that house an abundance of coral reefs. The park offers 2.5-hour **snorkeling tours** ($29.95 adults, $24.95 children) that leave for these reefs at 9am, noon, and 3pm. With depths of 5-15 feet, these snorkeling areas are rich with coral and tropical fish. At Dry Rocks reef, snorkelers can see Guido Galletti's 8.5-foot-tall bronze statue, **Christ of the Abyss,** extending its arms to the heavens from a depth of about 20 feet below the surface. This sight has drawn divers to this spot for more than 40 years. Scuba divers can avail themselves of the park's twice-daily deep-dive tours (9:30am and 1:30pm, $75 per person). Visitors who want a look at the vibrant marine life but would prefer to stay dry can head out to Molasses Reef on the *Spirit of Pennekamp,* a 65-foot glass-bottomed

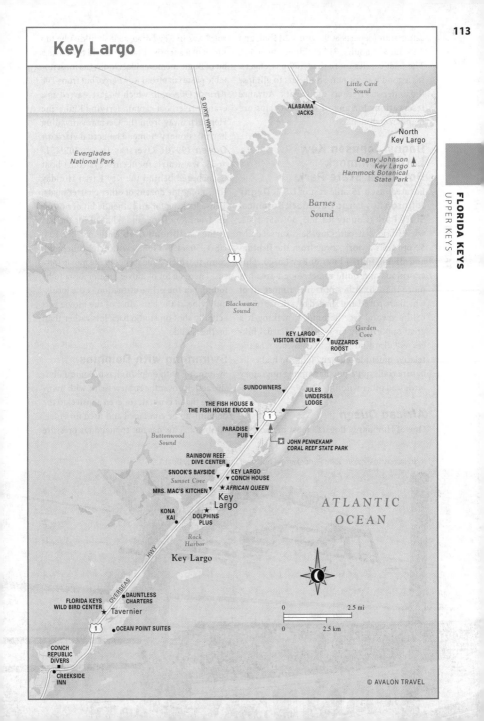

Key Largo

© AVALON TRAVEL

catamaran (departs at 9:15am, 12:15pm, and 3:15pm, $24 adults, $17 children under 12). The boat carries more than 100 passengers. It's a good way for non-snorkelers to glimpse the underwater beauty of the park. Advance reservations for any of the boat trips are highly recommended.

Dagny Johnson Key Largo Hammock Botanical State Park

Located just 0.25 mile east of US-1, **Dagny Johnson Key Largo Hammock Botanical State Park** (County Rd. 905, 305/451-1202, www.floridastateparks.org, 8am-sunset daily, $2 pp) feels a world away from the fishing-and-diving tourist buzz of Key Largo. This enormous and quite undeveloped area has more than six miles of trails, almost all of which are paved and shaded by a dense tropical hardwood tree hammock, making it a great opportunity for bicyclists. Casual hikers will also find plenty to enjoy here, as the relative quietude of Dagny Johnson makes its nature trails quite popular among migratory birds and other wildlife.

African Queen

One of Humphrey Bogart's most memorable roles was in *Key Largo,* so it shouldn't be too much of a surprise that the island town has a bit of Bogie memorabilia. Oddly, the most notable piece isn't from *Key Largo,* but from *The African Queen,* in which Bogart starred as a cranky riverboat captain ferrying Katharine Hepburn away from the Germans invading her missionary home. The actual *African Queen* (99701 Overseas Hwy., 305/451-4655, www.africanqueenflkeys.com) boat is anchored behind the Key Largo Holiday Inn, alongside dozens of other charter boats. Those looking for an authentic bit of nostalgia from *Key Largo* should head for the bar at the **Caribbean Club** (mile marker 104, US-1, 305/451-4466, www.caribbeanclubkl. com), in which some scenes in the movie were set. There's a lot of movie memorabilia to be found, but the prime attraction is the locals-only vibe at the bar. Most of the movie was actually shot on studio back lots rather than on the island.

Swimming with Dolphins

Swimming with dolphins has become a divisive activity over the last few years, with many saying that it is unfair (or even abusive) to the dolphins to be contained and used for entertainment. This has put tremendous pressure

A great way to explore John Pennekamp Coral Reef State Park is by boat.

on local businesses that work hard to provide educational and inspirational opportunities to interact with dolphins, but this activity is still seen by many as part of the quintessential Florida experience. **Dolphins Plus** (31 Corrine Pl., 305/441-1993, www.dolphinsplus.com, 8:30am-5pm daily) is one of the most notable attractions offering these swim-with-the-dolphins experiences. At the facility, there are structured and "natural" interactive experiences, seemingly designed for those who may be a bit nervous in the water with a dolphin, as contact is limited and the routines are closely guided by a trainer in the water with you. There are also looser, "natural" experiences that don't guarantee dolphin contact, but snorkelers are allowed to freely roam the dolphin swimming area, imitating the marine mammals in the hopes of some one-on-one interaction. The natural experience is less expensive ($125 for half an hour) and more adventurous; the structured experience ($195, 2 hours) avoids the chance of not getting near a dolphin. In addition to dolphin encounters, Dolphins Plus also offers other activities like swimming with sea lions and educational programs about marine biology.

Florida Keys Wild Bird Center

The **Florida Keys Wild Bird Center** (93600 Overseas Hwy., Tavernier, 305/852-4486, daylight hours daily, free) is a tiny bayside nature center that's dedicated to the rehabilitation of injured wild avian creatures. Unsurprisingly, there are scores of birds throughout the lush, if compact, grounds. There's a nice boardwalk and a coastal area where the birds love to congregate. Most visitors here are school groups, but a stroll through the property is both inspiring and educational and your donation helps keep the center running.

Sports and Recreation

As is the case throughout most of the Keys, a primary activity among many visitors to Key Largo is fishing. Accordingly, there are more than a few charters around willing to take you out and show you their "secret"

spots. **Dauntless Charters** (mile marker 97.5, US-1, 305/304-4551, www.dauntless-charters.com) is one of the more versatile in Largo, with boats equipped for deep-sea, inshore, and reef/wreck fishing.

Similarly, there are quite a few outfits offering packages and charters for divers. **Sea Dwellers** (99850 Overseas Hwy., 305/451-3640, www.seadwellers.com) is not only one of the most popular, it's also one of the best, with a wide range of packages ranging from kid-friendly scuba courses and snorkeling expeditions to two-tank, two-location trips out into John Pennekamp Park. The dive center has an abundance of gear for rent and for sale, as well as a repair shop and, of course, air fills; stay-dive package deals with the Holiday Inn are also available. Sea Dwellers has been a Key Largo institution for more than three decades, so its presence is hard to miss.

Rainbow Reef Dive Center (9701 Overseas Hwy., 305/451-5533, www.rainbowreef.us) is another well-established diving operation. Its fleet of boats is top-notch and the dive masters and staff are incredibly friendly (they even offer complimentary chocolate-chip cookies). Their landside operation is somewhat small.

Food

There are few places that claim to serve both superlative coffee and seafood, but ★ **Key Largo Conch House** (100211 Overseas Hwy., 305/453-4844, www.keylargoconch-house.com, 7am-10pm daily, from $12) does indeed make such a seemingly incongruous boast. Frankly, it's hard to argue: In the morning this former coffeehouse serves up decadent French toast, pancakes, Benedicts, and other traditional breakfast fare—plus some damn good coffee. Lunch sees the menu shift to paninis, wraps, and some highly touted fish tacos, and by the time dinner rolls around, the Conch House's transformation is complete, with fresh meat, poultry, and vegetarian entrées rounding out a menu packed with fresh, lightly prepared fish dishes, conch meunière, and richly sauced seafood pastas.

Best Restaurants

★ **Key Largo Conch House:** It really does feel like a house—complete with a porch—and serves exceptional coffee and decadent seafood dishes (page 115).

★ **Pierre's:** European fare is fused with local ingredients to create unique dishes such as hogfish meunière (page 121).

★ **Sunset Grille:** Standard beach-grill fare is enlivened by a boisterous atmosphere and amazing sunset views under the Seven Mile Bridge (page 127).

★ **Blue Heaven:** The whimsical tropical surroundings—painted picnic tables, an upstairs "tree house" dining room—are quintessentially Key West (page 147).

★ **The Cafe: A Mostly Vegetarian Place:** This cozy spot opts for a veg- and grain-based approach, rather than fake-out "meat" plates (page 147).

The atmosphere here is cozy, quirky, and decidedly unpretentious. The wraparound porch is a great place to relax with a glass of wine before or after dinner.

Two more great places in Key Largo to find seafood, conveniently enough, are located right next door to each other. **The Fish House** and **The Fish House Encore** (102400 Overseas Hwy., 305/451-4665, www.fishhouse.com, 11:30am-10pm daily, from $16) are built around the menu made famous by the original. The Fish House has been an institution in Largo since the 1980s, known for its fresh fish and seafood offerings. When a gift shop next door went out of business, the restaurant expanded its size and menu. The Fish House is an old-fashioned Florida seafood restaurant that stacks coleslaw, hush puppies, and corn on the cob beside your tuna steak. While Encore is more likely to accompany your dishes with steamed vegetables and rice, and there's a slightly more expansive and upscale selection of entrées as well as a sushi bar.

Other good options for seafood and steaks are **Sundowners** (103900 Overseas Hwy., 305/451-5566, www.sundownerskeylargo.com, 11am-10pm daily, from $18), **Snook's Bayside** (99470 Overseas Hwy., 305/453-5004, www.snooks.com, 11:30am-9:30pm daily, from $21), and **Ballyhoo's** (97860 Overseas Hwy., 305/852-0822, www.ballyhoosrestaurant.com, 11am-10pm daily, from $14). Snook's is probably the nicest of the three, boasting fantastic views and a boisterous tiki bar. The key lime pie at Sundowners is close to famous. But the food at all of them is quite good, if not incredibly inventive.

There's a pretty strong chance you'll want to get beyond seafood at some point during your trip. **Mrs. Mac's Kitchen** (99336 Overseas Hwy., 305/451-3722, www.mrsmacskitchen.com, 7am-9:30pm Mon.-Sat., from $12) is semi-legendary in the Keys, and serves up a splendid combination of meat-and-threes (get the meat loaf), relatively healthy sandwiches, and definitely not-very-healthy-but-still-excellent burgers, as well as seafood platters. Mrs. Mac's also has some of the best breakfast in Key Largo, and the place loves it when you get a glass of champagne with your three-egg omelet or churrasco-steak-and-eggs plate. Another spot that's as great for breakfast as it is throughout the day is **Evelyn's** (103360 Overseas Hwy., 305/451-1691, 6am-9pm Mon.-Sat., 6am-2pm Sun., from $7), which serves up coma-inducing plates of eggs-and-bacon as well as bursting-at-the-seams breakfast burritos all day long. Evelyn's also has a full menu of Mexican staples and diner-style dishes (burgers, meat loaf, pasta, Philly

The Fish House

cheesesteaks); make sure to get the huevos rancheros.

There are a handful of options for drinks and pub fare in Key Largo, and almost all of them offer some variety of burgers, oysters, wings, seafood baskets, and ice-cold beer. Whatever these joints lack in epicurean savoir-faire they make up for in their determined efforts to give locals and visitors places to drink; they are the extent of nightlife in Key Largo. The dive-bar atmosphere of **Sharky's Pub & Gallery.** (522 Caribbean Blvd., 305/453-0999, 7am-2pm daily) belies the convivial nature of the staff and the fact that they serve sushi and an exceptional fish taco. **Buzzards Roost Grill & Pub** (21 Garden Cove Dr., 305/451-4696, www.buzzardsroostkeylargo.com, 11am-9pm Mon.-Thurs., 11am-10pm Fri.-Sat., 10:30am-9pm Sun.) is just a bit more upscale, with steaks and ribs on the menu and a decent selection of beer on tap. Over in Card Sound (the waterway you'll cross over as you come from Miami to the Keys), is **Alabama Jack's**

(58000 Card Sound Rd., 305/248-8741, 11am-6:30pm daily), a legit slice of Old Florida that's almost as well known for its ice-cold beer and friendly, marina-style vibe as it is for the paper plates full of incredible conch fritters.

Accommodations

★ **Jules' Undersea Lodge** (51 Shoreland Dr., 305/451-2353, www.jul.com, from $400 pp) asks its visitors a simple question: Have you slept underwater lately? Since most people can't answer this question in the affirmative, Jules is truly and easily classified as a unique lodging experience. Guests have to swim to their guest rooms some 21 feet beneath the surface in an underwater research facility. There's a distinctly retro-futuristic vibe to the lodge, like the spy-movie "moon pool" where water comes right up to the floor, to the pod-like structure itself. Guest rooms are small, but a common room has a television and stereo as well as a mini kitchen. The lodge even has Wi-Fi. Most guests avail themselves of the services of Jules's "mer-chef," who dives down to prepare a gourmet dinner. You can also get pizza delivered from the nearby Tower of Pizza. Still, most folks who come don't spend their entire time cooped up in the sea pod and instead come and go as they please on scuba-diving expeditions in the area. The lodge provides unlimited air tanks for divers. (Note: You don't have to be a certified diver to stay here; Jules' offers a three-hour resort course to prepare you for the dive down, and, of course, while you're lodging here, you can take an extended certification course.) Although staying here is understandably pricey, the two guest rooms are often booked months in advance.

For something a little closer to the action in Key Largo, **Sunset Cove Beach Resort** (99360 Overseas Hwy., 305/451-0705, http://sunsetcovebeachresort.com, $130 d) provides an excellent balance of relaxing quietude and convenient location. Opening out onto the waters of Florida Bay, with grounds landscaped with thick, tropical vegetation, Sunset Cove is a cozy and welcoming property. There's a small but nice beach, a dock,

Best Accommodations

★ **Jules' Undersea Lodge:** Guests swim to their rooms in this unique underwater lodge (page 117).

★ **Casa Thorn Bed & Breakfast:** Each guest room is individually decorated in a playful theme, from the plush Moroccan Suite to the tropical Tiki Hut (page 122).

★ **Glunz Ocean Beach Hotel & Resort:** This comfortable and relaxed spot is a great, affordable lodging option (page 129).

★ **Conch House:** Enjoy classic Key West accommodations in this Caribbean colonial-style complex (page 149).

★ **Orchid Key Inn:** This modern, stylish version of a 1950s hotel offers a touch of luxury in Key West (page 150).

and complimentary canoe and kayak rentals. Lodging here is a varied mix of standard rooms and suites as well as a half-dozen cottages and, somewhat uniquely, a handful of full-outfitted RVs. All of these are priced extremely reasonably. While the accommodations certainly aren't all that fancy, they're comfortable and clean, with all expected conveniences.

Kona Kai (97802 Overseas Hwy., 305/852-7200, www.konakairesort.com, from $299 d) is considerably more luxurious, with 11 guest rooms set among bougainvillea, palm trees, and fruit-tree- and flower-filled gardens. Guest rooms are airy and large, with tile floors and large windows. The secluded resort has a freshwater pool that overlooks a private white-sand beach; most of the property's activities take place in this area, from lazy hammocks and barbecue grills to a Ping-Pong table and a hot tub. There's also a tennis court. Despite the insulated surroundings, the resort is surprisingly close to a number of restaurants along US-1. Worth noting: Kona Kai is an adults-only facility.

Families should head for **Ocean Pointe Suites** (500 Burton St., 305/833-3000, http://www.providentresorts.com/ocean-pointe-suites, from $175 d). With 150 different condo rentals available, sizes range from smaller kitchenettes to two-bedroom units, but all are suites. Décor varies, since each unit is individually owned, and some suites are more dated than others; make sure to ask for an updated one. There's a small white-sand beach as well as a freshwater swimming pool. A café and bar are on the property too. While this is a condo property, it feels more like a resort.

Information and Services

The **Key Largo Chamber of Commerce** operates a small **visitors center** (mile marker 106, US-1, 800/822-1088, www.keylargochamber.org, 9am-6pm daily) that can help with trip advice and advance planning as well as last-minute reservations.

Getting There

Key Largo is at mile marker 100 on the Overseas Highway (aka US-1), about 60 miles (1.5 hours) south of downtown Miami and about 100 miles (2 hours) north of Key West.

ISLAMORADA

Islamorada is the smallest of the four "big" towns in the Florida Keys. It's known as the Sportfishing Capital of the World. Like Key Largo, the main attractions on Islamorada are fishing, snorkeling, diving, and relaxing. The town has its share of tourist-oriented kitsch along with its friendly small-town Florida vibe.

Windley Key Fossil Reef Geological State Park

The geology at **Windley Key Fossil Reef Geological State Park** (mile marker 84.9, US-1, 305/664-2540, www.floridastateparks. org, 9am-5pm Thurs.-Mon., $2.50 pp) is not that of your average depleted quarry. In the early days of the 20th century, this plot of land was sold to Henry Flagler, who used the limestone here to help build his Florida East Coast Railroad. What remains are both the remnants of the quarry itself, namely, the giant quarry walls, and imposing sheets of fossilized coral. There are some short hiking trails that allow easy viewing of the property with informative signage explaining how Flagler used the rocks excavated from here. Some of the original machinery still remains. Guided tours are available (10am and 2pm Fri.-Sun., $2 pp). This is a fairly quiet state park, and will be most appreciated by history buffs or as a good spot for a picnic.

Theater of the Sea

The thing that draws most visitors to the hard-to-miss gates of **Theater of the Sea** (84721 Overseas Hwy., 305/664-2431, www. theaterofthesea.com, 9am-5pm daily, $32.95 ages 11 and up, $22.95 children 3-10, children 2 and under free) is the promise of up close marine-life encounters, including a swim-with-the-dolphins experience that is trumpeted all over the attraction's promotional literature. The general admission to the park allows guests to watch a handful of shows featuring trained dolphins and sea lions as well as to leisurely stroll through the tropical grounds. To get up close and personal with the sea animals costs quite a bit more. It's $55 to swim with rays, $135 to swim with sea lions, and a whopping $175 to swim with the dolphins; these sessions typically last 20-30 minutes.

History of Diving Museum

One of the coolest things inside the **History of Diving Museum** (82990 Overseas Hwy., 305/664-9737, www.divingmuseum.org, 10am-5pm daily, $12 adults, $6 children, children 4 and under free) is a huge display wall with dozens of antique diving helmets arrayed on it. The *Parade of Nations* exhibit, especially when accompanied by the distinctive audio

Theater of the Sea in Islamorada

narration by museum founder Joe Bauer, is both interesting and educational in its own quirky way. There are also exhibits dedicated to treasure hunters, the odd evolutionary path of helium diving, and a general overview of the history of underwater exploration from skin-diving to scuba.

Entertainment and Events
THE ARTS

Among the dive shops and tiki bars of Islamorada, there's a lively arts and crafts scene. The **Rain Barrel Village** (86700 Overseas Hwy., 305/852-3084, 9am-5pm daily) is an impossible-to-miss "artist village" that signals its presence with a giant lobster that faces US-1. In addition to the main gallery filled with pottery, several local artisans also ply their wares here in tiny gallery storefronts. It's also a none-too-shabby spot to grab a coffee or ice cream for the road.

FESTIVALS AND EVENTS

The weekend-long **Islamorada Island Festival** (305/664-4503, www.islamoradachamber.com, Apr.) takes place at Founder's Park (87000 Overseas Hwy.), with live music, arts and crafts, and the Taste of Islamorada contest in which local restaurants compete for various awards and the crowds get to sample their offerings.

Sports and Recreation
BEACHES

As is the case throughout most of the mangrove-thick coast of the Keys, sandy beaches are few and far between in Islamorada. The small oceanside swimming area at **Anne's Beach** (mile marker 73, US-1, sunrise-sunset daily) is about as good as they come. There are covered picnic pavilions, two parking areas, and restrooms. The water is fairly shallow and quite calm. Given the rarity of public beaches in the area, Anne's Beach is often incredibly crowded and far from relaxing. There is also a beach at **Founder's Park** (87000 Overseas Hwy., sunrise-sunset daily, free).

PARKS

The largest public park in Islamorada is **Founders Park** (87000 Overseas Hwy., sunrise-sunset daily, free), and it's a pretty impressive one. In addition to standard amenities like ball fields (soccer, baseball), it boasts a great swimming pool, five tennis courts, a marina, and a beach that, although bayside, is nonetheless quite nice and clean. The beach is often considerably less crowded than the tourist-heavy Anne's Beach. Founder's Park is also home to Islamorada's main visitors center.

DIVING

Diving is the primary recreational activity around Islamorada, and there are dozens of shops and charters that cater to divers. **Key Dives** (79851 Overseas Hwy., 305/664-2211, www.keydives.com, two-trip single-tank dives from $85, snorkeling excursions from $40 pp) is routinely cited as one of the best. The company's concierge approach to expeditions is designed to minimize headaches and maximize memorable underwater experiences. Their decades of history in the area mean they've got more than a few "secret" dive sites that will be considerably less crowded; they also offer spearfishing and wreck-diving excursions.

Nearby Tavernier (about halfway between Islamorada and Key Largo) has good dive shops and charter boats in the form of **Conch Republic Divers** (90800 Overseas Hwy., Tavernier, 305/852-1655, 8am-5pm daily, www.conchrepublicdivers.com, half-day trips from $60) and the **Florida Keys Dive Center** (90451 Overseas Hwy., Tavernier, 305/852-4599, www.floridakeysdivectr.com, 8am-5pm daily two-tank trips from $50, snorkeling excursions from $35). The only true difference between these two is the price.

FISHING

There are several sportfishing charters operating out of Islamorada. Captain Mike Bassett specializes in backcountry trips for snook, redfish, mangrove snapper, tarpon,

1935 Labor Day Hurricane

No single event is more significant in the history of the Florida Keys than the infamous Labor Day Hurricane of 1935. The unnamed storm was one of the strongest hurricanes to make landfall in the United States and is one of only three hurricanes to ever strike the United States with Category 5-strength winds. Category 5 hurricanes have winds in excess of 155 mph. The 1935 hurricane was estimated to have had 185 mph winds.

At least 400 people died in the hurricane—some estimates say that casualties could have been as high as 600. While that number is substantial on its own, it's important to note that at the time only about 1,000 people lived in the Keys. Among the dead were 259 World War I veterans employed in a government bridge-building program. Their work camps were woefully inadequate to withstand the storm's ferocity, a tragedy highlighted by a poignant essay by Ernest Hemingway titled, somewhat bluntly, "Who Murdered the Veterans?"

The hurricane made landfall directly over Islamorada. The damage there was incredibly severe. All the Keys were devastated, however. The loss of a railway connection to the mainland compounded the difficulty of relief efforts as well as reconstruction efforts, and it wasn't until the Overseas Highway was finally completed in 1938 that the Keys were really able to begin rebuilding. There's a touching memorial in Islamorada, at mile marker 82, dedicated to those who died in the storm.

FLORIDA KEYS
UPPER KEYS

and more. He runs a 19-foot skiff under the name of **Born & Raised Charters** (84000 Overseas Hwy., 305/853-5541, www.bornandraisedcharters.com). **Reef Runner Charters** (83413 Overseas Hwy., 305/852-3660, www.reefrunnerfishing.com) operates a 40-foot boat out of Whale Harbor Marina that can take fishing groups of up to six people. **Captain Bill Bender** (85932 Overseas Hwy., 305/664-8232, www.captainbillbender.com) runs a smaller 22-foot boat for light-tackle fishing a little closer to shore and specializes in sniffing out sharks. **Islamorada Sport Fishing** (www.islamoradasportfishing.com) is a good resource for anglers looking for more information on Islamorada charters.

Food

The crepes, pastries, and coffee at **Bitton Bistro** (82245 Overseas Hwy., 305/396-7481, from $8) make for a great way to start your day in Islamorada. This casual, French-style café is decidedly unpretentious, but the food that emerges from its kitchen is so consistently good that you would almost forgive a little snobbery. Beyond early morning noshes, Bitton also offers substantial quiches,

excellent sandwiches (built on fresh-baked French bread), and gelato throughout the day.

Despite its French-sounding name, ★ **Pierre's** (81600 Overseas Hwy., 305/664-3225, www.moradabay.com, 5pm-10pm Sun.-Thurs., 5pm-11pm Fri.-Sat., from $29) does not serve a strictly French menu. The preparations of fresh local seafood—for instance, a hogfish meunière or sea scallops served with veal jus—are distinctly continental. These dishes are accented by a smattering of Asian-inspired plates (tempura lobster, Wagyu beef, and daikon salad) and more traditional fare like grilled tuna and braised beef short ribs. Everything is served in the classically elegant atmosphere of a gorgeous two-story colonial-era building with wraparound verandas and marvelous sunset water views. Meals here are pricey, and reservations are essential.

Located on the same property as its sister restaurant, Pierre's, **Morada Bay Beach Café** (81600 Overseas Hwy., 305/664-0604, www.moradabay.com, 11:30am-10pm Sun.-Thurs., 11:30am-11pm Fri.-Sat., from $24) is a little more casual, although certainly not cheap. Traditional Italian, Caribbean, and American fare is the order of the day here, with dishes like veal piccata, filet mignon, broiled lobster, and coconut-crusted yellowtail snapper. Morada Bay is a nice choice for a classy lunch, with sandwiches and a limited selection of entrées for about half the price of dinner. The beautiful island-style atmosphere and top-notch kitchen combine for a great experience.

Those looking for an even more straightforward selection of sandwiches and seafood should head for the casual, Caribbean-style **Island Grill** (85501 Overseas Hwy., 305/664-8400, www.keysislandgrill.com, 11am-1am Mon.-Thurs., 11am-2am Fri.-Sat., 10am-midnight Sun., from $9). The festive decor and friendly atmosphere make this a fine place to attempt one of its Big Kahuna Burgers (a half pound of meat topped with bacon, pineapple, cheddar cheese, and hot sauce). If that's too intimidating, make sure you order a plate of the superlative tuna nachos and an ice-cold craft beer. There are excellent, relaxing views of Snake Creek from the bar area, and there's even an outdoor tiki bar/"beach" that makes Island Grill an exceptional experience.

The Gulf-side **Marker 88** (88000 Overseas Hwy., 305/852-9315, www.marker88.info, 11am-10pm daily, from $18) could probably thrive based solely on the incredible sunset views available from its dining room. Thankfully, unlike many Florida restaurants that boast beautiful vistas and mediocre food, the kitchen here is almost as impressive as the window seating. Marker 88's sublime coconut-coated hogfish should be a Keys staple, but given how hard hogfish are to catch (they're almost exclusively spearfished, rather than netted), you should indulge in this spectacular dish whenever you get a chance. The regularly appearing menu items are also pretty impressive. The restaurant sticks primarily to standard island fare like fish sandwiches, grilled mahi Caesar salads, broiled fresh catches, and more. Marker 88 is definitely not a fried-basket joint, as the presence of exceptional starters like lobster/mango guacamole and sides like Thai green beans should make clear.

Hogfish is a treat best had in the Keys, and the folks at **Chef Michael's** (81671 Overseas Hwy., 305/664-0640, 5pm-10pm Mon.-Sat., 10am-2pm and 5pm-10pm Sun., from $20) have pretty much staked their reputation on it. The restaurant's tagline is "Peace, Love, and Hogfish." If you're dead-set on indulging in this flaky, spear-caught specialty, Michael's is definitely a great place to go. The plates here are pretty incredible. You can get hogfish or any of the day's fresh catches prepared in a number of inventive and indulgent ways, from the Creole-style Ponchartrain (fish topped with crawfish and shrimp) to the lighter, more fish-forward Mediterranean approach of the Adriatic (grilled and dosed with olive oil and herbs). Michael's goes far beyond the blackened-broiled-or-fried approach of most restaurants. The restaurant also prominently features at least one substantial and thoughtful vegetarian dish daily. Sunday brunch is a decadent affair: shrimp-and-grits, thick egg-and-bacon sandwiches, omelets, and more.

Located in "downtown" Islamorada's tiny arts district is **Kaiyo Grill** (81701 Old Hwy., 305/664-5556, www.kaiyokeys.com, 5pm-10pm Mon.-Sat., from $14), an essential stop if all those "fresh seafood" signs around town turn your thoughts to sushi. While the sushi chef here seems to lean pretty heavily on the standards, Kaiyo also offers a surprising selection of inventive and locally inspired rolls. Do not leave without trying the Macadamia Hogfish roll and the fried-pork-belly-based Crazy Cuban. The kitchen fare is also exceptional, with fresh-catch preparations that cover the basics (grilled, blackened, etc.) as well as unique fusion approaches like a miso glaze. Kaiyo Grill also prepares incredible starters, like grouper cheeks, rice balls, and key-lime-juice-infused edamame.

Accommodations

The five guest rooms at the quietly luxurious ★ **Casa Thorn Bed & Breakfast** (114 Palm Ln., 305/852-3996, www.casathorn.com, from $89 d) are routinely booked solid, and it's easy to understand why. Each guest room is individually decorated in a playful theme, from the plush four-poster bed and Moorish chandelier in the Moroccan Suite to the tropical ambiance of the Tiki Hut. All of the guest rooms have Wi-Fi access, down comforters, and private patios. The refined elegance of the Secret Garden Room, complete with its own private entrance and courtyard, is the best choice. Children under 8 aren't allowed, but small pets are.

The quiet, clean, and basic rooms at the **Creekside Inn** (90611 Old Hwy., Tavernier, 305/852-2351, http://mycreeksideinn.com, from $109) are ideal for Islamorada visitors who intend to spend a good portion of their visit here diving; the inn is located just a few steps away from the Florida Keys Dive Center. The owners and staff do a good job of ensuring that all their guests have a nice stay, encouraging a friendly and convivial atmosphere as well as making sure that friendliness doesn't spill out into late-night, post-dive parties. The sunset views along the creek here are fantastic. There's a nice pool/barbeque area (complete with hammock). The inn is a short drive from several Islamorada sights and restaurants. Its location is pretty quiet and isolated, and the rooms are a great value.

The basic **OceanView Inn & Sports Pub** (84500 Overseas Hwy., 305/664-8052, www.theocean-view.com, from $159 d) is a fun and comfortable budget option. All seven of the guest rooms here are clean, bright, and equipped with mini fridges and microwaves. The pub is a good place to grab a greasy bite and knock back a few with the locals. The hotel is owned by two former National Football League players, so it's not that surprising that this is a preferred spot on Islamorada to catch the football game on Sunday.

Families traveling with small children should check out **Lookout Lodge** (87770 Overseas Hwy., 305/852-3035, www.lookoutlodge.com, from $150 d), which offers a variety of guest-room configurations ranging from basic studios to two-bedroom suites. Most of the spacious—if somewhat dated—guest rooms have full kitchens; the others have kitchenettes. All guest rooms have TV and central air-conditioning as well as free Wi-Fi and even free local and long-distance calling.

The **Postcard Inn Beach Resort** (84001 Overseas Hwy., 305/664-2321, www.holiday-isle.com, from $239 d) actually offers what its name implies: a beach! This is a rarity in the Keys, and the cozy spread of sand and palm trees here is a far sight cleaner, more comfortable, and more relaxing than the public wading area at Anne's Beach. Thankfully, the hotel itself doesn't require you to sacrifice your standards for the sake of having a beach; all the rooms here, from the oceanfront suites to the standard king- and queen-size rooms, have hardwood floors, flat-screen TVs, and Wi-Fi. They are all well-furnished, spacious, and stylishly tropical, and the hotel is also pet friendly. While some of the Old Florida vibe of the place has been lost to recent renovations, the feeling here is still quite relaxed.

Cheeca Lodge & Spa (81801 Overseas Hwy., 305/664-4651, www.cheeca.com, from $379 d) is a luxury-minded, family-oriented resort. The revamped resort stands as one of the best places in the Keys for high-end travelers and those looking for a relaxing splurge. Standard rooms are spacious and modern. The suites and roomy adults-only bungalows provide the most relaxing (and luxurious) stays. And while everyone can't put out for a 400-plus-square-foot beachfront bungalow while on vacation, the resort amenities available to all guests make Cheeca an enticing option. Perks range from excellent golfing and tennis facilities to spa treatments, fishing charters, and endless waterfront views. The resort is somewhat off the main drag and nearly completely self-contained, with a fine-dining restaurant (Atlantic's Edge), a family-style Italian bistro (Limoncello), an oceanside tiki bar, and even a sushi restaurant.

Information

The Islamorada Chamber of Commerce operates a **visitors center** (mile marker 87, US-1, 305/664-4503, www.islamoradachamber.com).

Getting There and Around

Islamorada is located 83 miles (about 1.5 hours) south of Miami, about 23 miles (30 minutes) south of Key Largo, and about 77 miles (2 hours) north of Key West. Enter the town from the north at about mile marker 91.

Lower Keys

The wildlife and outdoor activities on Big Pine Key, Marathon, and the other nearby islands of the **Lower Keys** are less than an hour away from Key West. The area has withstood hurricanes, pushed back against development, and maintained a laid-back lifestyle that's richly evocative of Old Florida's charms.

MARATHON

Marathon is one of the four big towns in the Keys, with a population almost as large as that of the second-biggest city, Key Largo. Still, it's worth noting that "big" is entirely relative down here; both Marathon and Key Largo are less than half as populous as Key West, and the population of Key West could barely fill a small college football stadium. (The fourth town, Islamorada, is the smallest of the group.) The attractions in Marathon are fishing, boating, diving, and relaxing. At its core, Marathon is still just a small town in a near-perfect setting.

Long Key State Park

Henry Flagler established the Long Key Fishing Club in the early 20th century, and it quickly became a preferred destination for saltwater fishermen with the means to visit it. In 1935, the great Labor Day Hurricane that ripped through the Upper Keys not only destroyed most of the rail and bridge work that Flagler had so heavily invested in but also obliterated the Fishing Club. Today, Long Key is **Long Key State Park** (67400 Overseas Hwy., 305/664-4815, www.floridastateparks. org, 8am-sunset daily, $4.50), and it's still a prime destination for anglers, although it is considerably less opulent than in Flagler's day. In addition to ample fishing opportunities onshore and in the lagoons, nature hikes, canoe and kayak trails through the mangroves, and oceanfront campsites provide ample opportunities for pastoral relaxation.

Dolphin Research Center

One of the more popular of the many places in the Keys that offer interactive dolphin experiences, the **Dolphin Research Center** (DRC, 58901 Overseas Hwy., Grassy Key, 305/289-0002, www.dolphins.org, 9am-4:30pm daily, $28 adults, $23 children, children under 4 free) is also one that's considerably more forthright in pronouncing its commitment to the health and well-being of the marine mammals in its midst. While many of the other swim-with-the-dolphins spots are certainly kind to their animals and dedicated to conservation issues, the fact that "research" is part of the name gives visitors some indication as to what the primary focus is. Many published scientific papers have originated in research done at the facility, most of which involves ascertaining dolphins' higher cognitive abilities. The DRC's Trainer for a Day program ($695) is one of the most, uh, immersive options, with groups limited to four people; guests spend the day interacting with both dolphins and trainers, getting a pretty thorough sense of the relationships that develop between them. Researcher Experience ($475) is another all-day program that puts visitors to work assisting with various projects around the center. More straightforward swim, play, meet, and even paint (!) with the dolphin experiences cost $65-200.

Curry Hammock State Park

The 260-acre **Curry Hammock State Park** (56200 Overseas Hwy., 305/289-2690, www. floridastateparks.org, 8am-sunset daily, $5/

carload, $4/single-occupant vehicle) opens up to both the bay and the ocean. The latter side is preferred by day-trippers, who flock to the small, clean beach, picnic and grilling area, and campground. The bay side is a bit rougher, with thatches of mangrove, hardwood hammocks, and kayak trails thick with flora and fauna (look up for tropical birds, look down for lolling manatees). There's also a 1.5-mile walking trail. The campground here is nice and will often have availability when other parks are full. The park is home to the annual **Florida Keys Birding & Wildlife Festival,** which takes place every September.

★ Crane Point Hammock

In 1989, the Florida Keys Land Trust made one of the largest conservation purchases in the group's history: a 63-acre tract of land that had been slated to be turned into a shopping mall and housing development. Walking around those 63 acres today, in their current form as **Crane Point Hammock** (5550 Overseas Hwy., 305/743-9100, www.cranepoint.net, 9am-5pm Mon.-Sat., noon-5pm Sun., $11 adults, $9 seniors, $7 children, children 5 and under free), you can only be convinced that it was a smart buy. The vast tropical landscape is one of the best places to

get a sense of the Keys's ecological diversity, with mangrove forests, tidal lagoons, thatch palm hammocks, wetlands, and hardwood hammocks. The natural beauty is exceptional. The operators of the Land Trust have taken care to make the area accessible via boardwalks and nature trails without diminishing the natural beauty of the property.

There are two museums on-site, the **Museum of Natural History** and the **Florida Keys Children's Museum,** which give further interpretive context to the flora and fauna throughout Crane Point. Archaeological spots like Cracker houses, wooden shelters built by early settlers, and a restored Bahamian village provide insight into the people who once lived here. A visit to Crane Point is not only personally edifying but also supportive of a great conservationist mission.

The Turtle Hospital

Sea turtles are a big deal in Florida. These creatures start their lives in the most fragile and perilous way: Mother turtles lay their eggs on a beach, cover the eggs with sand, and then head back to the ocean, leaving the eggs to incubate and hatch, followed by the tiny baby turtles making their way back to the water.

the educational and entertaining Dolphin Research Center

Since the arrival of humans to the coast of Florida, sea turtles have been increasingly endangered. Florida residents have sought for years to mitigate human impact on sea turtles by protecting and monitoring their nests. The tiny facility of **The Turtle Hospital** (2396 Overseas Hwy., 305/743-2552, www.turtlehospital.org, 9am-6pm daily, $22 adults, $11 children, reservations recommended) rescues, rehabilitates, and releases more than 1,500 injured turtles since opening in 1986. Alongside researchers from the University of Florida, the hospital staff studies viral diseases that inordinately affect sea turtles. The daily guided tours are illuminating, not only shedding light on the good work that the hospital itself does, but also letting people know the many small actions they can take to avoid harming sea turtles.

Sombrero Beach

Beaches are not the reason most people come to the Keys, as most are small, shallow, and sometimes even stinky. **Sombrero Beach** (end of Sombrero Beach Rd, 7:30am-sunset daily, free) isn't the best beach in the Keys (that honor goes to the beaches at Bahia Honda State Park), but it's a close second, with one of the largest, sandiest, and cleanest beaches around, and although it can get quite crowded (there's no entrance fee), it's both pleasant and friendly. Waves, when they exist at all, are tiny, so it's also quite safe for swimmers.

★ Pigeon Key National Historic District

When Henry Flagler was building his railroad between Miami and Key West and work was under way on its most notable feature—the Seven Mile Bridge—the tiny island of Pigeon Key made a perfect site for a work camp, as it was located at almost the exact midpoint of the bridge's span. The five acres of the island are now the **Pigeon Key National Historic District** (mile marker 45), a sort of trapped-in-amber ghost town that, thanks to the construction of the *new* Seven Mile Bridge, is ironically a little tough to get to. Visitors will need to park in a tiny lot on the north side of the bridge and walk out over the remnants of the old bridge for about a mile to get to the district. (Bicycles are permitted on the old bridge, but no motorized vehicles, due to the semi-perilous state of repair the bridge is currently in.) Alternately, the Pigeon Key Foundation offers guided tours that depart three times a day via ferry from a visitors

the Pigeon Key National Historic District

center in Marathon (mile marker 47, US-1, 305/743-5999, $12 adults, $9 children). Once here, you can explore the dozen or so buildings on the island, mostly cottages painted in Flagler's favorite color (yellow). There's also a visitors center with information about the island's unique history. There is a science center on the island, but it is mostly geared toward school groups and camps.

Sports and Recreation

Sea Dog Charters (mile marker 47.5, US-1, bayside, 305/743-8255, http://seadogcharters.net, half-day charters from $60 pp) has four boats in its fleet, ranging 30-41 feet in length. Their namesake boat is a 37-foot twin-diesel-powered sportfishing vessel that's able to run deep-sea routes as far away as the Dry Tortugas and the Bahamas. It's worth noting that Sea Dog is a "green" charter outfit that uses biofuels and recycled products.

The largest dive center in Marathon is **Tilden's Scuba Center** (mile marker 49.5, US-1, bayside, 305/743-7255, www.tildensscubacenter.com, 8am-6pm daily). The well-regarded crew here offers a large array of gear sales, rentals, and repairs, including hydrostatic testing, as well as air fills and Professional Association of Diving Instructors (PADI) certification classes, reef charters, and the only SNUBA (a combination of snorkeling and scuba diving) facility in the Keys.

For a water-based experience beyond diving or fishing, head for **Keys Cable** (59300 Overseas Hwy., 305/414-8245, www.keyscable.com, 11am-6pm daily, from $22/half-hour), a wakeboard park on Duck Key. There are two cable systems running through the seven-acre saltwater lake, allowing wakeboarders (and water-skiers) to reach some impressive speeds and, if they so desire, take a jump over one of the ramps scattered throughout the lake. Boards and helmet rentals are available for an additional cost; monthly, seasonal, and annual passes are also sold.

Food
The **Stuffed Pig** (3520 Overseas Hwy.,

305/743-4059, www.thestuffedpig.com, 5am-2pm Mon.-Sat., 6am-noon Sun., from $5) has been serving breakfast and lunch in Marathon since 1984. Grabbing a spot on the outdoor patio for a cup of coffee and a plate of gator tail and eggs or banana nut French toast should be an essential part of anyone's visit to town. Breakfast includes country-fried steak, fish and eggs, and a belt-straining four-egg omelet filled with sausage, ham, and bacon. The Southern flair of the breakfast menu extends to the barbecue sandwiches and conch fritters that sit alongside fried shrimp, burgers, dogs, and deli sandwiches (including a club sandwich that piles on ham, beef, turkey, and bacon).

The breakfast and lunch offerings at **Leigh Ann's Coffee House** (7537 Overseas Hwy., 305/743-2001, www.leighannscoffeehouse.com, 7am-6:30pm Mon.-Fri., 7am-5pm Sat., 8am-noon Sun., from $7) aren't as belly-busting as the Stuffed Pig. Fresh pastries, traditional American breakfasts, and frittatas and burritos are available in the morning, along with the Leigh Ann's excellent java. Lunch tends toward lighter fare like cold cuts, salads, quiche, and soups.

After your first time at the ★ **Sunset Grille** (7 Knights Key Blvd., 305/396-7235, www.sunsetgrille7milebridge.com, 8am-10pm daily, from $9), you may want to come back every night. What ensures that the Sunset Grille is packed evenings is the astounding vistas it offers right around, well, *sunset*. Right at the northern base of the Seven Mile Bridge, the Sunset Grille sits on one of the most beautifully scenic spots in all of the Keys, and the business here has predictably grown up around that. Instead of a simple dining room with panoramic windows, the vibe here is a boisterous mix of open-air dining room mixed with a sandy tiki bar area and a full-sized swimming pool. It's less a dinner spot than a prime locale for a several-hours-long food-and-beer party that culminates with a nearly perfect sunset every night. The food is standard beach-grill fare. You can get a plate of competently prepared fresh-catch fish or one of Sunset's dizzying variety of fried baskets or even a perfectly acceptable burger.

There are a couple of other restaurants near Marathon's end of the Seven Mile Bridge that are definitely worth checking out. The **7 Mile Grill** (1240 Overseas Hwy., 305/743-4481, www.7-mile-grill.com, 6:30am-9pm daily, from $7) is a super-friendly, family-owned diner specializing in Greek food as well as fresh-caught seafood. (Literally "fresh": You can bring your own fish in to be cooked.) The grill also has some of the best breakfast dishes in Marathon and some excellent pastries as well. A couple of doors away is **Porky's Bayside BBQ** (1410 Overseas Hwy., 305/289-2065, http://porkysbaysidebbq.com, 11am-10pm daily, from $12), which somehow splits the difference between being a scenic marina grill, a real-deal barbecue joint, and a locals bar custom built for day drinking. The staff here is great, the beer is ice-cold, and the fish dip/nacho platter is almost as great as the fantastic Carolina-style barbecue.

Although the **Cracked Conch Cafe** (4999 Overseas Hwy., 305/743-2233, www.conch-cafe.com, 7am-midnight Mon.-Fri., 11am-midnight Sat.-Sun., from $8) serves breakfast, the main reason folks stop into this old-school seafood joint is for the conch chowders, fritters, and offerings like conch Parmesan. For those who haven't quite developed a taste for these luscious mollusks, the café also offers a limited selection of steaks, poultry, and ribs, as well as sandwiches and salads. Start off with a cocktail and wrap up with a slice of key lime pie and a cup of Cuban coffee, all of which can be enjoyed in the shaded outdoor patio area.

For seafood served in a somewhat more formal environment, the **Barracuda Grill** (4290 Overseas Hwy., 305/743-3314, 6pm-10pm Mon.-Sat., $25-35) is a consistent favorite. The atmosphere—which, though more polished than many local seafood joints, is still Keys-casual—complements sophisticated preparations, with menu items that touch every base, from comfort food (meat loaf) to Floribbean (*ropa vieja,* grilled yellowtail with mango salsa). Known equally for its sky-high prices

and palate-singeing spicy seafood sauce, the Barracuda is worth a splurge visit.

Splitting the difference between craft-beer bar, highway seafood shack, and local family institution, **Herbie's Bar and Chowder House** (6350 Overseas Hwy., 305/743-6373, 11am-9pm Wed.-Sun., from $10) is unprepossessing and unlikely to enrapture big-city foodies, but it has great food and a great atmosphere. While it doesn't boast spectacular views (unless you really like looking at US-1), it does offer three distinct dining experiences: A screened-in porch area is designed to accommodate larger groups, a cozy dining room feels like a neighborhood diner, and the bar can seat about a dozen or so folks, either bar side or at a few high-top tables. Note: Each of these dining rooms has its own separate front door, and, despite having three individual dining rooms, Herbie's is a pretty intimate space. A wide selection of craft beer and cider complements a pretty standard bar-and-grille menu that's highlighted by some excellent smoked wings, robust burgers, conch fritters, and some locally legendary chowder.

El Molcajete (1622 Overseas Hwy., 305/780-7988, 10am-9pm daily, from $10) is the only Mexican restaurant in Marathon. The fare here is standard Tex-Mex, with burritos, enchiladas, tacos, and so on, but augmented with a not-insubstantial selection of more authentic Mexican fare like lengua tacos, fresh ceviche, and more. For those seeking a respite from seafood—or looking for something to soak up last night's overindulgence—El Molcajete is a great option.

Accommodations
During high season, accommodations in Marathon can get somewhat pricey. A good option for travelers on a budget is **Seashell Beach Resort** (57612 Overseas Hwy., 305/289-0265, from $119 d), a small, family-owned mid-century motel that's been maintained well and offers clean, basic rooms. Some rooms have kitchenettes and many have balconies with water views. The property has

a small, sandy beach (and Sombrero Beach is a short drive away), a pool, and a dock.

Another inexpensive and somewhat unique option would be the "floating rooms" at the **Sea Cove Motel & Marina** (12685 Overseas Hwy., 305/289-0800, www.floatingrooms.com, from $139 d). These "rooms" are boats that are docked at the Sea Cove's marina. Having a whole (stationary) boat to yourself for a few nights makes for a distinctly Keys holiday. That said, neither the motel-style efficiency rooms nor the boats are luxurious; while clean, the accommodations here are a little rough around the edges. Still, the staff is friendly and the price can't be beat.

One of the best bargains in Marathon is ★ **Glunz Ocean Beach Hotel & Resort** (351 East Ocean Dr., Key Colony Beach, 305/289-0525, www.glunzoceanbachhotel.com, from $155 d), a formerly unremarkable motel that's been given a complete makeover by its owners. From the comfortably stylish rooms, all of which have flat-screen TVs, ceiling fans, Wi-Fi, and Keurig coffeemakers, and the spacious suites (which add full kitchens and separate bedrooms) to the relaxed and welcoming vibe of the staff, the Glunz truly seems to have no other priority than making sure your stay here is a memorable one. There's no pretense of luxury, but all the basics are deftly handled, with small touches (a free lending library, onsite laundry, the staff's friendly attitude) combining to make this an exceptional (and affordable) place to stay.

The **Tranquility Bay Resort** (2600 Overseas Hwy., 305/289-0888, www.tranquilitybay.com, from $229 d) offers all the advantages of a beach house stay—fully equipped kitchens, separate bedrooms, laundry facilities—with the amenities of a high-end resort. The property has a small, secluded beach, two swimming pools (one of which is adults-only), a gym, a spa, and water-sports equipment rentals. There's an excellent restaurant, the **Butterfly Cafe**, as well as a beachfront tiki bar. The 87 "houses" are available in one-, two-, and three-bedroom configurations. They're spacious, airy, and quite luxurious,

with flat-screen plasma TVs, plush beds, and top-shelf linens. All the guest rooms boast waterfront views, though the pricier ones are located beachside.

At **Little Conch Key** (62250 Overseas Hwy., 305/289-1377, www.conchkeycottages.com, from $329 d), there are nine standalone cottages, three apartment-style rooms, and one regular hotel room, which makes this property on Walker's Island both intimate and able to accommodate a variety of needs. Each of the cottages is uniquely decorated in muted tropical tones. The small, waterfront one-bedroom cottages are the best option. Designed for two guests (but able to accommodate a family of four), these three tiny bungalows truly feel like a home away from home, with full kitchens, screened porches, and incredible ocean views.

Hawks Cay Resort (61 Hawks Cay Blvd., Duck Key, 305/743-3000, www.hawkscay.com, from $349 d) manages to balance a sophisticated island resort feel with kid-friendly amenities, making it a prime destination for families. While still amplifying the natural beauty of the Keys for moms and dads eager to hike, fish, or just relax, Hawks Cay also offers an array of kid-centric activities like day and evening camps for kids, tweens, and teens. Of course, a lot of kids don't need a room dedicated to their Xbox needs to have a good time in the Keys, and there are plenty of opportunities for them—and their parents—to dive, sail, fish, or just relax poolside. There are nearly 175 guest rooms and suites, all of which are decorated in muted Keys-classy styles with contemporary furnishings and large windows. Families gravitate toward the 100 or so two-, three- and four-bedroom villas, which have full gourmet kitchens, flat-screen TVs, dining rooms, and luxurious touches.

The smaller and more intimate **Lime Tree Bay Resort** (68500 Overseas Hwy., Long Key, 305/664-4740, www.limetreebayresort.com, from $279 d) has only 33 units, ranging from traditional hotel rooms and mini suites to full-sized, custom-decorated suites like the Zane Grey Master Suite, a two-story, two-bedroom, apartment-style guest room. The coolest guest room is the two-bedroom Treehouse Suite; located on the second story of the same building as the Zane Grey Suite, the Treehouse's greatest attraction is its wraparound windows and the beautiful porch that has, well, a tree growing through it. There are also three cottages with private entrances. The Lime Tree has two small sandy beaches on the property, a dock, a pool, and several grilling areas.

Campers have plenty of options in Marathon. **Curry Hammock State Park** (56200 Overseas Hwy., 305/289-2690) and **Long Key State Park** (67400 Overseas Hwy., 305/664-4815) both offer tent and RV camping facilities, and can be reserved well in advance (www.reserveamerica.com). The sites at Curry Hammock sit along a waterfront loop, although only about one-third have water views. The sites at Long Key are fantastic, with beautiful waterfront views and shaded camping areas.

For RV campers looking to commune with fellow travelers, there's **Grassy Key RV Park** (58671 Overseas Hwy., 305/289-1606, www.grassykeyrvpark.com, from $55/night) and **Sunshine Key RV Resort** (38801 Overseas Hwy., 305/872-2217, from $65/night). Both sites are built to handle all sizes of RVs, and have water access, swimming facilities, full hookups, Wi-Fi, and laundry facilities. The main differentiators are that Sunshine Key is an Encore facility on the south end of the Seven Mile Bridge, while Grassy Key is privately owned and more convenient to other sights in Marathon.

Information and Services

The Greater Marathon Chamber of Commerce operates the tiny but very helpful **Marathon Visitors Center** (12222 Overseas Hwy., 305/743-5417, www.floridakeysmarathon.com, 9am-5pm daily), where you can pick up information and brochures on area attractions and accommodations.

Getting There

Marathon spans seven islands: Boot Key, Crawl Key, Fat Deer Key, Grassy Key, Knight's Key, Long Point Key, and Key Vaca. The heart of town is located at the exact midpoint of the Keys at mile marker 50 on the Overseas Highway.

It's a 60-mile, 80-minute drive to get to Marathon from Key West. It's a 107-mile, two-hour drive from Miami to Marathon.

BIG PINE KEY

There's not much to the 10-square-mile island known as **Big Pine Key.** Home to the National Key Deer Refuge, it's one of the only places in the world to see the endangered Key deer. Nearby Bahia Honda State Park has one of the most gorgeous beaches in the Florida Keys.

★ National Key Deer Refuge

From the giant fences and countless signs warning you to slow down because of the presence of Key deer, you should know that these adorable little creatures are held in high esteem down here. The 30-inch-tall deer are an endangered species, currently estimated to have a population of less than 1,000, almost all of which live within the borders of the 8,500-acre **National Key Deer Refuge.** If you're passing through Big Pine Key in the morning or evening, you'll almost certainly see a handful of deer grazing along the road (hence the signs). The **National Key Deer Refuge Visitor Center** (28950 Watson Blvd., 305/872-2239, www.fws.gov, 8am-5pm daily) is a great place to get information on the deer and the other wildlife, including approximately 20 other endangered species, that live throughout the refuge. The visitors center is best used as a starting point for exploring the two hiking trails and other natural features of the refuge. Don't miss the Blue Hole, an abandoned quarry that is now the largest body of fresh water in the Keys.

★ Bahia Honda State Park

The three white-sand beaches at **Bahia Honda State Park** (36850 Overseas Hwy., 305/872-2353, http://bahiahondapark.com, 8am-sunset daily, $6/carload, $4/single-occupant vehicle, camping $36 per night, snorkeling tours from $30 pp, kayak rentals from $12/hour) are certainly the best in the Florida Keys. Many visitors to the Keys are disappointed by the relative lack of beaches on the islands, but a visit to Bahia Honda quickly disabuses them of the notion that the Keys are completely devoid of good places to splash around and sunbathe.

The largest beach area, **Sandspur**, is at the southeast end of the island and has three picnic pavilions as well as restroom and shower facilities. Most visitors head straight for it, as the 2.5-mile narrow stretch of white sand and calm blue waters is quite beautiful and surprisingly spacious. The shallow waters at the small **Loggerhead Beach** area are great for families; a sandbar just offshore is a nice place for kids to play during low tide. Still, the best beach here is **Calusa Beach**, which offers not only the beautiful sands and blue waters of the other beaches, but also a great view of the cars zooming by on the Overseas Highway bridge. Be advised that the underwater surface here quickly shifts from smooth, shallow sand to jagged rocks.

There are ample snorkeling opportunities just a few hundred feet from the shore of all three beach areas. Between the underwater beauty, the on-shore activities, and its relative isolation in the south Keys, this park more than earns its reputation as one of the best beach spots in the state. There are also snorkeling trips that can be arranged at the visitors center.

Beyond the beaches, Bahia Honda has plenty of opportunities for bird-watching and hiking along two fantastic nature trails, one of which takes visitors up to the ruins of the old Bahia Honda Bridge, a vantage point that provides fantastic views of the deep-blue ocean as well. Camping, fishing, and boating are popular activities here as well. The on-site nature center and the butterfly garden are both great educational detours for curious kids and adults. Overnight campers should make reservations well in advance, especially during the winter.

FLORIDA KEYS
LOWER KEYS

Key deer are the most important residents on Big Pine Key.

Food

No Name Pub (30831 Watson Blvd., 305/872-9115, www.nonamepub.com, 11am-11pm daily, from $5) has been serving up burgers and seafood baskets since the 1930s. The lived-in roadhouse vibe is instantly comfortable and definitively casual. The decor is best defined by the presence of paper towel rolls on every table, and a ceiling decorated with thousands of dollar bills. Whether tucking into one of the pizzas or some lip-puckeringly saline fish dip, you'll probably agree that this out-of-the-way spot was worth the drive. (Plus, you're pretty likely to catch a glimpse of a Key deer or two as you make your way through the neighborhoods you have to traverse to get to No Name Pub.)

The **Florida Keys Cafe** (30739 Overseas Hwy., 305/872-7030, 7am-2pm daily, from $5) is an unprepossessing diner serving generous portions of breakfast standards.

Accommodations

The **Barnacle Bed & Breakfast** (1557 Long Beach Dr., 305/872-3298, www.the-barnacle.net, from $175 d) consists of three guest rooms within a main villa and a separate one-bedroom cottage. The property is quirky and tropical, right down to the tiki hut out by the whirlpool tub. Guest rooms are decked out in colorful fabrics and paint schemes and have private baths, Wi-Fi, and mini fridges. This property does not allow children under age 16.

Campers, boaters, and anglers should head for **Big Pine Key Fishing Lodge** (33000 Overseas Hwy., Big Pine Key, 305/872-2351, www.bpkfl.com, $43-169), an excellent, family-owned marina/campground right on the border of the National Key Deer Refuge. The campground is huge, with 172 RV sites ($69), 75 tent sites ($43), and motel and cabin lodging (from $134). The marina is the focal point of activities here, but there are also hiking trails, a recreational area with a swimming pool, shuffleboard, a playground, and a camp grocery.

Getting There

Big Pine Key is 25 miles (30 minutes) north of Key West and 135 miles (2.5 hours) south of Miami, between mile markers 29.5 and 33 along the Overseas Highway.

Bahia Honda State Park

Key West

As you arrive in Key West via the Overseas Highway, the island might not be what you expect at first sight. The marinas, shopping centers, and fast-food joints of New Town are your first introduction to the "Conch Republic." It's in the historic district of Old Town where you'll find the romance and fun of Key West.

Historic buildings, tropical landscapes, quirky residences (and residents), and a deep sense of individuality combine to create a powerful atmosphere that's quite welcoming but that must be met on its own terms. From the grizzled mariners who live on houseboats in the historic marina to the flamboyant drag queens beckoning tourists into nightclubs, people here are strongly encouraged to be themselves. That extends to visitors as well, as long as you manage to be respectful of the fact that Key West is home to 25,000 people who were here before you arrived and will still be living here when you leave.

SIGHTS

One of the best ways to see Key West is on a guided tour. Hop on a bike and follow along with **Lloyd's Tropical Bike Tours** (601 Truman Ave., 305/294-1882, http://lloyd-stropicalbiketour.com, $39). These two- to three-hour tours are led by Lloyd, who knows unusual and interesting spots around Old Town and can add a unique perspective on many of them that's well worth the cost of the tour.

★ Duval Street

Running in a north-south direction right through the middle of Key West's historic district, **Duval Street** is often the only part of town that many visitors see. The northern end is a hive of activity, especially when a cruise ship is docked, with bars like Sloppy Joe's and restaurants like the Hard Rock Café competing for tourist dollars with dozens of souvenir shops, food stands, and tour guides. The crowds lessen a little farther south from

Duval Street welcomes everyone with its open and friendly party vibe.

Key West

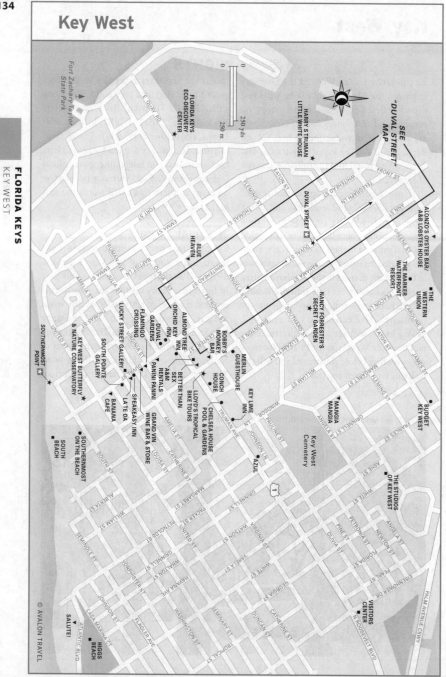

© AVALON TRAVEL

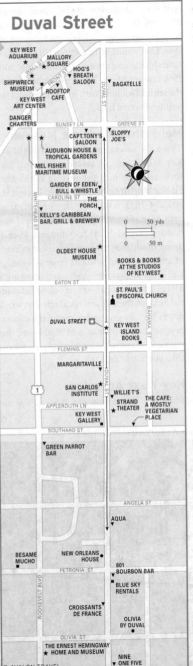

Duval Street

KEY WEST AQUARIUM
MALLORY SQUARE
HOG'S BREATH SALOON
SHIPWRECK MUSEUM
ROOFTOP CAFE
KEY WEST ART CENTER
BAGATELLE
DANGER CHARTERS
SUNSET LN
GREENE ST
CAPT. TONY'S SALOON
SLOPPY JOE'S
AUDUBON HOUSE & TROPICAL GARDENS
MEL FISHER MARITIME MUSEUM
GARDEN OF EDEN/ BULL & WHISTLE
THE PORCH
CAROLINE ST
KELLY'S CARIBBEAN BAR, GRILL & BREWERY
0   50 yds
0   50 m
OLDEST HOUSE MUSEUM
BOOKS & BOOKS AT THE STUDIOS OF KEY WEST
EATON ST
ST. PAUL'S EPISCOPAL CHURCH
DUVAL STREET
KEY WEST ISLAND BOOKS
FLEMING ST
MARGARITAVILLE
SAN CARLOS INSTITUTE
WILLIE T'S
APPLEROUTH LN
STRAND THEATER
THE CAFE: A MOSTLY VEGETARIAN PLACE
KEY WEST GALLERY
SOUTHARD ST
GREEN PARROT BAR
ANGELA ST
AQUA
BESAME MUCHO
NEW ORLEANS HOUSE
ROOSEVELT BLVD
PETRONIA ST
801 BOURBON BAR
BLUE SKY RENTALS
CROISSANTS DE FRANCE
OLIVIA BY DUVAL
OLIVIA ST
THE ERNEST HEMINGWAY HOME AND MUSEUM
NINE ONE FIVE
DUVAL ST
GREENE ST
WHITEHEAD ST
BAHAMA ST
© AVALON TRAVEL

this nexus, and the architecture and cultural style that defines the city becomes a little easier to see.

Although it's only about a mile long, Duval's range of shopping, dining, and drinking options can easily occupy an entire day, but make sure to take time to look at a few of the unique and beautiful buildings. The building that houses **St. Paul's Episcopal Church** (401 Duval St.) dates from 1901, although the parish has been on the property since the mid-1800s. The previous buildings were destroyed by the 1886 Great Key West Fire and several different hurricanes. The old **Strand Theater** (527 Duval St.) is currently a chain drugstore, but the building still evokes the glory of its 1930s roots. Built in 1871 by Cuban exiles, the ornate **San Carlos Institute** (516 Duval St.) is a museum, library, art gallery, and theater focusing on Cuban and Cuban American culture.

Nancy Forrester's Secret Garden

Tucked away on a side street a block or two away from the bustle of Duval Street, **Nancy Forrester's Secret Garden** (518 Elizabeth St., 305/295-0015, http://nancyforrester.com, 10am-5pm daily, $10 adults, $5 children, children under 5 free) is something of a poorly kept secret. Over the years, Nancy Forrester and her friends have reclaimed several lots in this residential neighborhood and turned them back over to nature, showcasing hundreds of species of tropical plants that are seldom seen in other gardens in the United States. The gardens only take up an acre, but visitors are immersed in a natural and pastoral experience complete with tropical reptiles, beautiful parrots, and even a few cats.

Harry S. Truman Little White House

Built in 1890 as the headquarters for the U.S. naval command, the **Harry S. Truman Little White House** (111 Front St., 305/294-9911, www.trumanlittlewhitehouse.com, 9am-5pm daily, $15 adults, $13 seniors, $4.50 children,

children under 5 free) gained its place in history as President Truman's favorite place to rest and rejuvenate. Truman took 11 working vacations here between 1948 and 1953, during which several momentous decisions were made, ranging from the creation of the Department of Defense to the recognition of the State of Israel. Truman's successors must have thought he was on to something, as it was also used by Presidents Dwight Eisenhower, John F. Kennedy, Jimmy Carter, and Bill Clinton. Other notable guests have included inventor Thomas Edison, General Colin Powell, and King Hussein of Jordan. Informative and enjoyable tours of the house, the grounds, and the botanical garden are given every 20 minutes.

Audubon House and Tropical Gardens

The first thing you should know about the **Audubon House and Tropical Gardens** (205 Whitehead St., 305/294-2116, www.audubonhouse.com, 9:30am-5pm daily, $13 adults, $10 students, $5 children 6-12, kids under 6 free) is that John J. Audubon never actually lived in the house. The residence was built in the 1840s for Captain John H. Geiger, a local harbor pilot. Audubon visited here a decade earlier, camping

on the grounds for six weeks as he painted wildlife in the area. Most of the focus here is on the 30-plus engravings Audubon made during his visit. This house and its gorgeous (if small) botanical garden are a beautiful window into mid-19th century life on Key West, right down to the sense of solitude just a few feet off from the well-trod tourist track.

Mel Fisher Maritime Museum

There are several museums that highlight Key West's role in treasure-hunting history, and the most interesting is the **Mel Fisher Maritime Museum** (200 Greene St., 305/294-2633, www.melfisher.org, 8:30am-5pm Mon.-Fri., 9:30am-5pm Sat.-Sun. and holidays, $15 adults, $12.50 students, $5 children). In addition to several excellent exhibits of antiquities and artifacts from slave ships and colonial treasure vessels—including quite a bit of actual treasure—there's also a substantial focus on the archaeological role that wreck divers play. By giving this material a context beyond the glimmer of gold doubloons, this museum is far more engaging and educational than you might expect.

Key West Aquarium

Built as a Depression-era Works Progress

Nancy Forrester's Secret Garden provides an avian oasis in a Key West neighborhood.

Sunset Cruises

Sunsets in Key West are a very big deal. After all, the island points directly into the western horizon, with expanses of water all around. Watching the sun dip below the ocean is a perfect, romantic way to punctuate the end of a day in the Conch Republic.

For a truly unobstructed view, head out on one of the many **sunset cruises** offered by nearly every charter company on Key West. Cruises with **Fury Watersports** (multiple locations, 888/976-0899, www.furycat.com) start at $35 and provide a friendly, party-boat atmosphere. Cruises offered by **Danger Charters** (235 Front St., 305/304-7999, www.dangercharters.com, from $75) are considerably more expensive, but are also much more intimate, with the boat's capacity limited to 20 people. Similarly low-key and personal is the sunset cruise offered by **Floridays** (Hyatt Resort, 601 Front St., 305/744-8335, www.floridays.org), which is both upscale and romantic, but also a bargain at $55 per person. All of these sunset cruises include complimentary wine and/or champagne.

There are options for landlubbers as well. Locals tend to vouch (publicly, at least) for the seventh-floor rooftop of the **Crowne Plaza La Concha Hotel** (430 Duval St.), where the nightly Sunset Celebration means drink specials and a lot of ooh-ing and aah-ing over the 360-degree views. If you don't mind crowds—or if you're pressed for time and need to get back to your cruise ship—head to the waterfront boardwalks of **Mallory Square** (400 Wall St.), where you can grab a drink and a bite to eat at one of the many nearby tourist spots.

Administration project, the **Key West Aquarium** (1 Whitehead St., 305/296-2051, www.keywestaquarium.com, 10am-6pm daily, $15 adults, $13 seniors, $8.50 children) was the island's first large-scale tourist attraction. Combining indoor and outdoor exhibits, the aquarium features a tank where guests can look at and feed sharks, a small touch tank where kids can pick up and observe starfish and other sea creatures, and several other small exhibits. The combination of the building's architectural charm and the conservation-minded exhibits make for a pleasant half-day visit. Do not expect a facility like California's Monterey Bay Aquarium (or even the Georgia Aquarium), as the Key West Aquarium is quite small and in some corners shows its age.

Oldest House Museum

Built in 1829 and moved to its current location in 1836, the residence of Captain Francis Watlington has withstood the various natural (and manmade) calamities that have befallen Key West over the years. Today, it's the site of the aptly titled **Oldest House Museum** (322 Duval St., 305/294-9501, www.oirf.org, 10am-4pm Mon.-Tues. and Thurs.-Sat., free), a small, but interesting museum filled with artifacts (some of which were Watlington's, but most of which are just period pieces). The knowledgeable staff members from the Old Island Restoration Foundation are more than happy to answer questions. Tours of the small house and grounds are self-guided.

Florida Keys Eco-Discovery Center

Located on the grounds of the National Oceanic and Atmospheric Administration's Nancy Foster Florida Keys Environmental Complex, the 6,400-square-foot **Florida Keys Eco-Discovery Center** (35 E. Quay Rd., 305/809-4750, http://floridakeys.noaa.gov/ecodiscovery, 9am-4pm Tues.-Sat., free) is heavy on scientific and educational aspects. The interpretive exhibits deliver an exceptional and detailed overview of the ecological work done throughout the Florida Keys National Marine Sanctuary and other nearby parks and wildlife refuges. There's also a beautiful Living Reef exhibit that features an enormous aquarium with live coral and tropical fish, along with a coral nursery.

Fort Zachary Taylor State Park

Although it can easily claim to have Key West's best beach, **Fort Zachary Taylor State Park** (300 Truman Ave., 305/292-6713, www.floridastateparks.org, 8am-sunset daily, $4 per single-occupant vehicle, $6/carload, $2/pedestrian or bicyclist) doesn't really have a whole lot of competition. Nonetheless, the small beach is quite pleasant. There are excellent snorkeling opportunities off the beach, where schools of parrot fish, snapper, and other fish can frequently be spotted among the coral reefs. Visitors can also enjoy fishing on the west side of the park, as well as biking and hiking along some pleasant short nature trails. The fort itself seems to be in a permanent state of rehabilitation. Still, park rangers offer daily guided tours during which you can poke around in the few open areas of the fort and see Civil War-era cannons and other military artifacts.

Key West Butterfly and Nature Conservatory

When you approach the **Key West Butterfly and Nature Conservatory** (1316 Duval St., 305/296-2988, www.keywestbutterfly.com, 9am-5pm daily, $12 adults, $8.50 children, children under 4 admitted free), you could be forgiven for thinking you've got the wrong address and are approaching someone's home. Once you get past the gift shop and the ticket counter and enter the humid environs of the glass-walled outdoor butterfly sanctuary out back, you could be forgiven for thinking you've landed in the middle of a nature film. The conservatory is filled with hundreds of beautiful farm-bred butterflies flying around an array of gorgeous tropical plants, with a few tiny birds for good measure.

★ Southernmost Point

The **Southernmost Point Buoy** (South St. and Whitehead St., a block east of Duval St.),

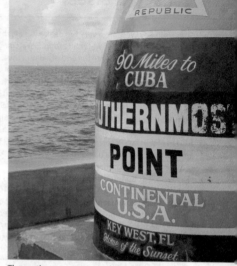

The southernmost point in the United States is in Key West.

brightly painted in black, red, and yellow, is close to the heart of historic Key West. Nearly all visitors make their way here for a snapshot, as it notes the fact that you're not only at the southernmost point in the continental United States, but also only 90 miles from Cuba. Although there is almost always a small crowd of people nearby waiting their turn to take a photo, you'll be in and out, photo taken, in less than five minutes.

Fort East Martello

A few blocks away from Smathers Beach, and set right alongside a beautiful waterfront view is **Fort East Martello** (3501 S. Roosevelt Blvd., 305/296-3913, www.kwahs.org, 9:30am-4:30pm daily, $7 adults, $6 seniors and locals, $5 children and students, children under 6 free), housed in a Civil War-era Union fort. This is a pretty unique museum, with an interesting mix of folk art and historical artifacts. Perfectly splitting that difference is Robert the Doll, a supposedly haunted doll dating from the early 20th century that was once owned

Hemingway in Key West

In 1928, on the advice of fellow author John Dos Passos, Ernest Hemingway and his new bride, Pauline, stopped in at Key West on their way back from Paris. Perhaps not surprisingly, the combination of tropical breezes and pioneer spirit appealed to Papa, and the couple decided to make the island home for a few years. They purchased a house, now known as the **Ernest Hemingway Home & Museum** (907 Whitehead St., 305/294-1136, www.hemingwayhome. com, 9am-5pm daily, $14 adults, $6 children), a few years after settling down. Visitors to the Spanish Colonial-style home are encouraged to take tours, which help put some perspective on the small number of artifacts and personal effects of Hemingway's that are in the house. Although the price of admission is a little steep, bibliophiles will doubtlessly enjoy soaking in the atmosphere of the as-is interior and the inspiring garden area.

Hemingway's influence on the island, as well as Key West's influence on him, went far beyond real estate. The writer finished *A Farewell to Arms* here. And in *To Have and Have Not* his intimate relationship with Key West is laid bare. Not only is the novel set here, but it manages to draw composite characters of Key West natives that still ring true today.

Beyond the house and museum, Hemingway aficionados will also want to check out **Casa Antigua** (314 Simonton St.). The property was originally an odd dual-use building with a Ford dealership downstairs and a hotel upstairs. That hotel, the Trev-Mor, was where the Hemingways first stayed in Key West.

In July, the **Hemingway Days Festival** takes place, with book signings, readings, fishing tournaments, and most hilariously, a Hemingway look-alike contest held at one of Papa's favorite watering holes, Sloppy Joe's.

by noted local artist Gene Otto. This is one creepy doll, whether or not the stories of it being possessed are true.

Key West Tropical Forest and Botanical Garden

There's a reason why "tropical" is part of the name of **Key West Tropical Forest and Botanical Garden** (5210 College Rd., 305/296-1504, www.keywestbotanicalgarden.org, 10am-4pm daily, $7 adults, $5 seniors, children under 12 free). This garden is proudly the only "frost-free" botanical garden in the continental United States. This means that most of the flora here is more clearly Caribbean in roots than what you might see at a garden even in Miami. The 11-acre facility is also proud of its several "champion trees," such as a Wild Dilly, a Locust-Berry, and a Black Olive. These trees are designated by both the National Register of Big Trees and the Florida Forestry Division as the largest living specimens of their particular trees. The largely undeveloped grounds are verdant and

peaceful. You're also likely to see lots of butterflies and birds.

SPORTS AND RECREATION
Water Sports

You shouldn't have much trouble finding a company ready to put you out on a boat with all the water gear you'll need. Up and down Duval Street, in front of restaurants, on street corners, and of course down near the port area, there are kiosks and sales booths touting the services of **Fury Water Adventures** (2 Duval St., 305/296-6293, www.furycat. com, snorkeling cruises from $40 pp, parasailing from $40 pp, sunset sailing from $37) and **Sebago Watersports** (205 Elizabeth St., 305/292-4768, http://keywestsebago.com, parasailing from $55 pp, snorkeling cruises from $49 pp, sailing from $39, Jet Ski tours from $150). Both companies offer an array of parasailing and snorkeling excursions, powerboat trips, Jet Ski tours, catamaran trips, and scenic cruises. The differences between their offerings are minimal, so just grab a few brochures and figure out which trip seems the most appealing to you and your group. **Sunset Watersports** (201 William St., 305/296-2554, www.sunsetwatersports-keywest.com, water sports activity cruise from $119 pp) offers similar activities but bundles it all in a "party boat" atmosphere. Your ticket price includes a day of Jet Skiing, sailing, windsurfing, waterskiing, kayaking, and more.

Like Fury, Sebago, and Sunset, it's hard to miss the advertising blitz employed by **Danger Charters** (407 Caroline St., 305/296-3652, http://dangercharters.com, snorkeling cruises from $75, sunset cruises from $75, kayak tours from $90). The sunset "wind and wine" sailing cruises, snorkeling excursions, and guided kayak trips offered are some of the best in town.

Also noteworthy are the passenger cruises available on *The Western Union* (202 William St., 305/292-1766, http://schooner-westernunion.org, sailing cruises from $65 pp, reservations required). The historic vessel was originally used to lay telegraph cable among Key West, Cuba, and the rest of the Caribbean and is a justifiable local landmark. In addition to the sunset cruises, *The Western Union* also offers day sailing and a thoroughly unique "stargazer" cruise that takes advantage of the area's relative lack of light pollution.

Kitehouse (1801 N. Roosevelt Blvd., 305/294-8679, www.thekitehouse.com, lessons from $200 for 4 hours) specializes in kiteboarding or kitesurfing lessons and excursions out to nearby flats where the winds are high and the shallow water is perfect for the sport. Although there are other kiteboarding outfitters in town, Kitehouse strongly advocates extensive training for beginners and has designed two-day and five-day courses with the right combination of instruction and activities to get novices comfortable with the sport.

Lazy Dog Charters (5114 Overseas Hwy., 305/293-9550, http://lazydog.com, kayak rentals from $20/half day, fishing charters from

$400/half day) and **Blue Planet Kayak Eco-Tours** (2933 Seidenberg Ave., 305/294-8087, http://blue-planet-kayak.com, kayak rentals from $30/half day, kayak tours from $50 pp/2.5-hour tour) also offer canoe and kayak rentals, guided nature tours, and flat-water fishing excursions.

Fishing

Finding a charter fishing excursion in Key West is about as difficult as finding a bar. There are dozens of single-boat operators like **Sea-Clusion** (5950 Peninsula Ave., 305/295-0774, www.seaclusion.com) and **Triple Time** (700 Front St., 305/296-8210, www.fishtripletime.com), which run large boats out into the deep water where snapper, cobia, barracuda, sailfish, and tuna reside. Larger charter companies like **Almost There** (5001 5th Ave., 305/295-9444, www.almostthere.net) offer a dozen boats that include flats boats, backcountry boats, and wreck-and-reef boats, providing a little more flexibility.

Diving

Though there aren't quite as many scuba and snorkeling charters as there are fishing charters, it's still pretty tough to swing a cat in Key West and not hit an air tank or a pair of fins. The biggest gear shop in town is **Divers Direct** (535 Green St., 305/293-5122, www.diversdirect.com). **Dive Key West** (3128 N. Roosevelt Blvd., 305/296-3823, www.divekeywest.com) also offers air, repairs, rentals, and gear, along with lessons and certification, custom charters, and dive trips (reefs, wrecks, night dives). **Reef Raiders** (617 Front St., 305/295-8748) is another good option, especially for visitors looking to get scuba-certified quickly. Its $175 resort course consists of two hours of pool instruction followed by two one-hour reef dives. It also offers custom charters, snorkeling excursions, deep-reef dives, wreck dives, and dolphin-spotting trips.

Golf

Unlike the rest of Florida, there's not much golfing going on in the Keys. The only course on Key West is the **Key West Golf Club** (6450 E. College Rd., 305/294-5232, http://keywestgolf.com, from $75). Here you can find an 18-hole Rees Jones-designed course that was renovated in 2007. The 6,500-yard par-70 course is beautifully landscaped with lots of tropical foliage.

Skydiving

Just outside of Key West proper on Sugarloaf Key is the tiny Sugarloaf Airport, which is home to **Skydive Key West** (mile marker 17, US-1, Sugarloaf Key, 305/745-4386, www.skydivekeywest.com, from $245 pp). Skydive Key West provides the wonderfully sadomasochistic service of taking you thousands of feet into the air into the beautiful skies of Key West, only to have you jump out of the plane. Hurtling toward the ground at 130 miles per hour is an incredible thrill no matter where you do it, but doing it over the scenic Lower Keys is a unique experience indeed. Skydivers are strapped, of course, to a trained instructor. All of the instructors are certified by the U.S. Parachute Association.

BEACHES

The beach at **Fort Zachary Taylor State Park** (300 Truman Ave., www.florida-stateparks.org, 8am-sunset daily, $3.50) is certainly the best in Key West, but none of the beaches on the island is particularly noteworthy. **Smathers Beach** (S. Roosevelt Blvd.) is by far the most popular beach in Key West, and it's also the most crowded. Smathers is small and unimpressive, but considering the dearth of options in Key West, it's a decent enough alternative for those looking for quick access to sand and sea.

Higgs Beach (Atlantic Blvd. at White St.) is also home to the **Key West AIDS Memorial.** Although the beach itself is nice and the picnic and park facilities are pleasant, there is a tendency for panhandlers to congregate.

ENTERTAINMENT AND EVENTS
Nightlife

Finding a place to have a drink in Key West is not a problem. Deciding which of the endless number of bars is right for you may be a bit harder. With the exception of a few places with very specific audiences, most every pub and club in Key West is personable and without pretense. Even when a cruise ship is docked and Duval Street seems flooded with tourists, it still seems as if most of the

Higgs Beach

barstools are taken up with yarn-spinning locals. Bars in Key West open very early and close very late.

There are a handful of adult-oriented businesses that have less-than-stellar reputations for a wide range of reasons. Do yourself a huge favor and avoid them; there are plenty of other opportunities for legal adult pleasures in Key West.

The clothing-optional **Garden of Eden** (224 Duval St., 305/296-4565, 10am-4am Mon.-Sat., noon-4am Sun.) is upstairs from the somewhat more traditional open-air environment of the **Bull & Whistle** (224 Duval St., 305/296-4545, www.bullkeywest.com, 10am-4am Mon.-Sat., noon-4am Sun.). The Garden of Eden's prohibitions against cameras and insistence on patrons' usage of towels on the deck chairs keeps the goings-on as decent as you could expect at a bar staffed by topless bartenders and populated with a mixture of the nude, the partially nude, and the blushingly curious. Frozen drinks seem to be the preferred libation.

The **801 Bourbon Bar & Cabaret** (801 Duval St., 305/296-1992, www.801bourbon. com, 10am-4am Mon.-Sat., noon-4am Sun.) is a multi-building entertainment complex for gay men. The Bourbon Street Pub is a massive bar that's all about drink specials, drag shows, and dancing. Upstairs is the all-male New Orleans Guest House. Across the street at the corner of Duval and Petronia Streets is the 801 Bourbon Bar, with its downstairs bar and upstairs cabaret shows, and a handcuffs-and-paddles leather bar known as the One Saloon.

Key West is legendarily gay friendly, and in addition to 801, nightclubs like **Aqua** (711 Duval St., 305/294-0555, www.aquakeywest.com), bars like **Bobby's Monkey Bar** (900 Simonton St., 305/294-2655), and even hotel complexes like **La Te Da** (1125 Duval St., 305/296-6706, www.lateda.com) strive to provide comfortable, fun, and safe environments. Gay men and women are unlikely to find much static in any of the bars and clubs along Duval Street, whether or not they're focused on a specifically gay clientele.

There are a few bars in Key West that are tourist magnets. **Hog's Breath Saloon** (400 Front St., 305/296-4222, www.hogsbreath. com, 10am-4am Mon.-Sat., 10am-midnight Sun.) and **Sloppy Joe's** (201 Duval St., 305/294-5717, https://sloppyjoes.com, 9am-4am Mon.-Sat., 9am-midnight Sun.) are on almost every day-tripper's drinking itinerary and are best avoided when a cruise ship is in port. At night, it's less crowded. Sloppy Joe's is the better of the two, not because of its 80-year history and Hemingway affiliations but because of its quiet and largely vacant backroom bar, where you can enjoy a midday beer or cocktail without lining up behind scores of tourists. **Captain Tony's** (428 Greene St., 305/294-1838, www.capttonyssaloon.com, 9am-4am Mon.-Sat., 9am-midnight Sun.) is actually at the original location of Sloppy Joe's and is a bar with its own unique half-century-long history. As you'll see from the number of barstools painted with the names of its many famous patrons, ranging from Hemingway (of course) and writer Truman Capote to Presidents Truman and JFK, it's long been a mandatory stop on serious drinkers' tours of Key West. Amazingly, it's actually a pretty decent bar still, popular with locals and those who want to gawk at the dense thicket of ladies underwear hung from the ceiling. Some of Jimmy Buffett's earliest gigs were here in the early 1970s. But, if you want to see him perform "Margaritaville," you're going to have to head over to **Margaritaville** (500 Duval St., 305/292-1435, www.margaritavillekeywest.com, 11am-midnight daily), which oddly (and somewhat awesomely) is the smallest and friendliest outpost in Buffett's chain of souvenir burger joints.

If you're looking for a less-touristy chapter in Buffett's Key West history, head for the **Chart Room** (inside the Pier House Resort & Caribbean Spa; 1 Duval St., 305/363-7478, 4:30pm-2am daily), which was the first bar the singer stopped in upon arriving on the island in 1971. Not only did Buffett have his first Key West drink here, it was also the first place he performed, becoming a regular fixture on the bar's tiny stage. Although the simple motel that once housed the Chart Room has metastasized into a much larger (and much more family friendly) resort, the bar retains the classic, quirky, dive-bar vibe that made it a haven for smugglers, treasure hunters, and other colorful locals. Drinks aren't cheap, but there are free peanuts, popcorn, and hot dogs, and the bartenders are more than willing to share endless stories.

The open-air bar at **Willie T's** (525 Duval St., 305/294-7674, www.williets.com, 10am-4am Mon.-Sat., noon-4am Sun.) is a far better option for visitors strolling the tourist strip who want a beer and to be able to watch the parade of humanity traipse by on Duval Street. The atmosphere here is personable and a little ramshackle. The bar serves great mojitos and even has a decent food menu. Alternately, head for the **Smallest Bar In Key West** (124 Duval St., 305/509-2904, 10am-4am Mon.-Sat., noon-4am Sun.), which is frequently packed and loud, though that isn't difficult to achieve, considering the place is about 6 feet wide by about 15 feet deep.

Locals tend to gravitate toward places like the **Green Parrot Bar** (601 Whitehead St., 305/294-6133, www.greenparrot.com, 10am-4am Mon.-Sat., noon-4am Sun.) that are

friendly, unpretentious, and somewhat off the beaten tourist track. Open since 1890, the bar is simple and fun with a great blues-filled jukebox and occasional live music.

Intimate craft-beer spots like **The Porch** (429 Caroline St., 305/517-6358, www.theporchkw.com, 11am-4am daily) tend to be primarily frequented by locals. Beer lovers should absolutely check out one (or both) of these places while in town. The Porch is in a (supposedly) haunted building, and its vibe is what I like to call "mansion-casual." The bar itself is located in a downstairs room of an incredibly large Key West residence, with a small, adjacent seating area. Although the staff is incredibly friendly and knowledgeable, you'll want to grab your Dale's or your Dogfish Head and immediately retire to the spacious front porch.

Somewhat more upscale is the **Grand Vin Wine Bar & Store** (1107 Duval St., 305/296-1020), a cozy, comfortable wine bar with a small but decent selection of bottles available for sale. Tastings are offered, and you can have your bottle opened for a relaxing drink on the gorgeous front porch.

The Arts

The best place to start exploring art in Key

Margaritaville's original location on Duval Street

West is right in the heart of the Mallory Square tourist district. The **Key West Art Center** (301 Front St., 305/294-1241, www.keywestartcenter.com, 10am-5pm daily, free) is the oldest gallery in Key West, and definitely has a homespun, art-in-a-tourist-town vibe. The folks who work at this nonprofit know the local arts scene and can help direct you to galleries that fit your taste. The Center also puts on the annual Key West Craft Show and the Old Island Days Art Festival.

Along Duval Street is where the bulk of the galleries is. **Key West Gallery** (601 Duval St., 305/292-9339, 10am-10pm Mon.-Fri., 10am-11pm Sat.-Sun.) and **Peter Lik Fine Art Photography** (519 Duval St., 305/292-2550, www.lik.com, 10am-10pm daily) are some of the best, dealing primarily in top-shelf art. The atmosphere at both is distinctly unstuffy and welcoming even with the high price tags and high quality of art. **Lucky Street Gallery** (540 Greene St., 305/294-3973, www.luckystreetgallery.com, 11am-6pm) is a bit more formal in its gallery approach, but still a fun spot to visit.

For more information and deeper insight into the Key West cultural scene, stop into **The Studios of Key West** (600 White St., 305/296-0548, http://tskw.org), which in addition to hosting regular workshops and exhibits also puts on musical events and other affairs on a regular basis.

Festivals and Events

The **Key West Songwriters Festival** (www.keywestsongwritersfestival.com, late Apr./early May) has been bringing acoustic-playing stool-sitters to venues throughout Key West, with the center of activity at the Hog's Breath Saloon. Sponsored by song-publishing company BMI, the festival features performances by the unsung heroes behind some of the charts' biggest hits as well as performers who made their own songs famous. There's a good-natured casual feel to the festival, befitting its locale, and the performances are as much storytelling sessions as they are concerts.

The **Cuban American Heritage Festival** (citywide, 305/295-9665, www.cubanfest.com, late May) is rather minimal, considering Key West's proximity to Cuba. The festival's dinners, dance parties, and other events are quite family focused.

Originally envisioned as a way to get tourists into town during the typically slow autumn season, **Fantasy Fest** (citywide, 305/296-1817, www.fantasyfest.com, late Oct.) has evolved into a defining event for Key West. Part Halloween festival, part debauched parade, part drinking marathon, this 10-day festival is decidedly adults-only. Wet T-shirt contests, lingerie parties, porn-star sightings, body-painting, costume contests, and more ratchet up the already decadent vibe of Key West into something stratospherically raunchy. Oddly, the event that kicks off the whole thing is the **Bahama Village Goombay Festival** (http://bahamavillagegoombay.com, late Oct.), which takes place in the cozy residential neighborhood of Bahama Village off Petronia Street. The Goombay Festival is incredibly fun, if somewhat low-key, focusing on Afro-Caribbean arts and crafts, food, and live music.

SHOPPING

South Pointe Gallery (1201 Duval St., 305/295-9354, www.authenticvintageposters.com, 11am-8pm daily) is a unique art store focusing on vintage posters from Hollywood's golden era, Jazz Age France, and the glamorous years of air travel.

Besame Mucho (315 Petronia St., 305/294-1928, www.besamemucho.net, 10am-6pm Mon.-Sat., 10am-4pm Sun.) sells an array of boutique soaps, lotions, and other personal-care products along with jewelry, classic Latin crafts, and unique domestic products. All of it is housed in a gorgeous tin-roofed bungalow that's almost as charming as its contents.

For a more literary experience, head for **Key West Island Books** (513 Fleming St., 305/294-2904, http://keywestislandbooks.com, 10am-9pm Mon.-Sat., 10am-6pm Sun.), a small but incredibly well-curated bookstore with a bountiful selection of new and used tomes. In keeping with its surroundings, the store has plenty of Florida-centric titles, and a substantial section of LGBT books. There are also lots of inexpensive newer titles. It's a decidedly (and determinedly) eccentric store, so you may not find exactly what you're looking for, but you'll definitely find something you didn't yet know you needed to read.

Also of note for book fans: legendary author Judy Blume (a part-time Key West resident) opened **Books & Books at the Studios of Key West** (533 Eaton St., 305/320-0208, 10am-6pm daily) in partnership with her husband and Miami Book Fair International cofounder Mitchell Kaplan. The store is a nonprofit enterprise, and offers a small—but wide and well-curated—selection of books in many different genres; the Floridiana and Key West selections are great, as is (unsurprisingly) the range of smartly written kids' books on offer.

FOOD
Breakfast and Brunch

Tucked into a verdant, shaded courtyard just off busy Duval Street, **Cuban Coffee Queen, Downtown** (5 Key Lime Sq., 305/294-7787, 7am-7pm daily, from $4) is exactly the sort of oasis you may need to shake the fog off from the night before and get your day started right. Pair your iced coffee (with ice cubes made from frozen espresso) with a "Cuban bagel" (Cuban bread pressed with cream cheese and topped with honey and sesame seeds). Note that this is one of two locations; the other location, at 284 Margaret Street, is the original, and lines there are often quite long (and unshaded).

Iguana Cafe (425 Greene St., 305/296-6420, 24 hours daily, from $4) overlooks Duval Street and serves everything from fried gator to conch burgers. The garden out back is a pleasant and quiet place to enjoy the traditional American breakfasts while sipping on a sweet and strong Cuban coffee. If you need some hair-of-the-dog to shake off last night's revelry, the Iguana also has a full bar.

The tiny **La Crêperie Café** (300 Petronia St., 305/517-6799, http://lacreperiekeywest.

com, 9am-10pm Thurs.-Tues., 9am-6pm Wed., from $5) is located in the Bahama Village neighborhood. The café's selection of freshly made crepes, both sweet and savory, along with one of their excellent espressos, will make it hard to forget. Grab one of their sidewalk tables and watch the tourists stroll by.

Need a pick-me-up and a chance to catch up with the office? **Sippin' Coffee House** (414 Eaton St., 305/293-0555, http://sippinkeywest.com, 7am-11pm daily, from $5) offers a pretty standard selection of espresso-based drinks, a menu of breakfast sandwiches and fresh-baked pastries, and wireless access to a T1 Internet line, a copy machine, and even photo-printing services.

Sunday brunch at **La Te Da** (1125 Duval St., 305/296-6706, www.lateda.com, 8:30am-3pm and 6pm-11pm daily, from $8, buffet brunch $30) is a pretty decadent affair as diners feast from a large buffet of omelets, seafood, steak, fruit, cheese, pastries, and more. The brunch is well worth the high price. The restaurant also offers a daily breakfast menu with all the expected standards at considerably lower prices. The restaurant, like its hotel, is a bit more elegant than many Key West establishments, and it is gay friendly. Unlike the hotel, however, the restaurant doesn't enforce an adults-only rule.

Lunch and Light Bites

Crowds pour into **Croissants de France** (816 Duval St., 305/294-2624, www.croissantsdefrance.com, 8am-4pm Wed., 8am-10pm Thurs.-Tues., from $7) for breakfast and brunch every day, feasting on the selection of crepes, pastries, brioche, and eggs Benedict dishes. Lunch here is truly exceptional. Skip the paninis, sandwiches, and even the quiches and head straight for the menu of galettes. Croissants de France stuffs these soft flatbreads with smoked salmon, roasted chicken, andouille sausage, or shrimp and brie, making it a richly flavored lunch treat.

You may not guess it from the name, but **Panini Panini** (1075 Duval St., 305/296-2002, www.paninikw.com, 10am-8pm Wed., 11am-9pm Thurs.-Tues., from $6) specializes in paninis. Located a few blocks from the Southernmost Point, this is a great spot to grab an excellent grill-pressed sandwich after posing in front of the buoy.

American

From a basic *pasta basilico* (linguine with basil, tomatoes, garlic, and olive oil) and filet mignon to fish dishes and grilled bison strip steaks, **Rooftop Cafe** (308 Front St., 305/294-2042, www.rooftopcafekeywest.com, 9:30am-10pm daily, from $18) has plenty on its menu to be proud of. The rooftop deck, thick with foliage and boasting great views of the city, draws the crowds in. Even the indoor seating area, with its wraparound windows and island-style ceiling fans, feels like an outdoor dining room.

The building in which **Bagatelle** (115 Duval St., 305/296-6609, www.bagatellekeywest.com, 11:30am-11:30pm daily, from $14) is housed dates back to the 1880s. The menu, with its combination of fresh seafood, tropical produce, French panache, and Southern flair, manages to trace the outlines of Key West's culinary traditions. There may be no other place in town that serves up a portobello and avocado egg roll like Bagatelle's. Even the simple modifications of classic dishes—sweet curry chicken, honey-fried lobster tail—are refreshingly decadent and thoroughly interesting.

The first tickets sold for Pan-American Airways were sold out of the Key West building that currently houses **Kelly's Caribbean Bar Grill & Brewery** (301 Whitehead St., 305/293-7897, www.kellyskeywest.com, noon-9:30pm Sun.-Thurs., noon-10pm Fri.-Sat., from $14). This fact is hard to escape from the minute you step onto the porch. You can almost imagine one of those 1920s seaplane pilots feasting on a bowl of conch chowder or one of Kelly's eight-ounce pork chops with andouille and cornbread stuffing. Fresh fish is prepared here in several different ways. One of

the best options is to get a filet encrusted with macadamias and banana rum butter.

Steak and Seafood

Alonzo's Oyster Bar (700 Front St., 305/294-5880, http://alonzosoysterbar.com, 11am-11pm daily, from $10) is a good choice for those looking for raw-bar selections and a respite from the constant buzz of Duval Street. Located on the waterfront at Key West Bight and downstairs from the much fancier A&B Lobster House, the evening happy-hour specials and fresh bivalves draw a considerable crowd here. Beyond oysters, Alonzo's offers soups, sandwiches (including a great lobster sandwich), and a standard array of fried pub grub.

Nine One Five (915 Duval St., 305/296-0669, www.915duval.com, 6pm-11pm daily, from $16) is a hip, contemporary tapas restaurant with a range of plates that includes Thai beef salad rolls, steak *frites,* grilled short ribs, seared whole snapper, and filet mignon carpaccio. The menu's blend of meat, fish, and even vegetarian small plates has a little something for everyone. The stylish atmosphere comes with an appropriately high price tag. Upstairs is Point5, a wine lounge with more than 20 wines available by the glass.

Located a few blocks from the most touristy parts of Old Town Key West, **Seven Fish** (921 Truman Ave, 305/296-2777, 6pm-10pm Wed.-Mon., from $18) is well worth the walk into this largely residential area. The striking, modern exterior of the restaurant is somewhat at odds with the menu's emphasis on simple, fresh seafood preparations (it offers three different fresh-fish dishes daily), pasta classics, and homestyle favorites like meat loaf and mashed potatoes. But while the menu may be straightforward, the kitchen puts extraordinary care into the dishes, focusing on quality, rather than flash.

Hogfish Bar & Grill (6810 Front St., 305/293-4041, 11am-midnight Mon.-Sat., 9am-midnight Sun., from $13) is something of a legend among locals. Tucked away among the scruffy residences and busy commercial marinas of Stock Island, the restaurant feels like a lost treasure of Key West's past. And although its vintage is fairly recent, Hogfish does an admirable job of maintaining a legit Old Florida vibe, from the chickee-hut exterior to the laissez-faire friendliness of the staff. Seafood here—especially the titular fish—is off-the-boat fresh and well-prepared; prices are surprisingly reasonable. Parking can be a challenge.

Italian

Located right on Higgs Beach, **Salute!** (1000 Atlantic Blvd., 305/292-1117, http://saluteonthebeach.com, 11am-10pm Mon.-Sat., 5pm-10pm Sun., from $14) has both indoor and outdoor seating available. On the menu are homemade pasta dishes, paninis, salads, and traditional Italian fare. The real attraction here is the exceptional view and relaxed atmosphere.

The ground-floor bistro **Mangia Mangia** (900 Southard St., 305/294-2469, www.mangia-mangia.com, 5:30pm-10pm daily, from $15) is located in a pleasant residential neighborhood. Locals come to enjoy freshly made pasta worked into dishes like New Zealand mussels with spaghettini or a picadillo pasta that features black-bean pasta shells in a Cuban-spiced red sauce.

French

Banana Cafe (1215 Duval St., 305/294-7227, www.bananacafekw.com, 8am-3pm and 6pm-10pm daily, from $19) delivers exceptional omelets and pastry in the morning and fresh salads and sandwiches for lunch. In the morning, plan on trying one of Banana Cafe's simple, sweet-and-fruit-filled crepes or a more complex savory crepe like "La Ber," which features sautéed scallops in a lime-juice-and-cream sauce. Any of the crepes on offer are worth the carb-and-calorie guilt trip you'll give yourself afterward. At dinner, the menu scales up considerably, with steaks and chops and a small selection of extra-special crepes.

Even though the dishes are a bit fancier after sunset, the vibe here is still quite casual and friendly. Reservations are definitely recommended for dinner.

Vegetarian and Vegan

Although certainly not strictly vegetarian, ★ **Blue Heaven** (729 Thomas St., 305/296-8666, www.blueheavenkw.com, 8am-10:30pm daily, from $8) offers a selection of tofu- and vegetable-based dishes alongside its fresh seafood and meats. Vegetarians will want to start with a carrot and curry soup and work their way through Blue Heaven's tofu stir-fry or a heaping plate filled with brown rice, grilled plantains, and black beans. Meat lovers will rejoice in the excellent jerk chicken, the legendary seared grouper, or any of the restaurant's daily seafood specials. The whimsical tropical surroundings—painted picnic tables, an upstairs "tree house" dining room—are quintessentially Key West.

There's a community-centric vibe at ★ **The Cafe: A Mostly Vegetarian Place** (509 Southard St., 305/296-5515, http://thecafekw.com, 11am-10pm Mon.-Sat., from $8). The cozy modern diner has seating at the bar area and at a few tables, and the low lights, hip music, and friendly staff make it incredibly comfortable. Although there are a few tofu dishes on the menu (like a fantastic barbecue tofu served home style with sautéed spinach and roasted potatoes), most of the plates here are vegetable- and grain-based. Asian stir-fries can be made with tofu, seitan, or tuna, but are best with just the brown rice and mixed vegetables that constitute the base. The Cafe's goat-cheese-topped polenta cakes are drenched in a chilled tomato sauce that makes for a great flavor-texture contrast.

Dessert

The homemade gelatos, sorbets, and frozen yogurts at **Flamingo Crossing** (1105 Duval St., 305/296-6124, 11am-11pm Mon.-Thurs., 11am-midnight Fri.-Sat., noon-11pm Sun.) are a Key West institution, and for good reason.

Key Lime Pie

In 1965, Key West's member of the Florida House of Representatives, Bernie Papy Jr., wrote a bill that would have fined anyone producing "key lime pie" with limes that weren't actually key limes. Papy's point was not lost on dessert aficionados. The tiny and super-tart yellow limes that are indigenous to the Florida Keys are quite different from the more common green Persian limes. A true **key lime pie** is one that utilizes that tang as a counterpoint to the pillows of light sugary meringue that top them. An even more legitimate key lime pie is one that conforms to the traditional recipe brought over to the Keys by Bahamian immigrants. Originally, a key lime pie was not baked. The chemical reaction between the acidic limes and the milk (always condensed milk and never the reduced-fat variety) "cooks" the pie in the same way that the lime juice in a ceviche "cooks" the fish. These unbaked pies are somewhat hard to come by, but there are some traditional Bahamian-style dessert shops that still make them this way.

Although Papy didn't get his bill passed, he would have doubtlessly been smiling in 2006 when the legislature passed a resolution deeming key lime pie the official dessert of Florida.

The Flamingo's kaleidoscope of flavors—from Cuban coffee and raspberry cappuccino to tropical tastes like mango and soursop—are devastatingly refreshing.

You shouldn't need to be told more than once to check out a place called **Better Than Sex** (926 Simonton St., 305/296-8102, www.betterthansexkeywest.com, 6pm-midnight daily, $8-13) for dessert. The emphasis here is on decadence, from the bordello-style decor to the dizzyingly decadent desserts on offer, which may make Better Than Sex a onetime outing for most couples (and a singular let's-sneak-away-from-the-kids experience for parents). It's definitely an outing you should have with your significant other. The dining room goes beyond "dimly lit" and firmly into "oh, my god, it's pretty dark in here," focusing your senses on the intensely sweet flavors before you. Desserts include the legendary chocolate grilled cheese (brie and dark chocolate on thick, buttered cinnamon toast) and a super-fluffy slice of key lime chiffon pie that would horrify purists (which is probably the point!). The restaurant has proven to be so popular in Key West that it's expanded to other cities in Florida.

ACCOMMODATIONS

There are scores of beautiful unique hotels in Key West, along with dozens of authentic and homey guesthouses that are available on a nightly basis. Visitors interested in extended stays should definitely look into renting a house. There are many rental homes available in the heart of Old Town that are charming and historic. Contact **Vacation Homes of Key West** (305/294-7358 or 888/404-2802, www.vacationhomesofkeywest.com) for a rundown of their available properties.

During the summer and fall off-season, rates for lodging can plunge to nearly half the high-season rates. Although a sizable chunk of the off-season also happens to be hurricane season, a late autumn visit to Key West can be a bargain and can also be beautifully uncrowded.

$150-250

A great place for one-stop shopping for some of Key West's most unique and affordable accommodations is **Key West Historic Inns** (305/294-5229, www.keywesthistoricinns.com). The company operates six historic bed-and-breakfasts on the island, all of which are located in charming, mostly residential neighborhoods. Each property has its own individual personality and offers surprisingly decent rates. Among the properties is the large, 33-room **Chelsea House Pool & Gardens** (709 Truman Ave., from $249 d); the spacious, quiet, and romantic **Key Lime**

Inn (725 Truman Ave., from $229 d), with 37 guest rooms; the aptly named but quite nice **Budget Key West** (1031 Eaton St., from $199 d), with 17 rooms; and the rustic, minimalist **Merlin Guesthouse** (811 Simonton St., from $240 d), which has 20 guest rooms. All of the properties are rented hotel-style via a central reservations system, but each accommodation is unique.

Olivia by Duval (511 Olivia St., 305/296-5169, from $199 d) is a pleasant, adults-only guesthouse in a central location. It has a clothing-optional pool and courtyard. The guest rooms are mainly efficiency suites, but they also have a two-bedroom and a one-bedroom unit. All guest rooms have ceiling fans, air-conditioning, TVs, and private baths.

Historic accommodations are abundant on Key West, and the history of the **Speakeasy Inn** (1117 Duval St., 305/296-2680, www.speakeasyinn.com, from $199 d) is evident both in its classic architecture and the downstairs rum bar. The inn was the 19th-century home of Raul Vasquez, a noted rum-runner. The one-, two-, and three-bedroom units are open and spacious, with hardwood floors and ceiling fans. Nearby is the **Avalon Bed & Breakfast** (1317 Duval St., 305/294-8233, www.avalonbnb.com, from $189 d). All of the rooms here are bright and airy, with "classic Florida" furnishings (including beds with flowing mosquito netting). The downstairs king-bed rooms and the exclusive King Cottage are the best bets, as they provide the most luxury and privacy.

Southernmost on the Beach (508 South St., 305/296-6577, http://southernmostresorts.com, from $249 d) adds a much-needed dose of contemporary luxury to the less-crowded southern end of the island. The nicest and newest guest rooms can run as much as $600 during high season, but bargains can be found during low season.

Duval Gardens (1012 Duval St., 305/292-3379, www.duvalgardens.com from $229 d) is a pet-friendly B&B with regular hotel accommodations (king, queen, and double queen) as well as one kitchenette-equipped guest room with a mini fridge, a stove-oven combo, a coffeemaker, and a microwave. Tiled bathrooms and four-poster canopy beds accent the beautiful tropical setting.

New Orleans House (724 Duval St., 305/293-9800, www.neworleanshousekw.com, from $229 d) is geared towards gay men. The atmosphere is all about the party. Although there are two buildings separate from the main facility, the booming nightclub activity at the downstairs Bourbon Street Pub goes until 4am, and the activity keeps the whole place hopping. The pool area is clothing optional. The guest rooms are basic and a bit worn, but sleeping seems to be the last thing on most guests' minds.

For the money, the excellent accommodations at the **Truman Hotel** (611 Truman Ave, 305/296-6700, www.trumanhotel.com, from $199 d) are an incredible bargain. While it's only a block away from all the action on Duval Street, the atmosphere here is surprisingly quiet and relaxing. There's a pleasant outdoor pool area, and all rooms are kitted out with modern, comfortable furnishings and conveniences. Although it's most definitely a hotel, the friendly and welcoming staff, the stylish decor of the rooms, and the complimentary continental breakfast make the Truman feel more like an upscale boutique B&B.

$250-350

The Inn At Key West (3420 N. Roosevelt Blvd, 305/294-5541, www.theinnatkeywest.com, from $259 d) is located in the downtown, "new" part of Key West, near the strip malls and more recent residential development. The waterfront views and tropical decor make it a decent option for those looking for a spot away from the hustle and bustle of Old Key West and closer to activities at Smathers Beach.

The Caribbean colonial-style ★ **Conch House** (625 Truman Ave., 305/293-0020, www.conchhouse.com, from $269 d) is a complex composed of four separate buildings. The nicest guest rooms are located in the two-story main building and the shotgun-style Delaney House. The tiny Casa Cabana room is the most private. All the accommodations are classic Key West. The wraparound porches and green shutters of the main house evoke Conch House's century-plus past. The owners have managed to combine historic charm with modern convenience and value.

Azul (907 Truman Ave., 305/296-5152, www.azulkeywest.com, from $279 d) offers adults-only accommodation and the atmosphere is decidedly upscale. The historic Queen Anne house is located on traffic-heavy Truman Avenue, a few blocks away from the activity along Duval Street. Nonetheless, the vibe is quiet and the views from the wraparound porches are gorgeous, especially those that look out over the pool area. Inside there are only nine guest rooms and two suites, all with flat-screen TVs, Wi-Fi, marble-floored bathrooms, and fashionable, contemporary furnishings.

Although the rooms at the **Almond Tree Inn** (512 Truman Ave., 305/296-5415, www.almondtreeinn.com, from $329 d) are incredibly well-appointed and quite stylish, it is a motel, albeit a beautifully renovated and modern one. The staff here is quite friendly and accommodating; the rooms are remarkably quiet, incredibly comfortable, and very luxurious; and the outdoor whirlpool tub/pool

area is as welcoming as it is relaxing. While you surely won't be disappointed by your stay here, there are other places in Key West that offer many more singular experiences for nearly the same cost, or less.

Over $350

Unlike most of the historic properties on Key West, the ★ **Orchid Key Inn** (1004 Duval St., 305/296-9915, www.orchidkey.com, from $399 d) doesn't evoke 18th-century opulence. The hotel is a modern, stylish version of a 1950s motel. From the neon sign to the crisp white paint and open layout, it looks as if it were transported from a Miami Beach fever dream. The four-star facility only has 24 guest rooms and suites, all of which have free Wi-Fi, plasma-screen TVs, plush beds, surround-sound audio, and other luxury touches. The boutique property is lushly decorated with tropical plants and water features throughout. The hip Orchid Bar is popular among guests and non-guests alike.

The Marker Waterfront Resort (200 William St., 305/501-5193, www.themarker-keywest.com, from $379 d) is a fairly recent luxury addition to the Key West lodging scene, splitting the difference between the larger-scale resorts and more intimate,

Azul is one of many lodging options that takes advantage of Key West's historic houses.

historic hotels. The compact property boasts a prime location, overlooking the waters of Key West Bight, in the heart of all the action around the Mallory Square area. With 96 bright and spacious rooms that are clean and modern in their design (and surprisingly quiet, given the location), the resort also has three swimming pools (one of which is adults-only), a cozy restaurant/lounge, and a small fitness center. Note that there is a resort fee ($37 per day at press time) and valet parking is also pricey ($30 per day plus tips)

INFORMATION AND SERVICES

The **Monroe County Tourist Development Council** (305/296-1552, www.fla-keys.com) is a valuable phone and Internet resource staffed with knowledgeable folks who can help with everything from advice to last-minute reservations.

TRANSPORTATION
Getting There

Key West is a three-hour drive from Miami along US-1 (a.k.a. the Overseas Highway).

Key West International Airport (EYW, 3491 S. Roosevelt Blvd., Key West, 305/296-5439, www.keywestinternationalairport.com) offers service via American, Delta, Southwest, and United.

Another option is to take the **Key West Express** (888/539-2628, www.seakeywest-express.com), a high-speed ferry with daily departures from Fort Myers on Florida's southwest coast. The ferry ride is about 3.5 hours (compared to the 5-hour drive), with round-trip fares costing $139 for adults and $75 for children.

Getting Around

Parking is a consistent hassle in Key West. Thankfully, most sights, restaurants, and clubs are centrally located on and around Duval Street, and the best way to get around is either on foot or on a two-wheeled vehicle. Bicycles, scooters, and jitneys are available from a number of different sources. Try

A and M Rentals (523 Truman Ave., 305/896-1921, www.amscooterskeywest.com) or **Blue Sky Rentals** (805 Duval St., 305/294-3900, www.keywestblueskyrentals.com) for the best selection and to make reservations.

★ DRY TORTUGAS NATIONAL PARK

One of the most unique destinations in the entire National Parks system, **Dry Tortugas National Park** (305/242-7700, www.nps.gov/drto, sunrise-sunset daily, Bush Key closed Feb.-Sept., seven-day pass $10 adults, under 17 admitted free) is a group of seven tiny isolated islands located about 70 miles west of Key West. Named the "Dry" Tortugas due to the absence of fresh water on the scrub-lined islands, these islands were used for most of the late 19th and early 20th centuries as the southern edge of the United States' naval defense strategy. Accordingly, the heart of the park, and the sole indicator of human habitation, is Fort Jefferson, one of the largest and most remote coastal forts in the country.

Taking over the entirety of Garden Key, Fort Jefferson was constructed in the mid-1800s as an adjunct to a lighthouse built two decades earlier as a means to ward off pirates. The addition of the fort was intended to bolster the navy's presence on the island. Eventually the difficulties with getting supplies (and fresh water) to the island proved too much for an ongoing mission here. By the 1930s, the fort was decommissioned and turned into a national monument. The fort is the largest masonry structure in the Western Hemisphere, with over 16 million bricks used in its construction. Ironically, despite all that, the fort remains technically unfinished (several ancillary areas of the fort were never completed).

The fort is the only artificially constructed sight in the Tortugas. If you've undertaken the voyage here, you'll probably want to see and do more than an afternoon traipsing around the old fort and lighthouse, regardless of how impressive they are. The majority of visitors to the Tortugas use their time here to explore the abundant marine life. Expansive coral reefs are home to blindingly colorful tropical fish and the predators who feed on them, as well as lobsters, anemones, sea turtles, and more. The park contains a recently established 46-square-mile Research Natural Area, basically a well-protected no-anchor zone, that provides endless opportunities for exploration in the clear blue waters and helps maintain this fragile ecosystem. There are also ample fishing and boating opportunities in and around the Tortugas, and camping is available at an 11-site campground located near Fort Jefferson. (Camping at Fort Jefferson is primitive. You need to bring all of your supplies, including water. The only forms of fuel allowed are self-starting charcoal and sterno cans. All 11 sites have a picnic table and grill. The fee is $15 per campsite, per night.) The National Park Service limits the number of outfitters who can provide services (dive charters, fishing trips, ecotours,

and so on) within the park. Check the park's website for an up-to-date list.

There are two ways to get to the park. The most commonly used way is by ferry boat. The only officially authorized ferry operator is **Yankee Freedom** (305/294-7009, www. yankeefreedom.com, full-day excursion $175 adults, $165 students/military/seniors, $125 children, children under 4 free), a 100-foot catamaran that operates out of Key West's ferry terminal (100 Grinnell St.). Yankee Freedom is a much more affordable option than the one offered by **Key West Seaplane Charters** (305/293-9300, www.keywestseaplanecharters.com, half-day excursion $329 adults, $263 children, children under 2 free, full-day excursion $578 adults, $462 children, children under 2 free). However, it should be noted that the ferry boat takes two-plus hours to arrive at Fort Jefferson, while the seaplane gets you there in 40 minutes. It's highly advised to purchase your tickets in advance for either the ferry or the seaplane, as the excursions can sell out.

Atlantic Coast

Look for ★ to find recommended
sights, activities, dining, and lodging.

Highlights

★ **Fort Lauderdale Beachfront:** These gorgeous and expansive beaches make up some of the largest and most beautiful municipal oceanfront in the state, with broad swaths of white sand merging into crystalline blue-green waters (page 162).

★ **Las Olas Boulevard:** This strip of boutiques, galleries, and restaurants is classy and charming, evoking Fort Lauderdale's history (page 165).

★ **Worth Avenue:** The "Rodeo Drive of Florida" is home to stores like Cartier, Hermès, Ferragamo, and Louis Vuitton, along with pricey art galleries, custom boutiques, and ritzy restaurants (page 176).

★ **Morikami Museum and Japanese Gardens:** It's one of the most peaceful destinations in South Florida, with a meditative museum and equally relaxing and well-curated gardens (page 184).

★ **Kennedy Space Center Visitor Complex:** This facility's location within sight of the NASA's launch pads makes it the closest most of us will ever get to extraterrestrial action (page 196).

★ **Canaveral National Seashore:** Bought by NASA to provide a security buffer for Kennedy Space Center, Canaveral has some of the state's most secluded and naturally beautiful coastline (page 200).

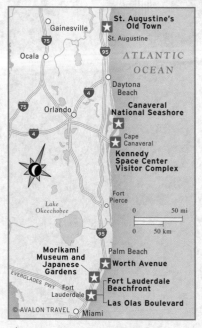

★ **St. Augustine's Old Town:** Enjoy the beauty of its 400-year-old buildings and narrow walkways (page 215).

On Florida's Atlantic Coast, cities like Fort Lauderdale, Palm Beach, and Vero Beach are charming and laid back, offering a bounty of beaches, cute boutiques, idyllic fishing spots, and plentiful sunshine.

Florida's Atlantic coast is deeply aware of its history, and more possessed of remnants of Old Florida than you are likely to find elsewhere. It's incredibly easy to step back in time in this part of the state.

Fort Lauderdale has a quiet charm that's as dependent on its high-end shopping, yacht-mooring, and art galleries as it is on its vibrant and diverse nightlife scene and mellow beaches. While it's definitely no longer the so-called spring break capital of the world, it's also far from the staid, sleepy town that some people perceive it to be.

A few dozen miles to its north is Palm Beach County, home to Palm Beach—one of the wealthiest towns in North America, and thick with top-dollar boîtes and boutiques—and the more proletarian West Palm Beach, which is a beneficiary of the largesse of the nearby millionaires but is far more accessible and friendly, not to mention affordable.

Along the Treasure Coast are scruffy beach villages like Fort Pierce, gamely trying to steady themselves after years of economic decline. By sprucing up long-neglected and infinitely charming downtown areas, these towns are drawing more new visitors, who are discovering the magnificent beaches and fishing opportunities that abound here. Farther north is the tidy and somewhat stuffy Vero Beach.

These beach towns are decidedly low-key, with friendliness and a laissez-faire parochialism taking precedence over big-city aspirations. There's plenty of gaudiness, seediness, and even a good bit of capitalism-fueled madness, but even these are executed with a bit of folksy flair. (And truthfully, much of the tackiness is concentrated in Daytona Beach.) By the time you get to Jacksonville, the state's largest and most northernmost city, the proximity to Georgia becomes quite clear, although the quiet barrier-island vibe on nearby Amelia Island feels very Old Florida.

Maybe it's the moss-draped oaks along

Previous: Fort Lauderdale Beachfront; downtown Delray Beach. **Above:** Palm Beach.

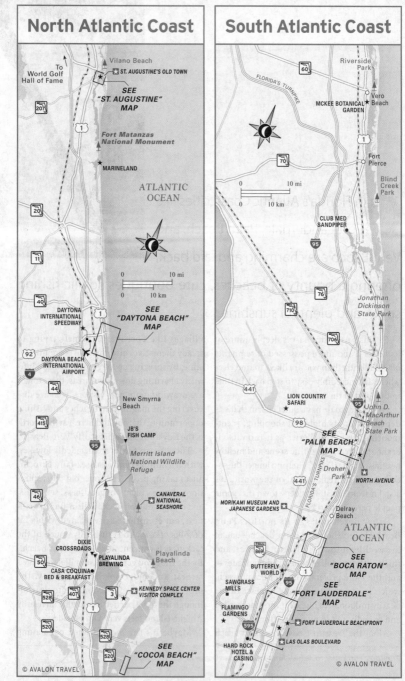

Three Days Along the Atlantic Coast

Las Olas Boulevard in Fort Lauderdale

More than 300 miles separate the southernmost (Fort Lauderdale) and northernmost (Jacksonville) areas covered in this chapter. Although those miles are mostly seamless, it's impossible to take in all that Florida's Atlantic Coast has to offer in just three days. However, if you've got a long weekend and want to explore the area's highlights, try the below itinerary, which takes in some of the best sights, beaches, and other experiences.

DAY 1

Spend the morning shopping the boutiques along **Las Olas Boulevard** in Fort Lauderdale, then take a **scenic drive** up **A1A** along the ocean to Palm Beach, where you can gawk at multimillion- dollar mansions and lunch with the local swells at **Testa's.** While away the afternoon strolling through the **Morikami Museum and Japanese Gardens** in Delray Beach, then drive another hour or so north to Vero Beach, where you can dine beachside at the Ocean Grill and spend the night at Gloria Estefan's stylish **Costa d'Este hotel.**

DAY 2

Get an early start for the 90-minute drive to **Merritt Island National Wildlife Refuge** for hiking and bird-watching; plan on cooling off at the beautiful beaches of nearby **Canaveral National Seashore.** Grab lunch and a freshly brewed craft beer at **Playalinda Brewing Company** in Titusville before heading further up the coast to enjoy the tourist kitsch of Daytona Beach and its Boardwalk area.

DAY 3

Explore historic **St. Augustine** in the morning before the weather gets too hot, since most of the sights here are only accessible on foot (or bike). Take an A/C break to tour **St. Augustine Distillery** and then hop across the street to the **Rype N Readi farmers market** to pack a picnic basket for an afternoon chilling on the beach in historic Fernandina Beach, which is about 90 minutes away. Plan on spending the night in nearby Jacksonville, with dinner at the **Bearded Pig** and nightlife in **Five Points** bars like **Raindogs.**

US-1, the vast stretches of undeveloped coast around the Kennedy Space Center, the sight of a heron alighting on a branch in the Halifax River, or the 17th-century architecture on display in St. Augustine, but this part of the state is a reminder of what Florida may have looked like had cigarette boats and mouse ears never become part of its cultural definition. The chance to look back at the state's Spanish history and forward to its space-exploration future is what makes this part of Florida so appealing.

PLANNING YOUR TIME

It's only a two-hour drive from the southern part of Fort Lauderdale to the northern edge of Vero Beach. Although the sights along the south Atlantic coast are concentrated in a fairly small geographic area, each of the areas in this chapter is worth a day or two of exploration. Add in a requisite few more days at the gorgeous beaches, and you could spend a full week here. Fort Lauderdale and the Palm Beach area each deserve two days, while the sights of the Treasure Coast can easily be seen in one day. If you're trying to take in the whole southern area at once, explore Fort Lauderdale and Palm Beach County from a base in downtown Fort Lauderdale and then move to a hotel along Vero Beach's Ocean Drive to check out the Treasure Coast.

As for the northern part of the Atlantic coast, the Space Coast is typically tacked on as an afterthought to vacations in nearby Orlando, with many visitors opting to take a day away from the theme parks to dip their toes in the ocean or check out Kennedy Space Center. Nonetheless, nature lovers will find the area to be a haven and should allow at least a full day each to explore the Merritt Island National Wildlife Refuge and the Canaveral National Seashore. A full day in St. Augustine's Old Town allows you to see most of what the town has to offer.

Fort Lauderdale

With temperatures that rarely dip below the high 50s and long stretches of beautiful coastline, it's no surprise that Fort Lauderdale is one of Florida's most popular tourist destinations. As early as the 1930s, the area was one of the top spring break locales in the United States, a title it held until the 1980s when city leaders decided they had had enough of drunken college kids falling from hotel balconies. While many students still head for the area in March to shake off the cold of the U.S. Northeast, the numbers are less than 5 percent of the quarter million or so who once flocked to the area.

Fort Lauderdale has achieved a nice balance among its traditional roles as a sun-and-fun destination, a popular location for yachters to lay anchor, and a modern growing city. There's an unmistakable undercurrent of big money in the city, but a vibrant youth culture and a long-standing beach- and boat-bum laissez-faire attitude keep the city from taking itself too seriously.

SIGHTS
Old Fort Lauderdale

Little of **Old Fort Lauderdale** is left. The tiny village maintained by the **Fort Lauderdale Historical Society** (219 SW 2nd Ave., 954/463-4431, www.fortlauderdalehistoricalsociety.org, 10am-5pm Tues.-Sat., noon-5pm Sun., $10 adults, $5 students, children 5 and under free; admission includes Museum of History and tour of King-Cromartie House) is tucked away in a corner of 2nd Avenue, bordered by the New River on one side and the nightlife district of Himmarshee Street on the other. Although the collection is not that extensive, this is a great place to take in some of the area's turn-of-the-20th-century history with a visit to the **New River Inn and Museum of History**

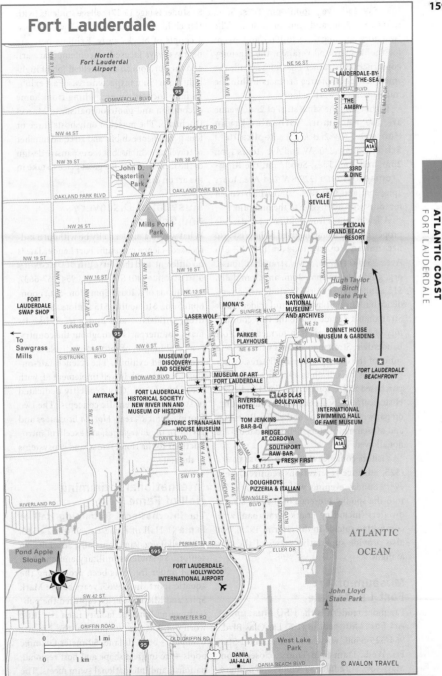

Fort Lauderdale

North Fort Lauderdale Airport

LAUDERDALE-BY-THE-SEA

THE AMBRY

COMMERCIAL BLVD

NW 31 AVE

NW 44 ST

NW 39 ST

33RD & DINE

John D. Easterlin Park

OAKLAND PARK BLVD

CAFÉ SEVILLE

NW 26 ST

Mills Pond Park

PELICAN GRAND BEACH RESORT

NW 19 ST

Hugh Taylor Birch State Park

NW 16 ST

FORT LAUDERDALE SWAP SHOP

MONA'S

LASER WOLF

STONEWALL NATIONAL MUSEUM AND ARCHIVES

BONNET HOUSE MUSEUM & GARDENS

To Sawgrass Mills

SUNRISE BLVD

PARKER PLAYHOUSE

LA CASA DEL MAR

FORT LAUDERDALE BEACHFRONT

MUSEUM OF DISCOVERY AND SCIENCE

MUSEUM OF ART FORT LAUDERDALE

AMTRAK

BROWARD BLVD

FORT LAUDERDALE HISTORICAL SOCIETY/ NEW RIVER INN AND MUSEUM OF HISTORY

RIVERSIDE HOTEL

LAS OLAS BOULEVARD

INTERNATIONAL SWIMMING HALL OF FAME MUSEUM

HISTORIC STRANAHAN HOUSE MUSEUM

TOM JENKINS BAR-B-Q

DAVIE BLVD

BRIDGE AT CORDOVA

SOUTHPORT RAW BAR

FRESH FIRST

SW 17 ST

DOUGHBOYS PIZZERIA & ITALIAN

SPANGLER BLVD

RIVERLAND RD

Pond Apple Slough

ATLANTIC OCEAN

PERIMETER RD

ELLER DR

FORT LAUDERDALE-HOLLYWOOD INTERNATIONAL AIRPORT

John Lloyd State Park

SW 42 ST

GRIFFIN ROAD

PERIMETER RD

0   1 mi

0   1 km

OLD GRIFFIN RD

West Lake Park

DANIA JAI-ALAI

DANIA BEACH BLVD

© AVALON TRAVEL

(231 SW 2nd Ave., noon-4pm Tues.-Sun., tours 1pm, 2pm, and 3pm Tues.-Sun.). The two-story building dates to 1905, and except for the wraparound veranda, the masonry construction is rather charmless. Still, the small collection of area artifacts within the museum is well worth a look.

Right along the same strip of 2nd Avenue are the **Philemon Nathaniel Bryan House** (227 SW 2nd Ave.), a **Replica 1899 Schoolhouse** (230 SW 2nd Ave., tours 1pm, 2pm, and 3pm Tues.-Sun.), and the **King-Cromartie House** (229 SW 2nd Ave., tours 1pm, 2pm, and 3pm Tues.-Sun.), which is open for tours with admission to the museum.

A few minutes from Old Fort Lauderdale proper, but still along the river, is the **Historic Stranahan House Museum** (335 SE 6th Ave., 954/524-4736, www.stranahanhouse. org, guided tours 1pm, 2pm, and 3pm daily, $12 adults, $11 seniors, $7 students), a residence built in 1901 by successful trader Frank Stranahan a decade before the tiny community of New River was transformed into Fort Lauderdale. Stranahan and his wife Ivy were some of the city's pioneering figures. A few years after Ivy's death in 1971, the house was purchased and restored by the Fort Lauderdale Historical Society. Its exhibits are interesting, on par with the displays at the New River Inn and Museum of History. Self-guided tours are not allowed.

Visitors come for the **river ghost tours** ($25, advance reservations required) held every Sunday evening, which not only delve into the spooky presence of the city's early dwellers (including Frank Stranahan, who committed suicide in the river in 1929), but also provide superlative views of the city at night.

Museum of Art Fort Lauderdale

Far more modern is the **NSU Museum of Art Fort Lauderdale** (1 E. Las Olas Blvd., 954/525-5500, www.moafl.org, 11am-5pm Fri.-Wed., 11am-8pm Thurs., closed Mon. May-Nov., $12 adults, $8 seniors and military,

$5 students (age 13-17) college students (with ID), children 12 and under free), which is just a couple of blocks away. Exhibits here are nearly always focused on contemporary art, and the curators do an excellent job of highlighting art in unexpected areas: Past exhibits have focused on everything from home decoration and photojournalism to Marcel Duchamp. The museum only hosts three or four permanent exhibits and an equal number of traveling exhibits, but the expansive design of the facility makes it a great place to take in the art on display.

Museum of Discovery and Science

What would a modern city be without a kid-focused science museum? Fort Lauderdale is no different, and the **Museum of Discovery and Science** (401 SW 2nd St., 954/467-6637, www.mods.org, 10am-5pm Mon.-Sat., noon-6pm Sun., $16 adults, $15 seniors, $13 children, children 1 and under free), like its many counterparts throughout the country, is a combination of interactive displays and eco-minded exhibits. The science-fair-on-steroids approach is well implemented, with areas like *Gizmo City* explicitly dedicated to straight-up scientific concepts. The two Florida-centric areas, *Florida Ecoscapes* and *Living in the Everglades*, are excellent introductions to the flora, fauna, and ecosystems of the state.

International Swimming Hall of Fame

The **International Swimming Hall of Fame** (1 Hall of Fame Dr., 954/462-6536, www.ishof.org, 9am-5pm daily, $8 adults, $6 seniors, $4 students, military and children 5 and under free) has been promoting the aquatic sport since 1965, years before Mark Spitz and Michael Phelps captured the public imagination. The facility itself is a little worn out, but the two pools at the Aquatic Complex—both 10-lane, 50-meter Olympic pools—are in great shape and host regional, national, and international swim meets. The

Sea Turtle Nesting

The Atlantic coast is popular for sea turtles to make their nests, and Florida is a particularly favored place. There are some 70,000 sea turtle nests made annually along the Florida coastline, and most of them are made by loggerhead turtles.

Sea turtles spend most of their lives in the ocean, only returning to land to dig into beach sand to lay their eggs, after which they immediately head back out to the ocean. This is a doubly dangerous proposition for the creatures. First, the sea turtles return to the same spot every year to make their nests, guided by the currents, stars, and most importantly, the light of the moon; development along the Atlantic shoreline has obviously resulted in a lot more light along the beach, which both disorients and imperils the turtles. Second, those nests are often dug in the very same beaches where crowds of sun-worshippers descend daily, which occasionally results in the nests being crushed. Even if the mama turtle makes her way to the right spot and the nest remains undisturbed long enough for the turtles to hatch, the baby turtles still aren't out of the woods, as they have to rely on the same combination of moonlight and stars to make their way back to the ocean. If lights along the shore disorient them, they can go the wrong direction and wind up trying to cross a highway instead of diving into the sea.

Obviously, coastal development has gone hand in hand with a steep decline in the sea turtle population. Thankfully, there are now numerous regulations barring humans from interfering with nests or turtles, as well as a number of common-sense reminders around the beach area to minimize light pollution during the summer nesting months. Groups like the Fort Lauderdale-based **National Save the Sea Turtle Foundation** (877/887-8533, www.seaturtle.org) are doing a great job raising awareness of the turtles' struggles and educating tourists and locals about what they can do to keep from being part of the problem. You can even support the foundation's mission by adopting a sea turtle nest. The **Museum of Discovery and Science** (401 SW 2nd St., 954/467-6637, www.mods.org) also hosts moonlight sea turtle walks in May, June, and July.

museum and library that are the heart of the Hall of Fame have old meet posters, photos from the last century of competitive swimming, and unique memorabilia like medals and swimsuits from the likes of Mark Spitz, Johnny Weissmuller, and Buster Crabbe.

Bonnet House Museum and Gardens

Hidden away behind a condo complex, the **Bonnet House Museum and Gardens** (900 N. Birch Rd., 954/563-5394, www.bonnethouse.org, 10am-4pm Tues.-Sat., noon-4:30pm Sun., $20 adults, $16 children, children 5 and under free, grounds-only admission $10) is a surprisingly restful oasis near the beaches of Fort Lauderdale. Built in 1925, the house itself is a Caribbean colonial-style complex that is charming despite its large size. The bedrooms, servants' quarters, and kitchen offer a glimpse into the past because many of the housewares and furnishings, including the china and the chairs, are original. The whimsical layout is far from stuffy, with a bamboo-walled bar area and bright high-contrast tropical colors throughout. If the house's history isn't appealing, a walk around the grounds, which are said to contain five distinct ecosystems, is a sublime treat. The dense tree canopy is still impressive despite damage from hurricanes, and it gives visitors isolation and quiet to transport themselves back in time.

Stonewall National Museum and Archives

Fort Lauderdale has been a preferred destination for gay and lesbian travelers for decades, so the presence of the **Stonewall National Museum and Archives** (2157 Wilton Drive, 954/530-9337, www.stonewallnationalmuseum.org, 11am-8pm Mon.-Fri., 10am-5pm

Sat., free, but $5 donation suggested) isn't surprising. The museum houses more than 5,000 items, ranging from magazines and photographs to social-science documents and the gavel used to repeal the Don't Ask, Don't Tell law. It's open to the public, and often hosts art exhibitions, lectures, and movies.

Butterfly World

Founded in 1988 by researcher and butterfly aficionado Ronald Boender, **Butterfly World** (3600 W. Sample Rd., Coconut Creek, 954/977-4400, www.butterflyworld.com, 9am-5pm Mon.-Sat., 11am-5pm Sun., $29.95 adults, $21.95 children, children 2 and under free) is a 10-acre complex that houses several butterfly habitats and is also home to hummingbird and lorikeet aviaries, botanical gardens, a butterfly farm, and research facilities. While you don't have to love butterflies to enjoy Butterfly World, you probably shouldn't go if you have a fear of winged creatures, as it's pretty hard to avoid them. The grounds are tropical and gorgeous. Admission is a bit steep, but the pastoral environment is an incredible oasis among the sprawl and traffic of South Florida, and visitors are almost certainly guaranteed a one-on-one encounter with some kind of flying beauty.

Flamingo Gardens

Flamingo Gardens (3750 S. Flamingo Rd., Davie, 954/473-2955, 9:30am-5pm daily, $19.95 adults, $12.95 children, children 2 and under free) is an enormous 60-acre facility that is somewhat basic, allowing the beauty of the animals and gardens to speak for themselves. There's a 25,000-square-foot free-flight aviary with dozens of birds and native plants. Other animal facilities include alligator, otter, panther, and, of course, flamingo habitats. There is also an impressive humid greenhouse with orchids and scores of rare tropical plants. The half-hour guided tram ride is a great way to take in the various natural areas and get an understanding of the diversity of animal and plant life. However, the best way to experience Flamingo Gardens is on foot and not in a rush.

BEACHES
★ Fort Lauderdale Beachfront

Looking out onto the wide expanses of soft white sand and blue-green Atlantic waters at the **Fort Lauderdale Public Beach** (State Rd. A1A between 17th St. and E. Sunrise Blvd.), it's not hard to understand why Fort Lauderdale was a prime spring break destination for years. The beach is as large as it

Fort Lauderdale Beachfront

is beautiful, and it can often get incredibly crowded. Today, those crowds are considerably more diverse than they were in Fort Lauderdale's spring break heyday. Still, the atmosphere here is festive and generally family-oriented. Because it is a city beach, the crowds can sometimes include some less-than-savory characters, but lifeguards and roaming beach patrols ensure a fairly high level of safety during the day.

If you want to bring your best animal friend to the shore with you, a few blocks north of the main beachfront area is **Canine Beach** (Sunrise Blvd. at State Rd. A1A, Fri.-Sun. only, $7 per dog), where dog lovers can bring their pooches for some wave romping on the weekends.

Hugh Taylor Birch State Park

Parking near the main Fort Lauderdale beach can often run as high as admission to nearby **Hugh Taylor Birch State Park** (3109 E. Sunrise Blvd., 954/564-4521, 8am-sunset daily, $6/carload, $4/single-occupant vehicle). While the former estate of Chicago attorney Hugh Taylor Birch doesn't offer the same sort of isolated experience as many of Florida's beachfront parks, the park offers more than just swimming and sunbathing: Canoe and kayak rentals are available to provide visitors with access to the mile-long freshwater lagoon, and there are hiking trails and an eco-minded visitors center.

Lauderdale-by-the-Sea

About 10 minutes north of Hugh Taylor Birch is the trapped-in-amber beach town of **Lauderdale-by-the-Sea,** which is both grubby and charming. Parking here is something of a challenge (especially on weekends). There are meters all over town; the ones near the beach cost $1 per hour. But keep in mind that they are enforced 24 hours a day. It's well worth the effort of finding a parking spot, as there's a huge live coral reef just 100 feet off the beach, making this an ideal spot for snorkeling and diving.

South Beach Park

A few blocks south of the main beachfront area is **South Beach Park** (1100 Seabreeze Blvd.), which offers the same beautiful white sands and azure waters but also has considerably more parking (still, you should arrive early), restroom and shower facilities, and even a playground.

Dr. Von D. Mizell-Eula Johnson State Park

Even farther south in nearby Dania is **Dr. Von D. Mizell-Eula Johnson State Park** (formerly John U. Lloyd Beach State Park; 6503 N. Ocean Dr., Dania, 954/923-2833, 8am-sunset daily, $6/carload, $4/single-occupant vehicle), which offers more of what you would expect from a beach state park. Taking up nearly the entire northern tip of a barrier island, the park is surprisingly isolated considering its proximity to the busy South Florida towns of Hollywood, Dania, and Fort Lauderdale. Snorkeling is great just offshore from the beach, and boating through the mangroves of Port Everglades Inlet is a popular pastime, with canoes and kayaks available for rent. The main beach can get crowded quickly, but the middle part of the park between the two main parking areas is worth the hike.

ENTERTAINMENT AND EVENTS
Nightlife

Nightlife in downtown Fort Lauderdale is fairly concentrated in the area around Himmarshee Street (a confusing name given to a two-block section of 2nd Street west of Andrews Avenue) and the adjacent Riverfront area. This critical mass makes barhopping something of an endurance sport on the weekends, and the crowds can get pretty intense at most of these spots.

For big-name live music, head for **Revolution Live** (100 SW 3rd Ave., 954/449-1025, www.jointherevolution.net), which hosts national and regional bands on a regular basis. Those looking for laid-back grunginess should check out **Poor House**

(110 SW 3rd Ave., 954/522-5145, www.poor-housebar.com, 9pm-4am daily), a decidedly low-rent but quite friendly pub, or the skate-punk-and-craft-beer vibe at **Original Fat Cat's** (320 Himmarshee St., 954/524-5366, 5pm-4am daily).

Away from downtown, but still centrally located, is the wonderful "no jerks, yes beer" vibe of **Laser Wolf** (901 Progresso Dr., 954/667-9373, 5pm-2am Mon.-Sat., 2pm-8pm Sun), which, despite its unassuming railroad-trackside location and tiny interior space, is one of the friendliest and coolest bars in the city. Specializing in craft beer (with a selection that's probably higher in number than the building's fire-code capacity for people), Laser Wolf also boasts a comfortable outdoor court-yard, the occasional street-side food vendor, and, if you're lucky, a vintage horror film on the indoor TV screens.

Of course, there are also a number of bars near the beach, including the **Elbo Room** (241 S. Atlantic Blvd., 954/463-4615, www.elboroom.com, 10am-2am daily), which has been a beachside institution since the 1940s. It was made famous by its appearance in Where the Boys Are and is now home to a party-hearty atmosphere, complete with bikini contests and loud rock and roll. The neigh-borly atmosphere at **McSorley's Beach Pub** (837 N. Ft. Lauderdale Beach Blvd., 954/565-4446, www.mcsorleysftl.com, 11am-2am Mon.-Thurs. and Sun., 11am-3am Fri.-Sat.) is a fine option, with a friendly bar staff, plenty of sports on the TVs, and sidewalk seating that looks onto the beach.

The pink roadside building that houses **Mona's** (502 E. Sunrise Blvd., 954/525-6662, www.monasbar.com, noon-2am Sun.-Thurs., noon-3am Fri.-Sat.) gives the bar the appear-ance of a decades-old dive. In reality, it's one of the friendliest gay and lesbian bars in Fort Lauderdale, with pool tables, frequent drink specials (including free drinks if you pick the number drawn every time a train rumbles by on the nearby tracks), and a welcoming pub-like atmosphere.

Eleven miles (20 minutes) southwest of downtown Fort Lauderdale is the **Seminole Hard Rock Hotel & Casino** (1 Seminole Way, Hollywood, 954/791-7600, www.seminolehardrockhollywood.com, 24 hours daily). With its on-the-reservation location, there's not much else to do in the area in the way of nightlife, so the Seminole tribe has gone to great lengths to create an insulated entertainment complex—dubbed "Seminole Paradise"—around the casino. In addition to poker, blackjack, and approximately eleventy-billion slot machines, there are more than a dozen restaurants, bars, and nightclubs on the premises. The whole thing feels a bit like a mall or a cruise ship. If you're not the gambling type, there are clubs dedicated to dancing, live music, jazz, comedy, and casual drinking, as well as tourist shops and chain-style restaurants.

The Arts

Fort Lauderdale's Las Olas Boulevard has some of the city's best galleries nestled among the boutiques and high-priced boîtes. The ritzy **New River Fine Art** (914 E. Las Olas Blvd., 954/524-1817, http://newriverfineart.com, 10am-10pm Mon.-Thurs., 10am-11pm Fri.-Sat., 11am-10pm Sun., free) focuses on top-dollar works, with originals by Dalí, Picasso, Chagall, and others, along-side the likes of Henry Asencio, Thomas Arvid, and M. L. Snowden. Despite its name, **Call of Africa's Native Visions Gallery** (807 E. Las Olas Blvd., 954/767-8712, www.nativevisions.com, 10am-10pm Mon.-Sat., 11am-9pm Sun., free) is not focused solely on African art. Instead, the gallery features landscape paintings, sculpture, and other works that are inspired by wildlife and na-ture scenes. Other great galleries along Las Olas include **Las Olas Fine Arts** (701 E. Las Olas Blvd., 954/767-0063, lasolasfinearts.com, 10am-9pm Mon.-Sat., noon-5pm Sun.), which specializes in contermporary fine art and the artist-owned **Jamali Gallery** (1018 E. Las Olas Blvd., 954-617-9990, jamali-gallery.com, 10am-10pm Mon.-Sat., 10am-8pm Sun.).

Most of the area's high-profile performing arts groups put on productions at the **Broward Center for Performing Arts** (201 SW 5th Ave., 954/462-0222, www.browardcenter.org). The Concert Association of Florida, Gold Coast Jazz Society, Miami City Ballet, Florida Grand Opera, and Symphony of the Americas all use this space, and it's also utilized for touring Broadway productions and national jazz and pop performances. The **Parker Playhouse** (707 NE 8th St., 954/763-2444, www.parkerplayhouse.com) is considerably smaller. It is a beautiful, 1,200-seat venue that hosts performances by artists, ensembles, and productions that are more appropriate for the smaller venue.

The one-screen **Cinema Paradiso** (503 SE 6th St., 954/525-3456, www.fandango.com) is an art-house theater housed in a beautiful turn-of-the-20th-century facility (formerly a Methodist church) that not only screens contemporary foreign and independent films but also puts on late-night screenings of cult classics and occasional educational lectures. The three-screen **Gateway Theatre** (1820 E. Sunrise Blvd., 954/763-7994, http://thegatewaytheatre.com) is a vintage 1950s-era movie house that typically shows an interesting mix of (decent and curated) mainstream features and lesser-known indie flicks, foreign films, and classics.

Festivals and Events

Like many South Florida destinations, the majority of festivals in Fort Lauderdale occur during the winter and early spring. Sponsored by the Fort Lauderdale Orchid Society, the annual **Orchid Show** (War Memorial Auditorium, 800 NE 8th St., 954/812-2231, www.flos.org, Jan.) is an old-fashioned opportunity for amateur and professional horticulturists to show and sell these delicate tropical flowers. The annual weekend-long **Pride Fort Lauderdale** (Holiday Park, 1150 G. Harold Martin Dr., 954/561-2020, www.pridesouthflorida.org, Feb.) is said to be Florida's largest gay pride festival. With the array of DJs, live musicians, and food, drink, and crafts vendors that crowd into Holiday Park for two days, as well as the numerous ancillary events in local bars and restaurants, it's easy to believe that claim.

The **Las Olas Art Fair** (600 Las Olas Blvd., 561/746-6615, www.artfestival.com, Jan.) benefits from the crisp January weather, which not only makes for a great backdrop for local and national artists and crafters to display their wares, but also makes this festival incredibly popular.

A benefit for the American Lung Association, the one-night **Las Olas Wine & Food Festival** (Las Olas Blvd., http://lasolaswff.com, April) features the fare of some of the city's best restaurants in booths and tents all along the closed Las Olas Boulevard.

One summer festival worth withstanding the heat for is **The Hukilau** (Bahia Mar Fort Lauderdale Beach, 801 Seabreeze Blvd., 954/243-7709, www.thehukilau.com, Jun.), which turns the Bahia Mar resort into a four-day bacchanal of tiki torches and Polynesian exotica. The celebration is a retro, irony-free party, which draws hundreds of visitors every year for super-sweet (and possibly smoking) cocktails, surf rock, and hula dances.

SHOPPING
★ Las Olas Boulevard

Dedicated shoppers should head directly for the upscale offerings and classy boutiques located along **Las Olas Boulevard,** where even those without high credit limits will likely enjoy window-shopping. While Las Olas is decidedly fancy, it feels less like an exclusive enclave than a well-to-do Main Street. Highlights include jewelry shops like **Carroll's Jewelers** (915 E. Las Olas Blvd., 954/463-3711, www.carrollsjewelry.com, 10am-6pm Mon.-Sat., noon-4pm Sun.); the high-end fashions at the European-styled **Moda Mario** (1200 E. Las Olas Blvd., Suite 104, 954/467-3258, http://modamario.com, 10am-6pm Mon.-Sat.) and the South Beach-inspired **Elektrik Boutique** (619 E. Las Olas Blvd., 954/306-2596, www.elektrikboutique.com, 10am-10pm daily); and the retro and vintage menswear found at **The Archives** (1015 E. Las Olas Blvd, 954/533-8201, archvs. com, 10am-9pm Mon.-Wed., 10am-10pm Thurs., 10am-11pm Fri.-Sat., 10am-8pm Sun.).

Sawgrass Mills

If the prices along Las Olas are a bit beyond your means, **Sawgrass Mills** (12801 W. Sunrise Blvd., Sunrise, 954/846-2300, www. simon.com, 10am-9:30pm Mon.-Sat., 11am-8pm Sun.) may be the option you're looking for. The eighth-largest mall in the United States, Sawgrass has more than two million square feet of shops, including brand names like Burberry, Coach, Ferragamo, Movado, and more.

Fort Lauderdale Swap Shop

Still not cheap enough for you? Hard-core bargain shoppers or anyone curious as to what exactly a combination flea market, farmers market, outlet mall, and 13-screen drive-in theater looks like will no doubt want to check out the **Fort Lauderdale Swap Shop** (3291 W. Sunrise Blvd., 954/791-7927, www.floridaswapshop.com, 8am-6pm Mon.-Fri., 7am-7pm Sat.-Sun.). The owners cheekily refer to it as Florida's second-biggest tourist attraction, and while that may only be true on a square-footage basis, the annual visitor count of 12 million certainly marks the Swap Shop as a notable destination in and of itself. The sheer size of the market means that you can get almost everything here, even if it happens to be an off-brand knockoff or gently used specimen. The truly dedicated arrive when the outdoor shops open (7am Mon.-Fri., 5am Sat.-Sun.), but even late risers can manage to find good, or at least interesting, deals.

SPORTS AND RECREATION
Jai-Alai

Jai-alai was once hugely popular in South Florida, and **Dania Jai-Alai** (301 E. Dania Beach Blvd., Dania, 954/920-1511, www. dania-jai-alai.com, free) has been one of the best places to catch the fast-paced game since

the fronton opened in 1953. The enormous 220,000-square-foot complex has ample seating to watch the games. Unlike at many other frontons, where the main attraction is pari-mutuel betting on other sports, the crowds—though smaller in years past—are actually here to watch jai-alai being played. Accordingly, matches are raucous and well fought, and newcomers who may be intimidated by the complexity of the game's rules can quickly and easily be schooled by the many old-time regulars. The Dania club also offers a wide array of pari-mutuel betting opportunities, with live simulcasts of thoroughbred and greyhound races as well as other sporting events; there's also a large poker room.

Water Sports

Deep-sea fishing charters can be booked with **All-Inclusive Sport Fishing** (801 Seabreeze Blvd., 954/761-8202, www.all-inclusivesportfishing.com) and **Reel Work** (301 Seabreeze Blvd., 954/522-9399, www. lauderdalefishing.com).

Sea Experience (801 Seabreeze Blvd., 954/467-6000, www.seaxp.com) offers an array of scuba and snorkeling charters along with training and Professional Association of Diving Instructors (PADI) certification classes. Sea Experience offers twice-daily snorkeling trips on its glass-bottom boat out to Fort Lauderdale Twin Ledges, a reef that's teeming with coral and tropical fish.

FOOD
Breakfast

The no-nonsense, cash-only, eggs-and-bacon atmosphere at **The Floridian** (1410 E. Las Olas Blvd., 954/463-4041, 24 hours daily, from $6) has been keeping this diner in good stead with Fort Lauderdale breakfast hunters for more than 60 years. The kitchen cooks up biscuits and gravy, homemade oatmeal, omelets, and other breakfast fare in a manner that's both lightning fast and of high quality. In keeping with the diner's Las Olas location, if you feel like you need to spend large amounts of money, go ahead and splurge on

Best Restaurants

★ **The Foxy Brown:** This wonderful place splits the difference between upscale neighborhood diner, locavore foodie spot, and louche brunch bar (page 168).

★ **Testa's:** Breakfast and lunch are surprisingly affordable at this Palm Beach institution; dinner is not (page 178).

★ **Café Boulud:** The Palm Beach location maintains the high standards of fresh French cuisine that defines the New York City original (page 178).

★ **Spanish River Grill:** Inventive, rustic Spanish and Portuguese dishes with an emphasis on strong earthy flavors are served here (page 202).

★ **J.B.'s Fish Camp:** This restaurant offers fresh seafood, sandwiches, ice-cold beer, and a great view of the Intracoastal Waterway (page 203).

★ **Casa Maya:** Enjoy a healthy approach to Mexican food, with fresh ingredients and interesting reconfigurations of traditional Mexican dishes (page 221).

the $300 Fat Cat breakfast; it feeds two and comes with a bottle of champagne.

Somewhat more in keeping with the surroundings on Las Olas is **La Bonne Crêpe** (815 E. Las Olas Blvd., 954/761-1515, www. labonnecrepe.com, 7am-10pm Sun.-Thurs., 7am-midnight Fri.-Sat., from $9), which serves fresh-fruit-topped waffles, enormous pancakes, French toast, omelets, and, yes, crepes. Lunch and dinner are served as well, but the pleasant bistro atmosphere and sidewalk seating make it a great place to start the day.

Lunch and Light Bites

The arrival of **Fresh First** (1637 SE 17th St.,

fishing charters

954/763-3344, www.freshfirst.com, 8am-5pm Mon.-Sat., from $9) has been a boon for folks with gluten sensitivities. Everything the café sells is gluten free. That means Fresh First has a substantial menu of juices, salads, and soups, but it also has an array of excellent sandwiches (on flax bread, waffle bread, or as lettuce wraps) and inventive bowls stacked with fresh veggies, proteins, and rice or quinoa.

American

★ **The Foxy Brown** (723 E. Broward Blvd., 754/200-4236, www.myfoxybrown.com, 11:30am-10pm Mon.-Fri., 9:30am-10pm Sat.-Sun., from $12) splits the difference between upscale neighborhood diner and locavore foodie spot, managing to serve up wonderfully fresh and inventive dishes in a super-friendly and unpretentious environment. A tightly curated wine list and craft-beer selection are perfectly complementary to a focused and creative menu that changes frequently; make sure to pay attention to the specials on offer, as they tend more toward "inspired chef" than "clean out the fridge." Brunch is a decadent and leisurely affair, running until 4pm on weekends and serving up huge, soak-up-the-poison selections of steak and eggs, benedicts, banana bread grilled cheese (!), and more.

Big City Tavern (609 E. Las Olas Blvd., 954/727-0307, http://bigcitylasolas.com, 11:30am-11pm daily, from $14) is an outpost of a small corporate chain, but the restaurant's somewhat conservative take on trendy urban fare is appropriate to its Las Olas location. A boisterous pickup spot during happy hour and later in the evening, dinnertime is a bit more subdued. A nice selection of gourmet sandwiches, fresh-ground burgers, and ample salads is complemented by a handful of mildly interesting meat, fish, and poultry dishes. The bar is open until 3am nightly.

A block away is gastropub **American Social** (721 E. Las Olas Blvd., 854/764-7005, www.americansocialbar.com, 11:30am-1am Sun.-Tues., 11:30am-2am Wed.-Fri., 11:30am-midnight Sat., from $11), which features a menu primarily stocked with filling small plates (mac-and-cheese skillets, ribs, truffle fries, ahi tuna) and gourmet flatbread pizzas, allowing patrons to focus on the wide variety of craft beer on tap and by the bottle.

Like all good barbecue restaurants, **Tom Jenkins Bar-B-Q** (1236 S. Federal Hwy., 954/522-5046, http://tomjenkinsbbq.net, 11am-8:30pm Tues.-Thurs., 11am-10pm Fri.-Sat., from $8) has a pretty simple and straightforward menu: You get a plate of meat (ribs, chicken, or brisket) or a sandwich with meat (sliced beef, chicken, sausage, or catfish) and put beans, fries, corn, greens, or slaw on the plate with it. The restaurant also offers a couple of salads, but it's hard to imagine anyone actually ordering one, as the aroma of smoked meat is so pervasive and tempting that it could spell disaster for a quavering vegetarian's ethics.

Steak and Seafood

With a great view of the yachts passing down the New River, the **Historic Downtowner Saloon & Steakhouse** (408 S. Andrews Ave., 954/463-9800, http://downtownersaloon.com, 11am-11pm Sun.-Thurs., 11am-midnight Fri.-Sat., from $16) feels like it should be fancier, but it has a lighthearted neighborhood-friendly attitude that's quite welcoming. The building has been a Fort Lauderdale fixture for almost a century, and the collection of pop-culture artifacts scattered throughout the restaurant makes it seem as if the Downtowner has been open that long. Even though it hasn't, the kitchen has a steady, practiced hand, dishing up a simple selection of American steak house classics like prime rib, sirloins, and ribs, as well as seafood, sandwiches, and raw bar selections.

For a superlative downtown raw-bar experience, head a little farther south for the even more welcoming **Southport Raw Bar** (1536 Cordova Rd., 954/525-2526, www.southportrawbar.com, 11am-2am Sun.-Thurs., 11am-3am Fri.-Sat., from $6). Located on a canal extension of the Stanahan River, Southport brings in a number of anglers who utilize their fish-cleaning services ("you catch it, we cook it"). Nonfishers can avail themselves of some fantastically fresh seafood, from raw oysters and clams to fried baskets and only slightly more fanciful preparations of grilled or blackened fish. Make sure you indulge in some of Southport's sweet, white Bimini bread.

There are quite a few tourist-oriented meat-and-fish shacks along State Road A1A at the beach, and the **Casablanca Cafe** (3049 Alhambra St., 954/764-3500, www.casablancacafeonline.com, 11:30am-1pm daily, from $16) is a great option for those looking for something a bit more intimate and elegant. Korean-style duck, walnut-crusted chicken, and decadently sauced pasta dishes round out an inventive menu of thick-cut steaks and fresh-caught fish. The comfortable Mediterranean-style dining room provides a stylish but unstuffy environment in which to enjoy the food.

The **Poke House** (666 N. Federal Hwy, 754-200-4555, www.thepokehouse.com, 11:30am-10pm Sun.-Thurs., 11:30am-midnight Fri.-Sat., from $9) adheres to the superchill, surfer-lunch vibe that so many other poke joints go for, and they stick to it so hard that even their bowls are themed after surf spots. The over-theming would be annoying if the food weren't so good; bowls here are stuffed with ultra-fresh fish, vegetables, and starches (rice, lotus root, and more). Of course, in addition to being able to order preset bowls, you can also customize your own.

Japanese

Downtown's **Sushi Rock Cafe** (1515 E. Las Olas Blvd., 954/462-5541, 11:30am-10:30pm Mon.-Fri., 5pm-10:30pm Sat., 4:30pm-10:30pm Sun., from $12) does a good job with the standard array of rolls, and features a few interesting entrées like grilled whole squid, sautéed pork, and more.

Italian

What stands out the most at **Doughboys Pizzeria & Italian** (829 SE 17th St., 954/761-7652, www.doughboysfla.com, 11am-10:30pm

daily, from $9) is the extent of the menu. While some may argue that the various combinations of tomato sauce, pasta, and cheese could be infinite, it appears that Doughboys has gone to great lengths to determine just how many ways hearty Italian fare can be prepared. The restaurant itself is a drab diner-style eatery, but the staff is friendly, and whether you dig into the enormous portions of pasta, the Sicilian or Neapolitan pizzas, or the array of sandwiches, wraps, and calzones, a meal at Doughboys is highly recommended.

Just as the name implies, **Noodles Panini** (821 E. Las Olas Blvd., 954/462-1514, http://noodlespaninirestaurant.com, 11:30am-3pm and 5pm-10pm Tues.-Fri., 11:30am-11pm Sat., 11:30am-9:30pm Sun., from $8) specializes in noodles and panini and offers an astonishing variety of both. The inviting bistro also serves several Italian meat and chicken dishes and has a surprisingly extensive wine list.

European

The miniature-castle architecture of **The Ambry** (3016 E. Commercial Blvd., 954/771-7342, http://ambryrestaurant.net, 11:30am-2pm and 5pm-10pm Mon.-Fri., 5pm-10pm Sat., from $17) is as inviting as the staff and food at this Fort Lauderdale German restaurant. Once inside, the place feels more like a family dining room than a proper restaurant. Although it's unlikely to win any accolades from contemporary style critics, the food is hearty and authentic. From the liver-dumpling soup and goulash to a dozen different schnitzels, brats-and-kraut plates, and wild-game dishes, the Ambry is one of the best places in town to indulge yourself into a decadent food coma.

Cuban and Latin

Café Seville (2768 E. Oakland Park Blvd., 954/565-1148, www.cafeseville.com, 5pm-11pm Mon. and Sat., 11:30am-2pm Tues.-Fri., from $16) is routinely awarded various superlatives in the Fort Lauderdale dining community, and it's not hard to figure out why: The restaurant consistently provides excellent Spanish cuisine

Best Accommodations

★ **Riverside Hotel:** This is one of Fort Lauderdale's nicest hotels with large, luxurious guest rooms (page 171).

★ **Pelican Grand Beach Resort:** A beautiful option for families, this large resort evokes Caribbean elegance (page 171).

★ **Seahorse Beach Bungalows:** These bungalows are cute and quiet, just steps from the beach (page 193).

★ **Costa d'Este:** Owned by Gloria and Emilio Estefan, this spot was designed to bring "South Beach Style" to sleepy Vero Beach (page 194).

★ **Night Swan Bed & Breakfast:** This B&B is a good choice for a more homespun and personal environment (page 203).

★ **Casa de Solana B&B:** Friendly elegance in a convenient location make this one of the best options in St. Augustine (page 222).

★ **Casa Monica:** This is the grande dame of St. Augustine hotels, centrally located across from Flagler College and next door to City Hall (page 222).

in a friendly and comfortable environment. The menu is extensive and features a fairly predictable spread of paellas, *cazuelas,* and tapas, along with steaks, chops, seafood, and poultry dishes. There are often several lunch or dinner specials worth exploring. Seville is incredibly popular, especially on the weekend, so reservations are almost a necessity.

ACCOMMODATIONS
$100-150

Located a few blocks back from the beach is the gay-friendly ★ **La Casa del Mar** (3003 Granada St., 954/467-2037, www.lacasadel-mar.com, from $165 d) bed-and-breakfast. The secluded Mediterranean-style buildings house guest rooms that have been renovated, decorated in muted contemporary tones with plush, stylish furnishings and tile floors. Although the guest rooms are small, they are well-appointed, with free Wi-Fi, wall-mounted TVs, and kitchenettes. Most guest rooms overlook the lush foliage of the courtyard and pool area.

Another good B&B option is the **Granada**

Inn (3011 Granada St., 954/463-2032, www.thegranadainn.com, from $165 d). Located a couple of blocks from the beach, the European-style Granada offers some of the same secluded luxury as La Casa del Mar, with a dozen well-furnished guest rooms overlooking a pool and courtyard area landscaped with palms and tropical plants. Breakfast is served poolside, and all the guest rooms have private entrances.

Located right on the beach, the **Sea Club Resort** (619 Ft. Lauderdale Beach Blvd., 954/564-3211, www.seaclubresort.com, from $185 d) has standard hotel rooms and suites in a building that looks like it was once a standard motel that has transformed into a comfortable family-friendly resort with a restaurant-lounge, gift shop, and outdoor pool. All of the guest rooms have mini fridges, TVs, and coffeemakers and are decorated in basic beachy colors, with furniture that's of relatively recent vintage.

$150-200

Designed in the 1950s as a corporate retreat

for General Motors bigwigs, the **Manhattan Tower** (701 Bayshore Dr., 954/564-1117, www.manhattantowerfl.com, from $199 d) boasts some highly original period architecture that's somewhere between South Beach's art deco and The Jetsons Go to Hawaii. The guest rooms are a bit more modern and luxurious, but the apartment-style accommodations still manage to have personality. Clean and contemporary decor accents bright and airy spaces with large windows and tile floors; all guest rooms have full kitchens. During high season there is often a one-week minimum stay; at other times the minimum stay is usually three days.

The **Cheston House** (520 N. Birch Rd., 954/566-7950, www.chestonhouse.com, from $179 d) is a clothing-optional gay men's resort located just a couple of blocks from the beach. Understandably secluded, with copious foliage and privacy fences around the pool area, the resort offers standard hotel-style guest rooms, suites, and one-bedroom apartments. All guest rooms have TVs and DVD players, refrigerators, in-room safes, and Wi-Fi; the apartments have full kitchens.

Aqua Hotel (3016 Windamar St., 954/565-5790, www.aquafortlauderdale, com, from $159 d) is one of several updated mid-century modern boutique hotels located in the North Beach Village area, and is a fantastic bargain considering the size of some rooms. While couples will be content with standard king and queen rooms, there are also larger suites and studios with kitchenettes and multiple beds. All 39 rooms boast crisp, white decor, and free Wi-Fi, there are two on-site pools, and the property is just two blocks from the beach.

$200-300

Located on fashionable Las Olas Boulevard, the ★ **Riverside Hotel** (620 E. Las Olas Blvd., 954/467-0671, www.riversidehotel.com, from $229 d) has been one of Fort Lauderdale's nicest hotels since it opened in the 1930s. Guest rooms are quite large and are located either in the original six-story building or in a newer 12-story tower. Although the guest rooms in the original structure are a bit more charming, the tower guest rooms have balconies with fantastic views either onto downtown Fort Lauderdale and the New River or eastward toward the ocean. Luxurious touches are present throughout the property, from the marble bathroom countertops and beautiful furnishings to the high-end dining options and cocktail lounge.

The **Flamingo** (2727 Terramar St., 954/561-4658, www.theflamingoresort.com, from $269 d) is a decidedly upscale resort that caters to gay men. The individually decorated guest rooms—with four-poster beds, dark wood furnishings, and crisp linens—give the Flamingo a bed-and-breakfast atmosphere. But the guest rooms are far more spacious and well-appointed than what you find in most B&Bs. Although the resort claims to be a "true five-star," that's not quite the case, as there's no on-site restaurant, lounge, or any other amenity beyond the tropical private pool. The Flamingo's high level of service and comfortable, secluded property, however, combine with the luxuriousness of the guest rooms to make for an exceptional lodging environment.

Over $300

The enormous ★ **Pelican Grand Beach Resort** (2000 N. Ocean Blvd., 800/516-4651, www.pelicanbeach.com, from $349 d) is a beautiful and luxurious option for families traveling to the area. Of the resort's 160 guest rooms, 117 are suite accommodations with separate bedrooms and pullout couches in the living area. All guest rooms are decorated in cool tropical styles with French doors that open onto private balconies. The Caribbean-style verandas evoke an elegance that contrasts with the hum of activity around the gigantic pool area. Family-friendly touches like an ice-cream parlor and a lazy river all but ensure that the resort is as dedicated to the needs of romantic beach couples as it is to sandy schoolkids, not to mention the fact that the hotel sits right on 500 feet of private beach.

The **Hard Rock Hotel** (1 Seminole Way, Hollywood, 866/502-7529, www.seminole-hardrockhollywood.com, from $329 d), 11 miles southwest of downtown, is one of the nicer hotels in the Fort Lauderdale area, with spacious modern guest rooms boasting plush furnishings and an array of technological amenities, a glamorous pool area, and decadent spa facilities. Unfortunately, it's 20 minutes away from anything other than the adjacent Seminole Hard Rock Casino, making it somewhat inconvenient for beach vacationers or business travelers.

INFORMATION AND SERVICES
Visitor Information

The **Greater Fort Lauderdale Convention & Visitors Bureau** (1850 Eller Dr., 954/765-4466, www.sunny.org, 9am-5pm Mon.-Fri.) offers a good array of planning resources in an office near the intersection of I-95 and I-595.

GETTING THERE
Air

Fort Lauderdale-Hollywood International Airport (FLL, 320 Terminal Dr., Ft. Lauderdale, 866/435-9355, www.broward.org/airport) has seen considerable growth over the past few decades, particularly among low-cost carriers. All major domestic carriers and several international airlines (Air Canada, Avianca, and others) also fly into the airport. Despite its growth, FLL is still quite easy to navigate and much less of a strain on your sanity than coming into the area via Miami International Airport (MIA). FLL is located six miles south of downtown Fort Lauderdale. Taxi fares are approximately $30 per trip for up to five people to downtown; shuttles are only slightly cheaper.

Car

I-95 and Florida's Turnpike both come through Fort Lauderdale. The city is approximately 30 miles (half an hour) north of Miami and about 47 miles (an hour) south of West Palm Beach. The southern terminus of I-75 is between Fort Lauderdale and Hollywood, and this part of Florida is the only place where the interstate runs east-west. On the 110-mile, two-hour drive between Fort Lauderdale and Naples, on Florida's west coast, the highway is a toll road known as Alligator Alley because it cuts through the northern part of the Everglades.

Train and Bus

The Fort Lauderdale **Amtrak** station (200 SW 21st St., www.amtrak.com) is located about three miles from downtown.

2017 has seen the debut of high-speed rail in Florida, in the form of the privately owned **Brightline,** which connects Fort Lauderdale, Miami, and other major cities in South Florida to Orlando; the ride from Fort Lauderdale to Orlando is projected to take less than three hours, and the route is expected to be complete in 2018.

The Fort Lauderdale **Greyhound** bus station (515 NE 3rd St., www.greyhound.com) is located about five not-very-walkable blocks from the downtown core.

GETTING AROUND

Traffic on I-95 can be something of a nightmare at the best of times, and during rush hour it would try the patience of a saint. Unfortunately, it's all but unavoidable if you are traveling more than a short distance in town. Downtown is easily navigable, although parking is sometimes a challenge. As in Miami, car rental rates are quite competitive; a week-long rental can frequently be had for less than $200. Public transportation is handled by **Broward County/BCT** (954/357-8355, www.broward.org/bct, fares from $1.75, 10-day passes from $15).

Palm Beach County

This part of Florida is associated with its namesake city, the winter enclave of Palm Beach. The area around greater **Palm Beach County** offers much beyond the mansions, private clubs, and upscale shopping of one of the nation's wealthiest cities. The beautiful Japanese pastoralism of the Morikami Gardens in the western suburbs, the quiet classiness of Boca Raton, and the cute Old Florida vibes of downtown Delray Beach are all quite charming, while West Palm Beach anchors the area with a business-first vibe. Though stucco subdivisions and anonymous strip malls pervade outside of these zones, Palm Beach County has retained its own character and personality.

PALM BEACH AND WEST PALM BEACH

Although they're only separated by the sliver of water known as Lake Worth, there's a world of difference between the cities of West Palm Beach and Palm Beach. West Palm is, well, sort of a regular city, while Palm Beach is thick with wealth, vacation luxury, and even a presidential residence, all jammed onto a narrow spit of sand facing out into the Atlantic with its back to the mainland. You'll want to explore both at the same time, as they're so geographically close, but be prepared for a distinct experience from both.

Palm Beach Sights
MAR-A-LAGO
Mar-A-Lago (1100 S. Ocean Blvd.) was the largest of heiress Marjorie Merriweather Post's several estates, built in the early 1920s as a winter home for Post and her then husband, financier E. F. Hutton. The elegant and enormous house is spread across 110,000 square feet and has 58 bedrooms, 33 bathrooms, a dozen fireplaces, and three bomb shelters. Despite being declared a National Historic Landmark, Mar-A-Lago is privately owned by President Donald Trump, who uses the property as an exclusive—and ethically controversial—resort club. Unfortunately, unless you're extremely well-heeled, you're unlikely to see anything but the outside, and given security issues due to Trump's presidency, you'll likely be unable to view the outside either. (Roads and waterways around the area are shut down when Trump is in town.) There are occasional public events held here, but they are black-tie fundraisers and only slightly less exclusive than membership in the club itself.

FLAGLER MUSEUM
The Beaux-Arts building that houses the **Flagler Museum** (1 Whitehall Way, 561/655-2833, www.flaglermuseum.us, 10am-5pm Tues.-Sat., noon-5pm Sun., $18 adults, $10 children 13-17, $3 children 6-12, children 5 and under free) was originally built as Whitehall, industrialist Henry Flagler's winter estate in Palm Beach. The grounds and architecture are gorgeous and elegant examples of Gilded Age excess. The museum component is somewhat nontraditional as the main attraction is the house itself, stuffed with the original furnishings and artwork that Flagler collected. As an homage to Flagler, though, the museum also serves as a repository of the history of Florida's development, as it was this railroad titan who drove the state's progress in the late 19th and early 20th centuries. Still, most visitors come simply to experience the grandeur of the 55,000-square-foot mansion.

BETHESDA-BY-THE-SEA
Bethesda-by-the-Sea (141 S. County Rd., 561/655-4554, www.bbts.org, 8am-4:30pm Mon.-Fri., free) is an Episcopal church housed in a gorgeous Gothic structure originally built in 1925. The congregation dates to

Palm Beach

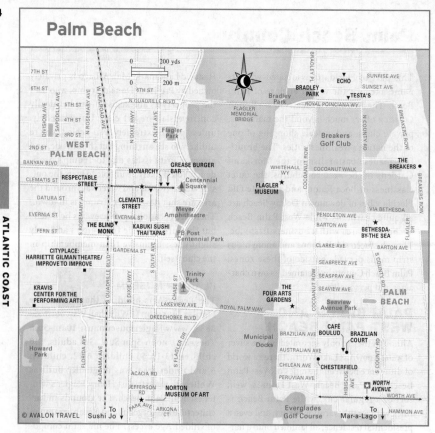

1889, the first Protestant church in southeast Florida. The building is open to the public for tours on two Sundays a month September-May, and one Sunday a month June-August. During the week, visitors can explore the beautiful Cluett Memorial Garden next door.

THE FOUR ARTS GARDENS

The Society of the Four Arts (2 Four Arts Plaza, 561/655-7226, www.fourarts.org, 10am-5pm daily, free) is primarily a location for performances, exhibits, and lectures, but the grounds and library are open to the public. The sculpture and botanical gardens are pastoral and beautiful, with a great view out onto Lake Worth.

West Palm Beach Sights
NORTON MUSEUM OF ART

The **Norton Museum of Art** (1451 S. Olive Ave., 561/832-5196, www.norton.org, 10am-5pm Mon.-Sat., 1pm-5pm Sun., closed Mon. May-Oct., $12 adults, $5 students, children 12 and under free) is a fantastic and expansive museum located just a few blocks from downtown, close to Lake Worth. The permanent collection is stocked with paintings by Mary Cassatt, Jackson Pollock, Stuart Davis, Robert Rauschenberg, Claude Monet, Paul Gauguin, and many other well-known artists, alongside impressive stashes of minimalist art, photography, contemporary sculpture, and much more. Visiting exhibits routinely are of the highest caliber. The museum is notably accessible and open, with architecture that serves the needs of the art as well as those of the visitor. Admission is free for Florida residents on Thursdays June-August.

DREHER PARK

Hugging the side of I-95 is **Dreher Park,** home to both the **Palm Beach Zoo** (1301 Summit Blvd., 561/533-0887, www.palmbeachzoo.org, 9am-5pm daily, $19.95 adults, $17.95 seniors, $14.95 children, children 2 and under free) and the recently renovated **South Florida Science Center & Aquarium** (4801 Dreher Tr. N., 561/832-1988, www.sfsciencecenter.org, 10am-5pm Mon.-Fri., 10am-6pm Sat., noon-6pm Sun., $16.95 adults, $14.95 seniors, $12.95 children, children 2 and under free). The 113-acre park is a destination on its own, with walking trails, fishing docks, playgrounds, and plenty of space to spread out a blanket and enjoy a sunny South Florida picnic. The conservation-minded zoo covers 23 acres and is home to many endangered species, including jaguars and Florida panthers; unusual creatures like tapirs, anteaters, and Chilean pudu deer; and more traditional zoo residents, like alligators, monkeys, birds, kangaroos, and horses. The science center houses an aquarium and planetarium, as well as a fairly standard (if Florida-centric) selection of permanent, hands-on science and conservation exhibits.

LION COUNTRY SAFARI

With such a respectable institution as the Palm Beach Zoo so close to central West Palm Beach, it may seem odd to suggest that visitors drive 20 miles (half an hour) out to the edge of the Everglades to visit **Lion Country Safari** (2003 Lion Country Safari Rd., Loxahatchee, 561/793-1084, www.lioncountrysafari.com, 9:30am-4:30pm daily, $35 adults, $31.50 seniors, $26 children, children 2 and under free), but this "cageless zoo" is a unique attraction that's well worth the trip. There are more than 800 animals living within the boundaries of

the 500-acre park, and many visitors choose to explore it by driving along the four miles of roadway through the animals' habitats, where giraffes, zebras, and other animals wander freely. More confrontational animals such as lions, tigers, and chimps are kept in confined areas by water barriers and unobtrusive fencing. The park's operators recommend that visitors arrive early in the morning or during a rain shower (hey, you'll be in your car), as the cooler weather is when the animals are more active.

Beaches

Most of the coastline in Palm Beach, not surprisingly, is the domain of multimillion-dollar estates, so public beach access is somewhat limited. At the intersection of **Ocean Boulevard and Worth Avenue,** however, there are a number of metered parking spaces with easy access to the shore. The beaches are fairly narrow and the water is prone to rip currents, but the views are unbeatable.

A couple of miles south is **Phipps Ocean Park** (2185 S. Ocean Blvd.), an isolated and natural park with a somewhat rocky beach but notably calmer waters than the rougher currents to the north. Snorkelers will find plenty to explore in the shallow waters just offshore.

The best beaches in the Palm Beach area can be found at **John D. MacArthur Beach State Park** (10900 State Rd. A1A, North Palm Beach, 8am-sunset daily, $5). Located about 17 miles (half an hour's drive) north of central Palm Beach, the coastline is largely undeveloped, and the 2 miles of unguarded beach offer plenty of pockets of privacy—so many, in fact, that the beach was once one of the state's top nude destinations. Today, naked folks are required to be outside of the park's boundaries. There are many mangrove trails to kayak along, a nature center, and plenty of nature-watching opportunities, but the wide natural beach is the main attraction. The water is fairly calm and shallow, making it great for snorkeling, and surfers manage to find good waves as well.

Shopping
★ WORTH AVENUE

More than 200 high-end boutiques line the four-block strip of **Worth Avenue** in central Palm Beach, and for years the street has been known as the "Rodeo Drive of Florida." While some Beverly Hills residents may sniff at the comparison, the concentrated presence of Chanel, Gucci, Cartier, Louis Vuitton, Tiffany, Ferragamo, Brooks Brothers, Hermès, and other luxury brands on the avenue certainly represents a high-dollar-value density that's unrivaled in the state. The stores are almost exclusively the stomping grounds of the well-heeled. There are shops along Worth Avenue that have roots going back seven or eight decades, and the architecture is as beautiful as the goods for sale, but bargain hunters will be pretty much out of luck.

WEST PALM BEACH

Across Lake Worth in West Palm, there are a couple of other shopping options that don't require six-figure credit limits. The open-air **CityPlace** (700 S. Rosemary Ave., 561/366-1000, www.cityplace.com, 10am-6pm Mon.-Sat., noon-6pm Sun.) has dozens of chain stores like Victoria's Secret, Bath & Body Works, and more. There are more than 25 restaurants, like Cheesecake Factory and Panera, to feed hungry shoppers, and the mall frequently hosts live entertainment.

Entertainment and Events
NIGHTLIFE

West Palm Beach's historic **Clematis Street** district is the area's prime nightlife destination, with a high concentration of bars, clubs, and restaurants within three or four blocks. A recently opened 600-space parking garage at the corner of Banyan and Quadrille Boulevards makes accessing the area quite convenient, and the best way to take on an evening of club-hopping is to park and walk and then take a cab home; parking is only $1 per hour Monday-Saturday and free on Sunday.

John D. MacArthur Beach State Park

Monarchy (221 Clematis St., 561/835-6661) is part of the "Clematis Street Live" project, and is an enormous 6,000-square-foot dance club with VIP tables and a unique royals-and-castles theme that's quite unusual for a club that books high-profile house DJs. The complex offers a variety of club themes and has been a big part of the resurgence of club life in the area, but the whole thing is a bit corporate and charmless.

More independent-minded folks will likely want to head for **Respectable Street** (518 Clematis St., 561/832-1570), an institution for live music in West Palm. The big space affords national and top local bands plenty of room to spread out. When the music isn't live, the DJs tend to play classic alternative and new wave.

Other good options in the neighborhood include the craft cocktails at food-forward gastropub **The Alchemist** (223 Clematis St., 561/355-0691) and the cozy Irish pub vibe at **Roxy's** (309 Clematis St., 561/296-7699), which also boasts a rooftop bar with views to Singer Island.

At the bustling open-air CityPlace mall, there are several places to grab a drink and relax, but unless you particularly enjoy drinking in a shopping mall, the only reason to head here is for a comedy show at the **Improv** (550 S. Rosemary Ave., 561/833-1812, http://palm-beach.improv.com).

THE ARTS

The **Kravis Center for the Performing Arts** (701 Okeechobee Blvd., West Palm Beach, 561/833-8300, www.kravis.org) is a large, modern performing arts center that hosts orchestra, opera, and Broadway performances as well as smaller-scale events like writers' lectures, film screenings, and poetry readings. **Harriett Himmel Gilman Theater** (600 S. Rosemary Ave., West Palm Beach, 561/835-1408) at CityPlace also features occasional classical and jazz performances.

FESTIVALS AND EVENTS

The **Palm Beach Jewelry, Art & Antique Show** (650 Okeechobee Blvd., 561/822-5440, http://palmbeachshow.com, Feb.) takes over the Palm Beach County Convention Center every Presidents Day weekend and is one of the largest shows of its kind. More than 200 exhibitors, including art galleries and antique dealers, showcase their collections in the hope that some of the 50,000 patrons who arrive at the public viewings are ready to do some one-stop shopping.

The **Palm Beach International Film Festival** (PBIFF, various theaters, 561/362-0003, www.pbifilmfest.org, Apr.) is a fairly young film festival. But in its 12-year history it has managed to host dozens of Hollywood stars and has been the site of more than 150 world premieres. The focus of the PBIFF is on accessible indie and international fare, and though few Sundance-sized deals are cut, the reasonably priced ticket packages make it a good opportunity for film buffs to get a glimpse of what are likely to be some of the year's most interesting films.

The annual **SunFest** (downtown West Palm Beach, 800/786-3378, www.sunfest.com,

Apr./May) is one of the area's biggest outdoor festivals. For three days, multiple stages host dozens of live musical acts of varied genres that are actually a few notches above the municipal-fair level most cities can afford. There are also arts and crafts vendors, food booths, and a kids' area. Past acts included Weezer, Flo Rida, Macklemore & Ryan Lewis, the Doobie Brothers, Cheap Trick, Counting Crows, and Alice in Chains.

Sports and Recreation

SPECTATOR SPORTS

Baseball fans will find plenty to keep them occupied at **Roger Dean Stadium** (4751 Main St., Jupiter, 561/630-1828, http://rogerdeanstadium.com), the spring training home of both the **Miami Marlins** and the **St. Louis Cardinals.** Spring training tickets start at $15. During the regular season, those teams' minor-league franchises play at the stadium. Minor league games start at $8.50 per seat.

The **National Croquet Center** (700 Florida Mango Rd., West Palm Beach, 561/478-2300, www.croquetnational.com, from $30/day) hosts tournaments throughout the spring.

FISHING AND BOATING

Blue Heron Fleet (389 E. Blue Heron Blvd., Riviera Beach, 561/844-3573, www.deepseafishingflorida.com, charters from $45 pp) specializes in deep-sea fishing charters, with three large boats—75 feet, 88 feet, and 101 feet—that depart both Palm Beach Inlet and Jupiter Inlet.

Palm Beach Water Taxi (98 Lake Dr., Palm Beach Shores, 561/683-8294, water taxi from $12 pp, guided cruises from $31 pp) offers a variety of charters and guided cruises throughout the waterways in and around Palm Beach.

Canoers and kayakers will want to head a half-hour or so to explore the **Loxahatchee River,** Florida's first National Wild and Scenic River. Surprisingly undisturbed and still quite beautiful, the river is home to a gorgeous 8.5-mile paddling trail that runs from Riverbend

Park in nearby Jupiter (9060 Indiantown Rd., Jupiter, 561/741-1359) to Jonathan Dickinson State Park in Hobe Sound (164540 SE Federal Hwy., Hobe Sound, 772/546-2771). The trail takes about 5-7 hours to complete, and ranges from tight, narrow pathways and cramped mangrove swamps to more spacious tidal basins. Canoe and kayak rentals are available at both parks.

Food
PALM BEACH

Located on one of Palm Beach's most classically beautiful stretches of road, ★ **Testa's** (221 Royal Poinciana Way, 561/832-0992, www.testasrestaurants.com, 7am-10pm daily, from $19) has been serving up quality food for more than 75 years. Though you might expect such a Palm Beach institution to be steeped in white-linen formality, the restaurant manages to balance a sense of history with a welcoming and friendly atmosphere. Breakfast and lunch are both surprisingly affordable, and the portions piled up by the kitchen are incredibly generous, whether they are the enormous pancakes or omelets for breakfast or the fish sandwiches and Reubens served at lunch. Dinner fare is more in line with Palm Beach standards both in terms of selection and price, and the richly flavored pastas, expertly cooked steaks, and various Italian specialties are excellent. Be sure to try the signature ricotta-stuffed eggplant.

Inventive reinterpretations of classic dishes can be found at ★ **Café Boulud** (301 Australian Ave., 561/655-6060, www.cafe-boulud.com, 7am-11am, noon-2:30pm, and 5:30pm-10pm Mon.-Fri., 7am-2:30pm and 5:30pm-10pm Sat.-Sun., from $32). The café is the brainchild of Chef Daniel Boulud, and the Palm Beach location maintains the high standards of fresh French cuisine that defines the New York City original. Provençal traditions like potato-leek soup are presented alongside dishes like "Austrian-inspired venison," a Vietnamese-style sub stuffed with duck confit and pâté, short rib ravioli, charcuterie plates, chickpea fries, and, yes, an $18 cheeseburger.

Theoretically a diner-cum-gastropub, **Buccan** (350 S. County Rd., 561/833-3450, buccanpalmbeach.com, 5pm-11pm Sun.-Thurs., 5pm-midnight Fri.-Sat., from $12) offers a dizzying range of dishes at a similarly disorienting range of prices. If you're in the mood to splurge for a $45 Wagyu beef short rib platter with gingered spinach and corn kimchee, you can do that; or, you know, if you want a hot dog pressed in a panini with sauerkraut and Gruyère cheese for $12, you can do that too. Pastas, pizzas, salads, and even sushi dishes round out the menu, but reconceived classics like roasted brussels sprouts doused in hot-wing sauce and the aforementioned hot dog panini are far more interesting.

The pan-Asian cuisine served at **Echo** (230 Sunrise Ave., 561/803-4222, www.echo-palmbeach.com, 5:30pm-9:30pm Tues.-Thurs. and Sun., 5:30pm-10pm Fri.-Sat., from $29) is created by a crew of skillful chefs overseen by the management of the Breakers. Echo isn't in the main Breakers complex, but it shares the same high level of service and atmosphere and brings together Japanese, Thai, and Chinese favorites, none of which are truly revolutionary but all of which are prepared with considerable focus. The sushi bar here is quite popular, as is the cocktail lounge.

WEST PALM BEACH

The spacious and airy two-story dining room at **Havana** (6801 S. Dixie Hwy., 561/547-9799, http://havanacubanfood.com, 11am-11pm Sun.-Thurs., 11am-1am Fri.-Sat., from $8) is a great place to enjoy an array of authentic Cuban dishes, all of which are priced quite reasonably. The extensive menu of fresh fish and seafood plates (try the broiled whole snapper), churrasco-style skirt steak, and other beef and poultry dishes as well as a range of grilled sandwiches goes well beyond the standard fare many Cuban restaurants dish up. Fresh desserts and *café Cubano* are a great way to end a meal here.

For a somewhat more raucous Cuban cuisine experience, head a bit down the street to **Don Ramon Restaurante & Social Club**

(7010 S. Dixie Hwy, 561/547-8704, http://don-ramonrestaurant.com, 11am-10pm daily, from $11). The bar and its two-for-one happy hour are popular with the afterwork crowd, but on the weekends, things get even more fun with the addition of live music. The massive menu is impressive both for its length and for the dependability and authenticity of all the dishes on it. Even if you're just stopping in for sangria on a hot Florida afternoon, make sure to soak it up with the Bandeja Don Ramon, a sampler platter of the restaurant's appetizers with everything from plantain chips and *croquetas* to fried cod and a spicy shrimp cocktail.

Miami native Joseph Clark is the "Jo" in **Sushi Jo** (319 Belvedere Rd., 561/868-7893, www.sushijo.com, 11:30am-11pm daily, from $12), but don't let the lack of a Japanese proprietor dissuade you from exploring the food at this excellent sushi spot. The restaurant claims to make "sexy sushi for sexy people," and the hip vibe at Sushi Jo is quite friendly and cozy. Jo takes his sushi pretty seriously, and some of the more exotic pieces of sashimi can justifiably run into double-digit prices. But traditional rolls and even some of Sushi Jo's specialty rolls (like the lip-puckeringly awesome kimchi and crab roll) are priced at more down-to-earth levels.

In the Clematis Street entertainment district, there are several good dining options. The sushi at **Kabuki Sushi Thai Tapas** (308 N. Clematis St., 561/833-6349, www.kabukiwpb.com, 11:30am-11pm Sun.-Thurs., 11:30am-midnight Fri.-Sat., from $11) is excellent and fresh, and the Thai dishes are also quite good. Kabuki's tapas are an extensive selection of (mostly) Japanese and Thai appetizers that has the kitchen playing to its strengths.

If you just need a burger, make sure to hit up the appropriately monikered **Grease Burger Bar** (213 Clematis St., 561/651-1075, http://greasewpb.com, 11:30am-midnight Sun.-Thurs, 11:30am-2am Fri.-Sat., from $8). Here, you can get a ground-beef beast like the "Ron Burgundy" (topped with a mushroom/burgundy reduction and Swiss cheese). Or

choose from a decent selection of bratwurst, accompany it with a heart-stopping plate of chili-cheese fries, then wash it all down with one of several craft brews on draft.

Tucked into a thoroughly nondescript downtown building just a few blocks from the thrum of Clematis St., **The Blind Monk** (561/833-3605, theblindmonk.com, breakfast/brunch 7:30am-11am Mon.-Fri. and 9:30am-1:30pm Sat.-Sun., dinner 4pm-midnight Sun.-Thurs. and 4pm-2am Fri.-Sat., from $12) is designed more as a bar than a restaurant, and the menu's emphasis on small plates (pate, bruschetta, banh mi, roasted vegetables, and more), a well-curated cheese list, and extensive wine and beer selections reflects that. That makes the Blind Monk an excellent stop in the afternoon or early evening. However, the secret weapon here is the breakfast menu, which, though relatively pricey—a $7 plate of biscuits would have made my grandma faint—is excellent, with quinoa bowls, avocado toast, *shakshouka,* pancakes, gravlax, and more.

Accommodations
PALM BEACH

It's possible (but not probable) to stay in Palm Beach during high season without spending a fortune. The best budget option on the island is the historic **Bradley Park** (280 Sunset Ave., 561/832-7050, www.bradleyparkhotel.com, from $229 d), which was built in the 1920s as convenient accommodations for gamblers at the Beach Club casino next door. (The casino is closed; the club is now an exclusive members-only property.) The Bradley has retained much of its decades-old charm and has standard guest rooms and small studios that are surprisingly affordable (you'll shell out the big bucks for the spacious condo-style suites). Guest rooms are clean and tidy, with tasteful and classically Florida furnishings; the suites feature full kitchens.

Another good, affordable option in Palm Beach is the aptly named **Palm Beach Historic Inn** (365 S. County Road, 561/832-4009, palmbeachhistoricinn.com, from $249). Located in the heart of "downtown" Palm

Beach, it's very close to shopping and restaurants and just a block from the beach. With only 13 rooms in this Spanish Colonial building, the vibe is cozy and friendly (and pet-friendly, too; the hotel has a "house" dog!), but the historic rooms are surprisingly spacious.

Those looking to splurge on their hotel room while in Palm Beach have more than ample opportunities to do so. The most famous upscale lodging is the iconic hotel at **The Breakers** (1 S. County Rd., 888/273-2537, www.thebreakers.com, from $499 d). With marble baths, plush beds, opulent furnishings, and an absurdly high staff-to-guest ratio, the Breakers more than lives up to its photo-shoot reputation, capturing all the glamour of Palm Beach's past and present. Every imaginable amenity is available and priced accordingly, including tennis courts, swimming pools, a private beach, nearly a dozen restaurants and bars, a shopping promenade, two championship golf courses, and a spa.

Few hotels can compete with the Breakers in terms of size, and though the rest of Palm Beach's best accommodation options would be the top places to stay in other cities, in the shadow of the Breakers, it's a little hard to stand out. That has not given inferiority

complexes to hotels like the **Chesterfield** (363 Cocoanut Row, 561/659-5800, www.chesterfieldpb.com, from $249 d), **Brazilian Court** (301 Australian Ave., 561/655-7740, www.thebraziliancourt.com, from $479 d), or the **Colony Hotel** (155 Hammon Ave., 561/655-5431, www.thecolonypalmbeach.com, from $399 d). Instead, the fact that these properties charge base rates that are close to those at the Breakers, despite the fact that none of them has the range of amenities or even beachfront locations, is a prime indicator of just how opulent they are. Each of these three properties offers small-scale luxury: Brazilian Court feels like a residential complex (which it still partially is); the Colony is a European-style boutique hotel; and the Chesterfield evokes the casual elegance of old-school Palm Beach. In their own way they provide an alternative to the wide-angle excitement of the Breakers.

WEST PALM BEACH

There are considerably more affordable accommodation options in West Palm Beach than in Palm Beach. Most of them are mid-scale chain hotels, but there are some highlights. **Biba** (320 Belvedere Rd., 561/832-0094, http://hotelbiba.com, from $175 d) is a friendly

The Breakers is Palm Beach luxury at its finest.

downtown hotel that manages to mash up historic Florida charm, Zen garden vibes, mod 1960s chic, and a walloping dose of whimsy. None of the 43 guest rooms could be described as massive, but they're spacious enough, and each is individually decorated with bold colors. The hotel's wine bar is a nice touch, and the quiet pool area is a great place to sweat out last night's bottle of Syrah.

For a cozier experience, check out **Grandview Gardens Bed & Breakfast** (1608 Lake Ave., 561/515-5833, grandviewgardens.com, from $225 d), a five-room B&B located less than a mile from West Palm's central business district and a couple of blocks away from the Norton Museum of Art. The Spanish Mediterranean-style building was built in 1925, is lushly landscaped, and boasts a relaxing and quiet swimming pool area. Rooms are spacious, clean, and stylish, and free Wi-Fi covers the property; two of the five rooms here are pet-friendly. Continental-style breakfast is served daily and is included in the room rate.

BOCA RATON

The city of **Boca Raton** has long been synonymous with the idea of retirement in Florida. Maybe it's because of the high concentration of northern snowbirds who have found their way to the condominiums along the coast. Whatever the reason, the city has done little over the past few decades to dispel the stereotype. Early-bird specials dominate the dinner routine, and the nightlife is typically confined to cocktails at a hotel or restaurant lounge. Still, the natural beauty of the area is attractive no matter what your age, despite the fact that Boca Raton doesn't offer a whole lot of glitz or electricity.

Gumbo Limbo Nature Center

The **Gumbo Limbo Nature Center** (1801 N. Ocean Blvd., 561/338-1473, www.gumbolimbo.org, 9am-4pm Mon.-Sat., noon-4pm Sun., $5 suggested donation) is a small eco-education center just across the street from the ocean. Although the center is mostly used for school field trips, it offers an inexpensive half-day's worth of appealing nature walks and exhibits. There's a boardwalk through a thick coastal hammock, several large indoor saltwater aquariums with sharks and tropical fish, and a special area dedicated just to sea turtles that houses half a dozen of the large reptiles. Walking around the 20-acre park, though, is the best way to spend your time here, as the park is seldom crowded, providing a pleasant and rustic way to while away a morning.

Boca Raton Museum of Art

You may not arrive with very high expectations, but the **Boca Raton Museum of Art** (501 Plaza Real, 561/392-2500, www.bocamuseum.org, 10am-5pm Tues.-Fri., noon-5pm Sat.-Sun., $12 adults, $10 seniors, children 12 and under free), despite its location adjacent to the Mizner Park open-air shopping mall, is a very good museum. The spacious floor plan allows comfortable viewing of the permanent collection, which includes originals by masters like Pablo Picasso, Henri de Toulouse-Lautrec, and Edgar Degas, as well as a healthy assortment of contemporary artists and artifacts from West Africa and the pre-Columbian era. The museum also hosts a small number of traveling exhibits.

Beaches

The beaches at **Red Reef Park** (1400 N. Ocean Blvd.) and **South Beach Park** (400 N. Ocean Blvd.) are the most central in Boca and provide ample parking and bathroom/shower facilities. They're also often the most crowded, although it must be said that a crowded day at the beach in Boca is often far less crowded that at many other beaches along Florida's Atlantic coast. **Spanish River Park** (3001 N. Ocean Blvd.) is the largest beach area in town, but parking is somewhat limited; there are street meters in addition to a pricey public lot.

Shopping

There's a museum, a cultural center, offices, and even apartments at **Mizner Park** (327 Plaza Real, 561/362-0606, www.

Boca Raton

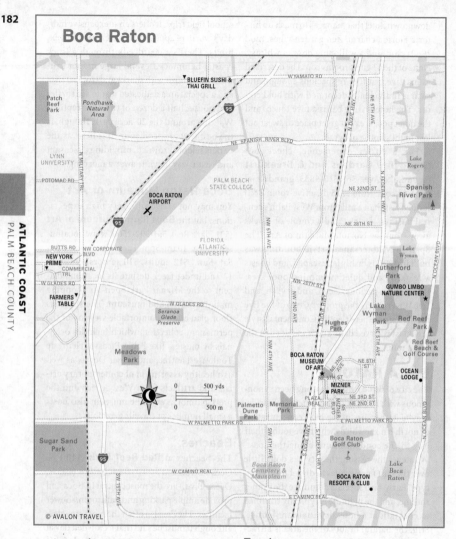

miznerpark.com, 10am-9pm Mon.-Sat., noon-6pm Sun.), but it's shopping that's the main draw here. Most of the stores are of the typical nice-mall variety, including Tommy Bahama, Les Bijoux, Mephisto, and others. But the wide-open residential-village vibe makes window-shopping those stores and other smaller boutiques a relaxing pastime. There are also a number of decent, if unspectacular, dining and drinking options available for hardcore shoppers.

Food

Located about 20 minutes due east from the beach is **Farmers Table** (1901 N. Military Trl., 561/417-5836, www.farmerstableboca. com, 7am-10pm Mon.-Thurs., 7am-11pm Fri., 8am-11pm Sat., 8am-9pm Sun., from $14), which, despite being located in a chain hotel in a pretty busy commercial area (big box stores, malls, etc.), manages to evoke a friendly, "healthy-eating" atmosphere. With a broad menu that includes breakfast, brunch, lunch, and dinner and covers a range of cuisines (everything from chicken wings and Cobb salads to cauliflower-and-brie flatbread, bison-meatball club sandwiches, and udon bowls), the overriding kitchen ethos seems to be fresh, flavorful, and (mostly) guilt-free meals.

Another restaurant that is worth the drive from the beach is **Bluefin Sushi & Thai Grill** (961 Yamato Rd., 561/981-8986, www.bluefin-sushi.com, 11:30am-3pm and 4:30pm-10pm daily, from $16) isn't the most conveniently located sushi restaurant in town, but it's certainly one of the best. The airy, stylish interior belies the strip-mall location, and the wide selection of non-sushi fare, including lobster curry, chili-drenched "volcano" shrimp, scallop curry, complements the superlative rolls and sashimi served up at the sushi bar.

New York Prime (2350 Executive Center Dr., 561/998-3881, www.newyorkprime.com, 5pm-11pm daily, from $34) is one of the Atlanta-based chain's three outlets, and the atmosphere forgoes the typically bland treatments of many chain steak houses, instead imparting a warm and comfortable sense of modern style. Thick hand-cut steaks, live lobsters, veal chops, and other steak-house staples are served in generous, expensive portions, and side dishes are of the classic steak-house variety (creamed spinach, potatoes, etc.).

Accommodations

Since the late 1920s the **Boca Raton Resort & Club** (501 E. Camino Real, 561/447-3000, www.bocaresort.com, from $329 d) has been the preferred destination for the area's many well-heeled visitors. The expansive property has done a fantastic job at maintaining its reputation for both first-class service and historical elegance. Originally built in 1926 as the Cloister Inn by Addison Mizner, a larger-than-life architect to the wealthy, the resort adheres to the "more is better" philosophy of luxury accommodations, both in terms of size (it sits on 365 acres), facilities (there are more than 1,000 guest rooms, 9 restaurant-bars, 5 pools, 18 tennis courts, a spa, a private beach, and even a marina), and service (the staff-to-room ratio is approximately 2:1). Mizner's Mediterranean revival-style architecture is still quite stunning, and all the accommodations, whether "simple" hotel-style guest rooms or private bungalows, are elegant and well-maintained. This is a Waldorf-Astoria property.

Located directly across the street from South Beach Park is the **Ocean Lodge** (531 N. Ocean Blvd., 561/395-7772, http://ocean-lodgeflorida.com, from $179 d), one of the few daily-rate beachside lodgings in Boca. There are only a dozen or so guest rooms in this motel-style accommodation, and given the supremely affordable rates, the high level of cleanliness is somewhat surprising. While the guest rooms themselves are far from modern (the TVs are a bit old, the furniture is a bit dinged), the friendly staff and excellent location more than make up for such shortcomings. For a slightly fancier guest room, be sure to book one of the recently renovated suites.

DELRAY BEACH

Often overlooked by visitors to the area, Delray Beach splits the difference between the flip-flops and sportfishing atmosphere of the Treasure Coast and the wealthy accoutrements of the rest of South Florida. The downtown area is quite charming and easily walkable, offering cafés and shopping, and the beaches here are relatively uncrowded and easily accessible. A 15-minute drive past the suburbs takes you to the Japanese pastoralism of the Morikami Gardens.

Cornell Museum of Art and History

The beautiful **Cornell Museum of Art and History** (51 N. Swinton Ave., 561/243-7922, www.oldschool.org, 10:30am-4:30pm Tues.-Sat., 1pm-4:30pm Sun., $5 donation) is located downtown in a circa-1913 elementary school building. The museum itself is somewhat small, with a few rotating displays of local history artifacts, traveling art exhibits, and an interactive children's area. The Old School complex where the museum is housed also includes the Crest Theatre in the old Delray High School and an outdoor pavilion where occasional concerts and events are held.

Sandoway House Nature Center

One of the only other non-beach sights in central Delray Beach is the **Sandoway House Nature Center** (142 S. Ocean Blvd., 561/274-7263, www.sandowayhouse.org, 10am-4pm Tues.-Sat., noon-4pm Sun., $5). The compact complex is situated just across the street from the ocean, and while the center isn't nearly as expansive as some municipal aquariums, the vibe here is friendlier and much more accessible. Geared primarily toward school groups, there's an educational bent to many of the exhibits—which are focused on marine life—but by far the most popular thing to do here is to take part in the regular shark-feeding exhibitions.

★ Morikami Museum and Japanese Gardens

About seven miles (a 15-minute drive) from downtown Delray Beach is the **Morikami Museum and Japanese Gardens** (4000 Morikami Park Rd., 561/495-0233, www.

morikami.org, 10am-5pm Tues.-Sun., $15 adults, $13 seniors, $9 children and students, children 5 and under free). The informative and spacious museum, designed to evoke a Japanese villa, is centered around an exhibit that documents the history of the Yamato Colony, a group of Japanese farmers who settled in the area in the late 19th century. The museum displays several thousand Japanese artifacts and pieces of art, including works of fine art and an enormous collection of items used in the Japanese tea ceremony. Even if you're not a Japanophile, the perfectly manicured and beautifully curated gardens on the grounds of the Morikami are certainly an appealing option. Several distinct garden areas reflect different styles of Japanese horticulture, and strolling through the bonsai, koi ponds, and pine forests is a sublimely transporting experience.

Beaches

The beaches in Delray Beach are beautiful and quite accessible. **Atlantic Dunes Park** (1301 S. Ocean Blvd.) is fairly quiet and surrounded by a wooded natural area with a boardwalk and short nature trail. The beach is fairly narrow but clean, and there are lifeguards on duty (9am-5pm daily).

Morikami Museum and Japanese Gardens

For a more social beach experience, **Delray Municipal Beach** (State Rd. A1A at Atlantic Ave.) is incredibly popular. The warm blue waters and wide sloping sandy beach bring big crowds on weekends and summer weekdays, but there's plenty of room to spread out along the 7,000 feet of beach, and paid parking is plentiful.

Food

The best places for a bite or a beer in Delray Beach are almost all centrally located along downtown's charming and pedestrian-friendly Atlantic Avenue.

The sidewalk seating and open-all-day atmosphere at **Boheme Bistro** (1118 E. Atlantic Ave., 561/278-4899, http://bohemebistro.com, 8am-11pm daily, from $7) make it one of the best places to kick back with a coffee or a glass of wine while nibbling on one of the bistro's omelets, Benedicts, healthy wraps, generous pasta dishes, or baguette sandwiches. More upscale but still casual and welcoming, the seafood-oriented ★ **City Oyster** (213 E. Atlantic Ave., 561/272-0220, 11:30am-2:30pm and 5pm-11pm Mon.-Sat., 5pm-11pm Sun., from $18) offers a number of more up-market entrées like crab-stuffed shrimp, caviar, and steaks, in addition to the expected array of raw-bar delectables.

Deemed Florida's most haunted pub by the Travel Channel, the **Blue Anchor** (804 E. Atlantic Ave., 561/272-7272, www.theblueanchor.com, 11:30am-2am daily, from $9) certainly doesn't feel ghostly, as the limited but well-chosen selection of beers combines with the airing of live soccer matches and a decent menu of pub fare to create quite a lively environment.

Out by the beach, **Caffe Luna Rosa** (34 S. Ocean Blvd., 561/274-9404, www.caffelunarosa.com, 7am-10pm daily, from $14) serves Italian cuisine in a beautiful, spacious dining room complete with strolling musicians. **Boston's on the Beach** and **Boston's Upper Deck** (40 S. Ocean Blvd., 561/278-3364, www.bostonsonthebeach.com, 11am-2am daily, from $9) are two connected but quite different dining experiences. The Upper Deck is a more upscale establishment with pricey seafood and steak dishes and beautiful views of the ocean, while Boston's on the Beach has a sports bar/casual dining atmosphere, with TVs, drink specials, and hot wings alongside pasta dishes and fried-seafood baskets.

There's also an outlet of the upscale chain **Burger-Fi** (6 Ocean Blvd., 561/278-9590, www.burgerfi.com, 11am-1am daily, burgers from $8) right at the beach, where you can grab an excellent custom burger, a craft beer, and one of the chain's renowned custards.

Accommodations

It's hard to miss the ★ **Colony Hotel & Cabana Club** (525 E. Atlantic Ave., 561/276-4123, www.thecolonyhotel.com, from $249 d), as the large 1920s structure is painted in bright shades of yellow and red, announcing its historic presence to all who pass by this Delray Beach icon. From the lobby to the guest rooms, the Colony indulges in its considerable history. The largely unaltered architecture is complemented by appropriate appointments and quite a bit of modern luxury. Although it's located in downtown Delray Beach rather than on the beach itself, the Colony offers scheduled complimentary transportation to its private cabana club, where guests can enjoy a beautiful 250-foot stretch of well-groomed private beach, changing and shower facilities, shuffleboard courts, a heated saltwater pool, and, of course, oceanfront cabanas.

For something a bit more intimate, the smaller-scale **Crane's Beach House** (82 Gleason St., 866/372-7263, http://cranesbeachhouse.com, from $219 d) offers a middle ground between bed-and-breakfast coziness and beach-town motel convenience. Crane's location a block from the beach and two blocks from buzzing Atlantic Avenue is just about ideal, and the secluded nature of the resort's design only adds to the quiet, comfortable feel. Guest rooms are bright, clean, and decorated with a bit of a tropical-heavy hand. Despite appearances, you're still in Delray, not in Key West, although the two small swimming pools, tiki bar, and courtyard area make the illusion hard to shake.

GETTING THERE AND AROUND

Palm Beach International Airport (PBI, 1000 Turnage Blvd., West Palm Beach, 561/471-7420, www.pbia.org) is the area's main commercial airport and is served by American, Delta, and United, and low-cost carriers like Southwest, Frontier, and JetBlue. The **Fort Lauderdale-Hollywood International Airport** (FLL, 320 Terminal Dr., Ft. Lauderdale, 866/435-9355, www.

broward.org/airport) is about 32 miles (1 hour) to the south.

I-95 and Florida's Turnpike both run through Palm Beach County. Getting around the area almost certainly requires a car, especially when traveling beyond the main tourist districts in Palm Beach and West Palm Beach. Heading south on I-95, Delray Beach is 21 miles and Boca Raton is 28 miles from Palm Beach and West Palm Beach.

There are also **Amtrak** stations in Boca Raton (1300 W. Hillsboro Blvd., Deerfield Beach, 954/421-1155), Delray Beach (345 S. Congress Ave., 800/872-7245), and West Palm Beach (209 S. Tamarind Ave., 800/872-7245), which are all on the Silver Service and Palmetto routes.

Treasure Coast

Named for the disproportionate number of shipwrecks that occurred off its reef-strewn shoreline, the **Treasure Coast** is a gentle segue from the shorts-and-sandals scruffiness of Florida's northern coast as you head toward the more stylish and cosmopolitan areas of South Florida. Coming from Palm Beach County, you'll first come across beach villages like Stuart and Jensen Beach. Continuing north alongside the scenic Indian River, you'll approach Fort Pierce, a town that's best known for the sportfishing activities that originate from its deep-water port. Fort Pierce is slowly but decisively recovering from decades of economic malaise. A few miles north of Fort Pierce is Vero Beach, a city that combines Old Florida charm and buttoned-down tastes.

SIGHTS
Fort Pierce

The mainland area of **Fort Pierce** struggles with economic issues, and there are parts of the city that are surprisingly dangerous. The small-town atmosphere that once made it one of the Florida coast's more livable locales is

striving to make a comeback, however, and an effort to redevelop the downtown waterfront district has yielded positive results. Stick to downtown and the beaches.

DOWNTOWN FORT PIERCE
If you're not in Fort Pierce to fish or go to the beach, the revitalized **downtown** area makes for a pleasant walkabout. Saturday mornings bring the activities of the **Downtown Fort Pierce Farmers Market** (772/940-1145, www.fortpiercefarmersmarket.com, 8am-noon Sat.) to the compact, pedestrian-friendly area near the **Fort Pierce City Marina** (1 Ave. A, 772/464-1245, www.fortpiercecity-marina.org). Visitors can stroll around and buy locally grown citrus or some of the goods offered by area artists while watching the fishing boats come in and out of the channel. The **Manatee Observation Center** (480 N. Indian River Dr., 772/466-1600, ext. 3333, www.manateecenter.com, 10am-5pm Tues.-Sat., noon-4pm Sun., limited hours July-Sept., $1, children under 6 free) is a small eco-education center located at the marina on the Indian River.

The Wreckage of the *Breconshire*

One of the Treasure Coast's most famous wrecks is the wreck of the steamer ship *Breconshire*. Captain Robert Taylor left New York City on April 25, 1894, en route to Tampa for a cargo pickup. Unfortunately, the nautical charts he brought with him were missing a vital section—the area of reefs and sandbars just beyond the shore of Vero Beach. The journey ended in disaster, with the *Breconshire* going under on the night of April 30, 1894. Today, the wreckage of the *Breconshire* is still visible from shore as a black blob in the water. The best place to see it is from the bar at the Ocean Grill (1050 Sexton Plaza, 772/231-5409, www.ocean-grill.com). However, every year on July 4 it becomes a bit easier to see as intrepid local divers make their way out to the sunken steamer to plant an American flag.

Next door is the **A. E. Backus Museum & Gallery** (500 N. Indian River Dr., 772/465-0630, www.backusmuseum.com, 10am-4pm Wed.-Sat., noon-4pm Sun., $5), a facility dedicated to the work of the man who taught most of the regional painters known as the Highwaymen. Legendary throughout Florida and American folk-art circles, the Highwaymen were mostly untrained, but adept at capturing the raw, prismatic beauty of South Florida landscapes. They were called Highwaymen because their "galleries" were typically ad hoc stands set up on the side of the road in areas heavy with tourists. If you're lucky, you may run across a Highwayman selling paintings alongside State Road A1A or US-1 in Fort Pierce, but if you don't, a stop into this gallery is essential.

Ghost-lovers should make sure to take a peek at the **Boston House** (239 S. Indian River Dr.). Although it's not open to the public except for clients of the law firm that's located inside, the house—formerly known as Cresthaven—is said to be haunted by the spirit of a woman who hanged herself in the attic. You're unlikely to see any spiritual activity, but the house itself is beautiful and is noted for its architectural blend of Georgian and neoclassical styles.

Just a few minutes out of downtown, en route to the beaches of Hutchinson Island,

A.E. Backus Museum & Gallery

is the small but worthwhile **Smithsonian Exhibit at the St. Lucie County Aquarium** (420 Seaway Dr., 772/462-3474, 500 N. Indian River Dr., 772/465-0630, www.sms.si.edu/smee, 10am-4pm Tues.-Sat., noon-4pm Sun., $4 adults, $3 children and seniors, children 3 and under free). Focused on the marine life of the nearby Indian River Lagoon and Atlantic waterways, the few exhibits here are unsurprisingly educational in nature, and the facility is staffed by a team that is friendly and knowledgeable.

NATIONAL NAVY UDT-SEAL MUSEUM

The **National Navy UDT-SEAL Museum** (3300 N. State Rd. A1A, 772/595-5845, www. navysealmuseum.com, 10am-4pm Mon.-Sat., closed Mon. May-Dec., noon-4pm Sun., $10 adults, $5 children, children 5 and under free) is very proud of the fact that it's the "only museum in the world dedicated exclusively to the elite warriors of Naval Special Warfare." The tiny museum is located in the parking lot of the popular Pepper Park beach, and would likely be of little interest to anyone without a very specific interest in the evolution of those forces, from frogmen to seals. There are a few amphibious craft in the outdoor area, and the small interior is filled with respectful remembrances of the various incarnations of the Navy's special ops teams.

Vero Beach

There are two Vero Beaches: the mainland town that boasts a cute and vaguely historic downtown area as well as sprawling suburban enclaves, and the compact oceanside attractions that are found on Orchid Island. Most visitors head straight for the beach to take in the shops and restaurants of Ocean Drive, also home to the majority of hotels. Beyond the beach there are interesting sights like the McKee Botanical Garden and the wide-open spaces of Riverside Park. There are a number of nice restaurants in downtown Vero.

DOWNTOWN VERO BEACH

There's not much in the way of sights in **downtown Vero Beach** beyond the **Vero Beach Heritage Center and Indian River Citrus Museum** (2140 14th Ave., 772/770-2263, www.veroheritage.org, 10am-4pm Tues.-Fri., free). The facilities house memorabilia and small exhibits tracing the history of the area and the citrus industry's profound impact on it. A tour won't take much more than an hour or so.

The area around 14th Avenue is tree-lined and home to lots of mid-century architecture, making for a pleasant walk. If it's shuffleboard season, you may even catch a match or two at the shuffleboard courts behind the Heritage Center.

RIVERSIDE PARK

The expansive and beautiful **Riverside Park** (Riverside Park Dr. at State Rd. 60) sits along the Indian River between mainland Vero Beach and the beaches of Orchid Island. In addition to open fields, sports facilities, playgrounds, and boat docks, the park is home to the **Vero Beach Museum of Art** (3001 Riverside Park Dr., 772/231-0707, www.vb-museum.com, 10am-4:30pm Tues.-Sat., 1pm-4:30pm Sun., $10 adults, $9 seniors, $5 students, children 17 and under and military free). The museum is housed in a large, beautiful building, and its permanent collection, primarily 20th-century American art, is somewhat small though well-curated. The park is also home to the **Riverside Theatre** (3250 Riverside Park Dr., 800/445-6745, www. riversidetheatre.com). Connected to the park by a walkway is the **Veterans Memorial Island Sanctuary,** a peaceful and reflective site dedicated to the memory of veterans from Indian River County; it's located on an island in the middle of the Indian River that was dredged specifically for this use.

MCKEE BOTANICAL GARDEN

Heading south on US-1 from central Vero Beach toward Fort Pierce, it's easy to pass right by the **McKee Botanical Garden** (350

US-1, 772/794-0601, www.mckeegarden.org, 10am-5pm Tues.-Sat., noon-5pm Sun., $12 adults, $111 seniors, $8 children, children under 5 free), but amateur horticulturists and anyone looking for a restful stroll through some astoundingly well-kept gardens would enjoy a visit.

Founded in 1929 as McKee Jungle Gardens, the site was a popular tourist attraction for decades but fell on hard times in the 1970s, when much of the original land was sold off. What was left was renovated and reopened in 2001 under a new, more pastoral-sounding name. Little of the site's ticky-tacky roadside past is left except the beautifully landscaped and lushly overgrown gardens. There are occasional exhibits, but the gardens themselves are a worthy draw, with lots of beautiful orchids, lilies, and exotic tropical plants.

BEACHES
Stuart

A relatively isolated beach experience can be had at the tiny **Fletcher Beach** (45 NE MacArthur Blvd.). The unsupervised area is preferred by anglers and low-key beachgoers. The parking lot only has seven spaces, so arrive early.

House of Refuge Beach (301 SE MacArthur Blvd.) is a decidedly unique experience, especially in Florida, due to the presence of several massive rocky cliffs that overlook parts of the 2,100-foot beach. The **House of Refuge Museum** (301 SE MacArthur Blvd., 772/225-1875, www.house-ofrefugefl.org, 10am-4pm Mon.-Sat., 1pm-4pm Sun., $8 adults, $6 children 2-12, free for children under 2) is interesting too. Houses of refuge were built in the late 19th and early 20th centuries as places for shipwrecked sailors and lonely travelers to spend the night. This particular house of refuge is Martin County's oldest building, and provided shelter for the survivors of an Italian ship whose dive-worthy wreckage is still 100 yards offshore. There is a tiny parking area here that is harrowing to pull in and out of, due to its location between two sharp curves in the road.

At the very end of the public portion of MacArthur Boulevard is **Bathtub Beach** (1585 SE MacArthur Blvd.), which is nice enough, but is often incredibly packed. This is something of a surprise given its rather out-of-the-way location. Parking here is a challenge due to the crowds and a lack of clearly defined spaces in the sandy lot. Snorkelers and skin divers will find it to be well worth the hassle once they get a few dozen yards offshore.

Fort Pierce

There are far more beachgoing options to the south, in Fort Pierce, and the beaches of Hutchinson Island are some of the best Atlantic beaches in the entire state of Florida, combining decent wave action for surfers, offshore snorkeling opportunities, and long, wide stretches of sand that can be virtually uninhabited in some spots.

The beaches at **Fort Pierce Inlet State Park** (905 Shorewinds Dr., 772/468-3985, www.floridastateparks.org, 8am-sunset daily, $6 per vehicle) are pretty much the opposite of uninhabited during the summer and on weekends, but on a late-spring weekday they provide plenty of space to stretch out. The majority of visitors come to enjoy the beach or to fish from the jetty. The 340-acre park, on the north side of Fort Pierce Inlet, is also great for hiking, biking, and bird-watching (avian aficionados should head for Dynamite Point, a former training site for Navy frogmen during World War II). The 0.5 mile of beach here is excellent and offers some of the best surfing in South Florida. There are picnic facilities, showers, and restrooms; lifeguards are on duty during summer months only.

Also popular is the public beach at **Pepper Park** (1 Ave. A, sunrise-sunset daily), with its tennis courts, picnic shelters, playground, six fishing piers, and an enormous 250-spot parking lot. Just 200 yards offshore is the wreckage of the 18th-century Spanish ship, the Urca de Lima, which is only 15 feet down, making it a popular snorkeling spot.

All along South Ocean Drive (State Rd. A1A) on Hutchinson Island, there are numerous tiny beach parks maintained by St. Lucie County. Almost all of them are little more than wide, unspoiled swaths of white sand, blue water, and a small parking lot. The best of these, and perhaps the best beach in the area, can be found at the end of the blink-and-you'll-miss-it driveway leading to **Blind Creek Park** (5500 S. State Rd. A1A, Hutchinson Island, sunrise-sunset daily). Out in the middle of nowhere, about eight miles south of Fort Pierce Inlet, the 335-foot beach has gorgeous soft, white sand that eases into shallow, warm, and blue waters. Often the only other people here will be laid-back anglers and the occasional local family, thanks both to its somewhat remote location and the fact that the parking lot only holds about 20 cars. Once you cross over the dunes on the boardwalk and survey the expanse of empty beach here, you'll wonder why you ever thought such things as lifeguards or restrooms were necessary for a perfect day at the beach.

Vero Beach

Although the town of *Vero Beach* is quite large, very little of it is actually on the beach. To get to the ocean, you have to cross from the mainland to Orchid Island. Once you're here, beachgoing options are somewhat limited. A lot of the shoreline is rough and rocky, and most of the rest is occupied by hotels and condo complexes. That leaves parks like **Humiston Beach Park** (3000 Ocean Dr., lifeguards on duty 9:10am-4:50pm daily) and the wide and comfortable **Jaycee Park** (4200 Ocean Dr., lifeguards on duty 9:10am-4:50pm daily) as just about the only areas where casual visitors can enjoy Vero Beach's beaches. Both can become rather crowded, but the long expanses of white sand at Jaycee Park provide many more places to stake out a spot.

There is also beach access in the heart of Orchid Island's business district, near **Sexton Plaza** (500-570 Beachland Blvd.), which has a parking lot that serves the beachgoing crowds as well as patrons of several local businesses.

Although this lot fills up quickly, you can often find parking less than a block away, along Ocean Drive.

ENTERTAINMENT
Nightlife

The nightlife scene along the Treasure Coast is limited and mostly consists of hotel lounges and beachside bar-and-grill locations. Down in Fort Pierce, an essential stop is the thoroughly rough-edged **Archie's Seabreeze** (401 S. Ocean Dr., Ft. Pierce, 772/461-3352, www.archiesseabreeze.com). One of the oldest biker bars in Florida, Archie's was originally just a beer shack that catered to soldiers in town for training. Today, it's a little bit larger, hosting live bands and expanded food and drink menus, but it still maintains its rustic, windblown attitude, while serving up some life-changing clam chowder.

In downtown Vero Beach, head for **Filthy's Fine Cocktails + Beer** (1238 16th St., 772/794-9512, www.drinkatfilthys.com, 2pm-1am daily), aka Filthy McNasty's, where local and regional rockers hit the stage to play for rowdy (but respectful) crowds. For something a little more sedate (and closer to the ocean), **Orchid Island Brewery** (2855 Ocean Dr, 772/205-2436, www.orchidislandbrewery.com, 2pm-10pm Tues.-Thurs., 11:30am-midnight Fri.-Sat.) offers a great selection of locally brewed beers and guest taps as well; try the citrus-infused IPAs and sours.

The Arts

There are several beautiful theaters along the Treasure Coast, and though they all schedule performances throughout the year, their calendars are packed during the winter months. **Riverside Theatre** (3250 Riverside Park Dr., Vero Beach, 800/445-6745, www.riversidetheatre.com) is located in Vero Beach's beautiful Riverside Park and has a primary auditorium that hosts touring Broadway productions and concerts, as well as a smaller black-box theater for more daring dramatic works.

In downtown Fort Pierce, the 1,200-seat **Sunrise Theatre** (117 S. 2nd St., Ft. Pierce,

772/461-4884, www.sunrisetheatre.com) is in a gorgeous 1920s-era art deco building. In its first incarnation it was the largest theater between Jacksonville and Miami; today it brings in most of the area's bigger performances, including adult-oriented pop and jazz concerts, musicals, and ballet performances.

Also dating from the 1920s is Stuart's **Lyric Theatre** (59 SW Flagler Ave., Stuart, 772/286-7827, www.lyrictheatre.com), which was originally a movie house but was redeveloped in the late 1980s to host musical performances. Today, you can see anything from a pop concert or an orchestra performance to a Broadway production.

SPORTS AND RECREATION
Spring Training

Despite still being home to "Dodgertown," the Los Angeles Dodgers no longer play their spring training games in Vero Beach, leaving the **New York Mets** as the only baseball team in the area still to be a part of the area's Grapefruit League games. The Mets, as well as their minor-league St. Lucie Mets, play at **First Data Field** (525 NW Peacock Blvd., Port St. Lucie, 772/871-2115, http://stlucie.mets.milb.com, from $7).

Water Sports

There are excellent diving and snorkeling opportunities along the Treasure Coast. **Bathtub Reef** (1585 SE MacArthur Blvd., Stuart) and **Coral Cove Park** (19450 State Rd. 707, Jupiter) are both great places to snorkel, but the expansive **Vero Beach Reef** that runs from Sebastian Inlet in the north all the way south to Fort Pierce Inlet is largely unbroken, quite close to shore, and about 0.5 mile wide. Intrepid divers can spot dozens of species of tropical fish, corals, turtles, manatees, rays, and even sharks. The best reef ledges are in the Vero Beach area, with enormous outcroppings and deep caves that provide superlative diving opportunities.

For gear, head to **Deep Six Dive & Watersports** (www.deepsixintl.com), which has locations in Vero Beach (416 Miracle Mile Plaza, 772/562-2883), Jensen Beach (3317 NW Main Ave., 772/692-2747), and Stuart (2791 SE Martin Square Corp Pwky., 772/288-3999).

For those who would rather explore marine life on top of the water, there are ample canoe and kayak routes along the Indian River/Intracoastal Waterway, with mangrove thickets, bird-watching opportunities, and lots of beautiful scenery along the way. **Indian River Kayak & Canoe** (3435 Aviation Blvd., Vero

Archie's Seabreeze

Beach, 772/569-5757, www.paddlefla.com, solo canoes and kayaks from $35 per day) can set you up with rental boats and maps.

Golf

Like the rest of Florida, the Treasure Coast has plenty of places for golfers to greet the morning sun. In Vero, the **Dunes at Sandridge Golf Club** (5300 73rd St., Vero Beach, 772/770-5000 for tee times, www.sandridgegc.com, $20-49) is one of the better public courses; it is owned by the county and offers very inexpensive greens fees. Farther south, try the **Fairwinds Golf Course** (4400 Fairwinds Dr., 772/462-4653 for tee times, www.stlucieco.gov/fairwinds, from $27) in Fort Pierce or the **Martin County Golf & Country Club** (2000 SE St. Lucie Blvd., 772/287-3747 for tee times, http://martincountygolfcourse.com, from $32) in Stuart. Both are priced to be accessible, and though they may not compare with Professional Golfers' Association (PGA) championship courses, they're reasonably challenging and quite scenic.

FOOD
Fort Pierce

Fort Pierce is not exactly a hotbed of culinary creativity, but the downtown area houses a handful of decent dining options. Near the marina, **Cobb's Landing** (200 N. Indian River Dr., 772/460-9014, www.cobbs-landing.com, 11am-10pm Sun.-Thurs., 11am-10pm Fri.-Sat., from $9) specializes in seafood dishes like lime-basted salmon and almond-crusted tilapia, as well as various meat and poultry items, while the waterfront views, small plates, and excellent wine list at **121 Tapas on the Water** (121 Melody Ln, 772/781-0943, www.121melody.com, 11am-10pm Tues.-Thurs., 11am-11pm Fri.-Sat., noon-9pm Sun., small plates from $6, entrees from $10) add up to a perfectly romantic night out. There's also a surprisingly good Vietnamese restaurant in the form of **Pho 16** (1009 Seaway Dr., 772/242-8065, 11am-9pm daily, from $10).

Out by the beach, the **Bluewater Beach Grill** (2025 Seaway Dr., 772/466-0023, www.bluewaterbeachgrill.com, 11am-10pm Sun.-Thurs., 11am-11pm Fri.-Sat., from $9) offers a nice twist on the standard beachside fare with unusual items like the Fiji Burger (a half pound of grilled ground beef with pineapple, green onions, and a soy-ginger glaze), meatloaf sandwiches, and fish tacos rounding out a menu of fried-seafood baskets, sandwiches, and raw-bar fare. Founded by a local surfer, the Bluewater has a distinctly laid-back feel and provides fast and friendly service.

Vero Beach

It shouldn't be surprising that Vero Beach has its share of high-priced, sit-down restaurants, and thankfully, places like the **Ocean Grill** (1050 Sexton Plaza, 772/231-5409, www.ocean-grill.com, 11am-9:30pm Mon.-Sat., 4pm-9:30pm Sun., from $9) and **The Tides** (3103 Cardinal Dr., 772/234-3966, www.tidesofvero.com, 4:30pm-9pm Mon.-Fri., from $16) do not disappoint. Both specialize in seafood, while the former also offers an excellent selection of prime steaks. The beachfront (and semi-casual) Ocean Grill offers perfect views of the Atlantic. While the Tides is set back a block or so from the beach, the classy dining room more than makes up for its non-oceanfront location.

For a quick and fresh lunch, **The Red Onion Eatery** (4069 Ocean Dr., 772/231-8837, http://redonioneatery.com, 10:30am-8pm daily, $6-10) is a tiny sandwich shop located directly across from the beach at Jaycee Park. A breathtakingly large menu of sandwiches, salads, and burgers is available, and everything from a simple BLT and a monstrous Dagwood sandwich to homemade potato chips is prepared to order with fresh ingredients.

On the mainland, **Avanzare Ristorante** (1932 14th Ave., 772/978-9789, www.avanzareverobeach.com, 5pm-9pm Tues.-Sat., $15-20) is a very nice dinner-only spot downtown that serves Italian dishes. Avanzare emphasizes the use of organic meat and homemade pasta, but this is definitely not a health-food restaurant as the portions are enormous and there are very few options for vegetarians.

In the downtown area there are several excellent restaurants, as well as most of Vero's international-food eateries, making a trip across the bridge from Orchid Island imperative if you want to tuck into something more than seafood or steak while you're here. **Kata** (1306 20th St., 772/564-8883, 11am-10pm daily, from $9) has excellent sushi, as well as Vietnamese and Thai dishes. **Taj Mahal Masala** (2050 11th Ave., 772/770-1120, http://tajmahalmasala.com, 11am-2pm and 5pm-9pm Mon.-Sat., 11am-2pm Sun., from $11) is friendly and has somewhat predictable Indian fare. For something a little more domestic in nature, head for the upscale-homestyle fare of **Southern Social** (1932 14th Ave., 772/205-2212, eatsouthernsocial.com, 5pm-10pm daily, from $13), where you can get shrimp and grits, chicken and waffles, dumplings, and mac and cheese as well as fusion dishes like brisket fried rice and barbeque bao buns. The best and cheapest breakfast in the area can be found at **Oslo Diner** (575 21st Ave., 772/569-1920, 7am-2pm Tues.-Sun., $3-8), a joint tucked into a corner of a strip mall. The surroundings are far from glamorous, but the friendly service, generous portions, and straightforward menu make it a great place to start the day.

ACCOMMODATIONS
Stuart

The **Inn Shepard's Park** (601 SW Ocean Blvd., Stuart, 772/781-4244, www.innshepard.com, from $175 d) is a cute, tin-roofed bed-and-breakfast located in the tiny historic downtown area of Stuart. It offers four rather frilly guest rooms that seem to be geared toward older couples.

The **Hutchinson Island Marriott Beach Resort & Marina** (555 NE Ocean Blvd., Stuart, 772/225-3700, www.marriott.com, from $249 d) is a large 200-acre resort that's right on the beach. Thirteen tennis courts, an 18-hole golf course, and a wide stretch of beautiful beach makes this property as popular with vacationing families as it is with conference-goers and deal-makers, and the decor makes a compromise between the two. Guest rooms are of decent chain-hotel-style quality and would be utterly unremarkable if not for the ocean views that many offer. The basic hotel rooms provide mini fridges and microwaves, and the one-bedroom suites offer full kitchen facilities.

Fort Pierce and Port St. Lucie

Lodging in Fort Pierce is dire, with options limited mostly to run-down motels along US-1 or freeway-hugging chain hotels. **Hutchinson Island Plaza Hotel & Suites** (1230 Seaway Dr., Fort Pierce, 772/595-0711, http://hutchinsonplazahotel.com, from $139 d) is one of the best choices in town and is located on South Hutchinson Island near the inlet and just a few blocks from the beach. There are standard hotel rooms and basic suites available. Although the guest-room decor is a bit dated, the hotel is clean and well maintained, with a small pool and hot tub area, laundry facilities, and a surprisingly copious continental breakfast buffet.

A much better option would be the ★ **Seahorse Beach Bungalows** (2502 Tamarind Dr., Fort Pierce, 877/321-5879, http://seahorsebeachbungalows.com, from $125 d), one of only a handful of by-night lodging options near the beach. This quaint, motel-style place (or, as the hotel calls it, "Key West-style") is cute and quiet. Rooms are far from fancy, but they're clean, and the entire property, which is located in a mostly residential neighborhood, is overrun with foliage and flowers. It's just steps from access to the beach.

The **Dockside Inn & Resort** (1160 Seaway Dr., Fort Pierce, 772/468-3555, www.docksideinn.com, from $89 d) is located on the water, but it's the waters of Fort Pierce Inlet, not the Atlantic. However, these suites and studios are spacious and clean, and only about 0.5 mile from the beach. Most folks who stay here are anglers who dock their boats at one of the inn's 34 slips. The Dockside offers complimentary breakfast baskets, laundry facilities, two swimming pools, and all the bait/tackle supplies you'd need for a successful day on the water.

The **Club Med Sandpiper** (4500 SE Pine Valley St., Port St. Lucie, 772/398-5100, www.clubmed.com, from $4,500 all-inclusive per couple, per week) is one of the all-inclusive giant's family-oriented resorts. The property boasts several exclusive kids' areas and daily programs designed specifically for the young ones. The 337 guest rooms range from straightforward hotel accommodations to apartment-style suites. The property has several swimming pools, a bocce ball pitch, golf, tennis, and a spa, and lessons are offered in everything from archery to in-line skating. The "beach" here is actually on the St. Lucie River.

Vero Beach

If you're vacationing in Vero Beach, you'll definitely want to stay at the beach. Along Ocean Drive there is a wide variety of accommodations to choose from. At the lower end are basic places like the **Islander Inn** (3101 Ocean Dr., 772/231-4431, from $139 d), a cute and comfortable family-owned spot across the street from the ocean. The basic accommodations are quite nice, with an airy tropical feel and a super-friendly staff. All guest rooms have mini fridges, while the efficiency apartments offer full kitchens that are perfect for extended stays.

If you want to be directly on the ocean, the **Prestige Hotel** (1526 Ocean Dr., 772/231-5218, www.prestigehotelverobeach.com, from $189 d) is a great moderately priced option, with clean and modern motel rooms, efficiencies, and small apartments. Set a bit back from the actual beach, the Prestige has a pleasant retro feel, with shuffleboard courts and tiki huts.

For something in the middle of the action (or at least what passes for action in Vero Beach), the **Driftwood Resort** (3150 Ocean Dr., 772/231-0550, www.thedriftwood.com, from $179 d) is a more centrally located beachfront "resort." From the weathered-wood exterior to the nautical theme throughout the property's interiors, it's as close to Old Florida as you're likely to get in Vero. The unique decor extends to the individual guest rooms, which range from villas and suites to regular hotel rooms. The poolside bar, called Waldo's Open Air Deck, is a great place for moms and dads to unwind in the evening as the kids splash around in the pool.

Owned by Gloria and Emilio Estefan, ★ **Costa d'Este** (3244 Ocean Dr., 772/562-9919, www.costadeste.com, from $339 d) was designed to bring "South Beach style" to the sleepy upper-crust environs of Vero Beach. While it certainly did its part, you can't help but notice just how incongruous such a stylish hotel is in this buttoned-down beach town. The property boasts an art deco-influenced white exterior that's complemented by guest rooms that are airy and modern with tile floors, contemporary bathrooms, and sleek furnishings. Wall-mounted flat-screen TVs and complimentary Wi-Fi provide the technological touches modern travelers desire, while the soft bedding and crisp linens all but guarantee a good night's sleep. It should be noted that on weekends, pool-facing guest rooms can be subject to the noise emanating from the poolside bar until late at night.

INFORMATION AND SERVICES
Fort Pierce

Part of the revitalization of Fort Pierce included the addition of the **Seven Gables House Visitors Center** (482 N. Indian River Dr., 772/468-9196, www.visitstluciefla.com, 9am-5pm Mon.-Sat., 1pm-4pm Sun., Nov.-Apr.). While the center offers the typical array of information and reservation assistance, its very location in the historic Seven Gables House makes it worth a visit even if you know your way around.

Vero Beach

The best way to get additional information on the area is from the **Indian River County Chamber of Commerce** (1216 21st

St., 772/567-3491, www.indianriverchamber.com). Although it doesn't operate a visitors center, staff members are very helpful and will send you a thick folder filled with information on request.

GETTING THERE AND AROUND
Getting There

This part of the state is notably short on airports. The small **Melbourne International Airport** (MLB, One Air Terminal Pkwy., Melbourne, 321/723-6227, www.mlbair.com), 37 miles (about a half-hour drive) north of Vero Beach, is the closest, but service is limited to a handful of connecting flights on national carriers. **Palm Beach International Airport** (PBI, 1000 Turnage Blvd., West Palm Beach, 561/471-7420, www.pbia.org) is 62 miles (about a one-hour drive) south of Fort Pierce and is served by American, Delta, and United, and low-cost carriers like Southwest and JetBlue.

I-95 and Florida's Turnpike offer the most direct routes to and through this part of the state. Vero Beach is about 100 miles (two hours' drive) southeast of Orlando, 28 miles (a half hour) north of Fort Pierce, and about 86 miles (90 minutes) north of Palm Beach.

Getting Around

I can't recommend highly enough **Indian River Drive** and the beach-hugging **State Road A1A** for north-south travels through the Treasure Coast. The former is a curving two-lane beauty that runs between Fort Pierce and Jensen Beach; it is one of the most beautiful drives in all of Florida.

The Space Coast

The construction of the Launch Operations Center at Cape Canaveral was authorized the same year—1958—that NASA was launched, and the growth of this part of Florida has gone hand in hand with the evolution of that center, now known as Kennedy Space Center. The cities along this stretch of Florida's mid-Atlantic coast have their fortunes tied inextricably to the space agency's missions. Though the area has plenty to offer in terms beach relaxation and natural beauty, it's interesting to note that much of the preservation of the natural beauty can be attributed to the security needs of NASA. Many of the Space Coast's towns feel less like hotbeds of engineering and technological progress than like military towns, so visitors expecting to see The City of the Future will be disappointed. Likewise, the cancellation of the space shuttle program and its thousands of attendant jobs has meant the area is undergoing something of an existential dilemma as it tries to reorient itself to the next space age.

TITUSVILLE AND COCOA BEACH

The sleepy town of **Titusville** is permanently intertwined with what happens at the Kennedy Space Center. Not only are NASA's operations just on the other side of the Indian River, but the beauty of the area's natural spaces, most notably the Merritt Island National Wildlife Refuge, is protected, mainly thanks to the space program's need for a security buffer. A little farther south, **Cocoa Beach** has built itself up as a tourist-friendly beach town that is more dependent on the cruise ships that come in and out of the nearby deepwater port than it is on NASA.

Merritt Island National Wildlife Refuge

Adjacent to the Canaveral National Seashore and next door to Kennedy Space Center, **Merritt Island National Wildlife Refuge** (entrance at east side of Max Brewer Causeway Bridge, Titusville, www.fws.gov/merritt-island, sunrise-sunset daily, visitor center

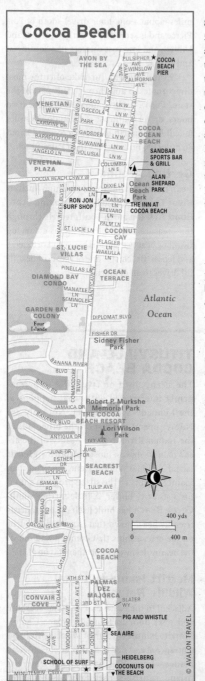

Cocoa Beach

8am-4:30pm Mon.-Fri., 9am-5pm Sat., 9am-5pm Sun. Nov.-Mar., $10 daily/vehicle, $40 annual pass) is blessed with abundant activities for hikers and nature watchers. Although there's no beach access here, the well-marked trails provide plenty of chances for spotting endangered turtles, scrub jays, or any of the other hundreds of species of birds, mammals, and plants within the refuge's boundaries. Pick up a trail map at the park gate. Strictly regulated fishing and hunting opportunities are also available. You can also access Playalinda Beach via the southern entrance to Canaveral National Seashore here.

★ Kennedy Space Center Visitor Complex

A visit to the Space Coast would be incomplete without a visit to the Space Center. The **Kennedy Space Center Visitor Complex and Astronaut Hall of Fame** (State Rd. 405 E., Titusville, 866/737-5235, www.kennedyspacecenter.com, 9am-5:30pm daily, $50 adults, $40 children; includes admission to Astronaut Hall of Fame) is as close as you'll be able to get to extraterrestrial action. NASA has translated the challenges and glory of space flight into something more than a museum and something less than a theme park. The exhibits are all about the innovative thinking that put humans into orbit. When you stand next to a full-sized rocket in one of the main exhibit halls, the effect is truly awe-inspiring. IMAX films and the daily "astronaut encounter," in which one of the 500 people who have ever flown in space shares stories and answers questions, help give visitors a real sense of the history of American space travel. The insightful guided tours of the complex and the virtual-reality launch simulator bring things to life. Although rocket launches aren't as frequent as they were during the shuttle era, if one is scheduled during your visit, you can now view them from the visitors center. Otherwise, you are still able to see the Vehicle Assembly Building, where the shuttles used to be prepared for launch, as well as the launch pads where rockets leave the earth. The shuttle program's legacy lives on in the $100 million exhibit featuring the Atlantis shuttle. KSC was one of a select number of locations to receive an actual shuttle for permanent display when the program ended. Kids also love many of the other exhibits, especially the stomach-churning reality of the launch simulator.

Cocoa Beach Pier

The **Cocoa Beach Pier** (401 Meade Ave., Cocoa Beach) has been around for decades and has become something of a tourist magnet. You can fish and relax on the beach, troll the gift shop, or wait an hour for a seat at a restaurant. All this activity in and around the pier has become a sort of rite of passage for visitors.

Beaches

Cocoa Beach does a great job at providing public beach access by spreading access locations throughout the city. There's metered parking all along Flagler Street, and there are also a number of beach parks. **Alan Shepard Park** (211 E. Cocoa Beach Causeway, Cocoa Beach) is the most centrally located and is therefore typically the most crowded. Paid

parking does little to inhibit the large influx of visitors on weekends and holidays.

For those looking for a slightly less crowded beach, head south to **Sidney Fischer Park** (4151 N. Atlantic Ave., Cocoa Beach), which is less busy but still hardly an oasis of calm. Even farther down the main drag is **Lori Wilson Park** (1500 N. Atlantic Ave., Cocoa Beach), a 32-acre park favored by locals. With an interpretive boardwalk, three pavilions, and a dog park (though no dogs are allowed on the beach), this is the place to go if being cheek-to-jowl with Orlando day-trippers isn't your idea of a pleasant day at the beach. If you go even farther south into "downtown" Cocoa Beach, there is copious three-hour street-side parking and you can walk right up Minutemen Causeway onto one of the area's best beaches.

Sports and Recreation

The relatively isolated **Savannahs Golf Club** (3915 Savannahs Tr., Merritt Island, 321/455-1377, www.golfthesavannahs.com, 7am-sunset daily, from $11 for 9 holes, from $15 for 18 holes) offers a par-72 Gordon Lewis-designed course that takes full advantage of the natural surroundings, with plenty of water hazards and a legendarily tough seventh hole. There's

Kennedy Space Center Visitor Complex

also a waterfront driving range, a practice range, and a putting green.

Red Zone Charters (1 A. Max Brewer Memorial Pkwy., Titusville, 321/302-9606, www.redzonecharters.com) runs a flats boat that's perfect for the shallow waters along Mosquito Lagoon. The small boat can only accommodate two passengers, but Red Zone's knowledge of the waters means a productive fishing day is almost certainly guaranteed. Bait and tackle are provided; food and drinks are not.

Adventure Scuba (2400 S. Hopkins Ave., Ste. A, Titusville, 321/383-1001, www.adventurescubafl.com, 8am-6pm daily) sells and services diving gear and does tank refills. They also offer scuba certification classes as well as lessons in underwater photography. Expeditions are available, but most are multiday trips outside of the immediate area.

Food and Drink

Hands down, the best place to eat (and drink) in Titusville is ★ **Playalinda Brewery's Brix Project** (5220 S. Washington Ave., Titusville, 321/567-5974, 4pm-10pm Mon.-Wed., 4pm-11pm Thurs., 3pm-midnight Fri., 11:30am-midnight Sat., 10am-9pm Sun., from $9). This is one of two Playalinda Brewing locations in Titusville; the original brewery opened in 2014 in a renovated 1910s-era hardware store in the historic downtown area (305 S. Washington Ave., 321/225-8978, 4pm-11pm Mon.-Thurs., 3pm-midnight Fri., noon-midnight Sat., noon-9pm Sun., from small plates from $5), serving small-batch on-site brewed beers and a concise menu of fresh and unique pub grub, while Brix Project opened two years later with an expanded food focus and craft cocktails. Although the menu at Brix isn't exactly expansive, at just two dozen items, it emphasizes fresh fare prepared with a unique touch; make sure you try the signature burger (locally farmed beef topped with brisket, beets, bleu cheese, and more) or the blackened red drum fish entrée. Either location will have great beer.

Dixie Crossroads (1475 Garden St., Titusville, 321/268-5000, www.dixiecrossroads.com, 11am-9pm Sun.-Thurs., 11am-10pm Fri.-Sat., from $9) is something of a love-it-or-leave-it place around these parts. Some locals contend that it's an overrated, overly busy destination restaurant more concerned with selling koozies and T-shirts than with delivering truly exceptional food. Others—me included—would fast for a week in order to make extra stomach room

Saturn V rocket model in the Kennedy Space Center Visitor Complex

for its delicious grilled rock shrimp. Those huge, succulent shrimp are what Dixie is best known for, and they are certainly delicious, especially when served with a basket of corn fritters dusted in powdered sugar. With a menu divided into "seafood" and "not seafood," the kitchen's strengths lie in frying and grilling creatures of the deep. While the knickknack-peddling is a bit wearying, and the unavoidable wait for a table can be dissuading, this place is an institution that actually deserves its must-eat-here status.

The **Sandbar Sports Bar & Grill** (4301 Ocean Beach Blvd., Cocoa Beach, 321/799-2577, www.sandbarsportsgrill.net, 11am-2am daily, from $9) is exactly what you would expect from a beachside sports bar: live music, drink specials, fried pub grub, and about a million people in line to get a table. Nonetheless, the Sandbar serves up a mighty fish taco, along with a decent selection of fresh seafood (oysters, shrimp, or crab are almost always part of a nightly special) and a fantastic view of the ocean. Likewise, **Coconuts on the Beach** (2 Minutemen Causeway, Cocoa Beach, 321/784-1422, http://coconutsonthebeach.com, 11am-11pm Sun.-Thurs., 11am-2am Fri.-Sat., from $8) is as notable for its perfect, on-the-sand location as it is for its excellent indoor/outdoor dining room and dependable (if not entirely exceptional) array of fried seafood platters.

Part British pub and part sports bar, the **Pig and Whistle** (801 N. Atlantic Ave., Cocoa Beach, 321/799-0724, www.pigandwhistlecocoabeach.com, 11am-2am daily, from $8) is extremely popular with locals, especially during football (and futbol) season. Standard English pub food—shepherd's pie, fish-and-chips, bangers and mash—is coupled with American sports bar fare like burgers and sandwiches. None of it is truly exceptional, but the atmosphere and the Ping-Pong tables make it a reliable spot for a pint and a quick bite.

For something a little more upscale and continental, head to **Heidelberg** (7 N. Orlando Ave., Cocoa Beach, 321/783-6806, http://heidelbergcocoabeach.com, 11am-10pm Tues.-Sat, 5pm-10pm Sun., from $12), which boasts a classy dining room, an extensive menu of German dishes, and an adjacent jazz club, Heidi's.

Accommodations

Cocoa Beach is pretty low-key, so don't let the name of the ★ **Surf Studio Beach Resort** (1801 S. Atlantic Ave., 4300 Ocean Beach Blvd., Cocoa Beach, 321/783-7100, www.surfstudio.com, from $135 d) fool you. This isn't a five-star, all-inclusive kind of place, but this family-owned apartment/motel-style resort is one of the friendliest and most comfortable spots in town. Owned and operated by the Greenwald family since 1948, the Surf Studio manages to maintain its rustic roots while providing clean and well-maintained lodgings beachfront. Things here aren't plush, but all of the rooms, from the most basic queen room to a one-bedroom apartment, provide kitchenettes, modern furnishings, laminate floors, Wi-Fi, and more. The sundeck and outdoor pool may make you think twice about taking the one-minute walk from your room to the beach, and that's just fine. This is one of the best places in Cocoa to spend the night or to spend a week.

With only 50 guest rooms set on a wide expanse of beach, **The Inn at Cocoa Beach** (4300 Ocean Beach Blvd., Cocoa Beach, 321/799-3460, www.theinnatcocoabeach.com, from $150 d) feels almost like a private resort. With a staff that seems to have had lots of training in personal hospitality, the inn tries hard to make guests feel at home, much like at a bed-and-breakfast. The guest rooms are priced reasonably, which means that advance reservations are a must. Most of the rooms have hardwood floors and all but a few have ocean views; the rest overlook the pool. All guest rooms have a private balcony or porch area. Airy and furnished in a panoply of different styles, the guest rooms are decidedly unique but consistently tasteful and comfortable.

Another good and inexpensive option in

Cocoa Beach is the **Sea Aire** (181 N. Atlantic Ave., Cocoa Beach, 321/783-2461, www.seaairemotel.us, from $90 d), which offers clean and decent motel-style accommodations at reasonable rates. The Sea Aire is near downtown, but is a beachfront property.

Lodging options are pretty limited in Titusville. Your best choice is the cute and tidy **Casa Coquina Bed & Breakfast** (4010 Coquina Ave., 321/268-4653, www.casacoquina.com, from $99 d), a nine-suite house with great views of the Indian River. It's a couple of miles south of central Titusville. But it's location right off US-1 means that it's an easy drive to get to Kennedy Space Center, Canaveral National Seashore, and Cocoa Beach.

Getting There and Around

Titusville and Cocoa Beach are about 33 miles (45 minutes) away from each other, separated by the east-west toll road State Road 528 (a.k.a. The Beachline), which is the quickest and most direct route to Orlando's airport and theme parks. FL-50 runs east-west across the entire state and terminates just south of Titusville; it's the best way to get to downtown Orlando.

From Cocoa Beach, it's about 23 miles (35 minutes) south to the **Melbourne International Airport** (MLB, One Air Terminal Pkwy., Melbourne, 321/723-6227, www.mlbair.com), which has daily service via Delta Airlines. Sixty miles (one hour) west of Cocoa are Orlando's attractions, theme parks, and **Orlando International Airport** (MCO, One Airport Blvd., Orlando, 407/825-2001, www.orlandoairports.net). The most convenient airport to Titusville is either Orlando's (about 40 miles or an hour west, via SR-528) or **Daytona Beach International Airport** (DAB, 700 Catalina Dr., Daytona Beach, 386/248-8069, www.flydaytonafirst.com), which is approximately 50 miles (an hour) north, via I-95.

A car is absolutely necessary in both cities because public transportation is quite limited.

NEW SMYRNA BEACH

Of all the towns along the Space Coast, **New Smyrna Beach** is the one that feels considerably less beholden to the presence of NASA. Still, the area's preeminent natural site, the Canaveral National Seashore, would unlikely be in such a great state of pastoral preservation were it not for its role as a buffer zone for the activities farther south at Cape Canaveral. The city of New Smyrna Beach (pronounced "New Suh-murna") combines beach-town mellow with occasional flashes of classy savoir-faire, making it one of the most attractive towns on Florida's mid-Atlantic coast.

★ Canaveral National Seashore

One of the best national parks in Florida, **Canaveral National Seashore** (visitors center at 7611 S. Atlantic Ave., New Smyrna Beach; southern entrance at 212 S. Washington Ave., Titusville, 386/428-3384, www.nps.gov/cana, 6am-6pm daily Nov.-Feb., 6am-8pm daily Mar.-Oct., $10/vehicle) is something of a unique experience. Combining isolated and near-meditative beaches, an expansive wildlife sanctuary, legendary fishing spots, and extensive hiking trails, Canaveral is a geographical snapshot of what Florida once was and a haven for those longing for an outdoors adventure. That it directly abuts NASA's Kennedy Space Center makes it kind of weird. The land on which Canaveral sits was purchased on the cheap (it was sparsely populated and of little agricultural value) as a buffer zone for the aeronautical activities at the space center. Soon, however, the area's biodiversity and unspoiled beaches became a point of pride in the region. Although quite a few people pass through the gates during the summer, even the busiest day at Canaveral never feels crowded. Whether making your way to Mosquito Lagoon for some fishing or sneaking off to the unofficial nude beach at the northern end of Playalinda Beach, the thing that impresses most about Canaveral is just how spacious and calming it is.

BEACHES

There are two easily accessible beach areas at Canaveral National Seashore. **Playalinda** is located at the southern end of the park, and this is the beach you'll encounter if you enter the park via Titusville. There are 13 parking areas, each of which has rudimentary toilet facilities, trash and recycling containers, and boardwalks to cross over the dunes. **Apollo Beach** is accessed via the northern entrance to the park on State Road A1A in New Smyrna, and has parking lots, fishing docks, restrooms, and concessions available at the visitors center. Between the two primary beaches is **Klondike Beach,** which is only accessible on foot or by boat. Needless to say, Klondike tends to be far less crowded, and, in fact, the southern part of Klondike just past the northern edge of Playalinda has for years been an informal and illegal nude beach.

HIKING TRAILS

There are half a dozen hiking trails around the park, all of which are brief, fairly easygoing, and well marked. The **Turtle Mound** trail is one of the best, as it not only winds through tidal flats and Mosquito Lagoon but also contains several shell mounds left by Timucuan Indians.

SCENIC DRIVES

Many visitors opt to drive along **Black Point Wildlife Drive,** a six-mile route that takes in marshland, wildlife, and slash pine copses. The drive takes about 40 minutes. Your best chance at wildlife sightings is 1-2 hours after sunrise and 1-2 hours before sunset.

FISHING AND BOATING

There are seven launch sites within the refuge that give boaters access. Most (five in the north, one in the south) provide access to Mosquito Lagoon. The launch at Haulover Canal gets you into the Indian River. Fishing is permitted in much of the park, although it is strictly regulated.

HUNTING AND CAMPING

Being a designated wildlife refuge, hunting is heavily restricted in Canaveral, but permits can be obtained seasonally for bagging migratory waterfowl. Primitive camping is allowed year-round on several islands in the park but nowhere in the refuge.

Flagler Avenue

New Smyrna Beach's historic downtown area along **Flagler Avenue** is touristy and adorable. While it has a requisite number of

Canaveral National Seashore

tchotchke dealers, it also boasts a lot of vintage buildings, easy beach access, and a variety of locally owned businesses. Bars like **Peanuts** (421 Flagler Ave., 386/423-1469, 11:30am-2am daily) and restaurants like **Flagler Tavern** (414 Flagler Ave., 386/402-8861, http://flagler-tavern.com, 11:30am-2am daily) are institutions, while the arts and clothing stores like **TaDa Gallery, Wild Side Beach & Surf,** and **Beachside Candy Company** make for a pleasant afternoon stroll. The district comprises about three blocks along Flagler Avenue.

Marine Discovery Center

The **Marine Discovery Center** (162 N. Causeway, 386/428-4828, www.marinediscoverycenter.org, 2-hour ecotours $29 adults, $26 seniors and students, $13 children, children under 4 free) is a nonprofit environmental education organization that primarily focuses on research and providing curriculum-based tours for school groups. Visitors to the area can also take advantage of a selection of ecotours. Although the big pontoon boat the center uses isn't the most pastoral transportation for a voyage through the lagoon backwaters, the knowledgeable guides help ensure a revelatory look at the wildly beautiful ecosystems in the estuary. For a quieter adventure, the center also provides kayak rentals and guided kayak tours.

New Smyrna Museum of History

The surprisingly large **New Smyrna Museum of History** (120 Sams Ave., 386/478-0052, www.nsbhistory.org, 10am-2pm Tues.-Sat., free) focuses on the various waves of inhabitants who called this area home. The few exhibits are well curated and adequately explained, giving visitors a sense of the area's evolution from the early Timucuan settlements and colonial-era explorers all the way through the 20th century. Of note is the attention given to the Turnbull Colony; in 1768, it was the largest settlement in America, and the museum

provides a good look at what life for those early settlers was like.

Bob Ross Art Workshop and Gallery

OK, sure, the **Bob Ross Art Workshop and Gallery** (757 E. 3rd Ave., 386/423-4346, http://bobrossartworkshop.com, 10am-6pm Mon.-Sat., free) is an art shop in a strip mall. But the smiling, soft-spoken man who taught so many PBS viewers on The Joy of Painting called New Smyrna Beach home when he died in 1995, and this official gallery of his work still functions as a working studio, where aspiring painters can come to learn. Classes are in full-day and half-day increments, and at the end of every Make It, Take It class, students have a finished painting they can show off to friends and family. The vibe is appropriately laid-back and commercial; guests can buy an array of branded supplies and prints.

Food

I love the ★ **Spanish River Grill** (737 E. 3rd Ave., 386/424-6991, www.thespanishrivergrill.com, 5pm-10pm Tues.-Thurs., 5pm-10:30pm Fri.-Sat., from $18) and have frequently driven an hour just to dine here. It may not seem exceptional at first: It's located in a strip mall, the prices are a little steep, and the menu is not all that unusual for the region. But there's a distinctly convivial atmosphere at the Spanish River Grill, one that encourages guests to relax and actually savor their meals. The rustic Spanish and Portuguese dishes prepared by chef Henry Salgado are exceptional and inventive, with an emphasis on strong, earthy flavors and no unnecessary filigree. An extensive wine list is perfectly complementary to the menu.

While seafood joints are about as easy to find as a T-shirt shop in the New Smyrna area, it's worth noting that the best casual dining experience in town is actually a couple of miles away from the beach. **NSB Sea Shack** (491 E. 3rd Ave., 386/428-8850, www.nsbseashack.com, 11:30am-10pm Mon.-Fri., 11:30am-11pm Sat.-Sun., from $11) offers a large outdoor dining area overlooking the marsh and an equally substantive indoor dining room. Look up and you'll see goldfish swimming around a see-through tube that circumnavigates the outdoor dining area. The brightly painted and playful environment disguises a frenetic kitchen. In addition to the expected fried seafood platters, NSB also has excellent calamari, steamed clams, crab cakes, pizza fresh from the wood-fired oven, and hot wings.

Offering a somewhat more sophisticated seafood environment, **Norwood's** (400 E. 2nd Ave., 386/428-4621, www.norwoods.com, 11:30am-10pm daily, from $15) 60-year history has afforded it iconic status in the area. The restaurant, however, doesn't have the feel of an institution resting on its laurels; the menu here is kept current, and the adjacent wine shop ensures that an excellent selection of interesting wines and beers are available. (Norwood's is one of very few restaurants in this part of the state that offers wine and beer flights with meals.) Norwood's specializes in crab legs and fresh wild-caught fish. Of course, fresh fish and seafood are the main draw, but corn-fed Black Angus steak is also a substantial part of the menu. Pasta dishes and salads are also available.

Blue crabs, oysters, and clams are the specialties at ★ **J.B.'s Fish Camp** (859 Pompano, 386/427-5747, www.jbsfishcamp.com, 11:30am-9:30pm daily, from $6), a rustic and raucous seafood joint located just a few miles south of the main action in New Smyrna. J.B.'s offers up dozens of variations of these, as well as pretty much any other edible aquatic creature you can think of, along with beef and poultry dishes and, somewhat incongruously, a bit of German fare. Sandwiches, ice-cold beer, and a great view of the Intracoastal Waterway make it a fine place to while away an afternoon. On the weekends, there's live music outside. But be warned: If there's a band playing, beer prices go up.

If you've had your fill of seafood, head for **Mon Delice French Bakery** (557 E. 3rd Ave., 386/427-6555, www.mondelicebakery.net, 8am-6pm daily, from $5), which also serves breakfast and lunch. Its menu is slightly limited and not terribly Francophile, with a couple of quiches and an egg sandwich for breakfast and a half-dozen sandwiches for lunch. But these few items, combined with a great selection of freshly baked French pastries and top-notch bread, are enough for pre-beach picnic-basket-filling.

Accommodations

Most visitors to the New Smyrna area opt for renting a beachside condominium rather than staying in a hotel. Although hotels are plentiful, they're thoroughly outnumbered by condos, especially along the beach. Quite a few properties are only offered on a monthly basis, but weeklies are available from **Ocean Properties** (386/428-0513, www.oceanprops.com, beachfront condos from $725/week); **RentCondos** (www.rentcondos.com, beachfront condos from $550/week) is a site used by individual New Smyrna condo owners to list their properties.

For a more homespun and personal environment, the 15-room ★ **Night Swan Bed & Breakfast** (512 S. Riverside Dr., 386/423-4940, www.nightswan.com, from $189 d) is a good choice. The Night Swan is in the tiny historic district and has a fantastic view of the Intracoastal Waterway. The three-story home was built in 1906 and is appropriately decorated in period-specific furnishings. The upstairs Captain's Suite is spacious, with two queen beds and a picture window overlooking the Intracoastal Waterway. As with many historic homes in the area, the expansive front porch here is a big draw.

The 21 wood-paneled guest rooms at the tiny **Seahorse Inn** (423 Flagler Ave., 386/428-8081, www.seahorseinnflorida.com, from $75 d) don't appear to have been updated in at least a couple of decades. This inexpensive motel offers decent enough budget accommodations right across the street from the beach, but they're definitely "budget." A far better—and slightly more expensive—option for beachside lodgings would be the **Islander**

Beach Resort (1601 S. Atlantic Ave., 800/831-1719, www.islanderbeachresort.com, from $90 d), a large, but friendly, 114-room resort with studios and one- and two-bedroom suites, all of which have full kitchens. While the rooms are somewhat small and the furnishings a bit dated, they're clean and well-maintained.

Getting There and Around

The coastal area of the town of New Smyrna Beach is located about seven miles (15 minutes) east of I-95 on State Road 44. Daytona Beach is about 24 miles (30 minutes) north of New Smyrna. Public transportation exists in the form of the Votran bus system (386/943-7033, www.votran.org), but visitors may find it somewhat inscrutable due to its locals-focused, indirect routes. It's far more optimal to rent a car and make your way to all the nearby sights.

Daytona Beach

If you're coming to Daytona Beach, it's likely for one of three reasons: a visit to the beach, a National Association for Stock Car Auto Racing, better known as NASCAR, race, or to show off your motorcycle during Bike Week. Daytona has an international reputation as a tourist-friendly destination and what seems like an endless array of bars and trinket shops.

SIGHTS
Daytona International Speedway

Because there can't be a stock car race every day or even every month, the **Daytona International Speedway** (1801 W. International Speedway Blvd., 386/681-6800, www.daytonausa.com) offers tours of the legendary race track throughout the year. The raceway used to be home to the *Daytona 500 Experience,* an interactive museum/tourist attraction dedicated to NASCAR, but the Experience closed in 2010 due to poor attendance. Some of the museum items remain in the lobby areas of the Speedway and are open to the public for free photo-ops, but the main draw on non-racing days are the behind-the-scenes tours. The **Speedway Tour** (11:30am, 1:30pm, 3:30pm, and 4pm daily, $18 adults, $12 children) is a half-hour, narrated tram tour around the Speedway, giving visitors a decent overview of how deeply Daytona and NASCAR's histories are intertwined. On the hourly **All Access Tour** (10am-3pm daily, $25 adults, $19 children), you get an additional 60 minutes of walking around pit areas, garages, and various other drivers-only sections. For hard-core fans, there's also the three-hour **VIP Tour** (1pm daily, $52, reservations recommended), which is more personalized and considerably more in-depth. True gearheads can undertake the **Richard Petty Driving Experience** ($135), which puts them in the passenger seat as a professional driver takes you out for three laps around the track. Well-heeled hard-core fans can actually get behind the wheel of a race car for 8, 16, or 24 laps around the track ($549-2,199). Specific tour dates depend on track availability, so call ahead.

Museum of Arts and Sciences

While certainly not substantial enough to build a trip around, the **Museum of Arts and Sciences** (352 S. Nova Rd., 386/255-0285, www.moas.org, 9am-5pm Mon.-Sat., 11am-5pm Sun., $12.95 adults, $10.95 seniors and students, $6.95 children, children 5 and under free) is a cute, populist institution. Permanent exhibits built around Cuban art and Florida history are augmented by visiting exhibits that range from Egyptian mummies to Barbie dolls. The oddly immersive and deeply nostalgic Root Family Museum exhibit features a hodgepodge of toys, race cars, Coca-Cola memorabilia, and even a

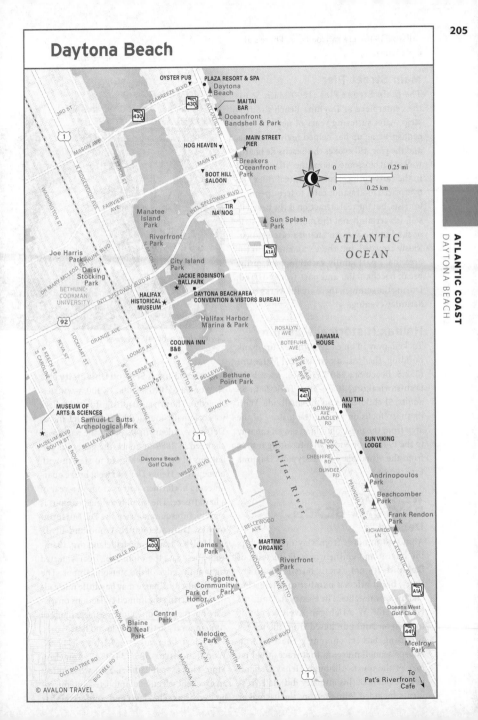

full-size 1940s-era railroad car. There's also a planetarium.

Main Street Pier

The **Main Street Pier** (1200 Main St.) is the centerpiece of Daytona Beach's tourist strip. After suffering years of neglect, a recent sprucing up has helped revive the area, and the pier still evokes the beachside boardwalks that blossomed along the Atlantic coast in the early 20th century. Carnival rides and overpriced food stands cater to free-spending tourists, but the real attraction is the beach itself. It's certainly not the most relaxing strip of sand in the area; in fact, it's often ridiculously crowded, but there's an energy to the area that's part family vacation, part spring break bacchanalia, and part Coney Island. During the summer, there are fireworks every Saturday evening.

Halifax Historical Museum

Tucked away in an early 20th-century bank building, the **Halifax Historical Museum** (252 S. Beach St., 386/255-6976, www.halifaxhistorical.org, 10am-4pm Tues.-Sat., $5 adults, $1 children) is on the small side. With its sharp focus on tracing the history of the area from the pre-Columbian era all the way to the 1940s, it provides an interesting respite from the visual blare of the typical Daytona experience.

WEST OF DAYTONA BEACH
DeLand

About 40 minutes from Daytona Beach is the quaint and eminently walkable city of **DeLand**. It's not exactly bursting with activity, but it offers a number of interesting and historical sights. The **Henry A. DeLand House** (137 W. Michigan Ave.) was built in 1886 on land purchased from the town's founding father; currently the building houses a small museum that traces the history of the town. Although Henry DeLand never lived here (his attorney did), later residents included John Stetson, the hatmaker

Daytona International Speedway

whose name graces **Stetson University** (421 N. Woodland Blvd., 386/822-7100, www.stetson.edu). The private Baptist-affiliated college was originally founded by Henry DeLand as DeLand Academy in 1883, but the name was changed in 1889 to honor the generous donations of Stetson, who had to step in with money after Henry DeLand went broke guaranteeing his farmers' citrus crops in a year of a hard freeze. The small tree-lined campus is both picturesque and friendly. The **Museum of Art, DeLand** (600 N. Woodland Blvd., 386/734-4371, www.moartdeland.org, 10am-4pm Tues.-Sat., 1pm-4pm Sun., free) is located right at the edge of the Stetson campus. The small museum's name may be a little misleading considering the limited collections on display, but there are often interesting exhibits of contemporary artists to be found here.

Grab a beer at **The Abbey** (117 N. Woodland Ave., 386/734-4545, 4pm-1am Mon.-Thurs., 4pm-2am Fri.-Sat.), which offers an excellent selection of imported and microbrewed beers. The classy and comfortable bar

NASCAR!

Beginning with **Speedweeks** in late January and wrapping up with the **Daytona 500** in mid-February, the **Daytona International Speedway** is where the NASCAR season kicks off every year. This is appropriate considering that NASCAR was born in a bar on Daytona Beach. Although the city had a storied history of car-racing on the beach, it wasn't until race promoter and beach track owner Bill France Sr. collaborated with drivers and car owners in 1948 to create a sanctioning body that codified rules and prize purses for races. In 1953, France put plans in motion to build the Daytona International Speedway, which opened in 1956 with the first running of the Daytona 500. Daytona is still considered one of the two most important racing cities in the United States, with the area around Charlotte, North Carolina, being the other.

NASCAR races only happen during the two weeks around the Daytona 500, when five other races are held, and around July 4, when the **Coke Zero 400** and the **Subway 250** occur. The month of March has a clutch of motorcycle races in conjunction with the legendary **Daytona 200**. A flotilla of RVs rolls into town, and nearly every hotel is booked to capacity, with more than 160,000 fans filling the raceway stands and many thousands more spilling over into Daytona bars to watch the race. It's festive, to be sure. For visitors disinterested in stock-car racing, the first couple of weeks in March are a good time to avoid Daytona.

area is a great place to get a lesson in Belgian ales. The sidewalk tables provide an ideal setting to relax and watch small-town DeLand slowly roll by.

Also worth exploring is **DeLeon Springs State Park** (601 Ponce DeLeon Blvd., DeLeon Springs, 386/985-4212, www.planetdeland. com, 8am-sunset daily, $6/carload up to 8 people). Although recreation areas pop up around many of Florida's natural springs, there is none that can claim what DeLeon Springs can: a restaurant where you can make your own pancakes at your table. The dining at the **Old Spanish Sugar Mill and Griddle House** (386/985-5644) is probably as much a draw for visitors as the 72°F waters. The waiters bring batter made from stone-ground grains to your griddle-equipped table, and you just add the fruit, chocolate chips, peanut butter, or whatever else you need to make the

the Old Spanish Sugar Mill and Griddle House

just-perfect pancake. Of course, activities in the large recreation area are a draw as well, but like many such developed swimming springs, the atmosphere is more like a public pool than a dip into nature's mystery. For that, there are ecotours and canoe or kayak rentals that will get you back into the Lake Woodruff National Wildlife Refuge, home to dozens of bird species and ample fishing opportunities.

Cassadaga

Less than 10 minutes away from DeLand is the community of Cassadaga, also known as the Psychic Center of the World. Such a title isn't bestowed idly, and Cassadaga more than lives up to, and trades off, its reputation as a home of spiritualists, psychics, mediums, and healers. **The Cassadaga Spiritualist Camp** (1112 Steven St., Cassadaga, 386/228-2280, www.cassadaga.org) traces its history back to the 1875 arrival of George P. Colby, a New Yorker who traveled around the country impressing people with his various healing and clairvoyant powers. Guided to this part of Central Florida by Seneca, his Native American spirit guide, Colby established the spiritualist community at Cassadaga in 1894. Today, the 57-acre "camp" (there is no actual camping here) is home to a few hundred permanent residents but sees a near-constant influx of true believers, curious onlookers, and folks just looking for a little spiritual comfort. Healers and mediums will analyze and attempt to correct your spiritual and physical ailments—for a price, of course. It looks just like a regular little community with some turn-of-the-20th-century buildings, houses, and shops, except as any one of the camp's residents will tell you, there's always more than meets the eye.

Mount Dora

The primary attraction in **Mount Dora** is its quaint village atmosphere. The gentle inclines of the town's downtown streets are about as close to "hilly" as one is likely to get in Central Florida, and they don't pose any challenge to the flocks of antiques-shoppers and casual strollers who descend on the town every weekend to take in the small-town vibe.

Sights

The cute **Inland Lakes Railway** (150 W. 3rd Ave., departures every 2 hours 11am-5pm Sat., $12 adults, $10 seniors, $8 children) gives visitors an opportunity to take a brief 75-minute ride on the Mount Dora Champion from the downtown train station, along the banks of Lake Dora, and into the nearby town of Tavares; the train then turns around and comes back.

Captain Doolittle's Eco-Tours (dock across from the Lakeside Inn, 352/434-8040, 10am and 2pm Mon.-Fri., 11am and 2pm Sat.-Sun.) boasts guides who know the local waters well, and you'll be able to spot a variety of wildlife along the banks, ranging from alligators and turtles to hawks, eagles, and other birds.

Shopping

Most visitors make their way to Mount Dora for one of two reasons: They either want to soak up the old-timey vibe or they seek bargains at the many antiques shops and boutiques.

The first stop most shoppers make is actually a mile or so outside of downtown Mount Dora, but **Renninger's Vintage Antique Center and Farmer's & Flea Market** (20651 US-441, 352/383-3141, flea/farmers market 8am-4pm Sat.-Sun., antique center 10am-4pm Fri., 9am-5pm Sat.-Sun.) has been drawing weekend bargain-shoppers from Central Florida and beyond for decades. The 117-acre property hosts two separate facilities, one an expansive (antiques mall and the other an even more expansive flea market-cum-farmers market. When at Renninger's it feels as if you could buy nearly anything on earth imaginable, from fresh produce and dollar-store castoffs to dusty electric organs and art deco furniture. The crowds (and parking) can be intense, but serious shoppers won't want to miss it.

While there are dozens of unique stores

situated within the gorgeous, walkable downtown area, no single shop sums up the quaint adorability of Mount Dora more succinctly than **Piglet's Pantry** (400 N. Donnelly St., 352/735-9979, 10am-5pm Mon.-Sat., 11am-5pm Sun.), a bakery dedicated to dog treats. If the offerings at the Pantry strike you as too specific, the 12,000-square-foot **Village Antique Mall** (405 Highland St., 352/385-0257, 10am-6pm daily) is home to the wares of more than 80 local antiques vendors.

If you're in need of liquid refreshment but still want to shop, **Maggie's Attic** (237 W. 4th Ave., Suite 2, 352/383-5451, 10am-5pm Sun.-Thurs., 10am-9pm Fri.-Sat.) is part beer and wine bar, part antiques store.

Food

Mount Dora's historic and decidedly unhip downtown district is home to one of the best and most interesting restaurants in Central Florida, ★ **1921 by Norman Van Aken** (142 E. 4th Ave., 352/385-1921, lunch: 11:30am-2pm Wed.-Sun., dinner: 5pm-9pm Tues.-Sun., lunch entrees from $11, dinner entrees from $19). Founded by James Beard Award-winner Norman Van Aken (who, since his start four decades ago in South Florida, has received international acclaim for his Florida-focused food innovations), 1921 goes for a somewhat rustic, Old Florida vibe that's almost casual, which may surprise those who are familiar with the fine-dining milieu Van Aken is most known for. However, just because the atmosphere is a bit more relaxed, the menu is still quite a splurge, but it's not only worthwhile, but practically essential for all foodies, as it takes "locavore" to new heights, focusing not just on locally sourced seafood, produce, and livestock, but on preparations that are essentially Floridian, reflecting the diverse multiculturalism of the state. Although the menu changes frequently, expect to find chili peppers, oysters, fresh fish, plantains, and other Van Aken staples somewhere on the menu.

The Beauclaire (100 N. Alexander St., 352/383-4101, 7am-10pm Mon.-Sat., 7am-2:30pm Sun., main courses from $19) acts as the main dining room at the Lakeside Inn, but its Southern charm and easy elegance make it a local favorite. The traditional American fare of steaks, chops, and poultry is far from adventurous, but the sunset views are tough to beat.

The fresh salads and piled-high sandwiches draw a lunch crowd to the **Goblin Market** (330 Dora Drawdy Way, 352/735-0059, lunch 11am-3pm Tues.-Sat., noon-4pm Sun., dinner 5pm-9pm Tues.-Thurs., 5pm-10pm Fri.-Sat., main courses from $10), but it's the European-inspired dinner menu—escargot, shrimp, and scallop fra diavolo, Gouda-stuffed chicken breast—that's worthy of a late-evening look. The dark and labyrinthine dining room feels more like a quirky salon than a four-star restaurant.

Accommodations

The large **Lakeside Inn** (100 N. Alexander St., 352/383-4101, www.lakeside_inn.com, from $639 d) overlooks Lake Dora and boasts a century-plus history to go along with its commanding views. In addition to historic guests like Thomas Edison and Calvin Coolidge, one of the oddest visitors to the hotel was an elephant brought in and trained to water-ski for a scene in John Schlesinger's 1981 film *Honky Tonk Freeway*. While some of the 86 guest rooms justifiably (and literally) creak with age, the vintage charm of the Inn is undeniable and irresistible to the antiques shoppers who descend on Mount Dora.

The six-room **Simpson's Bed & Breakfast** (441 N. Donnelly St., 352/383-2087, www.simpsonsbnb.com, from $150 d) is in the heart of downtown Mount Dora. There are two three-room suites and four two-room suites; all the suites have mini kitchens and are decorated simply. The B&B is within 2-3 blocks of almost everything Mount Dora has to offer.

Getting There and Around

Mount Dora is about 30 miles (an hour's drive) southwest of DeLand via scenic State Road 44.

Coming from Orlando, the 27-mile, 45-minute drive on U.S. 441 will take you through some of Orlando's bland suburbs before the rolling hills of Apopka and Zellwood put you in an appropriately rural mood.

Part of the joy of visiting Mount Dora is simply walking around and exploring the downtown area, but for those less inclined to wear out the soles of their shoes, guided tours can be had via **Segway of Central Florida** (140 W. 5th Ave., 352/383-9900, 1-hour tours $48) or the **Mt. Dora Trolley Co.** (departs from Lakeside Inn hourly 11am-2pm daily, $13 adults, $11 children).

BEACHES

There are surprisingly few delineated beach parks in Daytona. But as befitting a town with the word beach in its name, there's still plenty of sun and sand to be found. At low tide, the beach can be up to 500 feet wide, and despite the fact that hotels and condos loom over most of it, there are no private beaches in Daytona—only private parking.

Those looking for large crowds should head for the area around **Main Street Pier** (1200 Main St.) or **Sun Splash Park** (611 S. Atlantic Ave.), which features an interactive water fountain that's sure to keep the young ones entranced, as well as a playground, restrooms, and showers. More relaxed spots can be found closer to the less-dense areas near Daytona Beach Shores and other points south. There are more than 1,000 public parking spaces near the beach. In Daytona Beach proper, your best bet is to head for **Ora Street Park** (800 Ora St., near the Daytona Beach Bandshell), which is reasonably accessible and often uncrowded. In Daytona Beach Shores, **Frank Rendon Park** (2705 S. Atlantic Ave.) has almost 150 parking spots, a playground, and picnic and restroom facilities.

ENTERTAINMENT AND EVENTS
Nightlife

From the busy biker joints on Main Street and the shot bars booming out dance music until early in the morning to the cavalcade of strip clubs and package-store lounges, the nightlife scene in Daytona Beach isn't going to win any awards for elitism or innovation anytime soon. When it's race week, Bike Week, or spring break, drinking in Daytona becomes something of a competition, so expect rowdy crowds. Most other times, the locals are begrudgingly accommodating. Regardless of the time of year, you'd have to work pretty hard to go thirsty in Daytona.

As the sign at the **Boot Hill Saloon** (310 Main St., 386/258-9506, www.boothillsaloon. com, 11am-2am daily) reads, "It's better to be here than across the street." Across the street is the Pinewood Cemetery, and as any of the riders who pull up their motorcycles to this legendary biker bar will tell you, Boot Hill has plenty to remind folks that they are indeed still among the living. With bartenders that manage to be simultaneously gregarious and no-nonsense, an atmosphere that's somewhere between the Wild West and back-alley speakeasy, and a clientele that's half bikers and half gawkers, Boot Hill isn't quite as rough-and-tumble as its reputation. But the crowds, especially during Bike Week, are legendarily rowdy. As evidenced by the voluminous T-shirt and shot glass souvenirs for sale, Boot Hill is almost a tourist attraction in itself, but it's also a friendly (though not family-friendly) place to grab a cold one, whether you're on a bike or not.

Tir na nOg (612 E. International Speedway Blvd., 386/252-8662, www.tirnanogpub.com, 6pm-3am daily), or Land of the Young in Irish folklore, offers an excellent selection of domestic microbrews and hard-to-find import beers; in fact, it's one of the only places in town that bothers to stock more than the standard selection of big-brewery products. The staff is both friendly and knowledgeable. Pool tables, a decent jukebox, and a nonsmoking policy make this a prime spot for a quiet early evening pint.

Mai Tai Bar (250 N. Atlantic Ave., 386/947-2493, www.maitaibar.com/florida, 11am-2am daily) is part of a national chain

Driving on the Beach

Driving on the sand is a tradition on Daytona Beach.

People have been driving on the hard-packed sands of Daytona's beaches since there were cars to drive. That tradition has made it nearly impossible to impose anything beyond the most rudimentary restrictions on heading out onto the sand in your car. Some people may find this incredibly convenient; many other people find it incredibly annoying, as the constant hum of motors and car audio systems pretty much guarantees a day at the beach will be anything but quiet and peaceful. There are designated automobile areas, which are easy to spot by the presence of tollbooths where you flash your **annual pass** ($25 for Volusia County residents, $100 for nonresidents) or pay for a **day pass** ($10).

of "entertainment concept" spots, and is accordingly located among the Starbucks and Johnny Rockets of the ultra-touristy Ocean Walk Shoppes. The Hawaiian theme is unapologetically overplayed, but there's almost always a local band playing. The view of the ocean is hard to beat, especially as you sip one of the tropical concoctions the bartenders cook up. Despite the location, the Mai Tai is fairly popular with locals, especially late at night.

SPORTS AND RECREATION
Spectator Sports
The **Daytona Tortugas** baseball team plays at **Jackie Robinson Ballpark** (115 E. Orange Ave., 386/258-3106, www.daytonacubs.com,

from $8). This Class A affiliate of the World Series champion Chicago Cubs draws fairly substantial crowds, and the ballpark itself is an important part of baseball history. It was here in 1946 that Jackie Robinson stepped up to the plate for the first integrated spring training game in professional baseball. Robinson was playing for the Montreal Royals, the top-tier farm team for the Brooklyn Dodgers. He played for the Dodgers in 1947. Daytona Beach was the first city in Florida to allow Robinson to play; Jacksonville and Sanford refused to host the team because of Robinson's skin color. In 1990, the park's name was changed to Jackie Robinson Ballpark.

Boating and Fishing
Offering both boat rentals and guided

Bike Week

Since the early 20th century, Daytona Beach has been known primarily as a vacation destination. Beginning in 1905, the beach and a parallel road course were the site of car races, and in 1937, a motorcycle race, the Daytona 200, was launched. With the exception of a few years during World War II, the Daytona 200 took place on the beach annually until 1961, when it moved to the Daytona International Speedway. As motorcycle enthusiasts descended on the town every year for these races, an entire subculture developed to cater to them. Hotels, bars, restaurants, and shops all vied for the bikers' dollars.

Usually beginning the last week of February or the first week of March, nearly every restaurant and bar offers some sort of biker-friendly entertainment, and all along Main Street the energy and competition among the various bars is palpable. Highlights include convention-like vendor shows, demos, and displays at Daytona International Speedway, which even offers overnight camping during the week; pig-pickings; various boozy contests; and, of course, the running of the Daytona 200. This 10-day celebration of unchecked mufflers and souped-up two-wheelers is as much a part of Daytona Beach's identity as the Daytona 500. A smaller version of Bike Week happens in the fall in the form of Biketoberfest.

ecotours on a 40-foot pontoon boat, **Cracker Creek Canoeing** (1795 Taylor Rd., Port Orange, 386/304-0778, www.oldfloridapioneer.com) is located just outside Daytona in Port Orange. With access to Spruce Creek and the nearly 2,000 acres of the Spruce Creek Preserve and Recreation Area, Cracker Creek offers daily and hourly canoe and kayak rentals starting at $15; for those with their own nonmotorized boats, expect to pay a reasonable launch fee of $5.

Anglers should head for **Inlet Harbor** (133 Inlet Harbor Rd., Ponce Inlet, 386/767-5590, www.inletharbor.com, half-day boat charters from $50 per adult, fishing pier 6am-4pm Mon.-Fri., 6am-noon Sat.-Sun., $3 adults, $2 children, $5 pole rental) for pier fishing and deep-sea charters on boats ranging 36-65 feet. A restaurant and a gift shop are also on-site.

Golf

In a state filled with superlative courses, **Indigo Lakes Golf Club** (312 Indigo Dr., 386/254-3607, www.indigolakesgolf.com) proudly touts its consistent rating among Florida's top places to golf. With GPS-equipped carts and a par-72 course recently redesigned by Lloyd Clifton, Indigo Lakes is a popular, if somewhat understated, course.

Less understated are the courses at **LPGA**

International (1000 Champions Dr., 386/274-5742, www.clubcorp.com). The Rees Jones-designed par-72 Champions course is one of the hottest golf tickets in town, especially during the winter. As in demand is the par-72 Legends course, which is a little shorter and far more natural. Also available at LPGA is the practice facility, with 10 target greens, 6 putting greens, a place to practice bunker shots, and the three-hole Practice Academy course.

Don't feel like bothering with clubs? How about giving your throwing arm a workout with some disc golf instead? **Tuscawilla Park** (Orange Ave. and Nova Rd., 386/671-3400) offers 18 "holes" in a decidedly natural setting, with lots of trees and water hazards.

FOOD

Hog Heaven (37 N. Atlantic Ave., 386/257-1212, www.hogheavendaytona.com, 11am-10pm Sun.-Thurs., 11am-11pm Fri.-Sat., from $7) is just a block from the Boardwalk and within walking distance to the bars of Main Street, so it shouldn't even need to try to impress. But, boy, Hog Heaven still dishes up a mighty fine plate of smoked meat. The usual suspects are on the menu: ribs, chicken, beef, and pulled pork. For a truly finger-licking experience, try the Sloppy Hawg, a sandwich

Surf Florida

Florida may not be the first place that pops into surfers' minds when they're dreaming of perfect waves. The action along Florida's Atlantic coast can be brusque, choppy, unpredictable—or next to nonexistent. However, unlike some better known surf spots, Florida has warm waters much of the year, so surfers do hit waves along the mid-Atlantic coast. Here are some of the top spots:

- **Fort Pierce Inlet State Park** (905 Shorewinds Dr., 772/468-3985, www.floridastateparks. org, 8am-sunset daily, $6 per vehicle)

- **Anastasia State Park and Recreation Area** (1340 State Rd. A1A S., 904/461-2033, www. floridastateparks.org, 8am-sunset, $8/carload of 2-8 people, $4 for single-occupant vehicle)

- **John D. MacArthur Beach State Park** (10900 State Rd. A1A, North Palm Beach, 8am-sunset daily, $5)

A local surf culture has evolved here. Its most obvious manifestation is the impossible-to-ignore presence of **Ron Jon Surf Shop** (4151 N. Atlantic Ave., Cocoa Beach, 321/799-8820, 24 hours daily), with its round-the-clock store hours and ubiquitous presence on billboards along I-95. A formidable competitor, **Cocoa Beach Surf Company** (4001 N. Atlantic Ave., Cocoa Beach, 321/799-9930, 24 hours daily), has managed to not only survive but to thrive.

Don't know how to surf? Don't worry, **School of Surf** (259 Minutemen Causeway, Cocoa Beach, 321/406-0433) offers lessons ranging from daylong clinics (prices vary) to weeklong camps ($95/day or $350/week), and also offers private and semi-private lessons (from $50/hour). The staff are not only all professional surfers, they're also super friendly and super patient (which makes them great with kids).

stuffed with sauce-drenched beef, pork, and chicken; make sure to get a side of the deep-fried corn on the cob and some pork-seasoned collards too. The tiny dining room can't accommodate too many people, so it's best to drop in at nonpeak times.

Although it's somewhat out of the way, and although there's almost always a tremendous line, **Pat's Riverfront Cafe** (3300 S. Peninsula Dr., 386/756-8070, www.patsriverfront.com, 7am-2pm daily, from $5) is worth the effort in a town notably devoid of good breakfast spots. Massive pancakes, appropriately served one at a time, and overstuffed omelets are the marquee fare, but eggs-and-grits platters are done well and cheaply. Grab a free cup of coffee from the urn near the entrance and walk along the riverside marina for a while until it's your turn to be seated; you won't regret it. Pat's is cash only.

If you're going to name your restaurant the **Oyster Pub** (555 Seabreeze Blvd.,

385/255-6348, www.oysterpub.com, 11:30am-3am Mon.-Sat., 11:30am-midnight Sun., from $8), you'd better have a place that serves up good oysters and good times. This mainstay of Daytona's Party District has been around for almost 30 years. Though the interior is pretty utilitarian, with a wide-open, atmosphere-free space crammed with tables and TVs, the staff is pleasant and the oysters are always of high quality. When local bivalves are out of season, the pub flies them in from wherever they're fresh. The pub doesn't go out of its way to provide high-end preparations, but the kitchen staff does a fantastic job with basic oyster plates (Rockefeller, scampi, casino). A standard selection of burgers, cold sandwiches, fried seafood, and bar grub rounds out the menu. When there's a race or a big game on, be prepared to wait a while for a seat.

Located somewhat away from the bustle of the tourist strip, **Martini's Organic** (1821 S. Ridgewood Ave., 386/763-1090, www.martinischophouse.com, 5pm-10pm Tues.-Thurs., 5pm-11pm Fri.-Sat., from $18) is a sedate and sumptuous respite from the buzzing beachside. With sophisticated and luxurious interiors providing a perfectly complementary atmosphere for the decadently sized slabs of meat served, Martini's thrives as one of the few truly high-end restaurants in Daytona. Though some of the standard menu items will be familiar, like filet mignon, lamb, grilled salmon, and pork osso buco, they're carefully prepared and perfectly plated. (Yucca fries with skirt steak? Oh, yes.) More importantly, the menu is rounded out with seasonally appropriate dishes, most of which are sourced responsibly. Despite the emphasis on providing a rich experience, menu items are reasonably priced, and the waiters are as friendly as they are attentive and knowledgeable.

ACCOMMODATIONS

Most accommodations in Daytona Beach are either on or near the beach or in the area surrounding the Daytona International Speedway. And while the lodging scene has yet to be completely overtaken by international chains, many of the locally owned spots tend to be scrappy, run-down motels from the 1960s and 1970s; the guest rooms are affordable but not charming. There are, however, quite a few unique places to stay in the area.

It's on the beach; it's big; it's a resort, but somehow **Sun Viking Lodge** (2411 S. Atlantic Ave., 800/815-2846, www.sunviking.com, from $129 d) manages to have a personality. Maybe it's the giant Viking ship carved into the front of the hotel or the 60-foot waterslide, but the Sun Viking evokes an attitude of fun that's all too often missing from vacation spots. It is not the most modern or most luxurious hotel, but many of the Sun Viking's guest rooms have full kitchens, and all oceanfront rooms have balconies. The large outdoor pool and sundeck look out onto a wide stretch of beach. The Sun Viking is quite a good value for families. The nearby **Aku Tiki Inn** (2225 S. Atlantic Ave., 386/252-9631, www.bwakutiki.com, from $149

d) is a Best Western property with a kitschy vibe to its decor, recalling a 1960s-style fascination with pseudo-Hawaiian visuals.

The **Bahama House** (2001 S. Atlantic Ave., 800/571-2001, www.daytonabahamahouse.com, from $159 d) is another family-friendly resort spot with large guest rooms, all with balconies and most with kitchens, that are clean, comfortable, and well-maintained. Splurge for the reasonably priced king efficiencies; the ocean view, pull-out queen sleeper sofa, whirlpool tub, and ample space only run a few dollars more per night.

The **Plaza Resort & Spa** (600 N. Atlantic Ave., 386/255-4741, http://plazaresortandspa.com, from $159 d) aims to be the standard-bearer for upscale lodging in Daytona. With almost 350 guest rooms, the size of the hotel means it's far from an intimate experience. And its location in the heart of the tourist district and proximity to the convention center guarantee a near-constant hum of activity. With a history that stretches back to the late 19th century and its first incarnation as the Clarendon Hotel, the modern-day Plaza still retains much of its original architectural charm, although renovations to its public areas have given them a McMansion feel that's more plastic than classic. Rooms are spacious and very well appointed, with classy understated wood furnishings and modern amenities like flat-screen televisions.

INFORMATION AND SERVICES

The **Daytona Beach Area Convention & Visitors Bureau** (386/255-5478, www.daytonabeach.com) has two information centers. One is at its main office (126 E. Orange Ave., 9am-5pm daily). The other is at Daytona International Speedway (1801 W. International Speedway Blvd., 9am-7pm daily).

GETTING THERE

Daytona Beach is located at the intersection of I-4 and I-95, about 45 miles (45 minutes' drive) northeast of Orlando and about 58 miles (an hour) south of St. Augustine. The **Daytona Beach International Airport** (DAB, 700 Catalina Dr., Daytona Beach, 386/248-8069, www.flydaytonafirst.com) is small and is served by Delta, American, and JetBlue; for more options, **Orlando International Airport** (MCO, One Airport Blvd., Orlando, 407/825-2001, www.orlandoairports.net) is served by major and minor U.S. and international carriers.

If you're arriving by **Amtrak** (2491 Old New York Ave., 386/734-2322, www.amtrak.com), you'll have to hop off the train in DeLand and take a 20-minute bus ride to Daytona. The bus ride is included in your Amtrak fare.

GETTING AROUND

Most getting around in Daytona is done by car, especially traveling between the beach and land-side attractions. At the beach, the **Beachside Trolley** (386/756-7496, www.votran.org, noon-midnight Mon.-Sat., $1.25 adults, $0.60 seniors and children) operates along Atlantic Avenue. Fares are reasonable and it's an easy way to avoid having to find one of the increasingly rare parking spaces along the beach's main drag.

St. Augustine

As the oldest continually occupied city settled by Europeans in the United States, **St. Augustine** has a lot of inherent charm. Walking through Old Town, you'll see 400-year-old residences abutting beer bars, and gorgeous churches within sight of taco stands and wax museums. The narrow streets are remarkably well-preserved in some respects, and the dregs of tourist claptrap in others. This is what makes St. Augustine so fascinating. Of all the colonial sites on the East Coast, St. Augustine is the most intriguing.

SIGHTS

★ St. Augustine's Old Town

The most logical place to start a visit to Old Town is at the **Castillo de San Marcos National Monument** (1 S. Castillo Dr., 904/829-6506, www.nps.gov/casa, 8:45am-5:15pm daily, $10 adults, children 15 and under with adult free). Built in 1695 and constructed of coquina, the Spanish fort withstood the multiple attacks the English launched from Charleston, South Carolina, and Savannah, Georgia, and like many other territories in northern Florida, it changed hands often. When Confederate troops took the fort, it was manned by a single Union soldier who wouldn't surrender until he was given a receipt for turning it over. Today, the Castillo overlooks a much more peaceful Matanzas River. Reenactments and walking tours give visitors an opportunity to understand some of the area's complex history. Even better, there's a metered parking lot out front; cross the street and you're within the loosely defined boundaries of Old Town.

The **Colonial Quarter Museum** (53 St. George St., 904/825-6830, www.historicaugustine.com, 9am-5:30pm daily, $6.95 adults, $4.25 students, children under 6 free) is one of the first major sights you'll see. Like many other attractions in St. Augustine, it valiantly re-creates the life of the town's early colonists. The focus is on mid-18th-century Spanish families, and the staff here demonstrates activities like candle making, carpentry, blacksmithing, and more.

The **Cathedral Basilica** (38 Cathedral Pl., 904/824-2806, www.thefirstparish.org) looms large over Old Town and stands as a memorial to the city's 400 years of Catholic tradition. Built in 1797, after the destruction of two previous parish churches, and expanded in 1887 and 1966, the church is the oldest Catholic parish in the United States. Tours aren't given, but services are held regularly, and guests are welcome in the sanctuary.

St. Augustine

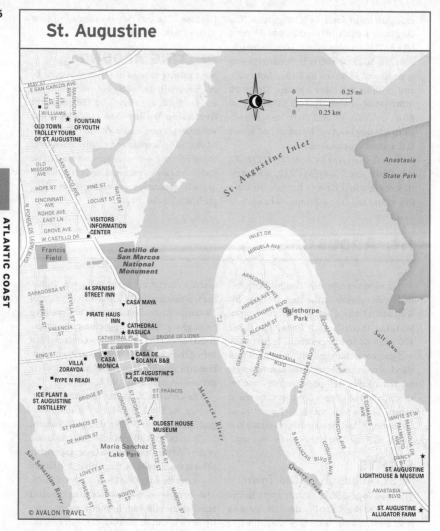

© AVALON TRAVEL

Half a dozen blocks away is the more whimsical **Villa Zorayda** (83 King St., 904/829-9887, www.villazorayda.com, 10am-5pm Mon.-Sat., $10 adults, $9 seniors and military, $8 students, $5 children 7-12, children 6 and under free). Located across the street from the beautiful campus of Flagler College, the Villa Zorayda was originally built in 1883 as a winter residence and modeled on a Moorish-era castle in Spain but at one-tenth the size. Audio tours provide a somewhat excessively

detailed history of the property and its many owners and renovations. A puzzling variety of artwork, antiques, and artifacts are on display. Accented in bright colors, the villa is hard to miss. Worth noting: Paid admission to the museum entitles you to a full day of free parking in its lot.

A block south of the Villa Zorayda is the **Lightner Museum** (75 King St., 904/824-2874, www.lightnermuseum.org, 9am-5pm daily, $10 adults, $5 children 12-18, children under 12 free). The three-story facility emphasizes its collection of Louis Comfort Tiffany stained glass and a wide range of Gilded Age antiques and oddities (particularly interesting are the odd turn-of-the-20th-century machines and musical instruments). The Lightner is somewhat refreshing in that it's one of the few historically oriented sites in St. Augustine that bridges the gap between the colonial era and modern times.

Two sights that make no such attempt are the **Ximenez-Fatio House Museum** (20 Aviles St., 904/829-5375, www.ximenezfatio-house.org, 11am-4pm Tues.-Sat., $10 adults, $8 seniors, students, and military) and the **Father Miguel O'Reilly House Museum Garden** (32 Aviles St., 904/826-0750, www.oreillyhouse.org, 10am-3pm Wed.-Sat., free). Located on the same narrow street just south of King Street, these are two of the more interesting "house museums" in Old Town. Of the two, the Father O'Reilly house is the oldest; in fact, it's the second-oldest building in St. Augustine after the Castillo de San Marcos. Both museums do an excellent job of putting the houses into St. Augustine's historical context. The O'Reilly House's lessons on the history of Catholicism in the city provide additional illumination.

Walking a few blocks farther south, you'll arrive at the **Oldest House Museum** (14 St. Francis St., 904/824-2872, www.staugustinehistoricalsociety.org, 9am-5pm daily, $8 adults, $7 seniors, $4 students, children 5 and under free), which, despite the nomenclature, does not contain the oldest house in St. Augustine; that would be the O'Reilly House. The house on this museum's property dates back only to the early 18th century, and the site has been continuously occupied since the early 1600s. It was once the site of the oldest Spanish colonial dwelling in the country. So, the "oldest house" designation is less inaccurate than it is misleading.

Outside of the main core of Old Town St. Augustine, but still within reasonable walking distance of the main sights is **St. Augustine Distillery** (112 Riberia St., 945/825-4963, tours 10:30am-5pm daily, gift shop open 10am-6pm daily, free admission), a relatively recent addition to the city's landscape, but one that manages to be unique and historical in its own way. Located in an old ice plant (a necessity in Florida before electricity), the distillery is renowned for its excellent small-batch spirits, especially its Florida Cane Vodka and New World Gin (which boasts a healthy dose

St. Augustine's Old Town

Henry Flagler: Founder of Modern Florida

Were it not for the expansionist entrepreneurialism of Henry Morrison Flagler, it's hard to imagine when, how, or even if modern Florida would have developed. Flagler was one of John D. Rockefeller's original partners in the founding of Standard Oil, and were that his only role in American history, it would have been a substantial one. However, with the money that Flagler made in that partnership, he was able to act on a flash of inspiration. Under doctor's orders to spend his winters in a more hospitable climate, Flagler began a series of vacations to Florida's east coast. In 1881, he honeymooned in St. Augustine and realized the potential that the city—and the state—had as a tourist destination; all it needed was a substantial investment in infrastructure.

Flagler made that investment quickly, first with the construction of the massive Ponce de León Hotel and the purchase and update of several small regional rail lines that were then connected to the main lines that led to the Northeast. From there, Flagler would go on to invest in and build hotels up and down Florida's east coast, including the 1,100-room Royal Poinciana Hotel in West Palm Beach and the Palm Beach Inn, now known as the Breakers, extending his rail network along the way. Flagler was directly or indirectly responsible not only for the development of St. Augustine and the northern Atlantic coast of Florida, but also for Palm Beach, Miami, and eventually the connection of the Florida Keys to the mainland with the construction of the Florida Overseas Railroad in 1912.

Today, Flagler's legacy is essentially the east coast of Florida. A more tangible monument to his impact on the state can be seen on the campus of **Flagler College** (74 King St., St. Augustine, 904/823-3378, www.legacy.flagler.edu, tours 10am and 2pm daily, $6 adults, $1 children 11 and under). The liberal arts school's hallmark building is Ponce de León Hall, which was originally the Ponce de León Hotel, the beginning of Flagler's long and influential role as one of modern Florida's founders. Designed by John Carrère and Thomas Hastings in the Spanish Renaissance style, the poured-concrete structures, with their red-tile roofs and arched windows, provided the visual foundation for much of the Mediterranean revival architecture that would come to dominate buildings in Florida for the next century.

of citrus in the mix). Distillery tours are free; the gift shop is not.

Across the Matanzas River

It's hard to decide what's coolest about the **St. Augustine Alligator Farm** (999 Anastasia Ave., 904/824-3337, www.alligatorfarm.us, 9am-5pm daily, $24.99 adults, $13.99 children). Is it the albino alligators? The gigantic vultures? The 15-foot-long behemoth saltwater crocodile known as Maximo? Or is it the even larger—but dead and stuffed—Gomek? Oh, choices, choices. In addition to 23 species of crocodilians, the Alligator Farm is also home to Komodo dragons, kookaburras, marmosets, and various other animals that don't get nearly enough marquee time at most zoos. One of the biggest attractions here, though, is the recently added zipline, which takes thrill-seeking guests high

above the ground across the alligator-thick farm grounds.

Across the street is the **St. Augustine Lighthouse & Museum** (81 Lighthouse Ave., 904/829-0745, www.staugustinelighthouse.com, 9am-6pm daily, $12.95 adults, $10.95 seniors and children, children 5 and under free). Guests can ascend to the top of the still-working lighthouse and, once 165 feet in the air, be afforded magnificent views in all directions, including out over the Atlantic Ocean. The museum consists largely of exhibits curated by the Lighthouse Archaeological Maritime Program, with shipwreck artifacts being the main attraction.

Fountain of Youth

The legend of a mystical well flowing with the waters of immortality is one that stretches back to the time of the Greeks. The story of explorer Juan Ponce de León setting off to find it and in the process finding Florida is the one that has captured imaginations in the New World since the 16th century. St. Augustine's **Fountain of Youth** (11 Magnolia Ave., 904/829-3168, www.fountainofyouthflorida. com, 9am-5pm daily, $15 adults, $14 seniors, $9 children, children 5 and under free), about three miles north of Old Town, unabashedly plays off that fascination. Legend has it that the park is located at the site where Ponce de León first landed in Florida. Although there is a fountain here (you can drink from it, but I wouldn't), the park goes to great lengths never to state explicitly that it is the actual font from which eternal youth springs (but wouldn't mind if you made such assumptions yourself). The kitschy nature of the park is more playful than deceitful, with strolling peacocks, creaky animatronic figures, and a black-light globe. It was founded in 1904 by Luella Day McConnell, who, no kidding, was known as "Diamond Lil." The park gamely attempts to make up for its archaeological shortcomings with displays of artifacts from the colonial and pre-Columbian eras, and though there are no tours, you can listen to a lecture about the area's history.

World Golf Hall of Fame

Located almost midway between St. Augustine and Jacksonville is the **World Golf Hall of Fame** (1 World Golf Pl., 904/940-4000, www.wgv.com, 10am-6pm Mon.-Sat., noon-6pm Sun., $20.95 adults, $19.95 seniors $10 students, $5 children 5-12, children 4 and under free). Fans of the game can explore the museum, which has a clutch of exhibits with artifacts and memorabilia from golf's history. However, there's also an IMAX theater that shows documentaries and Hollywood blockbusters and two outdoor courses for those so inspired: an 18-hole putting course and a recreation of the 17th hole at the Tournament Players Club in Ponte Vedra Beach. If you want to take the inspiration further, tee times can be reserved at either of the Hall's two par-72 courses.

Fort Matanzas National Monument

Heading south from St. Augustine on State Road A1A at the tip of Anastasia Island is **Fort Matanzas National Monument** (8635 State Rd. A1A S., 904/471-0116, www. nps.gov/foma, 9am-5:30pm daily, free). Overlooking Matanzas Inlet, the fort was constructed by the Spanish in 1740 to protect the southernmost water access to St. Augustine and was built at the site of two horrific massacres (matanzas is Spanish for "massacres"); in 1565, Spanish general Pedro Menéndez de Avilés slaughtered more than 200 Frenchmen who had surrendered to his forces. The fort itself is located across the inlet on Rattlesnake Island. A complimentary ferry leaves from the visitors center every 1.5 hours. Guided tours and small exhibits tell the story of the fort as well as the bloody history of the area. The drive here along State Road A1A from St. Augustine is gorgeous, with sand flats, massively wide beaches, houses on stilts, and a windswept geography that feels more like the Outer Banks than the Florida coast.

Marineland Dolphin Adventure

Marineland Dolphin Adventure (9600 Oceanshore Blvd., 904/471-1111, www. marineland.net, 8:30am-4:30pm daily, $16.95 ages 13 and up, $11.95 children 3-12, children 2 and under free) has a storied history. In 1938, Marine Studios opened as an "oceanarium" to which, the owners hoped, filmmakers would flock in order to film marine life. On opening day, an actual 20,000 guests came to see one of Florida's first theme parks. The park soon became a full-fledged tourist attraction. By the 1950s, Marine Studios was known as Marineland of Florida, and its trained dolphin shows and other aquatic attractions were one of the highlights of many families' visits to Florida.

With the opening of Walt Disney World in 1971, Marineland's attendance dropped precipitously and nearly went out of business. Today, the new Marineland's primary role is that of a Dolphin Conservation Center. Guests still have the opportunity to see dolphins, turtles, and sharks through thick-glass walls, but that's about all your general admission ticket will get you. The primary draw at Marineland now is the selection of hands-on experiences. These start at $75 for a 10-minute interaction with dolphins and range all the way up to $500 for six-hour "Trainer for a Day" programs.

BEACHES
Vilano Beach

In the 1920s, Sinclair Lewis rented a house at **Vilano Beach,** where he wrote Elmer Gantry, among other novels. It's quite likely that almost 100 years later, the author would still recognize the area. Although attempts at resort development have been made through the years, most notably with the 1920s construction of a casino, most of the projects have met with limited success, most notably the 1937 destruction of the casino by a tropical storm. Feeling like a pastoral fishing village, Vilano Beach is best known for its fishing pier. The beach at nearby **Surfside Park** (3070 Coastal Hwy.) has ample sandy access to the rough Atlantic, along with showers, restrooms, and picnic shelters.

Anastasia State Park

While the four miles of beach are what draw most people to **Anastasia State Park and Recreation Area** (1340 State Rd. A1A S., 904/461-2033, www.floridastateparks.org, 8am-sunset, $8/carload of 2-8 people, $4 for single-occupant vehicle), the park also has extensive nature trails that wind through hammocks and marshland. The wide beach access usually means that finding a spot isn't much of a challenge; though it's worth noting that, for some reason, the park allows visitors to drive their cars onto the sand. While such open-trunk beaching is expected in places like Daytona, in a more rustic setting like Anastasia, it's somewhat unsettling. Good surfing can be found north of the beach ramp, where cars make their way onto the sand. Despite the park's popularity, there are several areas to the south that are quieter but have much rougher water. Canoes, kayaks, and paddleboats can be rented at the on-site Island Joe's store, providing easy access to the tidal marshes.

St. Augustine Beach

Also on Anastasia Island, a few miles south of the state park, is the town of **St. Augustine Beach.** The main action takes place around the **St. Johns County Pier** (2106 State Rd.

Marineland Dolphin Adventure

A1A S., 904/471-1596), which provides a fishing pier along with a playground and volleyball courts. Public beach access, with vehicles allowed on the sand in most places, is available throughout town.

FOOD

Florida Cracker Cafe (81 St. George St., 904/829-0397, www.floridacrackercafe.com, 11am-2pm Mon., 11am-2pm and 5pm-10pm Tues.-Sun., from $9) is a pretty standard sandwich-and-salad spot in the Old Town, with a decent selection of burgers, hot dogs, and wraps. The addition of a handful of specialties like shrimp po'boys, fried gator tail, and a variety of fried seafood platters sets it apart.

Located in a labyrinthine little house just on the edge of the Old Town, ★ **Casa Maya** (17 Hypolita St., 904/823-1739, 8:30am-3:30pm Sun.-Thurs., 8:30am-3:30pm and 5pm-9pm Fri.-Sat., from $9) takes a healthy approach to Mexican food, with fresh ingredients and interesting reconfigurations of traditional Mexican dishes. With dishes like a Mayan soup (with *pico de gallo,* cilantro, cheese, avocado, and tortilla bits in an onion broth) and Mexican barbecue rather than the same old tacos and burritos, the fare here is as homey and comfortable as the surroundings.

The sandwiches and salads at **Café del Hidalgo** (35 Hypolita St., 904/823-1196, 9:30am-9pm Sun.-Thurs., 9:30am-10pm Fri.-Sat., from $6) are certainly decent enough; substantial portions of fresh vegetables and meats are piled onto paninis. But the main courses are just an excuse to try some of the café's desserts. In addition to cannoli, tiramisu, and even key lime pie, Hidalgo serves up a selection of its own in-house gelato, prepared fresh daily. Go for the Coppa to Share, which is a pile of 10 scoops of your choice into a dish with fruit, white and dark chocolate, nuts, and whipped cream.

With hearty soups and stews, light and healthy salads, tapas, omelets stuffed with everything from plantains and chorizo to blue crab, a sandwich menu that ranges from fantastic Cubans and *ropa vieja* to something

called the Elena Ruth (turkey with cream cheese and jelly on a sweet roll), **La Herencia Café** (4 Aviles St., 904/829-9487, http://laherenciacafe.com, 9am-4pm Fri.-Wed., from $7) has a menu that's nominally Cuban-Spanish but is not traditional. This family-run café has a nondescript dining room, but outdoor seating on Aviles Street more than makes up for that minor shortcoming.

Located in the same, converted ice plant as St. Augustine Distillery is a quite appropriately named restaurant, **The Ice Plant** (110 Riberia St., 904/829-6553, lunch: 11:30am-2:30pm Mon.-Fri., dinner: 5-10pm daily, brunch: 10am-2pm Sat.-Sun., bar open until 2am daily, from $14). Unsurprisingly, the cocktail bar here is excellent, serving craft cocktails ranging from perfectly done essentials to more imaginative (and seasonal) concoctions., and the beer and wine selections are great too. The food menu is Florida-centric, featuring local produce alongside grass-fed Florida beef, fresh fish, clams, fish dip, and more. Lunch items like a fried chicken BLT and a pork meatball banh mi are fantastic as well. The atmosphere here is decidedly unstuffy and cozy, but classy, historic, and incredibly romantic.

If you dig the produce from your Ice Plant meal, make sure to stop in across the street at **Rype N Readi Downtown Farm Market** (115 La Quinta Pl., 904/429-3070, 9am-6pm daily), an organic farm that doubles as a great local produce market that is one-stop shopping for a perfect beach picnic basket.

ACCOMMODATIONS
Old Town

There are several old St. Augustine residences reconfigured into hotel-cum-B&B accommodations. While some may veer toward preciousness or may overplay their hand when it comes to their historic nature, for the most part, these are some of the most unique lodgings you'll ever have the opportunity to stay in. Some good choices include **44 Spanish Street** (44 Spanish St., 904/828-0650, www.44spanishstreet.com, from $159 d), which is located a block or so away from the busiest parts of Old Town (but steps away from a couple of great restaurants and bars), and ★ **Casa de Solana B&B** (21 Aviles St., 888/796-0980, www.casadesolana.com, from $129 d), which is situated not just in the middle of the Old Town, but actually on the grounds of an old estate. Although its age and location might lead you to assume it would be either stuffy or affectatious, it's neither. Friendly elegance is the name of the game here, with brightly painted walls offsetting the treasure trove of antiques and furnishings. All guest rooms have private bathrooms and high-speed Wi-Fi available. The best bet, especially for winter travelers, is the Montejurra Room, a spacious well-lit second-floor room with a whirlpool, fireplace, and a majestic canopy bed.

The grande dame of St. Augustine hotels, ★ **Casa Monica** (95 Cordova St., 904/827-1888, www.casamonica.com, from $229 d) is centrally located across from Flagler College and next door to City Hall and the Lightner Museum. Built in a similarly grandiose Spanish style as its neighbors, the Casa Monica is the classiest building on a very classy block. Operated as a hotel by Henry Flagler 1888-1932, then serving as county courthouse for six decades, Casa Monica was reopened in 1999 as a modern hotel (now operated as part of the Marriott Autograph Collection) that manages to draw on its history and its legacy of luxury. While oak-and-stone magnificence abounds, there's a sense of small-scale intimacy at the hotel. Guest rooms are quiet, classy, and very comfortable, yet far from opulent. Still, given its location and legacy, the room rates are certainly justified.

Centrally located, staffed with friendly folks, inexpensive, and pirate-themed, the **Pirate Haus Inn** (32 Treasury St., 904/808-1999, www.piratehaus.com, from $99 d) isn't just the best lodging deal in St. Augustine, it's also a personality-rich place in a town where finding lodging with character isn't too much of a problem. Five private guest rooms have queen beds with extra bunk beds. The 1915 building is painted in various whimsical nautical themes. Although it's far from the most luxurious spot to stay in St. Augustine, it's comfortable, clean, family-friendly, and has free pancake breakfasts.

Vicinity of St. Augustine

Golfers and active luxury vacationers flock to the adjacent sister resorts of **Ponte Vedra Inn & Club** (200 Ponte Vedra Blvd., Ponte Vedra Beach, 904/285-1111, www.pvresorts.

Casa Monica in downtown St. Augustine

com, from $299 d) and the **Lodge & Club** (607 Ponte Vedra Blvd., Ponte Vedra Beach, 904/273-9500, www.pvresorts.com, from $399 d). Sharing two golf courses, multiple tennis courts, spas, fitness facilities, bike trails, swimming pools, equestrian facilities, and sailing and beaching opportunities, the two resorts feel less like hotels than they do residential country clubs. The inn opened in 1928, and the current facilities at the lodge date to 1989. Neither of them shows its age as both properties are exceedingly well-maintained. Guest rooms at the lodge are more spacious than those at the inn. However, neither resort could be accused of being anything less than luxurious, with everything from whirlpool tubs to turndown service available.

INFORMATION AND SERVICES

The city of St. Augustine operates the **St. Augustine & St. Johns County Visitors Information Center** (10 S. Castillo Dr., 904/825-1000, www.staugustinegovernment. com, 8:30am-5:30pm daily), conveniently located near the Castillo de San Marcos National Monument.

GETTING THERE AND AROUND

St. Augustine is located approximately 10 miles east of I-95, 45 miles south of Jacksonville, and about 58 miles (about an hour's drive) north of Daytona Beach.

The **Northeast Florida Regional Airport** (UST, 4900 US-1, North, St. Augustine, 904/209-0090, www.flynf.com) is a general aviation facility open only to private planes and charter flights, with the exception of one commercial route that connects to Trenton, New Jersey, via Frontier Airlines. **Jacksonville International Airport** (JAX, 2400 Yankee Clipper Dr., Jacksonville, 904/741-4902, www.jia.aero) has the largest range of commercial airline service, though good deals can occasionally be found on flights into **Daytona Beach International Airport** (DAB, 700 Catalina Dr., Daytona Beach, 386/248-8069, www.fly-daytonafirst.com).

The sights of St. Augustine's Old Town area are mostly only accessible on foot, and parking is fairly tough to come by near this part of town. **Old Town Trolley Tours** (167 San Marco Ave., 904/829-3800, www.trolleytours.com/st-augustine, $26 adults, $11 children 4-12, children under 4 free) and **Ripley's Sightseeing Trains** (170 San Marco Ave., 904/824-1606, www.ripleys.com, $25 adults, $11 children for "history by day" trains; $26 adults, $15 for children 6-12 for "ghosts by night" trains) offer trolley tours throughout, with tickets that grant access for three days.

Jacksonville

Jacksonville is big: Covering an area of 874 square miles, it's the largest city in the Lower 48. Owing to a 1967 consolidation referendum that effectively redrew the city limits at the much larger Duval County line (except for a few municipalities within the county), Jacksonville is also the third most populous city on the East Coast, topped only by New York City and Philadelphia. Bigger, however, doesn't always mean better. The consolidation order was approved not in an attempt to improve Jacksonville's position on ranking lists but to address a number of crises—racial tension, political corruption, industrial pollution—that threatened to sink the city completely, the aftereffects of which are still felt today.

To state the obvious, despite its size, Jacksonville has a long way to go before it's mentioned alongside Philly or the Big Apple on any other metric besides the census. Sprawling in every sense of the word,

Jacksonville spreads out for miles and miles beyond its tiny downtown core. Though beautifully bisected by the St. Johns River, the downtown area is dominated by banking and insurance interests during the day and left largely vacant during the evening, as those bankers and insurers head home to their suburban enclaves. Tucked away on the outskirts of this area, however, are a few interesting cultural pockets that are defiantly vibrant, struggling mightily against the waves of chain-store sameness and interstate off-ramps that dominate the growing—but still not entirely mature—city. Nearby Jacksonville Beach is a classic Southern beach town, low-key and a bit grungy; it's undergoing a decades-long process of revitalization yet somehow managing to keep its identity intact.

SIGHTS
Jacksonville Zoo and Gardens

The **Jacksonville Zoo and Gardens** (370 Zoo Pkwy., 904/757-4462, www.jaxzoo.org, 9am-5pm daily, extended summer hours, $17.95 adults, $15.95 seniors, $12.95 children, children under 3 free) is a moderately sized zoo located north of downtown Jacksonville. Covering 110 acres and providing a home for 2,000 animals, the zoo's marquee attractions are its Range of the Jaguar and Butterfly Hollow exhibits. Another exceptional and somewhat underplayed exhibit is the Australian Adventure, a great opportunity to see wallabies and kangaroos, and as in many other zoos, there's a free-flying aviary where guests can feed lorikeets. A substantial primate exhibit and the Wild Florida exhibit are also worth checking out. The zoo has two middling restaurants and a couple of snack bars in case you get hungry, and a children's play area with a small water park and petting farm.

Timucuan Ecological and Historic Preserve

The **Timucuan Ecological and Historic Preserve** and **Fort Caroline National Memorial** (12713 Fort Caroline Rd., 904/641-7155, www.nps.gov/timu, 9am-5pm daily, free) are northeast of downtown Jacksonville. Though the preserve itself is enormous, a visit to the reconstruction of Fort Caroline gives a taste of both the natural beauty of the Timucuan as well as something of a history lesson. Fort Caroline was established by the French in 1564 in one of their few unsuccessful bids to assert themselves colonially in what became the southeastern United States. The

The Friendship Fountain overlooks downtown Jacksonville.

fort only made it for a year; an attack led by Spanish governor Admiral Pedro Menéndez de Avilés, who had established the colony at St. Augustine, took out the French during a series of battles that culminated in a massacre 50 miles south at Matanzas Inlet. The fort here is a reconstruction built in the 1950s, so count on more of an interpretive-center experience than one of wandering through ruins. Extensive walking trails and observation areas in the 600-acre scrub-and-hardwood Theodore Roosevelt Area—where one can see shell mounds of the Timucua Indians—are complemented by an exhibit at the visitors center.

Anheuser-Busch Brewery

Jacksonville is home to one of the five **Anheuser-Busch Brewery Tours** (111 Busch Dr., 904/696-8373, www.budweisertours.com, 10am-4pm Mon.-Sat., free) available in the United States. Unfortunately, the Jacksonville brewery has little of the historic charm of, say, the St. Louis location; the glass-paneled office buildings and personality-free facilities here provide little of interest beyond learning about beer-making itself. (Heck, there aren't even any Clydesdales.) While Joe Sixpack may marvel at the enormous fermentation tanks, even the snootiest hop-head will likely get some sort of thrill from watching the production of factory beers, even if it's simply mocking the sterile precision of the whole affair. Tours are open to all ages, but you must be at least 21 years old to get a free beer sample after all that walking around.

Friendship Park

With a beautiful view of downtown Jacksonville, **Friendship Park** (1026 Museum Dr.) is on the south bank of the St. Johns River. The 200-foot-wide **Friendship Fountain** is the central and photogenic attraction here, with 17,000 gallons of water per minute coursing through dozens of jets up to 120 feet in the air. At night the fountain is gorgeously lit, and the area surrounding it provides a relaxing panoramic place to watch the boats traversing the waterway. Next door, the **Museum of Science and History** (1025 Museum Circle, 904/396-7062, www.themosh.org, 10am-5pm Mon.-Fri., 10am-6pm Sat., 1pm-6pm Sun., $12.50 adults, $10 seniors, military, children, children under 3 free) maintains a notably more naturalist bent than many other big-city science museums. A large number of the exhibits focus on regional flora and fauna as well as marine life, along with the requisite batch of hands-on science gimmicks for kids and a planetarium.

Riverside

One of the most beautiful neighborhoods in Jacksonville, the **Riverside** area blossomed after a tragic fire almost destroyed the entire city in 1901. Architects flocked to the area and lent their then-cutting-edge skills to the rebuilding process. The result was an area filled with a variety of stunningly designed—but eminently livable—houses and buildings, many of which survive to this day. The tree-lined streets have a gentle Southern charm to them, but a diverse mixture of residents and businesses gives the area an energy and sense of style that's largely missing from many other areas of the city.

The best place to start exploring the area is **Riverside Park** (753 Park St.), which is the heart of the neighborhood. Walking paths are shaded by century-old trees, stone bridges cross tiny duck-filled lakes, and despite the proximity of I-95, the vibe here is resolutely pastoral. The park is also home to arts fairs, farmers markets, and other local gatherings.

Nearby, the **Cummer Museum of Art & Gardens** (829 Riverside Ave., 904/356-6857, www.cummer.org, 10am-9pm Tues., 10am-4pm Wed.-Fri., 10am-5pm Sat., noon-5pm Sun., $10 adults, $6 seniors, military, and students, children 5 and under free) sits on the banks of the St. Johns River and is best known for its permanent collection of Meissen porcelain works. In addition, there's a strong focus on early 20th-century American art and European Old Masters. The two-acre garden complex overlooks the river, and there are several distinct plantings, all of which were conceived as residential gardens. With their selection of sculptures and statues, the gardens nicely complement the museum's artistic efforts.

Walking through **Five Points** (intersection of Park St., Lomax St., and Margaret St.) may not be quite as refined an experience as a stroll through the Cummer Gardens, but the area's quirky mix of shops, restaurants, and music venues gives it a definite pulse.

BEACHES

Jacksonville and Jacksonville Beach are often mentally intertwined, and many visitors often assume that the **beaches,** like many in other cities along I-95 in Florida, are just a mile or so from the downtown core. That's not the case; the beaches here are a half-hour drive and a world away from downtown Jacksonville. Jacksonville Beach was one of four municipalities that didn't take part in Jacksonville's 1960s consolidation, a streak of independence that nicely defines the tiny beach town's attitude. There's not much to do in Jax Beach besides go to the beach, and one gets the feeling that the residents and long-term visitors like it just fine that way.

The beaches here are reasonably wide but are often quite crowded and noisy. The soft beige sand and muddled rip-current-prone water are typical of most of the northern Florida coast. There is ample public beach access in town and a good amount of parking available. The two easiest places to head to are the centrally located **Front Park** (1st St. S. between 5th Ave. S. and 6th Ave. S., Jacksonville Beach) and farther south, **Hanna Park** (500 Wonderwood Dr., 8am-8pm daily, $3 pp 8am-10 am, then $5/car). Unsurprisingly, Ocean Front is the busier of the two, but visitors will find more nearby facilities; Hanna Park, however, is pet-friendly, if a little more remote. Be advised that weekend crowds during the summer are enormous; your best bet is to arrive early if you want any hope of finding a parking place or an empty bit of sand.

ENTERTAINMENT AND EVENTS
Nightlife

For a town of its size, Jacksonville's **nightlife** scene is fairly limited. A clutch of bars and dance clubs downtown provides predictable after-hours debauchery, but, thankfully, the Riverside/Five Points area offers some unique options like **Grape and Grain Exchange** (2000 San Marco Blvd., 904/396-4455, www.grapeandgrainexchange.com, noon-midnight Sun.-Thurs., noon-2am Fri.-Sat.), a speakeasy-style spot specializing in great cocktails and wine; and **Rain Dogs** (1045 Park St., 904/379-4969, 4pm-2am daily), a super-friendly, art-focused bar that, with its cozy seating, board games, and book exchange (!), feels more like a community hub than a trendy lounge.

Just beyond the outskirts of downtown is **Jack Rabbits** (1528 Hendricks Ave., 904/398-7496, www.jackrabbitsonline.com, hours vary by performance) one of the best places in town to catch live bands. Local, regional, and touring bands of the alternative and indie persuasion are onstage almost every night.

It's about a 20-minute drive from downtown, but if karaoke is your thing, you need to head for **Austin Karaoke** (5161 Beach Blvd., Suite 4, 904/399-1757, www.myspace.com/austinkaraoke, 5pm-2am Sun.-Thurs., 5pm-4am Fri.-Sat., $5 pp/hour). The rent-a-room setup is a bit more authentic than the style that many Americans are used to in which you give your slip to the DJ, but it also is a little less cordial, as you'll only be interacting with the group in your room rather than with a crowd of drunken singers. Beer and wine are available, as well as a nifty selection of Asian snack food. Reservations are recommended on the weekend.

SPORTS AND RECREATION
Spectator Sports

The big game in town is the National Football League's **Jacksonville Jaguars.** The team plays at **EverBank Field** (1 Stadium Pl.), which was also the home of Super Bowl XXIX in 2005. The stadium also hosts several high-profile college football games each year; the rivalry between the University of Georgia and the University of Florida plays out here, as well as the Atlantic Coast Conference championship and the Gator Bowl. The stadium was actually called the Gator Bowl before its retrofitting as an NFL facility in 1994.

Minor-league and college teams also have a substantial presence in Jacksonville; the **University of North Florida** basketball team plays at the **University of North Florida Arena** (1 UNF Dr.). A semipro rugby team, the **Jacksonville Axemen,** also plays on the UNF campus at **Hodges Stadium.** The **Jacksonville Jumbo Shrimp** (yes, really) are a minor-league outpost of the Miami Marlins; their games are played at the **Baseball Grounds of Jacksonville** (301 A. Philip Randolph Blvd.).

Fishing and Boating
Captain Jim Hammond (17184 Dorado Circle, 904/757-7550, www.hammondfishing. com) offers everything from surf fishing setups and ecotours to fly- and deep-sea fishing. Hammond has a wide variety of boats and is something of a local fishing celebrity thanks to his weekly fishing show.

Golf
Hyde Park Golf Club (6439 Hyde Grove Ave., 904/786-5410 for tee times, $28 Mon.-Fri., $38 Sat.-Sun.) was built in 1925 and designed by the legendary Donald Ross. The single par-72 course is beautifully landscaped and defined by its numerous old-growth trees. The par-71 course at **Bent Creek Golf Course** (10440 Tournament Rd., 904/779-0880 for tee times, $39 Mon.-Fri., $49 Sat.-Sun.) is similarly blessed with natural beauty, and has been certified as an Audubon Cooperative Sanctuary.

FOOD
Jacksonville
As the saying goes, in Florida, you head north to go South, and the excellent barbeque at **The**

Bearded Pig (1224 Kings Ave., 904/619-2247, thebeardedpigbbq.com, 11am-10pm Mon.-Sat., 11am-9pm Sun., from $9) is proof that you're pretty much in the South when you're in Jacksonville. Located in the San Marco neighborhood, convenient to downtown, the Bearded Pig has a cozy, cool vibe, with an outstanding outdoor dining area outfitted with picnic tables, and a giant chalkboard fence for kids to get their creative energies out. Specialties like smoked wings and brisket-topped poutine sit alongside standards like pork-seasoned collards, perfectly cooked brisket, ribs, and mac and cheese.

With locations in both the Riverside and San Marco areas, **Sake House** (1478 Riverplace Blvd., 904/306-2188; 824 Lomax St., 904/301-1188, www.sakehousejax.com, 11am-10pm Mon.-Wed., 11am-11pm Thurs.-Sat., noon-9pm Sun., main courses from $14) has a rather standard selection of sushi rolls along with teppanyaki, tempura, and katsu dishes. Everything is prepared well and reasonably priced, if unspectacular.

The **Mossfire Grill** (1537 Margaret St., 904/355-4434, www.mossfire.com, 11am-late, main courses from $9) has become something of a Riverside institution. With contemporary Southwestern-inspired dishes and a casual environment, it's a perfect fit with the laid-back vibe of the neighborhood. Few of the dishes here are daring or innovative, but with fresh ingredients and a menu that not only includes a number of Tex-Mex dishes but also seafood and even meat loaf, Mossfire is a solid choice. The upstairs lounge has an extensive tequila selection, and happy hour kicks off at 3pm.

Jacksonville Beach
What better way is there to close out a day at the beach than with some beer, barbecue, and blues? **Mojo Kitchen** (1500 Beach Blvd., 904/247-6636, http://mojobbq.com, 11am-9pm Sun.-Thurs., 11am-2am Fri.-Sat., main courses from $8) features live music on Friday and Saturday nights and dishes up top-shelf barbecue for lunch and dinner every day of the week. Smoked-meat connoisseurs will find

much to love here, as Mojo features Texas- and North Carolina-style preparations, along with country-kitchen fare like chicken-fried steak and catfish platters.

For meat cooked in a way that's a different sort of Southern, **Terra Gaucha** (528 N. 1st St., 904/246-1580, 5pm-10pm Tues.-Sat., 4pm-9pm Sun., main courses $20) is a Brazilian-style steakhouse where guests serve themselves sides and salad buffet style, and the wait staff brings out freshly grilled meat on skewers from the kitchen and circle the room. Ten different meats—from tenderloin and beef ribs to sausages and chicken breasts—will come your way, and will keep coming unless you ask the servers to stop.

ACCOMMODATIONS

For a city as large as Jacksonville, the variety of lodging options is disappointing. There are a lot of hotels in the city, but a shocking number of them are of the international chain variety. In the Riverside area, however, there are a number of tasteful B&Bs that can trace their history back to the first decade of the 20th century, providing a little bit of history and personality.

Jacksonville

Located in the beautiful Riverside district, the **St. Johns House** (1718 Osceola St., 904/384-3724, www.stjohnshouse.com, Nov.-Feb. and Apr.-May, doubles from $99 d) shares in the area's architectural uniqueness. Built in 1914 and converted into a B&B in 1992, the two-story house is as historical as it is comfortable. Classy without being stuffy, the three guest rooms here are smartly decorated with a notable lack of doilies. There's Wi-Fi throughout the house, and all guest rooms have private baths, telephones, and televisions.

Jacksonville's **Embassy Suites** (9300 Baymeadows Rd., 904/731-3555, www.embassysuitesjax.com, suites from $164) is ideally situated for families vacationing in the area. The chain is known for its free breakfasts and the one-bedroom-plus-sleeper-sofa setup in its guest rooms, but while this particular hotel

Casa Marina offers historic beachside accommodations.

isn't immediately convenient to anything, its proximity to I-95 on the south side of town means that all the sights in the region—the beaches, downtown, even Amelia Island and St. Augustine—are a lot easier to access and fairly equidistant.

Jacksonville Beach

Originally opened in 1925, the **Casa Marina Hotel & Restaurant** (691 1st St. N., Jacksonville Beach, 904/270-0025, www.casamarinahotel.com, from $169 d) has experienced several different lives in its extensive history: It served as military housing during World War II and was variously an apartment building, a retail store, a restaurant, and a tearoom. Reopened in 1991 to serve its original purpose, the Casa Marina does a marvelous job of reclaiming its former grandeur. Classy without being stuffy (this is Jacksonville Beach, after all), the Casa Marina has 23 guest rooms and suites, each of which is decorated in period style. The contemporary cuisine in the restaurant is complemented by an outdoor dining area that opens onto the Atlantic Ocean.

INFORMATION AND SERVICES

The **Jacksonville Convention & Visitors Bureau** has four easily accessible visitors centers: one at Jacksonville International Airport (in the baggage claim area, 9am-10pm daily), two downtown, at Jacksonville Landing (2 Independent Dr., 10am-7pm Mon.-Sat., noon-5:30pm Sun.) and at the bureau's office (550 Water St., Suite 1000, 8am-5pm Mon.-Fri.), and one in Jacksonville Beach (380 Paglo Ave., 10am-4pm Tues.-Sat.).

GETTING THERE
Air

Jacksonville is served by all major carriers via **Jacksonville International Airport** (JAX, 2400 Yankee Clipper Dr., Jacksonville, 904/741-4902, www.jia.aero). The airport is approximately 15 miles northeast of downtown.

Car

Jacksonville is located at the intersection of two of the nation's primary interstates, the east-west I-10, which goes all the way to Los Angeles, California, via the southern United States, and the north-south Maine-to-Miami I-95.

Train

The **Amtrak Station** (3570 Clifford Lane) is located approximately 8 miles from downtown and is served by the New York-Miami routes.

GETTING AROUND

Simply put, Jacksonville is a nightmare to navigate. The St. Johns River slices through the city, winding a course that's never clearly north-south or east-west, but usually a combination. This makes it difficult to fix your position relative to the water. Combine that with a maddening array of one-way streets and the meeting of two major interstates (the east-west I-10 and the nominally north-south I-95), and moving around town will often involve frequent bouts of disorientation and outright frustration. Unfortunately, the municipal government provides little relief; there is a downtown monorail, the **JTA Skyway**, but with only eight stops along a 2.5-mile track, your $0.50 fare won't get you very far. The **Jacksonville Transit Authority** public bus system is similarly vexing; though comprehensive in its route coverage, it's built on a hub system that means that unless you're traveling in a straight line, you'll likely be forced to route your trip through one of two primary downtown stations. If you're confining your trip to the downtown and Riverside area, taxis are an optimal choice, though they're difficult to hail; call **Gator City Taxi** (904/355-8294) or **Duval Taxi** (904/391-1616). Given the distances, excursions to the beaches or to sights to the north and south of town are best undertaken in a private car. Ride-sharing companies like Uber and Lyft also operate in Jacksonville.

Amelia Island

Though just about 35 miles (an hour's drive) away from downtown Jacksonville, **Amelia Island** is a world apart from that city's beige sprawl. Typically identified as a secluded vacation spot for the rich and richer, it's important to remember that Amelia Island is an entire island. Though the rarefied environs around the Omni Amelia Island Plantation and the Ritz-Carlton aren't meant for everyone, the rest of the island—namely the town of Fernandina Beach—is possessed of a down-home classiness that truly sets it apart. Whether driving under the tree-lined canopy of the Amelia Island Parkway, taking in the sights in historic downtown Fernandina Beach, gawking at the unusual mishmash of architectural styles along the beachside Fletcher Avenue, or simply whiling away a week or a month beside the ocean, visitors to Amelia Island don't have to be wealthy to feel rich.

SIGHTS

Downtown Fernandina Beach

Called the "Isle of Eight Flags" due to its strategic importance to a series of different colonial-era governments, Amelia Island—and specifically the city of **Fernandina Beach**— never really came into its own until after the Civil War, when the last of those eight flags, the U.S. flag, began to be flown. The shipping industry, and later a budding shrimping economy, grew up around the still-busy **Fernandina Beach City Marina** (1 S. Front St.). Across the street is the **Old Railroad Depot** (102 Centre St.), where shipped goods made their way into and out of Florida. Walking along Centre Street, there's a seamless blend of past and present, as many of the century-old buildings house shops selling antiques, art, books, and jewelry. Make sure to drop by the historic **Palace Saloon** (117 Centre St., noon-2am daily), which has been serving up drinks to thirsty travelers since 1903.

Amelia Island Museum of History

The tiny **Amelia Island Museum of History** (233 S. 3rd St., 904/261-7378, www. ameliamuseum.org, 10am-4pm Mon.-Sat.,

1pm-4pm Sun., $8 adults, $5 students and military) is situated in the old downtown jail. The "spoken history" museum displays artifacts from the last five centuries of the island's past, from the Timucuan Indians and the Spanish colonists to the Civil War and the island's role as a safe haven for escaped slaves.

Fort Clinch State Park

Built in 1847 and occupied alternately by both U.S. and Confederate troops until it was decommissioned in 1898, Fort Clinch was never the site of any major battles, which may account for its remarkable condition. However, most visitors to **Fort Clinch State Park** (2601 Atlantic Ave., 8am-sunset daily, $6/carload up to 8 people; overnight campsites $26) don't tarry too long at the fort itself, despite the tours and reenactments that the park offers. Instead, many head right for the beach, the fishing pier (which closed after receiving damage from Hurricane Matthew, but should be repaired by time of publication), or the six-mile hiking and biking trail.

BEACHES

If you're looking to see and be seen, the place to go is **Main Beach Park** (corner of Atlantic Ave. and Fletcher Ave.); situated at the beach

historic downtown Fernandina Beach

area's primary intersection, the park offers a large parking lot as well as bathroom and shower facilities. However, there is great public beach access all along Fletcher Avenue in Fernandina Beach, with metered parking lots. Even at its most population dense, there are relatively few houses along the road, meaning that most beaches are fairly empty. Giant dunes add to the seclusion, and the farther south you go, the quieter it becomes, especially the parking areas numbered 30-40.

The closer one gets to Amelia Island Plantation, the more difficult it becomes to find public beach access (although there are some "secret" access points near the Ritz-Carlton that lead to beautiful, relatively empty beaches). Beyond the plantation is the historically African American beach town of **American Beach,** founded in 1935 by the owner of the Afro-American Life Insurance Company as a vacation spot. Today, Atlantic Beach isn't much of a destination for anyone, but the expansive beach and relatively calm Atlantic make for a relaxing day. Be advised that driving is allowed on the sand, and be mindful to not get stuck in it. If that happens, though, don't be embarrassed to call 904/773-3877 for help; a very nice gentleman has posted a sign on the beach and charges a reasonable $50 humiliation tax to bail you out.

FOOD AND NIGHTLIFE

The **Surf Restaurant & Bar** (3199 S. Fletcher Ave., 904/261-5711, www.thesurfonline.com, 11am-midnight daily, main courses from $8) is a large multibuilding complex across the street from the beach. Despite its size, it always seems full. Live music, 23 televisions, and a drink while you wait on the outside deck that has a view of the Atlantic ease the pain of the seemingly eternal wait for a table. Once you finally get seated, you probably won't mind that the steak and seafood that the Surf dishes up aren't exactly anything to write home about; just sitting and eating is rewarding enough.

More upscale dining experiences can

be found in downtown Fernandina Beach. **España** (22 S. 4th St., 904/261-7700, www.espanadowntown.com, 5pm-10pm daily, tapas from $7, main courses from $19) features Spanish and Portuguese cuisine, with a wide selection of tapas plates and a full dinner menu as well. Dinner is served in one of two comfortable dining rooms and on a verdant outdoor patio.

ACCOMMODATIONS

The best way to stay on Amelia is to rent a house on a weekly or monthly basis. Few of the beach houses are fancy, but most are spacious, and nearly all are but a few steps from the beach. Contact **Amelia Island Vacation Rentals** (800/772-3359, www.ameliaisland-vacation.com) for rental information. When researching properties, you'll need to decide whether you want to stay near Fletcher Avenue in Fernandina Beach, in one of the numerous rental properties within the confines of Amelia Island Plantation, or in of the various condo communities on the south side of the island.

Short-term visitors should check out the well-appointed beach-view guest rooms at the **Seaside Amelia Inn** (2900 Atlantic Ave., 904/206-5300, www.seasideameliainn.com, from $109 d). Located at the northern tip of the island close to Fort Clinch State Park, the hotel offers clean contemporary guest rooms that are some of the newest on the island.

In downtown Fernandina Beach yet only a few minutes down State Road A1A from the beach is the **Hoyt House** (804 Atlantic Ave., 904/277-4300, www.hoythouse.com, from $299 d), a beautiful and unpretentious bed-and-breakfast. The inn's 10 guest rooms are housed in a 1905 home that's perfectly evocative of the historic district's lost-era elegance.

For a splurge, the **Ritz-Carlton Amelia Island** (4750 Amelia Island Pkwy., 904/277-1100, www.ritzcarlton.com, from $499 d) has all the frills one would expect from the chain. Bracketed by a dense copse of trees at the entrance and opening up to a wide private beach, the hotel offers secluded luxury. An on-site spa, two golf courses, three restaurants, and two lounges give you little reason to leave the property.

The original Amelia Island Plantation was one of the first "real" hotels on the island, offering luxurious isolation for those willing to make the trek out to the island. Today, it operates as the **Omni Amelia Island Plantation** (39 Beach Lagoon Rd., 904/261-6161, www.omnihotels.com, from $399), with all the expected accoutrements of an Omni property. The 400-plus rentals come in varieties ranging from standard rooms and family suites to luxurious oceanfront apartment-style lodging.

There are several pools, a spa, a fitness center, and multiple dining and drinking options on-site.

GETTING THERE AND AROUND

Head north from Jacksonville on I-95 and take the State Road 200 exit east, which leads directly to downtown Fernandina Beach. It is 35 miles to Fernandina Beach from Jacksonville, which takes just under an hour; from St. Augustine, it's approximately 75 miles (90 minutes). There is no public transportation on Amelia Island.

Walt Disney World and Orlando

Look for ★ to find recommended
sights, activities, dining, and lodging.

Highlights

★ **Magic Kingdom:** The heart of the Walt Disney World Resort is home to such icons as Cinderella's Castle, the Haunted Mansion, and Space Mountain (page 241).

★ **Animal Kingdom:** The combination of thrill rides, animal exhibits, and Disney magic has made it a wholly unique player on the theme-park stage (page 255).

★ **Islands of Adventure:** Between the superhero coasters and the Wizarding World of Harry Potter, this park is an essential, thrilling complement to Disney (page 272).

★ **Discovery Cove:** A day at this part island oasis, part eco-education center, and part pampering resort involves up-close interactions with dolphins (page 283).

★ **Loch Haven Park:** This park is home to several art museums, theaters, and the Orlando Science Center. The wide-open spaces are great for picnicking, and the numerous cultural opportunities make it well worth exploring (page 291).

★ **Downtown Winter Park:** Winter Park got its start as a resort town preferred by upper-crust New Englanders in the early 1900s. This tree-lined area is great for window-shopping and sightseeing (page 293).

© AVALON TRAVEL

A visit to Florida is incomplete without a trip to Orlando's world-famous theme parks. The city itself combines the urban flair of a growing metropolis and the tranquility of sprawling suburbs.

The Walt Disney World Resort is, of course, the theme-park center of gravity in the area. Not only was it the first, it's still the largest and most popular. The resort encompasses four "kingdoms," each of which offers a distinct take on Disney's family-friendly charm. The Magic Kingdom was the first park built in Orlando by Walt Disney. It takes the algorithm behind California's Disneyland and amplifies it into a self-contained universe filled with cartoon characters and immersive rides and attractions. At Epcot, Disney's vision of a futuristic city has been supplanted by science-fact displays of technology, a "parade of nations" voyage through the food and culture of several different countries, and a selection of thrill rides. At Disney's Hollywood Studios, the magic of Disney is combined with the magic of the movies. Disney's Animal Kingdom deftly blends live animal habitats, ecofriendly messages, and a handful of excellent rides. The resort also offers water parks,

golfing, shopping, nightlife, and a wide array of dining and lodging options.

There are two other major theme-park resorts in the Orlando area. Universal Orlando contains two distinct parks: Universal Studios Orlando is a Hollywood-themed park, with rides and attractions built around popular television shows and movies; Islands of Adventure is an amusement park with high-velocity coasters and thrill rides that pack in plenty of movie-studio synergy, including The Wizarding World of Harry Potter.

SeaWorld Orlando combines choreographed marine-mammal shows, sea-life exhibits, marquee coasters like Kraken, and an excellent eco-minded water park, Aquatica, as well as the exceptional Discovery Cove, which invites a limited number of daily guests for extended and close-up interactions with dolphins.

Although theme parks are a big part of Orlando's reputation among travelers, not

Previous: swans in Lake Eola Park; Wekiva Springs State Park. **Above:** Cinderella's Castle in the Walt Disney World Resort's Magic Kingdom.

Walt Disney World and Orlando

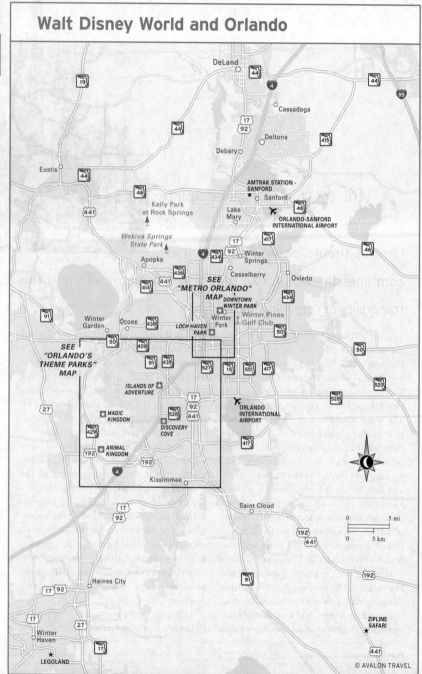

© AVALON TRAVEL

Orlando's Theme Parks

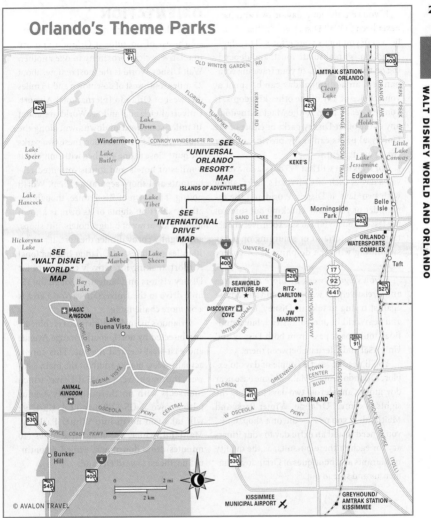

everyone who comes to the "City Beautiful" is interested in roller coasters and character breakfasts. Orlando's downtown area is compact, serving as a business hub during the day and a drinking destination at night. Immediately outside the core is where the city shines, with diverse neighborhoods housing everything from a bustling Vietnamese American district to art galleries, craft-beer bars, and a wide range of dining options.

PLANNING YOUR TIME

The seven major parks—the four Disney "kingdoms," the two Universal parks, and SeaWorld—each warrants at least a single day to explore. Trying to cram more than one into your day will not only be stressful and unrewarding, it will also be a decision that your feet will never forgive you for. Given the price of admission to the parks, it's best to get your money's worth out of each individual park.

If you've only got a day or two and have never been to Walt Disney World, that should be where you focus your efforts. The Magic Kingdom is an absolute must, and depending on the inclinations of your traveling companions, an additional day can be spent at your choice of any of the other kingdoms. If you've already been to the Magic Kingdom, any of the other Disney parks or either of the Universal parks can easily provide a day or two of excitement.

For trips that will last 3-5 days, allow yourself a day at each of Universal's parks, along with two days at Disney World and the remainder of your time checking out some of the lesser-known (and less-expensive) attractions like Gatorland or splurging on a day swimming with the dolphins at Discovery Cove.

If you've got a week or more in the area and a relatively fat wallet, I would still advise against trying to take in Disney, Universal, and SeaWorld in one go. Instead, buy a multiday multi-park pass from both Disney and Universal and alternate between them.

You'll need at least a couple of days to explore Orlando proper. Make a home base near downtown, and devote two days to seeing the sights of central Orlando, Winter Park, and Maitland. If you're a foodie or a shopaholic, you'll need to add an extra day to your itinerary for each of these pursuits, as the quality restaurants and boutiques of Orlando are numerous and spread out.

ORIENTATION

All of the main Orlando theme parks are southwest of downtown Orlando and are in relatively close proximity to one another. Walt Disney World is the most remote, about 25 miles southwest of downtown and 15 miles due west of Orlando International Airport. Universal Orlando and SeaWorld are about 10 miles southwest of downtown, along the International Drive corridor; these two parks are quite close to one another, with only about 5 miles of hotels and tourist-oriented restaurants and shops separating them. Worth noting: The town of Kissimmee, though relatively short on sights of its own, is known for its wide array of budget hotels, gift shops, and slightly corny dinner theaters. It's about 10 miles southwest of Orlando International Airport, making it relatively convenient for Disney visitors on a budget, although the 15-mile drive to the Universal/SeaWorld area is a bit more challenging.

Orlando's main downtown area is compact and bisected by north-south Orange Avenue and east-west Central Avenue. This core is actually a few blocks south of the main east-west thoroughfare, Colonial Drive, which intersects with north-south Mills Avenue (also known as US-17/92) and I-4. US-17/92 will take you north into Winter Park and Maitland, which are about five miles (10 minutes) from downtown, while I-4 continues northeast toward DeLand.

Three Days in Orlando

If you're traveling with kids or you've never been to Orlando's theme parks, a visit to this area would be incomplete without experiencing what Orlando is best known for. Plan on staying at one of Disney's resort hotels, either splurging for one of the top-shelf experiences like **Animal Kingdom Lodge** or protecting your budget by staying at one of the more economical spots like the **Pop Century Resort.** Either way, you'll be able to avail yourself of Disney's intra-resort bus system and monorails, saving yourself the headache of getting to and from the actual parks.

If theme parks are not on your agenda, plan to stay in downtown Orlando at the **Grand Bohemian** or in Winter Park at **The Alfond Inn,** where you can take in the drinking-and-dining scene available around these areas.

DAY 1

For your first day, the flagship **Magic Kingdom** park is a must-see, and to take in all the rides and attractions here, you should really devote most of the day to the experience. In the evening, head to the newly revamped and expanded **Disney Springs** to explore the wide array of shops and restaurants there.

DAY 2

If one day of Disney is enough (and it may well be!), spend your second day at Universal's **Islands of Adventure,** then take in the **Wizarding World of Harry Potter.** Afterward, the clubs and restaurants of **CityWalk** are a decent-enough option, but for better dining choices, head to nearby Restaurant Row and check out some of Orlando's better restaurants like **Amura.**

DAY 3

Dedicate at least one day to getting out of the theme-park maw and digging into the real Orlando by checking out **Loch Haven Park**'s museums, the **Harry P. Leu Gardens,** and the shopping available in downtown **Winter Park.**

Walt Disney World

TOP EXPERIENCE

When people say they're "going to Orlando," more often than not they mean that they're visiting **Walt Disney World**. The expansive resort includes four individually themed amusement parks, a few dozen hotels, and a raft of other distractions, from water parks to shopping. The place holds a captivating spell over children, but the resort also caters to grown-up tastes with exceptional fine-dining experiences, luxurious spas, and even award-winning cocktails.

None of it comes cheap, though. Currently, the price of a single-day single-park admission to the Magic Kingdom will set you back at least $105 (adults) or $99 (children 3-9),

while the other three parks are just $8 cheaper. However, Disney has recently implemented a tiered pricing system, dividing admission days into "peak," "regular," and "value" categories, depending on expected park capacity on that particular day. (The prices above reflect the "value" pricing, typically available for midweek, non-holiday days.) Moderately busy (but still crowded) days are "regular," and cost about $5 more, while the busiest days—national holidays, school vacation times, many weekends—fall into the "peak" category, bumping the single-day price nearly $20 above the "value" price. Confused? Sit back. It gets more confusing, as Disney offers a dizzying array of options—multiday/single-park

Walt Disney World

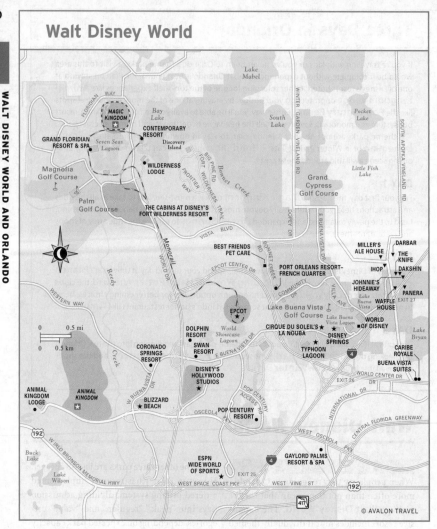

© AVALON TRAVEL

passes, multi-park/single-day passes, multi-day/multiday passes, none of which conform to the peak/regular/value structure—that can bring the price of park admission down to around $30 per day per person. These are what you should buy; I recommend going for the three-day Park Hopper pass that lets you jump around all four "kingdoms" for three days for $345 (adults) and $327 (kids). Keep in mind that the tickets expire 14 days after the first use. Admission to the water parks

can also be tacked on to any ticket for an additional, deeply discounted fee. Thankfully, Disney has a streamlined and easy-to-understand ticket purchase process on its website that clearly explains your options and lets you pick the ticket that's best for you.

For a truly unique Walt Disney World experience, guests can splurge on special access opportunities like the **Backstage Magic Tour** ($275), which gets you behind the scenes at all four parks for a guided seven-hour

Meeting Disney Characters

As soon as you enter the turnstiles of the Magic Kingdom, the very first gift shop you'll see is one that specializes in something that might seem peculiar for an amusement park: autograph books and pens. For children, and, frankly, for many adults, spending the day gathering the signatures of characters like Mickey Mouse, Winnie the Pooh, Snow White, or even Captain Jack Sparrow is a time-honored pastime.

There are two ways to meet the characters: by accident or on purpose. As you're strolling throughout the Magic Kingdom, you'll constantly be coming across throngs of children gathered around costumed characters and their handlers; simply get in line and wait your turn. In my opinion, this is the best way to approach the task, as the happenstance nature of the encounters only adds to the magical thrill your kids will get when you accidentally sight a beloved character.

There are scheduled appearances throughout the park during the day (consult the guide map), as well as opportunities to queue up in various lands to encounter a cavalcade of characters. There are also "character dining" opportunities at several restaurants throughout the Magic Kingdom and other parks. Reservations are essential for these; consult your guide map for specific locations and call 407/WDW-DINE (407/939-3463) to reserve.

tour. Deluxe tour opportunities are available through Disney's **VIP Tour Services** ($400-600 per hour, plus admission, six-hour minimum), which not only takes you behind the scenes but, perhaps more importantly, gets you right to the front of the line at all of the attractions.

★ MAGIC KINGDOM

The **Magic Kingdom** is what many people mean when they talk about going to Disney World. It's not only the resort's original park, it's also the one with the most signature attractions. From the spires of Cinderella Castle and the thrills of Space Mountain to meet and greets with Mickey Mouse and the halcyon Americana conjured up in Adventureland and Frontierland, this park most vividly bears the imprint of Walt Disney's clean-cut imaginative vision of what an American theme park should look, sound, and feel like.

Main Street, U.S.A.

The meticulous planning and affection for a more innocent time that was a fundamental element of Walt's vision for Walt Disney World is immediately apparent when you enter the park. The various hassles of parking, taking a tram, taking a monorail or boat, waiting in line, getting a ticket scanned, and passing through a turnstile all evaporate as soon as you make your way onto **Main Street, U.S.A.,** a nostalgic re-creation of late-19th-century and early-20th-century Americana. It's no accident that this is the very first thing a guest sees on entering the Magic Kingdom, as the friendliness, cleanliness, and innocence of Main Street are every bit as fantasy-derived as Tinker Bell or Dumbo the flying elephant.

Vintage fire engines, "horseless carriages," and even an omnibus roam Main Street. Guests can hop aboard a trolley here to be ferried along the street to Cinderella Castle. Guests can also board the **Walt Disney World Railroad,** which circumnavigates the park with stops at **Storybook Circus** and **Frontierland.**

The primary purpose of this part of the park is mood-setting, and there's very little to do other than shop, which you could say is an appropriate mood-setter in and of itself. A couple of outlets, like an ice cream parlor and the enormous **Emporium** (at 17,000 square feet, it's the largest gift shop in the Magic Kingdom), get the most attention. But there are a few truly unique places, like **The Chapeau** (monogrammed hats), **Engine Co. 71** (firefighter-themed gifts), and **Harmony Barber Shop,** where you can get an old-school shave-and-a-haircut as a for-real barbershop quartet sings along.

For the most part, though, guests just ooh and aah at the detailed buildings and the corny costumes and then weave their way through the crowds and the balloon sellers to get to the rides and attractions in the rest of the park.

Adventureland

Once you've made your way up Main Street, U.S.A., hang a left at the photo-ready sculpture of Walt and Mickey and head toward **Adventureland.** As with all the other "Lands" of the Magic Kingdom, this area of the park is "themed" down to the smallest detail. The overriding concept is a reflection of the daydreams of a boy who can't get enough of matinee heroes and literary tales of adventure.

The **Swiss Family Treehouse** is based on the 1960 Disney film *The Swiss Family Robinson,* and much like the movie itself, this attraction's charms are specific. Simply put, you'll be walking up and back down a 90-foot-high artificially constructed tree, gawking at the stranded family's survivalist inventions (a rope-and-pulley system used for hauling buckets of water, for example),

and wondering what exactly the fuss is about. Most guests skip it, which is understandable, but not every attraction need be a cavalcade of lights and animatronics, and personally, I think the Treehouse is sort of neat. My kids (and my wife, and everyone I've ever gone to Magic Kingdom with) vehemently disagree. If you're with someone who insists on ascending the tree but you'd rather not, or if you're physically unable to join him or her (this is the only non-handicap-accessible attraction in the park), enjoy one of the best snacks in the entire Magic Kingdom: a Dole Whip soft-serve pineapple ice cream from the **Aloha Isle** snack bar.

Little ones will flock to the **Magic Carpets of Aladdin** ride, which is essentially a repainted version of the Dumbo ride in Fantasyland; four people get into a "carpet" and the carpets rotate around the big lamp in the center. Riders can control both the up-and-down motion of their carpet as well as the pitch. Not exactly inventive, this ride seems more appropriate for a local carnival than for the place where dreams are supposed to come true. The fact that it's a note-for-note copy of another ride in the same park makes it doubly disappointing.

The Enchanted Tiki Room was the first

The riverboat ride evokes Walt Disney's vision of Americana.

FastPass+

Introduced in 1999, the FastPass system revolutionized theme park queue management with a very simple concept: Show up early at the ride you want to take, get a ticket with an appointment time (usually a window of about an hour), and then go do other stuff until it's time to board the ride. The paper ticket-based system was replaced with the FastPass+ system, which allows guests to make online reservations for experiences at the park up to 60 days in advance of their visit (after tickets have been purchased, of course). FastPass+ expands the reservation system beyond rides and now includes character greetings, entertainment, and viewing areas for parades and fireworks. Although guests are limited to three reservations per day (and all must be at the same park), making these FastPass+ reservations is essential to making the most of your time at a Disney park.

Disney attraction to fully incorporate animatronic technology, and it has been a nostalgic favorite for years. Copied from Disneyland for Walt Disney World's opening in 1971, the Tiki Room was more of a show than an attraction, as animatronic tropical animals cracked awful jokes and sang songs in an environment thick with 1960s exotica shtick. The 20-minute program was thoroughly overhauled in the last few years, and now elements from *The Lion King* and *Aladdin* have made their way into the show. The original four bird hosts are still on hand, though, and they still have the best zingers. Adults will enjoy the campiness of the entire routine, while somehow the jokes evoke massive belly laughs from the preteen set; those who fall in between those two categories will likely only be tempted by the lure of seats and ice-cold air-conditioning. Make sure to stop next door at the Sunshine Tree Terrace snack bar and get a soda in the famous "Orange Bird" cup.

Like the Swiss Family Treehouse, the **Jungle Cruise** is an Adventureland attraction that seems like little more than a leftover from a long-ago time. In this age of Discovery Channel documentaries, ecotourism, and, well, Disney's Animal Kingdom, the thrill of seeing fake zebras, snakes, rhinos, and tigers is limited. Still, this slow-moving boat ride makes up for its lack of live animals with a stream of well-rehearsed and ultra-corny jokes that issue forth from the mouth of your "tour guide." Still, in true Disney fashion the animatronic beasts are fairly realistic, and the well-choreographed river adventure is a sight to behold. Danger is around every corner as you make your way through four continents in 10 minutes, but you'll be laughing (or groaning) so much you'll hardly notice.

Oddly, before Johnny Depp smeared his eye makeup and boarded the *Black Pearl*, the **Pirates of the Caribbean** ride was often mentioned in the same breath as attractions like the Jungle Cruise or the Tiki Room. It was seen as little more than a fusty animatronic-heavy leftover from the park's opening, offering little more than nostalgia and a temporary air-conditioned reprieve from the Florida heat. Today, the ride has been lightly renovated to reflect its theatrical success, and several elements from the movie have been somewhat clumsily incorporated into it. But if you spend your time on the ride bemoaning the changes and playing "Spot Jack Sparrow" with your boatmates, you'll miss out on the essential reason for the attraction's enduring popularity: It's fun, it's a little thrilling, and it's even a little naughty. From the moment you board your boat and ride through the pirate battles and raids, the immersive genius of Disney's Imagineering team is evident. Even the most seasoned park-hoppers will get a thrill as their boat ascends a rapid and emerges onto a ship-to-ship battle, complete with cannon fire.

Liberty Square

The colonial-era theme of **Liberty Square** should make it a lot more exciting, but other than the hagiographic animatronics of **The

Hall of Presidents, there's little to do here but take snapshots of your loved ones in the stockade and grab a turkey leg on the way to other areas of the park.

The Haunted Mansion, though technically part of Liberty Square, doesn't fit in with the patriotic theme. Still, as it is situated between Liberty Square and Fantasyland, it seems that the park's planners thought it unwise to put all the ghosts and ghouls alongside Winnie the Pooh and Snow White. The mansion remains one of the Magic Kingdom's marquee attractions, and it's easy to understand why. Two-person "doom buggies" take guests on an eight-minute tour of this spook-infested mansion, from the ground floor to the attic. The sights along this ride are among the most intricately detailed in all of Walt Disney World, and from the wallpaper to the inscriptions on the headstones, there's always some new thing to notice. While inherently something of a scary experience—those graves aren't going to fill themselves—this ride has always managed to successfully balance thrills and humor. While some of the gags are a little dark and others are a little corny, all but the most knock-kneed young one will be able to muster a laugh long enough to chase away their fears.

Fantasyland

When people think of Walt Disney World, they almost immediately envision **Fantasyland.** As home to the iconic **Cinderella Castle,** as well as multiple rides and attractions built around beloved characters from decades of Disney movies, Fantasyland is the emotional heart that beats inside all the other areas of the resort. While certainly thick with its own peculiarly sneaky brand of consumerism, Fantasyland is the one "land" in the Magic Kingdom where the ratio of attractions-to-vendors seems most reasonable. Fantasyland is an essential stop on any Disney itinerary, whether or not you are traveling with young children, and a high-profile 2014 renovation of the area has emphasized its centrality to the Disney experience.

Entering from Liberty Square and the Haunted Mansion, the first attraction is **It's a Small World.** As something of an eternal punch line, the ride itself has become instantly associated with a headache-inducing repetition of its cloyingly simplistic theme song. There are even anecdotal reports of people (in my family!) being driven to near panic-attack states by the song. I don't believe any of it. The ride is sweet, as slow-moving boats give riders a tour of happy children all over the

The Many Adventures of Winnie the Pooh brings classic characters to life at Walt Disney World.

world. The ride itself was built for inclusion at the UNICEF pavilion at the 1964 World's Fair. A 2005 renovation did little to alter the ride's fundamentals; instead, a much-needed fresh coat of paint was applied throughout, some of the "children's" costumes were refurbished, and the soundtrack was given improved fidelity. Check your cynicism at the door.

As famous or infamous as It's a Small World is, it's the character-themed rides in Fantasyland that are the biggest draw, and which usually have the longest lines. On the face of it, **Peter Pan's Flight** and **The Many Adventures of Winnie the Pooh** are little more than motion-enhanced retellings of the classic tales. But in true Disney fashion, both of these rides are finely detailed and choreographed excursions that take riders deep into the story. The soaring sensation on Peter Pan's Flight and the goofy fun of riding around in one of Pooh's honey pots are immersive and highly enjoyable.

More invigorating is the **Seven Dwarfs Mine Train**. The steel coaster is like a pint-sized version of more classic Disney coasters like Big Thunder Mountain Railroad, taking riders on a track that travels both inside and outside in a "mine car" that sways back and forth.

In Fantasyland, two traditional and straightforward carnival rides are transformed into **Prince Charming Regal Carousel** and the **Mad Tea Party.** Neither is especially innovative, but both—especially the spinning teacups of the Mad Tea Party—are fun.

Little ones will also get a kick out of **Enchanted Tales with Belle,** a 20-minute show where they can hear the *Beauty and the Beast* heroine tell the tale of, uh, *Beauty and the Beast.* In true Disney fashion, there's plenty of audience interaction and lots of songs.

Mickey's PhilharMagic is one of several 3-D movie experiences at the Walt Disney World Resort. It's also on the grandest scale: The theater houses the world's largest seamless movie screen. The movie itself is equally grandiose, incorporating almost a dozen

classic Disney characters (from Mickey and Donald to Jasmine and Simba), sight gags, songs, and some very impressive 3-D effects.

Journey of the Little Mermaid is an extensive and expansive dark ride that takes guests on a clamshell ride through the story of *The Little Mermaid.* Even if you're not a fan of the movie, this immersive, six-minute ride, complete with a number of atmospheric changes that actually make you feel as if you're under water, is incredibly impressive.

Back when it was known as Mickey's Toontown Fair, **Storybook Circus** used to be the best place in the Magic Kingdom to meet Mickey and Minnie Mouse. Their "country houses" were located in this area. But the recent revamp of Fantasyland has made this once-isolated area of the park a more integral part of Fantasyland, and moved Mickey up to Main Street, U.S.A. Kids can still venture into **Pete's Silly Sideshow** to meet Minnie, as well as Goofy and Donald and Daisy Duck here, although they are in their circus-inspired avatars (Minnie Magnifique, the Great Goofini, the Astounding Donaldo, and Madame Daisy Fortuna). The circus theme extends to the revision of the long-running rides here, especially the **Dumbo the Flying Elephant** ride (which is ostensibly the inspiration for the circus atmosphere) and the **Casey Jr. Soak 'n' Splash Station,** a water-squirting fun house. The popular **Barnstormer** is a Goofy-themed rollercoaster that kids will want to go on again and again.

Tomorrowland

The retro-futuristic vibe at **Tomorrowland** was ratcheted up in the 1990s to reflect the reality that Walt's 1960s-era vision of the future was unlikely to come into fruition exactly as he saw it. This area of the park was themed to represent "the future that never was," a polished-chrome and rounded-edge future of rocket-ship cars envisioned by the sci-fi writers of the 1920s and 1930s. The theming is the most pronounced in attractions like **Tomorrowland Transit Authority** (a "people mover" that loops through Space

Mountain, the Carousel of Progress, the Buzz Lightyear attraction, and other points throughout Tomorrowland) and the elevated spinning rockets of the **Astro Orbiter.**

Most people flock to Tomorrowland for one reason: **Space Mountain.** Opened in 1975, the 2.5-minute-long, 28-mph indoor roller-coaster ride is far from the fastest coaster around, but for years the combination of quirky futurism, quick turns, and darkened thrills has been irresistible to roller-coaster fans. Space Mountain underwent a much-needed renovation in 2009. Lines stack up quickly here, so during high season a FastPass+ reservation is essential.

Monsters, Inc. Laugh Floor is a remarkable attraction. Based on the revelation of the titular film, in which the monsters discover that laughs, rather than screams, are more effective at producing the energy they need, there has been a comedy club set up that allows humans to come in and provide some laughs/fuel. The premise, however, isn't what makes this attraction work. Technology has been employed that allows the various computer-animated characters to interact with the audience in real time, meaning that every unscripted show is unique. The often-corny jokes are quite funny, and some are even submitted from audience members via text message. The Magic Kingdom hasn't had a lot of luck with attractions that it has put in this space, but given the technological innovations and interactive nature of the current occupant, that streak should change for the better.

Buzz Lightyear's Space Ranger Spin puts guests into a *Toy Story*-themed shooting game, riding around in "space cruisers" outfitted with laser guns. Riders can spin their cruisers in a full 360-degree rotation, allowing better sighting of the numerous targets. Points are racked up in eight different rooms leading up to a showdown with Buzz's nemesis, Zurg. The super competitive will want to aim for the diamond- and triangle-shaped targets, as they're worth the most points.

For all the dated retro-futurism of Tomorrowland, it's the noisy exhaust-spewing race cars of the **Tomorrowland Speedway** that actually seem the most anachronistic. Riders are allowed minimal speed-up/slow-down control but can't go faster than 7 mph as the cars meander along their respective rails on the 2,000-foot track. There are always inexplicably long lines for this ride.

Frontierland

If Tomorrowland is all about retro-futurism, then **Frontierland** is all about retro-retro-ism, evoking a halcyon vision of the Mild West. While you wouldn't expect to see cholera-infested wagon trains or massacres of Native Americans playing a huge role in an escapist theme park, the sheer audacious silliness of something like the **Country Bear Jamboree** is something that only Walt Disney could imagine as part of the pioneer experience. At Country Bear Jamboree animatronic bears sing cornpone songs that appeal to the very young and the very old.

There are thrills to be found in Frontierland, most notably at its two marquee rides. **Big Thunder Mountain Railroad** is a loud and rickety wooden coaster that takes riders on a high-speed run through an abandoned mining town. The careening coaster dips into dark caves and plummets down the mountain, tossing you from side to side as it makes its way along the track. The ride can be quite intense for younger riders.

Splash Mountain is a bit less exhilarating than Big Thunder Mountain, but the 10-minute log-flume ride themed around Br'er Rabbit and his compatriots from *Song of the South* can be deceptively calming. Multiple climbs and drops happen throughout the ride, and animatronic characters sing songs and tell the story of Br'er Rabbit in a series of densely detailed rooms. But it's the final soaking plunge of nearly five stories that ensures long lines on hot summer days.

Special Events

Mickey's Not-So-Scary Halloween Party (selected dates Sept.-Oct.) and **Mickey's Very Merry Christmas Party** (selected dates

Nov.-Dec.) are separately ticketed events that transform the park into a holiday-themed nighttime experience complete with special parades, shows, and fireworks displays. Most attractions and rides are operational during these events. Ticket prices change annually but are typically a little less than a single-day single-park admission ticket.

Food

Ironically, the crown jewel of the Walt Disney World Resort comes up rather short when it comes to dining. While all of the other parks have at least one truly remarkable restaurant option, the Magic Kingdom is notably lacking in this department. The best option is the prix fixe meals at **Cinderella's Royal Table** ($39-63 for breakfast, $44-75 for lunch and dinner). The intimate dining room feels regal, with its high, cathedral-like ceilings and windows that give a bird's-eye view of Fantasyland. Breakfast is an all-you-can-eat selection of eggs, bacon, yogurt, fruit, and other morning standards, while lunch and dinner are built around things like pan-seared salmon, roast chicken, grilled pork tenderloin, and more. As this is a character dining location, reservations are pretty much mandatory. Dinner includes a souvenir photo package with a shot of you and your party in the lobby. Tableside visits from princesses and free snapshots aside, the menu here is a bit drab and overpriced.

There are a couple of other alternatives to the seemingly endless offerings of hamburgers, hot dogs, and turkey legs throughout the Magic Kingdom. The **Liberty Tree Tavern** (hours vary, from $11.99) is a spacious sit-down eatery in Liberty Square. In keeping with its neighborhood's Early America theme, it offers fare ranging from clam chowder and roast turkey to pot roast, along with a few surprises like a vegetarian noodle bowl, a "William Penn Chicken Pasta," and a surprisingly healthful kids' menu. It's usually pretty easy to get a table.

Tomorrowland Terrace Noodle Station (hours vary, from $6.99) is a counter-service, open-air dining option sitting on the boundary of Main Street, U.S.A., and Tomorrowland. Noodle bowls are the centerpiece of the menu, along with a selection of Asian-inspired vegetarian dishes and, uh, chicken nuggets.

EPCOT

Divided into two slightly incongruous sections—the technology-driven Future World and the international expositions of the World Showcase—**Epcot** has taken a while to shake off its early identity crisis as the Disney park that doesn't seem like a Disney park. For much of its early life, visitors would arrive to Epcot expecting amusement-park rides and Mickey Mouse ears, only to be befuddled when confronted with Italian acrobats and the **VISION House**. Today, the park stands quite well on its own, with a combination of exciting attractions like **Mission: Space** and **Test Track**; interesting semi-educational pavilions that easily outclass your favorite science center; and the crash course in global culture that comes from a walk around the "world."

Future World

Half of the "permanent World's Fair" atmosphere of Epcot comes across in the inventions, innovations, and corporate sponsorships that are found throughout **Future World.** Putting forth a vision of an ecologically balanced, remote-controlled tomorrow, the various pavilions and attractions of Future World combine to create something like the world's biggest hands-on museum that just happens to have some really cool rides.

Spaceship Earth is not one of those cool rides. This is the iconic "giant golf ball." Although it underwent a thorough renovation in 2008, the ride inside the ball is far from the most exhilarating experience. Cars slowly make their way along the constantly moving track as animatronic figures and a narration by Judi Dench trace the history of communication from cave paintings and Roman couriers all the way through television and email. Afterwards, riders exit through "Project Tomorrow," an area with interactive games

Walt Disney's Vision of Epcot

Walt Disney's original plan for Epcot was for it to be a thriving independent city, built on a progressive platform of New Urbanism and technology-driven efficiency. Disney envisioned a village bustling with more than 20,000 residents who utilized monorails and PeopleMovers like the ones you can still ride in the Magic Kingdom on the Tomorrowland Transit Authority.

This vision was fundamental to Disney's original plans for the Florida Project he began work on in the late 1950s, as he had become increasingly distressed by what he saw as the deleterious effects of urban life as well as the anonymous effects of suburban sprawl. The meticulous planning that his staff employed at Disneyland, reasoned Disney, could simply be applied to the creation of a self-contained city.

Even though Disney passionately continued to work on plans for Epcot while on his deathbed, after he died the company's board didn't hesitate to put those plans aside, deeming them too expensive, too impractical, and not in line with the business's main mission: delivering family entertainment.

In the late 1970s, the idea was revived as a possibility, though it quickly transformed from a residential community into a sort of permanent World's Fair, with exhibitions of science and technology paving the way for the utopian cityscapes Disney so longed to create. The result was EPCOT Center, now known as Epcot, which opened in 1982. Although very little of Disney's original vision for Epcot is evident in the current park, the best place to see what it might have become is the town of Celebration, about 10 minutes from the main gate of Walt Disney World. Originally owned by the Walt Disney Company, the small village delivered on some of the retrofuturistic promise of Walt's original approach to Epcot—sans PeopleMovers and monorails. The community is mocked by some as a prefab Stepford-type town, but in the eyes of some architects and developers, it's acknowledged as a model of New Urbanism.

that highlight the technology of current sponsor Siemens.

Another giant ball at Epcot is the sphere that sits outside of **Mission: Space.** However, that's about the only similarity this ride has to the enervating journey one has on Spaceship Earth. If the many signs and cast-member admonitions warning away the pregnant, heart-troubled, and easily frightened aren't enough of a clue, be advised that Mission: Space is the most intense ride on Disney property. Built on flight-simulator technology, the ride is immersively themed as riders are transformed into a crew about to embark on a journey to the red planet. Of course, there is no actual launch, but the perfectly choreographed combination of computer animation, ride environment, and intense g-forces will very nearly fool your mind and body into believing that you've broken the bonds of gravity. In reality, you're just in a rapidly spinning centrifuge with your face plastered up against a tiny movie screen.

The two pavilions that make up the **Innoventions** plaza are stuffed with corporate-presented, educational-experimental exhibits like "Colortopia" (sponsored by Glidden). The most popular spot here is the Coca-Cola-sponsored "Club Cool," which features a half-dozen soda fountains stocked with non-American Coke products that are available as free samples, but, inexplicably, are not for purchase.

While Innoventions is one of the least-crowded areas of Epcot, the nearby **Test Track** typically boasts the park's most gruelingly long lines, which have only continued to grow. Advice: Don't be dissuaded by the crowds; abandon your group and head for the single-riders line, which is usually less than half the length of the standby line. Even if you have to stand in one of the longer lines, Test Track is not to be missed. Sponsored by Chevrolet, the attraction purports to recreate the design-and-test process that an automobile is put through before making its way to market. Digitally recreated testing grounds are the opening acts for a quick 65-mph ride down the steeply banked outdoor track; the last part only lasts for less than a minute, but it's a screaming bit of fun.

It's not exactly clear why the justifiably praised **Soarin' Around the World** attraction is in the agrarian-focused pavilion called **The Land,** but regardless of the incongruity of its location, this transplant from Disney's California Adventure in Anaheim has proved to be remarkably popular. Riders board a floorless flight simulator positioned in front of an enormous floor-to-ceiling movie screen. After liftoff, the seats move in tandem with the motion onscreen, realistically emulating the sensation of hang-gliding over various sights. A revamp of the ride transformed it from its all-California origin to a more global perspective that takes in sights like the Taj Mahal, Fiji, the pyramids at Giza, and much more. While it would have been nice if Disney had at least made Epcot's version of Soarin' a little Florida-centric, the thrill of fake flight is powerful indeed. Lines for Soarin' are nearly as outrageous as those for Test Track. With that in mind, the indoor line has been outfitted with motion-sensitive technology that gives guests an opportunity

to play interactive video games on screens overhead.

More appropriate to its location in The Land is, well, **Living with the Land,** a narrated boat ride expounding various methods of agriculture. Boring? Not so much. The combination of history lesson, ecological message, and the closing coup de grâce—a look at functioning futuristic hydroponic, aeroponic, and aquaculture labs, complete with gigantic gourds and Mickey-shaped cucumbers—proves to be surprisingly interesting. For an extra fee, guests can take the **Behind the Seeds Tour** ($20 adults, $16 children), a 45-minute close-up of Living with the Land's greenhouses.

The Seas with Nemo and Friends used to be a pavilion known as "The Living Seas," but given the success of *Finding Nemo,* the updated theme is a natural fit. The primary attraction here is a ride that is also called "The Seas with Nemo and Friends," an updated version of a more straightforward "sea cab" ride that used to guide visitors through the various features of the aquarium. Now, the sea cabs are "clamobiles," and animated versions of various characters from the film are projected to appear as if they're swimming with the inhabitants of the 5.7-million-gallon

Epcot's Test Track is a speedy thrill ride.

DiveQuest

Although the 5.7-million-gallon aquarium at the Seas pavilion provides plenty of aquatic beauty on the dry side of the thick-glass walls, scuba-certified individuals can get even closer to the sharks, fish, and rays by taking part in DiveQuest. The bulk of the three-hour program is a guided backstage tour of the aquarium facilities. The highlight is a 45-minute dive inside the coral reef habitat as tourists peer at you from the other side of the glass. Although the program is expensive ($175, theme park admission not required), it's quite a remarkable underwater excursion, combining perfectly controlled conditions and the typical Disney service (all dive gear is provided, as well as snacks afterward, and a DVD copy of footage of your dive is available for purchase). Divers must have current open-water adult dive certificates; in the case of kids age 10 and up, Junior Diver Certifications are also accepted. Reservations should be made at least a few days in advance (farther ahead during peak seasons) by calling 407/939-8687.

aquarium, the second-largest human-constructed saltwater tank in the world. While seeing characters Dory and Bruce may be appealing to the younger ones, it's that aquarium that holds the real stars of the Seas: more than 200 different species, including sharks, turtles, rays, tropical fish, and dolphins. The Sea Base area is set up like most public aquariums, and small educational stations are positioned throughout. If you've still got questions, a great place to get them answered is **Turtle Talk with Crush,** an animated and interactive show that utilizes the same technology employed at the Magic Kingdom's Monsters, Inc. Laugh Floor; an actor mimics the voice of Crush and responds to audience questions, while the animated turtle moves in real time, as if he can actually see the people in the crowd. It tickles kids to no end, and adults will be fascinated at the Imagineering prowess employed.

World Showcase

There are 11 countries represented in Epcot's **World Showcase.** Five are European, three are North American, two are East Asian, and tiny Morocco is left to represent the entirety of Africa and, I guess, the Middle East too. While nobody would attempt to argue that leaving out India and all of South America makes for a remotely representative way to showcase the world, this theme park section is as unique as it is improbable. There are very few actual rides or attractions in this part of Epcot, but the charming tourist-brochure image of each country that is represented makes for a fantastic way to spend an afternoon.

There are rides like Mexico's **Gran Fiesta Tour,** a lazy-river boat ride through various tourist sites (a 2007 update incorporated a *Three Caballeros*-era Donald Duck while excising some of the more 1980s-specific imagery), and Norway's **Frozen Ever After,** a briefly exhilarating boat ride that interpolates the location-agnostic Arendelle of the film *Frozen* into Norway. (This ride replaced the long-running Maelstrom ride, and utilizes the same technology and experience, just with different characters and visuals.) But these rides are the exceptions. Most countries highlight live-action performances like the Beatles tribute band in the UK pavilion, the **Dragon Legend Acrobats** in "China," or the demonstrations by **Miyuki** (who sculpts candy into animal shapes) in the Japan pavilion.

For the most part, the allure of the World Showcase is simply circumnavigating the lake, a pleasant walk that allows one to start in "Mexico" and end in "Canada," taking in food, drink, and tchotchkes from all over "Italy," "Germany," "France," "America," and more in the process. If this sounds like it would be boring for television-addled kids, it's actually not. Kids thrive on the wildly varying sights and sounds, and the cast members in each country take extra care to make

Eating and Drinking Around the World

A popular pastime at Epcot is to show up with an empty stomach, skip right past the rides and science exhibits of Future World, and eat and drink one's way around the world—or at least around the World Showcase. While this can be fun any time of the year, it's most enjoyable during the annual **Food & Wine Festival,** held late September-early November. In addition to the regular array of treats and tipples the World Showcase offers, the festival adds dozens of kiosks serving tapas-style nibbles and various beer and wine samples. Most of the regular World Showcase countries are represented with kiosks, but there are also more than a dozen additional countries serving food and drinks. The food samples usually cost $3.50-8, and drinks are typically $6-9.

their pavilions feel less like a World Cultures lecture and more like an animated adventure. In 2012, Disney launched the "Phineas and Ferb"-themed **Agent P's Showcase Adventure,** a Showcase-wide scavenger hunt that has kids digging up clues in each pavilion to track down Dr. Doofenshmirtz.

Special Events

In addition to the signature **Food & Wine Festival** (late Sept.-early Nov.), the annual **International Flower & Garden Festival** (spring) draws amateur horticulturists and backyard gardeners for topiary gawking as well as tips and workshops.

Food

Of all the Disney parks, Epcot is the one where, no matter what your culinary inclinations, you should have no problem finding something to eat. The Norwegian-themed **Akershus Royal Banquet Hall** (Norway pavilion) and the fresh-food-peddling **Garden Grill** (The Land pavilion) both offer character dining. The **Coral Reef** restaurant at the Seas pavilion offers fresh seafood, although you'll be surrounded by a saltwater tank and your kids will likely have just finished communing with Nemo, so it may actually be somewhat unsettling.

For quick-service dining, the **Sunshine Season** food court is far and away the best option. Located in the Land pavilion, it offers an array of ultra-fresh and veg-friendly dishes, ranging from sandwiches, soups, and salads to wok-tossed Asian dishes and noodle bowls, as well as rotisserie chicken and salmon cooked over a wood-fired grill.

The best of the nationalistic dining options is the exquisite **Bistro de Paris.** Reservations are mandatory at this dinner-only establishment, which also enforces a resort-casual dress code. Abstaining from flip-flops is a small sacrifice for the decadent (and expensive) dishes; while not strictly limited to French cuisine, the preparations are elegant and precise.

Less intimate but still serving remarkably good food is **Les Chefs de France,** which serves up traditional fare: quiche, crepes, goat cheese salad, and more. Also on the menu is a macaroni-and-Gruyère casserole that will have you forever foreswearing the blue-and-yellow boxes.

Also recommended would be the modern flair of Japan's **Tokyo Dining** and the **Rose and Crown** in the UK pavilion; the latter's menu options are limited to traditional pub food, but it's prepared excellently and the atmosphere is extra-friendly, even by Disney standards. Don't neglect to pick up a churro and a potent frozen margarita at Mexico's **San Angel Inn** or one of the signature frozen teas at the stand across from the China Pavilion.

DISNEY'S HOLLYWOOD STUDIOS

Disney's Hollywood Studios didn't exactly get off to a blockbuster start. Opened in 1989 as Disney-MGM Studios, it was the third park to open at Walt Disney World, hastily conceived as a response to the construction of Universal Studios Orlando. When the park opened, it only had four attractions. Today, the renamed park houses the two most thrilling attractions on Disney property: Aerosmith's Rock 'n' Roller Coaster and the Twilight Zone Tower of Terror. The setting combines Hollywood's Golden Age glamour with a sprinkling of Pixar's modern movie-making magic. Although it's still the lesser of the four parks, it has more than overcome its initial stumbles and now boasts plenty that's worth seeing.

Hollywood Boulevard

Just like the Magic Kingdom's Main Street, U.S.A., Hollywood Studios's **Hollywood Boulevard** is a mood-setting thoroughfare that allows visitors to slough off the outside world and transport themselves into the glory days of Hollywood. Appropriately, the only real "attraction" here other than an array of shops is **The Great Movie Ride.** One of the original attractions that opened with the park in 1989, this ride is definitely showing its age. Viewers ride on a tram that takes them through a sort of "living" high-light reel of the last 100 years of moviemaking. Extensive set pieces and animatronic figures recreate scenes from *Casablanca,*

Public Enemy No. 1, Alien, and more. The 20-minute ride culminates with a montage of great film moments, all set to a majestic and heart-tugging score.

Animation Courtyard

Several of the attractions in the **Animation Courtyard** continue the movie-museum theme of the Great Movie Ride. **Walt Disney: One Man's Dream,** and **Star Wars Launch Bay** are walk-through attractions stuffed with memorabilia and artifacts. Appropriately, One Man's Dream is the best of the three, and though predictably hagiographic, it does give a somewhat comprehensive look at the life of the man behind the mouse. The Star Wars exhibit, on the other hand, combines memorabilia with a cool meet-and-greet session with animatronic versions of the series's most iconic characters.

For the young ones who are less interested in movie magic and more interested in seeing their favorite characters, the **Voyage of the Little Mermaid** and **Disney Junior—Live on Stage** are two live action performances. The former is heavily dependent on some impressive special effects, while the latter is driven by audience participation and lots of singing and dancing.

Disney's Hollywood Studios

Pixar Place

Formerly an infrequently used and lightly trafficked part of the Animation Courtyard, **Pixar Place** now houses one of Hollywood Studios' most popular attractions, **Toy Story Mania.** This is a shooting ride, similar to the Buzz Lightyear ride at Magic Kingdom. However, Toy Story Mania has the added awesomeness of being in 3-D. While certainly not the most original ride concept, the execution of this attraction is flawless, from the heavily themed and interactive queue area where you become "toy-sized" to the impressive 3-D effects.

Echo Lake

Fans of the *Star Wars* movies may one day get the full-fledged theme park they've long pined for, but until then there's **Star Tours: The Adventures Continue,** a motion-simulator ride produced in collaboration with George Lucas. Of all the rides at Disney parks to undergo renovations, Star Tours was most in need of a revamp to take advantage of the 20 years of digital technology that have happened since it first debuted. In May 2011, *Star Wars* fans got their wish when the new ride opened, featuring an entirely new experience. The basic concept of the ride (you're aboard a starship for an excursion and things go awry, leading to unexpected adventure) is still in place, but the motion-simulation effects and 3-D visuals have been vastly improved. Even better, instead of a fixed, predictable voyage, there are now a number of different adventures possible, thanks to the hapless guidance of C3PO and R2D2. Although all riders face off with Darth Vader at the beginning, a ride could result in you on the ice planet of Hoth, taking part in a podrace on Tatooine, under the waters of Naboo, or several other possibilities. It's an impressive and immersive adventure. Although all four Disney resorts have a Star Tours attraction, only Orlando's Hollywood Studios has **Jedi Training: Trials of the Temple,** a live-action stage show that allows kids to interact with Chewbacca, Darth Maul, Darth Vader, and other characters from the films.

Sunset Boulevard

The two marquee attractions at Hollywood Studios are located within yards of each other at the end of **Sunset Boulevard,** so expect considerable congestion when making your way through the turkey-leg vendors and gift shops along this route. Your persistence will pay off, though, as **The Twilight Zone Tower of Terror** and the Aerosmith-themed **Rock 'n' Roller Coaster** are not just the two best rides at Hollywood Studios, they may be the two best rides on Disney property.

The Tower of Terror puts riders on a ghostly malfunctioning elevator inside the seen-better-days Hollywood Tower Hotel. The theming of this ride is incredibly impressive and detailed down to the last cobweb on the lobby's registration desk. While the *Twilight Zone* references may be lost on some generations of riders, there is a thrill in making your way through the hotel's 13 floors, dropping like a stone when your elevator malfunctions, and being jerked back up when it recovers, only to fall again and again. The drops are randomized, so riders never know when and how often they'll plummet.

The Rock 'n' Roller Coaster is an extremely fast indoor coaster that would be a screaming success even without the presence of aging rockers Aerosmith. The combination of the high-volume soundtrack, the 0-to-60-in-3-seconds launch, and a series of high-speed loops and corkscrews, all in neon-flecked darkness, makes for a chart-topping (*groan*) coaster experience.

For the less thrill-inclined, Sunset Boulevard is also home to **Beauty and the Beast—Live on Stage,** an extravagant stage production that distills the highlights of the animated film into a half-hour cavalcade of live action, songs, and dance.

Special Events

Star Wars Weekends (late May/early June) has become one of the resort's biggest annual

Best Restaurants

★ **The Hollywood Brown Derby:** An appropriately classic selection of dishes emulates the Golden Age of Hollywood (page 254).

★ **Sharks Underwater Grill:** It's the dining room that's the real attraction here: One wall is shared with the glass of an enormous shark-filled aquarium (page 282).

★ **Nile Ethiopian Cuisine:** International Drive is filled with tourist traps, but richly spiced meats and injera bread make Nile stand out (page 288).

★ **Pom-Pom's Teahouse & Sandwicheria:** More than two dozen varieties of hot and iced teas are available, along with an array of pressed sandwiches (page 303).

★ **The Ravenous Pig:** Exceptionally inventive and perfectly prepared dishes are the centerpiece of an environment that's part pub, part fine dining (page 303).

★ **Hawkers:** Numerous small plates of five-spiced meats and noodles and vegetables emulate Singaporean street food (page 304).

★ **Market on South:** This vegan food hall includes a bakery, kombucha brewery, and Southern comfort/soul food restaurant (page 305).

events, as fans of the sci-fi films flock to the park to look at exclusive memorabilia, costumed characters, and the occasional actual star from the films.

Night of Joy (Sept.) is one of two Christian music festivals that happen in Orlando-area theme parks; the other is the Rock the Universe night at Universal Studios, which is usually held on the same dates as Night of Joy. Appropriately, the Disney festival is a little more buttoned-down, focusing less on the sort of alt-rock Christian groups that play at Universal and more on pop-oriented acts.

Food

Disney's Hollywood Studios is home to several excellent restaurants, including the two best in-park dining experiences within the entire resort. ★ **The Hollywood Brown Derby** (11:30am-3pm and 3:30pm-10:30pm, from $19) is a little pricey but well worth the expense. Emulating the Golden Age of Hollywood elegance of its namesake, this Brown Derby serves an appropriately classic selection of dishes—strip steak, pork rib

chops, grilled salmon—along with more contemporary plates like ahi tuna and a coconut-tofu noodle bowl. And, yes, it makes a mean Cobb salad here. The atmosphere is upscale but also decidedly relaxed. In comparison to many other in-park restaurants, there's never a sense that you're being rushed to make room for the next wave of diners. The dining room, though large, is expertly partitioned to create a unique sense of spacious intimacy.

Even more intimate—in fact, homey—is the **'50s Prime Time Cafe** (hours vary, from $12). You'll be served by motherly waitresses who admonish diners to finish their veggies and keep their elbows off the table, while an array of black-and-white television sets shows clips from *Father Knows Best, The Donna Reed Show,* and, of course, *The Mickey Mouse Club.* Small dining rooms have Formica tables set out with blue plate specials like fried chicken, meat loaf, pot roast, and an absolutely mind-blowing chicken pot pie. In a not-so-subtle dig at the halcyon imagery of the decade, there's also a full bar adjacent to the dining room, serving everything from

The Tree of Life underscores the ecological vibe at Animal Kingdom.

classic cocktails and bottled beer to selections from "Dad's Liquor Cabinet."

★ ANIMAL KINGDOM

From the moment you pass through the turnstiles at **Animal Kingdom,** it's clear that this is a different kind of park. There's no expansive entryway with an icon like Cinderella Castle or Spaceship Earth announcing the park's intent; instead, the foliage-draped **Oasis** is a lush maze of animal habitats linked by gently flowing waters and the sounds of chirping birds and splashing mammals. It's a unique mood-setter, preparing you for a park built around eco-sensitive concepts and global conservation concerns. As any Animal Kingdom staffer will tell you, it is not a zoo. But the park is far more focused on observing and learning about animals than it is on delivering thrill rides and character interactions. Sure, you can ride a few great roller coasters here and get your picture taken with Tigger but the whole Animal Kingdom experience is definitely unique, making it not only the

newest of all the Disney kingdoms but also the one most worthy of repeat visits.

Discovery Island

Situated in the heart of Animal Kingdom is **Discovery Island,** which is home to the 14-story **Tree of Life,** an enormous replication of a baobab tree carved in such a way that images of nearly 400 animals comprise the "bark." The Tree of Life can be seen from throughout the park, but only by getting up close on Discovery Island can you see the intricate work that went into it.

The big attraction in this area of the park is located in the base of the Tree of Life. **It's Tough to Be a Bug** is a 3-D movie experience based on *A Bug's Life,* giving audience members a bug's-eye view of various insects. The 3-D effects are accentuated by seats that rumble and squirt water at unsuspecting viewers. There are a few startles and scares in this experience. Although it's directly targeted at younger crowds, the youngest in your crew may need a few reminders about the difference between movies and reality.

Africa

The **Africa** section of Animal Kingdom has a little bit of Kenya, a little bit of Zanzibar, a little bit of South Africa, and a little bit of Tanzania. Despite the broad sweep of the pan-African theming, there's a sensitivity and attention to detail in the central "village" of Harambe that's surprisingly effective.

The heart of Animal Kingdom is the **Kilimanjaro Safaris** ride, which puts visitors on a truck that goes out onto the savannas and jungles of the park's expansive animal habitats. There's a story about poachers told by every driver, and a few moments of melodramatic peril. But these bits of acting are entirely superfluous, as the stars of this ride are the dozens of animals on the safari. On busy days the safari ups the number of trucks that run the safari track, so some of the magic can be sapped away while waiting for the vehicles in front of yours to make their way through. Having the chance to get extremely close to giraffes, gazelles, lions, rhinos, and elephants who are just going about their business makes the traffic jams more than manageable.

After disembarking from the safari truck, make your way through the **Gorilla Falls Exploration Trail,** a walking trail through a five-acre habitat area filled with meerkats, antelopes, hippopotamuses, and silverback gorillas.

Asia

As ambiguous and all-encompassing as the Africa section, the **Asia** section of Animal Kingdom incorporates Chinese, Indian, Tibetan, Balinese, and Mongolian influences into the fictional kingdom of Anandapur. Just as Asia itself houses more than half of the world's population, you'll sometimes feel as if half of the day's Disney visitors are crammed into the sights and attractions of this part of the park. This is primarily due to the presence of popular rides like the white-water **Kali River Rapids** and the excellent **Expedition Everest** roller coaster. The former is a fairly standard theme-park soaker, accentuated by some environmental messages and some great special effects. As for Expedition Everest, the mere presence of the Abominable Snowman would be enough to make this coaster a

winner, but when combined with high speeds, a brief bit of backwards motion, and a 50-foot drop, it's no surprise that this ride is almost always subject to incredibly long lines.

Less adrenaline-pumping is the **Maharaja Jungle Trek,** another expertly themed walking tour through various animal habitats. This one features Komodo dragons, tapirs, fruit bats, peacocks, deer, and tigers.

Flights of Wonder is a 25-minute show featuring an array of trained hawks, falcons, parrots, and other birds. The plot of the show is silly and unnecessary, but the birds and their trainers are incredibly impressive.

Pandora: The World of *Avatar*

Developed in tandem with James Cameron and based on the 2009 blockbuster flick *Avatar,* **Pandora** opened in 2017 with great anticipation. Avatar isn't exactly the same sort of cultural touchstone that many Disney attractions are based on, but fans of the movie were eager to see how Disney "Imagineers" would translate Cameron's vision into an interactive world.

The optimistic curiosity was rewarded with one of the most innovative and immersive experiences on Disney property. Teeing off the environmental/conservation

Animal Kingdom's safari ride gives guests up-close views of many different animals.

undercurrent of Cameron's film (which is appropriate for Animal Kingdom), Pandora is a uniquely landscaped area that combines live plants from our own planet with more fantastic flora crafted by the Disney team, complete with jaw-dropping geographical features like floating mountains. There are also, of course, a couple rides here, and the thrilling virtual reality flight simulating *Avatar* **Flight of Passage** is the best of the two; however, the more standard boat ride **Na'vi River Journey** (which takes guests on a guided tour of Pandora's natural features) is also spectacular.

Dinoland U.S.A.

There's a distinct sense of incongruity that you experience when crossing the "Olden Gate Bridge" into **Dinoland U.S.A.** It's part carnival midway: **Chester & Hester's Dino-Rama** features themed-up versions of basic state-fair rides like the **TriceraTop Spin** and **Primeval Whirl.** And it's part playground: **The Boneyard.** The carnival and playground themes are clearly geared toward younger audiences. To that end, there's a live puppetry and dancing show, **Finding Nemo—The Musical,** that's sure to please the elementary school set.

All of this makes the presence of the **Dinosaur** ride something of a horrifying anomaly. After getting the kids all hyped up on the majesty and mystery of dinosaurs, they'll certainly be curious about this adventure. Bill Nye the Science Guy hosts visitors to the Dino Institute, where he invites them to hop on board a time machine to go back to the time of the giant reptiles. Of course, things go awry, darkness falls, meteors begin raining from the sky, and a giant carnivorous dinosaur begins chasing your vehicle. This ride is loud, dark, and incredibly intense, all of which is great for grown-up thrill seekers, but not for small kids, no matter how excited they are.

Rafiki's Planet Watch

Also known as the "the lines are too long in the rest of the park" area of Animal Kingdom, **Rafiki's Planet Watch** is well-intentioned but pretty inconsequential. Unfortunately, it's also pretty inconvenient. To get here, guests must board the **Wildlife Express Train** for a five-minute ride, only to be greeted by a five-minute walking trail to the actual site. The educational facility offers live animal encounters, a few interactive exhibits, and a peek at the park's behind-the-scenes veterinary work in the **Conservation Station.** There's also the **Affection Section** petting zoo.

Special Attractions

Although Animal Kingdom doesn't host any annual events, it does offer one unique experience. The **Backstage Tales** ($90 pp) experience is a great behind-the-scenes tour that gives guests a peek at the day-to-day maintenance and care of the many animals that live in the park.

Food

Africa's **Tusker House** (open all day, breakfast $18.99 adults, $10.99 children; lunch $19.99 adults, $10.99 children; dinner $26.99 adults, $12.99 children) is a buffet-style restaurant that hosts a unique breakfast, offering character dining in the form of "Donald's Safari Breakfast." The rest of the day features an incredible selection of pan-global dishes, ranging from couscous and vegetable samosas to Cape Malay curry chicken and spiced tandoori tofu, along with more routine plates like grilled salmon, rotisserie chicken, and for the kids, PB and J, mac and cheese, and more.

The **Yak & Yeti** (hours vary, $17-23) restaurant is actually two separate restaurants. Guests can take advantage of counter service for simple Chinese dishes like sweet and sour pork and kung pao beef, or they can sit down for a more extensive and expensive menu. Unfortunately, the food here has yet to live up to its location or its prices. Despite the beautiful theming of the restaurant, the Chinese fare—glazed roast duck, lo mein, crispy fish, stir-fried beef and broccoli—is nowhere near the quality you would expect for the price.

For light bites, head to the **Kusafiri**

MyMagic+

The **MyMagic+** program is a "vacation management system" intended to bring together a number of previously disparate elements: **hotel reservations, park admission,** and **FastPass** queue slots. The program is ambitious in both its technological implementation, via radio frequency identification (RFID)-enabled wristbands that allow everything from buying a Coke at a food vendor to getting into hotel rooms, and its data-mining possibilities. Your credit card information is attached to your ID, but more notably, the band allows park engineers to monitor and manage traffic flows throughout the parks. In development for more than a half-decade, the MyMagic+ program went through extensive tests in 2013 and 2014, first with park employees, then with resort-hotel guests, and went live in spring 2014.

While most of the advantage of MyMagic+ is in Disney's favor, there is plenty going for it for guests as well. Being able to schedule FastPass times at the parks' most popular rides is the most obvious advantage, of course, but the best part is being able to use the trip-planning elements of the program's website. You may end up spending more in the gift shops and restaurants than you planned, but you'll also be able to maximize your time at Walt Disney World. While scheduling your vacation to the hour may not seem like the most fun way to experience all that Disney has to offer, it's a good way to make sure you don't miss that must-see ride or restaurant.

Coffee Shop (hours vary) inside Tusker House for fresh pastries and coffee, or Asia's **Anandapur Ice Cream Truck** (hours vary).

There is also an outpost of the **Rainforest Cafe** (hours vary, from $15) at the park's entrance. Although the eco-theming is in line with the park's modus operandi, there's nothing spectacular about the menu here other than the eye-popping prices.

OTHER DISNEY RESORT ATTRACTIONS

Of course, there's a lot more to this 25,000-acre resort than just the four main kingdoms. Disney's ideal guest is one who arrives on Disney property and doesn't leave until it's time to go home, and to that end, there are dining and shopping areas, hotels, movie theaters, spas, golf courses, and pretty much anything else you would need to occupy your every recreational need for a week or more. The biggest attractions are the two water parks, Blizzard Beach and Typhoon Lagoon. During the summer they often fill up quite early in the day, forcing staff to prohibit new entries until a requisite number of people have departed. Fear not, though; even if you don't manage to make your way onto

the water slides before lunch, there are plenty of other diversions around the resort to hold your attention.

Blizzard Beach

The busier and more thrill-centric of Disney's two water parks, **Blizzard Beach** ($60 adults, $54 children) is all about breathtakingly high water slides. Sure, the snow-capped theming is amusing, but the focus here is on adventures like **Summit Plummet,** a 120-foot-high beast that propels riders at speeds nearing 60 mph. The **Slush Gusher** gets you going at "only" about 50 mph, and the competitive-minded can race each other on the inner tubes of the **Downhill Double Dipper.** Toboggan mat slides, tube slides, kid-friendly play areas, a lazy river, and a wave pool are also part of the park.

Typhoon Lagoon

Typhoon Lagoon ($60 adults, $54 children) may not offer slides of the same heart-pounding intensity as Blizzard Beach's, but with a water coaster like the impressive **Crush 'n' Gusher** and the 36-foot drop that sliders experience on **Storm Slides,** it's far from sedate. There's also a coral reef environment where guests can snorkel among live sharks and tropical fish, and a surfing-ready wave pool.

ESPN Wide World of Sports

The 220-acre **ESPN Wide World of Sports** is likely to be of little interest to park visitors who don't have a friend or relative participating in one of the many amateur athletic competitions that take place here. If your visit to Walt Disney World brings you here in March, you can catch the **Atlanta Braves** in spring training; in August, the **Tampa Bay Buccaneers** arrive at the complex for training camp.

Golf Courses

The Walt Disney World Resort is a prime **golfing destination** (407/939-4653, http://golfwdw.com), with four courses, all of which are certified wildlife sanctuaries. All of the 18-hole courses offer GPS-equipped carts; lessons and club rentals are available at all four courses. The **Magnolia** course (from $100) is impressive; the **Palm** and **Lake Buena Vista** courses (from $69) are slightly less expensive (and less challenging); and the **Oak Trail** (from $38) is a nine-hole walking course for those who want to get a quick half-round in.

Spas

There are three full-service **spas** at Walt Disney World, all of which are located in resort hotels. The **Grand Floridian Spa** (407/824-3000) is as luxurious as its surroundings, while the spa at **Saratoga Springs Resort & Spa** (407/939-7727) blends that property's old-timey vibe with contemporary massage and spa treatments. The decadent **Mandara** (407/934-4772) is at the **Dolphin Resort Hotel,** and it is thick with Southeast Asian ambiance. Of the three, Mandara is the only one that offers hair and nail services.

Food

Food courts and casual dining options abound throughout the resort. Most are lightly themed to align with the hotel or area in which they reside, and all deliver decent if thoroughly unspectacular food. When you're serving hundreds of thousands of plates a day, it's much more about being efficient than it is about being exceptional.

There are a handful of true destination dining options at the resort, however. They're all a bit pricey, but each is worth it. You'll need to make reservations for most of these restaurants, a process simplified by Disney's automated dining reservation system; just call 407/WDW-DINE (407/939-3463) as far as 180 days in advance. While it's likely that your schedule and budget can accommodate only one or two of these restaurants on a trip to Walt Disney World, any of them are worthy of a foodie's attention.

Jiko—The Cooking Place (Animal Kingdom Lodge, 5:30pm-10pm daily, $29-46) features an African-inspired menu, accented by Mediterranean and South Asian flavors. Finding quinoa, rocket pesto, figs, curry shrimp, ostrich filet, samosas, and short ribs on one menu may indicate the height of catch-all folly, but an emphasis on strong rustic flavors and rich earthy spices weaves together this broad selection of dishes.

From the moment you step into the LED-lit tunnel that leads you into **The Wave** (Contemporary Resort, 7:30am-11am, noon-2pm, and 5:30pm-10pm daily, $10.49-37.99), an atmosphere of stylish modernity is instantly established. This is technically a "casual dining" spot, offering breakfast, lunch, and dinner. Although all three meals feature somewhat circumscribed menus, the quiet atmosphere and expert preparation of meat and pasta standards, super-fresh salads, and a daily "sustainable fish" dish make it something of a well-kept secret. The bar is open until midnight.

Todd English's Bluezoo (Dolphin Resort, 5pm-11pm daily, $29-72) serves contemporary American cuisine in a sophisticated and modern environment. Of course, celebrity chef English probably won't be in the kitchen preparing your Cantonese lobster or bacon-wrapped tuna, but the crew on hand

The Hoop-De-Doo Musical Revue

At the **Hoop-De-Doo Musical Revue,** a long-running pioneer-themed dinner-theater experience at **Disney's Wilderness Lodge,** the jokes are corny, the music and jokes are corny, and the food consists of endless plates of fried chicken and corn on the cob (corny!), but somehow it all works, and if you're capable of shaking off the vestiges of ironic detachment and getting into the spirit of the show, it's an absolute must-do if you'll be on Disney property for more than a few days. The script for the show digs up every hoary joke, pun, and slapstick gag you can imagine and delivers them all in a lighthearted self-aware fashion interspersed with goofy, catchy songs that even the grouchiest attendee will find themselves enjoying. Even teenagers have been known to crack a smile during the show. The food is served in metal buckets that land on your table with a thud. The chicken, ribs, and other fare is comfort food done right, prepared excellently by a kitchen that could probably get away with doing a lot less.

There are three shows nightly, at 4pm, 6:15pm, and 8:30pm, and each show lasts about two hours from the time you're seated. There are three seating categories: the most expensive (from $72 adults, $43 children 3-9) gets you a table in the middle area closest to the stage; category 2 (from $67 adults, $39 children 3-9) still provides great seats, although they're a bit farther from the stage or in the middle of the balcony; and the "cheap" seats (from $64 adults, $38 children 3-9) have good visibility but are located along the sides of the balcony. The price includes appetizers, all-you-care-to-eat entrées, dessert, and soft drinks. Beer and wine are available for an additional charge. Reservations are essential (407/939-3463), and guests with special dietary needs are easily accommodated as long as those needs are made known at the time you make the reservation.

does a marvelous job nonetheless. The emphasis here is on fresh seafood—especially fish dishes—but beef, pork, and poultry are also available. Vegetarians are likely to find little here that they can eat.

Love great food? Hate crying babies? Head for **Victoria & Albert's** (Grand Floridian Resort & Spa, dinner seatings 5:45pm-6:30pm and 9pm-9:45pm daily, six-course prix fixe $145 pp, $210 pp with meal-specific wine pairing). Long the grande dame of Disney dining, Victoria & Albert's not only insists on a dress code (no jeans or capris, much less shorts or flip-flops; jackets are required for men), but also requires diners to be at least 10 years of age, the only restaurant in the park to have such a rule. While some may fuss over the indignity of not being able to have their toddler along for a six-course $145 meal, the result is a consistently exquisite restaurant experience. From the accompanying harpist and the complimentary rose for the women at your table to the personalized menus featuring anything from elk and *kurobuta* pork to duck and prosciutto-wrapped lamb, Victoria & Albert's is

classic fine dining. If the prix fixe offerings aren't quite extravagant enough for you, foie gras, caviar, and Kobe beef can be had for an additional charge. Also available for an additional charge (add $75 pp, $115 with wine pairing) is a seat at the chef's table in the kitchen, where the chef offers up various nibbles for you to sample and a maid and butler are on hand to tend to your needs.

Artist Point (Wilderness Lodge, 5:30pm-10pm daily, $28-52) combines an upscale menu with the rustic ambiance of a classic Pacific Northwest hunting and fishing lodge. The result is a menu of fresh and hearty fish dishes, like the cedar plank-roasted salmon, which is glazed in a pear-ginger reduction and served with a hash of pear and smoked pork belly. Steaks, chops, and pan-seared scallops are also on the menu. Vegetarians are restricted to potato-filled pot stickers served with edamame and wilted spinach.

DISNEY SPRINGS

The roots of **Disney Springs** go all the way back to 1975, when it opened as the small

Lake Buena Vista Shopping Village. Over time the village has grown considerably. In 1989 a nightlife area called Pleasure Island was opened (it closed in 2008), and by 1997 the original small shopping mall had expanded into two distinct areas, Downtown Disney's Marketplace and West Side. The site includes a (free!) parking garage and many shopping and dining opportunities. In addition to marquee entertainment spots like Cirque du Soleil's theater, House of Blues, a bowling alley, and one of Orlando's best movie theaters, there are restaurants, bars, and shops catering to a wide range of tastes (and price points).

The 24-screen **AMC Disney Springs** is a massive and modern multiplex movie theater, complete with a handful of "Dine-In Theatre" rooms where moviegoers (who must be 18 or older or accompanied by a parent or guardian) can dine on a limited menu of sandwiches and pizzas at their table/seat. There's also a bar, and the concession stand here is extensively stocked. Adjacent to the movie theater is **Splitsville Luxury Lanes** (10am-2am daily, from $15 pp/hour including shoe rental), a high-end bowling alley with 30 lanes spread over two levels. Despite the retro-kitschy 1950s decor, this ain't your granddad's bowling alley, as there's almost as much emphasis placed on the cocktails and craft beers, comfortable lounge areas, and expanded dining options as there is on the hurling of balls at pins.

Want to get away from the crowds? Take a ride on **Characters in Flight** (8:30am-midnight daily, $18 adults, $12 children), a hot-air balloon painted with the silhouettes of famous Disney characters that takes riders 400 feet above the bustle of Disney Springs for spectacular day or night views of the park and surrounding areas. The ride only lasts a few minutes, but is well worth the cost (and the wait).

Shopping

Think you've seen every possible permutation of mouse ears and magic wands in the seemingly endless array of gift shops throughout the Disney theme parks? You haven't. The 50,000-square-foot **World of Disney** (9:30am-11pm daily) purports to contain the largest selection of Disney merchandise in the world, and it's not hard to believe that claim. You'll find everything from key chains and coffee mugs to luggage, jewelry, and even kitchen goods stuffed into this enormous outlet.

Surprisingly, the majority of the shopping options at Disney Springs aren't specifically Disney-related. The fantastic **LEGO Imagination Center** is part building-block museum and part toy mega mart. Other well-known brands like **Columbia Sportswear, Uniqlo, Coca-Cola, Kate Spade, Lucky Brand, Sephora, Tumi** and more have outlets here, while there are many other shops focusing on niche items. Most stores in Disney Springs are open 10am-midnight daily.

Food

Part restaurant, part music venue, part tourist trap, **House of Blues** (11am-11pm Sun.-Mon., 11am-midnight Tues.-Wed., 11am-2am Thurs.-Sat., $11-28) is something of an attraction in and of itself. Like most of the chain's outlets, the one at Disney Springs maintains a faux-rustic atmosphere that's meant to convince guests they've stumbled upon some swampy roadhouse where the gumbo is hot and the blues are cool. The whole place runs like a well-oiled machine, and the shrimp po'boys, jambalaya, and fried chicken, though tasty, have considerably less personality than the folk art adorning the walls. On Sunday mornings, however, the restaurant extends its reach into the music hall and serves up a spectacular **Gospel Brunch** (seatings at 10:30am and 1pm, $40.50 adults, $22.25 children, children 2 and under free) with mountainous offerings of grits, fried catfish, mac and cheese, roast potatoes, biscuits and gravy, and pretty much any other comfort food you need to shake off Saturday night. The feasting is accompanied by top-notch gospel performances curated by gospel legend Kirk

Franklin; typically it's a local group, but occasionally the likes of the Blind Boys of Alabama grace the stage.

One of the most noteworthy additions to the new Disney Springs was **Morimoto Asia** (11:30am-midnight daily, $15-35), a fine-dining, pan-Asian restaurant helmed by Chef Masahura Morimoto of Iron Chef America. If you're looking for a splurge, indulge in the omakase experience ($150 pp), which treats you to a chef's selection of a half-dozen courses presented in a cozy setting. Reservations are essential.

Bongos (11am-10:30pm daily, bar until 2am, $8-29) gets quite a bit of attention due to its famous owners, entertainers Gloria and Emilio Estefan. The expansive Cuban menu ranges from light plates (media noche, Cuban sandwiches, pan con bistec) to hearty dishes like *ropa vieja,* pork loin, *chicharrones,* and more; all are rich and tasty, and some boast surprisingly complex flavor profiles. Service here can occasionally be poor, but once you're seated, the playfully stylish atmosphere, stiff mojitos, and nightly performances by a Desi Arnaz impersonator—yes, really—make for a memorable meal.

Irish food, when crafted solely as an accompaniment to whiskey and beer, can often be something of a nightmare. Accordingly, many "Irish pubs" in the United States, especially those targeted at thirsty tourists, are exceedingly liberal with their drink servings and exceedingly lazy in their kitchens. **Raglan Road** (11am-11pm, bar until 2am, $14-28) is certainly willing to pour you a stiff one or three, but the staff will make sure you've got some exceptional food to go along with the drinks. While including all the expected staples—shepherd's pie, bangers and mash, fish-and-chips—Raglan's kitchen also sneaks roasted ham, pork loin, lemon sole, pan-roasted chicken, and a number of other examples of atypical pub fare onto the menu. There's live Irish music and dancing nightly.

The food at **T-Rex Cafe** (11am-11pm daily, $13-20, buffet $28) isn't too special (burgers, sandwiches, pasta, steak, and seafood), but the atmosphere here is hugely attractive to kids who are obsessed with dinosaurs. Similar to the Rainforest Cafe (and owned by the same company), the decor is the main draw. Guests can not only gawk at massive animatronic dinosaurs but also witness meteor showers during which all the giant reptiles go crazy (a little morbid from the dinosaur's perspective), wander through an ice cave, and dig around a fossil-dig play area. It's complete sensory overload and totally fun at the same time.

ACCOMMODATIONS

The rates at most on-site hotels are a bit higher than at nearby places, but there are some distinct advantages to bear in mind. Guests who stay within the resort are entitled to take advantage of the complimentary Disney's Magical Express service, which picks them up from the airport and drops them and their bags at their hotel. Combined with the near-constant availability of bus transportation throughout the resort, guests who arrive intending to only explore Disney property will have all of their transportation needs taken care of, negating the need for a rental car.

Disney hotels are divided into three categories: value, moderate, and deluxe. But regardless of which tier you choose, the basics remain the same: an immaculately clean (if small) guest room located in a large, well-equipped hotel complex filled with swimming pools, dining options, recreational activities, and thousands of other tourists. As one ascends from "value" to "deluxe," the amenities and atmosphere scale accordingly, but even the most basic level of service on Disney property is in line with the best midrange national chain hotel. For on-site reservations, call 407/939-7429.

Resort Hotels

One of Walt Disney World's four "value" resorts, the **Pop Century Resort** (near Wide World of Sports; from $135 d) is the newest and the most fun. Ten blindingly bright motel-style buildings are painted in decade-specific themes, and the property is festooned

Best Accommodations

★ **Animal Kingdom Lodge:** Wild-roaming zebras, gazelles, giraffes, and other animals set this luxurious, safari-themed lodge apart (page 263).

★ **The Cabins at Disney's Fort Wilderness Resort:** Perfect for families or those planning an extended stay, these cabins are homes away from home (page 264).

★ **The Grand Floridian Resort & Spa:** Equipped with an award-winning spa and an excellent restaurant, this elegant hotel is worth the splurge (page 264).

★ **Hard Rock Hotel:** The best and most exciting of the three Universal Orlando resort hotels is this excellent rock-and-roll spot (page 278).

★ **Point Orlando Resort:** This is a surprisingly quiet all-suite resort in the thick of the I-Drive action (page 289).

with enormous renditions of pop-culture artifacts like yo-yos and Rubik's cubes. The buildings house an eye-popping 2,880 guest rooms, and accordingly the queues in the enormous food court and the crowds in any of the three pools can sometimes be daunting.

The "moderate" resorts (from $195 d) are best represented by the **Coronado Springs Resort** and the **Port Orleans French Quarter Resort.** Coronado Springs is large but charming and well-organized, with 1,900 guest rooms divided among "casita," "rancho," and "cabana" buildings, all of which are easily accessible from the main registration-dining-pool areas. The French Quarter resort has "only" 1,000 guest rooms but is laid out in a fashion that's very nearly quaint, with wrought iron fences and beautiful landscaping. It shouldn't be confused with the similarly named **Port Orleans Riverside Resort;** that one was formerly known as Dixie Landings, and its 2,000 guest rooms are spread out on a property enormous enough to be nearly unnavigable. All of the guest rooms in the moderate resorts are around 325 square feet.

Somewhat surprisingly, the majority of Disney's on-site accommodation options fall into their "deluxe" category. But again it's worth noting that the primary difference between these big-ticket guest rooms and their less-expensive counterparts is one of atmosphere and amenities. Beds are comfortable and guest rooms are clean throughout the entire resort. So, if you're just looking for a pillow to rest your park-wearied head on, there's little reason to splurge on the deluxe guest rooms. However, those who do indulge themselves will find the splurge memorable.

★ **Animal Kingdom Lodge** (from $310 d) is themed to emulate the experience of staying at a safari lodge. Employing lots of dark wood, natural light, and African craftwork, the ambiance is intensely evocative. Guest rooms are comfortably appointed, and a full-service spa, deluxe lounge, and enormous pool area add to the elegance. What's outside the back door truly sets this resort apart. The planners devised a way to re-create an African savanna, complete with wild-roaming zebras, gazelles, giraffes, and other animals. A recent addition to the property is the **Jambo House** (studios from $399, one-bedroom villas from $550, two-bedroom villas from $990), a collection of 216 villa-style accommodations that shares the amenities of the lodge but with larger units designed for extended stays.

The **Walt Disney World Swan and Dolphin Resort** (from $325 d) is actually two hotels, the "Swan" and the "Dolphin," logically enough. Operated by Starwood

Hotels and typically catering to well-heeled conventioneers and high-end travelers, the resort is stylish and modern. Boasting one of Disney's signature restaurants (Todd English's Bluezoo), as well as a Shula's Steak House, a Japanese restaurant (Kimono's, which also features a lively, after-hours karaoke scene), and the requisite activities needed to burn those calories off (a spa, health club, tennis courts, swimming pools), the Swan and Dolphin's level of luxury is almost high enough to make you consider forgoing rollercoasters and character visits for a day. The resort is located near Epcot, and, like all Disney accommodations, is serviced by Disney buses. An added bonus, though, is the boat service you can take directly to a secluded entrance into Epcot near the World Showcase.

For a truly upscale experience, the most well-heeled guests head for the ★ **Grand Floridian Resort & Spa** (from $549 d). From the stained-glass windows adorning the soaring atrium lobby and the enormous chandeliers to the spacious guest rooms, the Grand Floridian exudes Victorian elegance throughout its six buildings. Views across the Seven Seas Lagoon to the Magic Kingdom only add to the charm. The resort is also home to Disney's best restaurant, Victoria & Albert's, and an award-winning spa.

Though technically one of Walt Disney World's "moderate" offerings, ★ **The Cabins at Disney's Fort Wilderness Resort** ($375) are a truly unique lodging experience, and are strongly recommended for those traveling with children or those planning an extended stay. The 500-square-foot buildings won't be mistaken for mansions, but the idea of having a home away from home in your own freestanding building is certainly appealing. Spread throughout the campground are 409 cabins, and each has one bedroom with a bunk bed and a double bed, along with a Murphy bed in the living room; truly economical travelers can take advantage of the full kitchen and charcoal grill to prepare their own meals. The DIY ethos, thankfully, does not extend to toilet-scrubbing

the Walt Disney World Swan and Dolphin Resort

and bed-making, as each cabin is serviced daily by the resort's housekeeping crew. Fort Wilderness is somewhat remote, which is a blessing when you want to escape the crowds, but it also means you'll experience somewhat longer travel times to and from the parks.

Nearby Hotels

Buena Vista Suites (8203 World Center Dr., 407/239-8588, www.buenavistasuites. com, two-room suites from $149) and **Caribe Royale** (8101 World Center Dr., 407/238-8000, www.cariberoyale.com, from $209 d) are adjacent to one another, about a mile from Walt Disney World, and both are highly recommended. The 279 two-room suites at Buena Vista underwent a massive stem-to-stern renovation in 2013, and the result is a stylish and comfortable hotel with amenities like flat-screen HDTVs and granite countertops. More importantly, the affordable guest rooms are sparklingly fresh. Caribe Royale has more of a resort-convention center vibe, with a massive pool area and an endless array of meeting rooms tucked down its labyrinthine hallways. One-bedroom suites have microwave-fridge combos, while the two-bedroom villas are equipped with full kitchens.

For something a little more elegant, the enormous **Gaylord Palms Resort and Spa** (6000 W. Osceola Pkwy., Kissimmee, 407/586-2000, www.marriott.com, from $229 d) is an upscale facility geared more toward conventioneers and business travelers. One of the two pool areas is adults-only, and the recreation area is focused on croquet and a putting green rather than on merry-go-rounds and sandboxes. However, the other pool area is a raucous one, as screaming kids hurtle down the water slide. Families are clearly still welcome here, but there's a decidedly more adult feel than at any of the nearby resorts.

DINING OUTSIDE THE RESORT
Breakfast

There's not much in the way of unique or local breakfast spots near the main gate. For those folks unfortunate enough to not live in the southern United States, a visit here would be incomplete without a stop at **Waffle House** (12801 Kissimmee Vineland Rd., 407/239-6444, 24 hours daily, from $6), an iconic Southern diner institution that's certainly not fancy and certainly not healthy, but is definitely the friendliest, fastest, and cheapest place to get biscuits, eggs, and, of course, waffles. Hash browns are served "scattered" (spread out), "smothered" (with onions), or "covered" (with cheese).

There are also national breakfast/pancake chains like **International House of Pancakes** (12400 Kissimmee Vineland Rd., 407/239-0909, 24 hours daily, from $8), **Denny's** (12375 Kissimmee Vineland Rd., 407/239-7900, 24 hours daily, from $8), and **Perkins** (12559 Kissimmee Vineland Rd., 407/827-1060, 24 hours daily, from $9), but these spots offer neither the value nor the charm of a Waffle House. There is also a **Panera Bread** (8600 Vineland Ave., 407/842-1300, 6:30am-9pm daily, from $8) nearby for fresh-baked pastries, egg sandwiches, and espresso drinks.

American

Johnnie's Hideaway (12551 State Rd. 535, 407/827-1111, www.johnnieshideaway.com, 5pm-11pm daily, from $14) is located in a tourist zone directly across from one of Disney's main entrances, but somehow the restaurant manages a relaxed sophistication that proves a welcome respite from the surrounding area. Steaks are dry-aged on-site and are the big draw. In addition, a good selection of fresh seafood, including a raw bar, and "Floribbean" fare make for a well-rounded menu.

Similarly, **The Venetian Chop House** (8101 World Center Dr., 407/238-8060, www.thevenetianroom.com, 6pm-10pm Tues.-Sat., from $22) defies its location in the bowels of the Caribe Royale resort. Dark-wood furnishings and private dining alcoves make for a tremendously romantic atmosphere that's accentuated by white-glove service. The traditional epicurean fare—filet mignon, bouillabaisse, duck confit, lobster—is appropriate to the classic and classy atmosphere. Be advised that there is a dress code, and reservations are suggested.

For straightforward and somewhat reasonably priced pub fare, like burgers, sliders, and wings, head for **Miller's Ale House** (12371 Winter Garden Vineland Rd., 407/239-1800, www.millersalehouse.com, 11am-2am daily, from $10), a chain that is something of a Florida institution. Miller's serves predictable food that isn't going to win any culinary awards. Daily specials here are almost always incredibly inexpensive and incredibly filling, and Miller's is almost always a decent place to grab a drink and watch the game.

International

Across the street from a Disney entrance, **Dakshin** (12541 State Rd. 535, 407/827-9080, www.dakshin-indianrestaurant.com, 11:30am-2pm and 5:30pm-10:30pm Sun.-Fri., 5:30pm-10:30pm Sat., from $16) could probably easily get by on serving biryanis and chicken tikka to the throngs of tourists who want to try some Indian food on vacation. Instead, the restaurant specializes in south Indian cuisine—lots of seafood and Kerala-style spices—and presents it in an upscale environment decorated in brass, thick-carved wood, and elegant Indian art. A Kottayam fish curry is a menu highlight, as are the many different dosai that are available. Service can sometimes be slow, but the staff is friendly and the food is well worth both the wait and the price.

If you're looking for the North Indian fare most typically found in U.S. Indian restaurants, head for **Darbar** (12185 S. Apopka Vineland Rd., 407/238-7864, http://darbar-indiancuisine.com, 11:30am-2:30pm and 5:30pm-10:30pm Sun.-Fri., 5:30pm-10:30pm Sat., from $10), a decent place to grab chicken tikka or vegetarian thali.

Brazilian *churrascaria* places abound in Orlando, but **The Knife** (12501 State Rd. 535., 786/866-3999, www.thekniferestaurant.com, 11:30am-11:30pm daily, from $29) offers a unique, Argentinian take on the all-the-meat-you-can-eat model. The open-air *parilla* grill is repurposed as a self-serve area where you come to pick out your own cooked cuts. Make sure to try the chorizo and other surprising specialties like grilled sweetbreads and pork *pamplonas*. Desserts here are pretty excellent, and included in the price of the meal. Kids meals are, oddly, based on height: Children under 3 feet tall eat for free, children 3-4 feet tall cost $10, while 4-5-footers cost $14.

INFORMATION AND SERVICES

The one thing you'll never find lacking on Disney property is a smiling face ready to cheerfully answer whatever question you may have. Disney staff members are famously indoctrinated into a sort of cult of customer service, so anyone from the guy sweeping up in Tomorrowland and the ice-cream vendor at the Magic Kingdom to the manager of a gift shop is ready, willing, and able to point you (always with two fingers, never with one!) to whatever

and wherever you need, and if they can't, they'll be quick to find you someone who can.

Guide maps can be found throughout the parks at nearly every gift shop or concessionaire, and they contain the day's schedule of shows and character meet and greets. Dining reservations can be made from any restaurant (even if it's not for that restaurant) or by calling 407/WDW-DINE (407/939-3463).

Strollers and wheelchairs can be rented at any of the kingdoms, and baby feeding and changing stations are located near the entrance of each park.

Animals, with the exception of service dogs, are not permitted in any of the parks, hotels, or other public areas, but there are kennels near the entrance of each park as well as at Fort Wilderness Resort and Campground. The **Best Friends Pet Care** (near Magic Kingdom, 877/493-9738, www.bestfriend-spetcare.com, open daily one hour before park opening to an hour after park closing) is a standalone facility that offers top-notch boarding, day care, and grooming services.

Disney's website (http://disneyworld. disney.go.com) has reams of information about each park and the various other attractions within the resort, including restaurants and shopping opportunities; the **Disney Parks blog** (http://disneyparks.disney. go.com/blog) is also a great way to keep up with what's going on. There is also a **guest information line** (407/939-6244, 9am-10pm daily) where customer service staff is available to answer your questions, plus a Guest Services office at the front of each park, where endlessly friendly and helpful staff members assist with lost-and-found items, dining reservations, and general questions; these offices also have baby-changing stations.

GETTING THERE AND AROUND

Walt Disney World is located approximately 20 miles southwest of downtown Orlando and is accessed via five I-4 exits. All of these exits are well marked, giving appropriate guidance depending on which part of the park you're headed to. If you're arriving and heading for a hotel rather than a park, aim for the park that your hotel is associated with and follow the directions.

Parking at Disney parks is exorbitantly priced. It's currently $35 per car per day, although you are able to use your parking pass in multiple lots throughout the day. Parking is free at Disney Springs (although valet parking is available for a flat rate of $20) and the water parks. Add to that cost the fact that the lots are enormous, requiring trams to transport guests from the parking area to the main entrance, and using your car to get around the resort becomes a less-than-optimal solution.

I strongly advise the use of Disney's **intra-resort bus system** instead. For guests staying at Disney hotels, this is something of a no-brainer, as each hotel has its own bus stop with regular arrivals and departures. Even though resort guests (and annual passholders) get free parking at any of the parks, the buses are still the way to go. Even for day visitors it's an appealing option, as you can park your car once in the morning and use the buses to move between almost any two locations within the resort easily. The buses are free, and, more importantly, during the summer, they're frigidly air-conditioned.

Universal Orlando Resort

TOP EXPERIENCE

Tours of **Universal Studios** in Hollywood have been popular since the studio opened, and when those backlot peeks turned into a full-fledged theme park in the mid-1960s, Universal became the undisputed king of combining amusement-park attractions with movie-making glamour. It was only a decade after the Walt Disney World Resort opened that Universal began making plans to open a theme park in the Orlando area, and those plans came to fruition with the opening of the Universal Studios theme park in 1990. The original park was much more in line with the movie-magic concept of Universal Studios Hollywood. But the addition of Islands of Adventure in 1999, which focused more on thrill rides, has made the Universal Orlando Resort not just a formidable competitor to Disney but also a thematic complement. While Disney's image is all about halcyon Americana and the magic of imagination, Universal pointedly exhibits a bit of a rebellious streak, stressing its adrenaline-rush coasters, superhero experiences, and Hogwarts-themed fantasias. You won't find quite the same level of service or fastidiousness at Universal as you do at Disney, and in the shadow of the Mouse, Universal feels like nothing more than a couple of truly exceptional amusement parks. However, taken on their own merits, they easily outstrip every other non-Disney theme park in the country in terms of heart-pumping action and immersive imagination.

One-day one-park admission at Universal Orlando is $105 ($100 for kids), a price that's in line with admission prices at the Walt Disney World Resort. Getting a deal here requires far less commitment than at Disney: You can add a second park to a one-day pass for an additional $50, or get a two-day two-park pass for $235 (three-day and four-day passes are also available at additional discounts). Florida residents can get additional discounts, and annual passes are also quite a bargain.

UNIVERSAL STUDIOS FLORIDA

From its opening date in 1990, the theme at Universal Studios Florida has been an exhortation for guests to "ride the movies." That film-centric mission has since been expanded to include television shows, but the basic idea remains the same: This is the park where you go to see Hollywood come to life. There are

Universal Orlando Resort

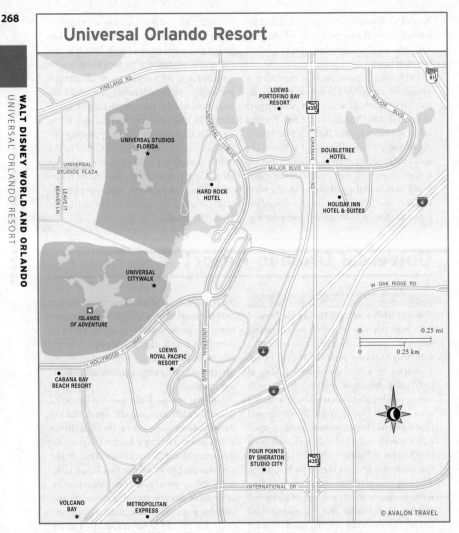

actual production facilities on-site (although they're not open to the public), and the various areas of the park are all designed to resemble either soundstages, backlots, or movie scenes come to life. While it doesn't quite capture the Hollywood action of its West Coast predecessor, there's a much more consistent cinematic theming to this park than at Disney's Hollywood Studios.

Production Central

Production Central is the first area guests enter when they come into Universal Orlando. It has also undergone the most renovations and revamps over the last few years. The oldest attraction here is **Shrek 4-D,** which debuted in 2003 and puts guests into a theater equipped with buzzing, bumping, and squirting seats to watch an amazingly effective and pretty hilarious film featuring Mike Myers, Eddie Murphy, and many of the other

Halloween Horror Nights

In 1991, Universal Studios Florida opened the temporary Dungeon of Terror haunted house as a way to drum up nighttime business during a traditionally slow part of the year. That lone haunted house in the queue area for the Jaws ride has since expanded to become one of the premier Halloween-themed events in the country, with nearly 20 haunted houses and "scare zones" transforming areas across both parks into a terrifying themed adventure. Costumed actors roam the fog-covered property, and visitors are never quite sure if that dark corner is hiding a blood-soaked character ready to chase them with a chainsaw. The houses and scare zones fully utilize the set-building and scene-setting prowess of Universal's creative team. Don't show up expecting the same sort of startles and screams you're treated to at your local haunted house.

The nature of Halloween Horror Nights makes it a decidedly adult affair, and in addition to the shrieks and scares, a lot of folks show up for the festive atmosphere and the grown-up beverages. Although some parents bring younger children, it's definitely not advised. Even if the ax murderers and serial killers don't give them nightmares, the occasionally inappropriate behavior of some park guests may leave their ears and eyes burning.

This event is incredibly popular, so the park gets crowded very quickly. It's best to check it out on a weekday evening, but even those crowds can be quite large.

Halloween Horror Nights runs early September-Halloween night and requires a separate admission (typically the same price as a one-day, one-park ticket). No costumes or masks are allowed.

---

voice stars from the *Shrek* films. The film's 3-D effects are impressive, and the physical gags the theater imposes on guests are a hoot, but what makes the attraction a winner is the smart-aleck humor from the characters. Across the way is **Despicable Me: Minion Mayhem,** a simulator ride that puts guests on an immersive ride through the world of Gru, Dr. Nefario, Margo, Edith, Agnes, and, of course, the Minions from Universal's super-successful *Despicable Me* cartoons. The pre-show here is great, setting the vibe by taking you through Gru's lab and his house, but ultimately, it's the eight-minute motion-simulating 3-D ride (which all takes place in one room) that's the highlight.

Next door is the most ambitious and adrenaline-pumping coaster on Universal property—when it works. While **Hollywood Rip Ride Rockit** may eclipse Islands of Adventure's Hulk when it comes to roller-coaster thrills, the ride has had something of a bumpy history, between an extended launch delay, various technical glitches which have taken it offline for weeks at a time, and even an unintentionally terrifying episode where riders were stranded mid-ride for a couple

of hours. On this ride, you can pick your soundtrack, one of six songs from one of five categories, before the coaster takes you 167 feet into the air and then drops you to the ground at 65 miles per hour. It is, to say the least, a thrilling ride.

The most recent addition to Production Central is **Transformers: The Ride,** which debuted in June 2013 to rave reviews. Similar in concept to the hugely successful Spider-Man ride at Islands of Adventure, Transformers is an immersive, 3-D dark ride that takes guests on an adventure onboard an Autobot named Evac as part of a mission to retrieve the AllSpark. The plot doesn't get much more complicated than that, but the 4.5-minute ride manages to not only cram in appearances by nearly all of the most well-known Transformers, but does so in a way that utilizes incredible 3-D effects with fog, lights, and intense motion-simulation that's incredibly believable. It's a must-ride experience.

Hollywood

Designed by director James Cameron, **Terminator 2: 3-D** is a fantastic attraction. Utilizing both live action and 3-D film work (not to mention the thespian abilities of *T2* stars Arnold Schwarzenegger, Linda Hamilton, and Edward Furlong), it's an incredibly immersive and often quite scary attraction, which is an impressive feat considering that there's no actual "ride." Guests visit the Cyberdyne plant on a tour, and as the action unfolds around them, it can be easy to forget that it's all make-believe.

The **Universal Horror Make-Up Show** is a scripted show about the use of makeup in horror movies, so it shouldn't be too surprising that it's kind of gross. It also has a few interactive elements and is pretty funny.

New York

Universal Orlando made up for its complete lack of roller coasters with the recent addition of **Revenge of the Mummy,** a bracingly fast (45 mph), indoor steel coaster that would be thrilling even without the effective scary Egyptian curse theme. Dark and intense, the ride also features a particularly frightening finale.

In one of the more bewildering displays of corporate synergy, **Race Through New York Starring Jimmy Fallon** brings the host of NBC's Tonight Show his own theme park ride. (NBC is owned by Comcast, which also owns Universal.) While Fallon is certainly beloved by many, it may be hard for late-night TV viewers to imagine what in the world he could bring to a ride. Well, it's the very same thing he brings to television: an affable, sure-why-not personality that's more than happy to host you through some absurd fun. While he is the face (and laughs) of the attraction, the real draw here is the adrenaline-pumping virtual ride through (and above) the streets of New York. This ride opened in the summer of 2017, taking the spot of the longstanding Twister attraction that opened in 1998.

The Wizarding World of Harry Potter–Diagon Alley

After the incredible success of Islands of Adventure's Hogsmeade area, **Diagon Alley** was added and connected by, of course, the Hogwarts Express. This expansion of the Wizarding World of Harry Potter is highlighted by **Harry Potter and the Escape from Gringotts**, an immersive, 3-D-effects-laden roller coaster. There are also puppet shows, a "Knight Bus" interactive attraction, and an array of shops fans of the franchise will recognize, such as Ollivander's Wand Shop, Weasley's Wizard Wheezes (a novelty shop), and Quality Quidditch Supplies (some of the

The Hogwarts Express brings fans' dreams to life at the Wizarding World of Harry Potter.

shop fronts are interactive for guests who purchase wands at Ollivander's). Note that guests can only traverse between Diagon Alley and Hogwarts via the Hogwarts Express, which requires a two-park ticket, although if you only have a Universal Studios Florida ticket, you can still explore Diagon Alley and all its attractions.

World Expo

Men in Black Alien Attack has one of the best-themed queue areas of any attraction at Universal Studios. Designed around the concept that visitors are coming to check out "The Universe & You" exhibition at the 1964 World Expo, the Disney-esque preshow abruptly segues into the "reality" that guests are taking part in a training exercise to become MIB agents. Peeks into labs and coffee-break rooms are funny, helping pass the time until you board your training vehicle. Once on board, the object is to shoot as many aliens as you can with your laser gun. Some, however, shoot back, causing your car to spin in rapid circles. Just like in the film, the aliens are often disguised, posing a greater challenge than you might expect.

The arrival of **The Simpsons Ride** at Universal Studios was greeted with mixed emotions by many park-goers. While many were upset to see the Back to the Future motion-simulator film ride disappear, the idea of a ride themed after the popular animated television series was quite promising. Thankfully, the Simpsons Ride is largely based on the same technology and ride concept as Back to the Future, except instead of hurtling through time with Doc Brown, riders are in Krustyland with the Simpsons family, trying to escape the sabotage efforts of Sideshow Bob. With the addition of 3-D effects and, it must be said, some rather cheesy computer animation, the motion effects of the Back to the Future ride are amplified, and the comedy factor is considerably improved. In 2013, Universal took upon a considerable expansion of the area surrounding the Simpsons Ride, resulting in **Springfield U.S.A.**, a highly themed and whimsical re-creation of the cartoon town, complete with Lard Lad donuts, Duff beer, and Krusty burgers.

Woody Woodpecker's KidZone

The preschool and elementary set will find plenty worthy of their attention in the **KidZone** area. Those without young ones will likely only be drawn here by **E. T. Adventure,** which puts riders on a bicycle "flight" through the world of the movie and onward to E. T.'s home planet, which is apparently populated solely by babies. Nearby, **Woody Woodpecker's Nuthouse Coaster** is a quick, unchallenging coaster with only two mild drops. Other kid-centric attractions here are **A Day in the Park with Barney** (which can be used to threaten your recalcitrant teenager) and two playgrounds: **Curious George Goes to Town** and **Fievel's Playland.**

Special Events

Universal's annual **Mardi Gras** (Feb.-Apr., $59.99 in advance, $74.99 at the gate) celebration brings a weekly live concert to the park, usually featuring a cavalcade of 1970s and '80s pop stars with a smattering of current hit-makers, as well as a bead-throwing New Orleans-style parade at the end of the evening. Purchase of a Mardi Gras ticket allows you entrance to the park after 5pm and admission to some of the cover-charging clubs of Citywalk after the park closes.

In the fall, the Christian-music-themed **Rock the Universe** (Sept.) festival happens, often on the same day as Disney's Night of Joy concerts. The musicians at Universal's concerts are typically more the alternative and punk bent, while those at Disney's are more pop-oriented.

During the Christmas season, the big event at Universal Studios is the daily **Macy's Holiday Parade,** but there are also Christmas-themed shows throughout the park.

Food

Beyond the standard array of popcorn stands and hamburger slingers, dining options at Universal Studios are quite limited. Nonetheless, **Finnegan's Bar & Grill** (New York, lunch and dinner daily, from $11) has Irish fare and a warm atmosphere that's surprisingly conducive to leisurely liquid lunches. It's even got daily happy-hour specials. Nearby, **Lombard's Seafood Grille** (San Francisco/Amity, lunch and dinner daily, from $11) is another decent spot for a sit-down meal, with excellent fish and seafood platters. For a great selection of breakfast pastries, **Beverly Hills Boulangerie** (Hollywood, open all day) is very close to the park entrance and provides the calories and caffeine you'll need to prepare for the day; it also serves sandwiches and desserts throughout the day.

The recent expansion of the Simpsons Ride into Springfield U.S.A. included the addition of some cool new food-and-drink experiences. Along Fast Food Boulevard, you can grab a beer at **Moe's Tavern** or some grub at the likes of **Cletus' Chicken Shack** (from $8) or **Krusty Burger** (from $8). True to the area's name, all of these spots are counter-service fast food, with the healthiest stuff (of course) available at **Lisa's Teahouse of Horror** (from $5). You can also get some decadent treats at **Lard Lad Donuts.** And there's even a food truck, **Bumblebee Man Taco Truck.**

★ ISLANDS OF ADVENTURE

Islands of Adventure is focused on rides and coasters and is the most thrill-oriented park in Orlando. Although several of the rides have movie themes, the park is far more unified by the adrenaline rushes to be had in each of its "islands." There are currently six islands, organized and themed in a fashion similar to the various "lands" at Disney's Magic Kingdom, with the most recent addition, The Wizarding World of Harry Potter, standing as the most completely immersive experience at either Universal park.

Marvel Super Hero Island

Two of the three best rides on the entire property are in close proximity to one another and among the first attractions you encounter in the park. To be sure, after experiencing the high-speed **Incredible Hulk Coaster** and the immersive 3-D simulations of **The Amazing Adventures of Spider-Man,** there is little question that Islands of Adventure is exponentially more thrill-focused than its next-door neighbor, Universal Studios. Unfortunately, the rest of the park has trouble living up to the high standard set by such an introduction.

the thrilling Incredible Hulk Coaster at Islands of Adventure

The Hulk coaster blasts riders out the launch area at 40 mph, and by the time the steel tracks have you hurtling through an underground tunnel from 100-foot heights, your speed has reached almost 70 mph. Two enormous loops and corkscrews ensure the ride never loses your full attention.

The Spider-Man attraction is equally engaging, as riders are sent out onto the villain-thick streets of New York, recruited by the cigar-chomping publisher of the *Daily Bugle* to get the story in high-tech "Scoop" vehicles. A combination of high-definition 3-D film effects, enormous set pieces, and fire and water effects make for a surprisingly visceral and believable ride that culminates in a heart-stopping "fall" from atop a skyscraper. This ride was renovated and updated in 2011; although there were no major changes to its plot or essential elements, the visual effects have been dramatically improved.

Toon Lagoon

"Lagoon" is an appropriate place name for this part of the park, as riders of either of its two marquee attractions are bound to get wet. Although many younger visitors are probably unfamiliar with much of the comic-strip theming (does anyone read *Krazy Kat* anymore?), the thrill of the splashing, soaking **Popeye and Bluto's Bilge-Rat Barges** river raft ride is pretty universal. And although the Bullwinkle cartoons that introduced previous generations to the uptight Canadian Mountie are no longer aired, **Dudley Do-Right's Ripsaw Falls** manages to update the idea of the log flume into a surprisingly heart-racing and butt-soaking thrill.

Jurassic Park

The theming of the Jurassic Park area of Islands of Adventure is pretty integral to the enjoyment of the premier attraction: **Jurassic Park River Adventure.** If you squint your eyes and take in this flume ride along with the nearby chairlift ride (**Pteranodon Flyers),** the **Camp Jurassic** playground, and the quasi-educational **Jurassic Park Discovery Center,** you can almost imagine that Jurassic Park is its own standalone amusement park. And, of course, that park is the same one in the book and films where things went horribly awry. Accordingly, the Jurassic Park River Adventure starts out as informative and relaxing and soon devolves into a pretty tense and very wet escape from some pretty scary dinosaurs.

The Amazing Adventures of Spider-Man is a virtual, 4-D thrill ride at Universal Orlando Resort.

The Wizarding World of Harry Potter–Hogsmeade

The Wizarding World of Harry Potter has completely redefined the concept of a visit to Universal's Orlando theme parks. This is the only section that, during peak season, often has queues just to get in the area, much less on any of the rides. Although the 20-acre site isn't completely dissimilar to the other "lands" in Islands of Adventure as far as size or number of attractions, the immersive and detailed theming here makes the Wizarding World much more impressive, rivaling (and perhaps even surpassing) Walt Disney World.

For this section, Universal re-created the fantastic environments of Hogwarts and Hogsmeade while simultaneously repurposing rides and real estate that had been active since the park's opening. Dueling Dragons is an inverted roller coaster on which riders come frightfully close to riders running on another "dueling" track, each of which utilizes a combination of inversions, loops, corkscrews, and rolls. This had long been one of the best coasters at Islands of Adventure, so it was wisely renovated to become **Dragon Challenge,** thanks to some re-theming of the coaster cars and the insertion of set pieces like Hagrid's house. Likewise, the **Flight of the Hippogriff** is a low-speed, low-thrill (but super-fun) roller coaster that used to be known as the Flying Unicorn. The Potter vibe on this one is pretty limited, but most of the kids who are young enough to be excited about this ride have probably had limited interactions with Harry Potter.

The main attraction at the Wizarding World is **Harry Potter and the Forbidden Journey,** a state-of-the-art attraction that's part dark ride, part immersive cinematic adventure, and part coaster. It's a fantastic experience that starts as soon as riders get in line. Perhaps anticipating the lengthy waits, the ride's designers went all out by having guests walk through Hogwarts for an in-depth look at the interiors of the castle. Though the ride only lasts 5 minutes, the 30-45 minutes most folks will spend queuing

are as much a part of the experience as the ride itself. But those five minutes on the ride pack in a lot, from Quidditch to Dementors to dragons and lots of magic, all of which puts riders in the heart of the action. If you ride nothing else at Islands of Adventure, make sure to ride this.

But the Wizarding World isn't just about the rides. It seems as though the park's designers paid nearly as much attention to re-creating the fantasy world that surrounds the rides. Shop in what is almost certainly the only theme park gift shop in the world that limits the number of people who can enter at one time: **Ollivanders,** where you can purchase a magic wand just as Harry Potter did, with a small group of fellow shoppers (restricted to 20 at a time), each of whom is chosen by their wand, rather than the other way around. And, of course, you can sneak a peek at the train that ferried Harry and his friends to school every year, the **Hogwarts Express.** Butterbeer at the **Three Broomsticks** is a must-buy. Then stop in **Honeydukes Sweetshop** for some treacle fudge and chocolate frogs.

Given the runaway success of the Wizarding World, Universal was quick to create an expansion: **Diagon Alley** opened next door at Universal Orlando, and guests with two-park passes can access it from Hogsmeade via a Hogwarts Express train.

The Lost Continent

A big chunk of the **Lost Continent,** including the Dueling Dragons coaster, was given over and re-themed to be part of the Wizarding World of Harry Potter, but this "land" still has a couple of attractions left. **Poseidon's Fury** is a walk-through attraction that combines live action and some stunning special effects. The dark passages, frequent scares, and the impact of the intense climax may be a bit much for younger visitors, but the occasional corny laugh lines delivered by your guide help to ease the tension. Stunt-show fans may be interested in **The Eighth Voyage of Sindbad,** but most other park guests take their seat in the theater just to get off their feet for a mildly entertaining half hour.

Seuss Landing

All theme parks have an area dedicated to small children, but Islands of Adventure's **Seuss Landing** is by far the most charming. The whimsical nature of the classic books elevates standard attractions like the **High in the Sky Seuss Trolley Train Ride**, the **Caro-Seuss-el**, and **One Fish, Two Fish, Red Fish, Blue Fish** (a Dumbo-like ride on which riders control the up and down motion of their vehicles as they spin around) into something altogether more engaging. **The Cat in the Hat** is a must-ride attraction for kids, parents, and even kid-free adults; the dark storytelling ride puts you right into the middle of the classic tale and is filled with spins, careening near-misses, and a sense of sly fun.

Special Events

Holiday festivities are somewhat limited at Islands of Adventure, but when you've got the most famous holiday curmudgeon on hand, what else do you need? **Grinchmas** is centered around daily performances of *How the Grinch Stole Christmas*. The real star of the show is the Grinch himself; kids and adults can get their picture taken with him throughout the day.

Food

While no sandwich at **Blondie's** (Toon Lagoon, lunch and dinner daily, from $7) quite comes close to the enormous ones devoured by Dagwood in the classic comic strip, it's a pleasure being able to get a fresh deli snack instead of the standard burgers-and-fries available throughout the rest of the park.

Diners seeking a somewhat more sophisticated theme-park repast should head straight for **Mythos** (The Lost Continent, lunch daily, dinner daily summer and Christmas, $15). Fresh ingredients and thoughtful preparation are key here. The menu, which generally leans toward Italian and contemporary fusion cuisines, changes frequently. All of it is accented by some stunning interior design, making for an exceptional dining experience. A meal for two, including wine, can be a bit pricey, but, hey, you're on vacation, right?

And, of course, there's the food available in the Wizarding World of Harry Potter. In addition to the must-have Butterbeer, the sit-down **Three Broomsticks** restaurant offers a traditional array of British pub fare.

VOLCANO BAY

Volcano Bay (10am-7pm daily, $67 adults, $62 kids) is Universal's first official foray into the waterpark wars (it purchased the iconic Wet 'n Wild, then closed it at the end of 2016), coming years after Disney's two and SeaWorld's one. And it is an impressive entry. With a 200-foot-tall faux-volcano (named "Krakatau") at its center, the park is visually striking, with the volcano's daytime waterfalls turning into "lava" fields at night. Of course, there are also the requisite wave pools, plunges, slides, and lazy rivers.

UNIVERSAL CITYWALK

The **CityWalk** concept was first explored at Universal's park in Los Angeles, which opened in 1993. When Universal Orlando expanded in 1999 with the opening of Islands of Adventure, CityWalk Orlando was part of that expansion. The entertainment and dining area is not dissimilar to Disney Springs, though there's far less emphasis here on Universal-themed places and products and a much larger contingent of known national chains. Local teenagers flock to CityWalk on the weekends to take advantage of the spacious 20-screen movie theater and the adjacent eateries, while adults flock to the several nightclubs and music venues.

Blue Man Group

Built, as so many things at Universal Orlando are, in response to a success at Disney (in this case, Disney Springs' Cirque du Soleil theater), the purpose-built Sharp Aquos Theater hosts daily performances of the **Blue Man**

Group (show times vary, daily, adult tickets start at $69, children at $29, children 2 and under free, but not recommended for children under 3). The Orlando production is one of seven permanent Blue Man productions, and the show here is something of a "greatest hits," incorporating various elements from different Blue Man shows. The oddball instrumentation, choreographed feats, physical humor, and general sense of amazement that the Blue Men are known for are amplified in the intimate theater setting. The 100-minute show is both hilarious and impressive.

Clubs and Bars

The variety of **nightclubs** at CityWalk has proven successful with both tourists and locals craving a safe and predictable entertainment environment. **CityWalk's Rising Star** (8pm-2am daily, 21 and over Fri.-Wed., 18 and over Thurs., $7) takes the karaoke bar concept to a new level; instead of singing along to plinky-plonky backing tracks, singers mount the stage to be accompanied by a live band. The **Red Coconut Club** (8pm-2am Sun.-Thurs., 6pm-2am Fri.-Sat., 21 and over, $7) was designed to capitalize on the ultra-lounge trend and emphasizes its fashionable atmosphere, VIP bottle service, and long martini list. DJs spin here, but dancing is best done at **The Groove** (9pm-2am daily, 21 and over, $7), an enormous hit-driven dance club.

Fans of live music should check out the lineup at **Hard Rock Live** (open only for concerts, ticket prices vary, all ages admitted). The huge modern venue hosts well-known touring bands and comedians and occasionally features local music as well.

Shopping

Although it sort of feels like an outdoor mall, there's actually not all that much shopping to be done at CityWalk. However, if you want to get a tattoo or just a tattoo-inspired T-shirt, **Hart & Huntington Tattoo Company** (11am-1am daily) has one of its three locations here. No, *Inked* isn't filmed here.

There are also outlets for **Fossil, Element,** clothing stores like **Fresh Produce** and **The Island Clothing Company,** and the Florida-based **Quiet Flight Surf Shop.**

Food

Nobody comes to a **Hard Rock Cafe** (11am-midnight or later daily, from $12) for the food, but grabbing an expensive and admittedly tasty burger at this one is a must-do for rock-and-roll fans. This outpost of the

Volcano Bay at Universal Orlando Resort

international chain is the world's largest, and, accordingly, it has a most impressive collection of memorabilia.

There's something a little disturbing about tucking into "The Whaler" (a tilapia sandwich) or a "Natty Dread" (vegetable patties) while your little one noshes on "Jamacaroni and Cheese" and flocks of tourists take part in the beer and booze specials of "Red Stripe Rastafarian Thursday." At least it's disturbing to me. Still, as jarring as the theming of **Bob Marley—A Tribute to Freedom** (4:30pm-2am daily, from $9) may seem, the kitchen serves up some surprisingly tasty Jamaican dishes. I just wish they'd change the name to "A Taste of Babylon" or something like that.

Emeril's (11:30am-2pm and 5:30pm-10pm daily, from $18) is, of course, one of celebrity chef Emeril Lagasse's 10 restaurants, and the menu is predictably a combination of New Orleans flavors and contemporary cuisine. The stylish dining room can sometimes be deafeningly loud. But dishes like an andouille-crusted redfish are worth the hustle and bustle.

If you're headed to CityWalk for a night of entertainment but are interested in some different on-site dining options, the resort's three hotels have some impressive restaurants.

Emeril's Tchoup Chop (Royal Pacific Resort, 5:30pm-10pm Sun.-Thurs., 5:30pm-11pm Fri.-Sat., from $18) is a more upscale and quieter fine-dining experience than Lagasse's CityWalk boîte, with prices and dress code to match. The Orlando outpost of famed New York steakhouse **The Palm** (Hard Rock Hotel, 5pm-11pm daily, from $20) successfully captures the elegance and classic American menu of its namesake. The recent addition of **The Toothsome Chocolate Emporium and Savory Feast Kitchen** (11am-11:00pm Sun.-Thurs., 11am-11:30pm Fri.-Sat., from $20) has given guests the chocolate-in-everything menu that's served in a whimsical steampunk setting they never knew they wanted. (It's great.)

ACCOMMODATIONS

Unlike Walt Disney World, Universal Orlando doesn't really mess around with "value" accommodations. Whether due to limited real estate or the fact that dozens of moderate and inexpensive chain motels are located less than a half-mile from the park's entrance, the result is four hotels that are unabashedly upscale. Guests staying at resort hotels can use their guest room keys as "Universal Express" passes, allowing them to bypass the line at

Drinks, dining, and even dancing bring nightly crowds to Universal Citywalk.

the theme parks' major attractions. This perk, along with the availability of discounted ticket-accommodation packages, make an on-site stay an attractive option for some visitors, but again, there are considerably cheaper hotels nearby, most of which offer complimentary transportation to the park (and the Disney parks) as well as their own discount packages. For on-site reservations, call 888/273-1311.

Resort Hotels

The best and most exciting of the three Universal Orlando resort hotels is the excellent ★ **Hard Rock Hotel** (from $309 d), which incorporates the chain's rock-and-roll theming with extensive touches of modern luxury. Flat-panel TVs, in-room stereos, and deluxe contemporary furnishings make the spacious guest rooms welcoming and comfortable. The 12,000-square-foot pool at the Hard Rock is as glam as it gets. With water piped in underwater, high-tech and sumptuous cabanas, whirlpool tubs, and a volleyball court, this pool is a destination in and of itself during the summer.

Universal's Cabana Bay Beach Resort (from $155 d), opened in 2014, occupies the only slot in Universal's "Moderate/Value"

segment. It has a mid-century modern vibe, with plenty of retro design and imagery.

The **Loews Portofino Bay Hotel** (from $339 d) is pricey, but also sedate and traditionally swanky. The re-creation of a waterfront Italian village is something of a stretch (the designers even installed cobblestone sidewalks), but for a moment you almost believe that you're not a few hundred yards from roller coasters on one side and the Florida Turnpike on the other.

At the "low" end of the deluxe resort hotel offerings is **Loews Royal Pacific Resort** (from $274 d). Ironically, it's also the most secluded and quiet. The Polynesian motif lends itself to long days lounging at the pool, sipping tropical drinks. The guest rooms, however, are decorated in neutral tones and dark woods, rather than tropical shades and lots of wicker.

Nearby Hotels

There is no shortage of moderately priced chain hotels near Universal Orlando. Most nearby hotels are located on the busy tourist strip of International Drive or the almost-as-overwhelmed Kirkman Road. Both the **Holiday Inn Hotel & Suites** (5905 Kirkman Rd., 407/351-3333, www.hiuniversal.com, from $89 d) and the **Doubletree Hotel**

The pool at the Hard Rock Hotel is a draw for visitors and locals alike.

(5780 Major Blvd., 407/351-1000, www.doubletreeorlando.com, from $129 d) are located immediately adjacent to the park. The quality of the Holiday Inn isn't that high, but it's a decent budget option. The Doubletree gets high marks all around.

A mile or so from the park entrance is the **Four Points by Sheraton Studio City** (5905 International Dr., 407/351-2100, www.starwoodhotels.com, from $139 d), which despite its Hollywood facade isn't all that glamorous. The hotel can often be crowded with tour groups; nonetheless, guest rooms here are clean and reasonably appointed.

DINING OUTSIDE THE RESORT

Orlando's Restaurant Row, home to a high concentration of upscale and midscale restaurants, is located in the tourist district along Sand Lake Road, near **International Drive** and the Orange County Convention Center.

INFORMATION AND SERVICES

As with the Disney parks, guide maps are easily available throughout any of the parks and can be found at restaurants, snack bars, and gift shops. The staff-to-guest ratio at Universal isn't quite as high as it is at Disney, and the crew here hasn't gone through the same sort of mission-critical training for customer service that Disney prides itself on. Each park has a Guest Services office near its ticketing area, where staff members can assist with lost-and-found items, dining reservations, and general questions.

Universal offers stroller, wheelchair, and locker rentals, and has a Family Services room at the entrance of each park with nursing facilities.

There's a day-boarding kennel facility located in the main parking garage; guests are required to provide food and occasionally come back during the day to walk their pets.

Universal Orlando's website (www.universalorlando.com) has information about hours, ticket prices, and the attractions and show schedules at both parks, as well as the dining and shopping options at CityWalk. It also offers reservations and package deals for the resort hotels. Call the **guest services information line** (407/224-4233, 8:30am-7pm daily) if you wish to speak to an agent with questions, to get more information, or to make dining reservations.

GETTING THERE

Universal Orlando Resort is located near the intersection of I-4 and International Drive, 16 miles (about 15 minutes) from **Orlando International Airport** (MCO, One Airport Blvd., Orlando, 407/825-2001, www.orlandoairports.net). The **Orlando-Sanford International Airport** (SFB, 1200 Red Cleveland Blvd., Sanford, 407/585-4000, www.orlandosanfordairport.com) is 35 miles (45 minutes) away.

GETTING AROUND

Due to its small size, Universal doesn't have an intra-resort bus service, although there is a boat that ferries resort-hotel guests to and from the parks, and any visitor not staying at one of the resort's hotels will need to park in the massive parking structure at the resort's entrance and undertake the long walk to the park entrances. Parking is $16 and you'll park in a garage that allows access to Universal Studios Orlando, Islands of Adventure, and CityWalk; Florida residents can park free after 6pm. I recommend, however, springing for valet parking ($15/2 hours, $30/more than 2 hours before 6pm, $25/more than 2 hours after 6pm), which brings you into the resort right at the entrance to CityWalk. The reduced walk may not seem like that big of a deal when you're first coming into the park, but the price difference will seem well worth it after a day on your feet.

SeaWorld Orlando

TOP EXPERIENCE

From its opening in 1973 to the launch of Epcot Center in 1982, **SeaWorld Orlando** was comfortably "the other Orlando theme park." It was the place to take the kids on a long weekend after the treasures of the Magic Kingdom had been exhausted, or the place you went if you couldn't quite afford the ticket prices at Disney. Even after Disney's other parks opened and Universal O

Orlando got off the ground, SeaWorld just went along its merry way, putting on Shamu shows and letting you ride an escalator through a shark tank. In 1998, though, it appeared that someone at the park realized SeaWorld was in danger of becoming an antiquated oddity, classed alongside old-school attractions like Gatorland. And so, Journey to Atlantis—SeaWorld's first thrill ride—was opened. After that first water coaster came the 65 mph, floorless Kraken steel coaster as well as a renewed focus on conservation messages in SeaWorld's animal exhibits. SeaWorld had renewed itself in terms

of vitality and relevance, and the expansion continued to include the dolphin-interaction experiences at Discovery Cove and the water-park fun at Aquatica.

While the resort is still definitely the lesser of the "big three," it certainly warrants consideration on almost any visitor's itinerary. The sea-mammal shows at the main park are truly unique.

Standard admission to SeaWorld is $99, but you can get a $20 discount if you order online at least one day before your visit. You can make your ticket a two-park ticket for a total cost of $109, or a three-park ticket for $119, choosing from SeaWorld Orlando, Aquatica Orlando, Busch Gardens Tampa Bay, and Adventure Island Tampa Bay. Multi-park tickets are valid six months from purchase date. Florida residents can get additional discounts and annual passes are also quite a bargain.

SeaWorld has no on-site accommodations, and as for nearby dining, you'll be heading for the International Drive area.

The Mako coaster is one of the newest thrill rides at SeaWorld.

SEAWORLD ADVENTURE PARK

This is the park people are referring to when they're talking about SeaWorld. There's the classic—and controversial—slate of trained animal shows featuring dolphins, sea lions, and orcas, as well as informative and educational sea-life exhibits and a steadily growing roster of thrill rides. While the park isn't quite as idyllic as you might hope from a nature-oriented attraction, it's lushly landscaped, and the animals all seem to be treated respectfully, with clean modern habitats.

Rides

Although most thrill-seekers head straight for the high-speed steel coaster known as **Kraken,** I have to give the nod to **Journey to Atlantis** when it comes to picking SeaWorld's best ride. Sure, dropping 145 feet at 65 mph makes for a winning ride by nearly any yardstick, but there's something about Atlantis's combination of the dark-ride theme, the log flume soaking, and roller coaster speed—not to mention the enormous fake out at the end—that makes the ride a truly unique experience.

A somewhat more sedate experience can be had at **Wild Arctic,** which combines a motion-simulator ride with a walk-through animal exhibit filled with polar bears, walruses, and beluga whales. **Antarctica: Empire of the Penguin** opened in 2013 and bears something of a thematic resemblance to Wild Arctic, but is much more interesting, combining live-penguin exhibits with a moderately exciting dark-ride experience.

A 140-foot-high flying steel coaster called **Manta** out-adrenalines Kraken, and is one of the best rides in the park, thanks to a combination of ride mechanics and live manta ray exhibits. **Mako** further upped the thrill quotient of SeaWorld's rides, offering a 200-foot-tall coaster experience billed as the "tallest," as well as the "fastest" (73 mph) and "longest" (4,760 feet of track) coaster in Orlando.

Shows

The heart of SeaWorld is its variety of **animal shows.** Although all are centrally focused on the amazing abilities of the animals—and the unique capabilities of the trainers and water acrobats that join them in the shows—each has a somewhat different premise and emphasis. **One Ocean** and seasonal shows are both held in the spacious **Shamu Stadium.** The enormous facility and its seven-million-gallon tank is needed to accommodate the iconic killer whales who star in the shows. Of the two, Shamu Rocks is definitely the cornier show, themed around a rock concert motif with a fantastic light show and less-than-fantastic tunes. One Ocean casts aside story and theme in favor of dazzling trainer-animal choreography and visual effects. The goofy **Clyde and Seamore Sea Lion High** show features a pair of sea lions, otters, and a Pacific walrus in the Sea Lion and Otter Stadium.

Animal Exhibits

Integral to SeaWorld's identity are the multiple animal exhibits, which allow visitors to get up close to various denizens of the deep. All are pretty self-explanatory. You can see manatees and penguins at the **Penguin Encounter,** and stingrays in the **Stingray Lagoon.** The chance to touch and feed the dolphins at **Dolphin Cove** and the thrill of traveling through an underwater tube while sharks swim overhead in the superlative **Shark Encounter** attraction make both of these exhibits must-sees.

Special Events

Seven Seas Food Festival (Feb. and March) is SeaWorld's take on Epcot's successful Food & Wine festival, featuring more than 60 different dishes, craft beer, wine, and live music by classic pop, rock, and country acts.

During the summer, SeaWorld stays open late for **Summer Nights** (late May-early Sept.), which allows guests to ride rides, do a little extra shopping, and see seasonal shows like Shamu Rocks.

On weekends in October, kids can don costumes and trick-or-treat throughout the

Other Nearby Attractions

LEGOLAND

Legoland Florida (1 Legoland Way, Winter Haven, 863/318-5346, http://florida.legoland. com, typically 9:30am-6:30pm daily, $93 adults, $86 for kids 3-12 and seniors 60 and older, with considerable discounts for early online purchase) made quite an impact when it was added to Central Florida's tourist landscape in 2011. Of all the Legoland theme parks throughout the world, Legoland Florida is the second-largest, covering 145 acres, including the Cypress Gardens botanical gardens. Several other attractions were held over from Cypress Gardens, including four roller coasters and the Splash Island water park (now Legoland Water Park, additional ticket upgrade $20). Despite all the attractions inherited from Cypress Gardens, Legoland Florida is a unique experience, with everything except the gardens themselves re-themed and re-imagined to reflect the kid-friendly vibe of the classic toys.

While it's still the coasters and thrill rides that command the most attention, the central area of the park, known as Miniland U.S.A., is the most obviously Lego-centric area, featuring tiny-brick re-creations of everything from New York City and Miami's South Beach to the fantastic galaxies of *Star Wars*. Throughout the park there are ample opportunities for kids to put their imaginations to work building Lego toys.

GATORLAND

Founded in 1949, **Gatorland** (14501 S. Orange Blossom Tr., Kissimmee, 407/855-5496, www. gatorland.com, 9am-5pm daily, $22.99 adults, $14.99 children) is a Central Florida icon, attracting Northern tourists who made their way down the once-scenic Orange Blossom Trail decades before the Magic Kingdom was even a glint in Walt Disney's eye. The basic premise is unchanged: Visitors tromp around decks that overlook lakes filled with gators, occasionally taking time out to watch one of the many feeding shows that happen throughout the day. There are also gator-wrestling exhibitions and an extensive trail-and-boardwalk system that winds through the 110-acre property.

park as part of **SeaWorld's Halloween Spooktacular.**

Food

The menu of pasta, steak, chicken, and, ironically, seafood at ★ **Sharks Underwater Grill** (lunch and dinner, from $17) is decent enough, but its the dining room that's the real attraction here: One wall is shared with the glass of an enormous shark-filled aquarium. If being surrounded by marine life all day has dampened your appetite for seafood, **Voyager's** (lunch and dinner, from $9) has a limited selection of home-style barbecue dishes served with watermelon and grilled corn on the cob, as well as salads.

There are several other fast-service options throughout the park. The **All-Day Dining Deal** ($32.99 adults, $17.99 children 3-9) is a pretty good deal if you're planning on spending the entire day at the park, as it covers all meals (one entrée, plus one side or dessert, plus one nonalcoholic beverage) at a half-dozen SeaWorld dining establishments.

You won't actually be in the tank when you **Dine with Shamu** (killer whale habitat, $29), but the poolside tables at this dining experience provide an up-close look at SeaWorld's star. The behind-the-scenes look is augmented by a decent (though limited) selection of local and organic fare, and a kids' buffet stacked with pasta, nuggets, and hot dogs.

AQUATICA

As far as water parks go, SeaWorld's **Aquatica** (5800 Water Play Way, hours vary seasonally, open year-round except select weekdays in winter, $59 at the gate, or $39 online at least one day in advance; steep discounts available when combined with SeaWorld Orlando

Gatorland is a classic Orlando attraction.

ZIPLINE SAFARI

Zipline Safari (4755 N. Kenansville Rd., St. Cloud, 866/854-3837, www.floridaecosafaris.com, groups depart hourly 10am-4pm, $85, participants must be at least 10 years old and weigh 70-275 pounds) is a great addition to the to-do list of active travelers in the area. It's the only zip line in Florida, and the only one in the world designed for flat land. The lines run through the forests and ranchlands of Osceola County, hurtling riders at speeds of up to 20 mph as they hang more than 50 feet in the air.

admission) is a solid selection. The added element of live animals, from Commerson's dolphins and tropical fish to a wide variety of exotic birds, even sets it apart from the two Disney water parks. But still, a water park's a water park, and Aquatica's main attraction is the number of opportunities it provides visitors to get wet.

Rides

By far the most unique slide at Aquatica is the **Dolphin Plunge,** which races you down one of two side-by-side tube slides right through a water habitat filled with dolphins. Although you'll likely be going too fast to really observe them at play, the underwater sensation is completely unique.

More traditional attractions at Aquatica include the side-by-side wave pools and sunbathing area of **Cutback Cove & Big Surf**

Shores, the splashing river rafting adventure of **Roa's Rapids,** and **Whanau Way,** an enormous, four-slide tower.

There's also the **Loggerhead Lane** lazy river and two kid-friendly areas.

Food

Dining options are fairly limited at Aquatica. The **WaterStone Grill** ($9) serves sandwiches and salads, and the **Mango Market** ($7) has pizzas, wraps, and chicken tenders. Guests committed to an entire day's visit tend to opt for the **Banana Beach Cookout,** which sells full-day passes ($18 adults, $13 kids), allowing unlimited noshing on barbecue, burgers, and hot dogs.

★ DISCOVERY COVE

There are no sky-high roller coasters or cartoon characters at SeaWorld's **Discovery**

Cove, but that's sort of the point. More a secluded natural oasis than a typical theme park, the marquee attraction here is the opportunity for one-on-one animal encounters, including a 30-minute swim session with dolphins, snorkeling among hundreds of brightly colored tropical fish, and wading in a lagoon filled with rays. In addition to the up-close animal interactions, the lush grounds also house an aviary and a beautiful temperature-controlled swimming area.

The point of a visit to Discovery Cove is to experience a day of exclusive relaxation, much as one might find when visiting a private island. As such, admission prices are all-inclusive; during the busiest days, it's $379 for a day that incorporates the dolphin encounter and $229 without it, although I can't imagine coming and not participating in this one-of-a-kind experience. (Substantial discounts are available during less-busy times, as low as $229 for the dolphin experience and $169 for non-experience admission.) Food and drinks throughout the day, gear rental for snorkeling, towels, lockers, beach chairs, and even sunscreen are included in the price of admission. (Private cabanas are available for an additional rental charge.) Even better, for an added $22, you can tack on unlimited access to SeaWorld Orlando, Aquatica, and Busch Gardens in Tampa. Reservations are required and should be made well in advance, as the park is filled to capacity most days.

INFORMATION AND SERVICES

There are guest service kiosks at the entrance of both SeaWorld and Aquatica, and park maps are readily available throughout both parks. Guests enjoying the day at Discovery Cove will find that from the moment they check in at the reservation desk, they will have attentive service throughout the day.

SeaWorld offers stroller, wheelchair, and locker rental as well as kennel service, located just outside the main entrance.

GETTING THERE AND AROUND

SeaWorld and the nearby hotels on International Drive are only about 15 minutes from **Orlando International Airport** (MCO, One Airport Blvd., Orlando, 407/825-2001, www.orlandoairports.net). The **Orlando-Sanford International Airport** (SFB, 1200 Red Cleveland Blvd., Sanford, 407/585-4000, www.orlandosanfordairport.com) is 45 minutes away. SeaWorld is located just off International Drive near the intersection of I-4 and State Road 528 (the Beach Line Expressway toll road).

Parking at SeaWorld is $19, and your parking pass can be used at both Aquatica and SeaWorld. Parking at Discovery Cove is free.

International Drive

Jammed side by side along the several miles of the strip known as **I-Drive** is a seemingly endless agglomeration of buffet restaurants, T-shirt shops, tchotchke dealers, miniature golf courses, go-kart tracks, cheap hotels, sports bars, and bargain steak houses. This strip is nearly unavoidable for visitors who venture out of the Disney cocoon for visits to Universal or SeaWorld. I-Drive is located alongside SeaWorld, and a block south of Universal.

ORLANDO EYE

Opened in 2015, the **Orlando Eye** (8401 International Drive, 866/228-6438, 10am-10pm Sun.-Thurs., 10am-midnight Fri., Sat., adults $25, children $20, discounts available for advance online purchase) has quickly become an iconic attraction. Not only is the 400-foot Ferris wheel visible from nearly everywhere in the area, its installation has revitalized the tourist-trap vibe of I-Drive. The 20-minute ride in enclosed viewing capsules is comfortable and impressive, providing views of both the surrounding theme park areas and even the city of Orlando.

SEALIFE AQUARIUM

Located adjacent to the Orlando Eye is the **SeaLife Aquarium** (8449 International Drive, 866/622-0607, 10am-9pm daily, adults $25, $20 children, online discounts available). While its relatively small scale means it isn't nearly as impressive as many urban aquariums—you can see the whole place in a little more than an hour—the exhibits are modern and informative, though they can get a little crowded. The highlight is a 360-degree walk-through tunnel that puts guests in the middle of a vibrant, teeming aquarium filled with multiple species of colorful fish.

WONDERWORKS

The garish upside-down building on the side of I-Drive? That's **WonderWorks** (9067 International Dr., 407/351-8800, www.wonderworksonline.com, 9am-midnight daily, adults $24.99, children $19.99), an attraction that features interactive exhibits frequently found in science centers and children's museums but without the educational content that usually accompanies them. The facility itself has seen better days, and the entertainment value hardly holds up for repeat visits, although as a rainy-day time-killer it's not too terrible. Games of laser tag can be appended to the admission fee for an additional $3. There's also a comedy and magic dinner show ($24.99 adults, $16.99 children). You can combine the exhibits, laser tag, and the dinner show ($44.99 adults, $34.99 children).

RIPLEY'S BELIEVE IT OR NOT!

It wouldn't be a tourist destination without a **Ripley's Believe It Or Not!** (8201 International Blvd., 407/351-5803, www.ripleys.com, 9:30am-midnight daily, $19.99 adults, $12.99 children, kids 3 and under free), now, would it? This "Odditorium" is much like other Ripley's outposts in other tourist-swarmed locales, featuring shrunken heads, a three-legged man, a Rolls Royce made out of matchsticks, a portrait of the Mona Lisa made out of burned toast, and other

the Orlando Eye on Orlando's busy International Drive

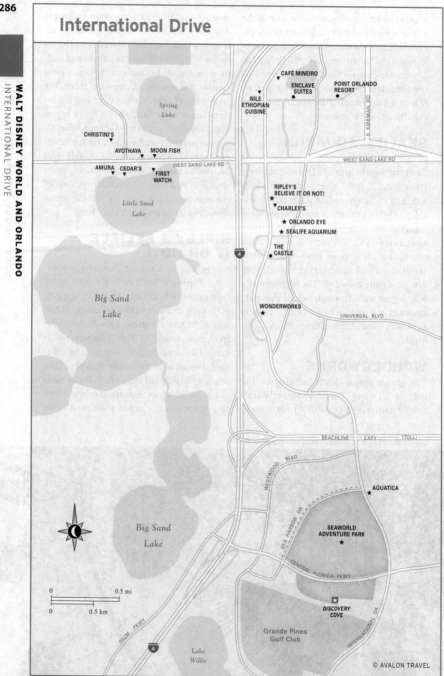

International Drive

CHRISTINI'S

AYOTHAYA   MOON FISH

AMURA   CEDAR'S   FIRST WATCH

CAFÉ MINEIRO

ENCLAVE SUITES

POINT ORLANDO RESORT

NILE ETHIOPIAN CUISINE

Spring Lake

Little Sand Lake

WEST SAND LAKE RD

S. KIRKMAN RD.

RIPLEY'S BELIEVE IT OR NOT!

CHARLEY'S

ORLANDO EYE

SEALIFE AQUARIUM

THE CASTLE

Big Sand Lake

WONDERWORKS

UNIVERSAL BLVD

BEACHLINE   EXPY   (TOLL)

WESTWOOD   BLVD

Big Sand Lake

AQUATICA

SEA HARBOR DR

SEAWORLD ADVENTURE PARK

CENTRAL FLORIDA PKWY

INTERNATIONAL DR

DISCOVERY COVE

Grande Pines Golf Club

PALM PKWY

Lake Willis

0   0.5 mi
0   0.5 km

© AVALON TRAVEL

sublimely ridiculous things. The building is hard to miss, as it appears to be sinking into the ground.

FOOD

It's somewhat ironic that a number of excellent restaurants have popped up in the shadow of three people-pleasing theme parks, but that's just what's happened along Orlando's own **Restaurant Row**, a strip of Sand Lake Road west of I-4. There are a couple dozen praiseworthy spots in this small area (which also happens to be close to the upscale neighborhoods of Dr. Phillips and Bay Hill), and, by all means, if you're wondering where to eat, aim your car here rather than the tourist strip of International Drive. Although there are a handful of neat spots on I-Drive, some of the best restaurants in Orlando are located along Sand Lake Road.

Breakfast

First Watch (7500 W. Sand Lake Rd., 407/363-5622, www.firstwatch.com, 7am-2:30pm daily, from $7) is a Florida-based chain that emphasizes fresh ingredients, a wide selection of healthy breakfast options, and unique preparations like "chickichanga," with scrambled eggs, chorizo, chilis, cheese, and avocado piled into a tortilla. Standard breakfast fare is also available in ample portions.

The locally owned **Keke's** (4192 Conroy Rd., 407/226-1400, www.kekes.com, 7am-2:30pm daily, from $6) specializes in waffles, and tops the Belgian beasts with any combination of fruit, nuts, and whipped cream you can come up with. Omelets, pancakes, and eggs-and-bacon plates are also available.

American

Bubbalou's Bodacious BBQ (5818 Conroy Rd., 407/295-1212, http://bubbalous.com, 10am-9:30pm Mon.-Thurs., 10am-10:30pm Fri.-Sat., 11am-9pm Sun., from $5) is a locally based chain that serves decent smoked-meat meals along with things like sausage sandwiches and fried catfish, which is all well and

good. However, the main reason to darken the door of this restaurant is its fried corn on the cob; the buttery, crispy treat is as near a perfect accompaniment to a pile of brisket as yet created.

Orlando is home to Darden International, the parent company of casual dining behemoths like Olive Garden and Red Lobster. So the opening of a new Darden concept restaurant in the area wasn't much of a surprise. But both the concept and the quality of **Seasons 52** (7700 W. Sand Lake Rd., 407/354-5212, www.seasons52.com, 11:30am-2:30pm and 5pm-10pm Mon.-Fri., 11:30am-11pm Sat., 11:30am-10pm Sun., from $16) were unexpected of the company behind the "never-ending pasta bowl." Every single item on the Seasons 52 menu clocks in at 475 calories or less, though it's far from an ascetic dining experience. The emphasis is on seasonal dishes, hence the "Seasons" of the name, and a menu that's tweaked for freshness on a weekly basis, hence the "52." The result is an exquisite and upscale dining experience that's actually about the food rather than about indulgence. Although the menu regularly changes, there's always an abundance of fish and seafood dishes as well as tasty and filling entrée-sized salads. Even steak and poultry manage to squeeze their way onto the calorie-restricted menu, and the rich and perfectly portioned desserts are served in shot glass-sized containers.

Steak and Seafood

In the I-Drive/Restaurant Row area, there's a Bonefish Grill, a FishBones, and then there's **Moon Fish** (7525 W. Sand Lake Rd., 407/363-7262, 5pm-10pm Sun.-Thurs., 5pm-11pm Fri.-Sat., from $22). If you're craving high-end preparations of seafood, the latter should be your destination. Asian touches abound on the menu, but there's also a solid selection of steaks and chops. The raw bar serves up phenomenal oysters.

There are a number of steak houses in the area, both of the traditional sort and of the *churrascaria* variety. For the traditional,

Charley's (8255 International Dr., 407/363-0228, www.charleyssteakhouse.com, 5pm-10:30pm daily, $16-65) is both the best and the longest-running, having served up thick, high-quality steaks (as well as alligator!) for years to tourists and locals who are more than willing to brave the crowds.

As far as Brazilian all-you-can-eat affairs, there are truly a surprising amount. But, you should head straight for the locally owned Café Mineiro (6432 International Dr., 407/248-2932, http://cafemineirosteakhouse.com, 11:30am-1am daily, from $20), which is both the most authentic and the most affordable. It's located in a repurposed Japanese restaurant.

Italian

If the baroque decor of the sumptuous dining room at Christini's (7600 Dr. Phillips Blvd., 407/345-8770, http://christinis.com, 6pm-midnight daily, from $30) doesn't clue you in that you're in for some old-school fine dining, then perhaps the strolling musicians or the gift of a red rose to female diners will do the trick. Owner Chris Christini prides himself on the classical atmosphere of his restaurant. Unfortunately, the kitchen prepares heavily sauced pasta and meat dishes that barely surpass the quality delivered in family-style chains.

For something a little more relaxed, the best pizza in the area is Flippers Pizzeria (6125 Westwood Blvd., 407/345-0113, www.flipperspizzeria.com, 11am-midnight Sun.-Thurs., 11am-1am Fri.-Sat., $14-23). With six theme-park area locations, you'll undoubtedly be able to get one of their fantastic pies to your hotel room door.

Asian

Ayothaya (7555 W. Sand Lake Rd., 407/345-0040, www.ayothayathaicuisineoflorlando.com, 11am-3pm and 5pm-10pm Mon.-Fri., noon-10pm Sat.-Sun., from $10) serves excellent Thai food in teak-heavy surroundings. In addition to the standard curries, soups, and noodle dishes, Ayothaya also offers a number of specialties like spicy duck and steamed fish.

Amura (7786 W. Sand Lake Rd., 407/370-0007, http://amura.com, 11:30am-2:30pm and 5pm-10pm Mon.-Fri., noon-3pm and 5pm-10pm Sat.-Sun., from $9) is consistently touted as one of the best sushi restaurants in Orlando, which is an opinion that's difficult to argue with. From the modern decor and the see-and-be-seen atmosphere, the vibe is decidedly hip and upscale. The eatery even refers to its sushi preparations as "high-definition." The staff is exceedingly friendly and will guide novices through the menu's wide range of options. Masterfully constructed rolls are brimming with flavor, and some of the more exclusive preparations, like the Coco-Mango roll (tuna, salmon, mango, coconut, and cilantro), are absolutely mind-blowing.

Other International

Cedar's (7732 W. Sand Lake Rd., 407/351-6000, http://orlandocedars.com, 11:30am-10:30pm Mon.-Fri., noon-2am Sat., noon-9pm Sun., from $16) presents a selection of authentic Lebanese dishes in a stylish atmosphere. Saturday nights feature live belly dance performances.

Finding an Ethiopian restaurant tucked away among the businesses of International Drive is something of a surprise, but right there, sitting among the T-shirt shops, is the family-run ★ Nile Ethiopian Cuisine (7048 International Dr., 407/354-0026, www.nile07.com, 5pm-10pm Mon.-Fri., 11am-midnight Sat.-Sun., from $12). Food is served family style and utensil-free, leaving you to sop up the richly spiced and delicious marinated meats and vegetables with the spongy sour injera bread. Although many of the dishes are based around poultry and beef, there are a number of vegetarian selections available as well. For a treat, finish off the meal with traditional Ethiopian coffee service.

ACCOMMODATIONS

The hokey architecture of The Castle (8629 International Dr., 407/345-1511, www.castlehotelorlando.com, from $150 d) fits right in with the overblown atmosphere of

International Drive. Although a stay here probably won't make anyone feel like royalty, the Renaissance-era styling and mass-market luxury touches make it one of the better values on the tourist strip.

Enclave Suites (6165 Carrier Dr., 407/351-1155, www.enclavesuites.com, from $79 d) is a pretty basic hotel, with decent, if slightly worn, guest rooms. About half of the guest rooms are regular hotel accommodations, the rest are kitchen-equipped suites in studio, one-bedroom, and two-bedroom sizes. There are four pools on the property, as well as a tennis court, game room, and playground.

For true budget travelers, the motel-style **Metropolitan Express** (6323 International Dr., 407/351-4430, www.orlandometropolitanexpress.com, from $60 d) is a good option. Although the guest rooms aren't going to win any awards for spaciousness or style, they've got all the basics, and the hotel has a free continental breakfast buffet and complimentary shuttles to the Disney parks.

The ★ **Point Orlando Resort** (7385 Universal Blvd., 407/956-2000, www. thepointorlando.com, studio suites from $109) is surprisingly quiet considering its location in the thick of the I-Drive action. The all-suite property has studio, one-, and two-bedroom "condotel" accommodations, all of which have full kitchens, flat-screen televisions, and laundry facilities. Guest rooms and public areas are clean and contemporary.

Those looking to escape the masses of budget travelers should head for the **JW Marriott** (407/206-2300, www.marriott.com, from $219 d) or the **Ritz-Carlton** (407/206-2400, www. ritzcarlton.com, from $239 d), both of which are located a few miles away at **Grande Lakes Orlando** (4040 Central Florida Pkwy., www. grandelakes.com), a 500-acre golf and convention resort set on a nature preserve. The combined amenities of the two five-star hotels include 11 restaurants, a spa, meeting facilities, a fly-fishing school, a Greg Norman-designed golf course, three tennis courts, bocce ball, carriage rides, and three pools. It goes without saying that the guest rooms and suites are up to the high standards set by each of the top-shelf chains.

Metro Orlando

Before there was Walt Disney World, there was a growing city called Orlando, a city that was beginning to make a name for itself as a center for aeronautical and military technology. Today, Orlando is immediately associated with theme parks and family fun, with little thought given to the impressive slate of sights, attractions, and cultural activities that have nothing to do with roller coasters or animated creatures. While the city's leaders have long been content to let tourism run the economic engine here, residents and adventurous travelers have learned that even without those theme parks to the south, the city is well deserving of attention.

Winter Park and Maitland, on the northern outskirts of Orlando, are located right next to one another, and both offer their own bit of Old Florida charm. Maitland is actually one of the oldest incorporated communities in Florida, but much of its history has been overtaken by its growth as a bedroom community. The town's "cultural corridor" gives a glimpse of its foundation and personality. Winter Park, established as a planned community for wintering members of the New England elite, has been far more fastidious about maintaining its history. Its thick canopy of oak trees hangs over brick-lined streets, hiding expansive mansions and the upscale shopping and dining of its downtown area.

SIGHTS
Downtown Orlando

Most visitors to downtown Orlando come for one of two reasons. Either they're conducting

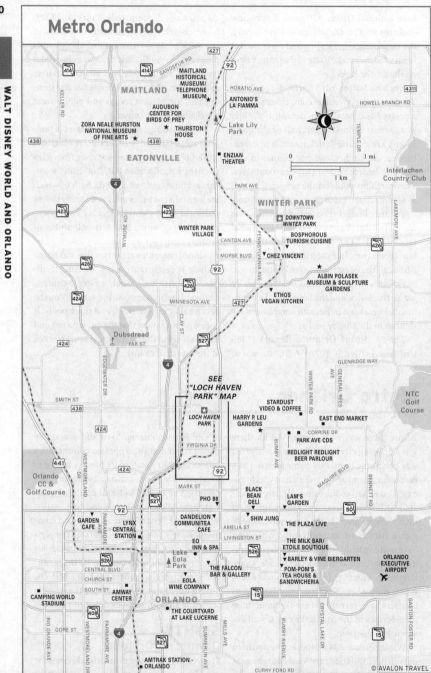

Metro Orlando

MAITLAND

MAITLAND HISTORICAL MUSEUM/ TELEPHONE MUSEUM

ANTONIO'S LA FIAMMA

Lake Lily Park

AUDUBON CENTER FOR BIRDS OF PREY

ZORA NEALE HURSTON NATIONAL MUSEUM OF FINE ARTS

THURSTON HOUSE

EATONVILLE

ENZIAN THEATER

Interlachen Country Club

WINTER PARK

DOWNTOWN WINTER PARK

WINTER PARK VILLAGE

BOSPHOROUS TURKISH CUISINE

CHEZ VINCENT

ALBIN POLASEK MUSEUM & SCULPTURE GARDENS

ETHOS VEGAN KITCHEN

Dubsdread

NTC Golf Course

SEE "LOCH HAVEN PARK" MAP

LOCH HAVEN PARK

STARDUST VIDEO & COFFEE

EAST END MARKET

HARRY P. LEU GARDENS

PARK AVE CDS

REDLIGHT REDLIGHT BEER PARLOUR

Orlando CC & Golf Course

PHO 88

BLACK BEAN DELI

LAM'S GARDEN

GARDEN CAFE

DANDELION COMMUNITEA CAFE

SHIN JUNG

THE PLAZA LIVE

LYNX CENTRAL STATION

EO INN & SPA

THE MILK BAR/ ETOILE BOUTIQUE

Lake Eola Park

BARLEY & VINE BIERGARTEN

ORLANDO EXECUTIVE AIRPORT

THE FALCON BAR & GALLERY

POM-POM'S TEA HOUSE & SANDWICHERIA

EOLA WINE COMPANY

CAMPING WORLD STADIUM

AMWAY CENTER

ORLANDO

THE COURTYARD AT LAKE LUCERNE

AMTRAK STATION - ORLANDO

© AVALON TRAVEL

0   1 mi

0   1 km

business or they've sought respite from the theme parks. The city center does not offer much but a few notable sights.

The city's crown jewel is **Lake Eola Park** (195 N. Rosalind Ave., 407/246-2827, www.cityoforlando.net, 6am-midnight daily, free). Walking along the trail that circumnavigates it is a pleasant way to while away an afternoon. But only once you've paddled out to the middle of the lake on one of the swan-shaped boats that are available for rent can you truly say that you've experienced Lake Eola.

History buffs should explore the **Orange County Regional History Center** (65 E. Central Blvd., 407/836-8500, www.thehistorycenter.org, 10am-5pm Mon.-Sat., noon-5pm Sun., $12 adults, $10 seniors/students/military, $9 children, children 4 and under free), located in a 1927 building that used to be the courthouse. Three floors of immersive and well-curated permanent exhibits are heavy on 19th- and early 20th-century artifacts. Although some of the museum's better material, particularly its Kerouac and Highwaymen exhibits, occasionally travel to other museums, this is still one of the better Florida-centric museums in the state.

★ Loch Haven Park

Located five minutes or so from downtown, **Loch Haven Park** (900 E. Princeton St., 407/246-2287, www.cityoforlando.net, 5am-sunset daily) is a rewarding destination, housing museums, theaters, and a science center on its expansive grounds.

The **Mennello Museum of American Folk Art** (900 E. Princeton St., 407/246-4278, www.mennellomuseum.org, 10:30am-4:30pm Tues.-Sat., noon-4:30pm Sun., $5 adults, $4 seniors, $1 students/children 6-18, military and children under 6 free) is housed in a beautiful, lakefront mansion. Founded in 1998 primarily as an exhibition space for a clutch of Earl Cunningham paintings donated by local philanthropist Marilyn Mennello, the museum diligently strives to give folk artists the respect they deserve. Cunningham's works still form the centerpiece of the Mennello, but a wide variety of visiting exhibits make it an essential stop for fans of somewhat nontraditional art.

The **Orlando Museum of Art** (OMA, 2416 N. Mills Ave., 407/896-4231, www.omart.org, 10am-4pm Tues.-Fri., noon-4pm Sat.-Sun., $15 adults, $8 seniors/students/military, $5 children 4-17, children 3 and under free) features a respectable collection of pre-Columbian

Loch Haven Park

Loch Haven Park

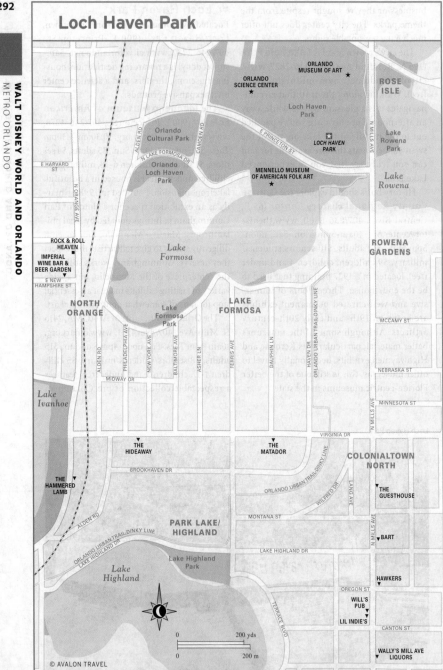

ORLANDO
MUSEUM OF ART ★

ORLANDO
SCIENCE CENTER ★

ROSE
ISLE

Loch Haven
Park

Lake
Rowena
Park

LOCH HAVEN
PARK

Orlando
Cultural Park

N LAKE FORMOSA DR

Orlando
Loch Haven
Park

MENNELLO MUSEUM
OF AMERICAN FOLK ART ★

Lake
Rowena

E HARVARD
ST

N ORANGE AVE

ALDEN RD

CAMDEN RD

E PRINCETON ST

N MILLS AVE

ROCK & ROLL
HEAVEN ●

IMPERIAL
WINE BAR &
BEER GARDEN ●

E NEW
HAMPSHIRE ST

Lake
Formosa

ROWENA
GARDENS

NORTH
ORANGE

Lake
Formosa
Park

LAKE
FORMOSA

MCCAMY ST

Lake
Ivanhoe

ALDEN RD

PHILADELPHIA AVE

NEW YORK AVE

BALTIMORE AVE

ASHER LN

FERRIS AVE

DAUPHIN LN

HAVEN DR

ORLANDO URBAN TRAIL-DINKY LINE

NEBRASKA ST

MIDWAY DR

MINNESOTA ST

THE
HIDEAWAY ▼

THE
MATADOR ▼

VIRGINIA DR

COLONIALTOWN
NORTH

BROOKHAVEN DR

ORLANDO URBAN TRAIL-DINKY LINE

WILFRED DR

LANG AVE

THE
GUESTHOUSE ▼

THE
HAMMERED
LAMB ▲

ALDEN RD

MONTANA ST

N MILLS AVE

BART ▼

PARK LAKE/
HIGHLAND

ORLANDO URBAN TRAIL-DINKY LINE
LAKE HIGHLAND DR

LAKE HIGHLAND DR

HAWKERS ▼

Lake Highland
Park

OREGON ST

Lake
Highland

WILL'S
PUB ▼

LIL INDIE'S ▼

TERRACE BLVD

CANTON ST

0   200 yds

0   200 m

WALLY'S MILL AVE
LIQUORS ▼

© AVALON TRAVEL

artifacts and American artwork by the likes of John Singer Sargent and Georgia O'Keeffe. OMA's African art exhibit is truly remarkable, presenting as artwork an array of fabrics, beadwork, masks, and other items that many museums would treat as anthropological items. Past visiting exhibitions have featured the works of Andy Warhol, Maya Lin, and many other notable contemporary artists.

After gawking at folk art and artifacts for a while, the kids in your posse will likely be tugging your arm, begging for a foray to the **Orlando Science Center** (OSC, 777 E. Princeton St., 407/514-2000, www.osc.org, 10am-6pm Sun.-Fri., 10am-9pm Sat., $20 adults, $18 seniors and students, $14 children, children 2 and under free). Like many such interactive museums, the exhibits at OSC are part hands-on fun, part subtle science lesson. The NatureWorks area is the most unique, with the complexities of various Florida ecosystems explained and illustrated, often with live animals. (Yes, those are alligators.) Other exhibits dedicated to dinosaurs and fun demonstrations of scientific principles, as well as the IMAX theater, planetarium, and a recently revamped and expanded KidsTown area—complete with a pint-size theater stage with props, climbing area, arts-and-crafts room,

and more—will be familiar to anyone who has visited other kid-centric science museums.

ViMi District

The burgeoning **ViMi District** is what's in and around Mills Avenue between Virginia Avenue at the north end and Colonial Drive at the south end. The area includes the Little Vietnam agglomeration of Vietnamese shops and restaurants at the southern end, as well as the bars, restaurants, and galleries along the Mills Avenue corridor.

The main sight in this area is the **Harry P. Leu Gardens** (1920 N. Forest Ave., 407/246-2620, www.leugardens.org, 9am-5pm daily, $10 adults, $3 children, kids 4 and under free, free 9am-noon Mon.), although its Forest Avenue address puts it a block or so north of the end of Virginia Avenue. The beautiful gardens house the largest formal rose garden in Florida as well as the largest camellia collection outside of California. Backyard greenthumbs can mine the three "idea gardens" for inspiration, while the less horticulturally inclined can simply enjoy the pastoral scenery that the 50 acres offers.

★ Downtown Winter Park

A visit to **downtown Winter Park** almost

Central Park in downtown Winter Park

always begins in the areas around **Park Avenue**. This brick-paved, tree-lined street is home to an array of high-end and not-so-high-end shops and eateries. Even if you're not looking to spend or eat, a walk down Park Avenue takes you through the heart of this little urban village for some great browsing and people-watching opportunities. If you're driving, take an hour or so to wander around the luxurious and historic neighborhoods immediately surrounding Park Avenue. If the price tags in the shops didn't seem expensive, some of these elegant and architecturally rich mansions certainly will. The 11-acre **Central Park** runs along Park Avenue and is home to various festivals and local events. The fountains and majestic oak trees practically beg you to spread out a blanket and have a picnic.

A fun way to get a peek at some of Winter Park's historic homes and beautiful scenery is the **Scenic Boat Tour** (312 E. Morse Blvd., 407/644-4056, www.scenicboattours.com, 10am-4pm daily, $10 adults, $5 children, children under 2 free), which takes passengers out onto the chain of lakes that wend through the city, offering a backstage view of the truly impressive residences that line them.

At the northern end of Park Avenue is the **Charles Hosmer Morse Museum of American Art** (445 N. Park Ave., 407/645-5311, www.morsemusuem.org, 9:30am-4pm Tues.-Sat., 1pm-4pm Sun., $5 adults, $4 seniors, $1 students, children under 12 free; free 4pm-8pm Fri. Nov.-Apr.), best known as the home of the world's most comprehensive collection of works by Louis Comfort Tiffany. Everything from Tiffany lamps and stained-glass windows to pottery and paintings is on display. The Morse extends its purview beyond Tiffany to include a number of other late-19th and early 20th-century decorative pieces, art pottery, and a number of paintings and prints by the likes of Mary Cassatt, John Singer Sargent, Maxfield Parrish, Edward Hopper, and more.

A few blocks west of Park Avenue is **Hannibal Square,** a historically African American neighborhood that has slowly seen its original residents replaced by boutiques and restaurants. While there's a nice commemorative marker at the corner of New England and Pennsylvania Avenues denoting the area's cultural history, the best way to get a sense of the neighborhood's past is to pay a visit to the **Hannibal Square Heritage Center** (642 W. New England Ave., 407/539-2680, www.hannibalsquareheritagecenter.org, noon-4pm Tues.-Thurs., noon-5pm Fri., 10am-5pm Sat., 10am-2pm Sun., free).

The area in and around the campus of **Rollins College** (1000 Holt Ave., 407/646-2000, www.rollins.edu) is well worth a visit. Located lakeside in the heart of the picturesque campus, the **Cornell Fine Arts Museum** (1000 Holt Ave., 407/646-2526, www.rollins.edu/cfam, 10am-4pm Tues.-Fri., noon-5pm Sat.-Sun., $5 adults) houses a fantastic permanent collection, with an emphasis on classical European and American art, including a handful of paintings from the Italian Renaissance and a number of 16th- and 17th-century portraits.

Also nearby is the **Albin Polasek Museum & Sculpture Gardens** (633 Osceola Ave., 407/647-6294, www.polasek.org, gardens, galleries, residence, chapel 10am-4pm Tues.-Sat., 1pm-4pm Sun. Sept. 1-June 30; gardens only 10am-4pm Mon.-Fri. July 1-Aug. 31; $5 adults, $4 seniors, $3 students, children 11 and under free, garden free). More than half of the works created by the Czech American sculptor are on display here. The beautiful expansive gardens are a near-perfect setting for these expressive sculptures. Polasek's small but emotionally intense *The 12th Station of the Cross,* however, is not at the Museum; it can be found at his grave site at **Palm Cemetery** (1005 N. New York Ave.).

Maitland Cultural Corridor

Downtown Maitland doesn't have the same level of charm as downtown Winter Park, but the area known as the **Cultural Corridor** can lay claim to two highly unique museums. The **Maitland Historical Museum and Telephone Museum** (221 W. Packwood Ave., 407/644-1364, www.maitlandhistory.

Zora Neale Hurston and Eatonville

The small town of Eatonville, located between Winter Park and Maitland, doesn't seem like much at first sight, but it was one of the first towns established after the Emancipation Proclamation to be a primarily African American city. Ironically enough, the town took its name not from one of its original African American leaders but from Josiah Eaton, the white landowner who sold the land that became the town.

That founding was described in Zora Neale Hurston's book *Their Eyes Were Watching God,* in which the protagonist Janie Crawford tells the story of her life growing up in early 20th-century Florida, a perspective that Hurston had quite a bit of authority on; she grew up in Eatonville. Every year the community pays tribute to its most famous former resident with the **ZORA! Festival** (http://zorafestival.org, late Jan.), dedicated not just to Hurston's work but also to a wide spectrum of African American art, culture, and music. Additionally, the small **Zora Neale Hurston National Museum of Fine Arts** (227 E. Kennedy Blvd., Eatonville, 407/647-3307, http://zoranealehurstonmuseum.com, 9am-5pm Mon.-Fri., donations accepted) features a couple of exhibits focused on Hurston's work and Eatonville history.

org, noon-4pm Wed.-Sun., $3 adults, $2 children, children 5 and under free) focuses on the history of the Maitland area with lots of photographs and historical documents. Oddly enough, it also focuses on the history of the telephone. Actually, the specific focus is on the founding of the Winter Park Telephone Company, which, you'll be reminded, happened in Maitland, along with a cluttered room filled with ancient telephone switchboards, phone booths, and other telephone-related detritus. This odd little museum is certainly not enough to build a day around, but it's a nice stop.

Nearby **Lake Lily Park** (701 Lake Lily Dr.) is home to the equally quirky **Waterhouse Residence Museum and Carpentry Shop Museum** (820 Lake Lily Dr., 407/644-2451, www.maitlandhistory.org, noon-4pm Wed.-Sun., $3 adults, $2 children, children 5 and under free). The Victorian-era home of builder William Waterhouse provides a snapshot look at life in the late 19th century, complete with a collection of hand-powered tools in the shed out back, otherwise known as the Carpentry Shop Museum.

Audubon Center for Birds of Prey

The **Audubon Center for Birds of Prey** (1101 Audubon Way, Maitland, 407/644-0190,

www.audubonofflorida.org, 10am-4pm Tues.-Sun., $5 adults, $4 children, children under 3 free) is primarily a rehabilitative center for eagles, owls, hawks, and other raptors. It's open to the public and offers occasional educational programs. The center rescues nearly 700 birds annually, with the goal of rereleasing them back into the wild. For that reason, the majority of the birds are kept away from human contact so they don't become acclimated to humans. Some, however, are so injured that they'll be living out the rest of their lives in captivity. These birds, representing some 20 species, can be seen in a beautiful aviary, along with accompanying information about their various struggles. Guided on-site tours are available for groups (10-30 people, $100 per group) with five-day advance notice.

SPORTS AND RECREATION

TOP EXPERIENCE

Parks

Florida is blessed with an abundance of beautiful and pastoral **freshwater springs,** those places where water bubbles up from the earth to feed rivers and provide sustenance. At **Wekiwa Springs State Park** (1800 Wekiwa Circle, Apopka, 407/884-2008, www.floridasateparks.org/wekiwasprings, 8am-sunset daily, $6/carload of 2-8 people, $5/single-occupant vehicle), *pastoral* isn't the first word that comes to mind. The year-round, 72-degree water means that there's almost always a crowd relaxing on the sloping banks and splashing around in the large water basin, making it feel more like a municipal swimming pool than the remarkable natural gift that it is. Beyond the main swimming area there are ample boating opportunities as the spring water flows into the Wekiva River, as well as well-marked hiking trails and numerous primitive, RV, and family campsites. The park closes to visitors when it hits capacity, so plan on getting here before 10am on weekends and holidays.

Kelly Park at Rock Springs (400 E. Kelly Park Rd., Apopka, 407/889-4179, 8am-8pm daily, $5/carload of 3 or more people, $3/single- or double-occupancy vehicle) has no pool-like area, as the springs immediately begin flowing into a briskly moving stream that proves irresistible to folks who want to go tubing. There are a number of tube-rental outfits near the park's entrance, most of which offer tubes for $3-5.

Excellent hiking and wildlife-viewing opportunities are available at **Black Bear**

Wilderness Area (5298 Michigan Ave, Sanford, 407/349-0679, http://www.seminolecountyfl.gov/locations/Black-Bear-Wilderness-Area.stml, dawn-dusk daily, free), just a 30-minute drive from downtown Orlando.

The more centrally located **Gaston Edwards Pk** (1236 N. Orange Ave., Orlando, 407/246-2283, 5am-sunset daily) is on Lake Ivanhoe near downtown. The preferred activities here are riding personal watercraft and waterskiing. Landlubbers typically stay onshore to enjoy a game of volleyball.

Spectator Sports
The National Basketball Association's **Orlando Magic** (407/916-2400, www.nba.com/magic, tickets from $15) and the East Coast Hockey League's **Orlando Solar Bears** (407/951-8200, www.orlandosolarbearshockey.com, tickets from $8) all play at the state-of-the-art **Amway Center** (400 W. Church St., 407/440-7000, www.amwaycenter.com). The city's most recent major-league addition is **Orlando City Lions,** a Major League Soccer team that plays at Orlando City Stadium, its own, purpose-built stadium downtown.

The seen-better-days **Camping World**

The cool waters at Wekiwa Springs State Park are a fantastic respite from the Florida heat.

Stadium (1610 W. Church St., no phone, tickets vary by event) was formerly known as the Florida Citrus Bowl, and is used for occasional marquee events, most notably the **Florida Classic,** a football showdown between two historically black colleges, Bethune-Cookman University and Florida A&M. The Classic brings tens of thousands of football fans to town in November for the game and, more notably, the legendary halftime show. The Citrus Bowl stadium also hosts the **Buffalo Wild Wings Citrus Bowl,** the New Year's Day game that pits the Southeastern Conference against the Big Ten Conference, and, a few days earlier, the **Russell Athletic Bowl** (Atlantic Coast Conference and Big Ten teams). It also hosted the **NFL Pro Bowl** in 2017.

The **Arnold Palmer Invitational** (www. arnoldpalmerinvitational.com, from $50/day) golf meet is held at the **Bay Hill Club and Lodge** (9000 Bay Hill Blvd., 407/876-2888, www.bayhill.com), which was owned by the late golfing great who called Orlando home. The tournament is held in late March, usually just a couple of weeks before the Masters, and most of the top golfers of the Professional Golfers' Association (PGA) show up to play.

For something a little more fast-moving, **Orlando Speed World** (19164 E. Colonial Dr., 407/568-1367, www.orlandospeedworld.org, from $12) has stock-car races, pickup-truck races, demolition derbies, and stunt shows nearly year-round. It's the Thanksgiving weekend "Crash-A-Rama," though, that brings out the big crowds for some truly riotous school bus—yes, school bus—races.

Golf
The city-owned **Dubsdread** (549 W. Par St., 407/246-2551, www.golfdubsdread.com, from $27) was originally designed in 1923, and it wears its history proudly. The relatively short par-72 course isn't all that challenging, but the sloping greens and water features are picturesque. The Tap Room restaurant is a local favorite among golfers and non-golfers alike. **Winter Pines Golf Course** (950 S. Ranger Blvd., Winter Park, 407/671-3172, http://winterpinesgc.com, from $15) is a small par-67 course located in a tidy Winter Park neighborhood and is routinely rated as one of the best golf values in Central Florida.

Water Sports
The chain of lakes that dot Orlando's landscape means that the area is a prime location for wakeboarding and waterskiing. **Orlando Watersports Complex** (8615 Florida Rock Rd., 407/251-3100, www.orlandowatersports.com, 11am-sunset Mon.-Fri., 10am-sunset Sat.-Sun.) takes full advantage of that, with two lakes dedicated to high-speed water activities. A series of cables runs above each lake, allowing boarders, wake-skaters, and waterskiers to career along at top velocity, jumping ramps and practicing their tricks at either 18 mph in the beginners' lake or at 20 mph in the advanced one. Ski boats also run on the lakes. There's a pro shop and a snack bar, and lessons and rentals are available.

ENTERTAINMENT AND EVENTS
Nightlife
While Orlando's **nightlife** scene is heavily weighted toward the downtown area, there are a number of great places only a few minutes' drive from downtown that greatly expand the palette of offerings. For the most raucous action and the highest concentration of dance clubs, downtown is surely your best option. But to catch interesting live music or knock back a pint or two of hard-to-find beer, you'll want to get away from the crowds on Orange Avenue and head to some of Orlando's other nightlife spots.

DOWNTOWN ORLANDO
Downtown Orlando's biggest centers of nightlife gravity—in terms of body count, at least—are the bars in the **Church Street** (Church St. at S. Orange Ave.) area and **Wall Street Plaza** (Wall St. at N. Orange Ave.), both of which cater to a demographic mix of just-legal college kids and young businesspeople.

Think 4-for-1 drink specials and body shots. However, as a brief glimpse at the crowds on Orange Avenue will tell you on any given night, there's much more to the downtown scene than that. With a few dozen bars and dance clubs scattered throughout the 10-square-block area, you're more than likely to find something to fit your taste.

For live music, the best options are **Back Booth** (37 W. Pine St., 407/999-2570, www.backbooth.com) and **The Social** (54 N. Orange Ave., 407/246-1419, www.thesocial.org), both of which regularly host touring indie, punk, and alternative bands.

The Beacham (46 N. Orange Ave, 407/246-1419, www.thebeacham.com) has been an Orange Avenue entertainment mainstay since the 1920s, first as a theater, and most recently as a combination live venue/dance club. Larger touring bands play here at least twice a week, and the elegant, historic space also hosts regular DJ nights. The Beacham was the epicenter of Orlando's 1990s heyday as a dance music mecca.

If you're determined to relive the alternative 1980s, the DJs at **Independent Bar** (70 N. Orange Ave., 407/839-0457, www.independentbar.net, 9pm-2am Wed.-Sat., 10pm-2am Sun. and Tues.) manage to weave New Wave, industrial, and synth-pop into a mix of contemporary indie hits and classic alternative music.

When London's legendary Ace Café decided to open their first North American location, they chose Orlando. But, tellingly, they opted out of the crowded tourist district, and selected a historic location in downtown Orlando (the site was originally a massive hardware/farming supply store owned by Harry P. Leu, and was later home to legendary Orlando music venue The Edge). The site is a fitting one for **Ace Café Orlando** (100 W. Livingston St., 407/996-6686, 11am-10pm Mon.-Wed., 11am-11pm Thurs., 11am-midnight Fri.-Sat., 10am-9pm Sun.), which not only allows visitors to soak in the motorcycles-and-classic-cars vibe of the original London location, but also plenty of space in which to enjoy surprisingly decent food and a wide selection of drinks.

Just looking for a drink? **Lizzy McCormack's Irish Pub** (55 N. Orange Ave., 407/426-8007, 2pm-2am daily) has fantastic happy-hour specials, a great selection of microbrews, and outdoor tables that are perfect for watching the night unfold on Orange Avenue.

The Courtesy Bar (114 N. Orange Ave, 407/450-2041, www.thecourtesybar.com, 5pm-2am daily) is one of several craft cocktail bars that have opened throughout Orlando.

Although located outside of what's normally considered downtown, the **Thornton Park** neighborhood is just on the other side of Lake Eola, and home to several great drinking spots that are pleasant alternatives to the buzzing debauchery along Orange Avenue. Oenophiles should hit up **Eola Wine Company** (430 E. Central Blvd., 407/481-9100, www.eolawinecompany.com, 4pm-12:30am Mon.-Wed., 4pm-2am Thurs.-Fri., 2pm-2am Sat., 2pm-12:30am Sun.) for an incredible selection and friendly staff. Art lovers will definitely want to check out **The Falcon Bar and Gallery** (819 E. Washington St., 407/423-3060, 6pm-midnight Mon.-Thurs., 6pm-2am Fri.-Sat., noon-midnight Sun.), a cozy bar whose walls are always filled with great, well-curated local art. And while it's routinely referred to as a dive, **Burton's** (801 E. Washington St., 407/425-3720, noon-2am daily) is the sort of friendly, drinking-is-the-point neighborhood bar that too few neighborhoods actually have.

A little farther east, but still in central Orlando is the **Milk District,** a small collection of bars and restaurants in the shadow of the TG Lee dairy plant. Of course, there's a bar called **The Milk Bar** (2424 E. Robinson St., 407/369-1701, http://themilkbarorlando.com, 2pm-2am Tues.-Sat.), but there's no milk. Instead, this intimate lounge specializes in craft beers and wine. **Sandwich Bar** (2432 E. Robinson St., 407/421-1670, 11:30am-2am daily) has sandwiches (and they're pretty good), but it's also a late-night bar, with a limited selection of craft drafts and frequent visits by excellent local DJs. **Bull & Bush** (2408 E. Robinson St., 407/896-7546, www.bullandbushorlando.com, 5pm-midnight daily) is a super-friendly British pub that hosts karaoke and comedy nights and serves amazing Scotch eggs to soak up the beer. **Barley & Vine Biergarten** (2406 E. Washington St., 407/930-0960, www.barleyandvineorlando.com, 4pm-2am Mon.-Fri., noon-2am Sat., noon-midnight Sun.) is an excellent choice for craft beers, with a friendly staff and a comfortable (and dog-friendly) outdoor patio area that hosts weekend brunches.

The Plaza Live (425 N. Bumby Ave., 407/228-1220, www.plazaliveorlando.com) is a live-music venue situated in one of Orlando's oldest movie theaters. It brings in a great mix of legacy acts (Lindsey Buckingham, Dr. John) and up-and-coming touring bands, as well as some of Orlando's bigger local acts.

VIMI AND AUDUBON PARK AREA

Still centrally located but well away from the downtown hordes are two roughly contiguous and amorphously defined neighborhoods: **ViMi** and **Audubon Park**.

ViMi (named after the intersection of Virginia Drive and Mills Avenue) is also known as Mills50 (for the slightly more southern intersection of Mills Avenue and SR-50/Colonial Drive). It has blossomed over the last couple of years, both in terms of quality and quantity of nightlife. The stalwarts here are Will's Pub and Wally's Mills Ave. Liquors. **Will's Pub** (1040 N. Mills Ave., 407/898-5070, www.willspub.org, 4pm-2am daily) is an Orlando institution and something of a home away from home for most of the city's musicians, thanks to its expansive and inexpensive craft beer selection and the wide variety of top-shelf rock and punk bands that play here. The bar is neatly subdivided into three rooms: a bar, a pool and game room, and a music room. Casual patrons can enjoy a pint without having to shout over the din of the music. Next door is **Lil Indie's** (1036 N. Mills Ave., no phone, 7:30pm-2am

daily), a speakeasy sister bar of Will's that only holds a few dozen people in its cozy, parlor-like environment, and features a rotating menu of unique craft cocktails, as well as beer and wine. A few stumbles south on Mills is **Wally's Mills Ave. Liquors** (1001 N. Mills Ave., 407/896-6975, http://wallysonmills.com, 7:30am-2am Mon.-Sat.), part of a dying breed in Florida: the combination package store/bar. On one side is a standard (if tiny) liquor store, while on the other is a cozy, smoky, no-bull bar that opens early enough for shift workers.

Nearby, **BART** (1205 N. Mills Ave., 407/796-2522, http://bartcade.com, 5pm-2am Tues.-Sun.) offers vintage arcade games and a decent selection of beer. Also nearby, **The Guesthouse** (1321 N. Mills Ave., 407/630-6574, 4pm-2am Mon.-Fri., noon-2am Sat.-Sun.) is a great spot for cocktails.

Over on Virginia is **The Matador** (724 Virginia Dr., no phone, 8pm-2am daily), which relocated from downtown for the more relaxed environs of ViMi. Along with the new address is a focus on craft cocktails and a vibe that's in keeping with the bar's boozy bordello decor. Also on Virginia, but more toward the Ivanhoe Village area is **The Hideaway** (516 Virginia Dr., 407/898-5892, www.thehideawaybar.net, 7am-2am Mon.-Sat., 11am-2am Sun.), a smoker-friendly, Miami Dolphin-fan paradise that some people consider a dive, but most folks consider to be Orlando's greatest sports bar. It's definitely home to one of the city's best burgers, and the outdoor patio is a perfect place to watch the game on an autumn afternoon.

More great nightlife options await in Ivanhoe Village, including **The Imperial Wine Bar & Beer Garden** (1800 N. Orange Ave., 407/228-4992, http://imperialwinebar.com, 5pm-midnight Mon.-Thurs., 5pm-2am Fri.-Sat.), a furniture-store-wine-bar.

A little to the northeast of the Mills50/ViMi neighborhood is Audubon Park, which, for years, offered little in the way of nightlife beyond **Stardust Video & Coffee** (1842 E. Winter Park Rd., 407/623-3393, http://stardustvideoandcoffee.wordpress.com,

7am-midnight daily), a cool coffee shop that hosts local artists and musicians, and **Big Daddy's** (3001 Corrine Dr., 407/644-2844, www.bigdaddysorlando.com, 4pm-2am Mon.-Fri., noon-2am Sat.-Sun.), a fun karaoke bar.

The biggest addition has doubtlessly been **Redlight Redlight Beer Parlour** (2810 Corrine Dr., 407/893-9832, http://redlight-redlightbeerparlour.com, 5pm-2am daily). With its late-night hours and large capacity, hop-heads are able to indulge with Redlight's exceedingly well-curated and internationally award-winning selection of microbrews and imports. Cask ales and small-batch craft beers are the specialties, and the bartenders are as helpful as they are knowledgeable.

WINTER PARK

While downtown Winter Park isn't exactly known for its raucous after-hours scene, there are a couple of interesting places. **The Wine Room** (270 Park Ave. S., Winter Park, 407/696-9463, www.thewineroomonline.com, 10am-10pm Mon.-Thurs., 10am-midnight Fri.-Sat., noon-7pm Sun.) utilizes the Enomatic wine-dispensing system, meaning patrons can indulge in over 100 different wines—one ounce at a time. Of course, an extensive selection of full bottles is available, ranging in price from reasonable to ridiculous. A handful of imported beers are also available on tap, and a well-stocked cheese case is staffed by folks knowledgeable about pairings.

The Arts

Nobody will mistake Orlando's art scene for New York City's or even Miami's, but marquee performing arts groups like the Orlando Ballet, Orlando Philharmonic, and a slew of smaller grassroots arts organizations maintain a cultural scene that's growing and vibrant.

THEATER

Located downtown in a beautiful new space, the **Mad Cow Theatre Company** (54 W. Church St., 407/297-8788, www.madcowtheatre.com) can't quite decide if it wants to be an edgy, urban theater or a crowd-pleasing night out for the blue-hair set. Production schedules have featured everything from Harold Pinter and Anton Chekhov to *The Glass Menagerie* and *The Fantasticks*.

Theatre Downtown (2113 N. Orange Ave., 407/841-0083, www.theatredowntown.net) isn't actually downtown but a couple of miles north near Loch Haven Park. The fare

Redlight Redlight Beer Parlour

here is usually just a step or two above community theater in terms of the repertory work performed, but the casts, sets, and direction are almost always top-notch.

Orlando Shakespeare Theater (812 E. Rollins St., 407/447-1700, www.orlandoshakes.org) is situated in beautiful Loch Haven Park. In addition to the expected slate of works by the Bard, which are almost always produced in unexpected ways, "the Shakes" puts on small-scale Broadway musicals and family-friendly fare.

MOVIES

The best place in town to catch a flick is definitely the **Enzian Theater** (1300 S. Orlando Ave., Maitland, 407/629-0054, www.enzian. org). The Enzian serves up art house and international fare on screen and has comfortable chairs and table service from a first-rate, inventive kitchen. Think mean roasted wild-mushroom salads or pizza Margherita instead of popcorn and nachos, and beer and wine instead of watered-down sodas. The Enzian's chalet-like building and its tree-canopied grounds are thoroughly romantic. Enzian's Eden Bar allows film fans to grab a cocktail before the movie starts.

Festivals and Events

The **Florida Film Festival** (FFF, 1300 S. Orlando Ave., Maitland, 407/629-1088, www. floridafilmfestival.com, late Mar./Apr.) happens at the Enzian Theater, and is one of the premier film festivals in the Southeast. The 10-day event not only features a superlative slate of independent and international movies, many of which have their national or regional premieres here, but also high-profile actors and directors as guests. The FFF recently added a food and wine component, bringing celebrity chefs like Anthony Bourdain and many local restaurants to the table for tastings and unique gastronomic tours of the area.

For years, the **Orlando International Fringe Theatre Festival** (Loch Haven Park, 407/648-0077, www.orlandofringe.org, mid-May) stuck to the format utilized by the original Fringe in Edinburgh, Scotland; dozens of empty storefronts and other spaces in downtown Orlando were turned into ad hoc theater venues, where an array of out-of-the-mainstream works could be presented in a playful and slightly competitive environment. Today, the Orlando Fringe retains its dedication to challenging or unusual theater pieces, but the whole affair has been moved to the area in and around Loch Haven Park, mainly utilizing the multiple established theater spaces there. While this circumscribed geography cuts down on the sense of exploration, it has actually made the 12 days of the festival much easier to navigate, allowing both the curious and hardcore theater fans easier access to these interesting works.

It started in 1991 as a form of loosely organized awareness-raising activity with gay and lesbian folks being encouraged to "wear red and be seen" at Walt Disney World on the first Saturday in June. Today, the annual **Gay Days** (Walt Disney World, 407/896-8431, www.gaydays.com, early June) celebrations last more than a week, bringing nearly 150,000 LGBT and LGBT-friendly visitors to the city. Events both official and unofficial have popped up throughout the city, few of which have anything to do with the ritual red-shirt visit to the Magic Kingdom. From a convention-like Expo and organized visits to the other Disney parks to comedy shows and all-night dance parties, Gay Days has become an integral part of Orlando's annual events calendar.

SHOPPING
Orlando

There's little shopping in downtown Orlando proper. **Etoile Boutique** (2424 E. Robinson St., 407/895-6363, www.etoileboutique.net, noon-8pm Mon.-Sat., noon-5pm Sun.), located in the Milk District, about one mile from downtown, is an essential stop for shoppers interested in locally designed clothes and crafts. Hip, modern, and defiantly pro-Orlando, Etoile features everything from unique soaps and candles to handmade bags, clothes, and vintage gear.

A mile or so on the other side of downtown, situated along Lake Ivanhoe, is Orlando's **Antique District**. While there is only about a block of actual antiques stores, the district extends about another block to include unique shops like the vintage vinyl of **Rock & Roll Heaven** (1814 N. Orange Ave., 407/896-1952, www.rock-n-roll-heaven.com, 10am-7:30pm Mon.-Sat., 11am-4pm Sun.). **Tim's Wine Market** (1223 N. Orange Ave., 407/895-9463, www.timswine.com, 10am-7pm Mon.-Fri., 10am-5pm Sat.) is a friendly and knowledgeable spot to pick up a singular bottle of wine.

In the Audubon Park Garden District, check out the stylish and affordable clothing (and make-your-own-jewelry) of **Dear Prudence and the BEAD Lounge** (2912 Corrine Dr., 407/894-8941, www.thebead-lounge.net, 10am-6pm Mon.-Fri., 10am-5pm Sat., 11am-4pm Sun.); fly-fishing gear at **Orlando Outfitters** (2814 Corrine Dr., 407/896-8220, www.orlandooutfitters.com, 10am-6pm Mon.-Fri., 10am-4pm Sun.); or the wide selection of vinyl, CDs, books, and toys at **Park Ave CDs** (2916 Corrine Dr., 407/447-7275, www.parkavecds.com, 10am-10pm Mon.-Thurs., 10am-11pm Fri.-Sat., 11am-8pm Sun.). A recent arrival to the district is **East End Market** (3201 Corrine Dr., 321/236-3316, www.eastendmkt.com, 10am-7pm Tues.-Sat., 11am-6pm Sun.), which is home to local dealers of fine foods ranging from fresh seafood and cold-press juices to coffee, cheese, and more. The quality here is exceptional, and nearly everything is local and/or organic, though it's priced accordingly.

Winter Park

Shopping is the activity of choice along Winter Park's **Park Avenue,** and it's hard to deny the appeal of spending an afternoon browsing the windows along this tree-lined street. Though populated with a few well-known stores like Pottery Barn, Williams Sonoma, and the Gap, the real draws on Park Avenue are the local boutiques like **Tuni's** (301 S. Park Ave., 407/628-1609, 10am-7pm Mon.-Sat., noon-6pm Sun.), which specializes in trendy, exclusive, and expensive women's clothing. It also has a selection of accessories and local jewelry. **Kathmandu** (352 N. Park Ave., 407/647-7071, www.tribalasia.com, 11am-8pm Mon.-Sat., noon-6pm Sun.), on the other hand, specializes in hippy-infused threads and knickknacks.

A few blocks away from Park Avenue in the Hannibal Square area are a handful of clothing and jewelry boutiques. The most unique is **Baraka Home** (123 E. Morse Blvd., 407/260-1400, 11am-6pm Mon.-Sat., noon-6pm Sun.), a gallery and shop focused on contemporary Middle Eastern and Arabic art and furnishings.

Nearby **Winter Park Village** (510 N. Orlando Ave., 407/571-2700, www.shopwin-terparkvillage.net, hours vary by shop) is an open-air shopping mall, with a handful of the usual retail suspects (Pier 1, LOFT, Jos. A. Bank) alongside specialty stores like REI, an excellent movie theater, and an extensive selection of restaurants ranging from P.F. Chang's and the Cheesecake Factory to Ruth's Chris and Mitchell's Fish Market.

Mall at Millenia

With outlets for Tiffany, Coach, Burberry, Chanel, and more, the annoyingly misspelled **Mall at Millenia** (4200 Conroy Rd., 407/363-3555, www.mallatmillenia.com, 10am-9pm Mon.-Sat., noon-7pm Sun.) considers itself "Orlando's destination for luxury brand shopping." And while it certainly is that, it also draws a number of tourists from the nearby theme parks who may just want to get a good deal on some American sneakers at the Vans store or pick up a new iPod at the gleaming Apple Store.

FOOD

Central Orlando and the Winter Park area are blessed with a number of excellent restaurants. These great dining options are outside of Orlando's Restaurant Row (located in the tourist district along Sand Lake Road, near Walt Disney World) and are usually far more adventurous and interesting.

Breakfast

Keke's (345 W. Fairbanks Ave., Winter Park, 407/629-1400, www.kekes.com, 7am-2:30pm daily, from $8) is an upscale diner with an emphasis on fresh and high-end ingredients. It offers decent plates of eggs and bacon and incredible waffles at the upper end of the price range. Service is excellent, and the food is uniformly good-to-great. Expect typically long waits on the weekend. The Winter Park location is convenient to local sights.

Lunch and Light Bites

The main focus at ★ **Pom-Pom's Teahouse & Sandwicheria** (67 N. Bumby Ave., 407/894-0865, http://pompomsteahouse.com, 11am-8pm Mon.-Thurs., 24 hours Fri.-Sat., midnight-6pm Sun., from $7) is sandwiches and tea. More than two dozen varieties of hot and iced teas are available, and the array of pressed sandwiches ranges from tuna melts and Dagwoods to various combinations of meats, cheeses, chutneys, fruits, vegetables, Asian slaw, and more. Breakfast is only served on the weekends, when the restaurant is open for marathon 24-hour sessions catering to the late-night and early morning crowds. Egg-and-cheese sandwiches, potatoes napoleon, crepes, and the standards of grits, bacon, and toast are available then. Owner Pom Moongauklang applies her quirky style to everything on the menu, resulting in a personality-filled restaurant that's a perennial favorite with locals.

Legendary among students at the University of Central Florida for its enormous slices and excellent beer selection, **Lazy Moon Pizza** (1011 E. Colonial Dr., 407/412-6222, 11am-midnight Sun.-Thurs., 11am-2:30am Fri., Sat.., from $5) recently expanded from its collegiate home base, opening a location near downtown in the Mills50 district. Even if the slices here weren't as big as your torso (a full pie measures 30 inches!), Lazy Moon would still be an excellent pizza choice, offering a wide array of fresh ingredients, and crust so perfect you can eat it as dessert (it even provides honey bears for you

to do just that). The beer taps always feature local crafts, and wine and cocktails are also available. There's even an indoor bocce ball pitch you can play on if the restaurant's not too busy.

The sidewalk seating at the too-cute-for-words **Briarpatch** (252 N. Park Ave., Winter Park, 407/628-8651, 7am-6pm Mon.-Sat., 8am-5pm Sun., from $6) along Park Avenue is a perfect setting to enjoy some of its rich cakes and homemade ice cream. The restaurant also serves breakfast and lunch.

American

★ **The Ravenous Pig** (565 W. Fairbanks Ave., Winter Park, 407/628-2333, www.theravenouspig.com, 11:30am-2:30pm and 5:30pm-10pm Tues.-Thurs., 11:30am-2:30pm and 5:30pm-11pm Fri.-Sat., from $14) serves exceptionally inventive and perfectly prepared dishes in an environment that's part pub, part fine-dining establishment. Braised pork belly, lobster tacos, steak tartare, raw-bar offerings, blue-cheese burgers, and truly divine truffle fries are just a few of the selections that have helped cement the Pig's reputation as a culinary destination. The carefully curated wine and beer lists and surprisingly friendly staff, not to mention the monthly pig roasts, have ensured a steady stream of regulars. Call ahead for a reservation.

The early 1990s decor and vibe at **Dexter's** (808 E. Washington St., 407/648-2777, www.dexwine.com, 11am-10pm Mon.-Thurs., 11am-11pm Fri.-Sat., 10am-10pm Sun., from $10) makes it feel like the wine bar from an episode of *Friends*. The menu is anything but stuck in the past, with plenty of inventive Asian-inspired seafood dishes, decadent appetizers like watermelon carpaccio, and steaks and pasta, as well as an extensive wine list.

Latin

An expansion of the Tampa institution **Ceviche** (125 W. Church St., 321/281-8140, www.ceviche.com, 11am-10pm Mon., 11am-2am Tues.-Fri., 5pm-2am Sat., from $14) in downtown Orlando completely eschews the intimate surroundings of the original restaurant for two massive, noisy dining rooms. Still, the bare brick and aged-wood furnishings have a certain romantic charm. The strength of the extensive and authentically Spanish tapas menu isn't diminished at all by the surroundings. There are more than three dozen hot and cold small plates available to choose from.

Near downtown Orlando, **Black Bean Deli** (1835 E. Colonial Dr., 407/203-0922, http://blackbeandeli.yolasite.com, 11am-9pm Mon.-Thurs., 11am-10pm Fri.-Sat., from $7) is one of the best Cuban restaurants in Orlando. The proprietors pride themselves on using fresh and local ingredients as much as possible while keeping prices accessible. The menu is chock-full of Cuban classics. While everything is excellent, the baked-chicken dinner is especially noteworthy.

Asian

If you're not Chinese or Vietnamese, odds are that when you settle into your seat at the semi-fancy **Lam's Garden** (2505 E. Colonial Dr., 407/896-0370, www.lamsgardenorlando.com, 11am-10pm daily, from $9) you'll be handed a green menu that comes with the expected array of *moo goo gai pan*, fried rice, and Americanized dishes. But ask for a red menu and select from a more thoroughly authentic Chinese experience, with dishes like ducks' feet, steamed fish, water spinach, and more. Lam's also has an excellent dim sum service on Sundays and holidays.

Orlando's Little Vietnam is home to a number of extraordinary Vietnamese restaurants. Head to the intersection of Colonial Drive and Mills Avenue, and you're likely to find a good Vietnamese eatery. One of the largest and most popular is **Pho 88** (730 N. Mills Ave., 407/897-3488, www.pho88orlando.com, 10am-10pm daily, from $7), which specializes in the traditional meat-and-noodle soup. It's not the most beautiful space and maybe not even the most authentic Vietnamese restaurant in town, but it's dependably great.

Tucked in among all the Vietnamese restaurants is **Shin Jung** (1638 E. Colonial Dr., 407/895-7345, www.shinjungkorean.com, 11:30am-10pm Mon.-Sat., 1:30pm-10pm Sun., from $15), an excellent eatery that happens to be one of the only Korean restaurants in Orlando. Although the tables are set up so you can barbecue your own meat at your seat in the traditional style, you needn't come prepared to cook. The kitchen dishes up soups and rice and noodle dishes, along with one of the best *dol sot bibimbap* bowls around. The atmosphere in this converted house, besides being thick with grill smoke, is friendly and comfortable, and it's almost always crowded.

A few blocks north of the core Little Vietnam district is the Singaporean street-food delight known as ★ **Hawkers** (1103 N. Mills Ave., 407/237-0606, 11am-10pm Mon.-Thurs., 11am-11pm Fri.-Sat., noon-10pm Sun., from $4). Although its menu is modeled on the fare found in hawker stalls throughout Southeast Asia, the atmosphere here is decidedly less chaotic. The numerous small plates of five-spiced meats and noodles and vegetables ensure that you'll need at least a few visits to fully appreciate everything on offer here.

French and European

The tiny ornate dining room at **Chez Vincent** (533 W. New England Ave., Winter Park, 407/599-2929, www.chezvincent.com, 11:30am-2pm and 6pm-10pm daily, from $15) has been a Winter Park date-night mainstay since it opened more than a decade ago. Its classic French cuisine once earned the restaurant a place on Zagat's "America's Top Restaurants" list. Yet, somehow, Chez Vincent manages not to feel like a stuffy stuck-in-the-past eatery. Maybe it's due to the cozy dining area or the way the kitchen makes standards like duck à l'orange seem interesting. The atmosphere is friendly and relaxed and the food is expertly prepared.

The modern-meets-traditional, east-meets-west atmosphere of **Bosphorous Turkish Cuisine** (108 S. Park Ave., Winter Park, 407/644-8609, http://bosphorousrestaurant.com, 11:30am-10pm Sun.-Thurs.,

11:30am-11pm Fri.-Sat., from $12) reflects many of the clichéd notions that come up whenever discussing Turkey and Turkey's beauty and sophistication. When dinner arrives, it's clear that the crew at Bosphorous is much more concerned with immaculately preparing an array of dishes built around vertically grilled meat (with a typically Turkish emphasis on lamb), fresh seafood, and inventive non-wrap uses of pita bread. A variety of hot and cold appetizers is also available for those who want to taste a range of different Turkish foods.

Antonio's La Fiamma (611 S. Orlando Ave., Maitland, 407/645-1035, http://antoniosonline.com, 11:30am-2:30pm and 5pm-10pm Mon.-Fri., 5pm-10pm Sat., from $18) serves exquisite and extensive Italian dishes that depend heavily on the use of a wood-burning oven. So, while you may have had a veal chop or fontina-stuffed chicken breast before, it's doubtful that you've had them imbued with the rustic flavor that so many of the dishes at Antonio's have. The decadently sauced and seasoned rice and pasta dishes are also homespun and hearty. The elegant atmosphere belies the reasonable prices and friendly service.

Vegan and Vegetarian

★ **Market on South** (2603 E. South St, 407/613-5968, www.marketonsouth.com, 8am-midnight Mon.-Sat., 10am-5pm Sun., from $10) isn't so much a vegan restaurant as it is a mini vegan food hall. Housing three separate businesses—a bakery (Valhalla), a kombucha brewery (Humble Bumble), and a southern-comfort restaurant (Dixie Dharma)—as well as a commissary for local chefs, it's an excellent place to indulge your palate. Whether jackfruit barbeque, biscuits and gravy, rich baked goods, or fresh veggies, the fare on offer here doesn't require any sort of sacrifice to keep with your plant-based diet.

Ethos Vegan Kitchen (601 S. New York Ave., Winter Park, 407/228-3898, www.ethosvegankitchen.com, 11am-11pm Mon.-Fri., 9am-11pm Sat.-Sun., from $8) has a comfort-food vibe, with lots of fresh and steamed vegetables, hearty soups, and mashed potatoes that are really just a starch bowl for the decadent gravy. Entrées like "sheep's pie" and pecan-crusted eggplant are joined on the menu by pasta dishes, sandwiches, and pizza, all of which are 100 percent vegan.

Dandelion Communitea Cafe (618 N Thornton Ave., 407/362-1864, http://dandelioncommunitea.com, 11am-3pm Mon., 11am-10pm Tues.-Sat., noon-6pm Sun., from $8) isn't completely vegan, but it's close. All of its sandwiches, soups, salads, and starters are vegetarian and built fwith fresh fruits, vegetables, and grains. Add to that a selection of all-organic teas and a palpable commitment to the local community and ecological causes, and it would be easy to assume that the vibe in Dandelion might be preachy or didactic. In fact, the opposite is true, and the environment is both welcoming and homey; in fact, it's in a gaily painted repurposed house.

ACCOMMODATIONS
$100-150

The **Courtyard at Lake Lucerne** (211 N. Lucerne Circle E., 407/648-5188, www.orlandohistoricinn.com, from $125 d) is another four-building accommodation set in a residential neighborhood. More traditional bed-and-breakfast-type guest rooms can be found among three beautifully restored early 20th-century buildings. But, it's the 15 stylish one-bedroom suites of the art deco Wellborn Suites building that set the Courtyard apart; though aimed at extended-stay business travelers (with desks, kitchenettes, and Wi-Fi), the rooms are comfortable enough for anyone visiting the area for more than a day or so.

Overlooking Lake Eola and downtown Orlando, the **Eo Inn & Urban Spa** (227 N. Eola Dr., 407/481-8485, www.eoinn.com, from $129 d) is a modern European-style boutique hotel aimed directly at luxury travelers. The rates are surprisingly affordable. The 17 guest rooms are Wi-Fi equipped and decked out with contemporary furnishings and super-soft beds with down comforters. With its relaxing rooftop whirlpool tub and a heavy emphasis on the various spa treatments available on-site, the Eo achieves a level of intimacy that's somewhat incongruous with its close proximity to downtown.

$150-200

The **Thurston House** (851 Lake Ave., Maitland, 407/539-1911, www.thurstonhouse. com, from $190 d) is an 1885 Queen Anne-style farmhouse set on a beautifully landscaped lot. There are only three guest rooms, all of which have free Wi-Fi, flat-screen televisions and DVD players, and private baths. The best is the O'Heir Room, which has a fireplace, a sleigh bed, and an enormous bay window looking out onto Lake Eulalia.

$200-300

The **Alfond Inn** (300 E. New England Ave., 407/998-8090, www.thealfondinn.com, from $239 d) is one of the most recent additions to Central Orlando's lodging scene, and was designed and built by nearby Rollins College to provide a place to stay for visiting prospective students, current students' families, and other college guests. But although Rollins guests may get first priority, this hotel is open to the public. It's just a couple of blocks from Park Avenue. The 112 rooms are in keeping with Winter Park's upscale and stylish vibe, and the atmosphere here is friendly. There's an on-site restaurant, pool, and even an art gallery. Early reservations are essential.

Formerly an extra-luxurious outpost of the Westin chain, the **Grand Bohemian** (325 S. Orange Ave., 407/313-9000, www. grandbohemianhotel.com, from $209 d) is now operated by the Kessler Collection (also the operators of the Casa Monica in St. Augustine). Though it has 250 guest rooms spread over 15 floors, there's a level of privacy and personal service here that's completely unmatched by other local hotels of this size. From the dark-wood furnishings and decadent velvet drapes to the same soft beds that made the Westin famous, much of the luxury of the hotel's former incarnation is intact, albeit with plenty of updates to ensure it stays modern. The bohemian vibe is maintained with a curated gallery, the downstairs Bosendorfer Lounge, which features tasteful live music nightly, and the award-winning Bohème restaurant, which is best known for its Sunday jazz brunch.

Transportation

GETTING THERE

Car

One of the reasons Walt Disney chose Orlando for the site of Walt Disney World was the opening of I-4, which connects Tampa (and I-75) on the west coast to Daytona Beach (and I-95) on the east coast. Orlando is right in the middle of the I-4 corridor, making it easily accessible via interstate.

Orlando is about three hours north of Miami via the Florida Turnpike (for a toll of about $15); opting for I-95 adds another half hour or so. Florida. From Tampa, via I-4, Orlando is about 90 minutes away, while the drive between Orlando and Daytona Beach on I-4 takes about 45 minutes.

Air

There are two public airports that serve the greater Orlando area. **Orlando International Airport** (MCO, One Airport Blvd., Orlando, 407/825-2001, www.orlando-airports.net) is one of the busiest airports in the United States and is served by nearly all major domestic and international carriers.

Disney recently introduced **Disney's Magical Express** at Orlando International, a program that provides complimentary bus transportation from the airport for guests staying at selected Disney resort hotels. It's incredibly convenient door-to-door service (the company even takes care of your luggage), especially if your visit to Orlando is going to be spent solely at Disney parks. Reservations for Disney's Magical Express must be made prior to arrival, typically when the hotel reservation is made.

The **Orlando-Sanford International Airport** (SFB, 1200 Red Cleveland Blvd., Sanford, 407/585-4000, www.orlandosanfordairport.com) in Sanford is used primarily for charter flights, although one low-cost carrier, Allegiant Air, has regularly scheduled year-round service from several small-market U.S. destinations.

Train

Amtrak has six stations in the greater Orlando area. The main **Orlando station** (1400 Sligh Blvd., Orlando, 407/843-7611) is located about a mile south of the core of downtown Orlando. The **Winter Park station** (150 W. Morse Blvd., Winter Park, 407/645-5055) is in the heart of downtown Winter Park, while the **Kissimmee station** (111 E. Dakin Ave., Kissimmee, 407/933-8293) is the closest one to Walt Disney World. All three stations are on the Silver Star and Palmetto routes, which reach to Jacksonville, Tampa, and Miami.

Other regular Amtrak stations servicing the areas covered in this chapter are the **Winter Haven station** (1800 7th St. SW, Winter Haven, 863/294-9203), near Legoland Florida, and the **DeLand station** (2492 Old New York Ave., DeLand, 386/734-2322). The sixth station is the **Sanford Auto Train station** (600 S. Persimmon Ave., Sanford), which is only serviced by the non-stop auto train that connects Washington DC and Florida.

Bus

Greyhound stops at an **Orlando station** (555 N. John Young Pkwy., Orlando, 407/292-3424) and a **Kissimmee station** (103 E. Dakin Ave., Kissimmee, 407/847-3911).

GETTING AROUND

Orlando is very much a car city, and public transportation here is abysmal. Although a local commuter rail, **SunRail,** went live in mid-2014, it's mainly designed to shuttle office workers between the suburbs and downtown, and doesn't operate on the weekend or on holidays. The city's bus system, **Lynx** (www.golynx.com, $2/single ride, $4.50 all-day pass), has extensive routes, but those routes seem to be remarkably indirect. It's designed primarily to get employees to work, not necessarily visitors to the city's sights. However, Lynx does offer a fantastic service in the form of **LYMMO,** which is a free circulator bus that runs throughout the downtown area; just hop on and hop off at the pink, well-marked stops.

There are bike lanes on most major roads, but Orlando is routinely ranked among the most dangerous cities in the United States for cyclists and pedestrians. Parking isn't much of a problem anywhere other than downtown. Although, there are several new parking garages in the downtown area, and fleets of pedicabs are often hovering outside the garages' exits. Taxi cabs are difficult to hail curbside but are just a phone call away; try **Yellow Cab** (407/422-2222). Most major ride-sharing services also operate in Orlando.

Tampa Bay Area

With theme parks, some of the best beaches in the United States, renowned museums, a rich architectural heritage, numerous opportunities for fishing and diving, and a nightlife scene second only to Miami's,

Tampa Bay is something of a microcosm of Florida.

Boasting some of the most consistently enjoyable weather in the state, and blessed by the maritime offerings of the bay itself, the Tampa Bay area is rich in outdoor activities. But this is no wilderness retreat: The area's nearly 3 million residents enjoy the major-league sports, top-shelf cuisine, big-business opportunities, and cultural offerings befitting one of the country's largest metropolitan areas.

Tampa is a bustling, sprawling city as rich in history as it is in urban amenities. From the redolent cigar leaves that have given Ybor City its atmosphere for decades to the neck-craning skyscrapers of downtown and the mansions along Bayshore Boulevard, it's a city that is as in touch with its past as it is with its future. St. Petersburg's downtown area is compact and pedestrian friendly, the proud home of the Salvador Dalí Museum and several turn-of-the-20th-century hotels. Clearwater may be

known to some as the home of Scientology, but the laid-back city has plenty of coastal charm and a steadily revitalizing downtown. The area's beaches are world-class, and the entire region is defined by the water that surrounds it, from the seemingly endless array of fishing options to the sponge-divers of Tarpon Springs and the manatee-filled springs in the Crystal River area.

While visiting the area, it's quickly apparent that visitors are warmly welcomed. Unlike some other parts of the state, however, you never feel as if the entire area was constructed purely for the enjoyment of tourists. Whether or not this means the locals like keeping their treasures a secret, the best way to get the best out of Tampa Bay is to relax and enjoy it like a resident.

PLANNING YOUR TIME

Given that the Tampa Bay area, like most of Florida, is a region that grew up in the age

Previous: Pass-A-Grille Beach; downtown Tampa. **Above:** sponges at Tarpon Springs.

Look for ★ to find recommended sights, activities, dining, and lodging.

Highlights

★ **Busch Gardens:** With high-adrenaline roller coasters and acres of animal habitats, Tampa Bay's marquee attraction manages to be both pastoral and thrilling (page 314).

★ **The Florida Aquarium:** This conceptually driven aquarium is designed to trace the path of a drop of water from underground springs to the ocean (page 316).

★ **Ybor City:** By day, dozens of active cigar-rollers ply their trade in the storefronts of beautiful historic buildings. At night, this is one of Tampa's most vibrant nightlife districts (page 319).

★ **Salvador Dalí Museum:** Home to more than 1,000 of Dalí's original works this museum has more of his massive surrealist masterpieces than any other museum in the world (page 335).

★ **Tarpon Springs:** Greek immigrants were drawn to the region in the late 18th century to work as sponge divers. Today, they'll take you out on a boat to show you how it's done (page 338).

★ **Caladesi Island State Park:** The quiet white-sand beaches on this small barrier island are at or near the top of many Best Beaches lists (page 340).

★ **Crystal River:** Snorkel with manatees that flock to the constant-temperature springs that feed the Crystal River (page 348).

of the automobile, you're likely to be doing a whole lot of driving here regardless of how focused your itinerary is. Thankfully, you'll seldom be much more than a half hour's drive away from the city of Tampa, which makes it the ideal home base. Although traffic on I-4 and I-275 in the city is a nightmare at rush hour, both freeways are generally easy to navigate. Allow yourself at least three days to take in major sights like Busch Gardens and the Florida Aquarium, the museums of St. Petersburg, a night out in Ybor City, and a day at the beaches near Clearwater to recover. A snorkeling excursion with the manatees in Crystal River, the northernmost area covered in this chapter, requires about 185 miles (three hours) of driving roundtrip but is well worth it.

It's worth noting that the theme parks of Orlando are only about an hour away, and many travelers opt to construct a monolith of a vacation that combines Orlando's offerings with Tampa's. While this may seem like an ideal way to maximize your time, it's inadvisable for two reasons. Tampa Bay isn't a very attraction-based area. It is much better enjoyed at a leisurely pace that allows you to soak in the culture and outdoor activities. The interstate between Tampa and Walt Disney World is a stretch of road that manages to make a 60-mile drive seem like 600, with bad traffic at either end, and a boring stretch in the middle.

One Day in the Tampa Bay Area

the Salvador Dalí Museum in St. Petersburg

The **Hampton Inn Ybor City** makes a good home base, as Ybor City is one of the neighborhoods that is most convenient to the interstate.

MORNING

If you're traveling with kids, you'll want to allocate at least half of your day to the rides and animal attractions at **Busch Gardens,** and then head back toward downtown for a few hours at the **Florida Aquarium.**

For those without kids, spend the morning on **St. Pete Beach** and hit the **Salvador Dalí Museum** afterward. On the way back to Ybor City, you can explore the shops and restaurants of **Hyde Park,** being sure to grab some modern diner fare for lunch from **Daily Eats.**

EVENING

In the evening, grab dinner and a movie in Ybor City. If you've still got energy, dig into the decadent late-night culture of Ybor City at dance clubs like **Prana,** live-music venues like **Crowbar** and you'll only have to walk a few blocks back to the hotel at night.

Tampa

Tampa has grown and changed considerably since Henry Plant opened the Tampa Bay Hotel in 1891. Despite the skyscrapers, Tampa has a much stronger sense of its past than any of Florida's other big cities. This history is found in both well-preserved pockets (Ybor City) and less so (some of the dilapidated warehouses and neighborhoods just outside of downtown) and is quite prevalent. While it suffers from its share of sprawl and freeway congestion, Tampa's vitality, fueled by its natural surroundings and by a vibrant and diverse community, is inescapable.

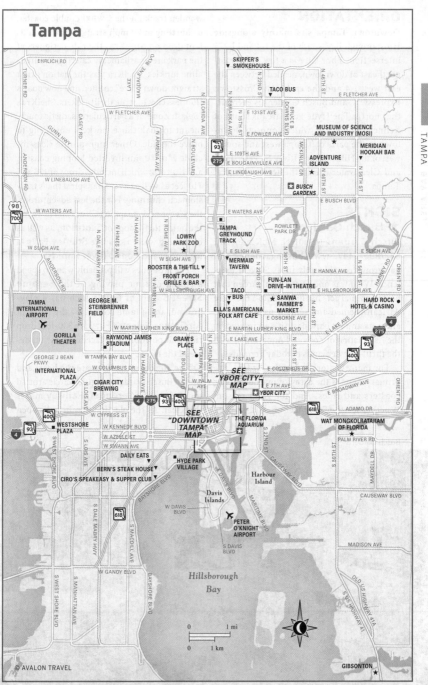

Tampa

EHRLICH RD

TURNER RD

W FLETCHER AVE

E FLETCHER AVE

SKIPPER'S ▾ SMOKEHOUSE

TACO BUS ▾

E 131ST AVE

E FOWLER AVE

MUSEUM OF SCIENCE AND INDUSTRY (MOSI) ★

MERIDIAN HOOKAH BAR ★

E 109TH AVE

E BOUGAINVILLEA AVE

ADVENTURE ISLAND ★

E LINEBAUGH AVE

W LINEBAUGH AVE

★ BUSCH GARDENS

E BUSCH BLVD

W WATERS AVE

E WATERS AVE

ROWLETT PARK DR

W SLIGH AVE

TAMPA GREYHOUND TRACK ▪

E SLIGH AVE

LOWRY PARK ZOO ★

MERMAID TAVERN ▾

W SLIGH AVE

E HANNA AVE

ROOSTER & THE TILL ▾

FUN-LAN DRIVE-IN THEATRE ★

FRONT PORCH GRILLE & BAR ▾

W HILLSBOROUGH AVE

E HILLSBOROUGH AVE

HARD ROCK HOTEL & CASINO ●

TACO BUS ▾

SANWA FARMER'S MARKET ★

TAMPA INTERNATIONAL AIRPORT ✈

GEORGE M. STEINBRENNER FIELD ▪

ELLA'S AMERICANA FOLK ART CAFE ▾

E OSBORNE AVE

W MARTIN LUTHER KING BLVD

E MARTIN LUTHER KING BLVD

GORILLA THEATER ★

RAYMOND JAMES STADIUM ▪

GRAM'S PLACE ●

E LAKE AVE

GEORGE J BEAN PKWY

W TAMPA BAY BLVD

E 21ST AVE

INTERNATIONAL PLAZA ▪

W COLUMBUS DR

E COLUMBUS DR

CIGAR CITY BREWING ▾

SEE "YBOR CITY" MAP

★ YBOR CITY

E 7TH AVE

W CYPRESS ST

SEE "DOWNTOWN TAMPA" MAP

E BROADWAY AVE

ADAMO DR

WESTSHORE PLAZA ●

W KENNEDY BLVD

THE FLORIDA AQUARIUM ▪

WAT MONGKOLRATARAM OF FLORIDA ★

W AZEELE ST

W SWANN AVE

PALM RIVER RD

DAILY EATS ▾

HYDE PARK VILLAGE ▪

BERN'S STEAK HOUSE ▾

Harbour Island

CIRO'S SPEAKEASY & SUPPER CLUB ▾

W DAVIS BLVD

Davis Islands

CAUSEWAY BLVD

PETER O'KNIGHT AIRPORT ✈

MADISON AVE

S DAVIS BLVD

Hillsborough Bay

0   1 mi

0   1 km

GIBSONTON ★

© AVALON TRAVEL

ORIENTATION

Downtown Tampa sits mainly alongside Hillsborough Bay, south of the I-4 and I-275 intersection. Ybor City is a few miles east-northeast of downtown, nestled between the east-west I-4 and the east-west Crosstown Expressway, and Busch Gardens is even farther north. The Hyde Park area is south of Kennedy Boulevard, which connects downtown to the parts of Tampa west and southwest of the Hillsborough River. St. Petersburg and Clearwater are to the west of central Tampa.

SIGHTS

★ Busch Gardens

Busch Gardens (10001 N. McKinley Dr., 888/800-5447, www.buschgardens.com) has grown considerably in its 50-year existence. What was once just a beer garden that hosted animal acts has grown into a 605-acre African-themed amusement park that balances its animal park past (it's accredited by the Association of Zoos and Aquariums) with the thrill-ride demands of today's crowds.

For many visitors to Busch Gardens, the primary draw is the array of marquee roller coasters and rides. And for good reason: Whether it's the 7,000 feet of skull-rattling

wooden track on the **Gwazi** double coaster, or hurtling at 70 mph straight down a 200-foot drop on **SheiKra,** the ride designers at the park are unashamedly catering to adrenaline junkies. SheiKra was the nation's first straight-down "dive" coaster, and now boasts floorless cars for true thrill seekers. SheiKra's "Splash Zone" is a particularly sadistic touch, meant to soak those gawkers unwilling to brave the ride. Other high-profile rides include **Montu,** an inverted looping coaster, and **Kumba,** which includes drops of 135 and 110 feet as well as a circular spiral that's truly stomach churning. For the less adventurous, there's the neck-snapping **Cheetah Hunt** and the quick-thrill loops of **Scorpion,** as well as drenching water rides like **Stanley Falls** (a log flume) and **Congo River Rapids.**

The little ones will probably want to spend a chunk of time playing in the **Sesame Street Safari of Fun,** which has a playground, and a tame coaster by the name of **Air Grover. Falcon's Fury** is a 300-foot drop ride that positions you facedown as you descend the tower.

The animal attractions are the heart and soul of Busch Gardens. A quick circle around the park on the **Serengeti Railway** makes this clear. As the old-timey train pulls open

Busch Gardens

cars around the park's **Serengeti Plain,** riders can gawk at zebras, giraffes, ostriches, antelopes, and many other animals. There's also a safari-like adventure ride, **Rhino Rally.** Ignore the canned and corny quips from the safari driver at your own risk, since the animal observations quickly turn into a string of navigational errors that result in some unexpected thrills. For a slower pace, take a walk through the numerous habitats. **Myombe Reserve** features gorillas and chimpanzees, and **Edge of Africa** has lions, hippos, and meerkats. Smaller animals can be found at **Lory Landing** (a bird enclosure).

The habitats in **Jungala** are more intimate. A Plexiglas tube allows visitors to get very close to the Bengal and white tigers on display in the Tiger Trail, while the residents of **Orangutan Outpost** are seemingly nonplussed by all the folks watching them go about their daily business. Jungala also features a large kids' play area and the **Jungle Flyers,** which let guests "hang-glide" along a zip line above the area.

Like most theme parks, the dining options at Busch Gardens are unremarkable, with one exception: the **Crown Colony Restaurant** ($12-18). While the food is of the institutional American sort with fried chicken, steak, and seafood, the wide-open views of the Serengeti Plain area from the dining room definitely improve the meal. There is also a **Serengeti Dining Safari** ($60 adults, $45 children) available for anyone over the age of 5. This option combines a meal at the Crown Colony with a 30-minute safari ride through the Plain in an open-air truck that seats only 20 people.

The park is open daily, but hours vary seasonally and by the day of the week. Summer hours are typically 9am-9pm Monday-Friday, 9am-10pm Saturday-Sunday. Winter hours are both more limited and variable; opening times fluctuate between 9am, 9:30am, and 10am, and the park closes at different times between 5pm and 8pm. Check the park's website for up-to-date opening hours.

Admission rates are also flexible, with a variety of discounts available for seniors, children, Florida residents, and frequent visitors. The walk-up rate for an adult ticket is $105 for all guests 3 and up, but there are considerable savings if you buy in advance on the Busch Gardens website. Keep in mind that your first-day ticket can also be used for a second visit within seven days. Tickets to Busch Gardens can also be upgraded to include visits to Adventure Island as well as Orlando theme parks like. Some of these combos even include shuttle service between Busch Gardens and Orlando, so there are plenty of ways to maximize your ticket money. Parking is $19. Preferred parking is available for an additional fee, but don't bother: Although your vehicle is closer to the entrance, you miss out on the convenience of a tram that drops you right at the front gate and end up actually walking farther.

Near Busch Gardens

Adventure Island (10001 Malcolm McKinley Dr., 888/800-5447, www.adventureisland.com) is a 30-acre water park located right next door to its sister park, Busch Gardens. It features 10 different slides, tubes, and flumes, as well as a 17,000-square-foot wave pool, a lazy river, and two kids' areas. The rides are standard water-park fare, but the 210-foot slide called **Gulf Scream** is a definite scream. For the little ones, **Splash Attack** is highly recommended, as it combines the fun of a tree house, a maze, and waterslides with the cackling glee that can only come from watching a 1,000-gallon bucket of water pour down on people walking below. Cabanas are available for rental, and visitors can also bring coolers (as long as they're not too big and don't contain glass or alcohol).

As with Busch Gardens, admission rates and opening hours are somewhat variable. The park is closed from mid-October-mid-March. During the peak summer season, hours are typically 9am-7pm Monday-Friday and 9am-8pm Saturday-Sunday. In the spring and early fall, hours are typically 10am-5pm Monday-Friday and 9:30am-6pm Saturday-Sunday. Check the park's website for up-to-date opening hours. Walk-up rates are $55 for guests 3 and older. These prices can be lowered significantly by purchasing a Busch Gardens ticket at the same time or by purchasing online. Florida residents can by a Fun Card that gets them into both parks for the rest of the calendar year for a deeply discounted price.

For an exceptional—and educational—indoor experience, the **Museum of Science and Industry** (MOSI, 4801 E. Fowler Ave., 813/987-6100, www.mosi.org, 9am-5pm Mon.-Fri., 9am-6pm Sat.-Sun., $26.95 adults, $25.95 seniors, $20.95 children) can't be beat. On the nearby campus of the University of South Florida, MOSI offers an array of hands-on science exhibits, including a harrowing high-wire bicycle ride that lets visitors propel a bike across a narrow cable more than 30 feet above the museum's floor. In between rapid heartbeats, you're supposed to learn something about physics. Exhibits on biology, chemistry, and even disasters are smartly curated and entertaining without being patronizing. Speaking of disasters, seek out the Gulf Coast Hurricane exhibit, which is actually hidden away in the courtyard outside of MOSI's main entrance. Guests sit inside an enclosed room, don eye and ear protection, and are then subjected to winds reaching and exceeding hurricane strength. Also outside the main museum is an enclosed free-flying butterfly garden. IMAX movies, both of the educational and the blockbuster sort, are also shown at MOSI daily.

If you couldn't get enough of the animals at Busch Gardens or if roller coasters just aren't your thing then the highly rated **Lowry Park Zoo** (1101 W. Sligh Ave., 813/935-8552, www.lowryparkzoo.com, 9:30am-5pm daily, $32.95 adults, $24.95 children, children 2 and under free) is a definite stop. The 56-acre public facility houses over 2,000 animals, from leopards, tigers, and elephants to warthogs, tapirs, and kookaburras. There is also an exceptional manatee exhibit.

★ The Florida Aquarium

More than any other locale that sought to revitalize an urban core with an aquarium, Tampa is particularly well suited to be the host of **The Florida Aquarium** (701 Channelside Dr., 813/273-4000, www.flaquarium.com, 9:30am-5pm daily, closed Thanksgiving and Christmas Days, $24.95 adults, $22.95 seniors, $18.95 children under 12, children 2 and under free). With water not only defining much of the Tampa Bay

The Florida Aquarium in downtown Tampa

Downtown Tampa

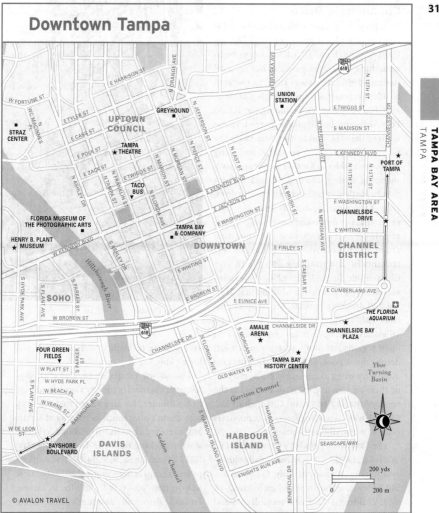

© AVALON TRAVEL

area but also most of the state of Florida, the designers of the 200,000-square-foot facility were free to create an environment that not only gives visitors the opportunity to gawk at marine life but also to learn quite a bit about the ecology of the state. The aquarium is designed in a way that traces the voyage of a drop of water from Florida's freshwater springs through its brackish coastal estuaries and out into the ocean.

Of course, the Florida theme doesn't explain the presence of penguins, but, boy, are they adorable. Sharks and a giant 300-pound grouper get a lot of attention. There are also alligators, sea turtles, river otters, eels, octopuses, and crustaceans galore. The aquarium also offers a unique dolphin-watching excursion as an add-on to museum admission (for a total of $49.90 adults, $44.90 seniors, $40.90 children under 12, children under 2 free); the excursion takes you into Tampa Bay on a 49-passenger boat.

Channelside Drive

Watching the cargo boats and cruise ships coming in and out of the **Port of Tampa** (1101 Channelside Dr.) had always been something of an area pastime. But up until the mid-1980s there was little in the area besides warehouses and shipping companies. Property owners, including the Tampa Port Authority, began promoting redevelopment of the area, and by the early 1990s the Channel District was created, combining attractions like the Florida Aquarium with shopping, dining, and nightlife geared both toward locals and cruisers on day excursions. It's not the most organically attractive part of Tampa, but one could easily wrap up the remainder of a day spent at the Aquarium at any of the tourist-friendly bars or restaurants in **Channelside Bay Plaza** (615 Channelside Dr., 813/223-4250, www.channelsidebayplaza.com). In addition to its dining and drinking options, the complex also has a **Splitsville** (813/514-2695, www.splitsvillelanes.com, open from 4pm Thurs.-Fri., open at noonSat.-Sun.), where you can eat, drink, shoot pool, and bowl. The area gets quite busy when a cruise ship pulls into port or there's a sporting event or concert at the nearby **Amalie Arena** (401 Channelside Dr., 813/301-6500, www.amaliearena.com), but is otherwise usually fairly quiet.

The **Tampa Bay History Center** (801 Old Water St, 813/228-0097, www.tampabayhistorycenter.org, 10am-5pm daily, $12.95 adults, $10.95 seniors, students, and children 13-17, $7.95 children 4-12, free for children 3 and under) spans more than 60,000 square feet, with more than 25,000 square feet of exhibits. The building itself is impressive. It is Tampa's first public building to receive Silver certification by Leadership in Energy and Environmental Design (LEED). The exhibits are both well-organized and impressively curated. Considerable attention is given to the area's earliest native residents, but also to the role that migrant culture has played in this port city. Interactive displays and tons of artifacts and memorabilia make the center just

the Tampa Theatre

as appealing to history buffs as hands-on-loving kids.

Downtown Tampa is crowded with skyscrapers, a symbol of the city's work hard-play hard attitude. This also means that the city's core doesn't offer much in the way of sights. Still, there are a handful of locations definitely worth checking out. The **Tampa Theatre** (711 N. Franklin St., 813/274-8981, www.tampatheatre.org) is in its original 1920s home. It was the first "air-cooled" building in Tampa. From the three-story marquee and the ornate lobby area to the luxurious main room, its historic charm is a striking contrast to the glass-and-steel construction that surrounds it. It's now a film and special events center, hosting screenings of art-house and classic movies and occasional concerts. It also hosts $5 balcony-to-backstage tours twice a month, giving insight to the theater's architecture and history.

Across the river is the University of Tampa, built around the former site of Henry Plant's Tampa Bay Hotel. Much of the original building is still here, restored by the university for its own purposes and home to the **Henry B. Plant Museum** (401 W. Kennedy Blvd., 813/254-1891, www.plantmuseum.com, Tues.-Sat. 10am-4pm, Sun. noon-4pm, $10 adults, $7 seniors, $5 children age 4-12). You'll see the towering steel-plated minarets as you're crossing the Kennedy Boulevard bridge and will likely be as awestruck as you are giggly. The audacious architecture behind Plant's hotel is just the beginning: Many of the antiques, artworks, and artifacts with which he stocked the original hotel are still here. While wandering through the Grand Hall or the Garden Room may not send you back in time, it's quite a lark nonetheless. For a free guided tour, show up in the main lobby by 1pm weekdays.

From the Plant Museum, it's only a few blocks south to **Bayshore Boulevard.** Hugging the side of Hillsborough Bay, this stretch of road is one of the most elegant in Florida, dotted with multimillion-dollar homes that maintain much of the architectural history of Tampa. There are no McMansions here. Running between Columbus Statue Park to the north and Gandy Boulevard to the south is also the world's longest continuous sidewalk, a 4.5-mile-long 10-foot-wide stretch of columned cement that's routinely filled with dog walkers, joggers, and bikers. This is one of the most scenic and beautiful spots in all of Tampa Bay.

About halfway down Bayshore, hang a right on South Howard Avenue. This will take you into the **SoHo** (named for South Howard Avenue) neighborhood of Tampa's Hyde Park area. The surrounding area is primarily residential, and the bungalow residences in this neighborhood, although not as palatial as those on Bayshore, are still character-rich. The strip of Howard Avenue that runs between Bayshore and Kennedy Boulevard to the north is filled with dozens of unique stylish shops and has cemented its reputation as Tampa's premier dining district.

★ Ybor City
Walking down 7th Avenue in Ybor City, the air has a note of the rich aroma of tobacco

leaves. The scent may come from the numerous cigar bars, like **King Corona Cigars and More** (1523 E. 7th Ave., 813/241-9109, www.kingcoronacigars.com, 8am-midnight Mon.-Wed., 8am-1am Thurs., 8am-2am Fri., 10am-2am Sat., noon-midnight Sun.), or the still-operating cigar factories, like the **Gonzalez y Martinez Cigar Store and Factory** (adjacent to the Columbia Restaurant at the intersection of 7th Ave. and 21st St., 813/248-8210, www.columbiarestaurant.com, 10am-5pm Mon.-Fri.), where you can stop in to watch the cigar rollers at work. More likely, it's still lingering in the bricks more than 125 years after Vicente Martinez Ybor moved his cigar business here from Key West.

Although Ybor City saw its heyday in the early part of the 20th century, the revitalization that has taken place in the area since the mid-1980s has kept much of the district's architectural flavor intact. It's known mainly for the numerous nightclubs and bars that keep the streets buzzing until the wee hours. But, you still get a rich sense of history just from walking around here during the day. Although many of the cigar factories and social clubs that defined the area in its prime are long gone, the buildings they inhabited mostly remain. The Centro Español social club, originally a gathering place for locals of Spanish descent, is now the **Centro Ybor** (1600 8th Ave., no phone, www.centroybor.com, hours vary by shop) shopping and entertainment complex. Some icons, however, remain intact still: The mosaic-tiled **Columbia Restaurant** (2117 E. 7th Ave., 813/248-4961, www.columbiarestaurant.com, 11am-10pm Mon.-Thurs., 11am-11pm Fri.-Sat., noon-9pm Sun.) has been serving up fine Spanish food since 1905 (its 1905 Salad is a local legend), but it's also home to a museum. The **Centennial Museum** (2117 E. 7th Ave., 813/248-4961, www.columbiarestaurant.com, 10am-5pm Mon.-Sat., noon-6pm Sun., free) is filled with small, artifact-heavy exhibits about the history of Ybor City.

For a less crowded look at Ybor City's

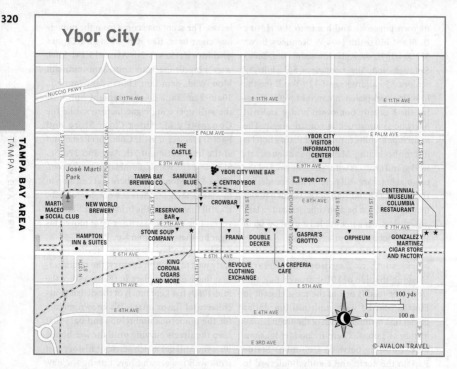

Ybor City

NUCCIO PKWY
E 11TH AVE
E 11TH AVE
E 11TH AVE
E PALM AVE
YBOR CITY VISITOR INFORMATION CENTER
E PALM AVE
THE CASTLE
E 9TH AVE
E 9TH AVE
José Martí Park
YBOR CITY WINE BAR
TAMPA BAY BREWING CO
SAMURAI BLUE
CENTRO YBOR
YBOR CITY
CENTENNIAL MUSEUM/ COLUMBIA RESTAURANT
MARTI-MACEO SOCIAL CLUB
NEW WORLD BREWERY
RESERVOIR BAR
CROWBAR
E 8TH AVE
E 7TH AVE
STONE SOUP COMPANY
PRANA
DOUBLE DECKER
GASPAR'S GROTTO
ORPHEUM
GONZALEZ Y MARTINEZ CIGAR STORE AND FACTORY
HAMPTON INN & SUITES
E 6TH AVE
KING CORONA CIGARS AND MORE
REVOLVE CLOTHING EXCHANGE
E 6TH AVE
LA CREPERIA CAFE
E 5TH AVE
E 5TH AVE
E 4TH AVE
E 4TH AVE
E 3RD AVE
0   100 yds
0   100 m
© AVALON TRAVEL

history, head to the opposite end. **José Martí Park** (North 13th St. at 8th Ave., 9am-sunset daily) is a tiny memorial containing a life-size statue of the hero of Cuba's independence movement. The park sits on the site where Martí lived while in Ybor City as he worked to mobilize workers in the local cigar factories (including the nearby Ybor Cigar Factory, which, grotesquely enough, now houses a Spaghetti Factory) to support the revolution. Interestingly, the park is actually considered Cuban territory; the country bought the site in 1957.

Also at the western edge of Ybor City is the **GaYbor District** (near 14th St. and 7th Ave., http://gaybor.com). Throughout the revitalization of Ybor City, this particular patch of land was routinely overlooked as bars and clubs fought for business just two blocks to the east. Soon enough, gay- and lesbian-oriented pubs and restaurants began sprouting up in the area, and in 2007 the GaYbor District Coalition was formed to promote the area as

not only gay friendly but also as a prime factor in Ybor's economic growth.

SPORTS AND RECREATION
Spectator Sports

There is a seemingly endless array of professional and collegiate sports happening in Tampa. Although the local Major League Baseball team, the **Tampa Bay Rays,** plays across the bay in St. Petersburg, stickball fans can get their fix watching **New York Yankees spring training** (www.legends-fieldtampa.com, from $17) in February and March at **George M. Steinbrenner Field** (1 Steinbrenner Dr., 813/879-2244, www.steinbrennerfield.com).

The National Football League's **Tampa Bay Buccaneers** (www.buccaneers.com, from $30) play in **Raymond James Stadium** (4201 N. Dale Mabry Hwy., 813/350-6500, http://raymondjamesstadium.com) in August-January underneath the shadow of a giant replica pirate ship. The stadium also hosts the annual New Years Day **Outback Bowl** (www.outbackbowl.com), which pits football teams from the Southeastern Conference and Big Ten Conference against each other. In August-November, the **University of South Florida Bulls** (www.gosfbulls.com) play their American Athletic Conference games in the stadium as well. The stadium has hosted two Super Bowls, in 2001 and 2009.

Ice hockey fans can catch 2004 Stanley Cup winners **Tampa Bay Lightning** (http://lightning.nhl.com, from $20) October-May at the **Amalie Arena** (401 Channelside Dr., 813/301-6500, www.amaliearena.com). The **Tampa Bay Storm** (www.tampabaystorm.com, Jan.-May), the area's Arena Football League team, plays at the Amalie as well. In January-March, **Krewe Rugby** (http://krewerugby.com, free) plays public home games at **Skyview Park** (6203 S. Martindale Ave., 813/832-1243) in southwest Tampa.

Water Sports

Not actually much of a beach, **Ben T. Davis Beach** is the sandiest waterside spot in the city. The small park offers picnic tables, grills, volleyball nets, a tiny little area to wade into the bay, and a few hundred feet of sand to lounge on. Nonetheless, this spot at the foot of the Courtney Campbell Parkway, which connects Tampa and Clearwater, is usually quite vacant on weekdays, save for a few anglers, making it an ideal spot for sunset-watching or just decompressing.

For more active engagements with the water, **Channelside Watersports Rentals** (700 S. Florida Ave., 813/226-2628, 9am-7pm daily) at the Marriott Waterside Marina downtown has boats, personal watercraft, and kayaks available for hourly, half-day, or full-day rental.

There's not much to 596-acre **Upper Tampa Bay Park** (8100 Double Branch Rd., 813/855-1765, 8am-6pm daily), and that's sort of the point. Given the fragile nature of this park's ecology, development of the area has been minimal at most. Facilities are limited to bathrooms, a few picnic areas, and an area to play sand volleyball. Come for the excellent opportunities to explore undisturbed wetlands, hardwood hammocks, and estuarine marshes. Fishing, kayaking, and canoeing are the primary activities here, along with hiking the several trails and boardwalks that allow for great wildlife viewing, ranging from birds and butterflies to tortoises and probably an alligator or two. The journey out here

Centro Ybor has restaurants, bars, and a movie theater.

The Elephants of Gibsonton

There are very few towns in the United States with zoning ordinances that allow for elephants to be kept in the front yard, but **Gibsonton** (a few miles south of Tampa on US-41) is one of them. In the heyday of traveling circuses, lots of carnival workers chose to winter in the town, and along with elephant trainers and trapeze artists were a number of "circus freaks." From the 8.5-foot-tall man known as "The Giant" (who was the town's police chief in the 1950s) and his 2-foot-tall wife, "The Half Girl," to the infamous "Lobster Boy," whose 1992 murder cast an unwelcome national spotlight on the town, Gibsonton was for years one of the oddest burgs in a state filled with oddities. Today, few remnants of Gibsonton's carnival history remain beyond the "dwarf counter" at the post office, a rusting circus trailer, and, yes, an elephant in someone's front yard.

takes more than 45 minutes from the heart of Tampa.

Golf
TPC Tampa Bay (5300 W. Lutz Lake Fern Rd., Lutz, 813/949-0090, www.tpctampabay.com, first start time 7am, $62-99) is located outside of town but is worth the drive for duffers who want to take a swing at this par-71 Bobby Weed-designed PGA Tour Club course. **Westchase Golf Club** (11602 Westchase Golf Dr., 813/854-2331, www.westchasegc.com, first start time 7am, $29-59) is in north Tampa and offers a 6,710-yard par-72 course designed by Lloyd Clifton. Both of these public facilities offer online tee-time reservations.

ENTERTAINMENT AND EVENTS
Nightlife
The center of gravity in Tampa's nightlife scene is Ybor City, and on weekend nights—heck, on any night—it has the decadent historical feel of a Bourbon Street bacchanalia. In other words, people don't really go out for drinks in Ybor; they come out to party. Some of the velvet-rope nightclubs like **Prana** (1619 E. 7th Ave., 813/241-4139, www.clubprana.com, 9pm-3am Wed.-Sat.) do their best to put a classy facade on things. But the idea behind a night in Ybor is to try to sample as many venues and cocktails as possible. Granted, this isn't as appealing to some people as it is to others, and, thankfully, that's not all that Ybor City has to offer.

In the thick of Ybor's club zone, locations like the Pabst Blue Ribbon- and Jäger-serving **Reservoir Bar** (1518 E. 7th Ave., 813/248-1442, www.resbar.com) and the heavy frozen mugs at **Gaspar's Grotto** (1805 E. 7th Ave., 813/248-5900, http://gasparsgrotto.com) all have unique personalities. Fans of live music can catch local and national underground bands at **Crowbar** (1812 N. 17th St., 813/241-8600, www.crowbarlive.com) and the **Orpheum** (1902 Ave. Republica De Cuba, 813/248-9500, www.statemedia.com).

If your dancing shoes tend to be of the spiked-heel-patent-leather type, the goth haven known as **The Castle** (2004 N. 16th St., 813/247-7547, www.castleybor.com) will be an essential stop.

More low-key drinking establishments like **Double Decker** (1721 E. 7th Ave., 813/248-2099, www.doubledeckertampa.com) and **Ybor City Wine Bar** (1600 E. 8th Ave., 813/999-4966, www.yborcitywinebar.com) emphasize quality over quantity, so you'll get higher-quality drinks here.

The tourist-friendly **Centro Ybor** (1600 8th Ave., www.centroybor.com) offers a multiplex movie theater, an arcade, and the **Tampa Bay Brewing Company** (1600 E. 8th Ave., 813/247-1422, www.tampabaybrewingcompany.com), a well-regarded brewpub. Beer fans will also want to check out the brewery and tap room for **Coppertail Brewing** (2601 E. 2nd Ave, 813/247-1500, wwwcoppertail-brewing.com), located just a few blocks outside of the main Ybor district. And, it should

Cigar City Brewing

be mentioned that a trip through Ybor City would be incomplete without a cigar and a stiff drink at one of the many cigar bars along 7th Avenue.

But not every night owl needs to endure the crowds of clubbers who flock to Ybor. The **Hard Rock Hotel & Casino** (5223 Orient Rd., 813/627-7625, www.seminole-hardrocktampa.com, 24 hours daily) looms high over I-4, beckoning travelers with the promise of riches gained via nickel slots. A very busy nonsmoking poker room (show up early, and prepare to wait on weekends and holidays) is tucked in the back. The majority of the vast floor space (which is definitely *not* nonsmoking) is given over to a seemingly endless array of slot machines, with some table games. Gaming isn't the only option at this casino; there is, quite obviously, a **Hard Rock Cafe** here that combines dining, gaming, and dancing and live music. On weekends, it's open until 5am, and it is the only nightclub in the area open after 3am. The 3am-5am time frame can get a bit crowded.

There's also a surprisingly decent selection of food here, ranging from food-court-style noshes to fine dining and Vietnamese fare.

Other gambling options include **Tampa Bay Downs** (11225 Race Track Rd., 813/855-4401, www.tampabaydowns.com, 11am-11pm daily), the only thoroughbred track on Florida's west coast, and **Tampa Greyhound Track** (8300 N. Nebraska Ave., 813/932-4313, www.tampadogs.com, 10am-2am daily), which no longer has live greyhound races. However, both facilities offer poker rooms and pari-mutuel betting on simulcast dog and horse races, as well as jai-alai.

In the dining district of SoHo and Hyde Park, the majority of the nightlife options centers around the area's restaurants, many of which double as late-night watering holes. **Ciro's Speakeasy and Supper Club** (2109 Bayshore Blvd, 813/251-0022, www.ciro-stampa.com, 5pm-1am Sun.-Thurs., 5pm-3am Fri., Sat.) is a prime example, serving up sharing-style plates of chicken and waffles, scallops, deviled eggs, and more alongside a robust menu of craft cocktails. **Four Green Fields** (205 W. Platt St., 813/254-4444, www.fourgreenfields.com, 11am-2am Mon., 11am-2am Tues.-Sat., 11am-midnight Sun.) is an Irish pub through and through, from its atypical selection of Irish cuisine and authentic beer selections to the live Irish folk that can be heard in the pastoral environs. At the opposite end of the spectrum is the **Hyde Park Cafe** (1806 W. Platt St., 813/254-2233, www.hydeparkcafe.com, 9pm-3am Tues.-Sat.), a high-energy dance club focused on the Red Bull-and-vodka set. Similarly, **The Kennedy** (2408 W. Kennedy Blvd., 813/259-9669, www.thekennedysoho.com, 10pm-3am Mon. and Fri.-Sat.) is a super-popular dance club that books big-name DJs.

Beer aficionados should assign a designated driver, because the two best beer bars in Tampa aren't really walking distance to anything. The tasting room at **Cigar City Brewing** (3924 W. Spruce St., 813/348-6363, http://cigarcitybrewing.com, 11am-11pm Sun.-Thurs., 11am-1am Fri.-Sat.), in a semi-industrial zone between the airport and Raymond James Stadium, is as much a gift shop as it is a bar. Given the seriousness of the Cigar City brewmasters and the high quality of their beer (not to mention the one-off specialty brews that you can only get in the tasting room), Cigar City Brewing is very much a haven for beer-lovers. (Note: If you can't fit a visit to the brewery into your itinerary, fear not; it has an outpost at the Tampa airport.) Over in the residential Seminole Heights area, the folks at **Mermaid Tavern** (6719 N. Nebraska Ave., 813/238-6618, 5pm-3am daily) don't brew their own beer, but they stock an amazing selection (along with a really good wine/champagne list and a classy bar-food menu to boot). Here, you can imbibe in a fun and casually stylish environment that's friendly and hip.

Near the University of South Florida, there's **Skipper's Smokehouse** (910 Skipper Rd., 813/971-0666, www.skipperssmokehouse. com, Tues.-Fri. 11am-11pm, Sat. 11am-midnight, Sun. 1pm-11pm), serving up smoked fish, cold beer, and live music. Despite Skipper's reputation as a blues club, the music tends toward the twin collegiate tastes of reggae and the Grateful Dead. Also drawing clientele from USF is **Meridian Hookah Bar** (11401 N. 56th St. Suite 20, Temple Terrace, 813/569-7701, www.meridianhookah.com, 9pm-3am daily, $12 cover). Meridian serves up water pipes filled with aromatic tobaccos, but no alcohol. The $12 cover charge gets you unlimited hookahs for the entire night.

If a movie's more your thing, a trip to the **Fun-Lan Drive-In** (2302 Hillsborough Ave., 813/234-2311, www.fun-lan.com, call for showtimes, $6 adults, $2 children 4-9) should be on your after-dark itinerary. First-run movies play on four screens as you tune into your FM radio for the soundtrack. An old-school snack bar keeps patrons greasily fed.

The Arts

Built downtown in 1987, the **Straz Center** (1010 N. W. C. MacInnes Pl., 813/222-1000, www.tbpac.org) is a 335,000-square-foot complex (formerly known as the Tampa Bay Performing Arts Center) that claims to be the largest performing arts complex in the South. The Center's enormous size allows for multiple local arts organizations to host performances in its five theaters. Ranging in size from a tiny playhouse that seats a few more than 100 people to the acoustically stunning Carol Morsani Hall (2,610 seats), the venues at Straz host everything from pop concerts and touring Broadway shows to performances by the local **Spanish Lyric Theatre** (813/936-0127, www.spanishlyrictheatre.com), **Opera Tampa** (813/222-1003, www.operatampa. org), and local theater groups.

The performing arts in Tampa are certainly not limited to those groups who rely on the Straz for space. The **Gorilla Theatre** (4419 N. Hubert Ave., 813/879-2914, www.gorilla-theatre.com) is located in an unprepossessing warehouse in the Drew Park district of town; every month the group puts on a new, contemporary work by a local or national playwright. Music, art, and dance provide the acronym for the **MAD Theatre of Tampa** (813/386-6173, www.madtheatre.com). Their productions of slightly edgier Broadway and off-Broadway fare (*Reefer Madness, Cabaret*) are appropriately staged in Ybor City venues like the **Ritz** (1503 E. 7th Ave.) or the **Marti-Maceo Social Club** (1226 E. 7th Ave.). Fans of contemporary dance should look into performances by **Moving Current** (813/237-0216, www.movingcurrent.com); the group typically performs at the University of South Florida.

Located downtown, the **Florida Museum of the Photographic Arts** (200 N. Tampa St., 813/221-2222, www.fmopa.org, $4 suggested donation) is a small gallery usually hosting only one exhibit at a time. The exhibits are well-curated, however, and usually quite extensive. The **Old Hyde Park Art Center** (705 Swann Ave., 813/251-3780, www. artgally.com) is situated in an old elementary school and operates both as a gallery and an art school. It has been run by a collective of local artists since 1968, and most of the art inside is by members.

Tampa's Most Famous Pirate

José Gaspar reigns over Tampa's mythology.

The first thing you should know about pirates in Tampa is that despite the buccaneer imagery of Tampa's National Football League franchise and the annual paean to piratical decadence that is the Gasparilla Pirate Festival, the Jolly Roger was a rare sight in Tampa Bay during the romantic heyday of Caribbean piracy. In fact, nobody is actually sure if Tampa's most famous pirate, **José Gaspar,** even existed. His legend, though, certainly lives on.

The tale begins with court intrigue at the palace of Spain's King Charles III, where Gaspar was the victim of aspersions cast on him by a rejected lover, forcing him to escape to the high seas, vowing revenge on Spain. This was done by looting every Spanish ship that came near the southwest coast of Florida. Other ships were supposedly victims too. It's said that Gaspar's ship was the one that looted the vessel transporting the $11.75 million that the United States paid France for the Louisiana Purchase. His treasure is said to be buried on Gasparilla Island (near Boca Grande) and his prison was on Captiva Island. After Florida passed into U.S. hands, Gaspar's ship was gunned down by an American naval vessel; the pirate leapt from his ship, anchor wrapped around his waist, proclaiming, "Gasparilla dies by his own hand, not the enemy's!"

Amazing stuff, right? It's almost certainly all fiction. Many of Gaspar's waterborne exploits were actually undertaken by a real pirate, the Haitian buccaneer known as Black Caesar, who plied the waters around Cuba and on Florida's east coast, stashing his treasure in the relatively untraveled areas southwest of Tampa Bay. Gaspar's legend is further clouded by its sources: Juan Gomez and Juan Gonzalez, two men who claimed to be the last living members of Gaspar's crew in the late 19th century. Gomez was notorious for telling tall tales, although his stories of life on the sea with Gaspar had a ring of truth to them, as he was able to lead a reporter to the burial site of one of Gaspar's supposed victims. Gonzalez said that he had helped to bury some of Gaspar's treasure on the banks of Lettuce Lake (near the University of South Florida). The booty was never discovered, but in Gonzalez's cabin, a jar of gold coins and a mysterious coded note were discovered. The note has yet to be decoded, and to this day nothing has been brought forward to prove that these stories were real. But that hasn't stopped Tampa Bay from reveling in the iconography and drinking habits of pirates; nor should it stop you.

Festivals and Events

The **Gasparilla Pirate Festival** (downtown Tampa, http://gasparillapiratefest.com, late Jan./early Feb.) is actually two separate events. The original **Gasparilla Pirate Fest** is put on by Tampa's own Ye Mystic Krewe of Gasparilla, a New Orleans-style civic organization formed in 1904. Every year since then, with only 10 wartime exceptions, the Jose Gasparilla pirate ship sails into Tampa Bay and the pirates "invade" the city, parade-style, tossing beads to increasingly inebriated partiers. Live music happens throughout the day on enormous stages, there's an amusement park-style midway with rides and games, and vendors are out in force. Note that the Mardi Gras similarities are intentional, and this is a decidedly bacchanalian event. It's not adults-only, by any means, although beads are tossed according to a very similar "barter system" as in the French Quarter, and young kids could get a little overwhelmed by the crowds of red-nosed grown-ups. The weekend before the Pirate Fest is the family-friendly **Gasparilla Extravaganza,** which features a children's parade and fireworks and is alcohol free.

With the area's phenomenal weather, it's not surprising that outdoor festivals are a regular occurrence. **Guavaween** (Oct.) happens the last Saturday of October in Ybor City. The Halloween theme is localized with Latin American influences, and the affair is nearly as legendarily decadent as Gasparilla. The day begins with family-friendly activities like trick-or-treating and costume contests. From 4pm on, live music, adult-oriented costume contests, and the legendary Mama Guava Stumble Parade draw some 80,000 people to the streets of Ybor.

Believe it or not, Tampa does host a number of festivals and events that aren't based around drunken revelry. The **Tampa Bay Black Heritage Festival** (citywide, 888/224-1733, ext. 3143, http://tampablackheritage. org, Jan.) and the **Cigar Heritage Festival** (1901 N. 13th St., Nov.) celebrate different aspects of the area's culture with plenty of good times but far less decadence than Guavaween

or Gasparilla. The **Gasparilla Film Festival** (citywide, 813/260-4433, http://gasparillafilmfestival.com, late Feb./early Mar.) and the **Tampa International Gay and Lesbian Film Festival** (citywide, http://tiglff.com, Oct.) focus on the cinematic arts. The annual **MacDill AirFest** (6801 S. Dale Mabry Hwy., Mar.) is one of the U.S. military's largest air shows; the two-day event brings out thousands of people to watch the Thunderbirds and other flight crews perform various aerial acrobatics.

SHOPPING
Hyde Park and SoHo

Hyde Park Village (1602 W. Snow Ave., 813/251-3500, www.hydeparkvillage.com, 10am-7pm Mon.-Sat., noon-5pm Sun.) is a multibuilding open-air mall that's somewhat at odds with the quirky vibe of this established neighborhood, offering urbane fare like Anthropologie, Brooks Brothers, lululemon, Sur La Table, West Elm, and more.

A stroll through the more localized shops of the nearby **SoHo** (S. Howard Ave.) area is likely to be far more rewarding, with stores like **The Other Side Antiques** (308 S. Howard Ave., 813/254-8799, www.otherside-antiques.com, 9am-5pm Mon.-Fri., 10am-5pm Sat., noon-4pm Sun.), the wittily named local craft gallery **Artsiphartsi** (2717 W. Kennedy Blvd., 813/348-4838, www.artsiphartsi.com, 10am-6pm Mon.-Sat.), or the homey independent-minded **Inkwood Books** (216 S. Armenia Ave., 813/253-2638, www.inkwood-books.com, 10am-9pm Mon.-Thurs., 10am-7pm Fri.-Sat., 1pm-5pm Sun.).

Ybor City

Stores like the vintage-hipster **Revolve Clothing Exchange** (1620 E. 7th Ave., 813/242-5970, http://revolve.cx, 11am-8pm Tues.-Thurs., 11am-11pm Fri.-Sat., noon-7pm Sun.) provide relief from the everyday. The **Columbia Restaurant Gift Store** (2117 E. 7th Ave., 813/248-4961, www.columbiarestaurant.com, 11am-10pm Mon.-Thurs., 11am-11pm Fri.-Sat., noon-9pm Sun.) is a

Best Restaurants

★ **Daily Eats:** This modern diner serves great breakfasts, lunches, and dinners every day of the week; try a "shredder bowl" (page 327).

★ **Ella's Americana Folk Art Cafe:** With a great vibe and fantastic local art, the Sunday soul food brunch is essential (page 328).

★ **Taco Bus:** This for-real restaurant hasn't lost its food-truck heart, leaning on a concise menu of authentic Mexican street food (page 329).

★ **The Moon Under Water:** This British colonial tavern serves up fish-and-chips as easily as it does jerk chicken and signature curries (page 344).

must-stop for souvenir shoppers and cigar lovers. If you're looking for fresh food to take on a boating or beach excursion, the outdoor **Ybor City Saturday Market** (Centennial Park, 8th Ave. at 19th St., http://yborfresh-market.ypguides.net, 9am-3pm Sat. Sept.-Apr., 9am-1pm May-Aug.) has locally and regionally grown produce as well as gourmet snacks and arts and crafts from local vendors.

West Shore Boulevard

International Plaza (2223 West Shore Blvd., 813/342-3790, www.shopinternation-alplaza.com, 10am-9pm Mon.-Sat., noon-6pm Sun.) is Tampa's more upscale mall, home to Apple, Burberry, Louis Vuitton, and Tiffany stores, along with luxe department stores like Nordstrom and Neiman-Marcus.

FOOD
Breakfast and Light Bites

La Creperia Cafe (1729 E. 7th Ave., 813/248-9700, www.lacreperiacafe.com, 10am-3pm Mon., 10am-10pm Tues.-Thurs., 10am-11pm Fri., 9am-11pm Sat., 9am-8pm Sun., $8-11) in Ybor City has an immense selection of crepes. The café serves fresh breakfast crepes, stuffed with eggs, cheeses, meats, and even fruit all day. Decadent morning selections like "La Versailles" (filled with butter, cream cheese, jam, and topped with powdered sugar) hint at how they can satisfy your sweet tooth throughout the day. The sweet crepes are

richly designed, utilizing various soft cheeses, fruit spreads, and ice cream. You can even get them flambéed. Croque monsieurs, paninis, and pasta dishes round out a selection of more substantial crepes.

Stone Soup Company (1517 E. 7th Ave., 813/247-7687, http://xsoup4u.com, 10am-9pm Mon.-Thurs., 10am-11pm Fri.-Sat., from $6.50) has a great location on the quiet end of Ybor City. Although the menu is pretty slim, with a few entrées, a few more sandwiches and salads, and a pretty good selection of soups, it's still a great place to grab a quick lunch or to shore up your belly before a night of drinking in Ybor. From borscht to bisque, Stone Soup will have your soup needs covered. Try a sampler, which gets you four five-ounce cups of whichever soups you choose. The pizzas (available on pita bread or cuban bread, rather than traditional Italian dough) and sandwiches (especially the Cuban) are also well worth digging into.

Weekend brunches are the calling card at ★ **Daily Eats** (901 S. Howard Ave., 813/868-3335, www.dailyeatstampa.com, 11:30am-10pm Tues.-Fri., 8:30am-10pm Sat.-Sun., $7). This modern SoHo diner also serves great breakfasts, lunches, and dinners every day of the week. Along with egg-and-bacon meals, Daily Eats plates up treats like coconut-crusted French toast with coconut honey cream cheese, and yogurt-fruit-granola bowls. For lunch and dinner, the "shredder bowls"—fresh fruits and vegetables along with shredded meats served atop a bed of brown rice and shredded lettuce—are the height of convenient comfort food. The selection of burgers, from a potato chip-crusted turkey burger to bison burgers, are thoughtfully reconfigured classics.

American

Housed in a 110-year-old Victorian abode, the **Front Porch Grill & Bar** (5924 N. Florida Ave., 813/237-5511, www.frontporchgrill.com, 4pm-10pm Mon.-Sat., $12) is best known for its award-winning meat loaf, a moist and substantial affair that's baked, briefly grilled, and then topped with a port wine demi-glace. The rest of the menu is similarly homespun. American classics like pot roast and catfish are available, along with pasta dishes and a goat-cheese-topped chicken breast. Enjoy a drink on the spacious front porch before you settle in at one of the nook-and-cranny tables inside. The Front Porch is far from ideally located, but it's one of Tampa's most unique eateries.

Bern's Steak House (1208 S. Howard Ave., 813/251-2421, www.bernssteakhouse. com, 5pm-10pm Sun.-Thurs., 5pm-11pm Fri.-Sat., $29-200) is a Tampa institution, and for good reason. Despite a stark exterior that looks like an abandoned dry cleaners, the inside is all Gilded Age excess, even though it opened in 1956. From the crystal-dripping chandeliers and the ornate staircase to the excessively decorated, deep-red walls, Bern's oozes a very particular and peculiar idea of elegance. The menu is similarly baroque. Allow yourself a good 15 minutes to read the various exegeses penned in honor of the steak house's meats, wines, and caviars, and then another 15 to decide between the multiplicity of ways you can have a slab of meat cut and prepared. Bern's takes its steak very seriously, and it shows, although the effect may be enhanced by the, uh, unique surroundings. Make sure to check out the downstairs dessert bar, where guests can sit in a hollowed-out wine cask and enjoy richly decadent sweets.

Rooster & the Till (6500 N. Florida Ave., 813/374-8940, www.roosterandthetill.com, 5pm-10pm Mon.-Thurs., 5pm-11pm Fri.-Sat., $18) is one of the marquee establishments in the burgeoning, hip neighborhood of Seminole Heights, managing to balance the area's low-key urbanity with the inevitable whiff of artisanal gentrification. The food here is simply sourced but sublime, featuring dishes like beef shank, oysters, foie gras, and duck breast, as well as incredible fresh pasta. Excellent service and cozy, comfortable décor provide a perfect complement to the farm-to-table menu, making this a standout among Tampa's rapidly evolving dining scene.

Here's the first thing you should know about ★ **Ella's Americana Folk Art Cafe** (5119 N. Nebraska Ave., 813/234-1000, www. ellasfolkartcafe.com, 5pm-11pm Tues.-Thurs., 5pm-midnight Fri.-Sat., 11am-8pm Sun., $8): It offers chocolate-covered bacon. Here's the second thing you should know: Service is notoriously sluggish. But, hey, you're getting chocolate-covered bacon! Or eggs-and-bacon pizza. Or chicken and waffles. Or a great fresh salad. And reasonably priced craft beer or inventive artisanal cocktails. And a great vibe and fantastic local art. The soul food brunch on Sundays is essential, though service is even slower then.

Latin and Caribbean

What started in 1997 as a romantic and cozy secret on the bottom floor of a SoHo apartment building has metastasized into a behemoth of Tampa Bay cuisine. **Ceviche** (2500 W. Azeele St., 813/250-0203, www.ceviche. com, 5pm-10pm Sun.-Mon., 5pm-midnight Tues.-Thurs., 5pm-1am Fri.-Sat., from $5) has long since outgrown its humble beginnings, opening plus-size outposts across Florida. The Tampa location has also grown, having moved (twice!) into a labyrinthine dining complex, which includes several dining rooms that attempt to re-create the intimacy of the original outdoor seating, and even a flamenco room. While most of the original charm is gone, the high quality of the tapas and Spanish

Sanwa Farmers Market

Sanwa Farmers Market is a great place to stock a global picnic basket.

If you're packing a picnic or loading up your vacation condo's fridge and need to get Colombian soda or instant curry mixes or Japanese snack foods or a 50-lb. bag of rice, then you need to make a beeline for **Sanwa Farmers Market** (2621 E. Hillsborough Ave., Tampa, 813/234-8428, www. sanwafarmersmarket.com, 4:30am-7pm Mon.-Sat., 8am-5pm Sun.). The market is divided into two sections: The front contains a stunning variety of nonperishables from Asia and Latin America, while the back is a massive area dedicated to fresh fruits, vegetables, herbs, meats, and seafood. While the market's main purpose is supplying local restaurants with the hard-to-find ingredients they may have trouble sourcing, it's a great resource for unique road snacks and reasonably priced fresh food. Located in an industrial zone across from the Fun-Lan Drive-In and Flea Market, it's not really close to many of Tampa's sights (although it is near the hip Seminole Heights neighborhood). However, Hillsborough Avenue is an easily accessible main drag and the market is close to I-275, making it a semi-convenient detour between the airport and downtown.

fare remains. Unlike many tapas restaurants, Ceviche's menu of hot and cold plates is both authentic and creative, as well as quite extensive, encouraging multiple visits. Do not leave without trying the sangria.

People have grown to expect friendly personal service at **Hugo's Spanish Restaurant** (931 S. Howard Ave., 813/251-2842, 8am-9pm Mon.-Fri., 7:30am-9pm Sat., $6-9) since it opened in 1973. Hugo's serves primarily Cuban food: excellent rice and beans, a decent Cuban sandwich, and a much-praised roast pork. It also serves breakfast and a small selection of Italian dishes.

Happy Fish (4046 N. Armenia Ave., 813/871-6953, www.happyfishtampa.com, 11:30am-8pm Mon.-Thurs., 11:30am-9pm Fri.-Sat., noon-8pm Sun., from $11) is a Peruvian restaurant located in a West Tampa strip mall, a few blocks away from Raymond James Stadium. While this means it's not exactly located in any of the city's dining hotspots, it is still well worth a visit. With an emphasis on seafood (hence the name), preparations here include a sublime mixed ceviche, a generous (and nongreasy) seafood fried rice, mussels, seafood soups, and stunningly fresh grilled fish dishes. Desserts like Peruvian picarones round out the fare.

★ **Taco Bus** (913 E. Hillsborough Ave.,

813/232-5889, www.taco-bus.com, 24 hours daily, from $7) started out as a converted school bus. The bus was a huge hit among everyone from street-food aficionados to late-night noshers, and today, Taco Bus has locations in Seminole Heights, downtown (505 Franklin St., 813/397-2800, 24 hours daily), the University of South Florida (2320 E. Fletcher Ave., 813/977-6808, 24 hours daily), and another in St. Pete. The original bus sits outside the Seminole Heights location, functioning as a kitchen. Although the business has grown, it hasn't lost its food-truck heart, leaning on a concise menu of tacos and authentic Mexican street food (opt for a torta and your life may well change for the better). Ingredients are fresh, the food is cheap, and it's served quickly and with a friendly smile, an approach that has helped make the Taco Bus a Tampa institution that's both beloved and dependable.

Seafood

Surprisingly, seafood restaurants aren't as common in Tampa as you might expect. **Skipper's Smokehouse** (910 Skipper Rd., 813/971-0666, www.skipperssmokehouse. com, 11am-11pm Tues.-Fri., 11am-midnight Sat., 1pm-11pm Sun., $10) serves up some fine oysters and smoked fish. **Oystercatchers** (at the Grand Hyatt, 2900 Bayport Dr., http:// hyatt.com, 813/207-6816, 11:30am-2:30pm and 6pm-10pm Mon.-Fri., 6pm-10pm Sat., 10:30am-2:30pm and 6pm-10pm Sun., $30) has been the go-to place for an upscale fish dinner for years. Adjacent to a bird sanctuary and overlooking Tampa Bay, the spectacular sunset views are complemented by a clean, modern interior design that allows you to quickly forget that you're in a hotel restaurant. The menu is seasonally variable and allows for fish dishes to be prepared in a variety of ways. The waitstaff is quick to make suggestions (sometimes even advising you to forgo some of the excellent sauces in favor of the fish's natural flavor). Of course, oysters are available, flown in fresh from Washington, Massachusetts, and elsewhere; Gulf oysters

are also available. They're all $3 a pop, so choose wisely. The restaurant also serves an exceptional weekend brunch.

Another good option for seafood is **Big Ray's Fish Camp** (6116 Interbay Blvd., 813/605-3615, www.bigraysfishcamp.com, 11am-9pm Wed.-Sat., 11am-8pm Sun., 11am-4pm Tues., from $10). There's not much parking and seating is limited to two indoor tables and a few picnic benches outside. Sometimes it closes without warning because it runs out of food. Regardless, this nondescript neighborhood fish joint has a distinct Old Florida vibe, and the food—especially the excellent fried grouper sandwich and the decadent lobster corn dog—is exceptional.

Japanese and Thai

In addition to traditional rolls and sashimi, **Ciccio Water** (10151/2 S. Howard Ave., 813/514-4426, www.watersushi.com, 6pm-11pm daily, sushi rolls and bowls average $9) shares a predilection with its sister restaurant, Daily Eats: They love to put things in bowls. Water Bowls are a bed of white or brown rice beneath an unrolled combination of the same ingredients that make up many popular sushi rolls. Imagine sushi as prepared by the same folks who came up with those KFC bowls, except, you know, good. This unique presentation allows the chefs considerable creative leeway, like eel with banana, resulting in a unique take on sushi.

Ybor City's **Samurai Blue** (1600 E. 8th Ave., 813/242-6688, www.samuraiblue.com, lunch and dinner Mon.-Sat., dinner Sun.) prides itself on its hipster-friendly vibe and modern take on sushi. Most of the dishes and rolls are old hat, but some surprises, like mussels baked with wasabi mayonnaise, also pop up. A substantial selection of non-Japanese meat and poultry entrées is available too. The sake bar is also very popular.

On Sundays, the ★ **Wat Mongkolratanaram of Florida** (5306 Palm River Rd., 813/621-1669, www.wattampainenglish.com, 10am-2pm Sun.) is the site of a Thai open-air market. The Buddhist temple, known as Wat

Best Accommodations

★ **Gram's Place:** This hostel's loose, festive vibe makes it a fun option, while strict quiet hours make families feel welcome (page 331).

★ **Inn On The Beach:** The tiny inn looks more like a cozy apartment than a hotel. The individually appointed rooms only add to the homey feel (page 347).

★ **Don CeSar Beach Resort:** Famous guests at this St. Pete Beach icon have included Al Capone and F. Scott Fitzgerald (page 347).

★ **Plantation at Crystal River:** This is a convenient choice for guests hitting the Plantation's golf links (page 351).

Tampa, is a beautiful sight in and of itself. And the many local vendors who turn out for the market make it a Thai food fan's dream come true. Fried taro, noodle soups, curries, and grilled meats are all on offer, and picnic tables are available for enjoying the low-priced food, as monks in saffron robes wander the grounds and local Thais socialize.

ACCOMMODATIONS
Under $100
There are hostels, and then there's ★ **Gram's Place** (3109 N. Ola Ave., 813/221-0596, www.grams-inn-tampa.com, $23-30 pp). Dedicated to the memory of country singer Gram Parsons, who was born in nearby Winter Haven, these two renovated houses north of downtown are linked via elevated decks, creating a place that's as whimsical as it is spiritual. Five dormitory rooms share musical themes, while one room is a toolshed-cum-tree house and the other is decked out like a railroad car. The owners keep the vibe loose and festive. Despite the BYOB "Parson's Pub," it's not a party hostel; quiet time is strictly enforced, and families will feel welcome. The rooms are appropriately rustic, but clean. All rooms are air-conditioned and have telephones and TVs.

$100-150
About 25 miles (30 minutes' drive) from downtown Tampa in tiny Lithia is the **Palmer**

House Bed-and-Breakfast (2221 Hinton Ranch Rd., Lithia, 813/654-0961 or 888/772-3348, www.palmer-house.com, from $139 d). There's not much to do nearby, and that's sort of the point. Guests are encouraged to relax in the spacious well-appointed rooms, which have Wi-Fi, TVs, mini fridges, and microwaves; wander the grounds; or take a dip in Palmer House's heated pool and whirlpool tub. Rooms adhere to the "country B&B" style of frilly decor, but owners Bob and Gail Palmer keep it tasteful.

$200 and up
Eleven floors of luxurious accommodations sit atop the gaming rooms at the **Hard Rock Hotel & Casino** (5223 N. Orient Rd., 866/502-7529, www.seminolehardrock-tampa.com, from $229 d). Their stylish, spacious decor shows what happens when you apply Hard Rock's fashion sense to an old bingo hall. The endless homages to 40-year-old rock songs may get a little wearying after a while, but the swank, high-tech rooms are unabashedly modern. They're also quite comfortable; thick person-size towels, Egyptian cotton sheets, and plush beds are designed to reinvigorate slot pullers. Nongamblers will certainly find much to love about the hotel as well. Although the Hard Rock isn't centrally located, its proximity to I-4 makes all of Tampa accessible within minutes.

Tampa's lodging situation is dominated

by chain hotels, and the **Hampton Inn and Suites** (1301 E. 7th Ave., 813/247-6700, www. hamptoninn.com, from $269 d) in Ybor City is worth noting. The hotel boasts a perfect location: It's only two blocks away from the buzz of Ybor City, which is exactly far enough away that the late-night partying shouldn't affect your sleep, unless guests bring the party home with them. Better still, it's a half block away from a trolley car stop. Rooms are clean and modern in keeping with the chain's standards.

The downtown **Le Meridien** (601 N. Florida Ave, 813/221-9555, www.lemeridientampa.com, from $349 d) is situated in the city's historic court house building, combining the chain's reputation for luxury with a bit of character in an area largely devoid of either.

INFORMATION AND SERVICES
Visitor Information
Tampa Bay & Company (615 Channelside Dr., Suite 101A, 813/226-0293, www.visittampabay.com, 10am-5:30pm Mon.-Sat., 11am-5pm Sun.) is the area's main visitors bureau. It operates a gift shop and visitors center in the Channelside complex, and the staff will gladly assist with maps, tips, and reservations. Their website contains lots of information and booking tools as well. If you're staying in Ybor City, drop by the **Ybor City Visitor Information Center** (1600 E 8th Ave., 813/241-8838, www.ybor.org, 10am-6pm Mon.-Sat., noon-6pm Sun.).

GETTING THERE
Car
Tampa and Orlando are almost directly connected by an 85-mile drive south on I-4, which takes just over an hour. Right before you hit downtown Tampa, I-4 ends, merging into I-275, which not only takes you to downtown Tampa, but also to Clearwater and St. Petersburg. US-41 is the Tamiami Trail, and its name stems from the fact that it connects Tampa and Miami. This route is highly recommended, as the Trail runs through the heart of nearly all of Southwest Florida,

including Sarasota and Naples. On the best day, this 275-mile drive takes about 6.5 hours. It's quite often a beautiful drive, but it's not exactly quick. Alternately, taking **I-75** will get you there in less than four hours.

Air, Train, or Bus
Tampa International Airport (TPA, 100 George J. Bean Pkwy., 813/870-8700, www. tampaairport.com) is huge and well served by all major domestic and international carriers.

Downtown Tampa's **Union Station** (601 N. Nebraska Ave., 813/221-7600, www.amtrak. com) is where Amtrak trains bring passengers from the Northeast Corridor (via Orlando and Jacksonville) and also to and from the east coast of Florida. Both Silver Star and Palmetto routes service this station.

The **Greyhound bus terminal** (610 E. Polk St., 813/229-8588, www.greyhound.com) is located just a few blocks away from Union Station.

GETTING AROUND
All the major **rental car** agencies are represented at Tampa International Airport; Hertz also has a conveniently located branch at the cruise-ship port. Visits to Busch Gardens or the SoHo neighborhood are much easier to undertake with a rental car. In-town traffic is usually quite manageable; if you'll be navigating freeways like I-4 or I-275, avoid rush hour if at all possible. There are no toll roads in central Tampa, and parking is generally easy to come by. In Ybor City and downtown parking can be expensive.

If your time in Tampa will mainly be spent in Ybor City, Channelside, and downtown, renting a car should be largely unnecessary, thanks to the **streetcar and trolley system** set up in the area. Operated by the **Hillsborough Area Regional Transit Authority** (813/254-4278, www.gohart.org), the interconnected system can get you to and from any point in these areas. The historic streetcars running through Ybor City travel a loop to and from the Channel District and the Tampa Convention Center, with several stops along the way at all the major sites. There is service at each stop every 15-20 minutes. The in-town trolley runs on two lines: one is a daytime line for weekday rush hour (6am-9am and 3pm-6pm Mon.-Fri., service every 10 minutes); another is designed for weekend revelers (6pm-2am Fri.-Sat., service every 10 minutes). One-way streetcar/bus fares are $2 (the trolley is only $0.25), although older kids and seniors ride for half price and kids age 4 and under ride for free. Only exact cash or fare card are accepted. Unlimited-ride cards are available in one-day, three-day, and 20-ride increments for a substantial discount.

Outside of hotels and busy tourist areas, it is difficult or impossible to hail a **taxicab.** Call **United Cab** (813/253-2424) or **Yellow** (813/253-0121) for a ride; it's $2.50 to start the meter and $2.50 per mile. Downtown Tampa is something of a ghost town after dark. If you're in the area for a movie at the Tampa Theatre or a show at the Straz Center, it's best to be very aware of your surroundings at night, especially if you're on foot.

St. Petersburg, Clearwater, and the Beaches

With a decidedly more low-key attitude than its go-getter sister city to the east, St. Petersburg offers lovers of history and art much to enjoy at a slow pace and in a friendly environment. The early 20th-century architecture that defines St. Petersburg's downtown speaks to the area's past as a prime tourist destination. Many of the same things that drew the area's first guests—beautiful weather, lively street-level shops, and cafés—are drawing younger crowds who are shuffling off the city's reputation as "God's waiting room." The beautiful, award-winning beaches that line a 25-mile-long barrier island are just as attractive, with communities that range from bustling to sedate.

ORIENTATION

St. Petersburg is on the southern tip of a peninsula, with the Gulf of Mexico to the west and Tampa Bay to the east, and it's connected to central Tampa via two east-west causeways, Gandy Boulevard and I-275. The city of Clearwater is on the northern end of the same peninsula, connected to Tampa via the Courtney Campbell Causeway, which turns into Gulf to Bay Boulevard within the city of Clearwater. St. Pete Beach is to the west of downtown St. Petersburg, along a lengthy connected strip of barrier islands that runs all the way north to Clearwater Beach.

SIGHTS
Downtown St. Petersburg

In the waterfront heart of downtown is **Straub Park** (Beach Dr. between 2nd Ave. and 5th Ave.), home to several interesting pieces of modern sculpture but utilized more often as the locale for festivals and weekend picnicking and sunbathing. Large oaks provide plenty of shade. There's also lots of space for activities. The view onto the Vinoy marina, as the yachts come and go, is perfect.

Adjacent to Straub Park is the **Museum of Fine Arts** (MoFA, 255 Beach Dr. NE, 727/896-2667, www.fine-arts.org, 10am-5pm Mon.-Sat., noon-5pm Sun., $17 adults, $15 seniors and military, $10 students and children, children 6 and under free). For a small Florida city with one exceptional museum in the form of the Dalí, the presence of the MoFA is noteworthy indeed. Permanent exhibits of 17th- and 18th-century European art and 19th-century American art are well curated and hit all the expected notes. Where MoFA shines is in its permanent collection of antiquities, ranging from pre-Columbian pieces to Asian fine art, and its dedication to photography. Bringing in

St. Petersburg, Clearwater, and the Beaches

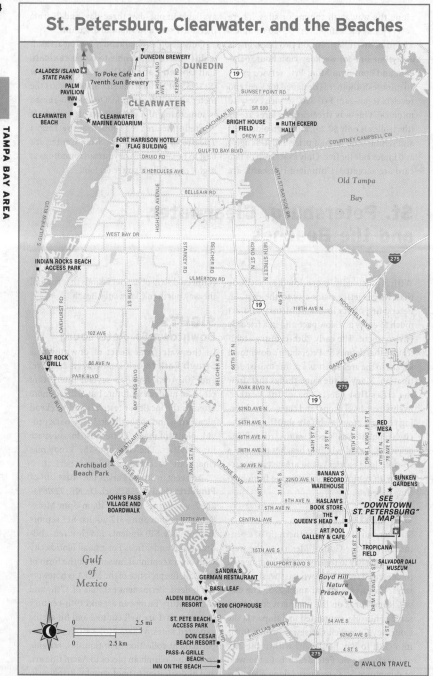

DUNEDIN BREWERY

CALADESI ISLAND
STATE PARK

To Poke Café and
7venth Sun Brewery

DUNEDIN

19

N HIGHLAND AVE
KEENE RD

SUNSET POINT RD

SR 590

PALM
PAVILION
INN

CLEARWATER

NE COACHMAN RD

CLEARWATER
BEACH

CLEARWATER
MARINE AQUARIUM

BRIGHT HOUSE
FIELD

DREW ST

RUTH ECKERD
HALL

COURTNEY CAMPBELL CW

FORT HARRISON HOTEL/
FLAG BUILDING

GULF TO BAY BLVD

DRUID RD

S HERCULES AVE

48TH ST/BAYSIDE BR

Old Tampa
Bay

HIGHLAND AVENUE

BELLEAIR RD

275

WEST BAY DR

S GULFVIEW BLVD

STARKEY RD

BELCHER RD

62ND ST N

58TH STREET N

INDIAN ROCKS BEACH
ACCESS PARK

ULMERTON RD

49 ST

ROOSEVELT BLVD

OAKHURST RD

113TH ST

19

118TH AVE N

102 AVE

SALT ROCK
GRILL

88 AVE N

66TH ST N

GANDY BLVD

275

PARK BLVD

BAY PINES BLVD

PARK BLVD N

GULF BLVD

BELCHER RD

62ND AVE N

54TH AVE N

46TH AVE N

38TH AVE N

24TH ST N

28 ST N

DR M L KING JR ST N

4TH ST N

78 ST N

RED
MESA

TOM STUART CSWY

PARK ST N

TYRONE BLVD

30 AVE N

58TH ST N

31 AVE S

22ND AVE N

BANANA'S
RECORD
WAREHOUSE

SUNKEN
GARDENS

Archibald
Beach Park

GULF BLVD

9TH AVE N

HASLAM'S
BOOK
STORE

SEE
"DOWNTOWN
ST. PETERSBURG"
MAP

JOHN'S PASS
VILLAGE AND
BOARDWALK

107TH AVE

CENTRAL AVE

5TH AVE N

THE
QUEEN'S HEAD

ART POOL
GALLERY & CAFE

16TH ST S

TROPICANA
FIELD

15TH AVE S

GULFPORT BLVD S

Gulf
of
Mexico

SALVADOR DALI
MUSEUM

SANDRA'S
GERMAN RESTAURANT

BASIL LEAF

Boyd Hill
Nature
Preserve

DR M L KING JR ST S

S 4 ST S

ALDEN BEACH
RESORT

1200 CHOPHOUSE

GULF BLVD

ST. PETE BEACH
ACCESS PARK

54 AVE S

DON CESAR
BEACH RESORT

62ND AVE S

0   2.5 mi

PASS-A-GRILLE
BEACH

PINELLAS BAYWY

4 ST S

0   2.5 km

INN ON THE BEACH

275

© AVALON TRAVEL

a wide range of exhibits, from Ansel Adams to Weegee, the museum shows a surprising fearlessness in balancing the old and the new.

The big highlight at the **St. Petersburg Museum of History** (335 2nd Ave. NE, 727/894-1052, www.spmoh.org, 10am-5pm Mon.-Sat., noon-5pm Sun., $15 adults, $12 seniors, $9 students, $9 children, children 6 and under free) is a walk through the First Flight Gallery, dedicated to Tony Jannus's historic first commercial airline flight. Similarly, the rest of the museum focuses closely on local history, with Native American artifacts and exhibits on the city's growth since the arrival of the railroad.

Also downtown is the **Florida Holocaust Museum** (55 5th St. S, 727/820-0100, www.flholocaustmuseum.org, 10am-5pm daily, $16 adults, $14 seniors, $10 college students, $8 students under 18, children 6 and under free). Originally founded in 1992 in nearby Madeira Beach, the museum expanded into its current location in 1998, and is now one of the largest Holocaust museums in the United States. The *History, Heritage, and Hope* exhibition is the cornerstone of the museum, and—like the rest of the museum—is both educational and respectful of the hate and horrors it documents.

★ Salvador Dalí Museum

Located just a few blocks outside the downtown core, the **Salvador Dalí Museum** (1 Dali Blvd., St. Petersburg, 727/823-3767, www.thedali.org, 10am-5:30pm Mon.-Wed. and Fri.-Sun., 10am-8pm Thurs., $24 adults, $22 seniors, $17 students, $10 children, children 5 and under free) is an essential stop for even the most casual art lover. The museum, just across from the Mahaffey Theater, houses the largest collection of the infamous surrealist's paintings in the United States. While such an important aggregation of 20th-century art might be expected to be found in New York or even in Miami, there's something perversely perfect about these still-provocative works being stashed away in this sedate waterfront town.

The entrance side of the building's exterior is just a stark concrete wall, the gray interrupted only by the slash of Dalí's signature engraved at the uppermost corner. The "back" side of the exterior is a complex tubular glass-and-metal piece that seems to bubble out from the building's foundation. Once inside, visitors travel chronologically and thematically through the substantial collection. Several of Dalí's more famous pieces are often traveling to other museums,

The Salvador Dalí Museum is a must-see in downtown St. Petersburg.

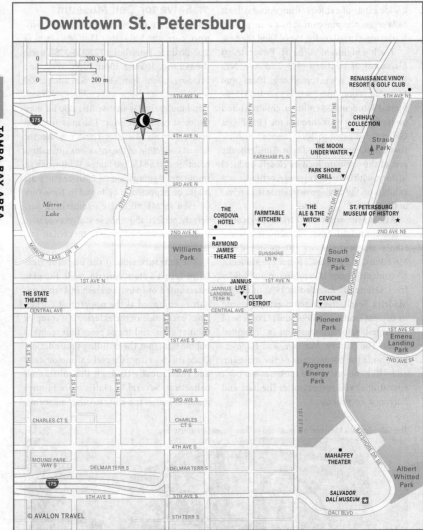

Downtown St. Petersburg

and others are not part of this collection, so don't have your heart set on seeing any specific works. What's most impressive is the spacious area devoted to the painter's large-scale masterworks, like the 14-foot-tall *The Discovery of America by Christopher Columbus.* Smaller pencil pieces and various sketches provide considerable insight into his formative years.

Sunken Gardens

Another venerable St. Petersburg attraction is **Sunken Gardens** (1825 4th St. N, 727/551-3100, www.stpete.org/sunken, 10am-4:30pm Mon.-Sat., noon-4:30pm Sun., $10 adults, $8 seniors, $4 children), known for its mature and well-kept botanical gardens and for the historical nature of the site. One of the first roadside attractions in Florida and one of the oldest tourist spots in the state, Sunken Gardens got its start in the 1920s when enterprising homeowner George Turner began selling fruit and flowers from his private "sunken gardens" (so named because he drained an on-site lake for planting) and charged visitors a nickel to admire his horticultural prowess. Almost a century later, the plants are accompanied by flamingos, reptiles, and a butterfly garden.

The Turner family acquired the main building in 1967 and made it part of Sunken Gardens. Sunken Gardens eventually fell into disrepair, prompting its rescue-purchase by the City of St. Petersburg. The gardens themselves are still much the same as they've always been, and they are a fine destination for school groups and amateur horticulturists.

Clearwater Marine Aquarium

Located in Clearwater Harbor, just off the causeway connecting downtown Clearwater to the beach, is the **Clearwater Marine Aquarium** (CMA, 249 Windward Passage, 727/441-1790, www.seewinter.com, 9am-6pm daily, $21.95 adults, $19.95 seniors, $16.95 children 3-12). It's more a marine animal rehabilitation center than a traditional public aquarium. Guests shouldn't arrive expecting slick displays and floor-to-ceiling tanks filled with scores of exotic fish. What they will find is a working facility that seeks to educate visitors on the unwitting impact humans have on underwater life. Staff members are friendly and informed. They are clearly enthusiastic about their work, and the animals, despite being a bit banged up, are obviously treated extraordinarily well.

In 2011, the aquarium added an exhibit in downtown Clearwater. **Winter's Dolphin Tale Adventure** (320 Cleveland St., 727/441-1790, www.seewinter.com, admission included with CMA admission, but visits must occur on same day) is an homage to the movie *Dolphin Tale,* which was about one of CMA's most famous residents, the tailless dolphin named Winter. It's a nice add-on, but it's only recommended for huge fans of the movie who

would enjoy spending a couple hours wandering around a renovated department store looking at stills and props from the movie. CMA provides free transportation between the aquarium and the downtown exhibit.

John's Pass and Village Boardwalk

If lounging on the white sands between Pass-A-Grille and Clearwater Beach isn't social enough for you, a visit to **John's Pass and Village Boardwalk** (150 Boardwalk Pl., Madeira Beach, 727/393-8230, www.johnspass.com, open daily) will allow you to fulfill your daily quota of people watching. The centrally located, reconstituted "fishing village" is still home to plenty of charter boats and fishing expeditions. But the primary draw is shopping in the dozens of tourist-kitsch shops, noshing on fried seafood, and catching a sunset.

Dunedin

For a more relaxed and charming outing, Dunedin maintains its Old Florida charm. In addition to being the gateway to Honeymoon Island State Park, the downtown area is home to a handful of unique local businesses. Stop into art galleries like **Clay and Paper** (350 Main St., 727/736-0934, www.claypaper.com, 11am-5pm Tues.-Sat.), and grab lunch or dinner at exceptional restaurants like the **Poke Café** (1140 Main St., 727/871-7653, http://pokecafedunedin.com, 11am-8pm Mon., Wed., Thurs., 11am-9pm Fri., Sat., 11am-7pm Sun., from $12).

Beer lovers probably already have Dunedin marked on their itinerary. Florida's oldest craft brewery, **Dunedin Brewery** (937 Douglas Ave., 727/736-0606, www.dunedinbrewery.com, 11am-11pm Sun.-Tues., 11am-1am Wed.-Thurs., 11am-2am Fri.-Sat., brewery tour $5), is well regarded throughout and beyond Florida for the wide variety of beers they brew onsite. The smaller, more focused Belgian beers coming out of **7venth Sun Brewery** (1012 Broadway, 727/733-3013, www.7venthsun.com, 5pm-midnight

Scientology

Scientology is impossible to escape in downtown Clearwater.

It's impossible to talk about Clearwater without talking about the Church of Scientology. The church quietly purchased the elegant **Fort Harrison Hotel** (210 S. Ft. Harrison St.) in 1975, when the building was a vacant shell of its former self. The Fort Harrison is the heart of Scientology's presence in the city members call their "spiritual headquarters." Next door is the site of the **Flag Building,** a 170,000-square-foot structure that has been under construction since 1998. Many downtown Clearwater businesses are owned by Scientologists, and through its many construction and commercial enterprises, it could easily be said that the church has performed a dramatic facelift on a once-dilapidated area. In addition to the city's many resident Scientologists, thousands of Church members come to Clearwater every year for religious retreats and training at the Fort Harrison. They often stay at the **Sandcastle Retreat** (200 N. Osceola Ave.) and **Osceola Inn** (211 N. Osceola Ave.), two luxurious-looking lodging facilities that unfortunately aren't open to non-Scientologists.

Tues.-Thurs., noon-midnight Fri.-Sun.) are also making a name for themselves.

For those who want to burn off some calories in advance of drinking, both sides of the **Dunedin Causeway** have ample parking, allowing access to the small sandy beaches that trail into St. Joseph Sound. This is a great location for fishing, wading, and Jet Skiing. Enter and exit southern Dunedin via Edgewater Drive; the view is gorgeous, with St. Joseph Sound on one side and beautiful historic homes on the other.

★ Tarpon Springs

In the late 19th century, Greek immigrants

began coming to the city of **Tarpon Springs** to work as sponge divers. Today, Tarpon Springs has more Greek American residents per capita than any other city in the United States. The sponging industry may not employ as many people as it did a century ago, but the folks in Tarpon Springs are more than happy to pretend that it does. Most of the sponging that occurs nowadays is for the benefit of tourists.

The beauty of the **St. Nicholas Greek Orthodox Cathedral** (17 E. Tarpon Ave., 727/937-3540, www.epiphanycity. org) is often overlooked by visitors eager to scarf down spanakopita. But the towering spires are definitely worth a lingering gaze. Afterwards, park at the **Sponge Exchange** (735 Dodecanese Blvd., 727/934-8758, www.thespongeexchange.com, 10am-9pm Mon.-Sat., 10am-7pm Sun.) to browse through the shops selling everything from tourist trinkets and candy by the pound to Greek fashion and Peruvian ceramics. From there you can make your way to the sponge docks, where you'll be invited by numerous touts to take a sponging excursion. You could do that, or you could just check out the unintentionally campy museum at **Spongeorama** (510 Dodecanese Blvd., 727/943-2164, www.spongeorama.com, hours vary but if there are tourists on the strip, it will be open; free), where you can watch a hilariously dated (but very informative) documentary on sponge fishing and then wander through the dusty exhibits on the Greek community's history in the area. There is, of course, a rather large gift shop.

Of the many Greek restaurants on the main drag, **Hellas Restaurant** (785 Dodecanese Blvd., 727/943-2400, http://santorinimediterraneangrill.com, 11am-10pm Sun.-Thurs., 11am-11pm Fri.-Sat., $9-22) is the best. Don't be fooled by the garish neon and mirrored walls, this is a solid Greek dining experience, with a menu that includes authentic Greek dishes as well as numerous fresh seafood entrées and an excellent bakery next door.

BEACHES

The 25-mile-long barrier island that starts with Clearwater Beach in the north and ends with Pass-A-Grille Beach in the south contains some of the most beautiful shoreline in all of Florida. Most of the towns along Gulf Boulevard have public beach access, but some (Indian Rocks Beach, Treasure Island) are more generous than others (Belleair Beach). True beach lovers will want to make the effort to get to the blissful environs of Caladesi Island, which is only accessible by boat.

Clearwater Area
HONEYMOON ISLAND STATE PARK
If you park at the north end of the large lot at **Honeymoon Island State Park** (1 Causeway Blvd., 727/469-5942, www.floridastateparks.org, 8am-sunset daily, $5 for up to 8 people per car) and walk down to the beach, you may wonder what all the fuss is about, as the beach at Honeymoon Island is consistently ranked among the best in the state. The shoreline is equal parts sand and rock, making it difficult to walk across, much less lie down on. A hundred or so paces south,

Tarpon Springs has sponges everywhere.

however, the rocks disappear, and large swaths of soft, white sand open up, leading into the warm shallow waters of the Gulf of Mexico. It is slightly more crowded but nonetheless charming. All along the beach there are restroom and shower facilities, and at the southern end there's a snack bar. There are also two excellent hiking trails here, the Osprey and Pelican Trails, which not only offer great walks through mangrove marshes and pine forest, but through an osprey rookery, giving hikers an opportunity to view nesting colonies of these birds.

★ CALADESI ISLAND STATE PARK

The only way to get to **Caladesi Island State Park** (727/469-5918, ferry 727/734-1501, www.floridastateparks.org, ferry $9 adults, $4.50 children, plus admission to Honeymoon Island State Park) is by boat. If you don't have your own watercraft, a ferry departs from near the entrance of Honeymoon Island State Park every hour beginning at 10am, with the last return trip, from Caladesi, at 4pm. The ride takes 20 minutes. The parks department caps daily admissions, and visitors are limited to four-hour excursions, so the park often reaches capacity by midday. It's recommended to call ahead and make sure that there's a seat available. Once you're at Caladesi, however, you'll appreciate those restrictions.

Four miles of unspoiled white-sand beaches provide plenty of space for beach activities and relaxed sunbathing. The views from nearly every vantage point on the beach are stunning. The shallow warm water is extremely calm, and the sand itself manages the soft whiteness expected of Gulf beaches while being firmly packed like many Atlantic-side beaches. Caladesi's perennial ranking at or near the top of every rundown of America's best beaches will immediately make sense, thanks to unspoiled views and the population-controlled atmosphere. You won't be roughing it, though; in addition to restroom and shower facilities, rental facilities are available to provide beach chairs (umbrella and 2 chairs $20 per day) and sea kayaks (from $10 per hour). The latter will come in handy for the verdant three-mile kayak trail that's excellent for bird spotting (owls, hawks, and even wild turkeys roam the banks).

CLEARWATER BEACH

The public beach at **Clearwater Beach** (metered parking at the end of Rockaway St.) is a perfect choice for those who want to stay a little closer to civilization. Clean, wide, and spacious, it seldom feels packed, even on busy summer weekends. There are a number of surf shops near the beach, including a Ron Jon location, but don't expect to catch any waves; the Gulf waters here are calm and smooth.

South of Clearwater

Pinellas County's **Indian Rocks Beach Access Park** (1700 Gulf Blvd.) provides 80 parking spaces as well as restroom and shower facilities. It's also incredibly crowded, especially on the weekends. There are two dozen other public beach access points located about once every block. The ones at 1st, 8th, 12th, 15th, 16th, 23rd, 26th, and 27th Avenues offer parking and showers, but only the main park has restroom facilities.

The town of Madeira Beach has fostered a low-key beach-party atmosphere for decades thanks to its laid-back vibe and its unique allowance of alcohol consumption on the beach. Some may choose to overindulge, but the spacious white-sand beaches are far more appropriate for those who enjoy sipping on their cold ones in relaxed moderation. **Archibald Beach Park** (15100 Gulf Blvd.), **John's Pass Park** (130th Ave. W.), and Pinellas County's **Madeira Beach Access** (14400 Gulf Blvd.) have ample parking, along with shower and restroom facilities. But the tiny lot at the **Kitty Stuart Pavilion,** on Gulf Boulevard between 140th and 141st Avenues, is a better option. Although it only has a handful of spaces and a shower, it's relatively quieter than the other big public-access points. Though, it is by no means pastoral. The city recently banned alcohol at all of its public pavilions, so the aggravation level at Kitty Stuart has dropped along with the crowds hanging out in the picnic shelters.

St. Petersburg Area

The four miles of beach at **St. Pete Beach** are largely taken over by beachside resort motels, although there's ample public beach access on almost every block. Sadly, the "access" consists mainly of a sandy walkway between the road and the sand; it's up to you to figure out where to park if you're not staying nearby. **St. Pete Beach Access Park** (4700 Gulf Blvd.) has 240 parking spaces as well as restroom and shower facilities. The slightly smaller **Upham Beach** (6700 Beach Plaza) has 189 parking spots and facilities. Keeping in mind that weekend and holiday crowds from the entire area pour into these spots in droves, neither of these two options is ideal for those seeking personal space.

Slightly farther south of St. Pete Beach and past the iconic pink Don CeSar Resort is **Pass-A-Grille,** a tiny beach community blessed with some of the most beautiful sunsets on the Gulf. Ample metered parking ($1.25 per hour, $8 per day, free after 8pm) is available along almost 20 blocks of Gulf Way. Clean, white sand and calm Gulf waters make this a popular spot all day long. When the tide rolls out, the geography of the beach results in long, shallow, canal-like tide pools that are perfect for little kids to splash around in. There are public restrooms and shower facilities at 10th Avenue. Make sure to take a drive or walk through this historic area; the houses are gorgeous slices of Old Florida.

The seven miles of beach at **Fort De Soto Park** (3500 Pinellas Bayway S., Tierra Verde, 7am-sunset daily, free) are only part of what brings visitors. This well-equipped county park also has a 238-site camping area, fishing piers, picnic shelters, a running and walking trail, a canoe trail, floating docks for launching boats, and 20 (!) public restroom buildings. All those amenities might make it sound like you'll be elbow to elbow with other people, but thankfully that's not the case. All the sights are spread out over 900 acres, and even the most crowded beaches manage to be pleasantly pastoral, if not private. The soft, powdery sand hides an abundance of seashells.

SPORTS AND RECREATION
Parks

Two St. Petersburg-area parks will appeal to hikers and bird-watchers. **Boyd Hill Nature Preserve** (1101 Country Club Way

beautiful St. Pete Beach

S, 727/893-7326, www.stpete.org/boyd, 9am-8pm Tues.-Thurs., 9am-6pm Fri.-Sat., 11am-6pm Sun., closed Mon., $3) has over three miles of trails through marshes and pine forests, is part of the Great Florida Birding Trail, and also has a small bird of prey aviary. The National Audubon Society has praised the bird-watching opportunities available at **Sawgrass Lake Park** (7400 25th St. N, 727/217-7256, www.pinellascounty.org, 7am-sunset daily, free); a mile-long boardwalk provides an excellent vantage point to spot herons, storks, and egrets, as well as the occasional alligator. Guided tours are available at both locations.

Egmont Key State Park (727/893-2627, www.floridastateparks.org) is the site of the ruins of the turn-of-the-20th-century Fort Dade and a still-operating lighthouse. Most visitors come to walk the trails—the island is a National Wildlife Refuge—and to fish and swim in relative solitude. There are no vendors, no lifeguards, and no bathrooms. Admission to the park is free, but it's only accessible by boat. **Tropical Island Getaway** (4630 29th Ave., 727/345-4500, www.dolphinshorkelingcruise.com) runs a four-hour snorkeling and dolphin-watching cruise ($40 adults, $28 children) from the Gulfport Marina in St. Pete Beach that takes passengers to Egmont Key.

Baseball

The area's Major League Baseball team, the **Tampa Bay Rays** (www.devilrays.mlb.com, from $20), plays April-October at **Tropicana Field** (1 Tropicana Dr., St. Petersburg, http://tampabay.rays.mlb.com), and baseball fans in the area can catch **spring training** February-March. Not only do the Rays open their spring games to the public, the **Philadelphia Phillies** (from $15) play in Clearwater at **Spectrum Field** (601 N. Old Coachman Rd., http://philadelphia.phillies.mlb.com) and the **Toronto Blue Jays** (from $15) take to the diamond in **Florida Auto Exchange Stadium** (373 Douglas Ave., www.milb.com) in Dunedin.

Water Sports

Tampa Bay Boat Charters (259 98th Ave. NE, St. Petersburg, 813/495-0646, www.tampabayboatcharters.com) offers motorized excursions to remote islands in and near Tampa Bay, as well as sunset cruises. Several fishing charters are available in the area. **Baracudaville Charters** (6701 34th St. S, St. Petersburg, 727/776-7335, www.baracudaville.com) has fly-fishing and flats-fishing trips, along with standard inshore and bluewater charters. **Pristine Florida Fishing** (1112 Gulf Oaks Dr., Tarpon Springs, 727/385-0382, www.pristinefloridafishing.com, half day from $325) has a 21-foot fishing boat for both snook and tarpon expeditions as well as ecotours. Several charters operate out of the downtown **St. Petersburg Municipal Marina** (300 2nd Ave. SE, 727/893-7329), offering a variety of sunset cruises and fishing expeditions.

Outfitter **Bill Jackson's** (9501 US-19 N, Pinellas Park, 727/576-4169, www.billjacksons.com) sells gear for fishing, kayaking, hunting, scuba diving, and much more. He frequently offers wreck-diving tours, scuba certification classes, and kayaking trips.

If you have your own canoeing or kayaking gear, head directly for **Weedon Island Preserve** (1800 Weedon Dr. NE, St. Petersburg, 727/453-6500, www.weedonislandpreserve.org, 7am-15 min. before sunset daily, free). The preserve occupies more than 3,000 acres of unspoiled waterways along Tampa Bay, and you can guide your craft through mangroves, estuary marshes, and wide-open water. There's also a small history center and several hiking trails too.

ENTERTAINMENT AND EVENTS
Nightlife

The area is well stocked with beach bars, but St. Petersburg is where most of the area's nightlife activity goes down. Many of downtown St. Pete's restaurants have vibrant, upscale bar areas that are active well after the kitchen closes. Serious drinkers will want to head to a spot like **The Ale & the Witch** (111 2nd Ave. NE, 727/821-2533, http://thealeandthewitch.com), a friendly and often quite busy craft-focused beer bar, or, on the other end of the spectrum, more dive-y joints like **Emerald Bar** (550 Central Ave, 727/898-6054) and **The Blue Goose** (48 9th St N, 727/201-9690), which keep the focus on drinks and conversation. If you want to knock back a few pitchers and watch the Rays or the Bucs, hit **Ferg's Sports Bar** (1320 Central Ave., 727/822-4562, www.fergssportsbar.com).

Top-tier local and national bands hit the big stages at the outdoor **Jannus Live** (16 2nd St. N, 727/896-2276, www.jannuslandingconcerts.com) and the former bank building now known as **The State Theatre** (687 Central Ave., 727/895-3045, www.statetheatreconcerts.com). Next door to Jannus Live is **Club Detroit** (16 2nd St. N, 727/637-2949), a recently resurrected smaller venue focused on regional and indie bands.

Want a different kind of show with your drinks? **The 4 Three Nine** (439 1st Ave N, 727/317-5858, the4threenine.com, 5pm-midnight Wed., Thurs., 5pm-2am Fri., Sat., 3pm-11pm Sun.) not only offers up an extensive wine and craft-beer list, but also boasts an actual trick-performing magician behind the bar.

The Arts

During the winter cultural season, the **Mahaffey Theater** (400 1st St. S, 727/892-5798, www.mahaffeytheater.com) in downtown St. Petersburg hosts touring Broadway productions and is also home to **The Florida Orchestra** (www.floridaorchestra.org). Also in downtown St. Pete is the **Raymond James Theatre** (163 3rd St. N, 727/823-7529), which hosts a variety of productions both challenging and mainstream by the **American Stage Theatre Company** (www.americanstage.org). The nationally renowned **Ruth Eckerd Hall** (1111 N. McMullen Booth Rd., 727/791-7400, www.rutheckerdhall.com) in Clearwater hosts live events year-round; winter brings ballet, Broadway, and symphony

performances, while spring and summer see pop and rock concerts from adult-oriented touring acts.

Open year-round, the **Chihuly Collection at the Morean Arts Center** (400 Beach Dr. NE, 727/896-4527, www.moreanartscenter.org, 10am-5pm Mon.-Sat., noon-5pm Sun., $14.95) is a 10,000-square-foot exhibition space dedicated to Dale Chihuly's renowned glassworks. It's not quite the Dalí Museum, but fans of the glass artist will definitely want to make a stop here. There's also a "hot shop" on-site where (for an additional $8.95) you can view glassblowers at work.

SHOPPING

Shopping doesn't draw a lot of people to the St. Petersburg-Clearwater area, but there are two unique places in St. Petersburg that are worth mentioning. **Banana's Record Warehouse** (2226 16th Ave. N, 727/327-4616, www.musicfinder.com, 10am-5pm Tues.-Sat.) is less a record store than, well, a warehouse with three million vinyl LPs and 45s. Owners Doug and Michelle Allen take excellent care of their stock and are more than likely to have the records you're looking for, as well as the ones you didn't know you were looking for. They also operate a more straightforward retail establishment a few blocks away that's very well stocked with vinyl, CDs, and more. But vinyl fans should head straight for the warehouse.

An equally excellent way to spend a day indoors is at **Haslam's Book Store** (2025 Central Ave., 727/822-8616, www.haslams.com, 10am-6:30pm Mon.-Sat.). Haslam's opened in 1933. With its 30,000 square feet of floor space, all quirkily arranged into nooks, crannies, and repurposed rooms, it houses 300,000 new and used titles. Haslam's is located in the increasingly vibrant Grand Central Art District near the historic Kenwood neighborhood. While there, you should definitely hop across the street to check out **Art Pool Gallery & Cafe** (2030 Central Ave., 727/324-3878, www.artpoolrules.com, noon-6pm Tues.-Sat.), which is part antique store, part vintage boutique, part coffee shop, part art gallery, and part beer garden. It's incredible and one of the friendliest, coolest places in all of St. Pete. The antiques are (relatively speaking) reasonably priced. Even if you're not shopping, you should stop in for a drink or a bite and soak up the vibe.

FOOD

St. Petersburg

Decked out like a British pub, ★ **The Moon Under Water** (332 Beach Dr. NE, 727/896-6160, www.themoonunderwater.com, 11:30am-11pm Sun.-Thurs., 11:30am-midnight Fri.-Sat., $8-15) is more an homage to the exploratory and slightly sodden nature of the Victorian Era. Billed a "British colonial tavern," the Moon serves up fish-and-chips and vegetarian shepherd's pie as easily as it does jerk chicken, tabbouleh, and a selection of signature curries. Despite the seeming incongruity of the menu items, it all makes sense, and the kitchen does a great job of juggling the varied cooking styles needed to pull off the variety of dishes. A solid selection of beers complement the menu, and tucking into a curry and a lager at one of the Moon's outdoor tables might be a Victoriana fan's dream come true. The outdoor seating provides excellent views onto Straub Park and beyond to the marina.

It's not the only excellent British pub in the area. **The Queen's Head** (2501 Central Ave., 727/498-8584, www.thequeensheadbar.com, 4:30pm-midnight Tues.-Thurs., 4:30pm-3am Fri., noon-3am Sat., 11am-10pm Sun., from $8) feels more contemporary with a food-oriented experience. The kitchen combines traditional pub fare like fish-and-chips with lamb sliders, chicken curry, bouillabaisse, and more. There is also a good selection of craft brews to be found here.

Another great option for beers and bites is **Engine No. 9** (56 Dr. Martin Lugther King Jr. St N, 727/623-0938, 11:30am-midnight daily, from $12). The menu here is sharply focused on rich, decadent burgers, crispy tater tots, and a wide range of craft beers. Ignore the TVs that seem to surround you and focus on the menu, which features more than two dozen burger variations that go far beyond the "which of four cheeses would you like?" selections you may be used to; get a Van Helsing (roasted jalapeños, roasted garlic bulbs, pepperjack, bacon), Alice in Pain (sriracha, pancetta, roasted red peppers, grilled pineapple, sweet chili), or the Marie Laveau (crawfish tails, andouille sausage, muenster cheese, green onions, creole sauce), and wash it down with one of the dozens of beers on tap here.

The **Park Shore Grill** (300 Beach Dr. NE, 727/896-3463, www.parkshoregrill.com, 11am-10pm Sun.-Thurs., 11am-11pm Fri.-Sat., $10-30) specializes in classics like filet mignon and lobster pasta, dishes served with flair. Little flourishes like chicken lettuce chili wraps give some indication of the Grill's contemporary leanings. The classy but unstuffy environment—along with those views—make this place a date-night staple, and the outdoor tables are fine for a casual lunch.

FarmTable Kitchen (179 2nd Ave N, 727/523-6300, 11am-10pm Mon.-Thurs., 11am-11pm Fri.-Sat., 11am-9pm Sun., from $15) is situated on the second floor of Locale Market, a "chef-driven" market focused on artisanal and locally sourced foods. Unsurprisingly, FarmTable Kitchen hews to these same ethics, offering an excellent—if slightly pricey—menu that frequently changes, dependent upon what is locally available. However, there are typically fresh seafood dishes available, as well as pizza and pasta, alongside cheese and charcuterie, beef, poultry, and pork dishes, and more.

Unwilling to settle for dishing up refried beans and tortillas in various configurations, **Red Mesa** (4912 4th St. N, 727/527-8728, www.redmesarestaurant.com, lunch and dinner Mon.-Sat., breakfast, lunch, and dinner Sun., $8-24) focuses on utilizing fresh ingredients in contemporary versions of traditional Mexican dishes. You might find a wild mushroom *fundido* or a roasted-pork tenderloin in ancho chili sauce on the menu. The seafood selections use mostly Gulf-caught shrimp and grouper. Red Mesa is pricier and more stylish than a bean taco.

Ceviche (10 Beach Dr., 727/209-2302, www.ceviche.com, 5pm-10pm Mon. and Wed., 5pm-11pm Tues. and Thurs., 5pm-midnight Fri., 8am-midnight Sat., 8am-10pm Sun., tapas plates $7-13) is the St. Petersburg outpost of the Tampa tapas powerhouse and serves a tantalizingly wide selection of authentic Spanish plates as well as remarkable sangria. This location is open for lunch and has a breakfast menu with pastries, croissant sandwiches, omelets, and *tortilla Española*.

Clearwater and Clearwater Beach

Clear Sky Beachside Café (490 Mandalay Ave., 727/442-3684, www.clearskybeachsidecafe.com, 7am-1am daily, from $10) serves breakfast, lunch, dinner, and a late-night menu, and somehow manages to excel at all of them. Lunch and dinner selections tend to focus on seafood (both upmarket preparations and fried baskets), sandwiches, and salads. The after-hours fare focuses the menu down to alcohol-soaking flatbreads, burgers, sandwiches, and sides. But it's in the morning hours, especially for brunch with Clear Sky's full bar, that this restaurant truly excels. French toast made with challah bread, blackened shrimp with smoked-gouda grits, chicken and waffles, lobster Benedict, and other indulgences sit alongside the expected bacon and eggs and bagels.

There are four Frenchy's restaurants in Clearwater Beach, all serving up a similar selection of casual seafood fare. But **Frenchy's Rockaway Grill** (7 Rockaway St., 727/446-4844, www.frenchysonline.com, 11am-midnight Sun.-Thurs., 11am-1am Fri.-Sat., $8-15) is both the biggest and the best. Located right on the beach, it's understandably a favored place among beachgoers looking for a lunchtime nosh. The extensive outdoor seating and to-go window caters to the flip-flop set. Indoor seating and a large bar area with live music day and night mean that Frenchy's is hopping from open to close. Most of the

dishes tend toward seafood specialties. Ribs, steak, poultry, and pasta plates are also available, all of which are prepared with surprising care in a kitchen that really doesn't need to try as hard as it does.

St. Pete Beach

Thick-cut steaks and generous seafood portions dominate the menu at the **Salt Rock Grill** (19325 Gulf Blvd., Indian Shores, 727/593-7625, www.saltrockgrill.com, 4pm-10pm Sun.-Thurs., 4pm-11pm Fri.-Sat., $15-35). Raw-bar selections, including freshly flown-in specialty oysters and grace notes like "Medibbean Shrimp" (sautéed in olive oil and garlic with olives and Feta cheese) and a chimichurri-topped veal porterhouse, have made this spot justifiably popular. And, along with **1200 Chophouse** (5007 Gulf Blvd., St. Pete Beach, 727/367-1300, www.1200chophouse.com, 5pm-10pm daily, from $15) farther south in St. Pete Beach, you've got at least a couple of solid, upscale steak house options if you get tired of the fried-seafood shacks along Gulf Boulevard.

PJ's Oyster Bar (7500 Gulf Blvd., St. Pete Beach, 727/367-3309, www.pjsoysterbar.com, 11am-11pm Mon.-Sat., 1pm-11pm Sun., $7-16) is a seafood shack worth a second look. Covering all the bases—oysters, wings, burgers, and seafood baskets—PJ's is set apart by its friendly atmosphere. Despite the fact that the large restaurant is constantly packed during high season, the staff always seems glad to see another guest come through the door. Family-run since 1985, PJ's is excellent for the casual seafood meal that so many crave while at the beach. There's also a location in **Indian Rocks Beach** (500 1st St.).

Outside of Italian and Mexican food, there aren't a whole lot of international dining options in the area, but what's available is pretty good. **Basil Leaf** (6395 Gulf Blvd., St. Pete Beach, 727/360-4000, www.basilthaisushibar.com, 11:30am-10:30pm daily, from $9) offers a straightforward selection of traditional Thai dishes along with some excellent sushi. **Sandra's German Restaurant** (7115 Gulf

The First Hooters

The infamous and now ubiquitous **Hooters** restaurant chain got its start in October 1983 when six Clearwater businessmen opened a restaurant devoted to "manly finger food" and scantily clad waitresses. Inspired by the sight of one of the founders' secretaries in her jogging outfit, the polarizing uniform of the Hooters Girl was first worn by a bikini-contest winner. Although Hooters is probably best known for its hiring practices and the pinup calendars that result from it, the restaurant's chicken wings kept crowds of males and females coming in, making the Clearwater restaurant a surprise success. It was so successful, in fact, that expansion occurred rapidly enough to catch the original owners off-guard. Franchising rights were sold to a group of investors who now oversee all the Hooters franchises worldwide. The original company still runs outlets in the Tampa Bay area, Chicago, and New York City. The first location is still open at 2800 Gulf To Bay Boulevard, its original Clearwater site.

Blvd., 727/363-4414, www.sandras-german-restaurant.com, 4pm-9pm Wed.-Mon., from $15) is a little pricey, but the intensely authentic German/Austrian fare here is well worth the price. On the menu are *shlachtplatte* and meatballs, liver dumpling soup, a coronary-inducing-but-possibly-worth-the-risk lumberjack platter, and, of course, a good selection of schnitzels and sausages.

ACCOMMODATIONS
St. Petersburg
Originally built in 1921, ★ **The Cordova Hotel** (253 2nd Ave. N., 800/735-6607, www.thepierhotel.com, from $169 d) achieves the unique grace note of being historical, comfortable, and extremely convenient. Located within easy walking distance of all of downtown St. Petersburg's sights, the hotel underwent an extensive renovation in 2000 that maintained its original charm while subtly incorporating modern conveniences. The era-specific decor in the lobby extends to the guest rooms. The staff is exceedingly friendly, and the complimentary evening happy hour is the perfect excuse to relax on the spacious front porch and chat with other guests.

The enormous **Rennaissance Vinoy Resort & Golf Club** (501 5th Ave. NE, 727/822-2785, www.marriott.com, from $369 d) is a Marriott property but has been a St. Pete institution since the 1920s. From the Mediterranean revival-style architecture that looms high over the nearby marina to the ornate and high-ceilinged lobby, the four-diamond facility is steeped in history and luxury. The guest rooms, however, are somewhat less charming as they're done up in business-friendly contemporary styles, which is nice but not exactly in keeping with the hotel's legacy. Multiple on-site restaurants and a private golf course cater to the hotel's steady stream of business meetings.

Clearwater and Clearwater Beach
The **East Shore Resort** (473 East Shore Dr., 888/449-3636, www.eastshoreresort.com, weekly rates from $880) is a charming old-school motel converted into one- and two-bedroom apartment suites. Catering more to anglers than beachgoers (it's just a few minutes' walk from the Clearwater Marina, but four blocks from Clearwater Beach), it's frequently booked solid. Suites are outfitted with TVs and full kitchens, and some even have screened porches. On-site amenities include a private 60-foot fishing pier and a swimming pool. What the East Shore lacks in modern decor, it more than makes up for in personality.

With an unbeatable location, **Palm Pavillion Inn** (18 Bay Esplanade, 800/433-7256, www.palmpavillioninn.com, from $130 d) doesn't have to be too fancy, and it's not. Rooms are on the small side, but they're clean and have all the basics (mini fridges, TVs, in-room safes). For beach lovers, though, the luxury of the room will surely be secondary to the fact that the Palm Pavillion is located just steps from the white sands of Clearwater Beach. In fact, it's located in the parking lot for the public beach. As most of the beachfront real estate in the area is taken up with high-rise resorts and condos, the Palm Pavillion is a rarity indeed.

For a considerably more upscale lodging experience, **Sandpearl** (500 Mandalay Ave., 727/441-2425, www.sandpearl.com, from $359 d) is a more recent addition to the beach. Plush mattresses, iPod docks, flat-screen TVs, and furnishings that reflect a classic Florida elegance make the 200 guest rooms exceptional. Fifty one- and two-bedroom suites occupy the top floor, providing particularly well-heeled guests with water views, private balconies, deluxe full kitchens, and in-room laundry facilities. The resort has two restaurants and a café, as well as a spa and fitness facilities.

St. Pete Beach

The tiny ★ **Inn On The Beach** (1401 Gulf Way, 727/360-8844, www.innonbeach.com, from $145 d) looks more like a cozy apartment building than a hotel, and the individually appointed rooms only add to the homey feel. Five of the accommodations actually are apartments with full kitchens and living rooms. The rest of the rooms are decked out in colorful hues with stylish quirky furnishings. You'll feel more like you're staying in a friend's large spare room than at a hotel and that friend is lucky enough to live right across the street from Pass-A-Grille Beach. The location means the beach's legendary sunsets can be viewed just by wandering out onto the inn's wraparound porch.

For resort accommodations with a little less legacy (and a little easier on the pocketbook), the **Alden Beach Resort** (5900 Gulf Blvd., 727/360-7081, www.aldenbeachresort.com, from $199 d) is an all-suite facility with 143 units, many of which are right on the beach. In either one- or two-bedroom configurations,

all of the suites have full kitchens and living rooms, along with standard amenities. The resort is arranged shotgun style, so staying in the quieter, less-populated area near the front lobby means you'll end up with a hike past two pools, a whirlpool tub, and the tennis courts before you hit the beach. Despite all the facilities on-site, the Alden doesn't tack on a resort fee; many other properties in the area do.

The shell-pink exterior of the ★ **Don CeSar Beach Resort** (3400 Gulf Blvd., 866/728-2206, www.doncesar.com, from $359 d) has become something of a St. Pete Beach icon. In the Jazz Age, notables like F. Scott Fitzgerald and Al Capone visited the "Pink Lady," but by the 1960s, it was a vacant eyesore scheduled for demolition. Rescued and reopened in 1973, the hotel was brought back to its original glory with extensive renovations throughout the 1980s. Unsurprisingly, the classic architecture and sense of history mean that the Don CeSar is high on the list for weddings and romantic vacations. For such luxe accommodations, the resort's kid-friendliness is noteworthy; not only are there extensive daily children's programs at "Camp CeSar," there's an ice cream shop downstairs. All 277 guest rooms have water views, some of the Gulf and some of Boca Ciega Bay. Two penthouse suites are also available.

TRANSPORTATION
Getting There

Most visitors fly into **Tampa International Airport** (TPA, 4100 George J. Bean Pkwy., Tampa, 813/870-8770, www.tampaairport.com), which is only a few miles from downtown Tampa but offers easy access to the St. Petersburg-Clearwater area. The airport is well served by major domestic and international carriers. Several low-cost carriers such as Southwest and Spirit fly into TPA also. It takes about 25 minutes to get to St. Petersburg from the airport.

Although it is closer, the smaller **St. Petersburg/Clearwater International Airport** (PIE, 14700 Terminal Blvd.,

Clearwater, 727/453-7800, www.fly2pie.com) is mainly served by charters and seasonal routes from Canada and the northern Midwest. However, low-cost carrier **Allegiant Air** (www.allegiantair.com) also utilizes the airport for flights to and from 15 cities.

Amtrak's *Silver Star* train arrives and departs daily at the **Amtrak station** (601 N. Nebraska Ave., 813/221-7600, www.amtrak.com) in downtown Tampa; the **Greyhound station** (610 Polk St., 813/229-8588, www.greyhound.com) is also in Tampa.

Getting Around

Navigating the area is fairly simple. Three causeways cross Old Tampa Bay, connecting Tampa to the St. Pete-Clearwater area. The Courtney Campbell Causeway provides a relatively direct route into downtown Clearwater, and the I-275 causeway is the fastest way to central St. Petersburg. Both are close to Tampa International Airport. The Gandy Boulevard Causeway follows a route similar to I-275 but connects to the southern end of Tampa. The beaches are all connected by the north-south Gulf Boulevard (State Rd. 699), which is easily accessible from Clearwater, St. Petersburg, and all points between.

In downtown St. Petersburg, hop on **The Looper** (www.loopertrolley.com, free), a trolley that makes stops near all the major sights about every 15 minutes. The Looper runs 10am-5pm daily, with service until midnight on Friday and Saturday evenings. The **Suncoast Beach Trolley** (727/540-1900, www.psta.net) runs up and down Gulf Boulevard, connecting Clearwater Beach to Pass-A-Grille with eight major stops along the way. Fares are $2.24 (exact change only) and the trolley has pickups every 20-30 minutes from 5:05am-10:10pm.

Crystal River Area

People come to **Crystal River** to fish, play golf, go freshwater diving, or go boating. But all of these things take a backseat to the area's primary attraction: manatees. Even if you don't come to Crystal River to look at a sea cow, chances are you'll end up searching for one during your time here.

SIGHTS

TOP EXPERIENCE

★ Crystal River

In the winter, when waters throughout the state turn chilly, **manatees** converge on the waters in and around the **Crystal River.** Thanks to nearby **freshwater springs,** the water is a constant comfortable temperature, and the clear water makes it a favorite spot for humans who want to observe the giant aquatic mammals. There are several local companies that provide manatee-watching excursions.

Crystal River Manatee Tour and Dive (36 NE 4th St., 888/732-2692, www.manateetouranddive.com, manatee swim tours $57 adults, sightseeing boat tours $42 adults) helps you either to commune with the gentle giants from the top of the water or by snorkeling alongside them. The company conducts tours year-round (some only provide services during the winter) and also offers rentals of canoes and kayaks.

Those rental watercraft will come in handy. While a guided excursion can be illuminating, one of the best ways to enjoy the Crystal River is on your own, and several of the best spots are only accessible by boat. Covering most of King's Bay, **Crystal River National Wildlife Refuge** (1502 SE Kings Bay Dr., 352/563-2088, www.fws.gov/crystalriver) is one such area. Once inside the 46-acre refuge, you'll be in one of the best places on earth to watch manatees go about their business. November-March, several areas are designated as no-entry zones, which means no boating, no diving, no swimming, and no fishing. This allows the manatees to eat and mate in peace for at least part of the year. During that time the area is so flush with sea cows you'd be hard-pressed to not find one in other parts of the wildlife refuge.

The **Three Sisters Springs** is a complex of three bright-blue springs near the wildlife refuge, although all the surrounding land is privately owned. The best place to put in a boat is at **Hunters Spring Park** (end of NE 1st Ave.). It's a popular public swimming area. From Hunters Spring, you're about 30 minutes' paddle from Three Sisters. The entryway to the springs is blocked by concrete pillars that prevent boats from going in; so, you'll need to take a canoe or kayak to that point and then swim in. Even if there are no manatees around, the setting is gorgeous and the snorkeling is outstanding.

Homosassa Springs

Homosassa Springs is a small town about 15 minutes south of Crystal River. It is known for the **Homosassa Springs Wildlife State Park** (4150 Suncoast Blvd., 352/628-5343, www.floridastateparks.org, 9:30am-5:30pm daily, ticket counter for boat rides 9:30am-4pm). Unlike many other natural state parks, the facilities here started as a full-fledged tourist attraction. Nature's Giant Fish Bowl opened in the 1940s, giving visitors a look at the vast underwater ecosystem. The park went through several owners and incarnations before being bought in 1984 by Citrus County and then turned into a state wildlife park in 1989. Although the environmental and ecological aspects of the park are amplified these days, the big draw is still the opportunity to catch a glimpse of fish, turtles, birds, and manatees in and around the 45-foot-deep spring. Boats depart regularly from the visitors center to viewing areas. While the experience at Homosassa Springs feels more like a zoo visit than a nature excursion, this giant fish bowl still thrills.

Weeki Wachee Springs State Park

One of the oldest and most iconic roadside attractions in Florida, **Weeki Wachee Springs State Park** (State Rd. 50 at US-19, 352/592-5656, www.weekiwachee.com, 10am-4pm daily July-Aug., hours and days vary in winter, $13 adults, $8 children) is where the mermaids have lived since 1947. The famous mermaid

Crystal River National Wildlife Refuge

shows still happen three times a day, and for some, watching a bikini-clad swimmer drink a bottle of Coke still provides a thrill. Most park visitors come to enjoy Buccaneer Bay, a water park that was added in an effort to boost attendance. Since the arrival of the interstate system—and to a greater degree, Walt Disney World—the park has struggled with attendance. In November 2008, Weeki Wachee was turned into a Florida state park, mermaid shows and all.

SPORTS AND RECREATION

If neither the mermaids nor the water slides are of interest, **Weeki Wachee Canoe & Kayak Rental** (State Rd. 50 at US-19, 352/597-0360, www.paddlingadventures. com, 9am-noon Mon.-Fri., 9am-11am Sat.-Sun.) is located at the back end of the parking lot to Weeki Wachee Springs. The convenient location allows boaters to put in close to the nearby springs. In the winter, the river is good manatee-watching territory.

Golfers in the area head straight to the **Plantation at Crystal River** (9301 W. Fort Island Tr., Crystal River, 352/795-4211, www. plantationinn.com), which has a 9-hole par-33 course and an 18-hole par-72 course.

Apollo Deep Sea Fishing (1340 NW 20th Ave., Crystal River, 352/795-3757, www. apollodeepseafishing.com) operates a 60-foot boat into the Gulf of Mexico for anglers looking for grouper and sea bass. Captain Don Chancey pilots a smaller 22-foot craft for **Flat Chance Charters** (groups meet at 5300 S. Cherokee Way, Homosassa, 352/303-9399) that allows for limited offshore runs and flats fishing.

FOOD

With a great waterfront location overlooking King's Bay, the food at **Cracker's Bar & Grill** (502 NW 6th St., Crystal River, 352/795-3999, www.crackersbarandgrill.com, 11am-11pm daily, $6-14) doesn't need to be exceptional. Standard fried-seafood plates are the name of the game, along with burgers and sandwiches. An expansive outside deck has its own bar and features live music on the weekends.

At **Grannie's** (1712 SE US-19, Crystal River, 352/795-8884, 5am-8pm daily, $3-7), some of the kindest waiters around serve gigantic portions of country breakfast all day long, with a decent selection of sandwiches available for lunch and dinner. Daily specials vary but are dependably of the Southern comfort-food variety.

the Plantation at Crystal River

For a slightly more upscale experience in Crystal River's tiny downtown area, **Vintage on 5th** (114 NE 5th St, 352/794-0004, 5pm-9pm Tues.-Thurs., 5pm-10pm Fri.-Sat., from $18) serves up classic American fare—with an emphasis on Southern dishes and fresh seafood—in a renovated church originally built in 1940. The atmosphere here is incredible, whether you're eating in the cozy dining room or al fresco on the covered porch, and the food—ranging from decadent chèvre-drenched mac and cheese or shrimp and grits to steak, lamb, and fish dishes—is consistently excellent, and often locally sourced.

ACCOMMODATIONS

Rooms at the ★ **Plantation at Crystal River** (9301 W. Fort Island Tr., Crystal River, 352/795-4211, www.plantationinn.com, from $184 d) are comfortable and contemporary, if character free, which is surprising given the antebellum-looking architecture of the main building. Guests are primarily concerned with hitting the Plantation's golf links. A beautiful pool deck overlooks one of the inlets to King's Bay, with manatees frequently trundling past during the winter. The hotel has meeting facilities and two bars, making it popular for business retreats.

The **Kings Bay Lodge** (506 NW 1st Ave., Crystal River, 352/795-2850, www.kingsbay-lodgefla.com, from $70 d) isn't much more than a motel, but it's right on the water with its own boat dock and fish-cleaning facilities. Guest rooms are clean and fully equipped mini suites with full kitchens. The friendly owners are often on the premises.

GETTING THERE

Crystal River is about 90 miles (1.5 hours' drive) from either downtown Tampa (via US-19/98) or downtown Orlando (via State Rd. 44). Visitors typically drive from either of those locales as there is no nearby airport. Public transportation is nonexistent, but if you need a taxi, try **Wayne's Taxi** (352/564-8294).

Homosassa and Homosassa Springs are about 10 miles south of Crystal River via US-19/98. Weeki Wachee is another 20 miles south of Homosassa Springs on US-19/98.

South Gulf Coast

A seemingly infinite selection of alluring white-sand beaches merges into the calm, blue waters of the Gulf of Mexico. Welcome to the Paradise Coast, offering pleasures unlike anywhere else in Florida.

You won't find theme-park attractions, spring-break bacchanalia, glitz, or glamour here. And that's what makes it so great. Even the little-known beaches here are fantastic, providing remote pastoral beauty, in-city access, or—amazingly—a combination of the two. The secret islands of Sanibel and Captiva are not so secret anymore. The bigger names like Siesta Key and Cayo Costa State Park routinely rank among the top choices of experts with the envious task of ranking beaches for awesomeness.

But the beaches are just the beginning. There are vast, open wildernesses here, ranging from rivers and forests ripe for exploration to undeveloped nature preserves ideal for bird-watching and hiking.

The gateways to the Paradise Coast offer their own attractions. Sarasota is an intimate city with a magnetism that makes all visitors potential future residents. It sustains a flourishing arts community of local creatives, moneyed snowbirds, and casual aficionados. Nearby, Naples similarly lays claim to a vibrant arts calendar and row of galleries that inspire envy in cities of similar size, as well as quirkier activities that will surprise you (swamp buggy races, anyone?).

PLANNING YOUR TIME

It's possible to take in the highlights of the south Gulf coast over the course of a long weekend. If sightseeing is your primary goal, make your first home base in or near downtown Sarasota, as most of the area's best attractions are nearby. Plan on devoting at least an entire day to exploring, with another full day devoted to beach going.

On your third day, head for the Fort Myers area. If you want a beach vacation with a couple of sights thrown in, make Fort Myers Beach your base of operations. If you want more emphasis on sightseeing, with a little beach time, pick a room near downtown Fort

---

Previous: Water abounds on the South Gulf Coast; J.N. "Ding" Darling National Wildlife Refuge on Sanibel Island. **Above:** Thomas Edison was an integral part of Fort Myers' history.

Look for ★ to find recommended
sights, activities, dining, and lodging.

Highlights

★ **Marie Selby Botanical Gardens:** This pastoral oasis' compact size and the smart curation of its impressive display of flora make exploration a breeze (page 360).

★ **Mote Marine Laboratory and Aquarium:** This research and conservation facility encourages visitors to engage with the vibrant Gulf-coastal ecosystem and the wide variety of marine life that calls it home (page 361).

★ **John and Mable Ringling Museum of Art:** John Ringling had an eye for fine art. The art museum on the grounds of his mansion has one of the best-curated collections of masterworks in the state (page 361).

★ **Siesta Key:** These wide beaches boast a combination of soft, snow-white sand, crystal-blue waters, and gentle wave action that's perfect for families with small kids and inveterate snorkelers (page 364).

★ **Edison & Ford Winter Estates:** Thomas Edison was so taken by Fort Myers that he not only built a large winter residence here, but also convinced his friend Henry Ford to do the same (page 383).

★ **Lovers Key State Park:** This state park has a secretive feel, with secluded and quiet beaches, nature trails, and out-of-the-way canoe and kayak opportunities (page 386).

★ **Cayo Costa State Park:** Accessible only by boat, this state park is home to nine miles of beautiful and peaceful white-sand beaches, five miles of hiking trails—and not much else (page 386).

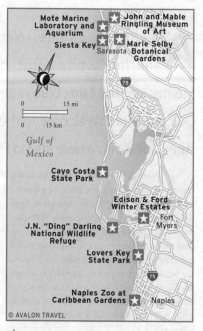
© AVALON TRAVEL

★ **J. N. "Ding" Darling National Wildlife Refuge:** Named after one of the early 20th century's most notable political cartoonists, the refuge has some of the best bird-watching in the entire state of Florida (page 397).

★ **Naples Zoo at Caribbean Gardens:** No other zoo in Florida is as beautiful and welcoming. The calm, lushly landscaped grounds are a joy to walk through (page 407).

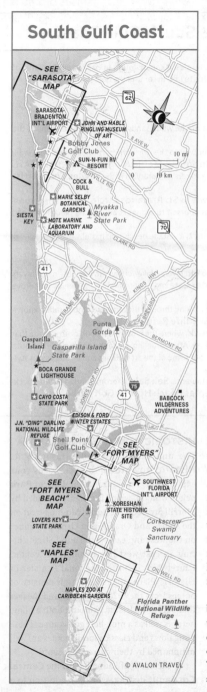

South Gulf Coast

Myers, which puts you less than a half hour away from the beaches and much closer to any of the sights in the area.

Alternately, you can spend a long weekend in the Naples area, particularly if you're continuing on to the Everglades.

Sarasota

The communities that surround Sarasota Bay are some of the most interesting places in Florida. There's a stunning amount of ecological diversity on display here, including award-winning white-sand beaches, dense flatwood forests, the beautiful Myakka River, and, of course, the waters of Sarasota Bay itself.

Although the **Sarasota** area doesn't boast the same sort of multicultural vibe as some of Florida's bigger cities, the confluence of college students, moneyed yuppies, growing families, and art-loving retirees makes for an interesting mix indeed.

The artistic bent of this region is most pronounced in Sarasota, which is by no means a big city. The Ringling College of Art & Design and the New College of Florida (the state's public honors college) draw a youthful crowd of students interested in the arts (both performing and fine). Residents here are enthusiastic patrons of the arts: Just check out the crowds at the impressive Ringling Museum of Art or at any local gallery opening. Even the ritzy shopping district of St. Armands Circle is punctuated by classical statues extolling the virtues of creativity and beauty. This love of the arts, combined with the abundant natural beauty of the area, ensures that visitors are likely to make Sarasota a repeat destination on future travels.

And then there are the beaches. Siesta Key's beaches are a work of art unto themselves, routinely awarded "best beach" status by whatever lucky judge it is that gets to make such designations. It's easy to understand why: The wide beaches boast soft, white sand that seamlessly merges into calm, crystal-blue

Two Days Along the South Gulf Coast

More than 100 miles separate Sarasota and Naples. It can be tough to pack in all the sights of this chapter into just two days, but it is possible to take in some of the best the area has to offer if you're willing to sacrifice total relaxation.

DAY 1

Start your morning by soaking up some rays on the white sands of **Siesta Beach,** one of the best beaches in the United States.

After a morning on the beach, make your way to the northern part of Sarasota for a walk through the grounds and galleries of the **John and Mable Ringling Museum of Art.** Then head toward downtown for more local and contemporary art at the **Towles Court Artist Colony.**

It's a quick drive over the Ringling Causeway to **St. Armands Circle,** where, after browsing the boutiques and shops, you can treat yourself to dinner at an upscale place like **Café L'Europe.**

Plan on crashing at the **Gulf Beach Resort,** a vintage beachfront motel.

DAY 2

Wake up early the next day for a drive south to Fort Myers. Make your way to downtown Fort Myers and see the historic **Edison & Ford Winter Estates** to get a feel for the genius that drove these two American industrial titans.

Spend a couple of hours on Sanibel Island walking through the bird-watching paradise known as the **J. N. "Ding" Darling National Wildlife Refuge.**

Grab a bite and a beer at **The Mucky Duck,** where the high-quality pub grub is made that much better by the gorgeous waterfront views. After refueling, make the one-hour drive south to Naples, where you'll still be able to check out some of the art galleries and boutiques on stylish **5th Avenue.**

Dinner at one of Naples's best seafood restaurants, **Sea Salt,** is recommended before checking in for the night at the luxurious **The Naples Beach Hotel & Golf Club.**

---

waters that are largely unaffected by tidal action (this is the Gulf, after all). This beauty extends to the beaches on Longboat Key and Anna Maria Island, as well, making the area around Sarasota one of the best in the state for beachgoers.

SIGHTS
Downtown and Bayfront

The sights of Sarasota are somewhat far-flung, but the downtown area offers quite a number of interesting spots to visit. The city's compact and comfortable downtown has history, arts, and beautiful scenery, as well as a few landmark attractions.

HISTORIC DOWNTOWN SARASOTA

The unheralded heart of Sarasota is its **Historic Downtown** district. Focus your explorations on areas like the **Laurel Park** neighborhood, which is roughly bounded by Morrill Street on the north, Mound Street on the south, and Orange and Osprey Avenues on the west and east, with Laurel Street cutting an east/west line through the center. Laurel Park is on the National Register of Historic Places due to the high density of homes from the 1920s and 1930s and the fact that Sarasota's first mayor built both a home here, as well as a nine-hole golf course. These bungalows and classic Florida homes are well maintained by their current residents.

To the north of Laurel Park is the **Central Cocoanut** district, which, in addition to a

Sarasota

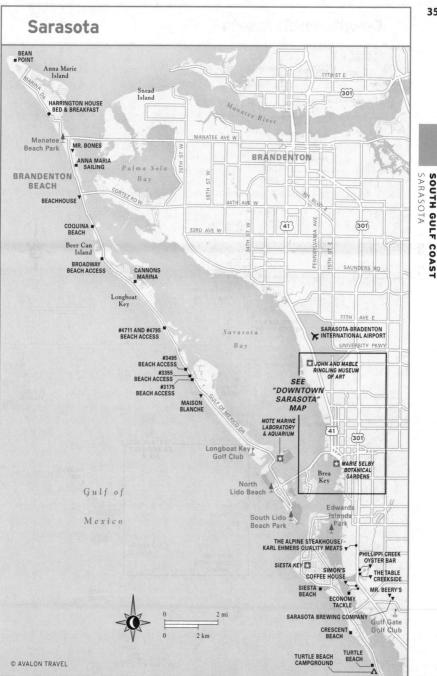

BEAN
POINT

Anna Marie
Island

Snead
Island

17TH ST E

301

Manatee River

HARRINGTON HOUSE
BED & BREAKFAST

MANATEE AVE W

BRANDENTON

Manatee
Beach Park

MR. BONES

ANNA MARIA
SAILING

Palma Sola
Bay

75TH ST W

59TH ST W

BRANDENTON
BEACH

CORTEZ RD W

44TH AVE W

301 BLVD E

15TH ST E

BEACHHOUSE

53RD AVE W

41

301

COQUINA
BEACH

34TH ST W

PENNSYLVANIA AVE

SAUNDERS RD

Beer Can
Island

BROADWAY
BEACH ACCESS

CANNONS
MARINA

Longboat
Key

77TH AVE E

SARASOTA-BRADENTON
INTERNATIONAL AIRPORT

UNIVERSITY PKWY

#4711 AND #4795
BEACH ACCESS

Sarasota
Bay

JOHN AND MABLE
RINGLING MUSEUM
OF ART

#3495
BEACH ACCESS

#3355
BEACH ACCESS

#3175
BEACH ACCESS

SEE
"DOWNTOWN
SARASOTA"
MAP

MAISON
BLANCHE

GULF OF MEXICO DR

MOTE MARINE
LABORATORY
& AQUARIUM

41

301

Longboat Key
Golf Club

MARIE SELBY
BOTANICAL
GARDENS

North
Lido Beach

Brea
Key

Gulf of

Mexico

South Lido
Beach Park

Edwards
Islands
Park

THE ALPINE STEAKHOUSE/
KARL EHMERS QUALITY MEATS

PHILLIPPI CREEK
OYSTER BAR

SIESTA KEY

SIMON'S
COFFEE HOUSE

THE TABLE
CREEKSIDE

SIESTA
BEACH

MR. BEERY'S

ECONOMY
TACKLE

SARASOTA BREWING COMPANY

Gulf Gate
Golf Club

CRESCENT
BEACH

0   2 mi

0   2 km

TURTLE BEACH
CAMPGROUND

TURTLE
BEACH

© AVALON TRAVEL

Downtown Sarasota

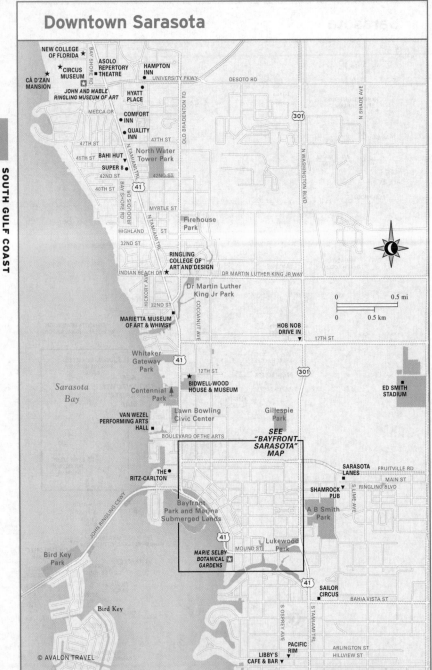

NEW COLLEGE OF FLORIDA ★

★ CIRCUS MUSEUM

ASOLO REPERTORY THEATRE

HAMPTON INN

CÀ D'ZAN MANSION ★

JOHN AND MABLE RINGLING MUSEUM OF ART

HYATT PLACE

UNIVERSITY PKWY

DESOTO RD

N SHADE AVE

BAY SHORE RD

OLD BRADENTON RD

301

MECCA DR

COMFORT INN

QUALITY INN

47TH ST

47TH ST

N WASHINGTON BLVD

45TH ST

BAHI HUT

SUPER 8

North Water Tower Park

42ND ST

42ND ST

BAY SHORE RD

N TAMIAMI TRL

41

40TH ST

MYRTLE ST

Firehouse Park

HIGHLAND

32ND ST

RINGLING COLLEGE OF ART AND DESIGN

INDIAN BEACH DR ★

HICKORY AVE

Dr Martin Luther King Jr Way

Dr Martin Luther King Jr Park

0   0.5 mi

0   0.5 km

22ND ST

MARIETTA MUSEUM OF ART & WHIMSY

COCOANUT AVE

HOB NOB DRIVE IN

17TH ST

Whitaker Gateway Park

41

12TH ST

Sarasota Bay

Centennial Park

BIDWELL-WOOD HOUSE & MUSEUM

ED SMITH STADIUM

301

VAN WEZEL PERFORMING ARTS HALL

Lawn Bowling Civic Center

Gillespie Park

BOULEVARD OF THE ARTS

SEE "BAYFRONT SARASOTA" MAP

THE RITZ-CARLTON

SARASOTA LANES

FRUITVILLE RD

MAIN ST

RINGLING BLVD

SHAMROCK PUB

S LIME AVE

Bayfront Park and Marina Submerged Lands

JOHN RINGLING CSWY

A B Smith Park

Bird Key Park

41

MARIE SELBY BOTANICAL GARDENS

Lukewood Park

MOUND ST

Bird Key

41

SAILOR CIRCUS

BAHIA VISTA ST

S OSPREY AVE

S TAMIAMI TRL

PACIFIC RIM

ARLINGTON ST

HILLVIEW ST

LIBBY'S CAFE & BAR

© AVALON TRAVEL

number of smaller, vintage residences from the early 20th century, is home to the 1882 **Bidwell-Wood House & Museum** (Pioneer Park, 1266 12th St., 10am-2pm Mon.-Fri., free), the oldest residence in Sarasota County, and the 1901 **Crocker Memorial Church** (Pioneer Park, 1266 12th St., 10am-2pm Mon.-Fri., free). Both of these are maintained and operated for the public by the **Historical Society of Sarasota County** (941/364-9076, www.hsosc.com).

TOWLES COURT ARTIST COLONY

One of the highlights of Sarasota's downtown area is the **Towles Court Artist Colony** (Adams Lane, between S. Links Ave. and Washington Blvd., 941/374-1988, www.towlescourt.com, most galleries open noon-4pm Tues.-Sun.). Originally part of the golf course that Sarasota's first mayor built in Laurel Park, the property was purchased in the 1920s by William B. Towles and turned into a residential district. Many of the bungalows from that era have been transformed into galleries, studios, and restaurants. At the heart of Towles are the many art establishments, like the **Elizabeth Stevens Gallery** and **Expressive Arts.** Additionally, there are salons, spas, and massage therapists, which help make it easy to while away an entire day on this beautiful property. On the third Friday of every month, the district holds an evening art walk, with live music, drinks, and vendors holding forth with their wares. With most of the establishments reliably open noon-4pm, afternoons are the best time to visit.

SARASOTA BAYFRONT

The **Sarasota Bayfront** (at Sunset Dr. and John Ringling Blvd.) is a great place to acclimate yourself to Sarasota's laid-back atmosphere. Watch the boats come in and out of the marina, and gawk at the downtown skyline. The calming waters of Sarasota Bay provide a great canvas for some spectacular sunsets. During the day, kids splash around in the playground fountains. For those brimming over with energy, the park also offers a running/walking trail with exercise way stations. Being Sarasota, those trails are also decorated with stunning modern sculptures. And no visit to this park would be complete without a photo op in front of J. Seward Johnson's three-story-high *Unconditional Surrender* (known more commonly as *The Kiss*), a romantic homage to the end of World War II.

Towles Court Artist Colony

Bayfront Sarasota

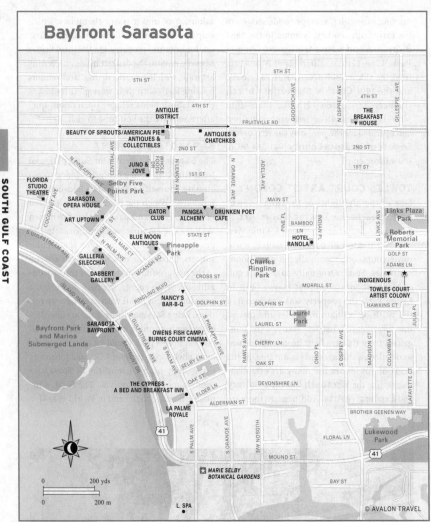

★ MARIE SELBY BOTANICAL GARDENS

Just a couple of blocks away from the Bayfront area and downtown are the **Marie Selby Botanical Gardens** (811 S. Palm Ave., 941/366-5731, www.selby.org, 10am-5pm daily, $25 adults, $15 children, children 5 and under free). This beautiful, 13-acre estate is an urban oasis. The garden houses 20,000 plants, including over 6,000 orchids, in its eight greenhouses, as well as scores of tropical plants lining the garden pathways. There's an emphasis on tropical plants, but there are lots of Asian influences here too. The plants are curated and arranged smartly. However, due to limited space, there are some incongruous areas nestled directly next to one another.

There is a good bit of space given over to the massive banyan trees. Only once you're up close can you truly understand how massive these twisted giants are. Your kids will take to them like monkeys, which is perfectly acceptable.

The first floor of the former Selby mansion is now a small museum with art exhibits, and there's a great little café that overlooks the main lawn, which serves coffee, ice cream, sandwiches, salads, beer, and wine. The Marie Selby hosts events throughout the year, so make sure to check the calendar for a current listing of events.

★ Mote Marine Laboratory and Aquarium

The **Mote Marine Laboratory and Aquarium** (1600 Ken Thompson Pkwy., 941/388-1720, www.mote.org, 10am-5pm daily, $20 adults, $15 children, children 3 and under free) takes up almost the entirety of tiny City Island, out between Lido Key and Longboat Key. Inside the facility, which couples as an open-to-the-public component with a working research operation, there are various marine habitats, including an enormous, 135,000-gallon saltwater shark tank, touch pools, a manatee exhibit, and the preserved 25-foot-long carcass of a giant squid. The most recent addition to the Mote is undoubtedly the cutest: Penguin Island, home to six black-footed penguins. The seabirds are

precocious and have taken quite well to their new home in Florida. There are some fantastic and informative displays at the Mote. Keep in mind, though, that the aquarium is just the public face of the Mote Marine Laboratory's research and conservation mission, so perhaps consider your ticket price to be a donation to some incredibly important work.

★ John and Mable Ringling Museum of Art

There are three museums on the grounds of the **John and Mable Ringling Museum of Art** (5401 Bay Shore Rd., 941/359-5700, www.ringling.org, 10am-5pm Fri.-Wed., 10am-8pm Thurs., $25 adults, $23 seniors, $5 children, children 5 and under free), and they couldn't be any more different. The primary attraction is John Ringling's impressive collection of masterworks in the massive, pink-tinted Museum of Art itself. Originals by El Greco, Diego Velázquez, Titian, Peter Paul Rubens, and many more are displayed in a gorgeous (if overwhelming) environment meant to evoke Florence's Uffizi Gallery. There are several re-creations of classic Italian fountains and sculptures in the courtyard, including Michelangelo's *David*. The re-creations extend beyond the artwork, though; two of

Marie Selby Botanical Gardens

the galleries in the museum—a salon and a library—are entire rooms purchased by Ringling from the Astor mansion in 1926. But the museum is definitely not all reproductions and recreations. In fact, it's the most active art gallery on the Gulf Coast. The curators keep most of the collections current, with new and notable exhibits rotating regularly. It's a fantastic art museum, well worth a day's visit.

John Ringling was, of course, the Circus King, so the collection of memorabilia at the **Circus Museum** (5401 Bay Shore Rd., 941/359-5700, www.ringling.org, 10am-5pm Fri.-Wed., 10am-8pm Thurs., admission included with Ringling Museum of Art admission) is both authentic and extensive. Everything from Ringling's private rail car to costumes, sketches, clown masks, and giant roller skates is on display. Interestingly, the most vital and engaging part of the Circus Museum isn't the actual memorabilia, but instead the massive scale model of a typical circus setup. The model is meticulous and incredibly detailed, including not just the three rings, menagerie, and sideshow, but also the performers' quarters, food-prep areas, and even the public bathrooms. It's impressive how extensive and massive the circus's operations were. This model does a great job of explaining how all of these elements come together for a single day's performance.

Built in 1926, **Ca' d'Zan Mansion** (5401 Bay Shore Rd., 941/359-5700, www.ringling. org, 10am-5pm daily, admission included with Ringling Museum of Art admission) is an example of Gilded Age immensity. John and Mable Ringling's Venetian Gothic mansion has 56 rooms spread across 36,000 square feet, all adorned in marble, gold, dark woods, and crystal. While Ringling surely felt that adding acres of gold leaf and antiques by the ton to this house would somehow endear him to the upper class, looking at the mansion today, one can only be struck by just how little restraint went into it. A mish-mash of global styles jams Morocco, Belle Epoque Paris, Singapore sitting room, and baroque filigree into the decor in a thoroughly ostentatious way that would have sparked revolt from his elephant trainers then and would probably spark revulsion today in anyone who has the slightest tendency toward minimalism. Nonetheless, it must be seen to be believed. Do not miss walking through this house.

BEACHES

When visitors talk about "the beach" in Sarasota, they're talking about the famous

the John and Mable Ringling Museum of Art

The Ringling Brothers

The seven sons of Heinrich and Marie Ringling are, after the Jackson 5, perhaps the most popular siblings in American pop culture history. The small circus they started in Baraboo, Wisconsin, in 1884 eventually became one of the two most popular circuses touring the country. With the 1907 purchase of the other most popular circus (the Barnum & Bailey Circus), it turned into a virtual three-ring monopoly. The circus's original winter home was in Bridgeport, Connecticut, but Sarasota, Florida, has been the cold-weather respite for the circus's animals, clowns, and equipment since the 1920s, a move inspired both by a tragic circus fire in Bridgeport, as well as the fact that John and some of his brothers had been vacationing in the area.

As the "advance man" for the circus, John Ringling was responsible for a number of the promotional gambits that made the circus so successful. His older brother Charles worked as the operations manager, keeping the circus running while it was on the road. These two had the most impact on Sarasota. Ringling Boulevard is named after Charles, who used his circus-derived wealth to invest in development and infrastructure projects throughout Sarasota. John wound up as the sole Ringling operating the circus after his six brothers died.

As you can imagine, one man running the nation's most popular circus amassed quite a bit of wealth. Though his **Ca' d'Zan Mansion** is the most obviously ostentatious display of his wealth, Ringling was also convinced that art was a mark of true civilization. With the stunning galleries at the **John and Mable Ringling Museum of Art** and his cofounding of what is now known as the **Ringling College of Art & Design,** John Ringling's impact on Sarasota is still felt to this day, although the legendary circus that bore his name is no longer around.

stretches of white sand on nearby Siesta Key. Those **beaches** are consistently ranked at the top of "best beach" lists, and for good reason. However, for folks who are close to central Sarasota, the beaches on Lido Key (just a five-minute drive from downtown across the gorgeous John Ringling Causeway) are "the beach." The beaches on Lido Key aren't just convenient second-stringers, either. They're broad, calm, and beautiful, and, thanks to the relatively restricted parking options on Lido Key, they're often less crowded than Siesta Key beaches. (That doesn't mean that they're empty.) Heading out on to the barrier islands and points northward, the beach-village vibe of Anna Maria Island and Longboat Key makes these beaches ideal long-term vacation spots.

Lido Key

Lido Beach Park (400 Ben Franklin Dr., sunrise-sunset daily, free parking) is the main beach destination on Lido Key, and the 400-space parking lot is a testament to that. Even though a summer Saturday often sees the lot filled to capacity before lunch, the beach itself manages to maintain a sense of calm, mainly because it's so huge. This is a people-watching beach, not a silence-and-solitude beach. The abundant facilities, which include a playground, showers, restrooms, a swimming pool, and (surprisingly tasty) concessions, are all optimized for big crowds.

Due to its immediate proximity to the shopping district of St. Armands Circle, parking at **North Lido Beach** (1 John Ringling Blvd., sunrise-sunset daily, parking $2/hour) can be difficult. There's a small lot with about 25 spaces and street-side parking as well (you'll pay at a meter station for any of these). All the parking spots fill up fairly early in the day. Once you actually get the car parked and get to the beach, you'll find the wide stretch of shell-filled sand is expansive enough that even a big crowd here never feels overwhelming. The farther north you walk, the less crowded it gets. (The northernmost points of North Lido Beach used to be popular nude sunbathing spots, however, nudity on the beach is illegal now.) Dunes and trees give the beach a

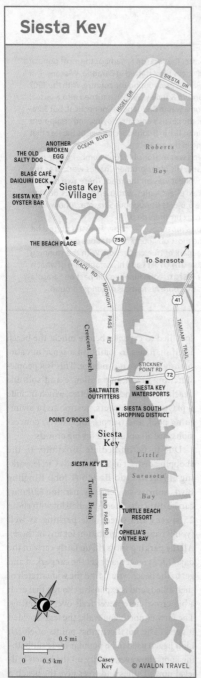

Siesta Key

wild and unspoiled feel, and the lack of facilities seems completely appropriate.

South Lido Beach Park (100 Taft Dr., sunrise-sunset daily, free parking) splits the difference between the wild solitude of North Lido and the massive crowds of Lido Beach Park. There are a few facilities here: restrooms, picnic tables, and a playground. The shady pine trees and walking trails provide ample opportunities for some alone time. The park is positioned at the lower tip of the key and is surrounded by four different bodies of water. The Gulf beach is the largest part. But boaters can dip their canoe or kayak into the waters of Sarasota Bay. Rip currents can be an issue here for swimmers, so use caution.

★ Siesta Key

The biggest issue with the marvelous beaches on **Siesta Key** is getting here. There are numerous beach access points, however, very few of them have dedicated parking. The main beach park has an epically huge parking lot and it often fills up fairly early on summer days and on almost every sunset-worthy evening. Still, since most visitors to Siesta Key are likely staying on the island, it's worth noting that the island is eminently walkable, and even if you're not staying right on the water, it's usually a none too challenging hike to get you and your stuff onto the sand.

The main beach here is **Siesta Beach** (948 Beach Rd., sunrise-sunset daily, free). Here, you'll find copious free public parking, bathroom and shower facilities, concessions, and lots and lots of people. Amazingly, the parking lot can feel like cars are stacked on top of one another, and the beach itself somehow still feels spacious. That wide-open beach vista is one of the biggest appeals of Siesta Key: The soft, white sand stretches out in all directions, providing ample space for all comers.

That said, those looking for a *little* more quietude might want to hit **Turtle Beach** (8918 Midnight Pass Rd., sunrise-sunset daily, free). It's still a pretty popular destination, thanks to the fact that it has a free public parking lot. But the lot is small, there are no lifeguards, and the somewhat rougher and narrower beach (and its out-of-the-way location on the south part of the island) self imposes its own form of population control.

A great destination for snorkelers and divers is **Crescent Beach** (at the western end of Point of Rocks Rd., sunrise-sunset daily, free). Parking is a living nightmare: you're restricted to a tiny handful of unmarked roadside spots; everything else in this residential neighborhood is emblazoned with No Parking signs. Your best bet is to make your way here on foot or by bike. (Be respectful of the folks who actually live here.) Once you make it to the beach, which is expansive and smooth, snorkelers should head to the southernmost tip. That's the titular "point of rocks," an outcropping of coral formations that's home to a wide variety of fish and marine life. The water here is gentle and easy to navigate, making it a prime destination for those who want to explore beneath the surface.

Longboat Key

The parking and public access issue on **Longboat Key** is almost hilariously frustrating. There are nearly a dozen public access points, but they're poorly marked and parking is limited to a small handful of spaces (and they're usually on the opposite side of the road from the actual beach). Do not park along the road. On the northern side of the island, the **Broadway** (100 Broadway St., Longboat Key) beach access provides the most parking and the easiest access, providing a boardwalk over the dunes to the waterfront. The beach itself here is very nice, if a bit crowded.

Almost all of the other public beach accesses are numbered to correspond with their addresses on Gulf of Mexico Drive. (Numbers increase going south to north.) On-site parking is available for **#3175** and **#3355,** and the accesses at **#3495, #4711,** and **#4795** offer on-site parking for people with disabilities as well. Please keep in mind that, although these beaches offer parking, it is very limited. Nonetheless, if you get here early enough to snag a spot, you'll be rewarded with a beach that's somewhat wilder than the ones found elsewhere in the area. Although the famed white sand and calm blue waters are in abundance, these are dune beaches, bounded by tall lines of sea oats that provide something of a barrier between you and the traffic whizzing by on the road.

Also on the north part of Longboat Key—right before you cross the bridge onto Anna Maria Island—is **Beer Can Island**

Siesta Beach is one of the best in Florida.

(sunrise-sunset daily, free). Not so much an actual island than an isolated spit of gorgeous white sand and swaying pine trees, Beer Can Island is a popular party spot for boaters, and is only accessible by boat.

Anna Maria Island

Beach access on **Anna Maria Island,** especially in the town of Bradenton Beach, is a breeze. Almost as soon as you cross the bridge from Longboat onto Anna Maria, you'll be greeted by the sight of the massive parking lot that serves **Coquina Beach** (sunrise-sunset daily, free). This lot also provides parking for the many anglers that come to the site to fish on the bayside. So, even if the lot seems crowded, the beautiful Gulf-side beach is often blissfully low density. There are lifeguards here, a small concession stand, and bathroom/shower facilities.

Coquina Beach segues somewhat seamlessly into the more northerly **Cortez Beach** (sunrise-sunset daily, free), which doesn't provide such a singularly large parking area, but instead offers multiple access points with generous and easily found lots. Both beaches are a little rougher than some of the other Gulf beaches. The sand is packed tighter and doesn't have the same "snowdrift" quality of

the beaches on Siesta Key and Longboat Key. Regardless, the skyscraping pine trees and expansive swaths of sand provide a spectacular backdrop.

Getting to the beach is a little tougher in the towns of Anna Maria and Holmes Beach due to the increased number of residences that line the Gulf. **Manatee Beach Park** (400 State Rd. 64, Holmes Beach, Anna Maria Island, sunrise-sunset daily, free) is popular and easily accessed. It can get very crowded, thanks to its copious amenities. There are bathrooms and showers, of course, but there's also a playground, a café and gift shop, and lots of picnicking space.

For something far more isolated, head to the very northern end of Anna Maria Island, where **Bean Point** (N. Shore Dr., Anna Maria Island, sunrise-sunset daily, free) awaits you. There is marked foot access at Fern Street and Gladiolus Street, and only limited roadside parking available. Bean Point marks the intersection of Tampa Bay and the Gulf of Mexico. Normally such a confluence of bodies of water would mean a tempestuous and rip-current-prone area, but the waters of Bean Point are remarkably calm, especially close to the shore. The sands are dense with shells, and the rough foliage of the dunes provides plenty of nesting

The beaches on Longboat Key are quiet and somewhat challenging to access.

opportunities for birds and other small wildlife. It's a beautiful and calm beach spot.

ENTERTAINMENT AND EVENTS
Nightlife

Downtown, the **Gator Club** (1490 Main St., 941/366-5969, www.thegatorclub.com, 4pm-2am daily, cover charge varies) is loved by the cover-band-and-cosmos set. The atmosphere is friendly and the vintage brick building that the club calls home provides its own ambiance. **Pangea Alchemy Lab** (1564 Main St., 941/953-7111, www.pangealounge.com, 4pm-2am daily, no cover) is stylish and unique but still relatively intimate. Check out the pharmacological-looking "liquid spice cabinet" that the bar uses to concoct its one-of-a-kind drinks. Just need a cool place to grab a pint downtown? Head for **Shamrock Pub** (2257 Ringling Blvd., 941/952-1730, www.shamrocksarasota.com, 3pm-2am daily, no cover) and check out its incredible beer selection.

The environment at **Sarasota Lanes** (2250 Fruitville Rd., 941/955-7629, www.sarasotalanes.com, 9:30am-midnight Mon.-Thurs., 9:30am-1am Fri.-Sat., 9:30am-9pm Sun., games from $3.50) is down-to-earth. Even if bowling isn't your preferred evening recreation, you should still check in here, as this is one of the most fun places to catch some of the area's good local bands.

A few miles south of downtown, and quite close to Siesta Key, is Gulf Gate, one of Sarasota's more concentrated dining and drinking areas. There is a wide variety of restaurants and bars here. One of the best spots is **Sarasota Brewing Company** (6607 Gateway Ave., 941/925-2337, http://sarasotabrewing.com, 11am-midnight daily, no cover), worth stopping by for its selection of handcrafted beers. There are usually a half dozen of the brewpub's beers on tap, and they're all quite good. However, true hop fans will want to head straight for **Mr. Beery's** (2645 Mall Dr., 941/343-2854, http://mrbeeryssrq.com, 3pm-1am daily), which offers one of the best beer selections on the Gulf Coast. Mr. Beery's

is staffed by a group of knowledgeable beer nerds who will enthusiastically guide you through their deep (and often-changing) menu. Make sure to avail yourself of the built-in-the-bar "Randall," which allows them to infuse your draft beer with various complementary flavors, or just more hops.

The **Bahi Hut** (4675 N. Tamiami Trail, 941/355-5141, www.goldenhostresort.com, 4:30pm-2am daily, no cover), located in (dangerously) close proximity to New College and the Ringling College of Art & Design, serves insanely, ridiculously, incredibly potent drinks. I would add more adjectives, but I really can't do much better than the "jet fuel" analogy many patrons make. This place has been slinging super-strong drinks for nearly 60 years, and has persisted in its location while the fortunes of the Tamiami Trail have gone through cycles of boom and bust. Accordingly, the staff here has a vintage attitude toward bar culture: Drink as many hair-burning drinks as you please, but whatever you do, don't use any profanity.

If you've got a designated driver, make the 15- or 20-minute drive from downtown out to the **Cock & Bull Pub** (975 Cattlemen Rd., 941/341-9785, 5pm-2am daily, cover charge varies). Although it's all the way out near I-75, the European-style pub specializes in offering an enormous selection of beer in a comfortable, rustic environment. The pub calls its beer menu a bible and it frequently hosts beer tastings and occasionally has beer dinners. Pretzels and pizza are offered most nights. It's also a great spot to catch live music.

Also in the area is Sarasota's first craft brewery (and one of the best on the Gulf Coast), **Big Top Brewing Company** (6111 Porter Way, 800/590-2448, www.bigtopbrewing.com, 2pm-10pm Mon.-Sat., noon-8pm Sun.). While their branding and theming nods toward the Sarasota area's long connection with the Ringling circus, these brewers aren't clowning around (sorry). The tasting room here is warmly appointed, clean, and staffed by incredibly friendly and knowledgeable folks. Make sure to try one of the standards

Arts Season

The arrival of winter heralds the **arts season** in most cities, and Sarasota is no different in this regard. However, like the rest of Florida—especially southern Florida—Sarasota also undergoes something of a population transformation during the colder months, as snowbirds make their way from the chilly climes of the north and the Midwest. In the case of Sarasota, many choose this city not just for its more temperate weather, but also for its vibrant cultural scene. Many of these snowbirds are of the deep-pocketed species, and they also tend to be extremely engaged in the arts, providing a huge boost of both encouragement and funds during the winter months. That said, Sarasota is an incredibly respectable arts city during the warmer months, too, thanks to the presence of New College and Ringling College of Art & Design, as well as the city's long history of support for the arts. It's just that when the temperature drops—even if only a little—the city's cultural life noticeably perks up.

like the Circus City IPA or the Trapeze Monk, but be prepared to have a flight or two of the rotating and experimental beers too; they're always super fresh (obviously, being brewed on site) and often utilize unique local flavors.

Located in the Burns Square district, **Burns Court Cinema** (506 Burns Ct, 941/955-3456, http://filmsociety.org) is operated by the Sarasota Film Society and is one of the best places in town to catch independent and under-the-radar films.

The Arts

Sarasota has a great arts scene, and it's one that's driven both by deep-pocketed snowbirds and adventurous year-round locals. So, although the winter definitely brings a sense of hyperactivity to the town's art scene, it manages to maintain itself quite well throughout the year.

GALLERIES

The area around South Palm Avenue is where many downtown galleries are located. **Galleria Silecchia** (12 S. Palm Ave. and 20 S. Palm Ave., 941/365-7414, www.galleriasilecchia.com, 10am-6pm Mon.-Thurs., 10am-9pm Fri.) is Sarasota's largest gallery, and it has a pronounced focus on sculpture, art glass, and ceramics. The **Dabbert Gallery** (76 S. Palm Ave., 941/955-1315, www.dabbertgallery.com, 11am-5pm Tues.-Sat.) features works by sculptors along with

modernist and realist painters from throughout the United States.

A block or so off Palm Avenue is **Art Uptown** (1367 Main St., 941/955-5409, www.artuptown.com, 11am-5pm Mon.-Thurs., 11am-9pm Fri., 10am-7pm Sat., noon-5pm Sun.), a co-op gallery that features works from local member artists. Pieces here range from abstract to realism, with a large contingent of porcelain and ceramics pieces too.

Combining the co-op vibe of Art Uptown and the community atmosphere of the Palm Avenue area, the tree-covered **Towles Court Artist Colony** (Adams Lane, between S. Links Ave. and Washington Blvd., www.towlescourt.com, most galleries open noon-4pm Tues.-Sun.) isn't just a great destination for arts lovers, it's a great destination, period, with fantastic restaurants and shops complementing the works that are found in the many intimate and friendly galleries here. There are more than 20 different galleries tucked into the bungalows that make up the Colony.

A few miles north of downtown is the Ringling College of Art & Design, home to six impressive galleries, including the **Selby Gallery** (2700 N. Tamiami Trail, 941/359-7563, www.selbygallery.org, 10am-4pm Mon. and Wed.-Sat., 10am-7pm Tues. Sept.-mid-Dec. and Jan.-Apr., 10am-4pm Mon.-Fri. May-Aug.), which is firmly focused on daring, contemporary art. Exhibits rotate fairly

The Van Wezel Performing Arts Hall

a sight to behold; as the Van Wezel folks say, it's "the world's only purple seashell-shaped theater." Renovations in 2001 improved the building without diminishing its unique character, heightening the impact of the near-flawless interior acoustics.

Florida Studio Theatre (1241 N. Palm Ave., 941/366-9000, www.floridastudiotheatre.org) is actually composed of three different on-site venues. The Keating Theatre is the main stage, where Broadway and off-Broadway plays are performed. The slightly smaller Gompertz Theatre is dedicated to more cutting-edge live theater fare. Most unique among the three is the Goldstein Cabaret, which, as the name implies, is a great place to catch big and brash musical numbers.

Although it's not located in the cultural hub of central Sarasota, the **Asolo Repertory Theatre** (5555 N. Tamiami Trail, 941/351-8000, www.asolorep.org) is nonetheless an incredibly important component of the Sarasota arts scene. With seasons that often pack in more than a dozen productions, collectively attended by more than 100,000 people, and supported by a partnership with Florida State University's Asolo Conservatory for Actor Training, the Asolo is the largest professional nonprofit theater in the state of Florida. Instead of focusing on pop-culture-driven Broadway rehashes, the Asolo resurrects classic musicals, produces and promotes lesser-known quality works, and puts on the occasional piece of work that could be considered daring. The productions themselves are top-notch, benefitting from the innovations and boundary pushing of conservatory students and the experience of the professionals who have been with the Asolo for decades.

Birthed in 1960 in the Asolo, the **Sarasota Opera** (www.sarasotaopera.org) moved downtown in 1979 to what is now the **Sarasota Opera House** (61 N. Pineapple Ave., 941/366-8450, sarasotaopera.org), a beautiful 1920s-era theater repurposed for the company's needs. Since then, the company has become one of the city's preeminent arts groups. The Sarasota Opera is probably

frequently in these modern spaces and the art on display is always superlative.

Nearby is the **Marietta Museum of Art & Whimsy** (2121 N. Tamiami Trail, 941/364-3399, www.whimsymuseum.org, 1pm-4pm Thurs.-Sat., free), a pleasant and personable place to visit, thanks to founder Mary Lee's ability to curate "happy" art. Some (okay, most) of the items verge toward kitschy (Lee even describes some of it as "goofy") and all of the items are for sale. Expect to see sculptures of dogs in primary colors, brightly painted cuckoo clocks, and even Christmas trees.

PERFORMING ARTS

The **Van Wezel Performing Arts Hall** (777 N. Tamiami Trail, 941/953-3368, www.vanwezel.org) is the crown jewel of the Sarasota arts scene, hosting touring Broadway productions, classical music, and pop concerts firmly aimed at senior citizens. The building was originally designed by Frank Lloyd Wright Foundation architect William Wesley Peters (Wright's son-in-law). The lavender exterior is best known for its ambitious, decades-spanning "Verdi Cycle" effort, during which the company plan performed every single one of Verdi's works, including alternate versions of his operatic works. Although the Cycle concluded in 2016, the Opera still balances consistency and innovation under the steady hand of artistic director Victor DeRenzi, who has been with the company since 1983. The Opera's season typically includes five productions.

The **Sarasota Ballet** (www.sarasotaballet.org) performs in multiple venues around town, primarily at the Sarasota Opera House, Van Wezel, and the Florida State University's Center for the Performing Arts (on the grounds of the Asolo). With a season that usually includes a half-dozen performances, the repertoire of the Ballet tends toward classics of relatively recent vintage. The quality of their performances of Frederick Ashton-choreographed pieces is well-regarded.

For a performing-arts experience that's uniquely Sarasota, be sure to check out a performance by the **Sailor Circus** (2075 Bahia Vista St., 941/361-6350, sailorcircus.org). The Greatest Little Show on Earth has its roots in a high school gymnastics class, and, to this day, middle and high school students train here in the circus arts. The Sailor was operated for decades by the Sarasota County School Board, but was recently transferred to a private, nonprofit company, Circus Sarasota. It's doubtful that this move will have much of an impact on the Sailor's operations, though, as educating young people and allowing them to perform is still the Circus's primary emphasis. The Sailor holds performances at its school throughout the year, as well as special performances at venues across Sarasota.

Festivals and Events

One of the newest events on the Sarasota cultural calendar has also become one of the most popular. The **Ringling International Arts Festival** (RIAF, 5401 Bay Shore Rd., box office 941/360-7399, www.ringlingartsfestival.org, Oct.) is a five-day celebration of visual and performing arts held on the grounds of the John and Mable Ringling Museum of Art. Launched in 2009 as a collaboration between the Ringling and the New York-based Baryshnikov Arts Center, the festival was an immediate hit, drawing more than 20,000 visitors over its first two years. There's an emphasis on surprisingly cutting-edge performances at the RIAF, with music, dance, and theater performances bringing out big crowds.

Despite the emergence of the RIAF, the **Sarasota Film Festival** (SFF, various locations, 941/364-9514, box office 941/366-6200, www.sarasotafilmfestival.com, Apr.) is still the preeminent cultural event in Sarasota. And for good reason: The SFF has grown considerably since its birth in 1999, not only in attendance and scope, but also in national acclaim. *Variety* magazine dubbed the festival "the acme of regional film festivals," based on the 10-day event's winning combination of independent film and marquee guests. Although the bulk of the festival is held at the downtown Regal Hollywood 20 multiplex, the SFF also includes beautiful locations like the Sarasota Opera House for various screenings and events. Recent years of the SFF included more than 200 films and featured guests like Todd Solondz, Penelope Ann Miller, Olympia Dukakis, and Sophia Loren.

The **Sarasota Chalk Festival** (S. Pineapple Ave., www.chalkfestival.com, late Oct./early Nov.) may sound like the sort of quaint, family-friendly event that peppers the calendar of small cities across America. But in arts-driven Sarasota, this temporary outdoor exhibition has become a weeklong highlight of the cultural calendar, bringing in street artists from all over the world and drawing more than 200,000 visitors. And sure, kids have an opportunity to bust out the chalk and decorate the concrete, but the main focus here is on internationally renowned street artists, who craft elaborate and often quite huge works (some as big as 180 square feet), all of which disappear at the end of the festival in a massive wash down.

Over the last 20 years, the **Sarasota Blues**

Festival (2700 12th St., 855/292-5837, www.sarasotabluesfest.com, Nov.) has consistently featured a mix of marquee national blues acts and local musicians. Although the festival changed hands and is now operated by a Texas-based concert promoter (and not the local promoter who produced it for most of its history), the daylong event at Ed Smith Stadium is still a highlight of blues aficionados in southwest Florida.

Taking over the entirety of the Sarasota Fairgrounds, the **Sarasota Medieval Fair** (Sarasota County Fairgrounds, 3000 Ringling Blvd., 888/303-3247, www.sarasotamedievalfair.com, mid-Nov.) includes jousting, medieval music, medieval village re-creations, comedy shows, a kids' area, pony rides, and, yes, even a pub.

Every May, kids and adults (but mostly adults) descend on the beach at Siesta Key to compete in the **Siesta Key Sand Sculpture Contest** (Siesta Beach, May). The contest has been featured on several cable TV travel shows, and for good reason. The soft, white sand at Siesta Key packs quite well but is also malleable enough to allow for considerable detail. These are no ordinary sandcastles. If you don't have the patience to watch folks pack, wet, carve, and repeat for hours upon end, come for the judging, which usually takes place around lunchtime. If you can't make the May sand-sculpting contest, there's another one in November. The **Siesta Key Crystal Classic** (Siesta Beach, www.siestakeycrystalclassic.com, Nov.) benefits sea turtle conservation. In addition to the breathtaking creations made on the sand, there are also food and beverage vendors on-site.

SHOPPING
St. Armands Circle

Shopaholics should head straight for Lido Key and the tony shops and boutiques of **St. Armands Circle.** Parking is something of a problem (especially on weekends, and especially on beach-worthy weekends), but, thankfully, the layout of the Circle is perfect for walking. Park your car at the first available spot and spend the rest of the day browsing the dozens of shops in the area. Clothing stores include chain operations like Fresh Produce, Lilly Pulitzer, and the Sarasota-based **Oh My Gauze** (352 St. Armands Circle, 941/388-1964, www.ohmygauze.com, 10am-9pm Mon.-Sat., noon-6pm Sun.). There also are other unique local options like **Dream Weaver Collection** (364 St. Armands Circle, 941/388-1974, www.dreamweavercollection.com, 10am-8pm daily), a classy and sophisticated boutique firmly focused on an upscale and somewhat adventurous clientele, with its beautiful and expensive dresses and outfits. **Casa Smeralda** (468 John Ringling Blvd., 941/388-1305, http://casasmeralda.com, 9am-8pm daily, extended hours on weekends) features everything from wedding gowns to belly dance outfits.

Proprietor Cleon Dixon owns two interesting shops: **Binjara Traders** (327 John Ringling Blvd., 941/388-3335, 10am-8pm daily) and **Ivory Coast** (15 N. Blvd. of Presidents, 941/388-1999, 10am-8pm daily). Both feature fashion and accessories from around the world. Binjara emphasizes floral fabrics and accessories from South and Southeast Asia, and Ivory Coast focuses on African textiles, leathers, and decor items.

There are also a number of jewelry stores ranging from traditional goldsmiths like **Armel Jewelers** (22 N. Blvd. of Presidents, 941/388-3711, www.armeljewelers.com, 10am-6pm Mon.-Sat.) to funky boutiques like **Uniquity** (21 Fillmore Dr., 941/388-2212, www.uniquityofstarmands.com, 10am-9pm Mon.-Sat.), which sells jewelry and interesting Sarasota-oriented gifts.

Downtown Sarasota

While shopping downtown isn't quite as cohesive an experience as heading to St. Armands, the array of boutiques and shops in central Sarasota are a nice complement to the many art galleries in the area. For clothing, try the eco-minded **Juno and Jove** (100 Central Ave., 941/957-0000, www.junoandjove.com, 10am-6pm Mon.-Sat.).

Antiques lovers will want to head to Sarasota's unofficial **Antique District** (Fruitville Rd., between Orange and Central Aves.), which skirts downtown. **American Pie Antiques & Collectibles** (1470 Fruitville Rd., 941/362-0682, 10:30am-5pm Mon.-Fri.) is jam-packed with books, glassware, furniture, artwork, miniatures, and lots more. **Antiques & Chatchkes** (1542 Fruitville Rd., 941/906-1221, www.antiquesandchatchkes. com, 10am-5pm Mon.-Fri.) feels like a miniature antiques mall. Although there are only three dealers here, the variety of goods for sale, ranging from wall art and sculptures to furniture and, well, tchotchkes, is impressive. A few blocks south is **Blue Moon Antiques** (134 S. Pineapple Ave., 941/365-0978, 10am-5pm Mon.-Sat.), which specializes in ornate, high-end European antiques.

SPORTS AND RECREATION
Canoeing and Kayaking

Between the calm waters of the Gulf of Mexico, the mangroves and wildlife to be found throughout Sarasota Bay, and the numerous smaller waterways in and around the city, small-boat lovers will find plenty of places to explore in Sarasota. If you can't travel with your own boat, kayak rentals are available at **Economy Tackle** (6018 S. Tamiami Trail, 941/922-9671, www.floridakayak.com, from $35/day), which also offers paddleboards, diving gear, fishing tackle, and tours. Another good option for rentals is **Almost Heaven Kayak Adventures** (100 Taft Dr., 941/504-6296, www.kayakfl.com, from $45/day). Both Economy and Almost Heaven offer multiday and weekly rates.

Edwards Islands Park (sunrise-sunset daily) is composed of three tiny islands in Roberts Bay, which is located south of the Siesta Key bridge and is bounded by Siesta Key and the mainland. Although it is technically a park, there are zero facilities here, and in fact, the area is quite wild, dominated by oyster beds and rough and rocky beaches and frequently visited by seabirds and dolphins.

Fishing is pretty good in the area. But most boaters prefer to visit here to make their way through the mangroves and canopies, and to take a land break walking through the quiet island trails. The park is restricted to day use, so camping and fires are prohibited.

For a spot that's even more isolated, head for **North Creek.** This narrow stretch of water runs roughly parallel to the Tamiami Trail before gradually widening and then dumping into Sarasota Bay near Osprey. There's a reason why North Creek isn't very busy: It's not only hard to find, it's also pretty tough to launch from. The best way to access it is to head to Vamo Drive (south of the Gulf Gate area of southern Sarasota) and trudge about 0.25 mile south of Vamo Road until you can begin making your way through the mangroves with your eyes set on a line of condos (your only real visual landmark); eventually, you'll hit the water, but only after traversing a foot-slashing oyster bed. Again, I said it wouldn't be easy. You'll probably curse a lot on your way there, and you may very well get a little lost. But once you hit the water (which, after a good rain, can get quite fast), you'll forget your travails and simply be able to soak in the quiet run.

Sailing and Fishing Charters

One look at the Sarasota Bayfront marina will let you know that this is a sailing city. And though you may not have the scratch to pull up to the marina with your own boat, there are nonetheless ample opportunities to sail around the bay. **Kathleen D Sailing Catamarans** (2 Marina Plaza, 941/896-6400, www.kathleend.net, call for reservations) offers charters aboard catamarans that can accommodate up to 20 guests. The outfit has been plying the waters of Sarasota, Longboat Key, Siesta Key, and elsewhere around the region for 25 years. It offers trips ranging from two and three hours ($40/person and $50/person, respectively) to half-day trips ($70/person). Food and drinks are included.

Sara-Bay Sailing School & Charter

(1505 Ken Thompson Pkwy., 941/914-5132, www.sarabaysailing.com, half day from $200/trip, full day from $300/trip, call for hours and rates) also offers charters. Additionally, it can provide rentals to qualified boaters. For those who aren't qualified but want to be, the school offers sailing courses for beginners and intermediate sailors.

Siesta Key Parasailing (1265 Stickney Point Rd., 941/586-1972, www.siestakeyparasailing.com, $75/person) and **Siesta Key Water Sports** (1536 Stickney Point Rd., 941/921-3030, http://siestakeywatersports.com, $75/person) both offer parasailing experiences over the beautiful Gulf waters. Siesta Key Water Sports also has personal watercraft and kayaks available for rent.

There are a half-dozen boats available for rent at **CB's Saltwater Outfitters** (1249 Stickney Point Rd., Siesta Key, 941/349-4400, http://cbsoutfitters.com, half-day fishing charters from $350, half-day boat rentals from $95). Those folks who don't want to bother with piloting their own boat should definitely avail themselves of CB's many fishing charters; it offers four-, six-, and eight-hour trips both into Sarasota Bay as well as inshore, nearshore, and reef trips. Full-day trips into Charlotte Harbor (about 40 miles southeast)

to hunt for snook, redfish, and more are also available.

For full-service boat rentals on Longboat Key, head for **Cannons Marina** (6040 Gulf of Mexico Dr., Longboat Key, 941/383-1311, http://cannons.com, half-day rentals from $160). It has half-day, full-day, and multiday rentals of a wide variety of fishing boats as well as sport and ski boats.

Wolfmouth Charters (Longboat Key, 941/720-4418, www.wolfmouthcharters.com, charters starting at $300/group) offers four- and six-hour fishing charters in Sarasota Bay (for snook, flounder, pompano, Spanish mackerel) and in the Gulf (for grouper, snapper, shark, tarpon, and more). Captain Wayne Genthner has over three decades of experience fishing in the area. Even if you're not interested in fishing, he can provide a great tour of area waters aboard the *Wolfmouth*.

Anna Maria Sailing and Boat Rides (Anna Maria Island, 941/580-1502, www.annamariasailing.com, from $30/person) departs from Bradenton Beach's Municipal Pier on Bridge Street with five different types of sailing excursions. Its most popular are the two sunset cruises, a three-hour cruise designed for larger groups ($40/person, drinks included), and another, more intimate,

the Sarasota Bayfront marina

four-hour trip for couples ($150/couple, meal included). It has full-day tours ($110/person, meal included) and a more economical three-hour trip in the daytime ($30/person), too.

Fun & Sun Parasail (402 Church Ave. at the Bradenton Beach Marina, Anna Maria Island, 941/795-1000, www.annamariaparasail.com) offers group packages and individual parasailing trips.

Golf

There are a number of public courses in and around Sarasota. The best by far is the **Bobby Jones Golf Club** (1000 Circus Blvd., 941/955-8041, www.bobbyjonesgolfclub.com, greens fees $5-12 for 9-hole course), a highly rated municipal club with two 18-hole courses and one 9-hole course. The 9-hole Executive course is a tremendous bargain. It was apparently designed for overscheduled business-people and can be played in about two hours. Another solid option is the 18-hole Red course at **Gulf Gate Golf Club** (2550 Bispham Rd., 941/921-5515, greens fees from $18).

Spectator Sports

For those with an eye to spectator sports, it's worth noting that the **Baltimore Orioles** (http://baltimore.orioles.mlb.com) play their spring training games at **Ed Smith Stadium** (2700 12th St., 941/954-4101, $8-27) throughout the month of March. If you're looking for something more than Cracker Jacks and fly balls, you can also check out matches at the **Sarasota Polo Club** (8021 Polo Club Ln., 941/907-0000, www.sarasotapolo.com, $10). Matches are played every Sunday at 1pm, mid-December-early April.

Spas

The premier spa experience in Sarasota has long been at **The Ritz-Carlton** (1111 Ritz-Carlton Dr., 941/309-2000, www.ritzcarlton.com, call for hours, massages from $135, spa treatments from $150). Offering an absurdly large menu of "rituals," ranging from a quick bath in essential oils to 80-minute massages, the spa at the Ritz is only available to members

and current hotel guests, which may be the right incentive to book a room here.

The **L. Spa** (556 S. Pineapple Ave., 941/906-1358, www.lboutiques.com, 9am-7pm Mon.-Sat., massages from $85, spa packages from $185) is an expansion of the L. Boutique that opened in Sarasota in 2004. The spa offers hair, makeup, and nail services, as well as massage and body treatments and a variety of packages for men and women.

FOOD
Breakfast and Light Bites

The Breakfast House (1817 Fruitville Rd., 941/366-6860, 7am-2pm Mon.-Sat., 9am-2pm Sun., from $7) is, literally, a little house. Even though it already gets points for its excellent and inviting setting, this restaurant does far more for breakfast than just a couple of eggs and a slab of bacon. With morning dishes that nod both to a Gulf Coast heritage (shrimp and grits) and the tropical weather (pancakes with pineapple, coconut, and macadamia nuts), the menu here is a great combination of tradition and innovation. Combine that with the whimsical decor and a convenient downtown locale and this is one of the best spots in town to start your day.

Opened more than 50 years ago, the **Hob Nob Drive In** (1701 N. Washington Blvd., 941/955-5001, www.hobnobdrivein.com, 6am-8:30pm Sun.-Thurs., 6am-9pm Fri.-Sat., from $5) doesn't seem to have changed all that much since it first started selling burgers, fries, and shakes back in 1957. Of course, the menu has expanded to include a full slate of standard breakfast fare, all of which is priced quite reasonably. You can get a good start to your day for less than four bucks with the basic morning menu: eggs, toast, bacon, potatoes, and pancakes. Plus, it's a classic drive-in, so if you can't make it for breakfast, you can still swing by and grab one of those burgers or shakes and sit outside and watch the traffic go by.

The friendly breakfast joint **The Broken Egg** (140 Avenida Messina, 941/346-2750, www.thebrokenegg.com, 7am-9pm daily,

Best Restaurants

★ **Indigenous:** One of the best restaurants in Sarasota focuses on a combination of updated classics and unique additions; nearly everything is locally or regionally sourced (page 375).

★ **The Table Creekside:** Enjoy exceptional takes on seafood, meat dishes, and fantastic side dishes (farro risotto, yuca mozzarella roll), with outstanding views (page 376).

★ **Mr. Bones:** Its dizzying selection includes ribs, wings, and brisket sandwiches, alongside Tex-Mex, Indian dishes, subs, salads, and curried rice (page 376).

★ **The Alpine Steakhouse and Karl Ehmers Quality Meats:** It's the home of the "terducken," but you can also get excellent dry-aged steaks, Kobe beef burgers, roast pig, and German delicacies (page 376).

★ **Bubble Room:** Dishes like the "Duck Ellington," the "Cluck Gable," and the "Salmon Davis Jr." are fun to order in this quirky local institution (page 402).

from $6) has a great patio area for dining, as well as a spacious inside dining room with lots of local artwork on the walls. It's a great choice for breakfast on Siesta Key, with standards supplemented by a selection of originals like an Egg Largo (a Benedict-style plate that substitutes sour cream, scallions, and tomatoes for hollandaise sauce), as well as massive omelets, blintzes, and Tex-Mex-styled breakfasts.

New American

Boasting a great location in the Towles Court Artist Colony, a casually upscale atmosphere, and a menu built around local ingredients, ★ **Indigenous** (239 S. Links Ave., 941/706-4740, www.indigenoussarasota. com, 5:30pm-9:30pm Mon.-Sat., from $15) is justifiably regarded as one of the best restaurants in Sarasota. Chef Steve Phelps focuses on a combination of updated classics—grass-fed burgers, braised short ribs—with unique additions like parmesan beignets. Nearly everything is locally or regionally sourced. Your server will not only tell you where your fish came from but also the name of the captain who piloted the boat that brought it in. With such attention to detail, the menu is subject to frequent revisions. (Hopefully, the roasted

peaches-and-lavender-creme biscuit that was on the dessert menu remains a permanent fixture.) The converted bungalow that houses the restaurant is decorated in a muted combination of rustic tones and cosmopolitan glamour, with a great patio and a separate cottage devoted to their wine bar. Service is unsurprisingly top-shelf.

A few blocks north of Towles Court is **Made** (1990 Main St, 941/953-2900, 11:30am-2:30pm and 4:30pm-11pm Tues.-Thurs., 11:30am-midnight Fri., 5pm-midnight Sat., 10am-3pm Sun., lunch from $8, dinner from $12, brunch from $13), one of the best and most unique restaurants in town. With a menu that's ostensibly "new Southern," Made nonetheless strips away much of the pretension that comes with that moniker. The kitchen enthusiastically serves up fried chicken, fried green tomatoes, mac and cheese, steak and eggs, meat loaf, and other standards that have been upgraded with fresh ingredients and creative recipe flourishes that do nothing to diminish these dishes' impact (on your taste buds or your waistline). The atmosphere is decidedly spirited, and the dining room is comfortable and cool but effortlessly so. Made also offers a fantastic brunch on Sunday mornings.

Another great spot for locally sourced and seasonal food is **Libby's Cafe + Bar** (1917 S. Osprey Ave., 941/487-7300, www.libbyscafebar.com, 11:30am-3pm and 5pm-close Mon.-Sat., 10:30am-3pm Sun., from $18). Emphasizing a fresh-from-market menu that changes seasonally (with tweaks on a regular basis), Libby's is a decidedly unstuffy purveyor of local produce, meats, and seafood. The restaurant's two bars are often quite crowded with folks socializing or watching the game. Libby's also serves lunch with a good selection of inventive sandwich interpretations rounding out small-plate versions of their dinner items.

The original location of ★ **The Table Creekside** (5365 S. Tamiami Trail, 941/921-9465, www.tablesrq.com, 4pm-10pm Sun.-Thurs., 4pm-10:30pm Fri.-Sat., from $15) was a big hit on the Sarasota dining scene, and locals were pretty upset when it closed in 2008 after an ownership change. However, in 2012, the original owner and chefs opened The Table Creekside at Philippi Creek. The dining room is stylish, boasting a retro-classic vibe, and there is a gorgeous outdoor deck overlooking the creek. But the views and decor are a distant second reason to come here; the menu features exceptional takes on seafood (wahoo ceviche, lobster ceviche, Brazilian shrimp and grits), meat dishes (short rib pot roast, a lamb chop served with spinach chimichurri), and fantastic side dishes (farro risotto, yuca mozzarella roll).

Burgers and Barbecue

Square One Burgers and Bar (1737 S. Tamiami Trail, 941/870-8111, www.squareonesrq.com, 11am-10pm daily, late-night hours on the weekends, burgers from $7.99) has an insane selection of burger combinations: certified humane Angus beef; hormone-free buffalo, lamb, and Wagyu; chicken and turkey; and homemade vegan patties. With one of those as your foundation, you can order nearly two dozen different burgers that incorporate everything from bacon and onion rings to fried jalapeños, porcini mushrooms, Brie, and much, much more. Beyond the burgers, Square One also serves up a decadent grilled cheese and a great array of fresh salads and side orders. A good beer selection and a dessert menu ensure that your diet will be busted after coming here. Don't worry, though, it's totally worth it.

Sarasota is a great city for eating, but there really just aren't a whole lot of barbeque joints. Thankfully, one of them is **Nancy's Bar-B-Q** (301 S. Pineapple Ave., 941/366-2271, http://nancysbarbq.com, 11:30am-9pm Mon.-Sat., sandwiches from $6.95). Nancy herself is often in the kitchen, and she loves North Carolina-style barbecue. (She also wittily notes on the menu that she's probably the only "white Jewish woman making pork barbecue." Well, she's definitely the only one in Sarasota.) Pork is the centerpiece here, with pulled pork coming to you on a bun or on a fantastic taco with salsa and cucumber-dill sour cream, as well as ribs, and pork sausage. Beef brisket, cured salmon, and chicken round out the menu, alongside sides, both standard (baked beans, coleslaw) and special (edamame succotash, cucumber salad), and desserts.

Holmes Beach is home to one of my favorite restaurants on Anna Maria Island. ★ **Mr. Bones** (3007 Gulf Dr. N., Anna Maria Island, 941/778-6614, www.mrbonesbbq.com, 11am-9pm daily, from $7) solves the age-old quandary faced in my house: when you love barbecue, but the rest of your family members are vegetarians exhausted by the corn on the cob and french fries that function as the meat-free selections at most barbecue joints. Mr. Bones serves up ribs, wings, and brisket sandwiches, but it also has a dizzying selection of other items that includes Tex-Mex, Indian dishes, subs, salads, and curried rice, and takeout is available.

Steak

The smoker at ★ **The Alpine Steakhouse and Karl Ehmers Quality Meats** (4520 S. Tamiami Trail, 941/922-3797, www.alpinesteak.com, 9am-9pm Tues.-Sat., from $9) produces a near-constant perfume that announces the meat-centric raison d'être here. This steak house doubles as a meat market (in the literal sense) and people are often coming and going picking up steaks and chops for home grilling. The casual, old-school vibe here is not to be missed. The Alpine has gotten a bit of attention for its turducken, turkey stuffed with duck stuffed with chicken, and it is attention the owners are certainly proud of, but the dry-aged steaks, Kobe beef burgers, roast pig, and German delicacies on the menu give diners plenty of other options.

Seafood

Phillippi Creek Oyster Bar (5353 S. Tamiami Trail, 941/925-4444, http://creek-seafood.com, 11am-10pm Sun.-Thurs., 11am-10:30pm Fri.-Sat., from $9) is one of Sarasota's best seafood options. Though decidedly unpretentious, this creek-side raw bar manages to serve up the freshest and most expertly prepared seafood in town. Those preparations are generally quite straightforward—fried, broiled, baked, or steamed—and mouthwateringly awesome. Big eaters, or hungry couples, should try a combo pot, which piles oysters, shrimp, corn on the cob, onions, and celery into an unglamorous but highly appetizing container.

Be forewarned: ★ **Owens Fish Camp** (516 Burns Ln., 941/951-6936, 4pm-9:30pm Sun.-Thurs., 4pm-10:30pm Fri., Sat., main courses from $10) is not an actual Florida fish camp. The real deal can be found all over the state, tucked away along docks and backwaters accessible only to boaters and boozers. Owens, however, is pretty easy to find (but not so easy to find parking for), in the heart of downtown Sarasota. Nonetheless, from the Old Florida decor to the friendly, slightly boozy vibe of the place, the proprietors have done a pretty good job at creating a reasonable facsimile of the real thing. While steaks and grilled fish and fried seafood dominate the menu, you can just ignore everything and head straight for Owens's low-country boil, which is actually more South Carolina than Florida, but it hardly matters. With crab claws, mussels, shrimp, potatoes, corn, and sausage delivered in copious quantities, it's the quintessential way to eat seafood, and Owens does a near-perfect job with it. Make sure you get one of the fried fruit pies for dessert.

European

15 South Ristorante Enoteca (15 S. Blvd. of the Presidents, 941/388-1555, www.15southristorante.com, 4pm-11pm daily, from $14) is located in the upscale St. Armands Circle shopping district. Though dinner can be something of a buttoned-down affair, the atmosphere here is surprisingly rustic and friendly. This is in keeping with the selection of traditional Italian country fare, like *pasticciata alla Bolognese,* risottos, stuffed cannelloni, and grilled veal chops. The dining room is beautiful and comfortable. Solo diners will definitely want to grab a seat at the marble-topped bar and let the bartender guide them through the selection of over 600 bottles of wine on offer at 15 South.

Café L'Europe (431 St. Armands Circle, 941/388-4415, www.cafeleurope.net, 11:30am-3pm and 5pm-10pm daily, from $35) has been a St. Armands mainstay for over 40 years. The way this place delivers a classy Continental dining experience leaves little doubt that it will probably be around for another few decades, at least. With white-linen service, an extensive wine list, and a menu of French and Italian fine-dining classics, the intimate and romantic environment of Café L'Europe is as perfect for a date night as it is for a luxurious vacation splurge.

Restaurant options in Longboat Key are somewhat limited, but the choices that are there are generally excellent. **Maison Blanche** (2605 Gulf of Mexico Dr., Longboat Key, 941/383-8088, www.maisonblancherestaurants.com, 5:30pm-9:30pm Tues.-Sun., from $31) is a superlative French restaurant, boasting a Michelin-starred chef and a beautiful, minimalist dining room. Unsurprisingly, the fare here tends toward modern interpretations of French classics, with an emphasis on local seafood. Reservations are imperative, even in the slow season, as foodies from downtown Sarasota are frequent visitors.

Japanese and Thai

Located downtown, the **Drunken Poet Cafe** (1572 Main St., 941/955-8404, www.drunkenpoetsarasota.com, 11am-10pm Sun.-Thurs., 11am-midnight Fri.-Sat., from $11) has been offering both Japanese and Thai food for the past few years. The dozen house rolls, including the Sexy Woman and the Chef Ginch, are exceptional. The kitchen menu is where the Thai flavors come forth, with well-known dishes alongside more unique preparations like salmon Panang and *gai bai teuy*. The cozy café is kind of tiny, and service is sometimes hit-or-miss.

Pacific Rim (1859 Hillview St., 941/330-8071, http://pacificrimsarasota.com, 11:30am-2pm and 5pm-9:30pm Mon.-Thurs., 11:30am-2pm and 5pm-10:30pm Fri., 5pm-10:30pm Sat., 5pm-9pm Sun., from $12) is a modern and stylish Japanese restaurant located just south of downtown. The atmosphere is pretty casual and the martini menu is almost as popular as the sushi bar. The sushi rolls are uniformly excellent, drawing large (and sometimes loud) evening crowds to the open dining room.

Vegetarian and Vegan

Simon's Coffee House (5900 S. Tamiami Trail, 941/926-7151, http://simonstogo.com, 8am-8pm Mon.-Sat., from $6) has a number of vegan and vegetarian options on its breakfast, lunch, and dinner menus. Though not strictly meat free, tempeh and tofu form the cornerstone of several of their meals. Expect everything from crepes and breakfast wraps in the morning; soups and sandwiches for lunch; and dinner dishes that include curry vegetables, panini pizza, tempeh meat loaf, and shrimp fettuccine. The whole food-oriented Simon's also serves coffee, smoothies, and even beer and wine.

A much better option for vegetarians, vegans, or anyone interested in organic and raw food is ★ **Beauty of Sprouts** (1474 Fruitville Rd., 941/350-8449, beautyofsprouts.net, 11am-3pm and 5pm-8pm Mon.-Sat., from $10). Centrally located in an unassuming storefront in the downtown antique district, the decor here is nothing to write home about—it's cute and cozy, but feels more like the living room at a quirky relative's house than it does a forward-thinking restaurant—but the constantly evolving menu more than makes up for any design shortcomings. Of course, there are excellent salads, soups, and smoothies, but where Beauty of Sprouts shines is with its hearty, all-natural, and mostly raw but still wonderful takes on classic comfort foods like pizza, taco salad, lasagna, and pad Thai. Instead of a simulacrum of "fake food," the dishes here are spectacular on their own accord, thanks to fresh ingredients and careful preparation. Don't miss dessert, especially a vegan tiramisu that may change your mind about dairy for good.

ACCOMMODATIONS
Under $100

Cheap lodging options are plentiful in Sarasota. Just taking a drive down the Tamiami Trail between the Ringling Museum and downtown will reveal what seems like dozens of cheap motels that hearken back to the days when the Trail was the primary tourist route through the area. Unfortunately, quite a few of these motels are difficult to recommend; many are pretty rough around the edges. Nonetheless, there are a handful of national budget chains with outposts here, and your odds of getting a clean, safe room are quite a bit better at them than at some of the more vintage motels. There's a **Quality Inn** (4800 N. Tamiami Trail, 941/355-7091, www.choicehotels.com, from $55 d) and a **Super 8** (4309 N. Tamiami Trail, 941/355-9326, www.super8.com, from $59 d) near the Ringling College of Art & Design that will suffice in a light-wallet pinch.

If you travel with your own hotel room, the **Sun-N-Fun RV Resort** (7125 Fruitville Rd., 941/342-6189, www.sunnfunfl.com, RV sites from $58) is a solid and inexpensive option.

Best Accommodations

★ **Gulf Beach Resort Motel:** The oldest hotel on Lido Beach is affordable with beautiful views (page 379).

★ **Hotel Ranola:** Its nine rooms are all decorated in a hip, playful, and urban style, with hardwood floors, checkerboard tiles, and bold color schemes (page 380).

★ **Silver Sands Villas:** The casual, colorful, and semi-residential atmosphere here is especially welcoming (page 395).

★ **Seaside Inn:** A casual, classic beach feel meets subtly upscale appointments and highly attentive service, resulting in one of the best places to stay on Sanibel Island (page 404).

★ **Gulfcoast Inn:** This is a fantastic budget option, especially in the off season (page 419).

★ **Inn of Naples:** This boutique family resort has fresh, bright paint and up-to-date appointments, enlivening decades-old hotel architecture (page 419).

★ **Inn on Fifth:** Here, boutique-style intimacy is combined with top-shelf grandeur (page 419).

★ **The Naples Beach Hotel & Golf Club:** The hotel combines Old Florida charm, 1950s glamour, and modern luxury in a way that manages to be friendly and accessible (page 420).

Although it's located a half-hour or so from downtown (a couple of miles east of I-75 on Fruitville Rd.), this resort has proven to be a preferred destination for motor home drivers. There are more than 600 RV sites, all of which include cable TV and 30- and 50-amp hookups. There are also sites for tent camping. Additionally, Sun-N-Fun offers rental homes in four different sizes and feature levels, with homes laid out close to one another. The resort has many amenities: an Olympic-sized pool, tennis and volleyball courts, a gym, and an activity center where guests can take classes in woodcarving, painting, or even computer skills. Obviously, this is a place optimized for folks who are going to be spending a big chunk of time here, most likely during the winter. It also has laundry facilities.

$150-200

Although it's a breeze to find hotels in this price range during the low season in Sarasota, finding a midrange-cost place to stay during the Sarasota high season can be something of a challenge. There are some consistently priced hotels near the airport, ranging from the basic **Comfort Inn** (5000 N. Tamiami Trail, 941/351-7734, www.choicehotels.com, from $100 d) to the nicer environs of a **Hampton Inn** (975 University Pkwy., 941/355-8140, http://hamptoninn3.hilton.com, from $159 d) and the **Hyatt Place** (950 University Pkwy., 941/355-8140, sarasotabradenton.place.hyatt.com, from $179 d), which opened in 2010. As these are chain hotels, you already know exactly what you're getting. If you need something at a reasonable cost during high season and don't mind driving a bit to see nearly everything Sarasota has to offer, then any of these hotels is a solid option.

For something more historically Sarasota, the ★ **Gulf Beach Resort Motel** (930 Ben Franklin Dr., 941/388-2127, www.gulfbeach-sarasota.com, from $160 d) is a much better choice. The fact that this place is as inexpensive as it is is something of a mystery to me.

It's the oldest hotel on Lido Beach, an area of Sarasota notably light on hotels already. And it sits right on a beautiful, quiet stretch of that beach. Sure, the TV only shows basic cable, and you have to get the remotes from the front desk, but, again, this is the oldest hotel on one of the Gulf Coast's best beaches. Who cares if you have to watch ESPN in standard definition? Go to the beach! Accommodations range from standard (and somewhat small) rooms to larger mini apartments complete with kitchenettes. Each room is individually decorated, and many guests have favorites that they return to every year. There's a heated pool, a beachside picnic area, and you can even play shuffleboard! The staff here is exceedingly friendly and helpful, making this place feel more like a family affair than a beach "resort."

About half a block from the beach on Lido Key is **Beau Lido Suites** (139 Tyler Dr., 888/5436-539, www.beaulido.com, from $150 d). This tiny, no-frills motel features somewhat outdated decor. The rooms range from the Guest Room, which holds a double bed and a TV, to a fully detached, two-bedroom house.

The unassuming outside of the ★ **Hotel Ranola** (118 Indian Pl., 941/951-0111, www.hotelranola.com, from $179 d) doesn't seem all that promising, but inside, this downtown boutique hotel is a real gem. Its nine rooms are all decorated in a hip, playful, and urban style, with hardwood floors, checkerboard tiles, and bold color schemes. They feel less like hotel accommodations and more like tiny apartments. All of the rooms are kitted out with flat-screen plasma TVs, free Wi-Fi, decadently soft bedding, and full (if small) kitchens. The basic rooms are around 400 square feet, but there are a couple of deluxe suites that top out at 600 square feet.

$200-300

The **Lido Beach Resort** (700 Ben Franklin Dr., 941/388-2161, www.lidobeachresort.com, from $219 d) is the largest beachfront property on Lido Key. Thanks to its somewhat labyrinthine layout, it feels surprisingly intimate. The waterfront tiki bar and restaurant are popular evening spots for guests and nonguests staying on the Key who don't feel like braving the high-season crowds in St. Armands Circle. The pet-friendly resort sits right on the Gulf, with a private beach area reserved for hotel guests. Facilities include volleyball, a fitness center, and two heated pools. The rooms are incredibly spacious, ranging from standard hotel-style rooms to kitchenette rooms and one- and two-bedroom suites. All rooms have flat screen TVs and safes, and there's Wi-Fi throughout the hotel.

Another good option on Lido Key is **Coquina on the Beach** (1008 Ben Franklin Dr., 941/388-2161, www.coquinaonthebeach.com, doubles from $209). Although it's lighter on the amenities than the Lido Beach Resort, the vibe is friendly, and the rooms are tidy and comfortable, if a little dated. The location provides great beach views from almost every room, and, if salt water's not on the agenda, the heated pool is a nice option. In addition to standard rooms, one-bedroom apartments are also available.

Operated by the Intercontinental Hotels conglomerate, the **Hotel Indigo** (1223 Blvd. of the Arts, 941/487-3800, doubles from $224) gamely attempts to pull off a boutique hotel vibe. The 95 small rooms are new and very brightly painted, and the corporate staff is well trained to provide fastidious service. There's a small pool and fitness center on-site.

Sarasota's **Ritz-Carlton** (1111 Ritz-Carlton Dr., 941/309-2000, www.ritzcarlton.com, from $269 d) overlooks Sarasota Bay and is just a few blocks away from the Van Wezel Performing Arts Hall. Accommodations here are typically Ritz-luxe, with featherbeds, Egyptian-cotton linens, a turndown service, and even a complimentary shoeshine service. The property opens into a marble-floored foyer, and there are three tennis courts, a pool, spa, and two fitness centers on-site. Guests also have access to the Members Beach Club on Lido Key. Somewhat surprisingly, the hotel is also pet friendly, permitting cats and dogs under 20 pounds to stay in specially designated rooms.

Vacation Rentals

For longer visits, **Timberwoods Vacation Villas** (8378 S. Tamiami Trail, 941/312-5934, www.timberwoods.com, villas $1,295 weekly) offer a good alternative to extended-stay hotels. The two-bedroom/two-bath villas are reasonably priced, clean, and comfortable, providing fairly easy access to Siesta Key and the food and nightlife of the Gulf Gate area. The complex, which feels like a somewhat-dated planned community, is located along the Tamiami Trail south of Sarasota.

INFORMATION AND SERVICES
Visitor Information

The local visitors bureau operates the official **Sarasota Visitor Information Center** (707 N. Tamiami Trail, 941/957-1877, www.sarasotafl.org, 10am-4pm Mon.-Sat.), which is conveniently located in the downtown area, near the Van Wezel Performing Arts Hall.

Medical and Emergency Services

Sarasota Memorial Hospital (1700 S. Tamiami Trail, 941/917-9000) is just a few minutes south of downtown, and is the closest hospital with a 24-hour emergency room. For prescriptions, there are dozens of branches of national chain pharmacies located throughout the city, including **Walgreens** and **CVS**, and prescriptions can also be filled at many **Publix** grocery stores.

GETTING THERE
Air

The **Sarasota-Bradenton International Airport** (SRQ, 6000 Airport Circle, 941/359-2777, www.srq-airport.com) is located in northern Sarasota, near the Ringling Museum and New College. The airport is serviced by Delta, American, Air Canada, JetBlue, and several charter services. Flights to SRQ are somewhat limited, and you'll definitely be able to find more flight options at the larger **Tampa International Airport** (TPA, 4100 George J. Bean Pkwy., 813/870-8700, www.tampaairport.com), which is about an hour away.

Car

By car, Sarasota is 60 miles (about an hour) south of Tampa Bay, via I-75 and I-275. The city itself is about 10 miles west of I-75. The historic Tamiami Trail runs through the city.

Siesta Key is six miles (about 15 minutes) south of downtown Sarasota via the Tamiami Trail, while the southern tip of Longboat Key is five miles (about 10 minutes) away from downtown, via the Ringling Causeway, which takes you through St. Armands Circle and Lido Key. County Road 789 is the main road that runs through the entirety of Longboat Key as Gulf of Mexico Drive; once you cross onto Anna Maria Island, its name gets shortened to just Gulf Drive. You can also access Anna Maria Island via Bradenton on Manatee Avenue or Cortez Road.

GETTING AROUND

Like most of the rest of Florida, Sarasota is a car city. Public parking throughout Sarasota is mostly metered, although there are many areas downtown where street-side parking is timed. Time violations earn a $15 parking citation.

The city government operates a decent bus system in the form of the unfortunately named **SCAT** (www.scgov.net), with fairly direct routes and a transfer station (1565 1st St.) located downtown. SCAT, in conjunction with Manatee County's **MCAT** (www.mymanatee.org), also operates trolley service to Longboat Key and Anna Maria Island. Routes are limited on Sundays and there is no service on major holidays. Single-ride fares for buses and the trolley are $1.25, but you can get unlimited-ride passes for $20/week or $50/month. **Lightning Bugz** (http://lightningbugzlsv.com, from $100/day) offers electric-golf-cart rentals on both Siesta Key (5253 Ocean Blvd., 843/478-7945) and Anna Maria Island (5347 Gulf Dr., Holmes Beach, 843/478-7945).

Fort Myers

The **Fort Myers** area is steeped in history. Even among Florida cities, the historical vibe here is unique. While some areas may boast of their past with pirates, conquistadors, and railroad barons, the discussion in this part of the state is about Thomas Edison, a utopian cult, and Native American shell mounds.

Fort Myers Beach is one of the best beach towns in all of Florida, with a low-key and welcoming vibe that's decidedly unsophisticated but tremendously relaxing. Despite being a tourist-friendly destination, the town never feels "touristy." Plus, the beach is absolutely gorgeous.

When coming into central Fort Myers via McGregor Boulevard, it's easy to understand why the city has been dubbed the City of Palms: The majestic, skyscraping palms that line the street seem to go on forever. The neat block houses give way to progressively larger and more unique abodes, and by the time you arrive at the city's proudest property—the Edison & Ford Winter Estates—there's little doubt as to why Thomas Edison was so enthusiastic about living in the city. From this vantage point, it's hard to imagine the city as being anything but perfect.

Beyond that somewhat idyllic stretch of road, Fort Myers is a little rough around the edges. It was hit hard by Hurricane Charley in 2004 and then again by the housing crisis that took hold in 2008. The economy has struggled and crime in the area is consistently above the national average. Nonetheless, the historic core of the city has undergone some spectacular revitalization over the past few years, and between the city's beautiful River District, some sights well worth visiting in the city's downtown area, and, of course, the Edison & Ford Winter Estates, Fort Myers offers plenty of reasons to visit.

SIGHTS
Imaginarium

The **Imaginarium** (200 Cranford Ave., 239/337-3332, www.imaginariumfortmyers.com, 10am-5pm Mon.-Sat., noon-5pm Sun., $12 adults, $8 students, children under 2 free) is a city-owned, kids-oriented science center. Much like other such municipal science

historic downtown Fort Myers

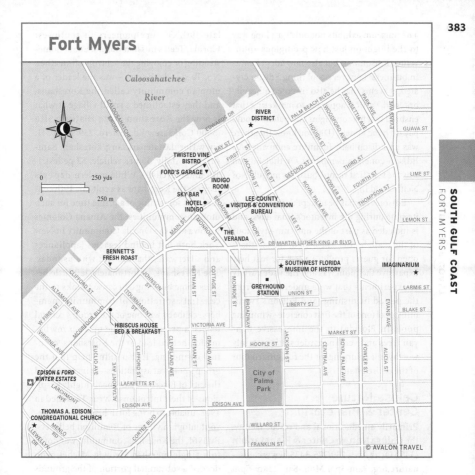

Fort Myers

centers, the Imaginarium is a collection of interactive exhibits intended to pique children's interest. The hands-on philosophy extends to several animal exhibits: Kids can touch different species of marine life in the "Sea to See" touch tanks.

★ Edison & Ford Winter Estates

Although there are dozens of historic and pedigreed homes throughout Florida, none captures the imagination or evokes an era as completely as the **Edison & Ford Winter Estates** (2350 McGregor Blvd., 239/334-7419, www.edisonfordwinterestates.org, 9am-5:30pm daily, admission to lab/museum: $12 adults, $5 children, children 5 and under free; home/gardens tour: $20 adults, $11 children, children 5 and under free; guided botanical tour: $24 adults, $10 children, children 5 and under free). Guests to the estates can explore the gardens, grounds, and houses themselves, as well as a 15,000-square-foot museum, filled with various inventions and memorabilia from both men's illustrious pasts. While Thomas Edison's house and labs are available to tour, Henry Ford's house is not. However, there is a Model T in the museum. This area is positively packed with inventions and educational displays, so much so that, at one point in your visit, you're likely to say "OK, I get it. Edison was a genius." And he certainly was.

The museum exhibits not only go a long way to shed light on just how prodigious an inventor Edison was, but also how adept he was in business. For every cool thing Edison created, it seems that he also invented a heavily branded, vertical approach to marketing that ensured that his copyrights and patents would pay off handsomely. (Did you know that there was an Edison baby furniture company? An Edison concrete company? Or that Edison was the very first record-business mogul? No? Neither did I.)

Edison's lab has been kept as is, reflecting its state during the inventor's final days, and is included as part of the museum-style tour of the main house. The area of the lab that's open for guests provides a feel for just how expansive the room was and the wide variety of experiments that were undertaken. From the period furnishings and Edison's swimming pool (one of the first concrete swimming pools in Florida) to the impressive banyan trees and verdant gardens, it's certainly worthwhile splurging for the full guided tour of the entire estate.

Calusa Nature Center & Planetarium

Primarily an educational and rescue facility, the **Calusa Nature Center & Planetarium** (3450 Ortiz Ave., 239/275-3435, www.calusa-nature.org, 9am-5pm Mon.-Sat., 11am-5pm Sun., $10 adults 13 and up, $8 children, children 2 and under free) sits on more than 100 acres near I-75. It has a butterfly garden, an aviary, and a small nature museum. The best reason to make the trek out here is to take in one of the facility's many daily educational programs, which allow kids (and adults) to get up close with butterflies, manatees, reptiles, and other animals. Make sure to allow enough time to walk along the rarely crowded, pine-shaded nature trails.

Koreshan State Historic Site

In 1894, Cyrus Teed moved to Estero, Florida. However, unlike many other late-19th century pioneers in southwest Florida, Teed's mission was not about homesteading or enjoying the subtropical weather. No, Teed—aka Koresh—was the leader of a utopian community called the Koreshans, and they established a small village at what is now the **Koreshan State Historic Site** (3800 Corkscrew Rd., Estero, 239/992-0311, www.floridastateparks.org/koreshan, 8am-sundown daily, $5 per vehicle, $2 pedestrians and bicyclists). While modern-day eyes may see the Koreshans as a cult, the 19th century was something of a prime time for such utopian communities; the Amana Colonies in Iowa and the Oneida Community in New York both left behind legacies (appliances and silverware) that are still with us today. The Koreshans, unfortunately, left little besides some buildings, because thanks to the celestial aspirations of community members, celibacy was one of the group's central tenets, a practice that, due to sheer mathematics, helped lead to the Koreshans' eventual dwindling. It also didn't help that the group's political aspirations—it incorporated the city of Estero—made locals highly suspicious of their intentions. Cyrus Teed died in 1908, unable to bring forth his vision of a devout, utopian village of 10 million believers. By 1961, the Koreshan community was down to a single member, Hedwig Michel, who deeded a substantial portion of the grounds of the community to the state of Florida under the precondition that it be used as a state park. (The remaining Koreshan land is controlled by the College of Life Foundation, which is historically connected to the original Koreshan community but has nothing to do with any Koreshan teachings.) Walking through the grounds today is fascinating, because thanks to the upkeep of the buildings by the state of Florida, one is able to get a fairly good picture of what life was like not just for Koreshan followers, but also for many of the early settlers to the area. On top of that, the actual grounds are beautiful, with walking trails and dense natural areas that,

Fort Myers Beach

while maybe not quite utopian (one can easily hear the whooshing of cars on the adjacent Tamiami Trail), is still very pastoral.

BEACHES
Fort Myers Beach

The beaches here are easily accessible and marked well, and there are two large **municipal parking lots** (1661 Estero Blvd. and 200 San Carlos Blvd., $2/hour) on the northern end of the island. All along Estero Boulevard are numerous, well-marked public-beach access points with small parking lots that fill up rather quickly. The farther south you go, the easier it is to find a parking spot; the access points are numbered in ascending order from south to north, and the best ones to head for are those with numbers lower than 20.

If you come off the Matanzas Pass Bridge and *don't* follow the flow of traffic heading left toward the busier, southern parts of Fort Myers Beach, and instead turn right, you'll come across **Lynn Hall Memorial Park**

(950 Estero Blvd., sunrise-sunset daily, free), which is located in the heart of downtown Fort Myers Beach. This park is quite popular and busy, and the parking lot fills up pretty early. Still, the beach here is great, and if you enjoy sharing your beach day with crowds, this is the spot for you. The iconic fishing pier is well-loved by anglers and by a colony of Brazilian Free Tail bats that lives underneath it, which makes sunsets here not only beautiful, but also kind of exciting.

Located at about the midway point of Fort Myers Beach is **Newton Park** (4650 Estero Blvd., sunrise-sunset daily, free), one of the newest and most unique public beach parks in the area. In addition to offering easy access to one of the quietest stretches of beach, the park is on the former grounds of Seven Seas, the beachfront residence of the late Jim Newton, a wealthy real estate developer who's actually best known as the author of *Uncommon Friends,* a book that detailed his relationships with the likes of Thomas Edison, Charles Lindbergh, Harvey Firestone, and other notable well-to-dos. Newton was friends with many of them during the 1930s. He hosted several of them (and many others) at Seven Seas during the 1950s.

★ Lovers Key State Park

For a rustic beach trip, **Lovers Key State Park** (8700 Estero Blvd., Fort Myers Beach, 239/463-4588, 8am-sunset daily, $8 per vehicle) is a fantastic option. Lovers Key initially gained its reputation and name because it was only accessible by boat, making its beach, um, extra private. Even though you can now pull into a parking lot and walk a few hundred meters to the beach, this park still has the feel of an isolated and secret location. Even during peak seasons, when there are concessionaires right at the boardwalk, you'll struggle to stifle a giggle that it's not any more crowded than it is. The beach here is two miles long, with the natural barrier-island setting and calm Gulf waters creating an instantly relaxing atmosphere. Renting a canoe or kayak from the concessionaire (from $32/half day for kayaks and $47/half day for canoes) allows one to traverse the intimate backwaters, while a bike rental (from $18/half day) makes the nature trails more easily accessible.

★ Cayo Costa State Park

Cayo Costa State Park (north of Captiva Island, 941/964-0375, 8am-sunset daily, $2) is all there is to La Costa Island, and that's

the boardwalk leading to the beach at Lovers Key State Park

just fine. The island (and the park) is only accessible by private boat or via the **Tropic Star Ferry** (13921 Waterfront Dr., Pineland, 239/283-0015, www.tropicstarcruises.com, daily departures at 9:30am and 2pm, with returns at 1pm and 3pm, round-trip ferry is $35 adults/$25 children), which departs from the Pineland Marina. There are nine miles of beautiful, white-sand beaches at the park, and snorkeling is fantastic just offshore. There are 30 tent campsites ($35/person) and 12 cabins (which are nearly impossible to reserve, given the park's popularity). The entire island is incredibly rustic, with facilities limited to a few public restrooms, outdoor showers, and a concession stand that sells insect repellent and sunscreen. In addition to beachcombing on the impossibly soft and sugary sand, visitors to Cayo Costa can also explore more than five miles of hiking trails that wind through hardwood hammocks and mangrove swamps.

ENTERTAINMENT AND EVENTS
Nightlife

The after-hours scene in Fort Myers is both limited and somewhat uninspired. There are plenty of sports pubs and dive bars, but outside of that the choices are pretty slim. The rooftop **Sky Bar** (239/332-7425), where DJs spin "South Beach style," is a popular choice, but for a more down-to-earth option, head for the **Indigo Room** (2219 Main St., 239/332-0014), which boasts a decent beer selection, pool tables, and a friendly atmosphere.

Gamblers should undertake the 45-minute drive out to the **Seminole Casino—Immokalee** (506 S. 1st St., Immokalee, 239/658-1313, www.seminoleimmokalee-casino.com, open 24 hours daily). Poker, blackjack, table games, and lots and lots of slot machines are awaiting your open wallet. There's a small counter-service deli, a café, and a lounge area.

There are dozens of places to grab a drink in Fort Myers Beach, and pretty much all of them are of the beach bar-and-grill variety,

like **Cottage Beach Pub & Grill** (1250 Estero Blvd., 239/765-5440, 11am-12am daily), which often has live music upstairs, but is mainly a great place to drink and watch the sunset. The top-floor lounge at the **Lani Kai Island Resort** (1400 Estero Blvd., 239/463-3111, www.lanikaiislandresort.com, 11am-midnight Mon.-Thurs., 10am-2 am Fri.-Sat.) is another bar and grill. If you can beat (or outlast) the dinner crowd, you can grab one of the gliding table/bench combos to sip on a cold one while watching the sunset from one of the best (and highest) vantage points on Fort Myers Beach. Downstairs at the same hotel is a beach bar that stays pretty busy throughout the day and picks up at night with DJs and occasional cover bands. Open containers are only allowed on the beach if it's right at the place that served them. For a down-and-dirty dive bar experience, head to **The Mermaid Liquors and Lounge** (1204 Estero Blvd, 239/765-9100, hours vary), a combination package store and bar staffed with some of the friendliest bartenders around. It's filled with regulars who have learned to tolerate the bewildered tourists who occasionally stumble in. **House of Brewz** (201 Old San Carlos Blvd., 239/463-9874) is a good choice for craft beer in downtown Fort Myers Beach; it also has a full bar and is conveniently located in the same space as a sushi restaurant (Zushi Zushi), so you can eat too. However, just a mile or so over the bridge in Fort Myers proper is ★ **Point Ybel Brewing Company** (16120 San Carlos Blvd, 239/603-6535, 4pm-9pm Mon., Wed.-Thurs., 4pm-10pm Tues., Fri. Sat., noon-7pm Sun.), a local microbrewery with expertly crafted beers that are served up super fresh in a clean and beautiful tasting room that occasionally features some great local and regional live music.

The Arts

Like the rest of southwest Florida, Fort Myers's arts scene gets a little boost in the winter, and it's then that most local performing groups ramp up their schedules. Both the

Thomas Edison in Fort Myers

Thomas Edison's Lab

Thomas Edison bought 13 acres of riverfront land in Fort Myers in 1885. In the following year, he began construction on the property where he and his new wife Mina would retreat to during most of the following winters. From the day that Edison first moved into the estate, the city of Fort Myers had practically fallen over itself to honor his part-time residence here (after all, if it weren't for Edison bringing his own electric dynamo to town, the city likely wouldn't have been electrified for another couple of decades).

Edison's winter home in what was then a swampy hinterland inevitably brought other high-profile guests, including Presidents Teddy Roosevelt and Herbert Hoover, naturalist John Burroughs, and industrialist Harvey Firestone. However, when auto manufacturer Henry Ford arrived in Fort Myers in 1914, he was so impressed with the area that he bought a home right next door to Edison's. Sixteen years after Edison's death in 1931, Mina deeded the estate to the city of Fort Myers. In 1988, the neighboring Ford Estate was purchased by the city, and today, the combined properties are the primary attraction in Fort Myers.

Southwest Florida Symphony (239/418-1500, http://swflso.org) and **Gulf Coast Symphony** (228/896-4276, http://gulfcoast-symphony.net) stage concerts at the **Barbara B. Mann Performing Arts Hall** (8099 College Pkwy., 239/481-4849, www.bbmann-npah.com), which also hosts a slate of touring Broadway musicals and pop concerts.

Musical theater is the main attraction at the **Broadway Palm Dinner Theatre** (1380 Colonial Blvd., 239/278-4422, www.broadwaypalm.com), which hosts touring versions of shows like *All Shook Up* and *Guys and Dolls*. The **Sidney & Berne Davis Art**

Center (2301 1st St., 239/333-1933, www.sbdac.com) downtown hosts classical concerts, dance performances, and lectures by authors and artists.

The community-oriented **Alliance for the Arts** (10091 McGregor Blvd., 239/939-2787, www.artinlee.org, 10am-4pm Mon.-Fri., 10am-1pm Sat.) is primarily a facility for classes, camps, and other arts-education events. It's also home to a gallery where local artists' works are displayed.

Festivals and Events

Sponsored by a local Kiwanis club, the annual

Medieval Faire (239/369-6881, www.medieval-faire.com) brings jugglers, jousting, turkey legs, and a human-sized chess match to the Lakes Regional Park every January.

In January and February, the city of Fort Myers honors its most famous part-time resident with the **Edison Festival of Light** (239/334-2999, www.edisonfestival.org), a monthlong celebration that includes weekends with live music, craft shows, a parade, and even a bed race. Also in February, the **Southwest Florida Wine & Food Fest** (239/513-7990, www.swflwinefest.org) finds more than 20 chefs and nearly a dozen vintners at the Miromar Lakes Beach & Golf Club for a weekend of upscale but accessible tastings. The festival also features chef dinners held in various homes in the area.

For more than 50 years, the **Fort Myers Beach Shrimp Festival** (www.fortmyersbeachshrimpfestival.com, Mar.) has been an institution in the area. The festival is a weekend-long event, with a huge area on the beach for food and crafts vendors, shrimp dinners, and the crowning of the Shrimp Festival Queen.

SPORTS AND RECREATION

Golf

The relatively new course at **Shell Point Golf Club** (17401 On Par Blvd., 239/433-9790, www.shellpointgolf.com, greens fees from $49) was designed by Gordon Lewis and opened in 2000. The course is a par-72, at 6,546 yards. Another Gordon Lewis-designed course is the par-72, 6,538-yard course at **Eagle Ridge** (14589 Eagle Ridge Dr., 239/768-1888, www.playeagleridge.com, greens fees from $49). This course is considered one of the more challenging ones in the area, and it is known for its beautiful, well-maintained greens.

The City of Fort Myers owns and operates two municipal public golf courses. **Fort Myers Country Club** (3591 McGregor Blvd., 239/321-7488, 6:30am-6pm daily, greens fees from $17.50) was designed by Donald Ross in

1916, making it one of the oldest courses in the region. It's also one of the prettiest, and, according to *Golf Digest,* one of the top public courses in the United States. The course here is an 18-hole, 6,421-yard, par-72 course. The city also runs the less historical **Eastwood Golf Course** (4600 Bruce Herd Ln., 239/321-7487, www.cityftmyers.com, 7am-6pm daily, greens fees from $30), which is located outside of the city center, closer to the airport. This is also a par-72, 18-hole course.

Tennis

The city-owned **Racquet Club** (1700 Matthew Dr., 239/321-7550, www.cityftmyers.com, 8am-8pm Mon.-Fri., 8am-2pm Sat., 8am-noon Sun., daily rates: $10 for nonmembers, $5 for juniors) has eight lighted clay courts and two hard-surface courts. Daily admission charges are incredibly reasonable. This is a well-maintained and clean facility, with lockers, showers, and a snack bar. Lessons are also available.

Boating and Fishing

Almost a dozen different boats are available for rent from **Snook Bight Yacht Club & Marina** (4765 Estero Blvd., Fort Myers Beach, 239/765-4371, http://snookbightmarina.com, rentals from $140/half day), ranging in size from a 17-foot Aquasport to a leisurely 24-foot pontoon.

Getaway Marina (18400 San Carlos Blvd., Fort Myers Beach, 239/466-3600, www.getawaymarina.com, half-day fishing charters from $55/person, four-hour boat rentals from $140) provides half-day fishing charters aboard a 90-foot bus-on-the-water vehicle called *The Great Getaway.* For a less crowded experience, you can also book one of several boats that are available for full-day charters. Getaway also offers nighttime fishing trips, sunset tours, and boat rentals.

Beachcomber Tours (708 Fishermans Wharf, Fort Myers Beach, 239/443-7456, sightseeing excursions from $30/person, four-hour private charters from $450) takes guests out on a 21-passenger catamaran for dolphin and shelling tours, as well as ecotours and sunset cruises. Kayak tours are also available.

If you're staying in central Fort Myers and don't feel like heading out to Fort Myers Beach to go fishing, the **Tarpon Street Fishing Pier** (700 Tarpon St.) is a quiet (and free) option located near downtown.

Kayaking

There are a half-dozen places on Fort Myers Beach where kayakers can put in and begin exploring **The Great Calusa Blueway** paddling trail. If you brought your own canoe or kayak, head for the Mound House or **Bowditch Point Regional Park** (50 Estero Blvd., 239/765-6794). If you need a rental, **Holiday Adventure Tours & Boat Rental** (250 Estero Blvd., 239/463-8661, www.holidayadventuretoursfmb.com) and **Salty Sam's Waterfront Adventures** (2500 Main St., 239/463-7333, www.saltysamsmarina.com) can set you up; both businesses also offer guided tours.

Spectator Sports

Two major-league baseball teams have their "Grapefruit League" spring training games in Fort Myers. The **Boston Red Sox** (http://boston.redsox.mlb.com, from $10) play at **JetBlue Park** (2201 Edison Ave., 239/344-5208). The **Minnesota Twins** (http://minnesota.twins.mlb.com, from $12) play at Hammond Stadium at the **CenturyLink Sports Complex** (14100 Six Miles Cypress Pkwy., 239/533-6472).

Everglades Tours

In southwest Florida, there are any number of ecotour companies that will take you out into the Everglades. One of the best is **Everglades Day Safari** (pickups at four locations in the Fort Myers area, 239/472-1559, www.ecosafari.com, 7:30am-5:30pm daily, full-day all-inclusive safari cost: adults $159, children 5-11 $139), which bases its west coast operations just outside of Fort Myers. Although Fort Myers isn't typically thought of as a launching point into the 'Glades, it's not but a short

drive away. Everglades Day Safari focuses primarily on full-day tours, giving customers the opportunity to take in the varied ecosystems of the Everglades via boat, swamp buggy, airboat, and on foot. Lunch is included. The 1.5-hour boat cruise is one of the best parts of Everglades Day Safari's tours, as it offers a unique vantage point to how important the Everglades are to the area's aquatic health. While most tours tend to focus on the swamps, this is one of the few Everglades explorations that gives a more well-rounded view of these ecosystems.

FOOD
Fort Myers
BREAKFAST

For a ridiculously decadent way to start your day, **Bennett's Fresh Roast** (2011 Bayside Pkwy., 239/332-0077, www.bennetsfreshroast.com, 6am-6pm Mon.-Fri., 7am-3pm Sat.-Sun., from $7) offers an insane menu of fresh doughnuts and breakfast pastries. You can get a pita bread breakfast sandwich stuffed with eggs, ham, and cheese, or maybe even a fruit salad or some fresh yogurt. But when there's maple-bacon doughnuts and peanut butter chocolate doughnuts and orange-coconut donuts available, why would you take the healthy route? Given this place's name, it shouldn't be all that surprising that the coffee here is exceptional. The coffee served is roasted within the last 24 hours, and ground and brewed within the last hour or so. Bennett's also serves a frequently updated selection of sandwiches and salads for lunch.

AMERICAN

Crave (12901 McGregor Blvd., 239/466-4663, http://cravemenu.com, 8am-9pm Mon.-Sat., 8am-2pm Sun., from $7) is a great, cooked-to-order modern diner that nails the standards of breakfast, lunch, and dinner, and it also manages to add more than a few impressive touches of flair throughout. So, yes, you can get a plate of eggs and sausage, a stack of fluffy pancakes, or some stupendous biscuits and gravy for breakfast, but you can also tuck into a tremendous omelet stuffed with shrimp, crab, asparagus, and shiitake mushrooms. Lunch and dinner are similarly exceptional, with an entire menu of classics available from noon that include such blue plate specials as chicken potpie, meat loaf, roast chicken, and pot roast. Those classics are augmented by an extensive selection of sandwiches, salads, and pub grub that manages to consistently include fresh and innovative ingredients. Even if you're not all that hungry, order a basket of the homemade bread, a light and crispy French bread seasoned with sea salt and black pepper. Crave's Sunday brunch is incredibly popular, and for very good reason.

The best, and most popular, restaurant downtown is **Ford's Garage** (1415 Dean St, 239-332-3673, fordsgaragefl.com, 11am-midnight Mon.-Thurs., 11am-2am Fri., Sat., 11am-10pm Sun., main courses from $10). The specialty here is burgers, and Ford's will cook them perfectly, whether in a classic, straightforward way or as one of its special versions (try the Kobe burger). The craft-beer selection here is exceptional (with lots of local specialties) as are sides like fried pickles, and the atmosphere—loud, convivial, and decorated to look like a Model T garage—is definitely fun.

If you're downtown and need a no-frills meal, stop into **Oasis** (1661 Estero Blvd. #7, 239/334-1566, www.oasisatfortmyers.com, breakfast from $5.95, lunch from $6.95), a nice, diner-style café that's been feeding Fort Myers office workers for more than a quarter century. Focusing on the basics—omelets, waffles, and eggs and bacon for breakfast; burgers, sandwiches, and salads for lunch and dinner—Oasis doesn't try to be fancy (one of the specialties is a fried-chicken wrap), and that approach serves them well. Prices are reasonable and service is ridiculously fast and friendly.

Another option for straightforward and super-filling grub is **Fancy's Southern Cafe** (8890 Salrose Lane, 239/561-2988, www.fancyssoutherncafe.com, 11am-9pm daily, main courses from $8), located near the airport and I-75. Unapologetically serving up heaping helpings of chicken and waffles, shrimp and grits, chicken potpies, meat loaf sandwiches, and more, Fancy's uses fresh ingredients and a made-from-scratch ethos that puts most meat-and-three spots to shame.

BARBECUE

It's sort of hard to describe where to find the best barbecue in Fort Myers. At the corner of Martin Luther King, Jr. Boulevard and Cranford Avenue is a completely nondescript house with a smoker outside and a screen-porch extension. There's no outdoor signage. There doesn't appear to be an actual name for the business either, but a placard inside says it's called **McCarter's BBQ & Catering** (2675 Dr. Martin Luther King Jr. Blvd., 239/690-0356, hours vary). To the cars zooming by, it's not even clear it's a business in the commonly accepted sense of the word. However, when the smoker's on, this corner is bustling with folks stopping in to pick up some masterfully rubbed and smoked St. Louis-style ribs and some incredible tomato-based sauce. Needless to say, this is a cash-only enterprise, and to-go boxes are definitely available, which is good, since there is pretty much nowhere to sit except on the ground.

FINE DINING

Located in a turn-of-the-century building in downtown Fort Myers, **Veranda** (2122 2nd St., 239/932-2065, www.verandarestaurant.com, 11:30am-2:30pm and 5:30pm-9:30pm Mon.-Thurs., 11:30am-2:30pm and 5:30pm-10:30pm Fri., 5:30pm-10:30pm Sat., from $28) has been one of the city's top dining destinations for more than three decades. The menu is traditional American fare (steaks, chops, and seafood) prepared with a unique touch that combines Italian seasonings and Southern flair. The Veranda's Chicken Orleans combines shrimp, crab, and chicken breast with a spicy, Cajun-styled beurre blanc. Their decadent, breadcrumb-coated veal chops are stuffed with buffalo mozzarella and prosciutto. All of it is served in an opulent, historic atmosphere by an attentive and friendly waitstaff.

SEAFOOD AND SUSHI

True sushi aficionados should head directly for downtown's **Blu Sushi** (13451 McGregor Blvd., 239/489-1500, www.blusushi.com, 11am-10pm Sun.-Wed., 11am-2am Thurs.-Sat., sushi rolls $5-15). Sushi rolls are expertly prepared and served in a modern, stylish environment that's unique in Fort Myers. The hip, urban vibe extends to Blu's drinks menu, which features treats like the Frank Zappacino (coffee-infused rum, *dulce de leche* liqueur, Frangelico), Zenergy (vodka, green tea liqueur, Red Bull), saketinis, and "saktails."

There are quite a few places in Fort Myers to get an expertly grilled piece of fresh fish, but if you're looking for a down-to-earth and tremendously filling seafood experience, head directly to **Clam Bake** (16520 S. Tamiami Trail, 239/482-1930, www.clambakefortmyers. com, 11:30am-8pm daily, from $8). This is an utterly unpretentious, family-owned seafood joint that specializes in fresh seafood that is served raw, broiled, steamed, baked, or fried. The dishes here tend to have a New England-style slant to their preparations, so you can grab a lobster roll, clam chowder, and even stuffed quahog. Shellfish (obviously) is a specialty, with great mussels, oysters, and clams. If they've got fresh grouper in, make sure to order their grouper Reuben, and then plan on taking a nap afterward.

EUROPEAN

The Italian menu at **Cibo** (12901 McGregor Blvd., 239/454-3700, www.cibofortmyers.com, 5pm-9pm Mon.-Thurs., 5pm-10pm Fri.-Sat., from $16) is kept simple and straightforward with a handful each of classic pasta, meat, and fish dishes, as well as an extensive antipasti menu. This allows the kitchen to focus its efforts on doing a few things excellently, rather than dishing up a wide range of mediocrity. Portions are reasonably sized, and presentation is exceptional. And, to the owners' credit,

once you step inside the cozy restaurant, the strip mall exterior melts away to reveal a stylish and comfortable interior that's definitely classy and intimate.

Austrian-German Restaurant (1400 Colonial Blvd., 239/936-8118, http://ag-restaurant.com, 11am-9pm Mon.-Sat., from $12) is a small, family-owned restaurant that is far and away one of the best German restaurants in all of Florida. The menu is simple and based on classics, with a selection of schnitzels, spaetzle, and potato salad served in massive portions. All of it is prepared from scratch by Chef Helga, one-half of the husband-and-wife team that owns and operates this restaurant. Ingredients are fresh and authentic (Helga uses Austrian pumpkin-seed oil as a salad dressing), and the atmosphere is incredibly convivial, making diners feel less like customers and more like houseguests.

Fort Myers Beach
BREAKFAST

Tuckaway Bagel & Wafel Cafe (1740 Estero Blvd., 239/463-5398, 7am-2pm daily, menu items from $4.50) serves extraordinary steamed bagels in a variety of flavors and with a seemingly endless array of fillings. Bagels are available for breakfast and lunch. The French owners also make some exceptional Belgian-style waffles in both sweet and savory editions. (Beware that if you say yes to whipped cream here, you are really saying, "Yes, lots!") In addition to its titular dishes, Tuckaway serves pastries and fresh coffee in the morning and a good selection of sandwiches and salads in the afternoon. There's outdoor, pet-friendly seating.

AMERICAN

The comfortable environment and rooftop dining area at the **Beached Whale** (1249 Estero Blvd., 239/463-5505, www.thebeachedwhale.com, 11am-2am daily, from $9) make it a popular spot around sunset time. It's also a great place to grab a quick bite or a drink any time of day. In addition to fresh fish and massive sandwiches, the Whale's relatively diverse menu has some impressive flatbread pizzas and fall-off-the-bone barbeque dishes.

FINE DINING

"Upscale" in Fort Myers Beach is a somewhat relative term. This is a beach town that takes "casual" pretty seriously, and, really, there are only a handful of restaurants that successfully attempt to move beyond the sandy shoes vibe. Of them, **South Beach Grille** (7205 Estero Blvd., 239/463-7770, www.southbeachgrille-fmb.com, 4:30pm-10pm daily, from $13) does it best. Near the marina, but incongruously located in the Santini Marina Plaza strip mall, this is one of the only—if not the only—fine-dining options in Fort Myers Beach. The atmosphere is in keeping with the area's friendly, low-key vibe and the service here is unpretentious. The food is classic fare, with steaks, chops, and fresh seafood prepared in a classic but thoughtful manner. If you brought good clothes to the beach, this is where you should wear them.

SEAFOOD

You're at the beach, so seafood is definitely on the menu. And while nearly every restaurant in the American cuisine categories will have a pretty good selection of fresh seafood on the menu, **The Fish House** (7225 Estero Blvd., 239/765-6766, www.thefishhouseres-taurants.com, 11am-10pm daily, from $8) is probably your best bet for a seafood-centric dining experience. Located right on the marina, this unpretentious, open-air restaurant specializes in stone crab claws, fried seafood baskets, and ice-cold beer. Get here early if you want a chance at getting a table, or even a barstool. And yes, it's worth it.

Another good choice is the **Smokin' Oyster Brewery** (340 Old San Carlos Blvd, 239/463-3474, www.smokinoyster.com, 11am-11pm daily, main courses from $8) which, yes, specializes in both oysters and beer, two of the most essential ingredients for a successful beach vacation. This is very much a casual, just-off-the-water-front beach bar, complete with live music

and potent cocktails, but the food is actually quite exceptional for a joint like this. The seafood is always super fresh, well chosen, and expertly prepared, and the other menu items like the burgers, sandwiches, and salads utilize fresh, local ingredients as much as possible.

INTERNATIONAL

International options on Fort Myers Beach are somewhat limited, but there are a few places to go to get beyond the burgers and shrimp baskets offered at so many spots here. **Zushi Zushi** (201 Old San Carlos Blvd., 239/463-9874, www.zushizushi.com, 11:30am-11pm daily, sushi rolls from $5.95) is a reliable sushi joint in the heart of downtown that has decent rolls as well as Japanese and Thai kitchen food at a reasonable price.

Yo Taco (1375 Estero Blvd., 239/463-9864, 11am-3am daily, menu items from $2.49) isn't a food truck, but it kind of feels like one, as the walk-up stand offers window service and a few tables in the parking lot. Fillings here are ultra-fresh, and the tacos and burritos are not only generously stuffed, but also surprisingly inexpensive, making this an essential lunch-time spot on a beach day.

Heidi's Island Bistro (2943 Estero Blvd., 239/765-8844, www.heidisislandbistro.com, 7am-9pm daily, main courses from $7) is a relatively new arrival to the Fort Myers Beach dining scene, offering authentic German and European food for breakfast, lunch, and dinner. Portions are huge, sandwiches (especially the Reuben) are fantastic, and you need to try the from-scratch strudel, no matter what time of day you stop by.

ACCOMMODATIONS
Fort Myers
UNDER $100

Although generally accommodations in the Fort Myers area aren't all that expensive, finding cheap and safe budget lodging that's conveniently located can be a challenge. Fortunately, the **Fountain Cottages Inn** (14621 McGregor Blvd., Fort Myers,

239/481-0429, www.fountaincottagesinn.com, from $80 d) is a clean and affordable option.

$100-150

Stepping up just a tiny notch into slightly more costly digs affords a better selection of inexpensive lodging. There are at least a dozen affordable chain hotels with outlets in and around Fort Myers. If you're looking for something more unique, the **Rock Lake Resort** (2937 Palm Beach Blvd., 239/332-4080, www.rocklakeresort.com, from $129 d) is where you should look first. Located just outside of downtown, Rock Lake is right on Palm Beach Boulevard, and less than a block away from the Caloosahatchee River. The property is quite a nice destination in and of itself. The actual lake is tiny, but the way these duplex units are ringed around the water makes it feel like a private and pastoral spot, where every room has a beautiful view. Rooms are spacious and clean, with all basic necessities accounted for: comfortable new beds, well-equipped kitchenettes, nice bathrooms, and tile floors. On the property, there's a heated pool, a tennis court, and even a horseshoe pitch. A nature trail, boardwalk, and shaded gazebo make it easy to find a peaceful moment to yourself. Easy access to the river is a godsend for those who want to go canoeing or kayaking.

The **Hibiscus House Bed & Breakfast** (2135 McGregor Blvd., 239/332-2651, www.thehibiscushouse.net, from $119 d) is situated on a beautiful stretch of historic McGregor Boulevard, close to the Edison & Ford Winter Estates. While it may not have quite the historical cachet of its nearby neighbor, the tree-covered property and small rooms inside are charming and beautiful. All five rooms have private bathrooms. Each room is decorated in a unique style that largely eschews the frills and lace expected from a B&B this close to the Edison house.

A fantastic choice for families who want to explore Fort Myers, Fort Myers Beach, and the islands of Sanibel and Captiva is the **Residence Inn Fort Myers Sanibel** (20371 Summerlin Rd., 239/415-4150, www.marriott.com, from $119 d). Located on the Fort Myers side of the Sanibel causeway (which means you'll only need to pay the sky-high toll when you want to head out to Sanibel) and about a 15-minute drive to Fort Myers Beach or downtown Fort Myers, the hotel is located next to a strip mall and across the street from outlet stores. Within the mall is a very nice Publix grocery store, which will come in handy for stocking the full kitchen that comes with each room. As with all Residence Inns, your room will be less like a standard hotel room and more like a tiny one-bedroom apartment. By some miraculous organizational feat, the designers managed to cram a comfortable living room, dining area, office, and kitchen into the non-bedroom space, leaving the sleeping area fairly spacious and comfortable. The staff is friendly and helpful. All expected site amenities—pool, fitness center, free breakfast, Wi-Fi—are available.

$150-200

Another great and reasonably priced option is **Hotel Indigo** (1520 Broadway, 239/337-3446, www.hotelindigo.com, from $149 d), which is fancier than Rock Lake Resort and more conveniently located in the downtown area. As with other Indigo locations (the brand is Intercontinental's boutique chain), the room count is low (74) and the style quotient is high. The smallish rooms have modern conveniences, with fresh bedding, up-to-date furnishings, flat-screen TVs, and some pretty luxe bathrooms.

The **Sanibel Harbour Marriott Resort & Spa** (17260 Harbour Pointe Dr., 239/466-4000, www.marriott.com, from $179 d) can boast of a location that's similarly convenient to that of the Residence Inn. It's right at the base of the Sanibel causeway in the relative isolation of Punta Rassa. There's a lot available on the resort property. Nearly 350 rooms (278 standard rooms, 69 suites) are stacked atop one another in giant imposing towers, and it seems like each one has a gorgeous view. There are five restaurants on site, and if that's not enough to choose from, you can also splurge on a dinner cruise aboard the resort's 100-foot yacht. A full-service spa and fitness center, three heated pools, tennis courts, volleyball, and a jogging trail mean you won't need to leave the property to get your exercise. However, if you need anything that's not available on the resort property, you're going to have to get in your car.

Fort Myers Beach
$150-200

There are plenty of accommodations to choose from on Fort Myers Beach, and among the best is the ★ **Silver Sands Villas** (1207 Estero Blvd., 239/463-6554, www.silversands-villas.com, from $149 d). It's as welcoming and unpretentious as the town in which it is located. The casual, colorful, and semi-residential atmosphere here definitely makes it feel like a home away from home. Twenty rooms are scattered about the property in cottages. Some are basic hotel-type accommodations; others are like tiny houses, complete with living rooms, multiple bedrooms, and kitchens. All of them are brightly painted and have beach-friendly hardwood or tile floors. Flat-screen TVs, soft towels, and deluxe bedding add a surprising touch of luxury. From the neighborhood cats that roam the property to the super-friendly staff, this choice spot is rather down-to-earth.

The **Beacon Beachfront Bed & Breakfast** (1240 Estero Blvd., 239/463-5264, www.thebeaconmotel.com, from $134 d) offers an economical and comfortable option very close to the heart of the action in Fort Myers. With 13 individually decorated rooms in various bedding configurations, two suites (one of which has a full kitchen), and a free-standing beach cottage, the Beacon is actually less than a proper bed-and-breakfast than it is a repurposed beachside motel. Although the rooms may not have the same sort of visual style as the pink-and-purple exterior of the building, they do all offer comfortable bedding, clean kitchenettes, and Wi-Fi.

$200-300

The all-suite **Edison Beach House** (830 Estero Blvd., 239/463-1530, www.edison-beachhouse.com, from $260 d) is a great option for couples or families. Rooms are large, apartment-style accommodations, with full kitchens, dinning areas, sitting areas that feature 47-inch flat-screen TVs, and balconies. The management is pretty fastidious about its cleanliness standards, extending them all the way out to the beach, which is raked every morning.

OVER $300

The expansive grounds of the 12-acre **Pink Shell Beach Resort & Marina** (275 Estero Blvd., 239/463-6181, http://pinkshell.com, suites from $329) pack a lot of amenities onto the property, with two restaurants, a spa, an enormous pool, and a specially designated kids' area. Reasonably modern and well-maintained suites and villas range in size from 650 square feet to over 1,000. There's even a private, old-fashioned beach cottage for rent. All the accommodations have full kitchens, dining areas, and separate bedrooms. The best bets here are the Captiva Villas; although they're not the largest, they boast the nicest furnishings and appointments and are in their own, quiet building.

INFORMATION AND SERVICES

The **Lee County Visitor & Convention Bureau** (2210 2nd St., Suite 600, 239/338-3500, www.fortmyers-sanibel.com) can help with information on Fort Myers, Fort Myers Beach, Sanibel and Captiva Islands, and any other destination in Lee County.

GETTING THERE AND AROUND
Getting There

The largest airport in the entire southwest Florida region is **Southwest Florida International Airport** (RSW, 11000 Terminal Access Rd., 239/590-4800, www.flylcpa.com), which, conveniently enough, is located just a few minutes away from downtown Fort Myers. It's serviced by most major American carriers, including Southwest. **Greyhound** offers service into the bus station (2250 Widman Way, 239/334-1011, www.greyhound.com).

By car, the nearest major highway is I-75, which connects the south Gulf Coast with the midwestern United States. Running roughly parallel to I-75 is the Tamiami Trail (US-41), which runs through Tampa, Sarasota, Fort Myers, Naples, and Miami.

Getting Around

Lee County operates **LeeTran** (239/533-8726, www.rideleetran.com), a bus company with decent route service throughout the county and the Fort Myers core. Its **Trollee** service can easily get you right to Fort Myers Beach from the heart of the city. Fares start at $0.50 per ride.

If you choose not to avail yourself of public transportation, you will need to have a car to get around central Fort Myers. Other than within the River District, this is not a pedestrian-friendly city. Attempting to bike around the city would be inefficient and dangerous, thanks to the not-insubstantial distances between sights and the lack of dedicated bike lanes along some of the busiest corridors.

Sanibel and Captiva Islands

It's said that you learn a lot about someone (or someplace) by how you're greeted. The first words you'll hear before crossing the only bridge onto **Sanibel** and **Captiva Islands** are, "Six dollars, please." Despite this rather begrudging welcome, the atmosphere and attitude on both Sanibel and Captiva are surprisingly low-key.

There are dozens of multimillion-dollar homes scattered throughout the islands, and some of the hotels and resorts charge high rates for relatively basic accommodations. But such upmarket accoutrements mask a beach bum's paradise. Both islands—but Sanibel in particular—are excellent for shelling and bird-watching. And the beaches are absolutely stunning.

SIGHTS
Sanibel Historical Village & Museum

The ironic thing about the **Sanibel Historical Village & Museum** (950 Dunlop Rd., 239/472-4648, www.sanibelmuseum.org, 10am-4pm Wed.-Sat. Nov.-Apr., 10am-1pm Wed.-Sat. May-mid-Aug., $5) is that the "village" itself is only about 20 years old. Although the eight buildings on this site date from 1898-1926, they were all at different places on the island until the 1980s, when they began to be relocated to this central location, refurbished, and opened as a historical attraction. The buildings themselves are quite interesting, ranging from a blue "kit" house bought from the Sears Roebuck catalog for $2,200 in 1925 and a gas-station-turned-tearoom to a one-room schoolhouse and a tiny post office. There's a small museum in the Rutland House with a collection of antiques and artifacts from around the area. The best way to get a feel for Sanibel's history is to go on one of the docent-guided tours of the village.

Bailey-Matthews Shell Museum

Shelling is a hugely popular pastime along the barrier islands of the southern Gulf Coast. The **Bailey-Matthews Shell Museum** (3075 Sanibel-Captiva Rd., 239/395-2223, www.shellmuseum.org, 10am-5pm daily, $15 adults, $9 children 12-17, $7 children 5-11, children 4 and under free) goes a long way to putting a serious tilt on an activity many folks undertake as a way to pass the time on a leisurely holiday. The large, modern building on the outskirts of the town of Sanibel has more than two dozen displays of shells and informative mini exhibits on their various uses throughout history. It may seem somewhat odd to devote so much attention to these temporary marine-life homes, but as the museum makes clear, there are extensive bio-science and anthropological implications to shells.

Center for the Rehabilitation of Wildlife (CROW)

The **Center for the Rehabilitation of Wildlife**, or **CROW** (3883 Sanibel-Captiva Rd., 239/472-3644, www.crowclinic.org, 10am-4pm Tues.-Sun., free), opened a visitor education center in 2013 to highlight the center's work in rescuing and rehabilitating the native wildlife of Sanibel. The center treats more than 4,000 animals annually. The primary role of the small visitors center is to raise awareness in order to bring that number down. Most of the displays are designed to simultaneously impress upon guests the diversity of the area's wildlife, while teaching them what they can do to reduce the number of animals injured or threatened by human development.

★ J. N. "Ding" Darling National Wildlife Refuge

The **J. N. "Ding" Darling National Wildlife Refuge** (1 Wildlife Dr., 239/472-1100, www.fws.gov/dingdarling, education center: 9am-5pm daily Jan.-Apr., 9am-4pm daily May-Dec., free; wildlife drive: 7:30am-sunset Sat.-Thurs., $5 per vehicle) is named after Jay Norwood "Ding" Darling, a political cartoonist in the early 1900s whose primary interests were political corruption and environmental conservation. As a hunter and fisherman, Darling was a fierce advocate for wise land use. He understood that intelligent regulations could insure the viability of wildlife for generations to come. His cartoons earned him three Pulitzer Prizes. But perhaps one of his greatest accomplishments was being tapped by President Franklin Roosevelt to head up the U.S. Biological Survey (the predecessor of today's U.S. Fish & Wildlife Service). In that position, Darling focused squarely on habitat preservation and restoration, as well as game management, all of which led to the establishment of national game refuges throughout the United States.

Darling often wintered on Sanibel and Captiva (he built a winter home on Captiva).

J. N. "Ding" Darling National Wildlife Refuge

So, it was only appropriate that one of the earliest national wildlife refuges—the Sanibel National Wildlife Refuge—was renamed in his honor. The J. N. "Ding" Darling National Wildlife Refuge is a permanent home or migratory stopover for more than 50 species of birds. In the winter, the mudflats and waterfront trees are thick with spoonbills, oyster catchers, storks, ibis, and others. There is a diversity of mammal and reptile life within the refuge, but bird-watching is one of the primary activities here.

To that end, the refuge's Wildlife Drive, a five-mile circuit that's open to automobiles, is quite popular, especially during the winter. It allows visitors a leisurely route through the park's mangrove forests and mudflats in their own vehicles. A tour company also provides tram tours along the Drive. There are several hiking trails and two canoe trails for those who wish to explore on their own. The visitors center is also an impressive sight, with exhibits that give a perspective on Darling's career, as well as the variety of wildlife within the refuge. Unlike many other National Wildlife Refuges, there's a pronounced sense of mission at the Darling facility. The staff and volunteers are exceedingly friendly and helpful, and their enthusiasm is contagious.

BEACHES
Sanibel Island

Causeway Beach (sunrise-sunset daily), along the bridge between Sanibel and Fort Myers, is quite nice, despite the traffic zooming by. Parking is free, and bathrooms and picnic tables are at the main beach area, right before the toll gate. The water here is a bit rougher than on the island, but it's shallow, and the sandy beaches are stocked with shells.

Once on the island, beach lovers should head directly for **Algiers Beach** (Algiers Ln. at W. Gulf Rd., sunrise-sunset daily, parking $4/hour). This isolated shorefront is named after a steamboat that ran aground and was used as a home for a while. This is a locals-favorite place, but the beach itself is seldom very crowded. Facilities include picnic tables, restrooms, and a paid parking lot. The sand here has a lot of shells and the water is smooth and shallow; leashed pets are allowed.

Another quiet option is **Bowman's Beach** (northwest on Sanibel-Captiva Rd., left on Bowman's Beach Rd., park is at the end of the road, sunrise-sunset daily, parking $4/hour). The parking lot is a bit of a hike from the actual beach. The general isolation of the location (it's quite a distance from any hotels or residences) gives it an insider's secret feel.

the lighthouse on Sanibel Island

However, the beach itself is fairly popular and the parking lot can fill up quickly. The white sand spreads out quite a distance from the entry point, so it's easy to find a quiet spot. It's a nicely equipped park, with picnic tables, barbeque grills, restrooms, a fitness trail, playground, and an outdoor shower.

Captiva Island
CAPTIVA BEACH

At the northern tip of Captiva Island is **Captiva Beach** (14790 Captiva Dr., 239/472-2472, www.leegov.com, 7am-7pm daily, parking $5/2 hours), a part of Alison Hagerup Beach Park, and one of only two publicly accessible beaches on the island. Captiva Beach's wide expanse of soft, white sand is quite popular. But the tiny parking lot here has the effect of limiting daily attendance. This is one of the most beautiful beaches on either island. Get here early to enjoy the shallow, blue waters or to explore for shells. Despite being a named park (Alison Hagerup Beach Park), the only facilities here are portable toilets. Although the beach along the main road is, technically, publicly accessible, there is absolutely nowhere to park to actually access it. So, unless you're renting a house nearby, there's no easy way to get to the beach.

BLIND PASS BEACH AND TURNER BEACH

These **beaches** (17200 Captiva Dr., 239/395-1860, www.leeparks.org, sunrise-sunset daily, parking $4/hour) are on either side of the bridge that links Sanibel and Captiva Islands. **Blind Pass Beach** is technically on the Sanibel side, but both beaches are closer to the action in Captiva than in Sanibel. Neither beach is particularly excellent for swimming; the undertow can be quite strong, especially near the bridge. But that same wave activity also makes for some incredible shelling at both beaches. The soft, white sand and crisp, blue water are absolutely gorgeous, making it a good place for sunbathing and a near-perfect spot for couples to catch the sunset. Fishing is quite popular at both beaches.

ENTERTAINMENT AND EVENTS
Nightlife

There's not much in the way of dedicated nightlife spots on Sanibel, but there's plenty of fun to be had at **Doc Ford's Rum Bar & Grille** (975 Rabbit Rd, 239/472-8311, www.docfordssanibel.com, 11am-10pm daily). Founded by noted Florida author Randy Wayne White (and named after the star of his series of area-located crime novels), it's much more of a restaurant and sports bar, with good food and a festive bar area beloved by locals and tourists alike.

The Arts

The arts scene on Sanibel pretty much falls under the umbrella of **Big Arts** (900 Dunlop Rd., 239/395-0900, www.bigarts.org, gallery hours 9am-4pm Mon.-Fri., 9am-1pm Sat.), the island's main (and only) dedicated cultural center. The center has a 400-seat performance hall, art gallery, sculpture garden, and classrooms. It's an impressive facility for such a small island. Big Arts maintains a pretty robust cultural calendar throughout the year, one that greatly expands during the high-season winter months. Classical music, theater, dance, jazz concerts, art exhibits, and more make their way here, and the offerings consistently manage to produce a comfortable, community-oriented atmosphere that's respectful without being stuffy.

Festivals and Events

For almost a quarter century, the **Sanibel Shell Fair & Show** (2173 Periwinkle Way, Sanibel, Mar.) has drawn beachcombers and shell aficionados to the island. Taking place over three days at the Sanibel Community House, it's an outdoor fair with shell-themed crafts and vendors. Inside, there's a show ($3 admission), where rare shells, jewelry, and juried exhibits are on display.

In November, local restaurants strut their stuff at **Taste of the Islands** (http://tastesanibelcaptiva.com). Live music and local craft

Shells Abound

Shelling on Sanibel Island goes far beyond the casual, exploratory pickings of a lazy day at the beach. Shells are serious business here. Sanibel and Captiva are known as the Shell Islands, and there's even the **Bailey-Matthews Shell Museum** on Sanibel dedicated to them. Thanks to a peculiar confluence of Gulf currents, and the geographical position of the island, Sanibel sees a large amount of empty marine-life homes washing up on its shores. Sanibel itself is positioned on an unusual east-west trajectory (rather than the north-south of most barrier islands in the Gulf of Mexico). More than 400 different species of shells—from bivalves to conchs—can be found on the beaches here. The shells are dug up by visitors of all ages who, by the end of their vacation, are suffering from what's known as "the Sanibel stoop."

vendors round out the offerings at this one-day event in Sanibel Community Park.

SPORTS AND RECREATION
Boating and Fishing

Tarpon Bay Explorers (900 Tarpon Bay Rd., 239/472-8900, www.tarponbayexplorers.com, fishing charters from $175/two people, kayak/canoe rental from $20/two hours) is located within the J. N. "Ding" Darling National Wildlife Refuge. It is the company that provides the tram tours of the refuge's wildlife trail. The company also offers a couple of guided kayak and canoe tours; fishing supplies; and kayak, canoe, and pontoon rentals. At the company's main location is a gift shop and visitors center with a touch tank that allows kids (and adults) to get hands on with hermit crabs, urchins, sea stars, and more.

Anglers interested in throwing a line in close to shore should head for the **Sanibel Island Fishing Pier** (112 Periwinkle Way, 239/472-3700, parking $2/hr). From here, you'll be able to land redfish, snook, sea trout, snapper, and grouper year-round. The spring and summer months bring tarpon, cobia, and pompano. Heavier tackle is recommended here. You can pick up any necessary supplies at **The Bait Box** (1041 Periwinkle Way, 239/472-1618, www.the-baitbox.com, opens 7am daily), located in the heart of Sanibel village.

Biking

There are ample bike trails throughout Sanibel, and the flat surfaces make biking on the island far preferable to driving. **Billy's Rentals** (1470 Periwinkle Way, 239/472-5248, bike rentals from $5, scooter rentals from $40) has bikes, surreys, and scooters for rent. It conducts Segway tours of the island too. Another good option for bike rentals and repairs is **Finnimore's Cycle Shop** (2353 Periwinkle Way, 239/472-5577, www.finni-mores.com, bike rentals from $14/day), which offers singles, tandems, and surreys, as well as beach gear, paddle boards, and kayak rentals.

FOOD
Sanibel
BREAKFAST

Nestled into the village-like atmosphere of eastern Sanibel Island, the **Lighthouse Cafe** (362 Periwinkle Way, 239/472-0303, www.lighthousecafe.com, 7am-3pm daily, from $8) claims to have the world's best breakfast. Breakfast here is not only pretty good, it's also pretty popular. In addition to morning-meal standards (eggs Benedict, omelets, and waffles), the Lighthouse slides in some interesting additions like frittatas and shrimp-and-crab omelets. The ingredients seem to be fresh, and the presence of Bloody Marys (made with sake) and mimosas can make for quite a leisurely take on the vacation breakfast or brunch.

The quaint and quirky **Island Cow** (2163 Periwinkle Way, 239/472-0606, www.sanibelislandcow.com, 7:30am-10pm daily, from $7) is a great place to grab a great meal any time of day. Breakfast seems to function with a theme of "more is more." Whether it's one of Island Cow's enormous pancakes, a belt-stretching seafood omelet (which combines shrimp, scallops, and crabmeat, and what seems like a half-dozen eggs and a quarter-pound of cheese), or a plate of eggs, grits, and home fries, there's absolutely no way you'll push back from the morning table feeling hungry. The lunch and dinner menus are no less satisfying, with quesadillas, po'boys, pasta, and seafood dishes. Beer and wine are served here too. But the beverages of choice come from the dairy bar, which whips up smoothies, milkshakes, floats, and even egg creams.

SEAFOOD

The best choice for seafood raw bar fans would be the **Lazy Flamingo** (1036 Periwinkle Way, 239/472-6939, www.lazyflamingo.com, 11:30am-1am daily, from $7). In addition to freshly shucked oysters and clams, the Flamingo also has a standard selection of fried seafood, conch fritters, sandwiches, salads, and wings. There's also a location on Pine Avenue (6520 Pine Ave., 239/472-5353, 11:30am-1am daily).

For dinner, the seafood preparations at **Gramma Dot's** (634 N. Yachtsman Dr., 239/472-8138, 11am-10pm daily, from $19) are uniformly excellent. A plate of coconut shrimp comes with gigantic and super-fresh prawns, coated perfectly with coconut shavings, and served with a rich, sweet pineapple sauce. Scallops, grouper, and mahi round out the seafood section of the small menu, which also has a few steak and chicken dishes.

AMERICAN

Just need a hot dog? Hit up **Schnapper's Hots** (1528 Periwinkle Way, 239/472-8686, www.schnappershotssanibel.com, 11am-8pm Sun.-Thurs., 11am-9pm Fri.-Sat., $5), a friendly, no-frills spot that serves franks, burgers, fries, pizza, and fresh ice cream.

FINE DINING

The best fine-dining option on Sanibel is the perfectly named **Blue Coyote Supper Club** (1100 Par View Dr, 239/472-9222, www.bluecoyotesupperclub.com, lunch: 11am-3pm Sun.-Fri., dinner: 5pm-9pm Tues.-Sat., main courses from $25). An extension of a members-only restaurant in Fort Myers, the Blue Coyote on Sanibel is open to anyone ... or at least anyone who's ready to shell out at least $50 on dinner for two. The food—a skillful and modern take on Continental cuisine with standards like beef tenderloin sitting alongside inspired comfort food like a seafood-and-sausage stew—is remarkable for its emphasis on consistency and quality rather than adventurous flourishes. However, the atmosphere, which has a variety of whimsically dark paintings at its heart and a friendly and attentive (but not obsequious) staff, ensures that this feels less like your grandparents' stuffy supper club and more like dinner at your artsy chef friend's house.

Despite a name that may conjure images of a classic rock-inspired bar-and-grill, **Sweet Melissa's Cafe** (1625 Periwinkle Way, 239/472-1956, www.sweetmelissascafe.net, 11:30am-2:30pm and 5pm-close Mon.-Fri., 5pm-close Sat., from $26) is, in fact, one of the best fine-dining options on Sanibel Island. The menu is extensive and varied. Executive Chef Melissa Talmage wisely invests her talents in presenting a wide array of nearly 20 tapas-style small plates. This allows diners to indulge in anything from a goat cheese crepe and bourbon-glazed pork belly to ricotta ravioli with Kobe beef-cheek *sugo*. Even the entrées—of which there are half a dozen—are available in small portions to basically make the entire menu a tasting menu. It's a smart and fantastic way to explore a range of flavors. Talmage incredibly seems to excel at all of the preparations.

The CIA and Sanibel

After a career in espionage, it's easy to imagine that, on retirement, one might want to while away his or her days on a small, quiet island devoid of international intrigue. For many Central Intelligence Agency (CIA) officers, Sanibel Island was that small, quiet island. For decades, Sanibel was known in government circles as one of the preferred retirement destinations for those leaving the CIA. In fact, Sanibel was so popular among retired spooks that, upon retiring from the agency's Directorate of Operations in 1971, Porter Goss moved to Sanibel. Goss's retirement was a medical necessity—he came down with a potentially fatal staph infection—and the urging of fellow retired CIA officers and the beautiful weather of Sanibel made it an easy choice for him to move here. Goss became a prime motivator behind the city's incorporation. In 1974, Goss was elected to Sanibel's first city council and, in 1975-1977, he served as the city's mayor. (All the while, he also was the publisher of a community newspaper on the island.) Goss's roles in Sanibel politics ultimately led to his election as the district's representative to the U.S. House of Representatives, and, in something of a full circle, he was appointed director of the CIA by President George W. Bush in 2004. There are probably still quite a few retired CIA operatives living on Sanibel—but you'll never know it.

Captiva

PUB GRUB

The Mucky Duck (11546 Andy Rosse Ln., 239/472-3434, www.muckyduck.com, noon-10pm Mon.-Sat., 3pm-9pm Sun., from $24) is a basic pub-with-grub place, serving up a somewhat unique combination of seafood platters and traditional English fare. Mucky Duck has an unbeatable location right on the sand. It boasts a fantastic outdoor dining area, with some of the best sunset views in the entire state of Florida.

FINE DINING

No visit to Captiva would be complete without a meal at the ★ **Bubble Room** (15001 Captiva Dr., 239/472-5558, http://bubbleroomrestaurant.com, 11am-3pm and 4:30pm-10pm daily, from $10). Perhaps not so much for the food, but for the sheer insanity of the decor. Imagine decades' worth of movie memorabilia, vintage toys, pop culture effluvia, and various kitsch from the 1930s, 1940s and 1950s jammed into a restaurant where the servers are dressed as youth scouts and you're halfway there. The Bubble Room is definitely quirky and has played on that reputation for years. What makes this environment so much fun is the sense that all that crazy clutter is here by accident, and not by design. It doesn't feel like a corporate-designed bit of weirdness; it is just weird. Dishes like the Duck Ellington, the Cluck Gable, and the Salmon Davis Jr. are fun to order and quite decent to eat. By far the best thing on the menu is the "bubble bread," a decadently sweet sticky-bun concoction that is perhaps the best finish-your-vegetables bribe ever invented.

The Green Flash (15183 Captiva Dr., 239/472-3337, www.greenflashcaptiva.com, 11:30am-9:30pm daily, from $26) offers some extraordinary views, thanks to its unusual-for-Captiva second-floor location. However, keep in mind that the windows are facing east, so this isn't a place to head for sunset drinks and dinner. The menu is focused squarely on seafood, with shrimp, crab, and multiple grouper preparations making up the bulk of the dinner menu. (The restaurant also serves veal and pork dishes.) Dinner can be an expensive endeavor, and the food is decent without being remarkable. The Green Flash is a much better bet for lunch, when you can grab a burger, a basket of fried shrimp, or one of its excellent veggie sandwiches for less than $10 while enjoying the view of the boats in Pine Island Sound.

ACCOMMODATIONS

During high season, "budget accommodations" on Sanibel and Captiva is a relative concept. Many places offer incredible values during the scorching summer months, but when the snowbirds descend November-April, overnight rates go through the roof, and at many places there are minimum stay requirements.

$150-250

Anchor Inn (1245 Periwinkle Way, Sanibel, 239/395-9688, http://sanibelanchorinn.com, from $229 d) is a centrally located property with a variety of room options available, ranging from basic hotel accommodations and one- and two-room efficiencies to a two-bedroom cottage. Rooms are cute and tidy, with tropical color schemes. The bright-yellow, two-story cottages have sleeping lofts and bedrooms. There's a heated pool and grilling/picnic area.

The tropical foliage that engulfs the **Kona Kai** (1539 Periwinkle Way, Sanibel, 239/472-1001, www.konakaimotel.com, from $199 d) does an admirable job of masking the traditional motel feel of this property. In addition to a handful of regular rooms, there are also efficiency and suite accommodations, as well as two small cottages. All of the rooms have garden views, with the exception of the pool cottage, which, logically, overlooks the pool. Furnishings here are, ironically, not quite as heavy on the tropical rattan-and-pastels theme that many other properties go for; instead, they're clean and contemporary.

On Captiva, **Jensen's "On the Gulf"** (15300 Captiva Dr., Captiva, 239/472-4684, www.gocaptiva.com, from $165 d) is a unique collection of 10 villas, cottages, suites, and beach houses. It has an intimate, boutique vibe. Each room is decorated differently, but all the furnishings are very nice and comfortable. One of the most interesting spots is the "Post Office Sweet," which was originally the Captiva Post Office but is now a semiprivate cottage. This is one of the few properties on Captiva that's directly on the beach. The Jensen family also operates the nearby Twin Palm Marina.

$250-350

'Tween Waters Inn (15951 Captiva Dr., Captiva, 239/472-5161, www.tween-waters.com, from $325 d) on Captiva has a decades-old past that has been updated to suit the needs of contemporary travelers. The property's history dates back to the 1930s, and although there are more than 100 units here, it's the 19 one-, two-, and three-bedroom cottages that exude the most nostalgic ambiance. With vibrant paint schemes outside, the cottages feature interiors decorated in rustic, hunting-lodge tones and are equipped with full kitchens, living and dining rooms, and separate bedrooms. Slightly less expensive are the spacious and contemporary hotel-style accommodations, available as regular rooms and suites. The well-groomed beach is where most folks will spend their day. There's also a large, sparkling pool, tennis courts, and discounted access to the Beachview Golf Club available to guests.

Located right on the beach, the perfectly named **Beachview Cottages** (3325 W. Gulf Dr., Sanibel, 239/472-1202, www.beachviewsanibel.com, from $279 d) is a great, reasonably priced option. A handful of cottages are lined up along a sandy pathway to the beach. These small, 1960s era lodgings are comfortable and clean, with full kitchens. Although the resort is situated among condos along West Gulf Drive, the Beachview feels like it is its own private village.

The **Song of the Sea** (863 E. Gulf Dr., Sanibel, 239/472-3181, www.theinnsofsanibel.com, from $329 d) is part of the Inns of Sanibel family of hotels. It is positioned to appeal to deep-pocketed visitors that crave charm and personality but don't want to sacrifice luxury and service. The pink-hued resort couldn't scream "romance" any louder, from its quiet, tropical atmosphere to the bottle of wine that greets guests upon arrival. There's a lot to love for couples here, without feeling like you've stepped into a champagne-glass whirlpool tub. There are only 30 rooms on the property, and all are comfortable and cozy without being cramped. Tile floors, ceiling fans, and wooden blinds give the rooms a classic tropical vibe. All the rooms and suites have their own kitchenettes and Wi-Fi.

Over $350

The ★ **Seaside Inn** (541 E. Gulf Dr., Sanibel, 239/472-1400, www.sanibelcollection.com, from $379 d) manages to combine a casual, classic beach feel with subtly upscale appointments and highly attentive service, resulting in one of the most luxurious and comfortable places to stay on Sanibel Island. Though built in the 1960s, the inn was completely renovated in the mid-2000s to meet the expectations held by many of the island's well-to-do visitors. The Seaside is part of the Inns of Sanibel family of hotels. From the daily in-room delivery of a continental breakfast (a basket of pastries, fresh fruit, juice, and coffee) to the plush in-room appointments, the Seaside is simultaneously charming and posh. The 32 units are spacious, ranging from standard guest rooms to studio cottages and three-bedroom suites, and they're all decorated tastefully, with muted tropical tones and contemporary furnishings. All rooms have at least a mini kitchen, and the cottages have full kitchens. DVD players (and a free rental library) and Wi-Fi are also available. More to the point, gorgeous blue waters are right outside your window.

GETTING THERE AND AROUND

The only way to drive onto Sanibel Island is via the Sanibel Causeway, which connects the island to Punta Rassa, just at the western tip of mainland Fort Myers. There's a $6 toll to go onto the island.

You can drive around Sanibel if you want to, but you really should ride a bike. There are 25 miles of wide, multiuse trails that run parallel to the main roads. Unless you're staying on the eastern tip of the island and want to make it all the way to the other end, the flat terrain is optimal for biking. Using a bike for your main mode of transportation also makes parking at crowded beach access points much easier.

The only way to get to Captiva is via Sanibel Island; the two islands are connected by a short bridge.

The downtown area of Captiva is walkable. However, that section of the island is really only about two blocks long by two blocks wide. The rest of Captiva has narrow roads with no sidewalks, making it something of a challenge for those on bikes or on foot. Parking is at a premium, so be mindful that you don't park in a private lot because you will be towed.

Naples

Although the art galleries and boutiques of downtown **Naples** provide wonderful, walkable window-shopping year-round, some of the best sights Naples has to offer are actually outside of that central core. Nature preserves and wildlife areas abound just outside of town, and longtime locals are eager to show them off to adventurous visitors. Even within city limits, the white, powdery sand of Naples's beaches are some of the best (and most underappreciated) in all of Florida. The Naples Zoo and the Naples Museum of Art are both exceptional and accessible.

Naples is a city that reveals part of its personality on the surface. Once you get past that initial impression, there's a lot more that's worth exploring.

SIGHTS
Old Naples

To get a real feel for Naples, the best place to start is **Old Naples** (public parking garages

Naples

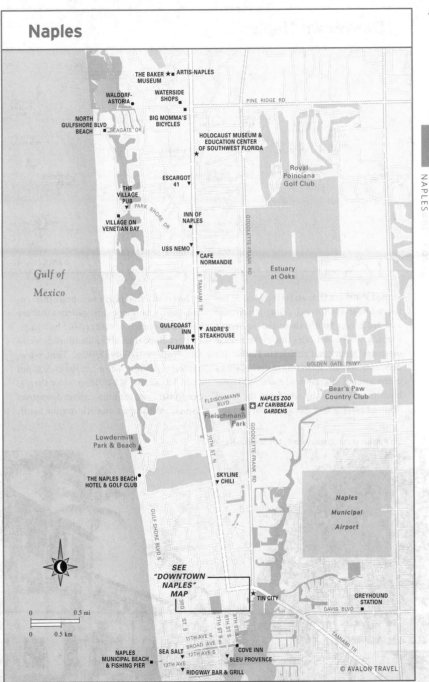

THE BAKER ★ ■ ARTIS-NAPLES
MUSEUM

WALDORF-
ASTORIA ●

WATERSIDE
SHOPS ■

PINE RIDGE RD

NORTH
GULFSHORE BLVD
BEACH ■ SEAGATE DR

BIG MOMMA'S
BICYCLES

HOLOCAUST MUSEUM &
EDUCATION CENTER
OF SOUTHWEST FLORIDA
★

Royal
Poinciana
Golf Club

ESCARGOT
41 ▼

THE
VILLAGE
PUB
▼ PARK SHORE DR

INN OF
NAPLES ●

VILLAGE ON
VENETIAN BAY ■

USS NEMO ▼

▼ CAFE
NORMANDIE

E TAMIAMI TR

GOODLETTE-FRANK RD

Estuary
at Oaks

Gulf of
Mexico

GULFCOAST
INN ●

▼ ANDRE'S
STEAKHOUSE

FUJIYAMA ▼

GOLDEN GATE PKWY

FLEISCHMANN
BLVD

NAPLES ZOO
AT CARIBBEAN
★ GARDENS

Bear's Paw
Country Club

Fleischmann
Park

10TH ST N

GOODLETTE-FRANK RD

Naples
Municipal
Airport

Lowdermilk
Park & Beach ⌁

THE NAPLES BEACH ●
HOTEL & GOLF CLUB

SKYLINE
▼ CHILI

GULF SHORE BLVD S

SEE
"DOWNTOWN
NAPLES"
MAP

3RD

★ TIN CITY

GREYHOUND
STATION ■

DAVIS BLVD ■

TAMIAMI TR

0   0.5 mi
0   0.5 km

NAPLES MUNICIPAL BEACH
& FISHING PIER ⌁

11TH AVE S

ST S

7TH ST S

8TH ST S

9TH ST S

BROAD AVE S

12TH AVE S

13TH AVE

SEA SALT ▼

● COVE INN

BLEU PROVENCE ▼

▼ RIDGWAY BAR & GRILL

© AVALON TRAVEL

Downtown Naples

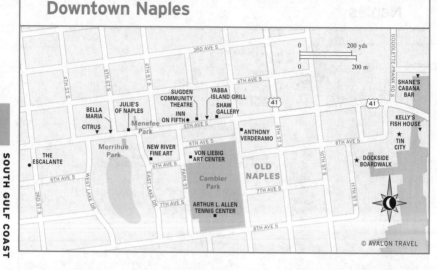

located at 400 8th St. S. and off 6th Ave. S., between 5th and 6th Aves.). Along 5th Avenue and 3rd Street South, there are numerous shops, galleries, and cafés that evoke a sense of tropical luxury that's unique in Florida. It's decidedly upscale, reflecting the sensibilities of the annual migration of moneyed snowbirds that flock to the area from the frigid Midwest every winter. Window-shoppers and art lovers will find plenty to capture their interest in the boutiques and galleries that are housed in dozens of century-old buildings. The tree-lined sidewalks are eminently walkable. **Naples Trolley** (239/262-7300, www.naplestrolleytours.com, 9:30am-5:30pm daily, $25 adults, $13 children older than 4, free reboarding) runs throughout downtown Naples, with stops along 5th Avenue South

5th Avenue is the upscale heart of downtown Naples.

and 3rd Street South, as well as in Tin City and other locations.

The Baker Museum

For a city with such a strong reputation as a place to view and purchase fine art, it's not surprising that **The Baker Museum** (5833 Pelican Bay Blvd., 239/597-1111, 10am-4pm Tues.-Sat., noon-4pm Sun., closed July-Oct., $8 adults, $6 children) is such an impressive facility. The building is beautiful. It's a three-story, 30,000-square-foot modern jewel located on the same grounds—dubbed Artis-Naples—as the Philharmonic Center for the Arts, with imposing metal gates designed by Albert Paley. The museum's permanent collections focus on modernism and sculpture. Seasonal exhibits are notably well-curated, with a balance of modern works from around the globe and more predictable fare. Photography, sculpture, and design work also figure prominently into the museum's ethos, making for an art experience that's somewhat surprising in such a buttoned-down city.

★ Naples Zoo at Caribbean Gardens

The 45-acre **Naples Zoo at Caribbean Gardens** (1590 Goodlette Rd., 239/262-5409, www.caribbeangardens.com, 9am-5pm daily, $22.95 adults, $21.95 seniors, $14.95 children, children 2 and under free) is an impressive combination of a conservation-minded zoo and a relaxed, informative botanical garden. Originally founded in 1919 as just a garden, the property is enfolded with stately palm trees and tropical foliage that enhance the immersive, natural experience. This experience is further amplified by the fact that the scores of animals on display are often no more than a few feet away from visitors at any given moment. From lemurs and lions and leopards to parrots, porcupines, and panthers, the zoo has an impressive, but not too expansive, array of animals. They are all housed in a relatively modern and very clean and comfortable environment. This zoo is one of my favorites; the shady pathways, the casual, animal-centric attitude of its design, and the breathtakingly beautiful array of plants make coming here very calming. It gives visitors the right mindset they need to take in the pro-conservation message the zoo is trying to impart.

Naples Botanical Garden

The **Naples Botanical Garden** (4820 Bayshore Dr., 239/643-7275, www.naplesgarden.org, 9am-5pm daily, $14.95 adults, $9.95 children 4-14, children under 3 free) got its start back in the mid-1990s as something of a community project spearheaded by local volunteers. Over the years, it has experienced considerable evolution and growth. In fact, in 2007, the garden closed for nearly 1.5 years to undergo extensive renovations and expansion. When it reopened in 2009, Naples Botanical Garden was the second largest botanical garden in Florida, with 160 acres of plant life representing more than 600 different species of flora in seven distinct garden environments. The Florida Garden is, obviously, dedicated to native Florida plants. The artful design of the Asian Garden, with its combination of beautiful flowers and tasteful architecture, makes it one of the best spots on the entire property. There's also a children's garden, where junior planters can get their hands dirty and burn off whatever excess energy they accumulated while you were investigating the plants and flowers in the other areas of the park. And, on some days (call for days/hours), you can even bring your dog; additional admission is $4.95, and all dogs must be current on shots and registration.

CORKSCREW SWAMP SANCTUARY

The **Corkscrew Swamp Sanctuary** (375 Sanctuary Rd. W., 239/348-9151, http://fl.audubon.org/corkscrew-swamp-sanctuary, 7am-5:30pm daily Oct. 1-Apr. 10, 7am-7:30pm daily Apr. 11-Sept. 30, $10 adults, $6 full-time college student with photo ID, $4 students ages 6-18, children under 6 free) is out of the way. Big time. Although it's only

Florida Panthers

When Congress passed the Endangered Species Act in 1973, one of the first animals listed as endangered was the Florida panther. A puma subspecies that used to abound in North and South America, the Florida panther is related to mountain lions, cougars, and catamounts. It's the only extant example of the species currently remaining in the eastern United States. In 1989, the panther population in Florida had precipitously fallen to only a few dozen animals, a situation brought about not so much by human predation than by habitat loss. The fast-growing South Florida region that these panthers used to freely roam has, over the past century, experienced such rapid and unchecked growth that the main Florida panther habitat is now the **Florida Panther National Wildlife Refuge** near Naples. Although the panther population has rebounded somewhat over the past two decades, thanks to captive breeding programs and the protection offered by the refuge, there are still fewer than 100 wild panthers left. It's a situation that will be difficult to remedy. The 26,400 acres of the refuge are somewhat limiting to a species in which the male typically can lay claim to up to 200 square miles of territory.

a half hour or so from downtown Naples, it's located at the end of a road at the end of a road at the end of a road that's off a rural highway. If getting away from the hustle and bustle is your goal, this is the place to do it. But, even if that's not what brings you out here, the voyage to Corkscrew is well worth it. Maintained and operated by the National Audubon Society, the sanctuary covers more than 11,000 acres of completely unspoiled land that, given its isolation and ecological diversity, is a perfect bird-watching spot.

Florida Panther National Wildlife Refuge

Don't arrive at the **Florida Panther National Wildlife Refuge** (13233 SR-29 S., 239/658-6163, sunrise-sunset daily, free) expecting to see any panthers. The endangered cats have had these 26,400 acres allocated to them for a reason; most of the refuge is off-limits to the public for the safety of both people and the panthers. There are, however, two public hiking trails. The Leslie M. Duncan Trail is a short, wheelchair-accessible trail

Make sure to explore the wild, quiet swamps of Corkscrew Swamp Sanctuary near Naples.

that loops for 0.3 mile through a hardwood hammock. The other, unnamed trail is longer (1.3 miles) and, though well-marked, is unimproved and can get quite muddy. Still, as fewer people make their way along this trail, wildlife is much more likely to be seen here.

Rookery Bay National Estuarine Research Reserve

Located between Naples and Marco Island, the **Rookery Bay National Estuarine Research Reserve** (300 Tower Rd., 239/417-6310, www.rookerybay.org, 9am-4pm Mon.-Sat., closed on Sat. May-Oct., $5 adults, $3 children, children under 6 free) is a mangrove estuary that is home to more than 150 different species of birds and other wildlife. The best way to get a feel for the wildlife within the reserve is to take a kayak tour; every Wednesday and Saturday, the facility offers guided kayak tours that take you out into the mangroves and waterways for two hours (10am-noon, $35, preregistration required). This experience provides an up-close look at the quietly vibrant ecosystem. The Visitor Center/Learning Center at the entrance of the reserve is large, but most of the 16,500 square feet is given over to working research labs and classrooms. The two-story area taken up by the actual visitors center isn't really worth the price of admission, as it only contains a few interactive exhibits and a large aquarium.

Marco Island

While you're on **Marco Island,** you're never very far from water, whether it's the Gulf, the Marco River, the bays that separate Marco from the mainland, or the scores of canals throughout the island's center. All that water explains why the island was so attractive to its earliest settlers. The coastal Calusa Indians were here during pre-Columbian times. Until the mid-1960s, it was a sleepy, isolated fishing village that, as far as most Floridians were concerned, was just past the edge of nowhere. As development in West Florida barreled southward in the 1950s and 1960s along I-75, some prescient real estate developers saw

Marco Island as a potential goldmine and began marketing it as a long-term destination for retirees from New York and New England.

Today, No Trespassing signs can be found dotting the landscape. The two best beaches are strictly reserved for residents. Still, slivers of Old Florida remain in the personality (and personalities) of the small fishing community of Goodland, a vibrant and friendly place. The accessible beaches of Marco Island, including Tigertail Beach, are some of the most beautiful in all of Florida. And, in the more historical area of Olde Marco, you can get a feel for Marco's low-key, predevelopment past. A quick boat ride out to Keewaydin Island provides an isolated and undeveloped slice of natural beauty. By taking advantage of the many charter boat tours available at most of Marco Island's marinas, it's possible to get a sense of both the physical beauty and natural isolation of this part of the Florida coast.

OLDE MARCO

Olde Marco was an island that was home to little more than a fishing village until the mid-1960s, when a full-fledged real estate boom turned it into a preferred destination for retirees from the northern and Midwestern United States. However, the spiritual remnants of that fishing village are still present in Olde Marco, which is basically the area of Marco Island north of Collier Boulevard. Here, the houses are smaller, high-rises are few and far between, and the vibe is more personable and inviting. The main sight is the **Rose Marco River Marina** (951 Bald Eagle Dr., 239/394-2502, www.marcoriver.com, 7am-7pm daily). There are several tour boats that operate out of the marina, the best of which is **Marco Island Princess Tours** (951 Bald Eagle Dr., 239/642-5415, www.themarcoislandprincess.com, 7am-7pm daily, cruises from $38.95), which offers various sightseeing cruises of the Ten Thousand Islands area and the Gulf.

GOODLAND

Another nice place to take in an Old Florida vibe is the tiny town of **Goodland,** located on the southeast corner of Marco Island. It's primarily a fishing village, and it's easy to imagine all of Marco Island having the same mellow, friendly vibe of this cozy community. There's not much going on here, but that's the way the few residents of this one-square-mile town like it. The annual Mullet Festival in February is the biggest event in town and the main business is **Walker's Hideaway Marina** (604 E. Palm Ave., 239/394-2797, www.walkersmarine.com, 8am-5pm daily). Stop in for lunch and a beer at the bayside **Stan's Idle Hour** (221 Goodland Dr., 239/642-7227, www.stansidlehour.net, 11am-late daily) and party like the locals do. You'll wonder why anyone would choose to live elsewhere on Marco Island when a convivial community like this is so close by.

BEACHES

The **beaches** here are fantastic. Large expanses of soft, white sand open onto calm, blue Gulf waters, as a constant, easy breeze flows off the water. They're very nearly perfect, and the citizens of Collier County know it. Though the beaches are certainly welcoming to visitors, it's worth noting that many of the parking lots aren't: all the best spots are reserved for residents; visitors are left to fight over spots usually a block or so away from the beach entrance. (And yes, you will be towed if you park illegally.) Still, ample metered parking is available, both in lots and along Naples' Gulfshore Boulevard. Most spots are ticket-metered, meaning you go to an automated booth near your parking spot, buy a ticket (usually $6 per day), and place it on your dashboard; weekly permits are also available ($50), but keep in mind that both of these options are only applicable toward beach parking.

Gulfshore Boulevard Beaches

The most centrally located public beaches in Naples are along Gulfshore Boulevard. **North Gulfshore Boulevard Beach** (81 Seagate Dr., sunrise-sunset daily, free) is close to the Village on Venetian Bay, and situated between two giant condominium complexes. There's a bit of a walk from the 38 available parking spaces to the beach entrance. Once on the beach, you should immediately start walking north for one of the more isolated beach experiences in town; just a few steps past the condos, it becomes almost deserted.

There is no such quietude to be found at **Lowdermilk Park & Beach** (257 Banyan Blvd., sunrise-sunset daily, free), perhaps the most popular of all the beaches in Naples. The central location and abundance of facilities (playground, restroom/shower facilities, picnic areas, a volleyball court, and over 100 parking spaces) draw huge crowds almost every day, and in the summer, you can wind up elbow to elbow with other sun worshippers. Still, the beach itself is gorgeous, and the water is warm and beautiful.

Surfers and anglers head for the **Naples Municipal Beach & Fishing Pier** (25 12th Ave., sunrise-sunset daily, free). A block south of the pier, the waves break as high as they're going to in this part of the state (which is to say, not very high at all), drawing determined boarders. The beach area in between the pier and the surfing spot is pleasant, though it can get a bit congested on holidays and during the summer. On a late spring weekday, though, this is one of the best places for a relaxing day at the beach.

Delnor Wiggins Pass State Recreation Area

Situated on a small barrier island a few miles north of downtown Naples, the **Delnor Wiggins Pass State Recreation Area** (11100 Gulfshore Dr., 239/597-6196, 8am-sunset daily, $6 per vehicle) offers a rustic and seminatural beach environment. Though quite popular, the park is also quite large. Once you pay your entrance fee, simply drive down the road until you find an appealing spot, pull over, and park. On the east side of the road are 80 acres of mangrove swamps, and on the west is one of the more beautiful beaches in the area. If you get here early enough, you can stake out a location all to yourself. It can get quite crowded around sunset time.

Marco Island

There's no easy public beach access facility for those who aren't staying on **Marco Island.** In fact, the main beach here is called Resident's Beach (it, as well as Sarazen Park South Beach, is reserved for Marco Island residents) and most of the other strips of sand are cordoned off by the towering condos and five-star hotels. Still, for $8 parking, **Tigertail Beach** (400 Hernando Dr., sunrise-sunset daily) is more than worth it. Isolated from the parking lot by dunes and a tidal lagoon, it's absolutely beautiful, with long, empty stretches of sand that beg you to wander along them for hours.

South Marco Beach (S. Collier Blvd., north of Winterberry Dr., sunrise-sunset daily, free) has basic facilities: a 70-space parking lot and bathrooms. It's a pretty beach, with a tree-lined sidewalk and tons of seashells in the sand. The water is clear and calm, and dolphin sightings are fairly frequent, especially in the winter months. There are a number of hotels right around South Marco Beach, so it can get pretty crowded.

Keewaydin Island (sunrise-sunset daily, free), located in Rookery Bay and part of the Rookery Bay National Estuarine Research Reserve, has a beautiful, naturally pristine beach. This island is only accessible by boat. There's a tremendous amount of ecological activity here, and the beach is monitored on a daily basis for sea turtle activity. Nests are marked to avoid being disturbed by human visitors. And, for a beach that's not terribly easy to get to, there are a whole lot of human visitors. Boaters come down from Naples and up from Marco Island to anchor and party, or to swim ashore and sunbathe on the white sand.

ENTERTAINMENT AND EVENTS
Nightlife

Most of Naples' nightlife takes place in bar-and-grill type places and sports bar settings like the **Foxboro Sports Tavern** (4420 Thomason Dr., 239/530-2337, www.foxboro-tavern.com, 10am-1am daily, no cover). There are also a few spots like the **Old Naples Pub** (255 13th Ave. S., 239/649-8200, 11am-10pm Mon.-Sat., noon-9pm Sun., no cover) and **The Village Pub** (4360 Gulf Shore Blvd., 239/262-2707, 11am-10pm Mon.-Sat., noon-9pm Sun., no cover) that serve decent pub grub, but mainly function as drinking establishments. **Shane's Cabana Bar** (495 Bayfront Pl., 239/732-6633, 11am-2am daily, no cover) is a neat spot to grab a drink, as it's little more than a bar, a roof, and some barstools, situated right on a relatively low-trafficked northern portion of Naples Bay. Shane's has great happy hour specials and friendly bartenders, although its relative status as one of Naples's few authentic bars means that it's often hard to grab a stool.

For an upscale take on the Naples nightlife experience, you should put on your best outfit and head for the decadent cigar bar BURN (9110 Strada Pl., 239/653-9013, www.burnbyrockypatel.com, 2pm-2am daily, no cover) and the low-key but high-class Avenue Wine Cafe (483 5th Ave. S., 239/403-9463, www.avenuewinecafe.com, 4pm-2am Mon.-Thurs., noon-2am Fri.-Sun., no cover), which, in addition to the titular wine you'd expect, also offers craft beer and cigars.

The Arts
GALLERIES

Naples is famous for its high-end art scene. The area in and around downtown is thick with galleries showcasing a wide variety of work. Along Gallery Row on 5th Avenue, well-known galleries like **New River Fine Art** (600 5th Ave. S., 239/435-4515, http://newriverfineart.com, 10am-5pm Mon.-Sat., extended hours in winter) display masterworks from the likes of Salvador Dalí, Joan Miro, and Auguste Renoir, alongside modern pieces from Frederick Hart, M. L. Snowden, Henry Asencio, and others, making it one of the most notable (and expensive) galleries on the Row. The **Four Winds Gallery** (340 13th

Ave. S., 239/263-7555, http://fourwindsnaples. com, 10am-5pm Mon.-Sat., extended hours in winter) takes a different approach, with carvings, jewelry, pottery, and other examples of modern Native American art. The atmosphere is both reflective and respectful of its artistic focus.

Shaw Gallery (761 5th Ave. S., 239/261-7828, www.shawgallery.com, 10am-6pm Mon.-Thurs., 10am-9pm Fri.-Sat., noon-5pm Sun.) has been a mainstay on 5th Avenue for more than two decades and specializes in sculpture, glass art, and paintings. It represents nearly 40 local, regional, and national artists. Although most of the art is both incredible and impressive, some of it is a little different from the standard offerings (the giant action painting of football quarterback Tim Tebow, for instance). Shaw Gallery is generally quite well regarded in the community.

A block south of 5th Avenue is the **Von Liebig Art Center** (585 Park St., 239/262-6517, 10am-4pm Mon.-Sat., $5 adults, $2 children) at the Naples Art Center, which combines exhibitions and gallery displays of the work of more than 400 local and regional artists. A little farther south, on 3rd Street between Broad and 12th Avenues, is another concentration of galleries. The **Darvish Collection of Fine Art** (1199 3rd St. S., 239/261-7581, 10am-5pm Mon.-Sat., limited hours in summer) is the second-oldest gallery in Naples; it focuses on 19th- and 20th-century artists.

PERFORMING ARTS

For those interested in the performing arts, the **Naples Community Players** perform a mix of crowd-pleasing musicals, kid-friendly fare, and even some more modern fare at the beautiful **Sugden Community Theatre** (701 5th Ave. S., 239/263-7990, www.naplesplayers.org). Ballet, classical music, and Broadway productions are performed at **Philharmonic Center for the Arts** (5833 Pelican Bay Blvd., 239/597-1900, www.thephil.org).

The robust arts scene in Naples includes live theatre.

Festivals and Events

Unsurprisingly, many of Naples's high-profile annual events are centered around art. Most occur during the peak of snowbird season, like the small-scale and craft-oriented **Naples New Year's Weekend Art Fair** and the much larger and more broadly curated **Downtown Naples Festival of the Arts** (Mar.), which are both hosted by the Naples Art Association (239/262-6517, www.naplesart.org) and held along Fifth Avenue South.

The trapped-in-amber vibe of the **Old Florida Festival** (239/252-8476, www.colliermuseums.com), held during the first weekend in March is a must-see for history buffs. Taking place on the historic grounds of the Collier County Museum, the Old Florida Festival divides the grounds up into camps populated variously by Native American tribes, Spanish settlers, British soldiers, Civil War soldiers, pioneers, and more. The result is a look at the many different phases of progress that Florida has seen throughout the years.

During the last two weeks of October, as the city prepares for the seasonal influx of snowbirds, the Naples **CityFest** (www.naplesnewsmediagroup.com/cityfest) brings a wide variety of art, dining, music, and shopping events to the downtown area, as well as seasonal stuff, like trick-or-treating. It's less a festival in the traditional sense than a rolling, multiday celebration that highlights the city's charms. The Stone Crab Festival is part of CityFest, and it's also worth noting that this may be the only festival in the country where a swamp buggy parade—now in its sixth decade—is a focal point of a municipal party.

Goodland's **Mullet Festival** (Stan's Idle Hour, 221 Goodland Dr., 239/394-3041, www.stansidlehour.net) is held every year on the weekend before the Super Bowl (because who wants to watch the Pro Bowl anyway?). The fine folks at the raucous and down-home Stan's Idle Hour seafood restaurant (and bar!) celebrate the local anglers who bring in mullet from the surrounding waters with bands, a beauty pageant (which names the Buzzard Lope Queen), and lots and lots of smoked and fried fish.

The **Marco Island Seafood Festival** (www.marcoislandseafoodfestival.com) in March is both more refined and less focused than the Mullet Festival. The festival draws thousands of folks to Marco Island's Veteran's Park (403 Elkcam Circle) for a weekend of food and music. Of course, there are dozens of folks selling seafood—freshly prepared, naturally—as well as typical festival fare like pizzas, sandwiches, and hot dogs. The music tends toward the adult-pop end of the spectrum. This festival can get really crowded, and jostling for a seat underneath the enormous dining tent can sometimes be a challenge. Still, it's definitely worth checking out. The profits go toward local charitable organizations.

SHOPPING
Downtown Naples

Interspersed among all those art galleries and cultural sites are a number of high-end (and not-so-high-end) shops. From candles and furniture to dog treats and Christmas ornaments, there is a wide variety of shops offering numerous ways to dispose of whatever disposable income you may have with you. **Julie's Of Naples** (533 5th Ave. S., 239/434-9761, www.juliesofnaples.com, 10am-6pm Mon.-Sat., noon-5pm Sun.) is a friendly, fashion-forward women's boutique, with highbrow casual wear, jewelry, and accessories. **Anthony Verderamo** (800 5th Ave. S., 239/403-7772, www.avgoldsmith.com, 10am-5pm Mon.-Sat.) specializes in luxe, custom-made gold jewelry that's as notable for its personal artistic touches as it is for its high-end appeal.

The Village on Venetian Bay

The **Village Shops on Venetian Bay** (4300 Gulf Shore Blvd., 239/261-6100, www.venetianvillage.com, 10am-7pm Mon.-Wed. and Sat., 10am-9pm Thurs.-Fri., noon-5pm Sun.) is an upscale, open-air mall, home to more than 50 stores, as well as a handful of restaurants and art galleries. The waterfront location makes it a bit more scenic than your average mall. Although there's a bit of an upscale tilt to most of the businesses here, there are accessible shops as well. Men's and women's clothing stores like **Diane's Fine Fashions** (239/213-4202), **Simply Natural** (239/643-5571), and **Teruzzi** (239/263-2252) dominate the offerings, along with a few decor and accessories shops, and five jewelers. The six restaurants (most of which are pretty high end) and a Ben & Jerry's easily put to shame any regular old mall's food court.

SPORTS AND RECREATION
Swamp Buggies

All those luxury cars, high-end boutiques, and five-star boîtes can't mask the fact that Naples is right next door to some pretty huge swamps. And there's no better way to get around those swamps than on a swamp buggy. These monstrous, open-air vehicles with giant tires and roaring engines were invented in Naples as hunting vehicles, but with the ban on hunting in the Everglades, resourceful drivers figured out something else to do with them. A great way to experience some swamp buggy fun is by heading out to **Captain Steve's Swamp Buggy Adventures** (22903 SR-29, Jerome, 239/695-2773, 9am-5pm daily, $97.50 adult for a half-day tour, children under 12 free). Located about a half hour east of Naples, right near the boundary of the Big Cypress National Preserve, Captain Steve's will take you out into the wild-and-wet in a buggy. The rides are more geared toward exploration rather than muddy adventure, so you'll have to count on wildlife sightings and the occasional close encounter with an alligator to get your adrenaline rush.

Golf

Naples is called the Golf Capital of the World for good reason: There are more than 80 courses in the immediate area. Driving down US-41, it almost feels like the entirety of Collier County outside of downtown Naples has been given over to fairways and retirement communities filled with golfers. However, many of those courses are private, which means visitors are relegated to hitting up an old-timer at the bar for an invite or making their way to one of the handful of decent public courses in the area.

Thankfully, those publicly accessible courses are impressive in their own right. Two of the three courses at **Lely Resort Golf & Country Club** (8004 Lely Resort Blvd., 239/793-2600, greens fees $35-167) are open to the public: Flamingo Island is a straightforward Robert "Trent" Jones Sr. course (7,171 yards); the Mustang course (7,217 yards) was designed by Lee Trevino, with lots of water hazards. The two Greg Norman-designed courses at **Tiburon Golf Club** (2620 Tiburon Dr., 239/594-2040, www.tiburongcnaples.com, greens fees $170-280) are pricey, but this club, which is home to the Merrill Lynch Shootout every December, is situated on an 800-acre, full-featured resort. The courses are routinely rated highly by guests.

Tennis

There are two fantastic publicly accessible tennis facilities in Naples. The city-operated **Arthur L. Allen Tennis Center** (239/213-3060, $12.72 for 90 minutes of play) is located in **Cambier Park** (755 8th Ave. S., 239/213-3058) and has a dozen lighted Har-Tru courts. Unlike many municipal courts, the ones here are very well maintained. They actually seem to exceed the standards held by many private and club courts. The additional touch of using chickees for shaded siting areas—rather than an awning off the side of the fence—is pretty nice. Cambier Park also has a great wooden playground, if you're toting your kids along with you.

The **Pelican Bay Community Park Tennis Facility** (764 Vanderbilt Beach Rd., 239/598-3025) is located in a somewhat exclusive residential area, but it also offers up usage of its excellent courts to the visiting public. Although community residents get first dibs at court reservations, guests can still often get a reservation on one of the eight Har-Tru courts, especially in the late spring and summer. Both of these tennis centers offer round robins, lessons, and clinics, as well as hosting multiple tournaments throughout the year.

FOOD
Breakfast

There are two decent spots to grab a morning bite in the arts district downtown. The appropriately monikered **Third Street Cafe** (1361 3rd St., 239/261-1498, 6:30am-3pm daily, from $6) has basic breakfast fare served in a pleasant environment. During lunch, it welcomes larger crowds for its deli selections. Even if you can't be bothered to make the walk, fear not, as the Third Street Cafe also delivers.

Jane's Cafe (1209 3rd St., 239/261-2253, www.janesnaples.com, 8am-5pm Mon.-Sat., 8:30am-4pm Sun., from $3) is a small, European-style café that specializes in pastries and lighter breakfast bites, as well as impressive omelets and a few vegetarian options.

It comes complete with a beautiful outdoor dining area.

The fine folks at Naples Cyclery are available to help get you onto a bicycle rental or, if you brought your own, perform maintenance or repairs on it. They're also available to fill up your personal combustion engine with **Fit & Fuel** (819 Vanderbilt Beach Rd., 239/514-3333, http://naplescyclery.com, 6:30am-5:30pm Mon.-Fri., 6:30am-2:30pm Sat., 7:30am-2:30pm Sun.), a small café attached to the bike shop where you can get fully caffeinated on fresh espresso or brew coffee before or after your ride.

American

You can get your burger cooked in dozens of different ways at **Brooks Gourmet Burgers and Dogs** (330 S. 9th St., 239/262-1127, www.naplesburgers.com, 11am-9pm Mon.-Sat., main courses from $6), a fact that is endlessly trumpeted throughout this great restaurant. In addition to artery-challenging monsters like a Donut Burger (cheese and bacon and a half pound of beef in between two glazed donuts) and the Todd's Way (a burger topped with fried egg, bacon, and two kinds of cheese), there are some more refined options, such as the Greek (red onion, Feta, olives, tomatoes and Greek dressing) and one topped with fresh pesto and goat cheese. Brooks Gourmet also has an array of similarly decadent hot dogs and sandwiches, but with so many ways to truly get a burger prepared your way, why bother with anything else? There's also a great selection of beer to wash it all down with.

I-75 connects Naples to the Midwestern United States, and cuts right through the heart of Ohio, bringing a large number of visitors from the area. Therefore, it shouldn't be surprising that when the Cincinnati institution known as **Skyline Chili** (710 N. 9th St., 239/649-5665, www.skylinechili.com, 11am-7:30pm Mon.-Sat., 11am-3:30pm Sun., from $5) was looking to expand beyond the Buckeye State, it chose to open an outlet here. Sure, you can get a wrap or a salad, but what would be the point when the rich, steaming chili Skyline is known for can be delivered atop a hot dog or even as part of a spaghetti dish?

New American

Citrus (455 5th Ave. S., 239/435-0408, http://citrusseafood.com, 11am-10pm daily, from $15) offers gorgeous al fresco dining and an extensive menu of fresh seafood dishes. But that could be said about a good number of restaurants in downtown Naples. What sets this place apart is its casually upscale vibe and amazingly extensive beer menu. While it may not present itself as a gastropub, Citrus almost certainly is one, as the food here is excellent and innovative without being precious, served in an atmosphere that's pleasant but not fussy. Flash-fried whole hogfish served atop a bed of jasmine rice is one of the specialties here; although whole fish is sometimes difficult to navigate gracefully, the hogfish's crispy outside easily opens up to reveal chunky, semi-sweet flesh. And, thankfully, since the atmosphere isn't all that uptight, nobody will notice (or care) as you pick your way through it.

Wine is one of the specialties at **Ridgway Bar & Grill** (1300 3rd St. S. #101, 239/262-5500, www.ridgwaybarandgrill.com, 11:30am-9:30pm daily, from $18), an intimate and beautiful establishment in downtown Naples. The wine list is *huge*, with over 600 selections, more than a dozen of which are served by the glass. It's not just the vino that sets Ridgway apart, though. The menus here are impressive, featuring a standard selection of meat, seafood, poultry, and pasta dishes that are prepared with fresh, locally sourced ingredients. Veal chops, snapper piccata, and braised short ribs may not sound too special, but the kitchen is thoughtful in its preparations. Those selections are complemented by a great array of comfort foods like meat loaf, chicken potpie, and fish-and-chips. Ridgway also offers two "simple" menus of seafood and meats, which allow you to select your steak, filet, or fish, and then add a side from choices like fried green tomatoes, ratatouille, grits cake, and other down-home specialties. If you're having trouble squaring "extensive wine list" with "fried green tomatoes," then the friendly, food-focused vibe at Ridgway may not be for you; however, those who enjoy indulging in kitchen-table standards prepared with flair and care will find a lot to love here.

There are few instances in this book where you'll be advised to head out of the heart of a city to eat at a strip mall, but, north of downtown, tucked into a mall between a Subway and a mattress store is **The Local** (5323 Airport Pulling Rd N, 239/596-3276, thelocalnaples.com, 11am-9pm daily, from $13), a farm-to-table experience that manages to be one of the best restaurants in town, despite its inconvenient location. Lots of vegetarian and gluten-free options, ultra-fresh seafood, soups, decadent chef-driven pork and poultry preparations, as well as an incredible wine list and a casual, laid-back vibe (the bar is actually a pretty great place to watch the game and have a decent beer and some great food) make The Local the kind of place that would be a no-brainer for an urban environment, but a pleasant surprise on the outskirts of Naples.

Steak

Naples is definitely a steaks-and-chops kind of town, and the **Pewter Mug Steakhouse** (12300 N. Tamiami Trial, 239/597-3017, www.pewtermug41.com, 11am-2pm and 4:30pm-10pm Mon.-Fri., 4:30pm-10pm Sat.-Sun., from $16) is one of the more popular (and populist) places in town to get a well-cooked slab of meat. The atmosphere is a bit old-fashioned, the portions are quite large, and the copious salad bar will help appease any guilt you may have about indulging in one of their 16-ounce prime ribs.

Andre's Steakhouse (2800 E. Tamiami Trail, 239/263-5851, www.andressteakhouseofnaples.com, 5pm-9pm daily, from $26) is a distinctly more upscale experience, with a dark and romantic dining room. Steaks are served New York style, coated in butter and plated with sides like creamed spinach and asparagus.

Seafood

Kelly's Fish House (1302 S. 5th Ave., 239/774-0494, http://kellysfishhousediningroom.com, 4:30pm-10pm daily, from $17) is the oldest seafood restaurant in Naples. This no-nonsense eatery has made a legend of itself not just by lasting a long time but by serving ultra-fresh seafood in traditional grilled/broiled/fried fashion. You can get raw bar treats like oysters and clams, along with expertly prepared takes on standards like shrimp, grouper, and crab, as well as a limited selection of chicken and steak dishes. The wood-paneled walls and kitschy, nautical bric-a-brac make it clear that Kelly's isn't going to try to impress you with its modern styling. The quality (and pricing) of the food and the waterfront views more than make up for any such "shortcomings."

On the other hand, the hyper-stylized (and hyper-stylish) **USS Nemo** (3745 N. Tamiami Trail, 239/261-6366, www.ussnemorestaurant.com, 11:30am-2pm and 5pm-9:30pm Mon.-Fri., 5pm-9:30pm Sat.-Sun., from $18) prides itself on delivering an exceptional atmospheric experience that is intended to make you feel as if you're underwater. This is done with blue-tinted windows covered by porthole-like contraptions and a bar that looks like a submarine galley. Thankfully, the food here lives up to the decor, with a focus on super-fresh preparations that are highly influenced by an Asian fusion approach. Sampler platters come in bento-box-type plates, and appetizers include tuna *tataki* salad and shrimp tempura.

The **Yabba Island Grill** (711 S. 5th Ave., 239/262-5787, www.yabbaislandgrill.com, 5pm-10pm Sun.-Thurs., 5pm-11pm Fri.-Sat., from $16) combines fresh and inventive seafood dishes prepared with a modern flair with a casual, beachside-bar vibe. Occasionally, the delicate plating and exotic cocktail concoctions get a bit too cute for their own good, but the Yabba is far from pretentious. It manages to be mellow and fun while serving up excellent and individual dishes.

The national upscale seafood chain **Trulucks** (698 S. 4th Ave., 239/530-3131, http://trulucks.com, 5pm-10pm Sun.-Thurs., 5pm-11pm Fri.-Sat., from $31) is a "proper attire required" experience with top-notch service and some of the best fresh-caught seafood. For a more local-oriented upscale seafood experience, head directly to **Sea Salt** (1186 3rd St. S., 239/434-7258, www.seasaltnaples.com, 11:30am-3pm and 5pm-10pm daily, from $22), a stylish downtown restaurant that specializes in innovative takes on the fresh seafood that abounds in the Naples area. The dining room is a little crowded, but beautiful; still, request patio seating (or even an indoor table near the patio) to have a little more breathing room. (Conversely, if you're feeling like splurging, go ahead and book the chef's table and get right in the middle of the action in the kitchen.) Organic and local ingredients are the focus of the menu, which changes with somewhat regular frequency. Unique among seafood-oriented spots is the extensive antipasto menu, complete with a half-dozen charcuterie selections, as well as raw oysters, carpaccio, cheese, olives, and shrimp cocktails. Making selections from that menu alone would make an evening at Sea Salt memorable, but there's also fresh pasta, high-end beef preparations, and limited (but select and specialized) seafood options. The artful preparations at Sea Salt—not to mention the restaurant's overall aesthetic—make it clear that although its seafood selections may not be numerous, they are where the restaurant's heart is.

French

Somewhat surprisingly, the best French restaurants in Naples tend to be focused on homestyle, classic French preparations rather than upscale, fine dining. That's not to say that these restaurants are cheap, but they are accessible, with dishes that are authentic, comforting, and well-prepared. **Bleu Provence** (1234 8th St. S., 239/261-3410, www.bleuprovencenaples.com, 5pm-10pm daily, from $16) makes it fairly explicit with its name that its specialties are its Provençal dishes, and the combination of seafood (mussels and scallops, especially) and Mediterranean flavors (tagine chicken and couscous) hits the spot. The menu also includes traditional dishes like steak tartare, veal chops, sweetbreads, and duck confit, as well as more locally inspired options like sesame tuna. Bleu Provence also serves up some fantastic steak frites.

Escargot 41 (4339 Tamiami Trail N., 239/793-5000, www.escargot41.com, 5:30pm-10pm daily, from $19) obviously has a soft spot for snails. Its menu is topped off with more than a half dozen different escargot preparations. A small selection of French-inspired beef, poultry, and seafood dishes provides the main bulk of the entrées, but if you focus on the escargot and the excellent selection of hors d'oeuvres (foie gras, pâté, salmon *fumé*), you can piece together a far more adventurous and exciting meal. The strip mall exterior belies a dining room that's beautifully decorated and elegant without being stuffy.

Crepes, quiches, sandwiches, and salads are the main attraction at **Cafe Normandie** (3756 Tamiami Trail N., 239/261-0977, www.cnnaples.com, 11am-3pm and 5pm-10pm Mon.-Sat., from $13), which is definitely the most casual of all of Naples's French restaurants. The café atmosphere is comfortable and friendly, and the kitchen is deft at dishing up an extensive selection of classic French comfort food at reasonable prices. This approach has made the café a popular lunch spot, but it shouldn't be overlooked as a dinner option. Although the menu is a bit richer in the evening hours, the focus—with dishes like beef bourguignon, veal stew, and roasted chicken—is still on homestyle cuisine.

Latin

Agave (2380 Vanderbilt Beach Rd., 239/598-3473, http://agavenaples.com, 11:30am-midnight daily, from $14.50) is a mid-scale Tex-Mex place near Vanderbilt Beach that opened in 2012. The menu includes a few dishes like bison chili and fresh ceviches,

Florida Stone Crabs

Stone crabs are abundant all along the coast of the Gulf of Mexico, down to the Keys, and then back up the Atlantic coast to North Carolina. However, the stone crabs that are prevalent along the southwest coast of Florida and in the Keys are known as Florida stone crabs, rather than Gulf stone crabs. Although any stone crab claw is highly prized in kitchens throughout the world, Florida stone crabs have a reputation as being both sweeter and meatier than Gulf stone crabs.

Stone crabs are harvested in Florida between mid-October and mid-May, and during that time, visitors to the area can avail themselves of some of the freshest crab claws around. (Frozen? Don't bother.) Stone crabs are incredibly abundant along the Gulf coast between Naples and Key West, and although demand has spiked in recent years, this fishery is still regarded by conservationists as a viable source for the crabs. During harvest season, crabbers head out on boats and launch crab pots baited with pigs' feet and other scavenge-like delights. Upon returning, the crabbers haul the crates to the boat, check for crabs with claws of legal length (2.75 inches minimum, about half the length that a mature stone crab claw can grow to), break the claw off at the knuckle so it can regrow, and then toss the now-amputated crab back into the water to grow another. It sounds brutal, and it is, but it's not a death sentence: a study of the practice determined that "only" 28 percent of the crabs who had a claw amputated died. Feasting on stone crab while in the area during harvest season is nearly mandatory. During Naples's **Stone Crab Festival** in October, if you don't try at least one of these succulent, meaty claws you're truly missing out. Try dipping one in mustard; it's better than butter.

which round out the expected selection of quesadillas, tacos, tamales, and entrée-style chicken and beef plates. Agave specializes in what it calls "plates on fire," which is basically an amped-up presentation of fajitas. Imagine if your local Mexican place served fajitas on a mobile cart, and prepared them tableside in a semi-theatrical, teppanyaki-inspired manner. Agave also offers tequila and margarita flights and has an ample selection of top-shelf tequilas on offer.

IM Tapas (965 4th Ave. N., 239/403-8272, www.imtapas.com.com, 5:30-10pm Mon.-Thurs., 5:30-11pm Fri.-Sat., 5:30-9pm Sun., tapas from $8) not only serves an expansive menu of hot and cold tapas with more than two dozen selections (including ostrich carpaccio, spicy octopus, and morcilla, among other surprises), but also dishes up awesome paella and *fideua* for those who want to eschew small plates for some family-style indulgence.

Another exceptional tapas option is **Lamoraga** (3936 Tamiami Trail N,

239/331-3669, www.lamoragarestaurant. com, 11:30am-10pm Mon.-Fri., 5pm-10pm Sat., Sun., tapas from $8), which tacks a sushi bar onto its tapas experience, making it a great place for small-plate explorations.

Japanese

Most popular with the birthday crowds that descend on the teppanyaki tables for the food-grilling show, **Fujiyama** (2555 N. 9th St., 239/261-4332, www.naplesfujiyama.com, 5:30pm-10pm Mon.-Fri., 5:30pm-11pm Sat.-Sun., from $15) also has one of the area's better sushi bars. On the north side of town, near Vanderbilt Beach, a similar, though pricier, teppanyaki and sushi place is **Daruma Steak and Seafood** (241 Center St. N., 239/591-1200, www.darumarestaurant.com, 5pm-10pm daily, from $14).

A more dedicated sushi experience can be had at **Tokyo Sushi** (3743 E. Tamiami Trail, 239/775-3388, 11am-10pm daily, from $9). It's located in a strip mall and also offers a carryout menu.

ACCOMMODATIONS
Under $100

Budget accommodations, especially during the winter, may be hard to come by in Naples. The **Sea Shell Motel** (82 9th St. S., 239/262-5129, from $99 d) is somewhat dated, but clean, reasonably well-maintained, and close to downtown.

$100-150

Each of the rooms at the **Lemon Tree Inn** (250 9th St. S., 239/262-1414, www.lemontree-inn.com, from $159 d) is individually decorated, which means you could end up with a plain hotel room with a gorgeous four-poster bed, or a gorgeous room with a plain bed. The best room here is the St. Croix Suite, with a separate entrance, two bathrooms, kitchenette, and hardwood floors. All the rooms open up to the courtyard and have mini fridges and microwaves. There's a pool onsite, which is where the daily continental breakfast is served.

The ★ **Gulfcoast Inn** (2555 Tamiami Trail N., 239/261-6046, http://gulfcoastinnnaples.com, from $139 d) is a fantastic budget option, especially in the off season. Located just behind a country club and just a five-minute walk to the beach, the inn offers surprisingly spacious rooms with kitchenettes and free Internet access. Some rooms have tile floors and are tropically decorated. All rooms overlook the large pool area and the poolside bar. There's also a Japanese restaurant on the property.

The **Lighthouse Inn** (9140 Gulf Shore Dr., 239/597-3345, from $135 d) is showing its age, but in a good way. It's a basic cinder-block motel, with super-clean and comfortable efficiencies and apartments that are some of the least expensive, decent accommodations near Vanderbilt Beach. There's a small heated pool, and each room has a television, but no telephone. Given the price and the Lighthouse's excellent location (and the fact that you've probably got a mobile phone anyway), who cares about the spartan amenities? There are only 15 rooms here, and they get booked incredibly early during high season.

$150-200

It bills itself as a "boutique family resort," and it's hard to argue with that self-assessment of ★ **Inn of Naples** (4055 Tamiami Trail N., 239/649-5500, www.innofnaples.com, from $179 d). Inside, the property has fresh, bright paint and up-to-date appointments masking decades-old hotel architecture. All rooms have private balconies and flat-screen TVs. In addition to hotel-style accommodations, there are also a handful of one- and two-bedroom suites. Though not located particularly close to anything, it's not exactly far away from anything either. It's situated on the busy Tamiami Trail. With swampy Sugden Park out its back door, the Inn of Naples has a surprisingly secluded feel.

The **Park Central Hotel** (40 9th St. N., 239/435-9700, www.naplesparkcentral.com, from $159 d) is a small hotel with only 30 rooms. It is situated in a convenient location just a few blocks away from the action on 5th Avenue. All of the rooms are uniquely decorated, and their tile floors give them a spacious feel that belies their somewhat smaller square footage. The rooms are quite nice, with flat-screen TVs, Internet access, wet bars, and new furnishings. The hotel's heated pool and lounge make it comfortable and relaxing. And, given those amenities and the hotel's location, the rates are something of a bargain.

$200-300

Perfectly located on 5th Avenue downtown, the historic ★ **Inn on Fifth** (699 5th Ave. S., 239/403-8777, www.innonfifth.com, from $279 d) combines boutique-style intimacy with top-shelf grandeur. The 76 surprisingly large rooms and 11 decadent suites are all decorated in a style that's not too ostentatious, with pillowtop bedding and nice touches like free Wi-Fi and iPod docks. The suites have whirlpool tubs and balconies. There's a beautifully landscaped pool in the back, and one of

Naples' best spas is on-site. The Inn on Fifth is an incredibly popular choice, and it's a challenge to get a room here on off-season weekends and pretty much any time during season; make sure to reserve early.

Right on Naples Bay is the thatched-roof **Cove Inn** (900 Broad Ave. S., 239/262-7161, www.coveinnnaples.com, from $229 d). As far south on 9th Street as one can go without falling into the water, the inn's location is its prime attraction. The clean, spacious rooms are a good value. With mini kitchens in the hotel rooms and full kitchens in the suites, each room in this condo hotel reflects the individual decorating choice of its owner. Accordingly, some of the rooms are bright and kitschy, while others are just stocked with the typical array of pastels and pelicans.

Over $300

With an excellent location that's very close to central Naples yet still feels out of the way (it's located in a predominantly residential area), ★ **The Naples Beach Hotel & Golf Club** (851 Gulfshore Blvd. N., 239/261-2222, www.naplesbeachhotel.com, from $329 d) is probably my favorite place to stay in all of Naples. And I'm not just saying that because they let me stay here free for one night. I'm saying that because the hotel combines Old Florida charm, 1950s glamour, and modern luxury in a way that manages to be friendly and accessible. Family owned since it opened in 1946, the Naples Beach Hotel & Golf Club is a little out of step with similarly outfitted resorts in the city. There's no sense of corporate gloss here. The buildings appear on the surface to have little to do with one another: The original hotel building looks like a fisherman's motel; one tower gives away its origins in the 1970s; while still another looks like an art deco apartment building. It may not be visually consistent on the outside, but all of the rooms share the same spacious, casual-tropical atmosphere and fresh decor. All rooms are decorated with prints by famed Everglades photographer Clyde Butcher and ceramics by Naples artist Jim Rice. The sunsets here can't be beat, and the friendly staff manages to make everyone feel welcome and pampered. All rooms have flat-screen TVs, wet bars, and mini fridges, and guests can avail themselves of the golf course (across the street) and the ample spa facilities. There is no resort fee.

Upscale lodging options abound in Naples. Although quite a few of the well-heeled types head directly for the **Ritz-Carlton Naples Resort** (280 Vanderbilt Beach Rd.,

The Inn on Fifth is one of the best places to stay in Naples.

239/538-3330, www.ritzcarlton.com/naples, from $429 d), there are several other impressive and luxurious places to stay in Naples. And though wrangling one of these plush beds during high season can be something of a challenge, off-season rates for those prepared to face the summer humidity are surprisingly manageable at most of them. This Ritz-Carlton is located right next to Vanderbilt Beach, so in addition to all of the typical amenities of a Ritz, guests here are treated to easy access to one of the most beautiful beaches in Florida. Also on-site: four tennis courts, a luxe pool with cabanas, several cool nature-based kids' programs, and a game room stocked with Wii, PlayStation, and Xbox consoles. Guests at the Vanderbilt Beach Ritz also have privileges at the 36-hole Tiburon Golf Course.

Serious luxury-minded duffers will want to book a room or suite at **The Ritz-Carlton Golf Resort** (2600 Tiburón Dr., 239/593-2000, www.ritzcarlton.com, from $379 d), which, though just a few blocks away from the main Ritz beach resort, puts guests right on top of those two Greg Norman-designed courses. The Golf Resort is a bit smaller, though far from intimate, with nearly 300 rooms and five restaurants. A good bit of the hotel's real estate is given over to conference facilities, and the vibe is definitely more wheel and deal than it is kick back on the coast.

If you can't decide between the Ritz's luxurious beach resort or the Ritz's luxurious golf resort, then the **La Playa Beach & Golf Resort** (9891 Gulf Shore Dr., 239/597-3123, www.laplayaresort.com, from $449 d) may be able to cover all your bases. Located just north of the Ritz-Carlton's beach resort, La Playa shares the same beautiful stretch of sand that is Vanderbilt Beach, albeit in a somewhat more secluded section. La Playa only has one 18-hole course, but the Robert Cupp-designed course is gorgeous. Rooms here are spread across multiple buildings, including two towers; request a beachfront room in the Gulf Tower for incredible views and easy access to the beach. Rooms in the Bay Tower are

also luxurious, but located across the street from the main resort; you'll get a decent view in upper-floor rooms, but you'll be somewhat away from the main action. The best rooms, though, are the 850-square-foot one-bedroom suites, which are not only huge and stylish, but also beachfront. All rooms at La Playa are airy and bright, decorated in a comfortably luxurious style that's tropical without being pastel-drenched. They offer all the amenities you would expect from a luxury hotel. The resort has two restaurants, a tiki bar, a spa, and a fitness center.

The Escalante (290 5th Ave. S., 239/659-3466, www.hotelescalante.com, from $429 d) is a boutique hotel that feels like a boutique hotel. The atmosphere manages to cross Mediterranean decor and a Key West-inspired tropical vibe, and it does so in a location that's right in the heart of Old Naples. The Escalante has just 11 rooms on its property, and all of them have some sense of individuality. There are two suites, a standalone villa, and eight small standard rooms, which have either a private patio or open up to the garden and pool area. The on-site restaurant, Dish, is equally intimate and exceptional.

For those looking for elegant beachside accommodations, the Hilton-owned **Edgewater Beach Hotel** (1901 Gulfshore Blvd., 888/564-1308, from $420 d) is an excellent option. All the rooms are recently updated and well-maintained. The property, though family friendly and perfect for a beach vacation, is nonetheless quite classy, with lavish, modern decorations.

INFORMATION AND SERVICES
Visitor Information

The infinitely helpful staff of the **Naples, Marco Island & Everglades Visitors Bureau** (www.paradisecoast.com) has an information center downtown at 800 5th Avenue South. You can pick up brochures and maps there, as well as make hotel reservations and get information on local events.

Medical and Emergency Services

NCH Healthcare System Downtown Naples Hospital (350 7th St. N., 239/436-5151) is the main hospital in the area; NCH also operates **NCH North Naples Hospital** (11190 Health Park Blvd., 239/552-7000), which is located in the Pelican Bay/Vanderbilt Beach area. Both hospitals have 24-hour emergency rooms. There are more than two dozen branches of national chain pharmacies located throughout Naples, including **Walgreens** and **CVS**, and prescriptions can also be filled at many **Publix** grocery stores.

GETTING THERE AND AROUND
Getting There
AIR

The main airport in the area is **Southwest Florida International Airport** (RSW, 11000 Terminal Access Rd., 239/590-4800, www.flylcpa.com) in Fort Myers. It's serviced by most major domestic carriers, including Southwest. Another option is to fly into **Fort Lauderdale-Hollywood International Airport** (FLL, 320 Terminal Dr., Ft. Lauderdale, 866/435-9355, www.broward.org/airport), which would require a two-hour drive along the toll stretch of I-75 known as Alligator Alley.

CAR

I-75 ends its north-south route running through the middle United States in Naples,

where it takes a sharp turn toward the east and Fort Lauderdale. Also running through Naples is the scenic Tamiami Trail (US-41), which connects Tampa and Miami via the Everglades.

BUS

Greyhound offers bus service into the **Central Park Bus Terminal** (2699 Davis Blvd., 239/774-5660, www.greyhound.com, 8:15am-10:30am and 1:30pm-5pm Mon.-Sat.).

Getting Around

Public transportation in Naples, via the county government's **Collier Area Transit** (CAT, 239/252-8192, www.colliergov.net, $1.50/trip or $4/day pass) is extremely limited, focused primarily on the Tamiami Trail and outlying areas. You'll definitely need a car, and parking can sometimes be a challenge. Please keep in mind that beach parking passes purchased from meter boxes are only valid for beach lots and not valid in the downtown area.

The only way to get to Marco Island is in your car. From Naples, it's about a half-hour drive, via the southbound Tamiami Trail and then Collier Boulevard, which takes you right onto the island. There is no public transportation on Marco Island, but, unlike Naples, it's pretty bikeable. You can rent bikes and scooters from **Island Bike Shop** (1095 Bald Eagle Dr., 239/394-8400, http://islandbikeshops.com, 9am-6pm Mon.-Sat., 10am-3pm Sun.). This is recommended, as parking is at a premium pretty much everywhere on the island.

The Panhandle and North Florida

Highlights

© AVALON TRAVEL

★ **Panama City Beach:** Simultaneously family-friendly and party hardy, Panama City Beach is probably best known for its tourist-trap vibe of T-shirt shops and five-for-one drink specials. Nonetheless, the stretch of white sand and warm blue waters manages to be as relaxing and beautiful as it is fun (page 430).

★ **Destin Beaches:** The beaches at Destin somehow feel softer and the water bluer. It's far easier to find a wide stretch of publicly accessible beach here than almost anywhere else along the Panhandle (page 435).

★ **University of Florida:** The campus is the defining characteristic of Gainesville. It's a quintessential college town, with a mixture of bohemianism and football fanaticism (page 457).

★ **Ocala National Forest:** With freshwater springs, extensive and rugged hiking trails, and lots of camping and boating opportunities, this vast landscape is the natural heart of north-central Florida (page 464).

★ **Equestrian Ocala:** Renowned as one of the top thoroughbred-breeding areas in the world, the Ocala manages to split the difference between salt-of-the-earth and blue-blood (page 466).

I t's often said that in Florida, you have to go north to go South. It's quite true that the northern part of the state has more in common with the American South than the rest of the state does.

The north-central part of the state encompasses the rolling hills and horse farms of the Ocala area as well as the college towns of Gainesville and Tallahassee, which is also the state's capital. Each of these areas has distinct flavors, but they're all deeply steeped in Southern tradition. Even if the low-key fishing villages and rural towns that line the marshy Gulf coastline of the state's Big Bend didn't immediately remind you of similar towns in, say, the South Carolina low country, you'd soon realize that you're humming an antebellum tune as you paddle down the area's main waterway, the Suwannee River.

Along the Panhandle, luxurious white-sand beaches and the rural atmosphere of the Old South combine to evoke a charm and natural wonder that the earliest travelers to Florida must have felt. While some beach towns like Panama City seem to have a corner on the market for tawdry tourist tackiness, a short drive will take you to one where it's easy to imagine spending the rest of your life whiling away the days on a shrimp boat. Cities like Pensacola and Destin depend heavily on tourism for survival and have invested accordingly over the past decade or so; amazingly the result has managed to provide a decent tourist infrastructure without any of these communities losing their drawling friendliness.

HISTORY

The modern history of Florida—indeed, the modern history of the United States—can be traced to the Panhandle region. In 1559, in Pensacola, Tristin de Luna y Arellano established the first European settlement in what would become the United States. Although the settlement was abandoned only two years later as Spanish colonists found their way to the east coast of Florida, the Panhandle region would play a prominent role in colonial politics for many years to come.

Florida was initially divided into two

Previous: marsh on Cedar Key; Manatee Springs State Park. **Above:** A historic sign welcomes visitors to Pensacola Beach.

The Panhandle and North Florida

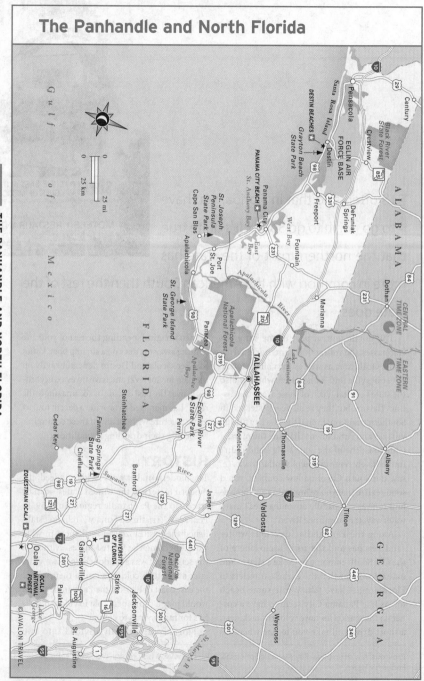

Gulf of Mexico

FLORIDA

ALABAMA

GEORGIA

CENTRAL TIME ZONE

EASTERN TIME ZONE

TALLAHASSEE

Pensacola
Century
Crestview
Black River State Forest
Santa Rosa Island
DESTIN BEACHES
Destin
Grayton Beach State Park
EGLIN AIR FORCE BASE
PANAMA CITY BEACH
Panama City
St. Anthony Bay
Freeport
DeFuniak Springs
Dothan
Fountain
West Bay
East Bay
Marianna
St. Joseph Peninsula State Park
Port St. Joe
Cape San Blas
Apalachicola
Apalachicola River
Apalachicola National Forest
Lake Seminole
St. George Island State Park
Panacea
Apalachee Bay
Econfina River State Park
Perry
Steinhatchee
Monticello
Thomasville
Albany
Fanning Springs State Park
Cedar Key
Chiefland
Branford
Suwanee River
Jasper
Valdosta
Titon
EQUESTRIAN OCALA
Ocala
OCALA NATIONAL FOREST
Gainesville
UNIVERSITY OF FLORIDA
Starke
Ocoloa National Forest
Palatka
Lake George
Jacksonville
St. Marys R.
Waycross
St. Augustine

0   25 mi
0   25 km

10
29
85
331
98
231
20
10
84
231
91
84
19
319
27
98
19
129
441
75
82
441
341
301
27
121
75
301
100
16
10
301
301
1
95
95

© AVALON TRAVEL

Two Days in the Panhandle

The **Panhandle** is not only culturally different from the rest of Florida—it's more like South Alabama than South Beach—it's also physically far away from the rest of Florida. Due to the relatively low population density north of Orlando and west of Jacksonville, the drive between the peninsula and the panhandle requires a few boring hours on the highway, which can feel interminable. And, once you've made the drive, you'll want to make it worth the time; here's an itinerary that takes in the rural charm, gorgeous beaches, and natural beauty of this unique part of the state.

DAY 1
Start at the eastern end of the Panhandle, in the state capital of **Tallahassee.** Explore the campus of **Florida State University** and the **Florida State Capitol complex** first, then head a half hour out of the city to hike through the **Appalachicola National Forest.** Afterward, cool off in the freshwater springs at **Edward Ball Wakulla Springs State Park.**

DAY 2
Destin is just a couple hours from Tallahassee, but it feels a world away from the hilly, tree-lined streets of the capital city. Boasting some of the most beautiful white-sand beaches in the state, Destin is a great place to spend an entire day, whether sunbathing on the beach, taking a boat into the Gulf of Mexico, or simply enjoying the slower pace of this Southern-style beach town.

DAY 3
For a somewhat more intense beachgoing experience, spend the final day at **Pensacola Beach,** which is stuffed with tourist shops, marinas, and, in nearby downtown **Pensacola,** a surfeit of overlooked historical sites.

THE PANHANDLE AND NORTH FLORIDA

territorial regions, East Florida and West Florida. West Florida was roughly defined as the Panhandle region, with the Apalachicola River as the eastern boundary and the Yazoo River as the western edge, and it also encompassed parts of what are now Mississippi, Alabama, and Louisiana. Sovereignty of West Florida was contested among the Spanish, British, and American governments for years until 1822, when Florida became a solely U.S. territory. At that point, the capital of the territory became Tallahassee, which was the midpoint between the capital of East Florida (St. Augustine) and the capital of West Florida (Pensacola). Before Florida became a state, though, there was one more burst of dispute over sovereignty when residents of the Panhandle voted to be annexed into Alabama in the early 1800s. Although the annexation never took place, in the area today it's not hard to understand that this part of the state is both more geographically proximate and culturally similar to the Yellowhammer State than it is to Florida cities like Miami and Orlando.

PLANNING YOUR TIME

Allow yourself a week, a month, or a year at any of the Panhandle beaches; it won't matter how long you stay because at the end of your visit, you'll be wishing you could stay a bit longer. There's very little to do along the Panhandle, with most of the sights and attractions a very distant second to the lure of the beach.

For the rest of the Northern Florida area, unless you're in Tallahassee on business, there's little to hold one's interest beyond half a day or so. Gainesville and Ocala each warrant a day or two on their own, and the camping, hiking, and canoeing options in the area will doubtlessly encourage outdoors types to extend their stay. The charming fishing village at Cedar Key is a great half-day respite from the bustle of the real world.

"The Spring Break Capital of the World"

Panama City Beach may promote itself to the world as the home of "the world's most beautiful beaches," but it's far more renowned for the somewhat less savory title of "the spring break capital of the world." It has recently become the latest Florida beach town to hold that questionable honor, after Fort Lauderdale in the 1970s and then Daytona Beach in the 1990s wearied of the endless hassle and emergency room overflow that inevitably occurs when college kids arrive with the sole intention of drinking themselves into oblivion and then sleeping it off on the sand the next day. In recent years, a massive crackdown by police, coupled with some high-profile tragedies, have dampened the bacchanalian mood somewhat among college students, and while plenty still flock to the area during spring break, the massive pool parties and all-night club nights that have defined PCB spring break for many college students are becoming less and less a focal point.

Panama City Beach

Spring-breakers, middle-class families, and unrepentant beach bums flock in droves to the beautiful white-sand beaches of **Panama City Beach** (PCB). While the town itself is perhaps one of the most inelegant oceanside tourist traps you're likely to see outside of Myrtle Beach, South Carolina, those gorgeous beaches more than make up for any shortcomings the city planners may have had. That being said, recent development along PCB's main drag of Front Beach Road has resulted in a number of posh hotels and high-rise condos that aim to alter the character of this scruffy beach village, and the jury's still out on whether those changes will actually be for the better. Part of Panama City Beach's charm is its utter charmlessness and its relaxed Southern take on the Florida beach vacation.

SIGHTS
Gulf World Marine Park

The trained-animal shows and marine life exhibits at **Gulf World Marine Park** (15412

Gulf World Marine Park

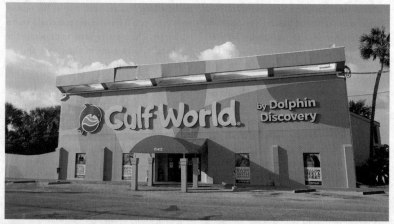

Panama City Beach

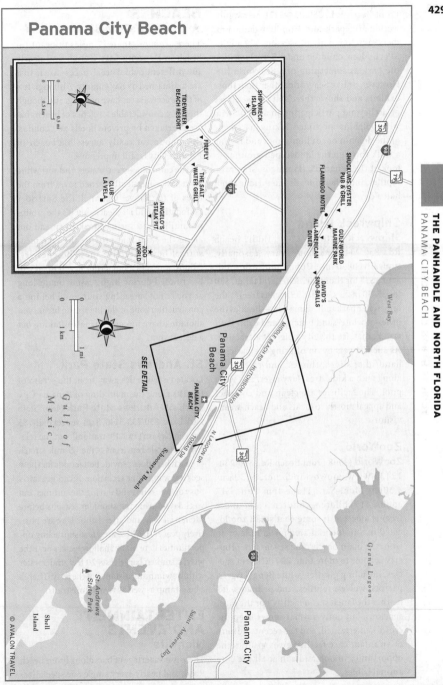

© AVALON TRAVEL

Front Beach Rd., 850/234-5271, www.gulf-worldmarinepark.com, 9am-4pm daily summer, 9am-2pm daily off-season, $29 adults, $19 children, children under 5 free) position the park as something of a SeaWorld lite. However, unlike SeaWorld, other than those exhibits and shows there's little else to see or do beyond participating in a $150 Swim with Dolphins encounter. Taking in a couple of the dolphin or sea lion shows and having a walk through the landscaped grounds to look at the penguins, flamingos, stingrays, reptiles, and other animals should take about half a day.

Shipwreck Island

Shipwreck Island (12201 Middle Beach Rd., 850/234-3333, hours vary seasonally, typically 10:30am-5:30pm mid-Apr.-mid-Sept., $35 for those 50 inches and taller, $30 for 35-50 inches, under 35 inches free) is the only water park in Panama City—besides the miles of white-sand beaches and calm Gulf waters that are the city's biggest attraction. As such, it gets by on offering the basics: a handful of slides, flumes, and river rides along with a kids' area, lazy river, and wave pool. The facilities are clean and compact and appeal mostly to locals and beach-weary visitors.

ZooWorld

ZooWorld (9008 Front Beach Rd., 850/230-1243, www.zooworldpcb.net, 9:30am-4:30pm Mon.-Sat., 11am-4pm Sun., $17 adults, $13 children, children 3 and under free) is a decent if somewhat small zoo located in a residential area just a mile or so from the main beach. The seven-acre property is home to more than 200 different species, including giraffes, white Bengal tigers, parrots, wolves, reptiles, and primates. It's neither the fanciest zoo facility nor the most spacious, but daily animal shows keep the crowds entertained, and the recent addition of an infant care facility gives visitors the opportunity to ooh and aah at all the cute animal babies.

BEACHES
★ Panama City Beach

There are more than 27 miles of beautiful beach in Panama City Beach and nearly 100 different public beach access areas that are maintained by Bay County. Although few of these access areas have parking, and though there are considerable stretches of beach that are overtaken by private hotels and condos, the amount of easily accessible beach in Panama City is still impressive.

The calm blue-green waters and soft white sand have consistently earned raves from the likes of the Travel Channel, the Surfrider Foundation, and Dr. Beach, but it's the groups of families and spring-breakers spread out along the sand that provide the true measure of how attractive these beaches are. Almost any spot along Front Beach Road will be crowded during high season, but as long as you're not spreading your towel behind a construction zone or during spring break, you shouldn't have too much trouble staking out a decent spot.

St. Andrews State Park

Located a few miles away from the scrum of tourists along the main drag of Panama City Beach, St. Andrews State Park (4607 State Park Lane, 850/233-5140, 8am-sunset daily, $5 per vehicle) isn't exactly tranquil, but the relatively unspoiled environs of the 1.5-mile stretch of beach here does provide better odds for those seeking waterfront seclusion. It can get fairly busy on weekends and during the summer, but weekdays during the shoulder seasons before Memorial Day and after Labor Day are positively peaceful. There are great snorkeling opportunities here in the shallow waters near the jetty; a sunken barge rests 20 feet underwater within swimming distance of the jetty. There's a boat ramp as well as two nature trails.

ENTERTAINMENT AND EVENTS
Nightlife

There is no shortage of bars along Front Beach Road, and nearly every single one specializes in cold beer and endless happy-hour specials. As interchangeable as all those places are, there is one place along the strip that is totally unique. The enormous waterfront **Club La Vela** (8813 Thomas Dr., 850/233-0226) is the self-proclaimed largest nightclub in the world and a spring break legend. With a capacity topping 6,000 people and 10 separately themed club-within-a-club "rooms," not counting all the action that goes down in and around the club's pool, La Vela is nothing if not excessive. Events from rock shows to wet T-shirt contests to teen dance nights occur in the club, but "party" (as a verb) seems to be the operative word when describing any of them.

Festivals and Events

Fans of smooth jazz fill the **Pier Park Amphitheater** (600 Pier Park Dr.) for the annual **Seabreeze Jazz Festival** (Apr.). The festival brings quiet-storm favorites to town for a weekend of concerts, including a Smooth Jazz Dinner Cruise.

SPORTS AND RECREATION
Fishing and Boating
Island Time Sailing Cruises (3605 Thomas

Dr., 850/234-7377, day cruises $35 per person, evening cruises $25 pp) takes up to 77 passengers out on a 55-foot catamaran for day cruises that include snorkeling and dolphin watching. It also offers two-hour sunset and dolphin-watching cruises.

Jubilee Deep Sea Fishing (3605 Thomas Dr., 850/236-2111, from $55 pp) runs two boats: the 60-foot *Treasure Island* and the smaller but faster *Jubilee*. The former is used for custom-scheduled trips for up to 40 people, while the *Jubilee* is a fishing "party boat" that goes out for 5-, 6-, and 8-hour trips. Fishing trips on the *Jubilee* include bait and tackle, and those who just want to ride along are only charged a nominal $20.

Golf

There are a few public courses in Panama City Beach. **Hombre Golf Club** (120 Coyote Pass, 850/234-3673, from $59 for 9 holes) has three whimsically named nine-hole courses: Ugly (3,427 yards, par 36), Good (3,170 yards, par 35), and Bad (3,393 yards, par 36). The **Holiday Golf Club** (100 Fairway Blvd., 850/234-1800, $75 for 18 holes) has a full 18-hole course (6,588 yards, par 72) and a tiny 9-hole (1,003 yards, par 27).

St. Andrews State Park near Panama City Beach

Best Restaurants

★ **Firefly:** With beautiful atmosphere and delicious fish, meat, and pasta dishes, Firefly stands out (page 432).

★ **The Fish House:** The fish here is good, but this downtown spot also offers other great dishes. Try a Soul Roll or the shrimp and grits (page 445).

★ **Food Glorious Food:** Emphasizing fresh, often organic ingredients and rich flavorful preparations, the menu has a comfort-food heart and a gourmet touch (page 455).

★ **Crane Ramen:** Sure, college kids love ramen, but the broth-based cuisine here is better than the college fare and a robust menu offers extensive options (page 461).

FOOD
Breakfast and Light Bites
The 1950s-style **All American Diner** (10590 Front Beach Rd., 850/235-2443, 7am-10pm daily, main courses from $5) is built to resemble a classic chrome-style diner, right down to the statue of Marilyn Monroe that greets guests as they enter. The fare is basic eggs-and-bacon plates, but the waitresses—though harried—are friendly, and the short-order cooks are fast.

David's Sno-Balls (13913 Back Beach Rd., 850/236-1998, 6:30am-8pm Mon.-Fri.) not only offers the New Orleans-style shaved ice-and-syrup treats that go down wonderfully on a hot summer day, but early risers can also stop by for fresh-brewed coffee and wonderful beignets.

American
In a dining scene crowded with fried seafood joints and casual dining options, the fine-dining experience at ★ **Firefly** (535 Beckrich Rd., 850/249-3359, 5-10pm daily, main courses from $15) truly stands out; even if the competition were stiffer, Firefly would certainly rank at the top. An impressive faux-outdoor dining room—punctuated by a giant tree lit by "fireflies"—makes for a beautiful environment in which to be served the fresh, locally caught fish that Firefly specializes in. In addition, there's an extensive selection of meat, poultry, and pasta dishes, all of which are prepared with a light modern touch. The two lounges make for a relaxing beginning or epilogue to an exceptional meal.

Angelo's Steak Pit (9527 Front Beach Rd., 850/234-2531, 5pm-10pm daily, Apr.-Sept., main courses from $18) is a straight-up, Western-style, old-school steakhouse. With the corny motto "You won't get a bum steer here and that's no bull" and the giant plastic bull outside, Angelo's is brimming with personality. The most exotic dishes on the menu—if you don't count the "ladies' top sirloin"—are the Greek salad and the "shish-kabob"; everything else is some variation of a fire-grilled steak or hickory-broiled barbecue.

Seafood
The **Salt Water Grill** (11040 Hutchison Blvd., 850/230-2739, 4pm-10pm daily, main courses from $17) is one of the best of Panama City Beach's upscale seafood options, offering extensive menus of fresh fish prepared in both classic and contemporary styles alongside grilled and broiled seafood platters and meat and pasta dishes. The modern, stylish atmosphere at Salt Water Grill includes an impressive 25,000-gallon saltwater aquarium as part of the decor.

At the other end of the seafood spectrum is **Shuckums Oyster Pub & Grill** (15614 Front Beach Rd., 850/235-3214, 11am-7pm daily, main courses from $10), which has been serving up oysters from this location for more than 40 years. Although the menu also includes steaks, sandwiches, and a few Southern specialties, the main reason to open the screen door here is to dig into the sautéed, baked, fried, and raw oysters that the Carter family shucks and serves by the bushel.

ACCOMMODATIONS

Most vacationers—especially extended-stay visitors—opt for renting one of the many beachfront condos that are available. The sparkling and luxurious high-rises like **Aqua** (15625 Front Beach Rd., 800/793-0057, www. aqua-gulf.com, from $1,300 weekly in summer) and **Tidewater** (16819 Front Beach Rd., 850/275-5060, www.tidewaterbeachresort. com, from $1,200 weekly in summer), are some of the fanciest, but there are also other more basic (and cheaper) options to choose from. Often, short-term lodging options like Airbnb and vrbo.com will be your best bet if you want to avoid chain hotels.

There are plenty of frowsy charmless little beach motels along Front Beach Road, many of which look like they have been subjected to frequent spring break abuse. Of those, **Andy's Motel** (8101 Surf Dr., 850/230-8999, from $69 d) is probably the best option, as it's inexpensive, clean, and relatively updated.

With a condo-like layout and well-equipped guest rooms, the **Flamingo Motel** (15525 Front Beach Rd., 850/234-2232, http://flamingomotel.com, from $89 d) takes up three buildings on two sides of Front Beach Road and is a popular destination for families. Accommodations range from standard motel rooms to suites in no less than half a dozen different configurations; amazingly, all but one of those configurations have full kitchens (and even that one is equipped with a microwave and mini fridge). This variety of layouts means that everyone, from couples to large families, can find an appropriate room. Although the guest rooms are clean and well-kept, they're also basic and unlikely to win any awards for design touches.

INFORMATION AND SERVICES

The office of the **Panama City Beach Convention & Visitor Bureau** is located at the corner of North Arnold Road and Back Beach Road/Highway 98 (17001 Panama City Beach Pkwy., 850/233-6503). Its website—www.visitpanamacitybeach.com—is quite informative and has information on current and upcoming events.

GETTING THERE
Air

The **Bay County International Airport** (PFN, 3173 Airport Rd., Panama City, 850/763-6751, www.pcairport.com) serves the Panhandle's beaches. It's located about a 10-minute drive from Panama City Beach and is served by Delta Connection and Northwest Airlink commuter jets that connect through Atlanta, Cincinnati, and Memphis.

Car

U.S. Highway 98 hugs the Panhandle shoreline, connecting Panama City Beach with Destin (42 miles, about an hour's drive to the west) and Pensacola Beach (130 miles, about 2.5 hours to the west). Tallahassee is about 130 miles (2.5 hours) to the east via State Road 231 and I-10.

GETTING AROUND

The **Pier Park Express** (www.pierparkexpress.com) trolley is one of the best ways to get around Panama City Beach. The trolley stops at six spots along Front Beach Road, arriving and departing every half hour. Unfortunately, the trolley only runs seasonally, and its funding—most of which comes from a grant from the Florida Department of Transportation—was in jeopardy as of this writing.

If you're driving, parking is limited, except at the few public beach lots, but there are sidewalks along Front Beach Road that make getting from place to place in the main beach area fairly easy.

Destin and Fort Walton Beach

Catering to a crowd that's slightly more upscale than the spring-breakers of Panama City Beach, **Destin** is struggling to maintain the hospitality and laid-back atmosphere that the Panhandle beaches are known for; thanks to the fact that it is home to some of the most gorgeous beaches in the state, Destin has seen incredibly rapid development in recent years, with lots of new condos and high-end strip malls popping up. **Fort Walton Beach** feels like a small Southern town that's seen better days, but it is kept vibrant by the activity in and around Eglin Air Force Base, which covers almost half a million acres to the north, east, and west of Fort Walton Beach; as a result, Fort Walton Beach feels more like a small, Southern base town despite being separated from the more luxurious Destin only by a 0.5-mile bridge.

SIGHTS
Fort Walton Beach

One of the first sights visitors encounter on the way in from the airport is the **Air Force Armament Museum** (100 Museum Dr., Eglin AFB, 850/651-1808, 9:30am-4:30pm Mon.-Sat., closed federal holidays, free). It's rather hard to miss, with a collection of vintage bombers and military aircraft dotting the grounds. Just walking around in the shadow of these enormous planes is interesting enough, as getting up close with B-52s, SR-71s, and other wartime flyers gives an impressive perspective. However, the inside of the museum is also filled with exhibits and interactive displays.

The **Indian Temple Mound Museum** (139 Miracle Strip Pkwy. SE, 850/833-9595, 10am-4:30pm Mon.-Sat. year-round, noon-4:30pm Sun. June-July, $5 adults, $3 children) is somewhat tricky to find, as it's situated in a copse of trees at a rather busy intersection in the city of Fort Walton Beach. As much as the setting camouflages the attraction, it also provides a perfectly pastoral environment for this step back in time. A replica temple is surrounded by a boardwalk with informative signs that give a history of the area's ancient settlers; it is accessible at all times. The museum is small and actually somewhat less

downtown Fort Walton Beach

impressive than the temple area. Outside, you can imagine the early inhabitants going about their business; inside, the glass-cased displays of artifacts are interesting but presented in ordinary fashion.

There are over a dozen different animal exhibits at **Florida's Gulfarium** (1010 Miracle Strip Pkwy. SE, 850/243-9046, www.gulfarium.com, 9am-6pm daily, reduced hours in winter, $21.95 adults, $13.95 children, children 2 and under free), ranging from saltwater aquariums filled with tropical fish and turtles to displays of sea lions, otters, sharks, stingrays, and even tropical penguins. There are also daily shows featuring trained dolphins and sea lions. With advance reservations, guests can take part in dolphin encounters ($75 for a 15-minute feeding session, $150 for a 30-minute in-water experience). The Gulfarium has been an attraction in the area for more than 50 years and does a good job keeping its facilities maintained and its mission in line with current conservation efforts.

Destin

The tiny **Destin History & Fishing Museum** (108 Stahlman Ave., 850/837-6611, 10am-4pm Tues.-Sat., $5 adults, $4 seniors and military, $3 children, children 3 and under free) is situated in a repurposed house and offers some interesting exhibits about the town's history and its long tradition of angling. There's a collection of antique rods and reels—including one of Ernest Hemingway's—as well as a 1920s-era fishing boat alongside displays of photographs and artifacts from Destin's past.

A few miles east of Destin is **Eden Gardens State Park** (181 Eden Garden Rd., Santa Rosa Beach, 850/231-4214, grounds 8am-sunset daily, guided tours hourly 10am-3pm Thurs.-Mon., $3 per vehicle). Unlike many state parks in the area, the biggest attraction here isn't the beach or the wildlife; rather it's the elegant white-columned antebellum Wesley Mansion—filled with one of the largest collections of Louis XVI furniture in the United States—that gets most visitors through the gates. Surrounded by mossy oaks and little else, the serene atmosphere at the house is only interrupted by the occasional Civil War reenactment that takes place on the grounds. Wander along the nature trails or open up your basket at the picnic area that hugs Tucker Bayou.

★ Destin Beaches

The Florida Panhandle is renowned for its

O'steen beach in Destin

Destin and Fort Walton Beach

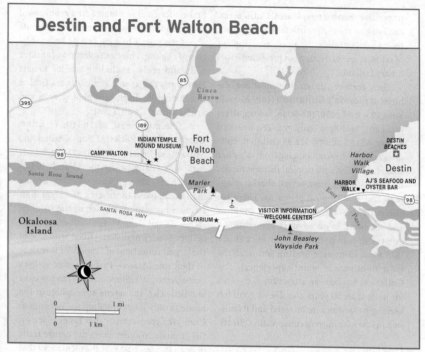

soft white-sand beaches, but nowhere is that sand whiter or softer than in Destin. In some places, the sand on these wide beaches can be so soft that it's difficult even to walk on; that's a small price to pay, though, for some exquisite beach going. Destin has 12 public beach access points in the city, only one of which—**Henderson Beach State Park** (8am-sunset daily, $4 per vehicle)—charges an admission fee. The rest offer limited parking and few facilities beyond a shower stand. Almost any of them make for a great day at the beach, but the easternmost accesses—**Norriego Point** (parking lot at the end of Gulf Shore Dr.) and **O'Steen** (park along the 300 block of Gulf Shore Dr.) tend to be the least crowded.

Crystal Beach (Hutchinson St. and Scenic Hwy. 98) is located along a highly developed strip of waterfront in western Destin and can be a complete zoo during the summer and peak season. Nearby Henderson Beach State Park is a bit more tolerable, but

an even better option is to continue driving west for another 20 minutes or so for the near isolation of **Grayton Beach State Park** (357 Main Park Rd., Santa Rosa Beach, 850/231-4210, 8am-sunset daily, $4 per vehicle). Although it's almost halfway to Panama City Beach, the rustic scenery and quiet atmosphere make it one of the best beach options in the area and the nearby Grayton Village is cute, historic, and has several good dining options.

ENTERTAINMENT AND EVENTS
Nightlife

The **Hogs Breath Saloon** (541 Hwy. 98 E., Destin, 850/837-1008) may be a Key West legend, but it actually got its start in this part of Northwest Florida; the Destin location embraces the same rowdy bikes-and-barbecue vibe as its more tropical cousin. For something a bit more low-key—but not much fancier—check out **The Red Door Saloon** (240

© AVALON TRAVEL

Harbor Blvd., Destin, 850/424-5974), which offers strong drinks, a raucously friendly vibe, and indoor and outdoor seating right on the water. The upscale jazz-and-cocktails crowd that shows up early at **Red Bar** (70 Hotz Ave., Santa Rosa Beach, 850/231-1008) starts cutting loose as the night progresses, but it's still a pretty straitlaced place.

Festivals and Events

The family-friendly **Billy Bowlegs Pirate Festival** (June) has been an annual tradition in the Fort Walton Beach area for more than half a century. The event brings buccaneer lovers out for parades, live music, arts and crafts, and, of course, a pirate ship—captained by Billy Bowlegs—coming into Fort Walton Beach Landing.

The **Destin Seafood Festival** (Oct.) also enjoys a long history, having kicked off in 1979. The weekend-long event brings out tens of thousands of people to HarborWalk Village in Destin, and in addition to the array

of seafood-eating opportunities, there are live bands, crafts vendors, and a kids' play area.

Down the road in Santa Rosa Beach, the **Flutterby Festival** (Oct.) is a two-day event that celebrates the annual migration of thousands of monarch butterflies through the area.

SPORTS AND RECREATION
Fishing and Boating

Just Chute Me! (404 Harbor Blvd., 850/200-2260, 8am-sunset daily, Apr.-Aug., flights from $45) offers parasail excursions high above Destin Harbor, ranging from 10-minute flights at 400 feet to 15 minutes soaring at 800 feet. Nonflying observers can come along for the boat ride for $20.

Sweet Jody (210 Harbor Blvd., 850/650-2500, www.fishing-destin.com, rates from $45 pp) is one of several charter fishing boats operating out of Destin. The 57-foot double-deck vessel has a snack bar and a knowledgeable crew. In addition to open-boat tours that run 4-10 hours, private charters are also available.

Those with their own boats should head for **Rocky Bayou State Park** (4281 Hwy. 20, Niceville, 850/833-9144, 8am-sunset daily, $4 per vehicle). Situated at the northern end of Choctawhatchee Bay, with access to the Rocky Bayou Aquatic Preserve, canoeing and kayaking in and around this park is an exceptional experience. Boat rentals are also available.

Parks

The primary function of **Longwood/ Poquito Bayou Park** (4 Bay St., Shalimar, 850/689-5084, sunrise-sunset daily) is for anglers to put in their boats as they head out into Poquito Bayou, but the picnic tables and small swimming area at this somewhat remote park make for a quiet getaway.

Kids with energy to burn should get to the **BMX & Skateboard Park** (126 Jet Dr. NW, Fort Walton Beach, 850/796-2326, 4pm-9pm Mon.-Thurs., 4pm-10pm Fri.-Sat., 4pm-8pm Sun., also 9am-noon June-July) in Fort Walton Beach; the 9,000-square-foot street course is great for skaters, and there's a BMX track and dirt jump area.

Golf

Sandestin Resort (9300 U.S. Hwy. 98, Destin, 866/285-6152, from $45) is the primary destination for duffers in the area. With four award-winning 18-hole courses—one designed by Robert Trent Jones Jr., one by Rees Jones, and the other two by Tom Jackson—as well as 15 tennis courts, a marina, and various water activities available on-site at the resort, many guests come to play and stay; the public is welcome to reserve tee times at the four courses.

While the **Emerald Bay Golf Club** (4781 Clubhouse Dr., Destin, 888/465-3229, from $57) only has the single Robert Cupp-designed, 6,802-yard, par-72 course, the facility's singular focus on golf makes it an appealing option for players uninterested in the resort atmosphere of Sandestin.

FOOD
Breakfast

Another Broken Egg Cafe (104 Hwy. 98 E., Destin, 850/650-0499, 6am-2pm daily, main courses from $8) has several locations in the area (it's a small Southeastern chain), but the food and service make it a far more attractive option than any of the Waffle Houses in the area. In addition to massive portions of standard breakfast dishes, ABE also has some specialties like huevos rancheros and *castines*.

If you're willing to queue up for some, the doughnuts at the locally legendary **Donut Hole** (6745 US Hwy 98 E., 850/2567-3239, 6am-10pm daily) are well worth the wait. The eatery also serves a regular sit-down breakfast too.

American

The views of Destin Harbor from the outdoor dining area of **Louisiana Lagniappe** (775 Gulf Shore Dr., Destin, 850/837-0881, dinner 5-10pm daily, brunch 11am-2pm Sun., main courses from $19) counter the fact that this excellent restaurant is located in a condominium complex. Lagniappe's take on New Orleans cuisine is less about po'boys and gumbo than about richly sauced and vibrantly seasoned seafood dishes. While you can tuck into a shrimp étouffée or some crab cakes, it's dishes like the grouper meuniere, blackened swordfish, and crab-and-shrimp au gratin that set this establishment apart.

There are plenty of casual dining options in the area, but the outdoor tiki bar-style dining area and relaxed vibe at **Fudpuckers** (11am-midnight daily, main courses from $7) makes it a good choice. Offering a standard array of pub grub (sandwiches, salads, seafood, and steak), Fudpuckers also gives diners the opportunity to watch live gators cavort in a pond in front of the restaurant.

Seafood

Dewey Destin Seafood Restaurant & Market (9 Calhoun Ave., Destin, 850/837-7575, 9:30am-8pm daily) is, quite literally, a

Best Accommodations

★ **Henderson Park Inn B&B:** Enjoy romantic, classy accommodations in a convenient location (page 440).

★ **Noble Manor:** Featuring modern amenities with a historic, lovely exterior, this downtown Pensacola spot is a great lodging option (page 446).

★ **Governor's Inn:** Far and away the best place to stay in Tallahassee has uniquely decorated rooms named after Florida's governors (page 456).

★ **Sweetwater Branch Inn B&B:** This multibuilding complex offers immaculate grounds and comfortable rooms (page 461).

Destin institution. The family that owns it is the same family that gave the city its name, and, not surprisingly, the focus here is on traditional preparations of fresh local seafood. Steamed, fried, or grilled are about your only options, but casual outdoor dining overlooking the Choctawhatchee Bay makes for a quintessential Destin experience.

AJ's Seafood & Oyster Bar (116 Hwy. 98 E., Destin, 850/837-1913, 11am-10pm daily, bar until 4am daily, main courses from $10) is less a restaurant than an all-in-one waterfront experience. With everything from a raw bar and an outdoor tiki lounge/sports bar with live music to charter boat rentals and dolphin cruises available on-site, AJ's surprisingly manages to put together a pretty good plate of seafood in its downstairs restaurant area. Expect massive crowds on weekends, during spring break and summer, and, well, pretty much any time.

Buster's Oyster Bar and Grill (125 Poinciana Blvd., 850/837-4399, main courses from $7) is located in a strip mall across from an outlet mall, but the bland surroundings are certainly not reflected in the quality of the oysters, shrimp, scallops, crab, and other seafood dishes served. There's not a lot of energy expended on creating innovative preparations, but by keeping it simple Buster's also keeps it good. It's been a local favorite for most of its 20 years in business, and the casual atmosphere

and excellent and reasonably priced fare makes it easy to understand why.

ACCOMMODATIONS
Vacation Rentals

For one-stop rental shopping, **ResortQuest** (850/275-5060, www.resortquestdestinvacations.com, studios from $1,100 weekly, larger units more) lists a wide variety of condos and rental homes throughout the Destin area with pictures, rates, and detailed descriptions. Its database is searchable by date, unit size, or location.

Both the **Silver Shells Beach Resort & Spa** (15000 Emerald Coast Pkwy., 850/337-5100, http://silvershells.com, 1-bedrooms from $225 daily, larger units more) and **Sandpiper Cove** (775 Gulfshore Blvd., 850/837-9121, www.sandpipercove.com, 1-bedrooms from $215 daily, larger units more) offer direct booking via their websites.

Hotel Accommodations

The **Hilton Sandestin Beach** (4000 S. Sandestin Blvd., 850/267-1816, 1-bedroom villas from $279 daily, larger units more, hotel from $229) offers a combination of condo rentals and hotel accommodations spread out among five different areas of the resort. Although the variety of lodging options and outdoor activities makes this resort a popular destination, it must be said that the huge property is largely free of character and easy to get lost in. If you're not coming to golf, there are better beachfront properties that offer a more comfortable experience.

On the other end of the spectrum is the beautiful and intimate ★ **Henderson Park Inn B&B** (2700 Scenic Beach Hwy. 98, Destin, 850/654-0400, from $259 d). Located at the end of a street that butts up against the boundary of Henderson Beach State Park, this historic B&B exudes romantic charm. Though very close to the hectic goings-on at Crystal Beach, the atmosphere here is subdued and classy. The two buildings house an array of suites, each of which is decked out in plush linens and antique furniture; rates include full breakfast, a boxed lunch, and even a complimentary bottle of wine.

The nearby **Beachside Inn** (2931 Scenic Beach Hwy. 98, Destin, 888/232-2498, www.destinbeachsideinn.com, from $210 d) is a beautifully renovated former motel, with stylish and sophisticated guest rooms that have kitchenettes.

Although it's not located beachside, the waterfront views from the **Inn on Destin Harbor** (402 Hwy. 98 E., Destin, 800/874-0470, www.innondestinharbor.com, from $145 d) are still impressive, and the well-appointed hotel rooms are clean, contemporary, and remarkably affordable.

GETTING THERE AND AROUND

The **Northwest Florida Regional Airport** (VPS, 1701 State Rd. 85 N., Elgin AFB, 850/609-4750, www.flyvps.com) serves the Panhandle's beach towns, and its location north of Fort Walton Beach makes it not only a good choice for this area but also for visitors going to Pensacola or Panama City Beach, as both towns are within an hour's drive. VPS is served by Delta, American, United, and Allegiant.

I-10, which runs east-to-west along northern Florida, is about 25 miles (45 minutes' drive) north of Fort Walton Beach.

Little of Destin is comfortably walkable, given that U.S. Highway 98 is the primary thoroughfare in town; thankfully, most destinations around the area have ample parking. Fort Walton Beach isn't very pedestrian friendly either. The **Okaloosa County Transit Authority** (850/689-7809, $1 per adult) operates a trolley service along the Destin beachfront during the summer months that provides a convenient and inexpensive alternative to driving and parking.

the Henderson Park Inn B&B

Pensacola

Pensacola was the first European settlement in the United States, and the village area downtown highlighting this history is interesting and quite a nice contrast to the bland midsize city that surrounds it. Most visitors to the area are here for the white sand of Pensacola Beach. With enormous dunes that threaten to erase roadways and long stretches of open blue water, the community is defined by its close relationship to the Gulf of Mexico and a thorough sense of relaxed individualism, as evidenced by some of the unique houses (think UFOs) along the main

drag. Development here has been slower than in some of the Panhandle's other beach towns, and the majority of the buildings here are low-slung and residential, resulting in a beachfront that's blissfully light on high-rise condominiums and hotels.

SIGHTS
Gulf Breeze Zoo

Spreading out across 30 acres and home to nearly 1,000 animals, the **Gulf Breeze Zoo** (5701 Gulf Breeze Pkwy., Gulf Breeze, 850/932-2229, 9am-5pm daily, $11.50 adults,

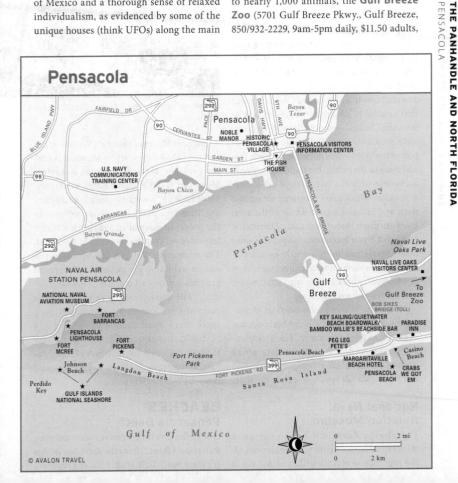

$8.25 children, children 2 and under free) should be a prime destination, but the facilities here are somewhat outdated, and the zoo has continued to struggle with a number of animal-care problems, including dozens of deaths. The problems are so acute, in fact, that the American Association of Zoos and Aquariums revoked the zoo's accreditation in 2006. The relentless marketing campaign that the zoo undertakes makes it hard to ignore its presence in the area—which is why it is included in these listings—but even a casual visitor is likely to notice the generally shabby conditions.

Historic Pensacola Village

There are 22 buildings and museums that comprise **Historic Pensacola Village** (205 E. Zaragoza St., Pensacola, 850/595-5993, 10am-4pm Tues.-Sat., $8 adults, $4 children, children under 4 free), ranging from cottages and churches to a Museum of Commerce and the beautiful T. T. Wentworth Jr. Florida State Museum (housed in the old Spanish mission-style Pensacola City Hall). With the exception of the Wentworth museum, which is free and open to the public, the buildings are only accessible with the purchase of an admission ticket, which allows entrance for up to a week and includes a guided tour of the area; tours are given three times a day. Despite the somewhat Byzantine admission process, once inside, you'll find the village to be quite interesting due to the historical architecture, most of which dates back to the early 19th century, and the verdant surroundings.

History buffs should also consider exploring the nearby North Hill Neighborhood, just a few blocks from downtown. The Victorian-era homes and lush, hilly streets aren't "sights," per se, but offer a unique glimpse into an Old Florida not typically seen in the state.

National Naval Aviation Museum

The Florida Panhandle has an extensive military aviation history, as evidenced by the presence of facilities like the Air Force

the famous beach ball on Pensacola Beach's Casino Beach

Armament Museum near Fort Walton Beach and the U.S. Army Aviation Museum at Fort Rucker. The **National Naval Aviation Museum** (1750 Radford Blvd., Pensacola, 850/452-3296, www.navalaviationmuseum. org, 9am-5pm daily, free) is not only one of the oldest (it opened in 1963), it's also the largest naval aviation museum in the world. There are more than 300,000 square feet of indoor exhibit space as well as 37 acres of grounds housing all manner of military aircraft. The most stunning exhibit is in the main atrium, a seven-story glass-ceilinged space that's home to four Blue Angel A-4 Skyhawks, but other exhibits on World War II flight-deck aviation, displays of memorabilia, and more make this an interesting—and free—half-day adventure.

BEACHES
Pensacola Beach

One of the first things you see when entering **Pensacola Beach** from the Bob Sikes Bridge is a giant beach ball. It's not just any ordinary giant beach ball but a 10-story-tall water tower painted to resemble a green, orange, and white beach ball with the words "Pensacola Beach" gaily painted across it. Overlooking the popular Casino Beach area and the Pensacola Beach Gulf Pier, the water tower is a playful reminder that these vast stretches of soft white sand and calm blue Gulf waters are the area's primary attraction. The beaches—whether packed with umbrellas and towels or isolated and quiet—are uniformly excellent and well-deserving of their reputation as some of the best in the United States.

For ease of access and availability of facilities, **Casino Beach** is the best option. The heavily trafficked location and popularity of the pier among anglers mean that there are not only several restaurants and shops directly on the beach but also a massive parking lot and easily accessed restroom facilities.

All along the dune-covered roadway of Pensacola Beach Boulevard are numerous spots to pull off and enjoy the beach, but head about seven miles west of town for the quiet stretch of sand called **Opal Beach.** You'll sacrifice facilities (there are portable toilets and parking spots, and that's about it), but you'll get a sublimely relaxing beach experience in return.

Gulf Islands National Seashore

The Pensacola area is home to the Florida portion of the **Gulf Islands National Seashore** (visitors center at 1801 Gulf Breeze Pkwy., Gulf Breeze, 850/916-3010, hours vary seasonally, generally 8am-sunset daily, $3). The expansive parkland ranges from marsh to mangroves to soft white beaches, with the most accessible swimming area near **Johnson Beach** on Perdido Key. Walking east from the parking area, you find a vast empty stretch of sand; the farther you go, the fewer people are around. Closer to the visitors center and Pensacola Beach is **Fort Pickens.** Completed in 1834, it's the largest of four forts constructed to protect the Pensacola area. It was decommissioned after World War II, and reopened by the National Park Service in 1976; with its relatively remote location within the Gulf Islands National Seashore, the fort is often deserted, but it is a great place to explore, and the cannon batteries provide some beautiful vantage points to look out over the bay. More importantly, there are some beautiful white-sand beaches just beyond the fort's walls that are vacant on most days. Worth noting: Neither of these beaches is particularly easy to get to—especially given the tendency

Gulf Islands National Seashore near Destin

of the roads around here to disappear under sand dunes—but both are worth the effort.

ENTERTAINMENT AND EVENTS
Nightlife

Most of the drinking spots in Pensacola Beach are of the beach-town pub variety, offering cold beer, big TVs, and fried food. From the legendarily boozy "Bannanawhacker" at the **Sandshaker Lounge** (713 Pensacola Beach Blvd., Pensacola Beach, 850/932-2211) to the picnic tables in the sand at **Paradise Bar & Grill** (21 Via de Luna Dr., Pensacola Beach, 850/916-5087), they all seem to be vying to be the most laid-back and beachy spot in the area; they're all uniformly friendly and packed on the weekends and during high season. For something a bit more sophisticated, head into downtown Pensacola, where spots like **Union Public House** (309 S. Reus St., Pensacola, 850/607-6320) pair their excellent drink lists and rustic ambiance with gastropub fare.

Festivals and Events

The **Gulf Coast Renaissance Faire** (Mar.) takes over the Pensacola Interstate Fairgrounds (6655 Mobile Hwy., Pensacola) for a weekend of jousting, sword fighting, puppetry, dancing, juggling, jesting, fire-breathing, and more. I would give almost anything to see this event done in conjunction with the annual **Interstate Mullet Toss** (last full weekend in Apr.). Folks gather at the Flora-Bama Lounge (17401 Perdido Key Blvd., Pensacola, at the Florida-Alabama state line) and throw fish from Alabama into Florida while bikini-clad women measure their abilities. It's more fun than it sounds, and it's a fund-raising event but also an excuse to drink, eat, hang out at the beach, and have a somewhat ridiculous time. The record for mullet tossing, by the way, is 189 feet.

In keeping with the somewhat underappreciated Cajun influence in the area, the **Pensacola Crawfish Creole Fiesta** (early May) is held in downtown Pensacola at Bartram Park (211 W. Main St.) and claims to be one of the largest crawfish boils in the state. Live Creole and Cajun music, crafts vendors, games, and tons of crawfish, po'boys, fried gator, jambalaya, and more culinary treats are on tap.

Held in Seville Square in downtown Pensacola, the **Great Gulf Coast Arts Festival** (Nov.) is a three-day event with free admission. There's a juried art show as well as a number of folk art displays. Crafts vendors and live music round out the offerings; held in adjacent Bartram Park (211 W. Main St.) during the same time is the **Children's Art Festival.**

SPORTS AND RECREATION
Fishing and Boating

Most anglers head straight for the **Pensacola Beach Gulf Pier** (41 Fort Pickens Rd., Pensacola Beach, 850/934-7200, 24 hours daily, $7.50 to fish, $1.25 to observe). At almost 1,500 feet long, there's always a decent spot to put a line in, with everything from flounder and mackerel to cobia and bonito swimming around in the water. For those uninterested in fishing, it's also a great place to catch a sunset. There's a tiny food stand with hot dogs and snacks as well as a bait and tackle shop.

For those who want to get out into deeper water, charter outfits like the **Snapper Trapper** (850/455-4662, www.snappertrapper.com) and **Chuck's Charters** (850/435-7363, www.chuckscharters.com) offer bottom fishing, cobia runs, spear fishing, and other options.

For those who want to learn to sail their own boats, **Lanier Sailing Academy** (850/432-3199, www.laniersail.com) offers courses as short as three hours or as extensive as weekend-long classes. They also have a variety of cruises and tours available.

Parks

In Pensacola near the I-10 overpass along the Pensacola Scenic Bluffs Parkway is **Bay Bluffs Park** (sunrise-11pm daily), a 32-acre nature preserve situated on enormous (at least by Florida standards) coastal bluffs. With wooden boardwalks and walking trails through dense pine forests, it's a great natural escape, and the views of Escambia Bay from the park are astounding.

The **Roger Scott Athletic Complex** (4601 Piedmont Dr., Pensacola, 305/912-4103, 9am-9pm Mon.-Fri., 9am-6pm Sat.-Sun.) has 18 tennis courts, baseball and soccer fields, restrooms, and concession facilities.

Golf

Marcus Pointe Golf Club (2500 Oak Pointe Dr., Pensacola, 850/484-9770, www.golfmarcuspointe.com) is a semi-residential public course designed in 1990 by Earl Stone. The relaxed and eminently playable 6,700-yard par-72 has been praised as a good value by *Golf Digest* readers.

The city-owned **Osceola Golf Course** (300 Tonawanda Dr., Pensacola, 850/453-7599, www.osceolagolf.com, from $21) is a par-72 6,366-yard course; there's a practice green and driving range on-site, as well as locker rooms and a restaurant.

FOOD
Breakfast

Breakfast is in something of a dire situation, as most locals and visitors seem content to eat at home or in one of the many Waffle Houses in the area. Nonetheless, **Native Cafe** (45 Via de Luna Dr., Pensacola Beach, 850/934-4848, 7:30am-3pm Mon.-Wed., 7:30am-8pm Thurs., 7:30am-10pm Fri.-Sat., 10am-8pm Sun., main courses from $6) serves huge omelets and from-scratch pancakes in a friendly environment, along with more hearty fare like *croque madame*, omelet paninis, and traditional American breakfasts.

American

Hemingway's Island Grill (400 Quietwater Beach Rd., Pensacola Beach, 850/934-4747, 11am-10pm daily, sandwiches from $9, main courses from $16) is considerably more upscale, with dishes like Havana Gun Club

Steak, Jack's Hurricane Shrimp, and Ketchum Idaho Rib Eye designed to evoke Papa's rugged outdoor attitude and masculine appetites. (We're supposed to forget, I suppose, that Ernest Hemingway killed himself in Ketchum.) This place is officially sanctioned by the Hemingway estate, along with its line of decorative pillows, marinades, and candlesticks, and trades heavily on Hemingway's personality to the point of it almost being a tourist attraction itself. The result is a warm and stylish atmosphere and decent if somewhat overpriced food.

Despite its name, the specialty at downtown Pensacola restaurant ★ **The Fish House** (600 S. Barracks St., Pensacola, 850/470-0003, 11am-10pm daily, main courses from $15) isn't seafood. Instead, the food here is delectable modern Southern cuisine. If you get nothing else here, stop in for a drink and a plate of Soul Rolls, in which chicken, collard greens, peach chutney, and brown sugar, pecan, and creole mustard sauce are stuffed into a spring-roll wrapper. Also a must-try: the Fish House's "world famous" shrimp-and-grits plate; grits thickened by melted smoked gouda cheese are topped with creole-spiced shrimp, sautéed spinach, bacon, portobello mushrooms and a heaping dose of awesome. There are seafood dishes available—salmon, fresh Gulf catches, and even sushi—and next door is the Atlas Oyster House for raw-bar fanatics, but the restaurant's exceptional perspective on Southern cuisine is another ample reminder that in Florida, you've got to go north to get to the South.

Seafood

Peg Leg Pete's (1010 Fort Pickens Rd., Pensacola Beach, 850/932-4139, 11am-10pm daily, sandwiches from $8, main courses from $13) is a straightforward family-casual beach-grub spot, with sandwiches, burgers, and pasta dishes rounding out a menu of fried seafood baskets and grilled and broiled specialties. The place got its start as an oyster bar, and there are plenty of shellfish options available as well as two friendly bars that are favored by locals.

Crabs We Got Em (6 Casino Beach Blvd., Pensacola Beach, 850/932-0070, 11am-10pm daily, main courses from $15) overlooks the Gulf of Mexico and has plenty of breezy outdoor seating. Crabs are the focus here, making for a somewhat more expensive menu than some of the other seafood places in town; still, for those who don't care to, uh, shell out the big bucks for Dungeness or king crab legs, the restaurant also has fresh Gulf-caught fish that it wisely offers naked preparations of. The sweet honey buns served as bread are decadent and delicious. The restaurant area is huge and even boasts an outdoor play area for kids.

International

Cabo Grill (400 Quietwater Beach Rd., Pensacola Beach, 850/916-2226, 11am-10pm daily, main courses from $13) has positioned itself as an upscale Mexican dining option on Pensacola Beach; considering that there aren't that many downscale Mexican dining options, the fare at Cabo doesn't have to do much to set itself apart. The fresh fare—from mahi-mahi-filled fish tacos to grilled salmon served with prickly pear salsa—is certainly a cut above expectations. Cabo Grill is also very proud of its extensive tequila selection and treats its margarita list the way some bars treat their martini menu.

There are a number of excellent sushi restaurants in downtown Pensacola, but **Dharma Blue** (300 S. Alcaniz St., Pensacola, 850/433-1275, 5pm-9:30pm daily and 10am-2pm Sat.-Sun., entrées from $12, sushi rolls from $4) is by far the best. Dharma offers a tightly curated and expertly executed selection of sushi as well as a few traditional Japanese entrées, serving it all up in a cozy environment that—thanks to its knickknack-heavy décor and airy front porch—is more evocative of Old Florida than Old Kyoto.

ACCOMMODATIONS
Vacation Rentals

One of the best ways to stay in Pensacola Beach is to rent a house or a condo and shack up for a week. Although there are several decent hotel accommodations in town, the casual family-friendly vibe in Pensacola makes it a naturally attractive destination for those coming for long weekends or full holiday weeks, and having your own kitchen—and your own bedroom—can make such a stay all the more relaxing. Both **Pensacola Beach Properties** (www.pensacolabeachproperty.com) and **Our Gulf Coast** (www.ourgulfcoast.com) have a wide variety of condos and some houses.

Hotel Accommodations

Paradise Inn (21 Via de Luna Dr., Pensacola Beach, 850/932-2319, http://paradiseinn-pb.com, from $129 d) is a nice, clean, and fairly up-to-date option that's located on the water's edge at Santa Rosa Sound. Be advised, though, that the Paradise is also home to a popular watering hole; though the guest rooms are insulated from the activity there, the property can get a bit crowded on the weekends.

Next door is the **Soundside Holiday Beach Resort** (19 Via de Luna Dr., Pensacola Beach, 850/934-2500, from $199 d), which houses 28 two-bedroom two-bath condo units, available for nightly and weekly rentals. All the units have full kitchens and laundry facilities and are individually decorated and appointed.

One of the last buildings at the easternmost edge of Pensacola Beach is the recently rebuilt **Portofino Island Resort & Spa** (2200 Via de Luna Dr., Pensacola Beach, 877/484-3405, www.portofinoisland.com, from $479 d). The luxury condominium complex has rentals available by the night and on an extended basis; the condos here are large (either 1,333 or 2,034 square feet) and gorgeously appointed with master suites, whirlpool baths, gourmet kitchens, laundry facilities, and stylish furnishings. There's a fitness center and a 40,000-square-foot spa on-site.

Located in downtown Pensacola's historic North Hill neighborhood, ★ **Noble**

Manor (110 W. Strong St., Pensacola Beach, 850/434-9544, www.noblemanor.com, from $139 d) offers its own brand of luxury with only four guest rooms, each of which is meticulously decorated and quite beautiful. The Tudor exterior of this century-old mansion belies the modern textures of the three guest rooms within—there are flat-screen TVs and Wi-Fi, along with claw-foot tubs and rich wood appointments. The fourth guest room is a carriage house suite with its own private courtyard entrance. It's about a 15-minute drive to the beach from here, but this location also puts visitors closer to the more diverse dining options of downtown.

INFORMATION AND SERVICES

As soon as you cross into Pensacola Beach on the Bill Sikes Bridge, the **Pensacola Beach Visitors Information Center** (735 Pensacola Beach Blvd., Pensacola Beach, 850/932-1500) is directly on your right, in the shadow of the giant beach ball water tower. It's stocked with brochures for hotels, restaurants, and local attractions along with a single friendly staff member who will be more than happy to proffer advice and directions.

GETTING THERE AND AROUND

Pensacola is midway between Mobile, Alabama, and the next closest Florida town of Destin, so in addition to the daily flights that come into **Pensacola Regional Airport** (PNS, 2430 Airport Blvd., Pensacola, 850/436-5000, www.flypensacola.com)—which is served by all the major U.S. carriers as well as low-cost carrier AirTran—there may be other cheaper options at the **Mobile Regional Airport** (MOB, 8400 Airport Blvd., Mobile, Alabama, 251/633-4510, www.mobairport.com) or even at the more limited **Northwest Florida Regional Airport** (VPS, 1701 State Rd. 85 N., Elgin AFB, 850/609-4750, www.fly-vps.com) north of Fort Walton Beach.

For those arriving by car, I-10 runs through the city of Pensacola, connecting it to Mobile, New Orleans, and Houston to the west and Tallahassee and Jacksonville to the east. Pensacola Beach is about 15 miles (a 20-minute drive) south of downtown Pensacola via U.S. Highway 98 and the toll-charging Bill Sikes Bridge.

The main part of Pensacola Beach, near the pier and the Casino Beach area, is pretty walkable and cyclable, and there's a large public parking lot. The best option around the beach

Noble Manor in historic downtown Pensacola

THE PANHANDLE AND NORTH FLORIDA
PENSACOLA

is the free **Pensacola Beach Trolley,** which operates Friday-Sunday Memorial Day-end of September. For other destinations, driving is essential; be advised that downtown Pensacola experiences some surprisingly heavy rush-hour traffic.

Tallahassee and Northern Florida

As hard as it is to believe, there are still large swaths of Florida that are mostly undeveloped and quite unpopulated. And all of them, it seems, are in the area of the state known as the **Big Bend**. Named after the curve in topography that connects the panhandle to the peninsula, the Big Bend is home to little more than marshy coastal communities without beaches, long-forgotten small towns, and, well, the state's capital city. Although there are some areas of profound natural beauty in this part of the state—particularly around the great Suwannee River—they're separated by large stretches of rural nothingness. This is where going north definitely equals "going South." Getting anywhere seems to take forever, but a day fishing off Cedar Key or canoeing down the Suwannee makes the effort worthwhile.

CEDAR KEY

This tiny fishing village is both historic—the town and much of the surrounding area are on the National Register of Historic Places, thanks to the numerous archaeological finds in the area—and charming. Having much the same laid-back attitude as the tropical Keys below Miami, **Cedar Key** boasts a compact and rustic waterfront area along Dock Street as well as a historic downtown area with buildings dating back to the late 19th and early 20th centuries.

Sights

Since the main attraction in Cedar Key is fishing, it's not much of a surprise that the **Cedar Key Marina** (12780 State Rd. 24, 352/543-6148) is the town's primary attraction. The full-service marina offers boaters storage, supplies, and repair facilities, and

the fishing pier at Cedar Key

Tallahassee and Northern Florida

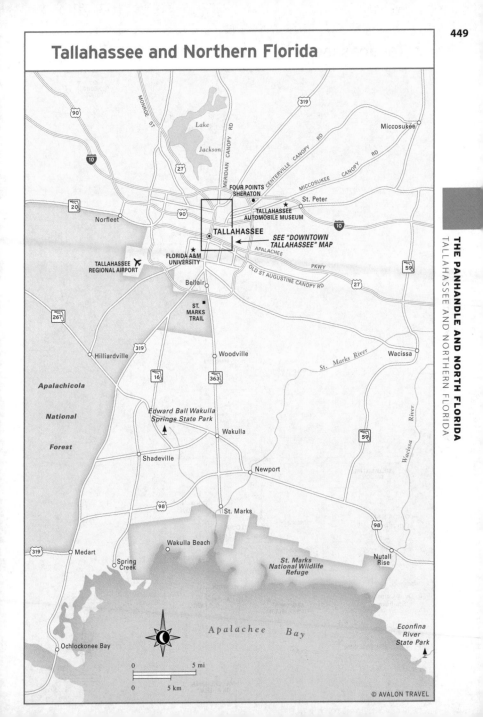

© AVALON TRAVEL

Tallahassee

FOOD GLORIOUS FOOD ▼

Lake Ella

W 10TH AVE
GIBBS DR
PROCTOR ST
JACKSON ST
MILTON ST
MARTIN LUTHER KING JR ST
MONROE ST
MERIDIAN ST
COLONIAL ST

W 7TH AVE

W 6TH AVE
BRONOGH ST
DUVALL ST
ADAMS ST
LEON PUB ▼
5TH AVE
THOMASVILLE RD
INGELSIDE ST

OLD BAINBRIDGE RD
W 4TH AVE
MARTIN ST
PINE ST

W 3RD AVE
MACOMB ST

MCDANIEL ST

GOVERNOR'S MANSION ★

BREVARD ST
CALHOUN ST
GADSDEN ST
MICCOSUKEE RD

GEORGIA ST

CAROLINA ST
DUVALL ST
ADAMS ST
MONROE ST

VIRGINIA ST

TENNESSEE ST

BULLWINKLE'S SALOON ■

CALL ST
MERIDIAN ST
FRANKLIN BLVD

FLORIDA STATE UNIVERSTY

Ponce de Leon Park ★
PARK AVE
PARK AVE
PARK AVE
MACOMB ST
DOWNTOWN MARKETPLACE

JEFFERSON ST
VISITORS CENTER ■
MLK JR ST
GOVERNORS INN ●

PENSACOLA ST
CITY HALL ■
To Doak Campbell Stadium
ST AUGUSTINE ST
NEW CAPITOL
APALACHEE PWY
MUSEUM OF FLORIDA HISTORY ★
DUVALL ST
OLD CAPITOL ★
CALHOUN ST
LAFAYETTE ST

MADISON ST

RESIDENCE INN ●
WAHNISH WAY
GAINES ST

BRONOGH ST
SOUL VEGETARIAN ON WHEELS ▼

© AVALON TRAVEL

0   250 yds
0   250 m

boat rentals are available as well. Anglers can pick up tackle here and charter boats that will take them out for fishing expeditions into the coastal flats and deep Gulf waters. The village area around the marina is thick with restaurants and gift shops.

About 10 miles (15 minutes' drive) from Cedar Key is the southern boundary of the **Lower Suwannee National Wildlife Refuge** (County Rd. 326, off County Rd. 347, 352/493-0238, www.fws.gov/lowersuwannee, accessible 24 hours, 365 days). The 53,000-acre refuge is a combination of pine forests, swamps, salt marshes, tidal flats, and more than 26 miles of Gulf coast frontage. There's an abundance of wildlife to be found within the refuge's borders; wildlife spotters are likely to encounter alligators, manatees, ducks, bears, wild turkeys, bald eagles, and lots of freshwater fish. There are extensive hiking and kayaking opportunities throughout the refuge, but one of the best spots to stake out the fauna is at **Shell Mound Unit,** near the site of a Native American shell mound, where crabs skitter along the muddy flats and there's a quiet boardwalk from which you can observe birds and other wildlife. There's a parking area, a small put-in for boats, and a portable toilet, but no other facilities, making this spot far more pastoral than the nearby county-owned **Shell Mound Park,** which you pass on the way into the refuge; that park has 20 campsites, shower facilities, a boat ramp, a playground, and lots of people launching their motorboats.

About 43 miles (an hour's drive) north is the 200-acre **Fanning Springs State Park** (18020 NW Hwy. 19, Fanning Springs, 352/463-3420, www.floridastateparks.org/fanningsprings, 8am-sunset daily, $6/carload of 2-8 people, $4/single-occupancy vehicle), which is a hub of the Suwannee River Wilderness Trail. The 12-foot-deep springs that give the park its name are a big draw, with a clearly marked swimming area that brings in large crowds during the summer; scuba divers also enjoy diving in these springs. There also are several hiking trails and a boardwalk as well as a handful of rental cabins available for overnight stays. It's also possible to rent a canoe or kayak and take a quick trip down the Suwannee to nearby **Manatee Springs State Park** (11650 NW 115th St., Chiefland, 352/493-6072, www.floridastateparks.org/manateesprings, 8am-sunset daily, $6/carload of 2-8 people, $4/single-occupancy vehicle), although you'll need to arrange with your outfitter for return transportation. Manatees

Cypress trees crop up from the ground at Manatee Springs State Park.

are abundant in both parks during the winter, and when the sea cows are around, swimming isn't allowed.

Food

Tucked away on the side of Highway 24 as you're heading into town, the **Blue Desert Cafe** (12518 State Rd. 24, 352/543-9111, 5pm-9pm Tues.-Sat., main courses from $8) would be easy to miss if it weren't so flamboyantly painted in an array of tropical colors. Although there's not much emphasis on speedy service—you won't get out of here in less than an hour—the pasta, pizza, burritos, and unique nonfried seafood preparations are worth the wait, and the good beer selection makes it easy to pass the time.

Carlin's Steakhouse & Waterfront Pub (490 Dock St., 352/543-8004, 11am-9pm Wed.-Sun., main courses from $8) has fantastic Gulf views and strong cocktails that more than make up for a pedestrian menu of decent steak, above-average seafood specialties, burgers, and sandwiches.

In a town filled with seafood restaurants, **Tony's Seafood** (597 2nd St., 352/543-0022, 11:30am-8pm Sun.-Thurs., 11:30am-10pm Fri.-Sat., main courses from $13) has made a name for itself as one of the best. Although there are a handful of fried platters on the menu, most of the dishes here are grilled and steamed specialties, and Tony's clam chowder is semi-legendary. The preparations aren't incredibly inventive, but they are expertly done and built around some super-fresh seafood. Despite having a beautiful dining room in downtown Cedar Key, the restaurant also does a booming to-go business and even delivers meals in a cute little electric car.

Accommodations

Other than a handful of places in Cedar Key, the majority of lodging options in the Big Bend area are of the highway-motel and low-budget-chain variety. Unless you're renting a coastal condo or state park cabin, Cedar Key is by far the best place to stay because of the unique nature of some of the hotels and the

generally more pleasant and relaxed atmosphere that's prevalent in the village.

The **Dockside Motel** (491 Dock St., 352/543-5432, $84 d) is one of several places to stay right next to the marina, and as the name implies, it's right along the dock, with most of Cedar Key's restaurants and shops no more than 100 yards away. With only 11 guest rooms, the family-owned motel is friendly, and the guest rooms, though tiny and basic, are immaculate. Situated in "downtown" Cedar Key, the **Island Hotel** (373 2nd St., 352/543-5111, www.islandhotel-cedarkey. com, $100 d) was built in 1859 and is on the National Register of Historic Buildings. For some, the main attraction of the hotel is its supposedly haunted history and the quaint charming rooms; for me, what truly makes the Island a superlative experience is the fact that there is no television in the bar area. While the Island trades considerably on its past, it's definitely more a casual past than one of antebellum elegance, so guests should arrive expecting a unique stay but not a luxurious one.

Getting There and Around

Cedar Key is 136 miles (three hours' drive) north of Tampa and 71 miles (two hours) west of Ocala. The closest major highway is U.S. 19, which runs along Florida's Gulf coast; take State Road 24 west from U.S. 19 in Otter Creek.

The small town is quite walkable, and parking is easy to come by along Second Street and Dock Street.

TALLAHASSEE

Tallahassee is a beautiful city, and its hilly tree-lined streets make it somewhat anomalous in Florida. As the seat of state government and home to Florida State University (FSU), it sees massive seasonal population swings. During the summer, when school's out and the legislature is out of session, the city is nearly empty; in the winter, when bills are being debated and term papers being written, it buzzes with its own peculiar energy. Unfortunately, unless you're a student, a Seminole football fan, or have some sort of government business, there's little reason to recommend a visit to the city, thanks to its oddly remote location and dearth of interesting sights.

The State Capitol

A visit to the grounds of the **Florida State Capitol** (Apalachee Pkwy. and Monroe St.) is an essential stop if you are in Tallahassee, not because the grounds are particularly beautiful or because you can get a sense of government in action, but simply because you have to see one of the most hideous, almost phallic pieces of government architecture in the United States. The Old Capitol Building (10am-4:30pm daily, guided tours by request, free, donations requested) still stands on the grounds and is worth a look, but the 22-story "new classicist" building that functions as the state's current capitol is a charmless and lifeless office tower.

Florida State University

Coming up the hill on West College Avenue, the **Westcott Building** is the first glimpse you get of **Florida State University,** and the view is quite impressive. The campus is verdant and self-contained, with a handful

of historic and architecturally interesting buildings like the collegiate Gothic-style **Dodd Hall,** which boasts a beautifully ornate stained-glass window at its west end, and the sculpture garden on **Sandels Green.**

TOP EXPERIENCE

Edward Ball Wakulla Springs State Park

Located 14 miles south of Tallahassee is the **Edward Ball Wakulla Springs State Park** (550 Wakulla Park Dr., Wakulla Springs, 850/926-0700, 8am-sunset daily, $6/carload of 2-8 people, $4/single-occupancy vehicle). Of course the premier attraction is swimming in the **freshwater springs.** 400,000 gallons flow here daily. The 180-foot opening draws cave divers while the demarcated and lifeguarded swimming area appeals to less adventurous aquanauts. There are also three distinct trail networks throughout the pines, wetlands, and swamps of the park as well as an abundance of wildlife ranging from manatees and alligators to wild turkeys and deer.

Named after the DuPont family's money manager—who had the foresight to build a lodge in the 1930s at these enormous springs—the 6,000-acre park is designated a National

the capitol building complex in downtown Tallahassee

THE PANHANDLE AND NORTHERN FLORIDA
TALLAHASSEE AND NORTHERN FLORIDA

Rosewood

About 10 miles outside of Cedar Key, along the side of State Road 24, there's a marker designating the former site of the town of **Rosewood.** Like many such markers, it's easy to miss, and even if you spot it, it's somewhat difficult to figure out what could possibly be notable about this patch of grass and abandoned buildings. In January 1923, however, this was the site of one of the most horrific incidents of racial violence in the United States.

Rosewood was one of very few predominantly African American communities in Florida, and the small town boasted a school, two stores, three churches, and an African American population of about 345. In a state that openly practiced segregation and turned a blind eye to the presence of the Ku Klux Klan in its larger cities, it shouldn't be that surprising that in this rural village, discrimination and oppression were a very real part of these 345 people's daily lives.

On New Year's Day 1923, Fannie Taylor, a young married white woman, reported to her husband that she had been beaten by a black man. As events unfolded—mostly fueled by rumors and second-hand reportage—violence soon descended on Rosewood, beginning at the house of one of the suspects and soon spreading through the entire village. Hundreds of whites from around the area—and from out of state—descended on Rosewood over the following days, and by January 7 every building had been burned to the ground, dozens of African American residents had fled the town, and eight people—six blacks, two whites—were dead.

It took more than a half century for the survivors and victims' families to get something approaching justice. In 1994, after almost a year of investigations by historians and researchers, Governor Lawton Chiles signed a bill authorizing $2.1 million in compensation, citing the government's failure to protect its own citizens. Three years later, noted director John Singleton's film *Rosewood* presented a dramatized but riveting account of what happened during that horrible week.

Natural Landmark and, thanks to the still-operating antebellum lodge (from $95 d), is also on the National Register of Historic Places.

Apalachicola & Cape San Blas

Farther south—about 65 miles from Tallahassee—is the small town of **Apalachicola**, known best for the oysters that come from Apalachicola Bay. However, the region offers more than just tasty bivalves. **Apalachicola National Forest**) is the largest national forest in Florida, spanning nearly 1,000 square miles between Tallahassee to the north and the Gulf of Mexico to the south. The forest contains several unique outdoor opportunities, including the Leon Sinks Geological Area which boasts impressive sinkholes and limestone caverns and the Apalachee Savannahs Scenic Byway, a driveable way to explore the unique subtropical grasslands of the region; the Fort Gadsden Historic Site is at the southern end of the Byway, near the town of Sumatra. On a small peninsula that juts out

into the waters of St. Joseph Bay—to the west of Apalachicola Bay—is the small vacation village of **Cape San Blas**. The white-sand beaches here are becoming more and more well-known, but it's still a quite secluded and special spot; there's not much in the way of shopping or restaurants and you'll most likely be staying in a vacation rental rather than a hotel, but there's plenty of pristine beach and wildlife-viewing opportunities, and that's how the locals and longtime visitors prefer it.

Other Sights

The **Tallahasee Automobile Museum** (6800 Mahan Dr., 850/942-0137, 8am-5pm Mon.-Fri., 10am-5pm Sat., noon-5pm Sun., $17.50 adults, $11.75 students, $8 children 5-8, children 4 and under free) is more a roadside attraction than a feature of central Tallahassee, as it's located along I-10 some 8 miles (20 minutes) from downtown. Fans of antique cars may want to dedicate a half day to exploring the museum.

Gadsden County, the "Coca-Cola" County

About 40 miles west of Tallahassee, nestled along the Florida-Georgia border, is **Gadsden County.** The county is unique not only in that it's the only predominantly African American county in Florida, but also because of its reputation as a "Coca-Cola county." In the early 20th century, the Coca-Cola company opened a bottling plant in Quincy, and many residents of the area bought stock in the nascent soda company at rock-bottom prices. As the daughter of one early Coca-Cola believer put it, "Daddy liked the taste and figured folks would always have a nickel for a Coke." That sort of instinct served many of the residents of Gadsden County well, and it's estimated that nearly 100 "Coca-Cola millionaires" live in this rural community of antebellum mansions and tobacco plantations. It's even said that more Coca-Cola stock is held within Gadsden County than anywhere else in the United States, although I'm sure there are some residents of Atlanta who would contest that fact.

The **Museum of Florida History** (500 S. Bronough St., 850/245-6400, 9am-4:30pm Mon.-Fri., 10am-4:30pm Sat., noon-4:30pm Sun., free) is a small facility with a handful of interesting interpretive exhibits about the state's history, from the pre-Columbian era to the present day.

Nightlife

Being a college town and a government town, Tallahassee is inundated with drinking establishments. Endurance drinkers head for the many bars in and around "the strip" along Tennessee Street, where bars like **Bullwinkles** (620 W. Tennessee St., 850/224-0651) cater to a collegiate clientele intent on cutting loose. The smoky hipster-friendly **Leon Pub** (215 E. 6th Ave., 850/425-4639) offers a great beer selection in a more relaxed neighborhood setting. For a unique nightlife experience, music fans should take the drive out to the **Bradfordville Blues Club** (7152 Moses Lane, 850/906-0766); located about 13 miles from downtown down a tiki-torch-lit dirt road, the cinder-block shack serves cold beer and hot blues every weekend. The atmosphere is unbeatable, and the touring blues musicians that frequent the tiny joint make for a truly exceptional night out.

Food

For an indulgent, comfort-food breakfast (or brunch), head to **Maple Street Biscuit Company** (1600 W. Call St., 850/391-1512, 7am-2pm Mon.-Thurs., 7am-3pm Fri.-Sat., from $9), a small, north Florida-based chain that specializes (obviously) in thick, flaky biscuits that are coupled with everything ranging from thick-cut bacon and deep-fried chicken breasts to goat cheese, scrambled eggs, sausage gravy and more. With two locations in Tallahassee, **Soul Vegetarian on Wheels** (200 S. Duval St., 809 Railroad Ave., 11am-3pm, 5:30pm-10pm Mon.-Fri.) offers quick-service vegan soul food cooked up by African Israelites. Its versions of mac and cheese, cornbread, collard greens, and even barbecue (with tofu) are hearty, filling, and guilt-free. Those looking for some great food and the opportunity to eat it while sitting down should definitely head for ★ **Food Glorious Food** (FGF, 1950 Thomasville Rd., 850/224-7279, lunch 11am-2:30pm Mon.-Sat., brunch 10am-2:30pm Sun., dinner 5:30pm-9pm Tues.-Sun., main courses from $14). Though not a vegetarian restaurant, FGF emphasizes fresh, often organic ingredients and rich flavorful preparations. From sautéed rock shrimp and pan-grilled quail to cheese grits and fried green tomatoes, the menu has a comfort-food heart and a gourmet touch. The dessert list is similarly amazing. **Bella Bella** (1215 E. 5th Ave., 850/412-4114, 11:30am-10pm Mon.-Fri., 5:30pm-10pm Sat., main courses from $12) is a solid selection for massive portions of well-made Italian food.

Apalachicola Oysters

Seafood chefs from Miami and New Orleans to Charleston and New York City probably don't agree on much, but one thing they don't argue about is the superiority of the **oysters** that come from Apalachicola Bay, about a 90-minute drive southwest of Tallahassee. This area's bivalves have earned a sterling reputation due to their size—the meat is thick and plump, and you rarely run the risk of shucking open a shell to reveal a stringy piece of flesh—and their simple succulent flavor. These oysters taste like oysters, with a direct richness that's less saline than oysters from Louisiana or Chesapeake Bay. Despite their noteworthy quality, oysters from Apalachicola don't command the same sort of astronomical prices that many "boutique" oysters fetch, and at places like **Boss Oyster** (in the Apalachicola River Inn, 125 Water St., 850/653-9364) in Apalachicola's famed Oystertown district, you can pull up to the bar and indulge yourself in a dozen freshly shucked raw oysters for under $6.

Accommodations

It's impossible to get a guest room at the ★ **Governor's Inn** (209 S. Adams St., 850/681-6855, www.thegovinn.com, from $169 d) when the legislature is in session, but the rest of the year this centrally located and historic boutique hotel is far and away the best place to stay in Tallahassee. Each of the hotel's 41 guest rooms is uniquely decorated, and each is named after one of Florida's governors. While the basic guest rooms—with four-poster beds, 15-foot ceilings, and flat-screen televisions—are nice enough, larger suites, including some with lofts and fireplaces, are designed for extended-stay comfort. The exposed brick and wood beams of the hotel's architecture add to its charm, and the staff is friendly and attentive.

Located alongside I-10, the **Four Points Sheraton** (1978 Village Green Way, 850/671-2020, from $150 d) has spacious, modern guest rooms that stand out among the other highway offerings. Although there are other chain hotels located more conveniently to downtown, this property's fresh, modern design and clean, well-maintained facilities make it one of the nicer options in the area.

Getting There and Around

Tallahassee isn't really close to anything. Orlando is 300 miles away and Tampa is 245 miles, each about four hours' drive. The closest major city is Jacksonville, 165 miles to the east, via I-10. The closest Panhandle beach is Panama City Beach, about 130 miles (2.5 hours) to the west, also via I-10. **Tallahassee Regional Airport** (TLH, 3300 Capital Cir. SW, Tallahassee, 850/891-7800, www.talgov. com) is served by six major airlines, with most flights connecting through hubs in Atlanta, Charlotte, Miami, or Orlando. The airport is located about 10 miles from the city center; many downtown hotels offer complimentary shuttle service, and taxis (Yellow Cab, 850/575-1022, approximately $25) and shuttles (Capital Transportation, 850/580-8080, approximately $15) are available for door-to-door service. The **Greyhound** station (112 W. Tennessee St., 850/222-4240) is located in the heart of downtown, just five blocks north of the capitol.

You'll definitely need a car to get around the city, and parking in and around the Florida State University campus and the downtown capitol area can be something of a hassle, although there are several parking garages and public lots.

GAINESVILLE

Although unmistakably a college town, the verdant environs of **Gainesville** make it a beautiful city to use as a home base for exploration of the surrounding area. Routinely ranked as one of the best cities to live in the

United States, Gainesville seamlessly blends collegiate cool, outdoor scenery, and Old Florida atmosphere.

Sights

★ UNIVERSITY OF FLORIDA

The campus of the **University of Florida** (UF) spreads across 2,000 acres of Gainesville and is the defining element of the town. Blue and orange color schemes predominate in a way that any other city would find offensive, and the number of Gator-themed businesses is stunning. The tree-lined central campus is home to many of the historic buildings from throughout the university's 100-year history; the Gothic-style Thomas Hall dates from its 1905 founding, while more recent buildings like Dauer Hall and the Century Tower trace the evolution of the campus' architecture.

Still, most visitors don't show up to admire the architecture; the crowds pour into Gainesville on football weekends and for basketball games, hoping the Gators will repeat their recent National Championship success. For those disinclined to observe the athletics, head for the museums at the **University of Florida Cultural Plaza** (SW 34th St. and Hull Rd.). The **Florida Museum of Natural History** (10am-5pm Mon.-Sat., 1pm-5pm Sun., $6 adults, $5 Florida residents, $4 seniors and students, $2 children 3-12) houses exhibits focusing on the state's ecosystems and a fantastic look at the state's biogeological history through fossils; also on-site is the excellent four-story-high butterfly habitat, housing hundreds of beautiful plants and butterflies. The **Harn Museum of Art** (11am-5pm Tues.-Fri., 10am-5pm Sat., 1pm-5pm Sun., free) is located in a beautiful facility with permanent exhibits of Asian and African folk art as well as a contemporary collection of works by Claude Monet, Georgia O'Keeffe, Auguste Rodin, and more.

KANAPAHA BOTANICAL GARDENS

Located a bit of a hike from downtown, the sprawling **Kanapaha Botanical Gardens** (4700 SW 58th Dr., 352/372-4981, www.kanapaha.org, 9am-5pm Mon.-Wed. and Fri., 9am-dusk Sat.-Sun., $8 adults, $4 children, children under 6 free) are well worth a visit for plant lovers. With more than a dozen distinct gardens about the densely foliaged property containing everything from herbs and hummingbirds to roses and ferns, the well-marked paths are as conducive to leisurely walks as they are to educational forays into gardening.

Downtown Gainesville

DEVIL'S MILLHOPPER GEOLOGICAL STATE PARK

The centerpiece of the 67-acre **Devil's Millhopper Geological State Park** (4732 Millhopper Rd., 352/955-2008, www.floridastateparks.org/devilsmillhopper, 9am-5pm Wed.-Sun., $4 per vehicle) is a 117-foot-deep 500-foot-wide sinkhole. A set of steps, boardwalks, and an observation deck make it possible for visitors to descend into the limestone-walled sinkhole, which has a completely contained mini ecosystem of springs, waterfalls, and plant life. Guests can picnic near the hole and hike throughout the other 67 acres of the park.

SANTA FE COMMUNITY COLLEGE TEACHING ZOO

For a unique zoological experience, the **Santa Fe Community College Teaching Zoo** (3000 NW 83rd St., 352/395-5601, www.dept.sfcollege.edu/zoo, 9am-2pm Mon.-Sat., $6 adults, $5 children and seniors, children 3 and under free) can't be beat. Boasting "the premier wild animal technology program in the United States," this zoo is less focused on gawking at animals than on getting an understanding of what goes into making a good zoo. Instead of arriving and wandering through the exhibits like at most zoos, visitors are taken on tours of the property; the tours are given by students in the zoo technology program, and in addition to learning about the birds, monkeys, kangaroos, deer, and other animals, guests gain insight on how exhibits are constructed and how the animals are cared for. Tours during the week need to be scheduled at least three days in advance; on the weekends no appointment is necessary as tours are given every half hour. Although you can walk around the zoo on your own, it's highly recommended that you take the touring option.

ICHETUCKNEE SPRINGS STATE PARK

In 1972, the head spring of the Ichetucknee River was declared a National Natural Landmark, but Floridians would have told you long before then that the spring and the beautiful river it feeds are one of the beating, natural hearts of the state. **Ichetucknee Springs State Park** (12087 SW US Highway 27, Fort White, 386/497-4690, 8am-sundown daily, $6/carload of 2-8 people, $4/single-occupant vehicle) celebrates that. While the park encompasses several beautiful wild habitats perfect for hiking (the 0.75-mile Trestle Point Loop is

the Harn Museum of Art on the grounds of the University of Florida

a gorgeous—and shaded—trail) and picnicking, but the main attraction here is the water, namely the 72°F springs and a river run that's a legendary tubing destination. Swimmers and scuba divers will want to enjoy the head springs and the deep waters of the Blue Hole area, while tubers will relish the leisurely flow of the river along a six-mile run; make sure to bring $5 for the tram service that gets you back to the main park area from the southern terminus of the tube run.

Entertainment and Events
NIGHTLIFE

Being a college town, Gainesville has more than its fair share of drinking establishments. **The Swamp** (1642 University Ave., 352/377-9267, 11am-2am daily) is located directly across from, uh, "the Swamp," aka the University of Florida's legendary Ben Hill Griffin football stadium. Although it is a full-service restaurant, the place's size and availability of outdoor seating (but perhaps not the quality of food and drink) make it a popular gathering place even when the Gators aren't playing across the street.

Located downtown, **Whiskey House** (60 SW 2nd St, 352/510-5534, 5:30pm-2am daily) obviously has a great whiskey selection (more than 200), but also offers a decent selection of wine and craft beer, and an exceptional cocktail menu. **The Bull** (18 SW 1st St., 352/672-6266, 4pm-2am Mon.-Sun.) is a great respite from the crowds, with a cozy, art-focused vibe, a solid (if small) food menu and a great selection of beer and wine.

Both the Whiskey House and the Bull offer live music occasionally, however, more dedicated music fans should head directly for **High Dive** (210 SW 2nd Ave., 352/372-7230, hours vary by performance), which sits on the sacred ground of legendary G-ville venues the Covered Dish and Common Grounds, and does a decent job at honoring that legacy by hosting a diverse array of local, regional, and national indie, alternative, and underground bands.

FESTIVALS AND EVENTS

The **Gainesville Improv Festival** (Jan.) takes over the black-box theater at the University of Florida's Philips Center for the Performing Arts (315 Hull Rd.). The punk-oriented **Fest** (late Oct.) is held in downtown music venues with hundreds of regional and national bands bashing it out for crowds of appreciative fans. The annual **Downtown Festival & Art Show** (mid-Nov.) has been a

"The Swamp" (Ben Hill Griffin football stadium) at the University of Florida

Surviving a Home Game Weekend

University of Florida Gator football is a century-old tradition, and between current students, alumni, and visiting teams, there is considerable demand for these autumn Saturday match-ups. Tickets for games are usually sold out years in advance, so getting face-value admission is very nearly impossible, and you should plan on paying at least $100, or even more for a game against another Southeastern Conference team or another big rival. Keep in mind, the truly big game on the Gators' schedule—Florida versus the Georgia Bulldogs—is held on neutral territory in Jacksonville; the annual Florida/Florida State University Seminoles rivalry game alternates between Tallahassee and Gainesville. While one can almost always find tickets on eBay or a ticket-broker website, a far better option—believe it or not—is to just show up in Gainesville on Friday afternoon with a wad of cash and start asking around. Students often have tickets they won't be using, or they may know someone who has extra tickets. If you have no shame, you can even submit yourself to wandering around University Avenue in Gainesville on the morning of the game with a sad sign explaining your plight. If neither of these tactics succeeds, you can always hit up the scalpers, keeping in mind that their prices will plummet around halftime.

If you're planning on coming to town on a game weekend but have no intention of watching the gridiron action, you'll probably find the effort necessary to procure a hotel room, dinner reservation, or parking spot anywhere downtown or near campus not to be worth the hassle.

Gainesville fixture for nearly three decades, and was recently ranked one of the nation's 25 best art shows by the craft-show magazine *Sunshine Artist*. Regional artists and craftspeople ply their wares along the streets of downtown, and there are several performing-arts and musical events as well.

SPECTATOR SPORTS

Spectator sports in Gainesville comes down to two words: "Go Gators." Even before the University of Florida's football team won two national championships within three years (2006 and 2008), scoring one of the 90,000 tickets into **The Swamp,** aka Ben Hill Griffin Stadium (University Ave. and Gale Lemerand Dr.), was a challenge. The lion's share of attention is heaped on the football team, but the rise of the UF men's basketball team over the past decade—including back-to-back championships in 2006 and 2007—has seen attendance boom at the O-Dome, aka "the house of horrors," aka **The Stephen O'Connell Center** (University Ave. and Gale Lemerand Dr., adjacent to the football stadium). The Gators also field teams in baseball, softball, soccer, volleyball, golf, tennis, gymnastics, and lacrosse.

Food

BREAKFAST, LUNCH, AND LIGHT BITES

Bagels Unlimited (2022 SW 34th St., 6:30am-3pm daily, main courses from $5) serves bagels but also has a good selection of eggs-and-bacon dishes along with some vegan and vegetarian selections like a tofu scramble. Service is frustratingly slow but friendly.

Volta Coffee (48 SW 2nd St., 8am-11pm Mon.-Fri., 9am-11pm Sat., 9am-7pm Sun.) prides itself on carefully pulled espresso shots and precisely blended coffee drinks—no rack of sweet syrups here—along with a well-curated selection of gourmet chocolates and homemade bakery goods.

AMERICAN

The Coop (1620 W. University Ave, 352/505-5772, 11am-9:30pm daily, from $9) focuses on doing one thing right: chicken. Okay, maybe two things: chicken and waffles. But the chicken is the star here, and the menu at the Coop is incredibly simple, with tenders, wings, a handful of chicken-based sandwiches/wraps/biscuits, and, of course, a decadent selection of waffles. The best dish on the menu is the straightforwardly indulgent chicken and waffles, which brings the Coop's best elements together perfectly, resting three juicy, crispy chicken tenders atop a thick, fluffy Belgian waffle drenched in syrup. They may not do much here, but what they do, they do very, very well.

A bit more variety can be found at the **Paramount Grill** (12 SW 1st Ave., 352/378-3398, 11am-9:30pm Mon.-Thurs., 11am-10:30pm Fri., 5-10:30pm Sat., 10am-9:30pm Sun., main courses from $12). The menu is concise and seasonally updated with a focus on contemporary American cuisine with some Mediterranean and Asian accents. Lunch offerings can include anything from a grilled duck BLT to the Paramount's legendary blue-cheese Angus burger, while dinner can feature crab-stuffed baked chicken, jerked grouper, and sides like poached tomato quinoa salad. Sunday brunch is often packed thanks to delectable treats like pecan-encrusted French toast and monstrous omelets.

An even larger menu can be found at one of Gainesville's most-loved (and, often, most-packed) restaurants, **The Top** (30 N. Main St, 352/337-1188, 5pm-2am Tues.-Sat., 11am-2pm and 5pm-2am Sun., from $12). Despite its extremely casual vibe, food is taken pretty seriously here, and no matter what you're looking for, you're likely to find it on the menu … and it's likely to be prepared excellently. While the fare ranges from burgers, brunch standards, and corn nuggets to pepper-crusted steaks, mouthwatering tofu and vegan dishes, rich desserts, and more, the kitchen staff manages to do a great job with all of it. Tack on a lively and reasonably priced bar with a great selection of crafts and cocktails, and it's not much of a surprise that there's often quite a wait to get in here.

INTERNATIONAL

Tucked into an unassuming location along a tree-lined downtown street, ★ **Crane Ramen** (16 SW 1st Ave, 352/727-7422, lunch 11am-4pm daily, dinner 5pm-11pm daily, from $13) might be easy to miss … if it weren't for the fact that everyone in Gainesville and everyone who had recently been to Gainesville hadn't told you to make sure to go there. While "college town ramen place" may seem like the most obvious cliché, and while the ramen here may not meet the exacting standards of West Coast ramen aficionados, the enthusiastic response Crane has received for its inventive and diverse take on broth-based cuisine should let you know that it's doing quite a bit more with its ramen than you did while a poor undergrad. A robust menu with several broth styles (chicken, dashi, miso, sweet potato, pork-bone, and more) and a wide array of accompaniments ranging from egg, pork belly, and enoki mushrooms to snow crab, kale, roasted pumpkin, and more as well as an excellently curated cocktail menu and reasonably priced craft beers has made this spot incredibly popular; even better: if you're traveling with kids, Crane features kid-sized portions and are family friendly (at least as family friendly as a college-town ramen spot can be expected to be).

Legendary among local students and musicians, **Reggae Shack Cafe** (619 W. University Ave., 352/377-5464, reggaeshack-cafe.com, 11am-10pm daily, from $9) serves up affordable and richly seasoned Jamaican food in an unassuming environment. Catering to both carnivores (the oxtail is amazing, as is the jerk chicken) and vegetarians (vegan options abound, and the curry palm hearts are a must-try), Reggae Shack manages to offer an extensive and authentic menu that's as wholesome as it is fulfilling.

Accommodations

The vast majority of the lodging options in Gainesville are geared toward parents moving their kids into school and Gator fans bunking down the night before and after a big game; as such, the emphasis is on economical chain options. However, there is a handful of exceptions. The ★ **Sweetwater Branch Inn B&B** (625 E. University Ave., 352/373-6760, www.sweetwaterinn.com, from $144 d) is a multibuilding B&B complex located close to downtown. There are two main buildings and some cottages with a total of 18 different lodging options. The most attractive are the six cottages, all of which have private entrances, cozy front porches, and full kitchens. All guest rooms have central air, sumptuous antique furnishings, televisions, and Wi-Fi, and most guest rooms have fireplaces. The grounds are immaculately kept, and despite the proximity to the collegiate buzz of central Gainesville, the tree-draped property is quite peaceful. Another cozy B&B that's convenient yet away from the heart of the action is the six-room **Camellia Rose Inn** (205 SE 7th St, 352/395-7673, camelliaroseinn.com, from $125 d), which is cute and comfortable in a "grandma really likes pink" kind of way; there's also a private cottage available, and full breakfast, all-day snacks, and happy hour libations are on the house.

The **Hilton UF Conference Center** (1714 SW 34th St., 352/371-3600, from $179 d) is located near a somewhat remote corner of campus, closer to the Cultural Plaza than to the football stadium, and is probably the nicest national chain option in town, as it is geared both toward the typical Gainesville visitor as well as conference planners. Another decent chain option is the **Holiday Inn— University Center** (1250 W. University Ave., 352/376-1661, from $139 d), which is just a couple of blocks from the football stadium and walking distance from much of downtown's dining and nightlife options. The location pretty much guarantees that weekends—especially football weekends—will be noisy. The super-cheap **Gainesville Lodge** (413 W. University Ave., 352/376-1224, from $55 d) has no-frills guest rooms that are reasonably clean, if quite worn, although it's definitely not recommended for families or single female travelers.

Getting There
AIR
The **Gainesville Regional Airport** (GNV, 3880 NE 39th Ave., Gainesville, 352/373-0249, www.gra-gnv.com) is small and easily navigable, served by American and Delta via connections through Charlotte and Miami. There are more flight options into the large international airports nearby in **Orlando** (MCO), **Tampa** (TPA), and **Jacksonville** (JAX). **Gator Express** (www.gatorexpress. com, 352/528-6048) offers shuttle service from JAX ($70 one-way) and MCO ($80 one-way).

CAR
Gainesville is located along I-75, about 115 miles (two hours' drive) northwest of Orlando via Florida's Turnpike and I-75, 130 miles (about two hours) northeast of Tampa via I-75, and 72 miles (90 minutes) southwest of Jacksonville via I-10 and US Hwy. 301.

Getting Around
Central Gainesville is fairly compact and arranged on a grid, so getting around is quite simple. Numbered avenues run east-west, with University being zero; numbered streets run north-south, with Main street being zero. The university is in the southwest quadrant.

Public transit is limited to the bus routes operated by **Regional Transit System** (RTS, www.go-rts.com), and with frequent and late-night service in the area around campus, this is often a good inexpensive option. Taxicabs also offer quite reasonable fares, but you'll probably have to call **Safety Cabs** (352/372-1444) or **Gainesville Cab Co.** (352/371-1515), as hailing one curbside is next to impossible. Ride-sharing is available here, too.

OCALA
The two defining features of **Ocala** are somewhat contradictory. On one hand, there are the rolling hills of the horse farms just outside of town filled with elegant thoroughbreds and the unique mixture of hardworking hired hands and moneyed landowners who have made this area one of the preeminent equestrian districts in the United States. And then there's the garish theme park that has popped up around the artesian springs at Silver Springs, tucked away off the side of a highway dotted with worn-down motels and tourist-trap shops. Both are beautiful and unique in

their own way, and right in the middle is the downtown area, which melds historical architecture and small-town charm.

Sights

DOWNTOWN OCALA

There's not much to downtown Ocala, but walking around the compact shopping and dining district at the intersection of Silver Springs Boulevard and Magnolia Avenue makes for a pleasant afternoon distraction. The sculpture-dotted central plaza is surrounded by artists' studios and historic buildings like the **Marion Theater** (50 S. Magnolia Ave.). A few blocks away is the **Fort King Street** neighborhood, with dozens of beautiful historic houses that have wraparound porches shaded by enormous oak trees.

APPLETON MUSEUM OF ART

The **Appleton Museum of Art** (4333 E. Silver Springs Blvd., 352/291-4455, www. appletonmuseum.org, 10am-5pm Tues.-Sat., noon-5pm Sun., $8 adults, $6 seniors, teachers, and students, $4 children, children under 10 free) is located between downtown Ocala and the Silver Springs area. Despite an aggressive billboard campaign throughout Central Florida and one of the most architecturally beautiful museum facilities in the state, it is often overlooked by visitors, which is truly a shame as the Appleton houses an astonishing art collection, ranging from pre-Columbian and contemporary art to Oriental figurines, Islamic pottery and weaving, African folk art, and ancient Mediterranean artifacts.

SILVER SPRINGS STATE PARK

Located just a couple of miles from downtown Ocala at the gateway to Ocala National Forest, **Silver Springs** has been a Florida tourist attraction for almost as long as Florida has been a state. A mere 15 years after the state was admitted to the Union, glass-bottom boats were navigating the waters. Almost 550 million gallons of water per day flow from the artesian springs, one of the largest in the world, and those boats are one of the best ways that visitors can observe their natural beauty. Over the years, the attraction expanded to include a theme park and a water park adjacent to a more nature-focused state park, but, eventually, attendance at the former dwindled, so these days, Silver Springs is once again focused on the natural beauty in and around the springs and the Silver River and, yes, there are still glass-bottom boats.

The state park once known as Silver River

Ocala National Forest

State Park is now the primary attraction, and is now called **Silver Springs State Park** (1425 NE 58th Ave., 352/236-7148, www. silversprings.com, 8am-sunset daily, $2). With 5,000 acres and 20 miles of river flowing through it—and yes, a few springs of its own—the park provides a look at the old natural Florida. There's a great interpretive center on-site that recreates an original cracker village, and the 3.5-mile Sinkhole Trail that winds through the park provides a great look at the variety of ecosystems, but the main attractions are canoeing and kayaking, and, of course, taking one of the classic, 90-minute glass-bottom-boat tours ($11 adults, $10 for seniors and kids, free for kids 5 and under). Swimming is not allowed on the property.

DON GARLITS DRAG RACING MUSEUM

Drag racing legend Don Garlits was the first driver ever to win three National Hot Rod Association national titles and three world championships. He's also the only driver to have one of his cars in the Smithsonian's National Museum of American History. So one can forgive the **Don Garlits Drag Racing Museum** (13700 SW 16th Ave., 352/245-8661, 9am-5pm daily, $20 adults, $15 seniors and children, $10 students, children under 5 free) for having a bit of a hagiographic feel to it. There are nearly 200 cars crammed into this enormous museum alongside numerous parts and memorabilia attesting to Garlits's feats of 0.25-mile success. The man earned the right to boast about himself, and boast he does—often in person, as he lives right next door to the museum. The museum is next to I-75 and is about 15 miles southeast of downtown Ocala.

★ Ocala National Forest

The second-largest national forest in Florida and the southernmost forest in the continental United States, **Ocala National Forest** covers 373,000 acres between the Ocklawaha and St. Johns Rivers. It's an incredibly popular destination for camping, mountain biking, and hiking expeditions, although the voluminous amounts of water that course through the forest make canoeing and fishing the preferred activities. Keep in mind that hunting and fishing activities are regulated by the state's Fish & Wildlife Commission, and licenses and permits are required. Day visits to swim in springs like Alexander Springs are a great way to beat the heat, but keep in mind that during summer months, these parks reach capacity quite early.

VISITORS CENTERS

The **Ocklawaha Visitor Center** (3199 NE County Rd. 315, Silver Springs, 352/236-0288), 21 miles southeast of Ocala, is the most visited of the park's three visitors centers, and it is the closest to Ocala. There are also the **Salt Springs Visitor Center** (14100 N. State Rd. 19, Salt Springs, 352/685-3070), 31 miles northeast of Ocala, and the **Pittman Visitor Center** (45621 State Rd. 19, Altoona, 352/669-7495), 44 miles southeast of Ocala. You can also check in with rangers at the **Lake George Ranger District** (17147 E. State Rd. 40, Silver Springs, 352/625-2520).

TRAILS

The **Florida Trail** has three main access points, at **Salt Springs Visitor Center** (14100 N. State Rd. 19, Salt Springs, 352/685-3070), the **Alexander Springs Recreation Area** (State Rd. 445, approximately 35 miles east of Ocala) and **Juniper Springs** (State Rd. 40, approximately 25 miles east of Ocala). The trail runs north-south for about 67 miles, traversing all of the park's diverse ecosystems—prairie, pine forest, swamp (there are boardwalks), and hardwood hammocks. The trail is very well-marked and has numerous campsites along the way.

There are also three loop trails that don't require quite as much commitment. The two-mile **Salt Springs Observation Trail** (near the Salt Springs Visitor Center) is both low impact and quite scenic, running along the water's edge, allowing views of numerous species of wading birds. The 8.5-mile **St. Francis**

Trail (near the Pittman Visitor Center) runs partially along the banks of the St. Johns River and takes hikers through swamps and hardwood hammocks as well as the site of the long-gone town of St. Francis. The **Lake Eaton Loop Trail** (parking lot and trailhead off Forest Rd. 79, south of State Rd. 314) is a two-mile trail through hardwood hammocks.

Nearby is an underappreciated trail, the **Lake Eaton Sinkhole Trail** (parking lot and trailhead on State Rd. 314, approximately 25 miles northeast of Ocala), which is actually three trails that all lead to the Lake Eaton Sinkhole, a 450-foot-wide 80-foot-deep dry sinkhole, the second largest in the state.

There are also two extensive trail systems dedicated to off-road vehicles, with trailheads at Big Scrub (intersection of Forest Roads 588 and 573 in the Seminole Ranger District) and Lake Delancy (3 miles west of State Road 19 on Forest Road 75 in the Lake George Ranger District).

TOP EXPERIENCE

FISHING, BOATING, AND SWIMMING

There are more than 600 rivers, **freshwater springs,** and lakes in the Ocala National Forest, making **boating, fishing,** and **swimming** among the most popular pastimes.

Canoes can be rented from concessionaires at the **Alexander Springs Recreation Area;** the crystal-blue waters of the springs—which offer great swimming and diving opportunities—flow into a rather slow-moving river with several landings along the five-mile route. Along the **Lower Ocklawaha** and **Upper Ocklawaha,** access points are fairly limited, but outfitters like **Ocklawaha Canoe Outpost and Resort** (15260 NE 152nd Pl., Fort McCoy, 352/236-4606, 8am-6pm Wed.-Mon.) can rent you a canoe or kayak and provide drop-off and pickup services.

Anglers come to the forest to chase down Florida largemouth bass, which have been known to grow as large as 10 pounds in the waterways, but the natural and generally slow-moving waters are also home to sunfish, catfish, and crappie. People can fish on riverbanks, lakeshores, and in boats, but fishing near swimming beaches and spring heads is prohibited.

CAMPING

There are 11 campgrounds within the Ocala National Forest. The two largest are at **Salt**

Alexander Springs Recreation Area is worth the short drive from Ocala.

Springs (197 sites, including RV hookups) and **Alexander Springs** (65 sites, including RV hookups). Smaller primitive sites are available at **Lake Eaton** (14 sites) and **Hopkins Prairie** (21 sites, near Salt Springs). Camping in the RV-ready campgrounds and developed tent sites costs $6-50, depending on the amenities; camping at the primitive sites is free, as is pitching your tent anywhere in the park.

There are also two cabins—at **Lake Dorr** and **Sweetwater Spring**—that can only be reserved if you win a lottery held every year for next year's calendar. If you're feeling lucky, call 352/625-0546 for more information.

Sports and Recreation

There are two city-owned golf courses in Ocala, the **Ocala Golf Club** (3130 E. Silver Springs Blvd., 352/401-6917, from $16) and **Pine Oaks of Ocala** (2201 NW 21st St., 352/401-6940, from $14). Both are par-72 courses; Pine Oaks is a bit longer with more natural hazards, while the Ocala Golf Club is a more traditional course. Pine Oaks recently added **The Preserve at Pine Oaks,** an 18-hole disc-golf course.

The **Ocklawaha Canoe Outpost and Resort** (15260 NE 152nd Pl., Fort McCoy, 352/236-4606, 8am-6pm Wed.-Mon.) is located approximately 20 minutes from central Ocala, but for river rats it's well worth the drive. Offering daily canoe and kayak rentals (from $32) as well as overnight accommodations in well-outfitted cabins (from $89), the Outpost is staffed by friendly folks who know their way around the nearby waterways. A trip down the Ocklawaha River is a great way to get a glimpse at gators, birds, turtles, and other wildlife, and there are several areas along the route to get out for picnics or rope-swinging into the water.

★ EQUESTRIAN OCALA

Almost 10 percent of the race horses born every year in the United States are born in Ocala, and the scores of working horse farms in the area attest to the town's claim to be the horse capital of the world. Driving the winding roads that branch off of U.S. 27 northwest of downtown Ocala, you'll see expansive farms that vary from low-key family ranches to picture-perfect plantation-style farms, all of which are dotted with barns, haystacks, and more beautiful horses than you're likely to see south of Kentucky. Because many of these farms are working enterprises concerned with breeding and caring for the next big winner, those who come to town looking for the opportunity for a leisurely horseback ride may be disappointed, but there are a few places that offer rides. The family-run **Young's Paso Fino Ranch** (8075 W. Hwy. 326, 352/867-5305, 10am-2pm Mon.-Sat., $7.50 pp) offers farm tours that give riders an hour or so atop its gentle and beautiful horses; it's best to call in advance to reserve a time.

Food & Drink

In the heart of downtown are several good restaurants. Breakfast at **Brick City Café** (10 NE 1st St, 352/629-4700, 6:30am-6:30pm Mon.-Fri., from $5) is basic diner fare, but it covers the essentials in a friendly, clean, and inexpensive environment. The similarly named, but not so similar **Brick City Southern Kitchen & Whiskey Bar** (10 S. Magnolia Ave. 352/512-9458, 11am-11pm Tues.-Thurs., 11am-2am Fri.-Sat., 11am-10pm Sun.-Mon., from $12) serves up excellent (and decadent) comfort food like fried chicken, Southern sausages, mac and cheese, fried pickles, ribs, and incredible barbecue. For evening indulgences, there is a full bar that includes an extraordinary whiskey selection; this is probably Ocala's best restaurant and Ocala's best bar. **The Ocala Wine Experience Bistro** (36 SW 1st Ave., 352/369-9858, 10am-6pm Mon.-Thurs., 10am-midnight Fri.-Sat.) is a wine and gourmet food shop downstairs with a cozy little bistro upstairs that serves 12-inch pizzas ($15), appetizers (from $8), cheese-and-fruit plates (from $15), and desserts (from $5) in addition to a routinely updated selection of wines and beer; it's a great place to stop and stock your picnic basket if you're headed out on a canoeing or horseback excursion. Just a few blocks outside of downtown is **Café Havana** (923 N. Magnolia Ave., 352/351-4853, 8am-4pm Mon.-Sat., from $7), where you can grab some fantastic, authentic Cuban fare at an incredibly reasonable price. The strip mall location and Styrofoam plates don't earn a lot of style points, but the food is excellent.

Accommodations

Most of the accommodations in the area fall into one of two categories: interstate-hugging chain hotels or indistinguishable budget motels around the Silver Springs area. Those interested in the former should head directly to the recently renovated **Holiday Inn Hotel & Suites** (3600 SW 38th Ave., 352/629-9500, from $129 d); the beautiful open atrium gives it an upscale sensibility that's accented by the inclusion of Tempur-Pedic beds in all guest rooms. The motels are something of a crapshoot; despite the vintage vibe at most of these places, the facilities are basic and in some cases quite dirty. There are, however, a small handful of unique lodging options, including the cute **Shamrock Historic Inn** (215 S. Pine Ave., 352/867-8858, shamrock-historicinn.com, from $78 d), which is close to downtown; although it's built on the bones of a typical roadside motel, the rooms are all cozy, very clean, quite well-maintained, and updated with all mod cons, and the property is safe, well-lit, and pleasantly decorated with outdoor seating, and verdant landscaping.

Getting There and Around

Ocala is located about 37 miles (45 minutes' drive) south of Gainesville on I-75. Ocala International Airport (OCF) is a general aviation facility, so unless you've got a private plane, you'll need to fly in to **Gainesville** (GNV), **Jacksonville** (JAX, 163 miles or three hours away), **Orlando** (MCO, 90 miles or 90 minutes' drive), or **Tampa** (TPA, 108 miles or two hours).

You'll need a car to get around Ocala, as none of the major sights are within walking or even taxicab distance of one another, and public transit is limited.

Background

The Landscape

GEOGRAPHY

Florida's **geography** is deceptively complex. Despite the understandable preconception that the state is little more than a flat palette of beaches, scrublands, and swamp, there is considerable variation in different regions. After all, the state covers more than 65,000 square miles. More than 20 percent of that area is water, in the form of springs, rivers, swamps, wetlands, and lakes, making Florida the third-wettest state in the country.

With the exception of some gently rolling hills in the north-central part of the state, Florida can generally be described as "flat." Sea-level coastlines hug the outline of almost the entire state, while the swampy peninsula interior is at—and in some cases, it seems, below—sea level, and the mean elevation of the state is just 100 feet above sea level. The highest point in the entire state is Britton Hill, in the Panhandle, which juts into the sky all the way to a majestic 345 feet.

There are three formal geographical regions in the state. The **Atlantic Coastal Plain** extends all the way north to Cape Cod, Massachusetts, and encompasses the entirety of Florida's east coast. It's an area defined by low, flat topography and features like sandy beaches, scrub-flecked ranchlands, the swamps of the Everglades and Big Cypress, and the marshy wetlands of Central Florida. This region of the state connects seamlessly to the **East Gulf Coastal Plain** that runs along Florida's west coast. In the south-central part of the state, this region shares the swampy characteristics of the 'Glades and Big Cypress; the Gulf beaches see far less wave action from the gentle Gulf of Mexico, resulting in powdery white-sand beaches that are quite legendary. The northern peninsular Gulf coast is primarily marshy deltas that lead to the white-sand beaches of the Panhandle. In that part of the state is the third distinct geographic region, the **Florida Uplands,** which resemble the pine forest landscapes of the American South and are home to what little elevation the state has.

CLIMATE

There are three basic **climate** zones in Florida. **North Florida**—roughly the Panhandle across to Jacksonville and dipping south into the Ocala-Gainesville area—sees four-season weather patterns similar to the rest of the American South: brutally hot and humid summers, chilly and largely snowless winters, and temperate, unpredictable springs and autumns.

The **Central Florida** region—between Daytona Beach and Vero Beach on the Atlantic coast and Cedar Key and Sarasota on the Gulf coast—sees its seasons reduced to three. Summer defines the area and lasts about late April-late September, bringing blisteringly hot and humid days in which a thunderstorm is almost guaranteed to occur every afternoon. A brief, blissfully beautiful autumn brings mild temperatures and clear skies early October-mid-December. It's then that "spring" begins, an indecisive season of dry air, sunny days, and temperatures generally hovering in the mid-60s to mid-70s; in Central Florida spring is occasionally interrupted by brief periods of winter that can bring temperatures down to the mid-30s. Northerners will cackle at the panic that grips Central Florida when a freeze warning is issued. These bouts of frigidity are unpredictable and often only last a few days at a time;

Previous: Pelicans hitch a ride on an airboat; Storms can move in quickly in Florida.

days with highs of 50°F or lower typically number less than a dozen a year.

Finally, tropical **South Florida** sees only two seasons: oppressive and pleasant. Summer lasts a little longer in South Florida—mid-March-mid-October—and has the same tendency as Central Florida to be dizzyingly humid and hot with daily thundershowers. But as a reward for sweating it out for half the year, South Floridians enjoy a picture-perfect other half, with an autumn-winter-spring season that sees consistently sunny, warm, and dry days with highs in the mid-70s-low 80s and lows clicking in comfortably around 60°F every night. Although some nights can get a little chilly and there are a handful of days when a light jacket might be necessary to ward off a cool mid-50s breeze, South Florida's weather between Halloween and Valentine's Day is about as perfect as you could hope for.

Throughout Florida, temperatures on the coast are usually 5-10 degrees cooler than inland, thanks to constant sea breezes; conversely, humidity in the inland parts of the state can seem twice as heavy and thick as it does on the coast.

Those same coastal weather patterns also bring the threat of **hurricanes.** The official season for Atlantic hurricanes is June 1-November 1, but the peak of activity is usually in August-September. The Florida Keys and South Florida are most often in the direct path of the storms that form in the Atlantic basin. Although almost every region of Florida has been impacted by hurricanes—most notably in 2004, when an unprecedented four hurricanes hit the state, including three that crossed the normally untouched Central Florida region—it's the Keys and South Florida that generally assume they'll be hit. Conversely, residents in the rest of the state—including the oft-impacted Panhandle—tend to assume they won't be hit. While many times they have been proven correct, the fact remains that Florida is a hurricane magnet, and when the storms do hit, they hit hard. If there is a hurricane warning announced for the area you're vacationing in, you need to leave immediately. Don't let local naysayers sway your decision with talk about how "it wasn't so bad the last time" or "it'll curve to the right like they always do." The terror of 70 mph or higher winds is an entirely different experience when you're living it rather than watching it on the Weather Channel, and even storms with midrange winds can often bring flooding downpours that are incredibly dangerous. Despite their best efforts, hurricane

mangroves in the Everglades

trackers are usually wrong, or at least not completely right, and these storms are large and unpredictable. Don't be a hero; don't be a know-it-all; don't be brave; just leave. The state will hopefully still be here when you come back.

ENVIRONMENTAL ISSUES

Florida's **environmental issues** can be distilled into one simple word: *growth*. With a relatively young history that has most of its roots in the state's development as a tourist destination, Florida's complex and beautiful ecology has been the victim of unplanned and unchecked development through the last century, and until very recently, environmental concerns took a very distant backseat to the demands of real estate speculators, construction interests, and the tourism industry. Entire portions of the state's most singular ecological treasure, the Everglades, were drained, dredged, and built on to satisfy the expansion of South Florida's suburbs and the needs of the mighty sugar industry; likewise, the ground on which Walt Disney World sits was once an intricate and delicate combination of marshland, hammocks, and waterways. (To Disney's credit, however, the vast majority of that land is still undeveloped and designated a wildlife preserve.) Coastal development has demolished dunes, and even the seemingly inhospitable Palmetto Prairie in the south-central portion of the state is beginning to experience the beginnings of far-flung suburban residential developments.

Beyond the impact of development on the state's ecology, the fast-growing population has spread out in all directions, resulting in low-density cities surrounded by dozens of commuter towns. The net effect is a deeply entrenched car culture and endless miles of roadways surrounded by cookie-cutter subdivisions that eat into land that was previously agricultural or undisturbed home to wildlife. While there are still great swaths of untamed land in Florida, those areas are slowly being eroded by development.

PLANTS AND ANIMALS
Plants
TREES

To the surprise of many, Florida isn't just home to swaying palm trees and orange groves. In the northern part of the state, one can find fruit-bearing hardwoods like cherry and apple trees. Scrub pines and slash pines are common throughout the state, particularly in the midsection, and that stereotypically Southern tree, the sweet magnolia, is also prevalent. Along the coastline, especially the northern Gulf coast and in the Florida Keys, mangroves are prevalent, and black mangroves can soar up to 50 feet in height. Some unique native Florida **trees** include West Indian mahogany trees, which can be found in southern Florida and the Keys, and pond apple trees, which grow in the state's swamps. Florida is most commonly identified with palm trees, but even though they are common throughout the state, the massive coconut palms that say "tropical vacation" to so many people are not a native species. The true Florida palms are the equally tall if somewhat less glamorous Sabal palm trees.

FLOWERS

The official flower of Florida is the orange blossom, and for the early part of the 20th century, a drive through the orange groves of central and southern Florida as the fragrant **flowers** bloomed was one of the high points of a vacation. Of course, the tropical and subtropical climate throughout most of the state means an abundance of gorgeous flowering plants can be seen almost year-round. Invasive species like bougainvillea, jasmine, gardenias, birds of paradise, and oleander have taken their place alongside native beauties like mistletoe and the puffy-flowered sweet acacia to make Florida one of the most beautifully—and naturally—landscaped parts of the country. Note that although they are somewhat common throughout South Florida, wild orchids cannot be collected as they're protected by law.

ANIMALS
Mammals

Florida is home to two unique and endangered mammal species, the Florida panther and the tiny Key deer, both of which have come quite close to extinction in recent decades. Preservation efforts have been effective in keeping the species around, but the drastically limited numbers of both animals mean that there's still quite a bit of work to be done. Somewhat more common in Florida are bobcats, which are smaller than panthers and can be seen in the hardwood swamps and hammocks that are so prevalent throughout the state. The two mammals you're almost certain to see while in Florida are armadillos and opossums; unfortunately, you'll likely only see these nocturnal creatures in a postmortem state on the side of the road.

Sea Life

With the majority of the state nestled against either the Atlantic Ocean or the Gulf of Mexico, it's none too surprising that Florida is a great place for spotting sea creatures. Pods of bottlenose dolphins are easy to spot from shore, and farther out to sea it's possible to see pilot whales. Offshore snorkelers find an abundance of coral reefs and the attendant schools of colorful tropical fish that live in and around them. Most iconic of all of Florida's water creatures is the West Indian manatee. These gentle "sea cows" feast on the mangrove leaves, algae, and turtle grass that are common throughout Florida's waterways, and the state's warm waters are the manatees' preferred place for wintering and mating. Crystal River, on Florida's Gulf coast, is a fantastic place to see manatees in the winter, as it has one of the greatest concentrations of the creatures. The rivers of South Florida are also home to a large number of manatees.

Birds

Florida is one of the best places in the United States for bird-watching. In addition to numerous native species—kites, osprey, spoonbill herons, scrub jays, and even bald eagles call Florida home throughout the year—the original snowbirds were the scores of northern species who make their winter homes here. Any of the dozens of nature preserves are ideal for bird-watching in the winter, but perhaps the best year-round spot is the J. N. "Ding" Darling Wildlife Refuge on Sanibel Island.

Insects and Arachnids

In 1845, the Central Florida region saw one of its first big public relations moves when its largest county was renamed Orange County after the sweet citrus that was becoming so popular in the United States. The county's previous name? Mosquito County. While certainly not as endearing, the name was certainly accurate, as Central Florida—especially toward eastern Orange County—is dense with the bloodsucking bugs, particularly during the summer. Coastal breezes make mosquitoes less of a problem in many parts of the state, but there are few areas of inland Florida where you won't find one feasting on your platelets.

Insects are prevalent throughout the warm and muggy state, and besides pesky skeeters and the painful bites of fire ants, there are also beautiful butterflies, especially in South Florida and the Keys, and elegant buzzing dragonflies.

Reptiles and Amphibians

Florida's most famous reptile is the alligator. If there's a body of water, it's likely home to at least one gator. The Everglades is thick with them, but even lakeside residences in urban Orlando and Tampa have been the sites of alligator encounters. These animals are incredibly dangerous, so you should use all due caution in or near any freshwater area in Florida. Venomous snakes are also common

Manatee Preservation Efforts

manatees at Blue Springs, near Orlando

As they like to inhabit the same waters that Florida's many boaters enjoy recreating on, manatees face their single biggest threat from the propeller blades of fast-moving boats. Injuries sustained by contact with boats have resulted in thousands of manatees dying a most gruesome death. Even manatees that aren't struck by boat propellers have been threatened by the deleterious effects of fishing gear (nets, hooks, etc.) that they swallow while feeding on sea grasses and algae.

Federal law prohibits harming a manatee (they are currently listed as "vulnerable to extinction"), which has resulted in something of an uneasy standoff on Florida's waterways. Boaters feel they have every right to roam the rivers at whatever speed they feel is appropriate and safe, while wildlife officials have gone to great lengths to cap speed limits on large stretches of water in the hopes of giving manatees an opportunity to avoid colliding with the boats. While the majority of boaters are respectful of the regulations and empathetic to the manatees' plight, a recent government study that found the sea cows' position was improving led many to note that such improvement was grounds for relaxing the regulations.

throughout the state, including native species like the diamondback rattler and foreign breeds that have been "liberated" into the swamps and forests. These dangerous species are far outnumbered by the ranks of nonvenomous snakes, though, and king snakes and black snakes are quite prevalent.

The most common reptiles in Florida are lizards and geckos, which can be seen skittering about during the day, sunning themselves and chasing down food. They seldom grow to any great size, and most are less than six inches long. Salamanders are also bountiful, especially in South Florida.

History

ANCIENT CIVILIZATION AND EARLY HISTORY

The first residents of Florida were Paleo-Indians who moved into the peninsula around 12,000 BC. These groups were largely nomadic, following their food sources. The first permanent settlements weren't established until around 5000 BC, when Early Archaic groups established fishing villages along the Gulf and Atlantic coasts. Between that time and about AD 500, these groups began segmenting into the distinct regional groups that would give way to Native American groups, which had a cultural identity similar to that of the Mississippian peoples. The major groups in Florida were the Ais (along the mid-southern Atlantic coast), Apalachee (mid-Panhandle), Caloosahatchee or Calusa (southwest Gulf coast), Mayaimi (around Lake Okeechobee), Tequesta (modern-day Miami-Dade County), and Tocobaga (middle Gulf coast). The Timucua people lived throughout central and northeastern Florida, but were connected more by a common language than by cultural traits. The Seminole people didn't develop until the late 18th century, when members of the Creek nation began migrating into Florida from Georgia and Alabama as a result of an internecine conflict; their numbers included members of other far-flung nations as well as freed African American slaves. The Micosukee people also migrated to Florida in the late 18th century, and its members are related to the Seminoles due to their shared Creek lineage, but they speak a different language and originally hail from Tennessee.

COLONIALISM

Juan Ponce de León, on the hunt for the legendary Fountain of Youth, landed on the east coast of Florida on April 2, 1513. This is widely considered to be the first European landing in Florida, although De León claimed to have met an Indian who already spoke Spanish. The land was named "La Pascua Florida" (the flowery Easter) in honor of the date on the religious calendar. Spanish exploration of Florida continued in earnest for the next half century, although attempts at settlement

Indian mounds, like this one in Crystal River, remind visitors of Florida's ancient history.

were continually thwarted by native people who wanted nothing to do with these interlopers. The first European settlement in what is now the United States was in Pensacola, but it only lasted for two years (1569-1571). The Spanish had better luck with the establishment of St. Augustine in 1565, which is now regarded as the oldest city in the continental United States. It was the point from which the Spanish began launching Catholic missions throughout the region.

By this time, the Spanish exploits in Florida had caught the attention of other European powers. French explorers Jean Ribault and René Goulaine de Laudonnière founded Fort Caroline near modern-day Jacksonville, and the English launched an ill-fated expedition to colonize the area that never even made it across the Atlantic. This left the French and Spanish to duke it out for the next half century, all the while contending with assaults from Native Americans. English settlers finally began arriving in the mid-17th century, although they were migrating south from colonies in Carolina and Virginia.

By 1702, the English government took a much more concerted interest in Florida, and Colonel James Moore banded together with the Yamassee people to attack the Spanish fort at St. Augustine. Although the attack failed, it signaled the beginning of the end of exclusive Spanish rule over Florida. The French captured Pensacola in 1719, extending their sovereignty from Louisiana, and the British continued their attacks on St. Augustine and other Spanish outposts in North Florida, finally wresting control of the region from Spain in 1763. The outbreak of the Revolutionary War diverted Britain's attention from Florida, and Spain was able to regain control in 1783; this last reign was both unenthusiastic (there were no settlements or missions established) and temporary (the Adams-Onís Treaty of 1819 ceded control of Florida to the United States in exchange for all claims that the United States had to Texas).

American control brought organization to the frontier land. The separate colonial states of East Florida and West Florida were merged, and the capital was established at Tallahassee, midway between the two former state capitals of Pensacola and St. Augustine. Migration of Americans from the north soon began in earnest, but early settlers were greeted none too warmly by Native Americans. In particular, the Seminoles had grown increasingly powerful in between the colonial powers' tugs-of-war and had increasingly irritated the leaders of Southern states by providing refuge to escaped slaves who had made their way to Seminole land. Among other conflagrations, this ignited the Second Seminole War (the first had happened when Spain had control of Florida), and it wound up being the costliest and bloodiest war in history between the U.S. government and a native tribe. The war lasted nearly seven years and ultimately resulted in the permanent establishment of the expansive Seminole Reservation as well as the exodus of thousands of Native Americans out of Florida into Oklahoma.

CIVIL WAR

Florida became the 27th state in 1845, and not too long afterward, it experienced considerable upheaval, first with the three-year Third Seminole War and then with its adoption of the Ordinance of Secession in 1861, which saw it separating from the United States along with the rest of the Confederate States of America.

Given the state's considerable history of violent shifts in control, it's somewhat surprising just how small a role Florida played in the Civil War. The only major battle was the Battle of Olustee near Lake City, a Confederate victory in early 1864 that resulted in nearly 300 deaths, 2,000 wounded soldiers, and a decision by the Union that battles in Florida were strategically unnecessary to win the war. Although they continued to maintain naval blockades around the state in order to prevent supplies from flowing northward, there was little effort by the Union army to retake Florida.

Florida Crackers

Some of the original American pioneers in Florida began arriving as early as the 1760s, when Great Britain began a brief stint as the controlling colonial force in the region. These men and women staked out inhospitable territory and were greeted by clouds of mosquitoes, acres of scrub, and hostile Native Americans. Nonetheless, these pioneer families were able to establish cattle ranches and sparse agricultural settlements in the state, and many of Florida's most notable citizens—from former Governor Lawton Chiles to astronaut-senator Bill Nelson—can trace their families' roots back to these daring and resilient settlers.

There is some debate as to why these pioneers were referred to as Crackers. Some tales have the origin of the term pointing to the cowboys' usage of whips to herd cattle—the *crack* of the whip being something of a clarion call—while others give it more pejorative origins. The Spanish colonialists in the region maintained that their towns were the height of civilization and that these hard-edged interlopers were not only culturally inferior but also spiritually lacking. The term *quáquero* (a bastardization of "Quaker") referred to any Protestant but was used with particular animosity toward these American settlers.

TURN OF THE 20TH CENTURY

After the Civil War, modern Florida's history began in earnest, with developers and speculators descending on the state and kick-starting a real estate boom and the beginning of Florida's tourism industry.

Along the east coast of Florida, Henry Flagler—an original partner in Standard Oil with John D. Rockefeller—bought up several regional rail lines and connected them to the main arteries of the rest of the country. In the process, he began heavy investment in hotels and infrastructure projects. Eventually, the Florida East Coast Railway extended all the way from Jacksonville to Key West, with several of Flagler's notable hotels—the Ponce de León (St. Augustine), the Royal Poinciana (West Palm Beach), the Palm Beach Inn (now the Breakers in Palm Beach), and the Royal Palm Hotel (now the site of the DuPont Plaza Hotel in Miami)—conveniently providing lodging for customers of the railroad.

On Florida's west coast, Henry Plant was busy buying up small rail lines to connect them to other rail lines he had purchased at bargain-basement postwar prices in Savannah, Georgia, and Charleston, South Carolina. Eventually, the Atlantic Coast Line Railroad had Florida operations that extended from Jacksonville and Fernandina Beach in the northeast to Tampa and St. Petersburg in the southwest. Like Flagler, Plant smartly constructed a destination-worthy hotel along his lines; today the Tampa Bay Hotel is the site of the University of Tampa, but its unique and slightly ostentatious Moorish-Spanish design still marks it as one of the area's more unusual sights.

As tourists began pouring into the area, so did real estate developers, some of whom had visions of turning Florida into a modern and sophisticated place. Most of them, however, saw the swamps and scrublands as a piggy bank ready to be raided. Acres and acres of land were sold by speculators to gullible northern investors sight unseen, who then intended to resell the property at a profit to folks who were ready to move to America's new promised land. (Sound familiar?) As Florida's tourism industry kicked up its own marketing and promotion efforts, the paradisiacal images of orange groves, palm trees, and blue seas were amplified by the potential dollar signs promised by real estate investors, and while hundreds of thousands of people did move to Florida and established several of its major cities, many more simply turned around and went back north when they discovered that the little slice of heaven they purchased was little more than a patch of cabbage palms infested with mosquitoes and unbearable heat and humidity. The boom finally went bust in mid-1925, a deflation that was compounded by a devastating 1926 hurricane in Miami and the 1929 stock market crash.

WORLD WAR II

Like the rest of the country, Florida was highly dependent on the military-industrial complex for its struggle back to prosperity after the Great Depression. As Florida's agony was compounded by the effect of the real estate bust, it had a lot further to go to climb back than many of its other Southern neighbors. Thankfully, the state offered flat terrain and expansive stretches of coastline that were particularly conducive to the needs of the air force and the navy's aviation program. Several bases were established in Florida during this time, including Eglin Air Force Base (in the Panhandle), MacDill Air Force Base (in Tampa, currently the home of the U.S. Central Command), and the Naval Air Station Jacksonville (which, incidentally, is near the site where a submarine manned by eight Nazi spies came ashore at Ponte Vedra Beach).

In the postwar years, Patrick Air Force Base and Cape Canaveral were chosen to be the sites of the military's missile-launch facilities, a development that quickly led to the initiation of the space race and the buildup of Cape Canaveral as the home of the National Aeronautics and Space Administration (NASA).

Contemporary Times

Florida's contemporary history is deemed by many to have started on the day in 1971 when the Walt Disney World Resort opened. On that day the state was transformed from a somewhat quirky land of beaches, swamps, and roadside attractions into one of the world's foremost tourist destinations. While the impact was felt most immediately in the Central Florida region, it also upped the ante throughout the state when it came to attracting tourists. Many cities also focused on other areas: Miami struggled with the impact of waves of Cuban immigration throughout the 1960s and again in the 1980s, the latter period representing a population explosion that would have been difficult enough to deal with even if Miami hadn't seen its economy falter and its crime rate skyrocket due to drug violence. Jacksonville had extensive issues with segregation as late as the 1980s, and cities like Tampa and Fort Lauderdale witnessed their urban cores implode—and then steadily regentrify—as suburban sprawl (and its reversal) irrevocably altered their geographic and cultural identity.

Still, through it all, people just keep coming to Florida. Even the recent real estate boom and bust—which again hit Florida disproportionately hard due to rampant speculation—has been proven a temporary setback. After all, the lure of swamps, gators, scrubland … I mean, blue skies, gentle breezes, and swaying palm trees is eternal.

Government and Economy

GOVERNMENT
Governmental Structure

Like most U.S. states, Florida has three branches of government: an executive branch headed by the governor; a judicial branch headed by the Florida Supreme Court, which has seven justices on the bench; and a legislative branch consisting of the 120-seat House of Representatives and the 40-seat Senate. The state government does most of its business while the legislature is in session, which is for one 60-day period beginning in March; often, though, special sessions are called in order to complete unfinished business.

On the local level, there are 67 counties and 379 municipalities in the state.

Politics

As anyone who watched the 2000 presidential election recount can attest, Florida is somewhat schizophrenic politically. In geographic terms, the vast majority of Florida is Republican; it is up for debate whether this is due to the constant inflow of retirees or the fact that the state has way more cowboys and good ol' boys than most people think. Still, the more densely populated areas even the scales somewhat. With younger populations and culturally diverse immigrants, Florida's cities tend to be less conservative. Thus, cities in South Florida are dependably Democrat, while Orlando and Tampa are more evenly split (blue in the city core, purple-to-red in the suburbs); beyond those enclaves, the rest of the state tends to vote Republican.

ECONOMY
Agriculture

To many people's surprise, Florida has an extensive history as cattle-ranching territory. Most of the middle of the peninsula, from south of Orlando to north of Lake Okeechobee, is given over to dairy and beef pastures. In fact, Florida's cattle industry is one of the 20th largest in the United States, although that ranking has been increasingly threatened as residential development encroaches on grazing lands.

Of course, the most famous product of Florida's farms are its oranges and other citrus fruits, and groves spread out from below the frost line (which cuts through the state roughly around Orlando) all the way south to the Everglades. In and around the Everglades, sugar is the number-one crop, although the environmentally intensive methods used to harvest and process sugar cane have caused so much damage to local ecosystems that the state government has offered to buy out the U.S. Sugar conglomerate in hopes of rescuing the Glades.

Industry

Florida's main **industry**—by an exponential factor—is tourism, which is estimated to bring in almost $60 billion a year. Agriculture is a close second, along with international trade due to the large number of deepwater ports and proximity to Central and South America. Technology is also a big part of Florida's economic mix, although the $4.5 billion space industry is a substantial chunk of that. During years of real estate boom, the construction industry in Florida is one of the nation's busiest; when the economy contracts, it still plays a big role in the state's economy.

Distribution of Wealth

Florida is a defiantly middle-class state; with personal income of around $36,000 per capita, the state is ranked 20th in the United States. Like many of its Southern neighbors, it's also a defiantly antilabor state. There wasn't a minimum wage in Florida until 2004, and the state is considered a right-to-work state, meaning employment can be terminated at any point for any reason, which in turn means that collective bargaining and union membership is all but irrelevant. There is no personal income tax in Florida, homeowners receive a "homestead exemption" on their personal property tax bill, and food and medicines are exempt from an already low 6 percent sales tax. This has been one of the primary economic drivers in attracting the state's large population of retirees, as they can relocate from the industrial high-tax north and live out their days paying relatively little in taxes. Throughout the state there are pockets of extreme poverty and pockets of extreme wealth, and in South Florida one can find the two extremes butting up against one another as a road through one glamorous neighborhood may soon lead you to a bombed-out community. Generally speaking, though, the Panhandle and Northern Florida have the lowest income levels, and as you move south toward Miami, you'll find increasing levels of wealth as well as increasing levels of income disparity.

People and Culture

DEMOGRAPHY

Florida is the third-most-populous state in the United States, with approximately 20.5 million people calling the state home. Population growth has slowed considerably since a migration boom in 2005 made it the fifth-fastest-growing state in the country; today, it's estimated to be about 30th. The most densely populated areas are within the Miami-Fort Lauderdale, Tampa, and Orlando regions, while there are parts of the Panhandle that have population densities of less than 1 person per square mile.

The largest racial group is a varied mix of non-Hispanic Caucasians, who make up approximately 60 percent of the state's population. Hispanics—primarily from Cuba and Puerto Rico—make up about 18 percent, a number that increases every year. Black residents comprise about 16 percent, with the highest concentration in Jacksonville and the Panhandle; most claim direct ancestry from Southern slave states, but there is a large population of Haitians and Afro-Cubans as well. Asians account for about 2 percent, with Native Americans and other groups making up the rest of the state's diverse cultural "salad bowl." The largest ethnic enclaves in Florida can be found in Miami (Cuban American, Haitian, Italian), Orlando (Puerto Rican, Vietnamese), Tampa Bay (Greek, Puerto Rican), and the Naples area (German).

RELIGION

Baptists, Methodists, and other Protestant faiths make up nearly half of the religious affiliations of Florida residents, and nearly one-quarter of the state's population is Roman Catholic. The state's Jewish residents only total about 5 percent of the total population, but their numbers are disproportionate in Miami, which is has the third-largest Jewish population of any American city. There are a number of "crystal cathedral"-type mega-churches in the state, particularly in Orlando and South Florida, and the headquarters of the Church of Scientology is located in Clearwater.

LANGUAGE

English is the predominant **language** in Florida, with more than 75 percent of the state's school-age children using it as their first language at home. Given the cultural diversity of the state and the large population of immigrants from Latin America, Spanish is widely spoken, and many government documents are available in both English and Spanish. Additionally, French Creole, spoken primarily by the Haitian population, is also quite prominent. All Florida educators must be certified in teaching English for Speakers of Other Languages (ESOL).

THE ARTS
Literature

Well-known works created by Florida authors include Zora Neale Hurston's *Their Eyes Were Watching God,* based on Hurston's youth in Eatonville; Ernest Hemingway's writing—it's estimated that Papa did some 70 percent of his life's work in Key West; and Marjorie Kinnan Rawlings's *The Yearling* was written at and inspired by her citrus farm in north-central Florida. Additionally, hard-boiled fiction books by Elmore Leonard and Carl Hiaasen combine cop drama action and sun-baked strangeness that could only come from Florida, and the gritty and grisly tales told in the novels of Harry Crews are uniquely products of this place.

Visual Arts

One of the most interesting **visual arts** stories in Florida is that of the Highwaymen. This group of 26 African American painters hailed from the Fort Pierce area. The nearly 200,000 works that were produced by the members of this loose-knit group were sold out of the backs of their cars along State Road A1A and U.S. 1 during the 1950s and 1960s. Many of the painters were taught by fellow Fort Pierce artist and renowned landscape painter A. E. Backus, but the outsider art they created didn't capture the interest of galleries or collectors until the late 1990s, and in 2004 all 26 of the recognized Highwaymen were inducted into the Florida Hall of Fame.

Pop art legend Robert Rauschenberg split his time between New York City and a home studio on Captiva Island for years, and from 2003 until his death in 2008 he worked solely from Captiva.

Frank Swift Chase, one of the founders of the Woodstock Artists' Association, also founded the Sarasota School of Art and taught there occasionally for more than a decade. Of course, everyone's favorite soft-spoken painting instructor, public television's Bob Ross, called New Smyrna Beach home until his death.

Music

Florida has been the birthplace of dozens of famous musicians, although most of them secured their fame elsewhere. Punks like Sonic Youth's Thurston Moore and Blondie's Debbie Harry made their names in New York City, while a rocker like Jim Morrison had to leave Gainesville to make it big in Los Angeles with the Doors—although one of his career's most infamous moments occurred when he was arrested for indecent exposure in Miami. Country legend Gram Parsons was born in Winter Haven, but didn't find success until moving to Los Angeles.

There are a few homegrown talents that Floridians are justifiably proud of. Tom Petty and the Heartbreakers got their start in Gainesville, and Lynyrd Skynyrd waved the flag for Jacksonville throughout their Southern-rock career. On the counterculture front, the roots of heavy metal's underground offshoot known as death metal had its genesis in the Tampa Bay area, and the raunchy rhymes and club-filling beats of Miami rap go beyond Luther Campbell's First Amendment battles all the way to the chitlin circuit post-disco grooves of acts like Blowfly.

There are quite a few chart-toppers that may not qualify for Sunshine State Hall of Fame status quite yet. Rap-rockers Limp Bizkit hail from Jacksonville, and the entire boy band scene of the 1990s—Backstreet Boys, 'N Sync—emanated from recording studios in suburban Orlando, as did the arena-rock stylings of Creed.

Essentials

Getting There and Around

CAR

There are three major interstate highways that get you into Florida. **I-95** runs down the entire eastern seaboard, the famous "Miami to Maine" route. It enters the state north of Jacksonville and hugs the Atlantic coastline through St. Augustine, the Space Coast, the Treasure Coast, and the Palm Beach-Fort Lauderdale-Miami megalopolis. **I-75** connects Florida to Atlanta, Georgia; Knoxville, Tennessee; Cincinnati and Toledo, Ohio; and Detroit, Michigan, and enters the state south of Valdosta, Georgia. From there, it shoots down the middle of the state via Gainesville and Ocala before heading west through Tampa Bay, Sarasota, and Naples; in Naples it makes a hard east turn toward Fort Lauderdale via the northern section of the Everglades. **I-10** runs along the southern edge of the United States and terminates in Jacksonville. Driving west from Jacksonville on I-10, you'll go through Tallahassee and the Florida Panhandle before exiting the state en route to New Orleans, Louisiana; Houston and San Antonio, Texas; Tucson and Phoenix, Arizona; and finally, Los Angeles, California.

The only other major interstate highway in Florida is **I-4,** which cuts across the state from Daytona Beach in the northeast to Tampa Bay in the southwest. Florida's Turnpike is a toll highway that connects to I-75 in Ocala and goes through Orlando on the way to the Treasure Coast before running parallel to I-95 and terminating in southern Homestead.

The other major highways in the state are **U.S. 1,** which runs along the East Coast and continues on to the Florida Keys; **U.S. 41,** aka the Tamiami Trail, which runs from Miami through Naples, Sarasota, and Tampa and north into the midsection of the state on a path roughly parallel to I-75. **U.S. Highway 19/98** is the main highway along the Gulf coast north of Tampa; U.S. 98 splits off in the Big Bend to run along the Panhandle shoreline. Also, beach lovers need to remember that State Road A1A is the main road through most of Florida's Atlantic beach towns.

All major car-rental agencies have offices at Florida's major airports as well as numerous city offices. Many of them frequently offer specials for Florida visitors, but even without such discounts, car-rental rates in Florida are some of the least expensive in the country. This is a good thing, given the dearth of public transportation and the lack of population density in most of Florida, as you will almost certainly be driving.

AIR

The international airports in Miami (MIA) and Orlando (MCO) are two of the busiest in the country, and they are served by major and minor domestic and international carriers. American Airlines has a hub in Miami, and Delta has a substantial presence in Orlando. Tampa Bay International (TPA) and Jacksonville International (JAX) are both large and quite busy airports, with service from most major carriers as well as several low-cost carriers, but international and direct flights into both of those airports are somewhat limited.

There are three small regional airports that serve the Panhandle—Pensacola (PNS), Fort Walton Beach-Destin (VPS), and Panama City Beach (PFN)—mostly via connecting flights on Delta and American. A good option in South Florida for avoiding the crowds at MIA is the growing facility at

---

Previous: Sunscreen, umbrellas, and other protection is vital on Florida's beaches; Outdoor dining is a great option in the cooler months.

Fort Lauderdale-Hollywood International (FLL), which has major airlines but is best known for its selection of low-cost carriers. Additionally, there are other small regional airports throughout the state—in Daytona Beach, Melbourne, Palm Beach, Fort Myers, Sarasota-Bradenton, Key West, and Tallahassee—that may get you closer to your destination than one of the big airports, but almost always via a connecting flight, and the fares are generally more expensive.

TRAIN

Amtrak (800/USA-RAIL--800/872-7245, www.amtrak.com) runs Palmetto and Silver Service trains connecting the state to rail lines along the New York-Washington DC, corridor as well as to Charleston, South Carolina. There are Amtrak stations in Jacksonville, Winter Park, Orlando, Kissimmee, Tampa, West Palm Beach, Delray Beach, Fort Lauderdale, and Miami, as well as smaller stations along the route. Connecting bus service adds Ocala, Sarasota, and Fort Myers to the list. Also available is Amtrak's **Auto Train,** which is a nonstop train between the Washington DC area and Sanford, just north of Orlando. The

service allows you to pack your automobile onto a freight car, obviating the need for a car rental when you get to Florida.

2017 has seen the debut of high-speed rail in Florida, in the form of the privately owned **Brightline,** which connects Miami and other major cities in South Florida to Orlando; the ride from Miami to Orlando is projected to take just three hours, and the route is expected to be complete in 2018.

BUS

Greyhound (800/231-2222, www.greyhound.com) has bus service into more than 50 Florida cities and towns. See the website for information on rates and routes.

BOAT

There are four major cruise ports in Florida—Miami, Fort Lauderdale (Port Everglades), Tampa, and Port Canaveral. Smaller terminals can be found in Jacksonville, Key West, and Palm Beach. Marinas dot the entire Atlantic and Gulf coastline; the Coast Guard's District 7 is responsible for the Atlantic coast, the Keys, and the lower Gulf coast, while District 8 covers the Panhandle west of Panama City.

Sports and Recreation

OCEAN SPORTS

Florida is surrounded by saltwater on three sides, so water sports are a big part of any vacation. The only parts of the state that are truly devoid of proper beaches are the Big Bend area, which is more of a marshy delta plain with occasional forlorn bits of sand; the similarly swampy and largely inaccessible southern tip of the state, where the Everglades dump into the Florida Straits; and much of the Florida Keys, although somewhat ironically, the sandy beaches that do exist in the Keys are fantastic. Other than that, the 2,200 miles of shoreline the state has are possessed of some of the greatest beaches in the world. Shelling along the west coast is a popular

pastime, while along the Atlantic, coral reefs and sunken ships make for great snorkeling opportunities, and surfing, though not up to California standards, can also be enjoyable. Divers also enjoy heading out to the deep water beauty off the Florida Keys.

CANOEING AND KAYAKING

The best place for small boating in Florida is throughout the backwaters and slow-moving rivers of the Everglades, as a jaunt there combines the meditative nature of a canoe trip with the ever-present danger of being swallowed by an alligator. There are also excellent rivers like the Silver and the Ichetucknee in the northern part of the state for **canoeing**, **kayaking**, and tubing. However, Florida is nearly 25 percent water, so finding a place to put in and paddle will be the least of your challenges.

FISHING

Florida is one of the most popular **fishing** destinations in the United States, due to the miles and miles of rivers and lakes throughout the inland area and the seemingly infinite possibilities for deep-sea fishing off the shoreline. The massive Lake Okeechobee is a hot spot for bass fishing, and saltwater anglers enjoy heading out into the open ocean for tuna, kingfish, marlin, and mackerel. Backwater fishing among the mangroves can yield tarpon, mangrove snapper, snook, and more.

HIKING

The primary destination for hikers in Florida is the 360,000-acre Ocala National Forest, aka The Big Scrub, but there are also fantastic trails throughout the Withlacoochee State Forest in Brooksville, the Everglades National Park, and Myakka River State Park near Sarasota. The terrain throughout the state is largely flat, so most **hiking** here is for watching nature, particularly to check out migratory birds in the winter, or for sheer endurance-testing during the hot summer months.

GOLF

There are almost 1,500 **golf** courses in Florida, from the northwestern tip of Pensacola all the way to the southernmost locales of Key West. The Professional Golfers' Association (PGA) Tour has its home offices in Ponte Vedra Beach. The Ladies Professional Golf Association (LPGA) has its home offices in Daytona Beach. There are six PGA tournaments held in the state throughout the year; if that's not enough to give you an idea of how important golf is in Florida and how important Florida is to golf, know this: Tiger Woods and Arnold Palmer live in the same Orlando neighborhood.

Needless to say, finding a place to hit the links in Florida is far from a challenge. The state's courses are almost all beautiful and challenging enough to command private membership fees. A substantial number of them are indeed private, and a good number of those are surprisingly reasonably priced. Keep in mind that at some of the better courses mentioned in this guide, tee-time reservations are not only mandatory but should be made as far in advance as possible, especially during winter in South Florida.

FESTIVALS AND EVENTS

There are numerous and varied festivals throughout the year in Florida. The following is a list of some of the premier events throughout the state; for more details on each, as well as a broader listing of each city's festival events, consult the individual destinations.

January

Gasparilla Pirate Festival (Tampa, last weekend in Jan.): For more than a century, Tampa has been "invaded" by pirates who sail into the bay and, thankfully, are more into tossing beads and knocking back booze than pillaging the village. This rowdy festival is a bit bacchanalian, so families may prefer the more low-key **Gasparilla Extravaganza,** held the weekend before.

ZORA! Festival (Eatonville and Orlando, last week in Jan.): Eatonville is one of the oldest African American communities in the United States, and this weekend festival honors the work of its most famous resident, author Zora Neale Hurston.

February

Edison Festival of Light (Fort Myers, throughout Feb., most activities on the 3rd weekend): The city of Fort Myers honors inventor Thomas Edison with this monthlong celebration that includes live music, craft shows, and a parade.

Daytona 500 (Daytona Beach, 2nd or 3rd Sun. in Feb.): The racing season of the

National Association for Stock Car Auto Racing, better known as NASCAR, kicks off with the Daytona 500, which also acts as the culminating event of the Speedweeks events at the Daytona International Speedway.

Palm Beach Jewelry, Art & Antique Show (West Palm Beach, Presidents Day weekend): The moneyed residents of the Palm Beach area fill the city's convention center during this weeklong exhibition of high-end artistry.

South Beach Wine & Food Festival (South Beach and Miami, last weekend in Feb.): Although many of the tastings and seminars at this festival are somewhat pricey, gourmets and casual foodies alike can find plenty to indulge in.

Bike Week (Daytona Beach, last week in Feb.): Daytona Beach without Bike Week—a 10-day "gathering of the tribe" that's all about loud pipes and louder parties—is like Daytona Beach without the Daytona 500.

March

Old Florida Festival (Naples, 1st weekend in Mar.): Although the Civil War-era reenactments are the most popular events here, this festival takes an interactive look at all phases of Florida's history.

Sanibel Shell Fair & Show (Sanibel Island, 1st Thurs.-Sat. in Mar.): The beaches of Sanibel Island are renowned for their splendid shell-gathering opportunities—there is a Shell Museum here, after all—and this weekend festival brings collectors and craftspeople together to display their wares.

Calle Ocho (Miami, 2nd weekend in Mar.): Held in Miami in the predominantly Cuban area of Calle Ocho, this festival is something of a pan-Latin event, with food, crafts, and music from across the Latin American spectrum.

Pride Under the Sun (Fort Lauderdale, 3rd weekend in Mar.): This weekend-long celebration is purported to be Florida's largest gay pride festival, featuring an array of DJs and live music, plus food, drink, and crafts.

Florida Film Festival (Orlando, last week in Mar.): This 10-day event is one of the premier film festivals in the Southeast, and is by far the best film festival in the state, bringing independent and international movies to the picturesque Enzian Theater.

April

Interstate Mullet Toss (Pensacola Beach, last full weekend in Apr.): It's exactly what you think it is: people tossing fish over the Alabama/Florida state line, for the admiration and applause of the beer-sodden crowds gathered to observe. It's also an uproariously good time.

SunFest (West Palm Beach, last weekend in Apr.): Many cities host music festivals, but SunFest books talent a notch or two above most similar such concerts.

May

Key West Songwriters Festival (Key West, first weekend in May): You may hear a song or two you know at this festival, but odds are you'll only hear "Margaritaville" as part of a punchline, as many of the acoustic performers here are established songwriters in their own right.

Siesta Key Sand Sculpture Contest (Sarasota, first Sat. in May): The sand here may not be any better or more castle-ready than that found on other Gulf coast beaches, but the sculptures that emerge from this annual contest have made the event quite famous.

Orlando International Fringe Theatre Festival (Orlando, mid-May): This 12-day festival is dedicated to challenging and unusual theater pieces, bringing out the best of Orlando's thespians, as well as shows from throughout the country and beyond.

June

Gay Days (Orlando, 1st week in June): Gay Days brings thousands of LGBT and LGBT-friendly visitors to Orlando for parties, consumer expos, comedy shows, concerts, and a traditional red-shirted Saturday visit to Disney's Magic Kingdom.

July

Hemingway Days Festival (Key West, last full week in July): Although fans of Papa's writings will find plenty to enjoy in the readings that take place during Hemingway Days, it's Ernest Hemingway's other pursuits—fishing and drinking—that are most popularly celebrated at this festival.

August

Key Largo Food & Wine Fest (Key Largo, first week in Aug.): This festival features wine-tasting events, progressive wine dinners, cooking demonstrations, and special menus at local restaurants.

September

Food & Wine Festival (Epcot Center, Walt Disney World Resort, late Sept.-early Nov.): Epcot's World Showcase offers a wide range of international food and drink throughout the year, but this festival more than doubles the offerings; other food-related events (such as tastings and cooking lessons) also take place.

October

Destin Seafood Festival (Destin, first weekend in Oct.): Almost 30 years old, the Destin Seafood Festival brings out tens of thousands of people to enjoy just about every possible version of fried, baked, grilled, and boiled crustacean, fish, and shellfish imaginable.

Fantasy Fest (Key West, Halloween week): Very much an adults-only event, Fantasy Fest celebrates the end of hurricane season with a debauched week of fun that culminates in one of the most eye-popping, decadent parades this side of Mardi Gras.

November

Pirates in Paradise Festival (Key West, last weekend in Nov.): As with many other buccaneer-flavored festivals throughout Florida, there are parades, food, and concerts, along with re-created pirate attacks; this particular festival, however, is more PG-rated than some of the adult-oriented swashbuckling that occurs at other festivals.

December

Art Basel (Miami, first weekend in Dec.): Begun as an auxiliary event of the original Art Basel in Switzerland, this early winter event focuses the art world's attention on Miami Beach for a weekend of exhibits, premieres, and artist appearances.

Travel Tips

VISAS AND OFFICIALDOM
Entering the United States

Non-U.S. citizens will need the following to enter the country:

- a valid passport (make sure it's valid for at least six months beyond your travel date)
- a valid visa or visa waiver (check with the U.S. embassy or consulate to find out if your country is one of the 27 with whom the United States has a reciprocal agreement on visa waivers; otherwise, you'll need to apply for a tourist visa in advance at your local U.S. embassy or consulate)
- a return ticket or proof of sufficient funds to support yourself while in the United States

Contact the U.S. embassy in your country for further details, as enforcement of restrictions has tightened considerably since September 11, 2001. You can also consult the U.S. Immigration and Citizenship Services online at www.uscis.gov.

Entering Florida

The primary restriction on entering Florida from Georgia or Alabama is that the import of nonnative produce, livestock, and plants is tightly monitored. If you have any of those items in your vehicle, you need to check in at the Agricultural Inspection Station at the state line.

ACCESS FOR TRAVELERS WITH DISABILITIES

Along with California, Florida is one of the leaders in making public places accessible to people with disabilities. Even the beaches and nature trails have wheelchair access, and visitors who are hearing-impaired or blind will find that most of the major attractions have the technology to make them not only accessible but enjoyable. Although there may be some locations that are less accessible than others, particularly some historic buildings, by and large, travelers with disabilities will find Florida both accommodating and welcoming.

TRAVELING WITH CHILDREN

At its core, Florida is a family-friendly destination. Although there are numerous opportunities for adults to indulge themselves in grown-up activities and sophisticated pursuits, every major city in Florida has at least a few attractions expressly designed to capture the interest of children. Most hotels—especially those in Central Florida and the Atlantic and Panhandle beaches—have lodgings designed with families in mind, ranging from multi-bed suites to full apartment-style lodging. Kids' menus are commonplace in all but the most upscale restaurants. The only places where children aren't accommodated or allowed are in some small romantic lodgings in the Keys.

WOMEN TRAVELING ALONE

Women traveling alone in Florida should exercise the same caution they would in any major city. With the exception of some bars during spring break or some of the more decadent aspects of Bike Week, women should feel comfortable traveling anywhere in the state.

SENIOR TRAVELERS

Not surprisingly, Florida is among the most prepared states in the country when it comes to the needs of senior travelers. Some destinations like Naples and Miami Beach seem to have been expressly designed for them. Almost every attraction and hotel offers discounted rates for senior citizens, and Florida's sizable population of retirees guarantees that activities and dining options designed for older visitors are available widely.

GAY AND LESBIAN TRAVELERS

Fort Lauderdale, Key West, and South Beach are some of Florida's most noted gay and lesbian travel destinations, and there are dozens of gay-owned and gay-friendly hotels, restaurants, and nightclubs in each of those cities; Orlando, Tampa, and, honestly, most of the rest of Florida is generally quite tolerant, and with the exception of rural areas and parts of the Panhandle, gays and lesbians should encounter very few problems.

The **International Gay and Lesbian Travel Association** or IGLTA (800/448-8550, www.iglta.org) is a great resource for information on gay- and lesbian-friendly accommodations and businesses around the world, and maintains an online-accessible database.

CONDUCT AND CUSTOMS

Behavior

Florida is considerably less courteous than its Southern neighbors to the north. Unsolicited greetings are usually frowned upon, and smiles are seldom yielded without provocation. People here drive like they're the only person on the road, and the odds are pretty low that someone will voluntarily hold the door open for anyone beyond a fragile elderly person or a pregnant woman with three bags of groceries and two children in her arms. However, "less courteous" doesn't necessarily equal "rude." Floridians tend to have a laissez-faire approach to most everything, and that extends to their interactions with other people, resulting in a seemingly blinkered unawareness that falls away as soon as someone actually needs assistance. Otherwise, they're going to stay out of your business and would hope that you do the same for them. Keep in mind, none of this applies to the Panhandle. That part of Florida is far more like the rest of the South than it is like Florida, and you're likely to get into a 10-minute conversation about your day with the checkout girl at the drugstore.

Dress

Florida is generally laid-back. Most restaurants don't have dress codes, and people tend to leave the house dressed as casually as they can get away with. Of course, business meetings, formal gatherings, and a handful of top-notch five-star restaurants require getting dressed up, but beyond that, a clean shirt, some sort of pants or shorts, and a pair of shoes is about all you need to gain admittance to most places. At the beach, flip-flops and shorts are fine just about anywhere, and anywhere else, slacks and a collared shirt would be considered getting cleaned up to go out.

Smoking

Smoking in restaurants and public buildings is prohibited, and in private outdoor spaces like Orlando's theme parks, it's highly restricted. The only indoor spaces where you're able to light up legally is in a bar or nightclub, although more and more have begun enacting no-smoking policies.

FOOD

The destination-by-destination selection of local restaurants, diners, boîtes, cafés, rib shacks, fish camps, and other sundry dining options listed in this guide should hopefully provide all but the fussiest eaters with some excellent options throughout the state. I also understand that sometimes, nothing beats picking up a bag of groceries and whipping up something on your own in your kitchen-equipped hotel room. Although I've gone out of my way not to include chain restaurants and fast-food peddlers, I am fully aware that driving through this massive state sometimes requires a grab-and-go meal so you can get back out on the road. To that end, I've included a small list of grocery stores and fast-food options that should serve you well.

Grocery Stores

The Lakeland-based **Publix** chain of grocery stores is a Florida institution and for decades was something of a secret that we Crackers kept to ourselves. The stores have a strong emphasis on customer service—they'll take your groceries to your car and cannot accept tips for doing so—and have recently undertaken a great expansion of their organic and all-natural selections. Many stores have full delis and bakeries, as well as a wide selection of ready-made meals and side dishes. The quality is uniformly excellent. There are also many natural and organic food stores throughout the state, with **Whole Foods, Lucky's,** and **Trader Joe's** in most major cities.

Fast Food

The Gainesville-based **Sonny's BBQ** is omnipresent in Florida and much of the rest of the South, and its barbecue is far better than it should be, coming from a chain restaurant and all. The **Tijuana Flats** chain is a fast-growing enterprise, serving up excellent fresh Mexican food in a friendly and quirky environment with a theme that seems to depend on cute collegiate waitresses and eye-melting hot sauces. A bit more sedate is the

Cuban and Caribbean fare one can pick up at the drive-through of a **Pollo Tropical,** which specializes in grilled chicken dishes, rice and beans, plantains, and other Latin American comfort food.

Oh, and no mention of chain restaurants in Florida would be complete without noting that Orlando is the corporate headquarters of Darden, the masterminds behind the fast-casual behemoths known as Olive Garden and Yard House, as well as the Caribbean-themed Bahama Breeze, all of which can be found throughout Florida.

HEALTH AND SAFETY

One of the biggest health problems people encounter in Florida is sunburn; the long-term health effects of a brutal sunburn are potentially pretty serious. The sun here is tropical, and while you're cavorting around a theme park or soaking up the ocean breezes, you're unlikely to notice just how badly you're getting burned. *Bring sunscreen,* and lots of it.

That same sun can affect you in other ways, namely in the form of heatstroke. Make sure to drink plenty of water (not beer; water) during the day and especially while engaging in outdoor activities.

It's also worth noting that mosquitoes and stinging insects like bees and wasps are quite common throughout Florida. People with allergies to the latter should consult their doctor before coming to the state and pack a dose or three of strong antihistamines. About the only thing you can do to avoid getting bitten by a mosquito is to pack some insect repellent; if you're heading into any of Florida's state parks or backwaters, its inclusion should be mandatory. The importation of the mosquito-borne Zika virus from Latin America hit Florida quite hard, and, although municipalities throughout the state have since upped their mosquito control programs, vastly reducing the population, mosquitos (and, theoretically, Zika-carrying mosquitos) are a fact of life in Florida. However, do know that, as of late 2016, there are no "active" Zika zones in Florida, which means no areas of active transmission.

Snakes and alligators are also common. Snakes are most often encountered in wilderness areas, but in the case of gators, if you're south of Jacksonville, you should assume that any natural body of water larger than a mud puddle will likely have an alligator in it. If you see one, don't stand, don't gawk, and don't tease. Just get yourself, your children, and any pets away from the site as quickly and quietly as possible.

WHAT TO TAKE

Generally speaking, it's worth remembering that a visit to Florida is not a visit to the outback. You'll be able to find almost anything you need within a 5- or 10-minute drive of nearly anywhere, so if you forget something, don't sweat it, because you'll certainly be able to get it when you arrive.

Clothing

Unless you're particularly fastidious about your fashion (or are headed for South Beach), it's important to note that Florida is a very casual state, so pack for comfort; one dressy outfit in a suitcase filled with sundresses or shorts and beachwear is probably plenty. Be sure to pack at least one pair of closed-toe shoes, as the many non-beach outdoor activities in the state, such as hiking the Everglades, are not ideally done in flip-flops or sandals.

Sporting Equipment

The many public golf resorts and tennis clubs in the state are accustomed to accommodating tourists, and rental equipment of a fairly high quality is often available; unless you're particularly attached to your racket or your clubs, there's probably little need to pack them. Likewise, in almost every beach town—and many of the state parks—there are at least a couple of facilities where you can rent beach chairs, bikes, umbrellas, and beach toys.

Personal Care

If you're going to be spending any time out-doors—and you probably will—pack sun-screen, as the tropical sun is merciless. Make sure to bring a copy of all your vital prescriptions as well as your eyeglass or contact-lens prescription. If you have a Walgreens or CVS in your town, it might be a good idea to make sure any of your medicine prescriptions are on file there, as that will expedite the process if you need to get a prescription refilled at any of those pharmacies' numerous Florida locations.

Information and Services

VISITOR INFORMATION

For in-depth information on specific locations, consult the local visitors centers or tourism bureaus listed in each chapter. For information on the entire state, the hardworking folks at the state's tourism marketing board, **Visit Florida**, are available via telephone (888/7-FLA-USA, 888/775-2872) and online (www.visitflorida.com). They can provide maps, trip-planning tools, and information on hotels and attractions.

MONEY

Currency

The U.S. dollar is the coin of the realm throughout Florida. Currency exchange facilities are available in all of the state's major international airports—Miami, Orlando, and Tampa—as well as in tourist districts near the Orlando theme parks and Miami's South Beach area.

Banks and ATMs

Major U.S. banks are well-represented throughout the state; Bank of America, SunTrust, Wells Fargo, and Chase branches are quite easy to find, as are a number of regional and state banks and credit unions. These banks also have ATMs at their branches, as well as many freestanding ATMs in heavily touristed locations. Many international banks (especially those with large Latin American presences) can be found in Miami, Tampa, and Orlando. Independent ATMs are at many attractions, bars, and convenience stores, although they often carry exorbitant fees. Many grocery stores accept ATM debit cards and will give cash back, usually up to $50-100 at a time, with purchase for no additional fee.

Credit Cards

Visa and Mastercard are widely accepted everywhere from theme-park food stands to gas stations; many places also accept American Express. Diners Club and Discover cards are sometimes accepted, but their usage is far less common.

Taxes

The statewide sales tax is 6 percent, but many counties and municipalities levy additional local option sales taxes, ranging 0.5-2 percent on top of the state tax. Hotel taxes range 9-12 percent on the room rate in addition to sales tax.

Tipping

For the most part, gratuities and service charges are not included on restaurant bills, although in some instances—South Beach lounges, tourist-heavy restaurants—you should check your bill first, especially if you are part of a large group. A 15 percent tip is considered the baseline for acceptable service, although 20 percent for restaurant bills and cab fares and $1 per drink on bar tabs is far more common. $1 per bag is normal for hotel porters.

COMMUNICATIONS AND MEDIA

Internet Access

Broadband Internet is available throughout

Florida, although many rural areas have limited access. Many hotels offer wireless Internet access, if not in guest rooms then at least in public areas, and coffee shops and bakeries like Starbucks and Panera Bread also have Wi-Fi.

Telephones

In most Florida locales, 10-digit dialing is standard, meaning the area code must be dialed before the main number. Pay phones are all but nonexistent. Cell phone coverage, however, pretty much blankets the state. In all but the most remote areas of Florida, you'll be able to get at least a couple of bars on your phone—even in the heart of the Everglades. AT&T, T-Mobile, Sprint, and Verizon have towers all over the state as well as dozens of stores and service centers in most major cities.

Media

There are five major television markets in Florida—Jacksonville, Miami-Fort Lauderdale, Orlando-Daytona Beach, West Palm Beach-Fort Pierce, and Tampa-St. Petersburg-Sarasota—as well as smaller markets in the Keys and Panhandle. Each market carries the four U.S. networks (NBC, CBS, ABC, FOX) as well as PBS, Univision, Telemundo, and community programming.

Radio in Florida is fairly flavorless, with a standard assortment of rock, pop, country, and public stations on the FM dial, and talk and sports on the AM dial. In Tampa, Orlando, and Miami, there are also several stations that play Latin music, as well as superlative college stations that suffer from limited wattage.

Florida is home to two of the best newspapers in the United States—the *Tampa Bay Times* and the *Miami Herald*—a fact that's made that much more impressive by the presence in those markets of competitive dailies. Single-paper towns like Orlando, with its *Orlando Sentinel,* and Jacksonville, with the *Florida Times-Union,* do fairly well also. Thankfully, each of Florida's major cities boasts a solid (and free) alternative weekly, like *Miami New Times, Creative Loafing,* and *Orlando Weekly.*

Resources

Suggested Reading

NONFICTION

Burt, Al. *The Tropic of Cracker*. Gainesville: University of Florida Press, 1999. Former *Miami Herald* columnist Burt did Florida natives a great service when he wrote *The Tropic of Cracker*. By reminding readers that the state would be nothing without the farmers, homesteaders, and pioneers who made this swamp livable (or at least bearable), Burt draws a bright line between the warm, organic, and occasionally quirky heart of Florida's traditional residents and the hucksters and opportunists who have sought to exploit the state for a quick buck.

Carlson, Charlie. *Weird Florida*. New York: Sterling, 2005. While nearly every state in the Union has its own weird sites and stories, Florida undoubtedly has more than most. Carlson has done a great job in collecting and organizing the weirdest and most wonderful, and for those looking for a sort of alternate-reality tour through the Sunshine State—or simply looking for a good chuckle—this book is essential reading.

Douglas, Marjory Stoneman. *The Everglades: River of Grass*. New York: Rinehart, 1947. This seminal treatise on the Everglades was originally assigned as a piece on the Miami River for Rinehart's *Rivers of America* series; instead, Douglas's research took her to the vast waterways and swamps of the Everglades, where she found a diversity of flora, fauna, and delicate ecosystems that was wholly unique and under threat from nearby development. By all accounts, Douglas's evocative and accessible writing in *River of Grass* laid the foundation for the contemporary conservation efforts underway in the Glades, as she painted a portrait of a natural area that was a distinct national treasure, worthy of protection.

Gannon, Michael. *Florida: A Short History*, revised edition. Gainesville: University of Florida Press, 2003. Histories of Florida, both comprehensive and condensed, abound. None, however, is as compelling and engaging as Gannon's 190-page narrative. Cramming five centuries of discovery, exploration, exploitation, and growth into an easy-to-read and stylistically enjoyable tale, Gannon's book dusts away the dry studiousness of most history texts and presents the state itself as the main character in an epic tale.

Pittman, Craig. *Oh, Florida!* New York: St. Martin's Press, 2016. Florida's reputation as the weirdest state in the Union may be well-deserved (see: Florida Man), but it's also somewhat misunderstood. Pittman's background as a newspaper reporter helps put it into context, threading history with more recent news to paint a picture of a state that's always been a magnet for grifters and dreamers alike and how the state's uniqueness has impacted not just its residents but the rest of the country and world. As Pittman likes to say, if there's a piece of strange or scandalous news somewhere, there's almost always a Florida connection.

FICTION

Crews, Harry. *All We Need of Hell.* New York: Harper & Row, 1987. A great introduction to the wild world of Crews's novels, at just over 150 pages and crafted with his typical concision, *All We Need* is one of the intense author's most lighthearted works. That's not to say that it's easy reading—the protagonist is Gainesville lawyer Duffy Deeter, who derives most of his life's pleasure and exercise from starting fistfights—but the interplay between Crews's well-drawn characters and their oppressive, humid surroundings is an engrossing introduction to the author's often-imitated style.

Hemingway, Ernest. *To Have and Have Not.* New York: Scribner, 1937. Although Papa wasn't particularly fond of this work—it was cobbled together from two short stories, a novella, and some additional writing; film director Howard Hawks reportedly said Hemingway referred to it as a "bunch of junk"—but it's still a remarkable look at early 20th-century life in the Keys. The protagonist is Harry Morgan, a smuggler who works the water between Cuba and Key West, and in telling Harry's story, Hemingway paints a vivid picture of just how lawless and adventurous this part of Florida was up until just a few decades ago.

Hiaasen, Carl. *Tourist Season.* New York: G. P. Putnam's Sons, 1986. Hiaasen's first book may not be his best; that honor has to go to 1991's *Native Tongue.* But the template the author set out here for his books is unmistakable and revolutionary in terms of Florida literature. Hiaasen has a reporter's knack for weaving a story out of multiple threads of corruption, crime, and craven carnality, and he does so with a steady dose of wry humor. One critic called him a cross between Elmore Leonard and Dave Barry, but his work is far more nuanced and less pulpy than Leonard's, and despite sharing a background in newspapers, Hiaasen and Barry's writing styles couldn't be more different. One of the only authors to capture the insanity, beauty, depravity, and deep-seated weirdness of the Sunshine State, Hiaasen is clearly in love with Florida, and uses each of his novels to jab at the moneyed interests that threaten to pave over it entirely.

Hurston, Zora Neale. *Their Eyes Were Watching God.* New York: J. B. Lippincott, 1937. Widely acknowledged as one of the best American novels, Hurston's classic is also a landmark in African American literature. Although written while Hurston was an integral part of the Harlem Renaissance, the book draws heavily on her experiences growing up in Eatonville, Florida, one of the first towns in the United States to be incorporated as an all-black municipality. The book's central activities take place in Eatonville, and the story follows protagonist Janie Crawford throughout her life in different cities in the state.

McGuane, Thomas. *Ninety-Two in the Shade.* New York: Farrar Straus & Giroux, 1973. "Nobody knows, from sea to shining sea, why we are having all this trouble with our republic," is not an expected opening line for a novel about a Key West fishing guide, but *Ninety-Two in the Shade* isn't a typical novel, nor is McGuane a typical writer. This book put McGuane on the map and set the stage for him to become the celebrity novelist nicknamed Captain Berserko, yet despite all the author's personal eccentricities and 1970s excess, this book's legend is well-deserved. Illustrating the roguish heart of the Keys, the ongoing moral implosion of the state of Florida, and at its core the story of a man who just wants to do the right thing, *Ninety-Two* is engaging and thought provoking, and often quite hilarious.

Rawlings, Marjorie Kinnan. *The Yearling.* New York: Simon & Schuster, 1938. This Pulitzer Prize-winning young-adult novel is, putatively, about a little boy and his pet fawn, but Rawlings sketches a beautiful portrait of rural north-central Florida in the Cracker era. Although most of us read the story of Jody Baxter and his farming family in grade school, rereading Rawlings's book now reveals it to be a rather harrowing and intense tale, as evocative of the realities of its time and place as some of Mark Twain's best work.

Smith, Patrick. *A Land Remembered.* Sarasota: Pineapple, 1996. Smith's sprawling novel covers more than a century of Florida history, told from the perspective of three generations of the MacIvey family. From the Civil War and the early 20th-century land boom and bust through the massive wealth amassed by Old Florida families through the 1960s, the book tends to get lost in its melodramatic sweep but captures and crystallizes the growth and change of the state.

White, Randy Wayne. *The Man Who Invented Florida.* New York: St. Martin's, 1993; Dorsey, Tim. *Florida Roadkill: A Novel.* New York: William Morrow, 1999. In the wake of Carl Hiaasen's success with telling the story of Florida from a slightly off-kilter and ultimately more realistic perspective, a number of other Florida writers got attention. White and Tim Dorsey are two of the most prolific and, thankfully, also two of the best. White's series of Doc Ford adventures—of which *The Man Who Invented Florida* is the third, best, and strangest—takes place on Florida's Gulf coast, which lends the proceedings more of a swampy backwoods-noir feel, but the crime and current issues at play keep the books from being standard potboilers. Like Hiaasen, Dorsey loves writing about shenanigans in Miami, and *Florida Roadkill* is his first and funniest book. Though he doesn't have the stylistic skills of Hiaasen, Dorsey's books are insanely good fun, barreling the reader through a cast of oddball characters and perilous situations.

Internet Resources

GENERAL INFORMATION
Visit Florida
www.visitflorida.com
Operated by the state's tourism board, this site is content rich. In addition to basic information on many of the state's attractions, as well as weather reports and event calendars, Visit Florida also offers trip-planning tools, blogs, video features, and reservation services. While the site is unflinchingly positive about everything (of course), it's surprisingly informative and an excellent resource if you're in the initial stages of planning a trip.

NEWSPAPERS
Daily Newspapers
To keep up with daily news in Florida, the websites for four papers in the state are good resources.

Miami Herald
www.miamiherald.com
Covers Miami and South Florida.

Tampa Bay Times
www.tampabay.com
Covers the Tampa Bay area.

Orlando Sentinel
www.orlandosentinel.com
Covers Orlando and Central Florida.

Florida Times-Union
www.jacksonville.com
Covers Jacksonville and St. Augustine.

Alternative Weekly Newspapers

For arts, entertainment, and event calendars, alternative weekly papers are the best resource.

Miami New Times
www.miaminewtimes.com
Covers South Florida.

Broward-Palm Beach New Times
www.browardpalmbeach.com
Covers South Florida.

Creative Loafing
http://tampabay.creativeloafing.com
http://Sarasota.creativeloafing.com
Covers Tampa Bay and Sarasota.

Orlando Weekly
www.orlandoweekly.com
Covers Central Florida amusements beyond the theme parks.

Folio Weekly
www.folioweekly.com
Has listings for the areas around Jacksonville and St. Augustine.

PARKS AND RECREATION
Parks and Camping
Florida State Parks
www.floridastateparks.org
A fantastic resource for every possible bit of information you could need on any of Florida's 160 state parks.

National Parks Service
www.nps.gov/state/FL

This site offers information on all 10 national parks in Florida, with hours, seasons, entrance fees, and other vital information.

Reserve America
www.reserveamerica.com
Most of the state, national, and privately owned RV parks in Florida use Reserve America to process campground reservations.

ACTIVITIES
Florida Rambler
www.floridarambler.com
This regularly updated blog doubles as an outdoor activity guide and love letter to wild Florida, with a focus on uncovering unique and less-frequented outdoor spots. Kayaking, canoeing, and hiking options get a lot of attention, but out-of-the-way sights and itineraries are also highlighted.

Florida Sportsman
www.floridasportsman.com
An essential resource for anglers and boaters, Florida Sportsman gear reviews, fishing reports, and even recipes. Hunters and divers have their own dedicated areas of the site, as do different regions of the state and the various types of fishing available here (inshore, offshore, freshwater, etc.).

Ross's Central Florida Surfing Reports
www.cflsurf.com
Surfers should point their browsers to Ross's for up-to-date information on conditions on the central Atlantic coast around the Cocoa Beach area; the site also has links to webcams and surf-report sites throughout the rest of the state.

Index

498

WXYZ

List of Maps

Photo Credits

MAP SYMBOLS

Symbol	Name	Symbol	Name	Symbol	Name	Symbol	Name
═══	Expressway	○	City/Town	✈	Airport	⚑	Golf Course
═══	Primary Road	◉	State Capital	✕	Airfield	P	Parking Area
───	Secondary Road	⊛	National Capital	▲	Mountain	⬟	Archaeological Site
- - -	Unpaved Road	★	Point of Interest	✦	Unique Natural Feature	⌂	Church
───	Feature Trail	•	Accommodation			⛽	Gas Station
- - - -	Other Trail	▼	Restaurant/Bar	≈	Waterfall		Glacier
⋯⋯	Ferry	▪	Other Location	♠	Park		Mangrove
═══	Pedestrian Walkway	△	Campground	⊓	Trailhead		Reef
▨▨▨	Stairs			⚡	Skiing Area		Swamp

CONVERSION TABLES

°C = (°F – 32) / 1.8
°F = (°C x 1.8) + 32
1 inch = 2.54 centimeters (cm)
1 foot = 0.304 meters (m)
1 yard = 0.914 meters
1 mile = 1.6093 kilometers (km)
1 km = 0.6214 miles
1 fathom = 1.8288 m
1 chain = 20.1168 m
1 furlong = 201.168 m
1 acre = 0.4047 hectares
1 sq km = 100 hectares
1 sq mile = 2.59 square km
1 ounce = 28.35 grams
1 pound = 0.4536 kilograms
1 short ton = 0.90718 metric ton
1 short ton = 2,000 pounds
1 long ton = 1.016 metric tons
1 long ton = 2,240 pounds
1 metric ton = 1,000 kilograms
1 quart = 0.94635 liters
1 US gallon = 3.7854 liters
1 Imperial gallon = 4.5459 liters
1 nautical mile = 1.852 km

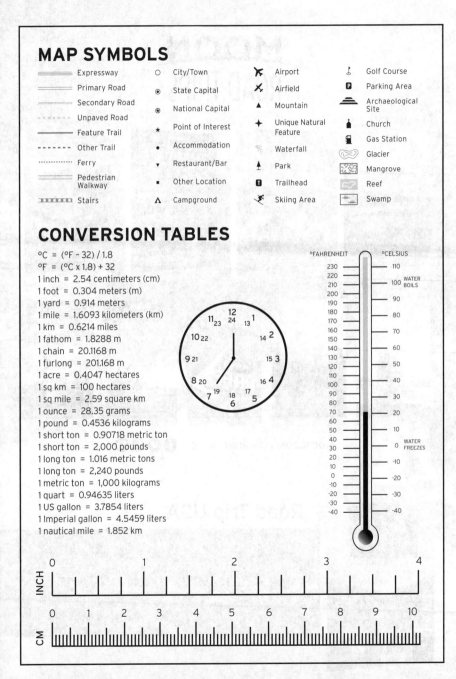